# 1-2-3™:
# The Complete Reference

Mary Campbell

Osborne **McGraw-Hill**
Berkeley, California

Osborne **McGraw-Hill**
2600 Tenth Street
Berkeley, California 94710
U.S.A.

For information on translations and book distributors outside of the
U.S.A., please write to Osborne **McGraw-Hill** at the above address.
A complete list of trademarks appears on page 883.

**1-2-3™: The Complete Reference**

Screens for this book were created using PRINT SCREEN™ by Domus
Software Limited, 303 Waverley Street, Ottawa, Ontario, Canada K1P
OV9.

567890 DODO 8987

ISBN 0-07-881005-1

Jean Stein, Acquisitions Editor
Mella Mincberg of Applied Computer Consulting, Oakland, California,
    Technical Reviewer
Lyn Cordell, Project Editor
Judy Wohlfrom, Text Design
Bay Graphics Design Associates, Cover Design

# CONTENTS

## PART TWO   Data Management, Graphics, and Macros

I wish to thank the following individuals, without whom this book would not have been possible:

Jean Stein, senior editor, Osborne/McGraw-Hill, whose ideas substantially enhanced the manuscript, and who coordinated the resources needed to complete the writing.

Mella Mincberg, technical reviewer, whose perspective and attention to detail greatly improved the quality of each chapter.

Lyn Cordell, project editor, Osborne/McGraw-Hill, who coordinated the production phase and provided error-free copy that made the author review process easy.

Lisa Yount, copy editor, whose expertise and hard work produced a quality product. Lisa did an excellent job of finding the right words when, at times, they escaped me.

Karen Hinkle, typist, who was asked to decipher the indecipherable and did so in a timely manner.

Caroline Camougis and Brenda Langburt of Lotus Development Corporation for their valuable assistance.

I dedicate this book to my husband, Dave.

# PREFACE

Although 1-2-3 has been available for several years, it is still one of the best-selling microcomputer software packages. Individuals who are new to computing are anxious to gain the same benefits that other users have realized from the package. Organizations that have been using 1-2-3 for years are purchasing additional copies for use in new departments and new applications.

The introduction of release 2 of 1-2-3 in the fall of 1986 added a new level of sophistication to the package. Users who had begun to stretch the limits of the 1A version found a product that added greater memory capabilities, more sophisticated analytical techniques, new built-in calculating abilities, and an expanded macro command language with all the flexibility of a true programming language.

## Uses of This Book

*1-2-3: The Complete Reference* is designed to serve the needs of both new and experienced 1-2-3 users. Beginning users should start at the beginning of the book and work through the first six chapters. After reading these chapters, they may want to enter some of the chapter examples into their systems for practice. Users already familiar with 1-2-3 basics will want to review the table of contents and focus on chapter topics with which they are less familiar, such as data management features, keyboard alternative macros, and command macros.

Experienced users will also find this volume to be a valuable reference tool, describing all of 1-2-3's many features in detail. Both release 1A and release 2 commands are covered. If you are using both versions of 1-2-3 in your organization, you will be able to look to one source for the answers to your questions about both releases. Each topic has working examples in addition to a description of the feature. Boxes in the text highlight important summary information, and a thorough index will help you find the precise topic you are looking for. Reference sections at the end of many of the chapters provide a quick alphabetical guide to commands.

In addition to its thorough coverage of 1-2-3, this book provides information on several add-on products. 1-2-3 Report Writer, a Lotus add-on to expand the reporting features of the package, is covered in detail in Chapter 14. Chapter 15 contains information on several products offered by other vendors.

## Organization of This Book

This book is divided into three parts. Part One covers the worksheet and all the commands you need to create efficient worksheet models. Part Two focuses on database and graphics commands. Part Three expands the basic 1-2-3 features with the power of macros and add-on products. An outline of the chapters follows:

- Chapter One, An Introduction to 1-2-3, will get you started with the 1-2-3 package. It covers installation as well as hardware options for the package.

- Chapter Two, The Access System, Display, and Keyboard, provides an overview of the package by introducing you to some of its most important features. You will learn all about 1-2-3's display.

- Chapter Three, Entering Data in 1-2-3's Spreadsheet, gets you started in creating worksheet models. You will learn all about the types of entries that can be made on the worksheet.

- Chapter Four, Changing the Appearance of the Worksheet Display, introduces you to the flexibility 1-2-3 allows in formatting data. You will learn how to override the default display characteristics to create the exact display you want.

- Chapter Five, Printing, provides explanations and examples of all 1-2-3 printing features. It shows you how to do everything from printing formulas to adding borders to a printed report.

- Chapter Six, Basic Worksheet Commands, covers all the command options pertaining to the worksheet. You will learn how to determine the worksheet status and change options to suit your needs.

- Chapter Seven, 1-2-3's Built-in Functions, lists and describes each of 1-2-3's built-in functions. You can read about just the ones you are interested in or survey them all to discover new uses for the package.

- Chapter Eight, Working With Files, covers everything you will need to know to save and retrieve files. You will also learn how to consolidate files and save just a section of your worksheet.

- Chapter Nine, Data Management, introduces you to

the sort and query features 1-2-3. You will learn how to sequence data in any order and extract particular data for any purpose.

• Chapter Ten, Using Data Management Features in the Spreadsheet Environment, introduces you to the power that the data management features can add to spreadsheet models. You will learn about the tools needed to perform a sensitivity analysis, generate matrices, and sort formula entries.

• Chapter Eleven, Working With 1-2-3's Graphics Features, provides examples of graphic display for your data. You will learn how easy it is to change numeric data into graphics and charts.

• Chapter Twelve, Keyboard Macros, shows you how to save keystrokes for menu selections and other activities in worksheet cells. These keystrokes can then be reused at will.

• Chapter Thirteen, Command Language Macros, covers the powerful new command language available in release 2. Each macro command is described and illustrated with an example.

• Chapter Fourteen, Using 1-2-3 Report Writer, takes you on a tour through the menu options in Report Writer. You can use this review to determine whether this product would be a worthwhile addition for your applications.

• Chapter Fifteen, Extending 1-2-3 With Add-on Products, looks at a few add-on programs that can really increase the power of 1-2-3. Learn how you can enhance your graphics, audit your worksheet, save disk space, print across your paper, create better reports, and document your worksheet with the products discussed.

• Appendix A, A History of 1-2-3, explains 1-2-3's popularity in the context of previous spreadsheet solutions.

• Appendix B, 1-2-3 Keyboard Guides, shows how the keyboards of several popular microcomputers differ from that of the IBM PC/XT.

Most of the models used in this book are available on a set of disks. You will find that using these disks can save time, especially if you plan to use the volume for training other users in your organization. The disks may be ordered directly from Campbell & Associates at the following address:

Campbell & Associates
P.O. Box 358
Gates Mills, OH 44040

|  | Price Per Set | Quantity | Subtotal |
|---|---|---|---|
| Accompanying disks for *1-2-3: The Complete Reference* | $37.95 | _____ | _____ |

Ohio residents add 5% sales tax

**TOTAL ENCLOSED** _____

Checks should be made payable to Campbell & Associates.

# 1-2-3 Worksheet Reference

# PART ONE

# An Introduction
# To 1-2-3

**Your Equipment**
**Installing 1-2-3**

# ONE

This chapter is designed to serve as an introduction to Lotus 1-2-3 for new users. It will cover 1-2-3 installation on various types of equipment. Whether you use a hard disk or a floppy disk, you will find detailed instructions to ensure that the installation process proceeds smoothly.

Before beginning with 1-2-3 specifics, this chapter will introduce the hardware options for 1-2-3 and the various system components. It is not possible to install 1-2-3 if you do not have at least some general knowledge about the system you will be using. In order for the Install program to configure your copy of 1-2-3 to run with the specific hardware components you have, you must be able to tell the program what those components are.

1-2-3 is designed to run on a personal computer from AT&T, Compaq, or IBM. A number of certified compatibles are also able to run 1-2-3 successfully. The Zenith Z-100 and 248, the TI Professional, and the Wang Professional are just a few of the many systems with which the package will work. Since the compatible market is constantly changing, you will need to check with your dealer for the most up-to-date list of certified compatibles. In case of doubt, have the dealer demonstrate 1-2-3 on the machine you are considering.

Throughout this chapter we will assume that you have an IBM PC or XT. If you have an IBM AT or an AT&T, refer to the keyboard conversion instructions in Appendix B. If you have a certified compatible, look at the keyboard of your machine and the peripheral devices such as disk drives to determine which of the listed machines most closely matches your configuration.

## Minimum Configuration

The minimum system configuration required for 1-2-3 is listed in Figure 1-1. An optimal configuration for your application may require more equipment. Notice the differences in memory and disk drive support between version 1A and version 2. The minimum memory under release 2 has been increased to 256K from 192K for release 1A and 128K for release 1. Also, release 2 can be used with one double-sided diskette, whereas release 1A requires either two diskettes or a hard disk and one double-sided diskette.

### Keyboard

You will begin using the keyboard in this chapter as you work with the Install program. Any directions given will refer to key names on the keyboard for the IBM PC. The same keyboard configuration is used for the IBM PC/XT, the IBM Portable, and the Compaq. There are some differences

|  | Release 1A | Release 2 |
|---|---|---|
|  | IBM PC, XT, AT, or Compaq | IBM PC, XT, AT, Portable, or PCjr<br>Compaq Portable, Plus, or Deskpro<br>AT&T 6300<br>Certified compatibles |
|  | Keyboard | Keyboard |
|  | 192K | 256K |
|  | 2 double-sided/double-density<br>diskettes or 1 hard disk<br>and 1 double-sided/double-<br>density diskette | 1 double-sided/double-density<br>diskette |
|  | Monochrome or color monitor | Monochrome or color monitor |

**Figure 1-1.** Minimum configuration

between this configuration and the keyboards of other popular systems that work with 1-2-3. Appendix B describes some of these differences.

## Monitor

Monitors come in two basic varieties, color and monochrome. Monochrome implies one color. This may be white, green, or amber on black. Normally a monochrome monitor will display only text, although you can add cards such as an Enhanced Graphics Adapter or a Hercules card. Even with the graphics adapter, a monochrome monitor will display one-color graphs. A color monitor can display graphs in color as well as utilize color for highlighting some of the 1-2-3 screens, for example, using red for the error indicator and blue to highlight menu choices.

## Expansion

With the minimum configuration you will be able to load the 1-2-3 package and use most of its features. You may find that you want to expand beyond the minimum configuration for convenience and to obtain maximum benefit from the package features, however.

### Adding Memory

The models you create will be limited by the amount of memory on your system. Operating 1-2-3 at the lowest level possible, you will be able to use all of the package features but will be restricted in the size of your data files and spreadsheet applications. If you plan to build large models, you will want to consider expanding the memory of your machine. The standard memory expansion can take your PC up to 640K. A variety of multifunction boards can be added in an empty slot of your PC to achieve this memory expansion. Frequently these cards will offer other functions, such as a battery-operated clock to keep track of the time, a print buffer, or additional printer or communications ports.

With release 2, you also have the option of expanding memory beyond the standard 640K. To do this you will need to select a card that conforms to the Lotus/Intel Expanded Memory Specification, such as the Above Board card. With these cards you can expand memory by as much as 8MB (approximately 8,000,000 characters), although 1-2-3 is designed to access only 4MB. This expanded memory will allow you to build large data files and spreadsheets with the 1-2-3 program.

Release 2 also supports the addition of a math coprocessor. Both the 8087 and the 80287 coprocessor chips are supported and will be automatically recognized once they are installed. Spreadsheet models with a significant number of calculations will be calculated much faster with one of these chips added to the motherboard of your machine.

## Adding Disk Drives

Although release 2 can be used with one disk drive, a frequent user will find the disk swapping required to be quite cumbersome. Data cannot be stored on the System Disk containing the program and help files, so you will find yourself changing disks frequently.

If you have two drives, one drive can be used for the program and the other can be used for data. This will work whether both drives are floppy drives or one is a hard disk and one is a floppy. The best configuration for using 1-2-3 is to have a hard drive along with a floppy so that you can load all the 1-2-3 programs onto the hard drive and have the flexibility of storing data files on either the hard disk or a floppy. You will then be able to switch from 1-2-3 to Translate or PrintGraph without having to search for the proper diskette, since all three programs will be on your hard drive. Also, with a hard drive you will be able to store files that exceed a floppy diskette's 360K capacity. Hard drives are available with capacities from 10MB to 40MB or more. At present the most popular size is a 20MB drive.

## Adding a Printer

1-2-3 will support a wide variety of printers. In the installation program you will be able to select from a menu listing an assortment of makes and models. 1-2-3 will even support separate printers for text and graphics if you desire, but it is important that the printer type chosen for either graphs or text be on the installation list. Although a different brand may in fact emulate one of the listed models, you will want to verify the support at the time you purchase the printer rather than after you have taken it to your office if the printer type does not appear on the list.

1-2-3 supports both a text and a graphics printer because some text printers will not print graphs. A letter-quality daisy wheel printer may be used to print your text, for example, but this printer could not support printing graphs. A dot matrix printer can print both text and graphs in either draft or near-letter-quality mode in most cases. Laser and ink jet printers are also gaining in popularity and are supported by release 2 of 1-2-3.

If you have both a dot matrix and a letter-quality printer, you may want to use the letter-quality device for text and use the dot matrix to print graphics. To connect either of these printers to your system, you will also need a cable and an available port. It is possible to connect printers to both parallel and serial ports as long as they are compatible, but there are some special settings if you use a serial connection. First, you must set the printer's baud rate to control the speed of data transfer. At any baud rate except 110 you should also set 1 stop bit, 8 data bits, and no parity. With a speed of 110 there should be 2 stop bits. Once the program is loaded, use the Worksheet Global Default Printer Interface command and select the baud rate matching your printer's rate. This is done by typing /**WGDPI**, pointing to the baud rate you need, and pressing ENTER. This change is saved with the Worksheet Global Default Update command (/WGDU). With PrintGraph a similar change must be made with Settings Hardware Interface. If you are purchasing your system at the same time you acquire 1-2-3, your dealer will normally assist you with this installation.

## Adding a Plotter

A plotter provides another option for producing graphs. With most devices you can use either paper or transparencies in your plotter with the appropriate pens to create the display medium of your choice. Since 1-2-3 supports only a limited number of plotters, you will want to ensure that the one you are considering purchasing is on the acceptable list; otherwise it may not function with 1-2-3.

## The Operating System

The operating system is the control program that resides in the memory of your computer regardless of the software you are working with. It controls the interface between the various devices and establishes the format for data storage on disk. The different releases of 1-2-3 are compatible with different versions of the DOS operating system. Since DOS is absolutely essential to utilizing your computer and its software, you will want to make sure you have a version of DOS that is compatible with the release of 1-2-3 you have.

Release 1A of 1-2-3 was designed to run under DOS 1.1 or 2.0. With release 2 the version number depends on the type of system you have. For the IBM PC, PC/XT, Portable, P, and 3270-PC you will use DOS 2.0, 2.1, 3.0, or 3.1. For the IBM PC/AT you will use 3.0 or 3.1. Using the IBM PCjr with the Utility program requires DOS 2.1. With the Compaq machines use 2.02 or 2.11, and with the AT&T use 2.11. All this may seem a bit confusing, but your dealer can advise you based upon your configuration. The dealer can also give you information about new versions of DOS that may be introduced.

## Noting Your Equipment

You are now ready to proceed with the steps needed to install your 1-2-3 disks. First, however, make a note of your hardware configuration. Figure 1-2 provides a convenient form for doing this. You will want this information available when you use the Install program.

## Installing 1-2-3

The purpose of installation is to tailor your 1-2-3 disks to run with your specific hardware configuration. If 1-2-3 only ran with one type of hardware this step would not be necessary. Since it is, you should remember that it offers you an advantage: You can continue to use the package even if you change your hardware configuration to include a plotter, a new printer, or a color monitor.

**HARDWARE**

| | |
|---|---|
| Computer manufacturer | _____ |
| Computer model | _____ |
| Graphics card | _____ |
| Monitor | _____ |
| RAM | _____ |
| Printer manufacturer/model | _____ |
| Printer interface (serial or parallel) | _____ |
| Plotter model | _____ |
| Plotter interface (serial or parallel) | _____ |
| Disk drives—number and type (Hard versus Floppy) | _____ |

**SOFTWARE**

| | |
|---|---|
| DOS version number | _____ |
| Lotus 1-2-3 version | _____ |

Figure 1-2.    Configuration worksheet

## Preliminary Steps

When you purchase 1-2-3, the package you receive contains an envelope with several diskettes. With release 2 you receive the System Disk, the Backup System Disk, the Utility Disk, the PrintGraph Disk, the Install Library Disk, and A View of 1-2-3. With release 1A you receive only five disks; there is no Install Library Disk in the earlier release. Release 1A has a Tutorial Disk in place of release 2's A View of 1-2-3.

The disk you use most often will be the *System Disk*, since it contains the 1-2-3 program and the Lotus Access System. The Backup System Disk is an exact duplicate of this disk. The second disk is needed because the System Disk cannot be copied. (Although you might be successful in copying each of the files, your new disk would not run because of a special protection scheme.) Lotus would not want you to be unable to use your 1-2-3 system because of a damaged System Disk.

The *Utility Disk* contains two important routines. The first is the Install program, which copies drivers from the library disk to your other disks so they will work with your individual equipment configuration. Drivers are files that contain information concerning the interface requirements for your specific equipment. For example, 1-2-3 will interface differently with a laser printer than with a dot matrix model. Once these driver sets are installed, you will not have to be concerned further with equipment needs unless you change your system. Placing these driver files on your diskettes or hard drive is a critical step if you plan to use the printer or other output device for worksheets and graphs.

The second application on your Utility Disk is the Translate program. This program allows you to maximize the benefit from data recorded in another program such as dBASE III or VisiCalc by translating the data to a format that 1-2-3 can use.

The *Install Library Disk* contains the driver files for all the equipment Lotus supports, including printer drivers, plotter drivers, and display drivers. When you run the Install program and indicate your equipment selection, the drivers will be copied from the library disk to your other disks.

*A View of 1-2-3* is new with release 2. It replaces the Tutorial Disk provided with release 1A and is more comprehensive. You will find this to be an excellent tutorial whether you are a new user wanting to get a feel for the package or an experienced user wanting a quick look at some of release 2's new features. It is organized into lessons to allow you to spend a few minutes or a few hours with the program.

The *PrintGraph Disk* is essential for printing copies of

graphs created with the package. It supports interface with a wide variety of graphics printers and plotters. It also allows you to access a variety of fonts for titles on your graphs.

You will want to complete several preliminary steps with this set of disks before running Install. First, locate your DOS disk, the keyboard guide, all six 1-2-3 disks, and five blank formatted diskettes (unless you have a hard disk). Since the steps required for installation with a hard disk are different from those required with diskettes, the procedures will be covered separately.

## Installing With Diskettes

Use the instructions in this section if you have a system with one or two diskette drives but no hard drive (see Figure 1-3). The basic steps in installation in this case are making backup copies of four of the Lotus disks, copying critical DOS files to the disks, and running the Lotus installation program. It is important to note that for release 2, these preliminary steps will not allow you to make the System Disk a bootable disk as was true with earlier releases. Since release 1A is no longer being marketed, the installation instructions given here are for release 2. If you have an uninstalled version of 1A, read the instructions at the front of your Lotus manual, as there are a few differences in the installation process between release 1A and release 2.

### Making Backup Diskettes

You already have a backup copy of the System Disk, and the hidden protection scheme will not allow you to make additional backup copies. The disks you will be backing up, therefore, are the Utility Disk, the PrintGraph Disk, the Install Library Disk, and A View of 1-2-3. It is worthwhile to back up all the diskettes, even if you think you will not use some of them. After completing the backup, store the original disks in a safe place and use the backups.

One floppy disk drive

Two floppy disk drives

One floppy and one hard disk

**Figure 1-3.**    System configurations

The procedure for backing up the disks is as follows:

1. Create an appropriate label for each of the disks: Backup PrintGraph, Backup Utility Disk, and so on.

2. With DOS loaded in your system, place the Print-Graph Disk in drive A and a formatted blank diskette in drive B.

3. Type **COPY A:\*.\* B:** /V and press the ENTER key. Lotus recommends the use of the Copy command rather than Diskcopy because the /V parameter for Copy causes DOS to verify each file after it is copied to ensure that it matches the original exactly.

4. With a one-drive system, DOS will prompt you to take the disks in and out several times, since DOS can copy only a limited amount of data at one time.

5. Once the first disk has been copied, remove both the original and the copy from the drives and apply the label to the newly copied disk. Then proceed to copy the other three disks.

If you use the copies and store the originals, a failure in one of the copies can be remedied by making another copy from the original disk. If the System Disk should fail, use the Backup System Disk and refer to the instructions in the Lotus Customer Assurance Plan for obtaining a replacement.

### Copying COMMAND.COM
### To Your Diskettes

Although it is not possible to place all of the DOS files on your Lotus disks because of space limitations, you may want to place the DOS COMMAND.COM file on the disks. This will prevent an error message from appearing every time you exit 1-2-3 or one of the other programs. If you elect to omit this step, you will see the error message "Insert disk with /COMMAND.COM in drive A and strike any key when ready" every time you exit 1-2-3 or an auxiliary program.

You will probably want to add COMMAND.COM to the System Disk, the Backup System Disk, A View of 1-2-3, PrintGraph, and the Utility Disk. Placing COMMAND.COM on the disks will not make the disks bootable, however, so you will have to load DOS into your system before beginning to work with any of these programs. The following directions for copying COMMAND.COM are for a two-drive system, but you can easily adapt them to a one-drive system by using the backup copy model in the preceding section.

1. Insert your DOS disk in drive A and boot your system if the DOS A> prompt is not on your screen.

2. Place your System Disk in drive B without a write protect tab.

3. Type **COPY A:COMMAND.COM B:** /V and press ENTER. This will copy COMMAND.COM to drive B and verify the copy to ensure that it is correct.

4. Remove the System Disk. Repeat the procedure for the Backup System Disk, A View of 1-2-3, the Utility Disk, and PrintGraph.

You are now ready to install 1-2-3 for your equipment. Make sure you have your completed equipment configuration worksheet (Figure 1-2) handy.

### Running Install With a Floppy Disk System

It is possible to use your 1-2-3 package without running the Install program, but without it you will not be able to use a printer or display a graph. Since you are bound to want to do at least one of these things eventually, you might as well get the installation completed now. You will want to start the Install program directly from DOS, so make sure the DOS disk is in drive A. Then boot your system.

1. Check for the A> prompt on your screen and reboot if it is not there. Next, place the Utility Disk in drive A. Type **Install** and press ENTER.

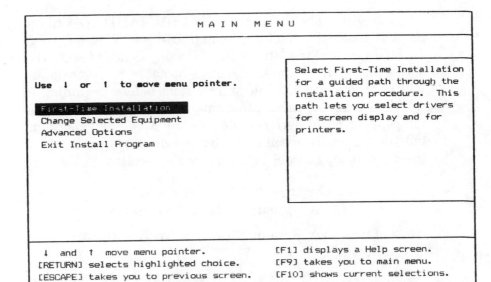

```
                    M A I N   M E N U

                                          ┌─────────────────────────────┐
                                          │ Select First-Time Installation │
                                          │ for a guided path through the  │
   Use ↓ or ↑ to move menu pointer.       │ installation procedure.  This  │
                                          │ path lets you select drivers   │
   ▐First-Time Installation▌              │ for screen display and for     │
    Change Selected Equipment             │ printers.                      │
    Advanced Options                      │                                │
    Exit Install Program                  │                                │
                                          │                                │
                                          │                                │
                                          │                                │
                                          └─────────────────────────────┘

   ↓  and  ↑  move menu pointer.       [F1] displays a Help screen.
   [RETURN] selects highlighted choice.  [F9] takes you to main menu.
   [ESCAPE] takes you to previous screen. [F10] shows current selections.
```

**Figure 1-4.** Installation options

2. Follow the directions on your screen for disk swapping. Install will repeat its message if you should accidentally place the wrong disk in the drive.

3. Since this is a first-time installation, select that option from the menu screen presented to you (see Figure 1-4). 1-2-3 will then take you on a guided tour through the entire installation process. Refer to the earlier section on the keyboard if you wish to make selections described at the bottom of the screen and are uncertain of the location of keys on your keyboard.

4. You will be asked to select the monitor and the text and graphics printers in your configuration. Figures 1-5, 1-6, and 1-7 show several of the selection screens that will be presented to you during installation. Refer to the equipment configuration you listed on your worksheet to supply the correct selections.

5. If you are creating only one set of installation parameters, you will want to save your selections as 123.SET. If

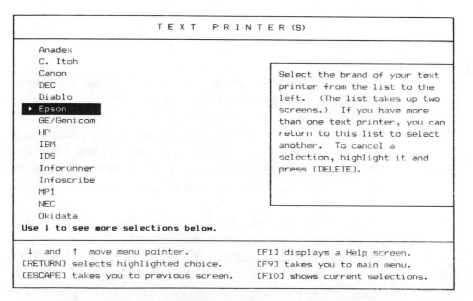

```
                    S I N G L E   M O N I T O R

 Hercules card (80 x 25)
 Hercules card (90 x 38)
 IBM color card, single-color monitor      Select this for an IBM
 IBM color card                            monochrome monitor with a
 Plantronics ColorPlus card                Hercules graphics card if
 Enhanced Graphics Adapter                 you want a standard 80 x 25
 AT&T 6300, single-color monitor           screen display.
 AT&T 6300, color monitor
 AT&T 6300 (80 x 50)
 IBM 3270-PC, color monitor
 IBM 3270-PC, monochrome monitor
 IBM 3270-PC/GX
 COMPAQ, single-color monitor
 COMPAQ, color monitor
 IBM Portable Computer
 Use ↓ to see more selections below.

   ↓  and  ↑  move menu pointer.        [F1] displays a Help screen.
 [RETURN] selects highlighted choice.   [F9] takes you to main menu.
 [ESCAPE] takes you to previous screen. [F10] shows current selections.
```

**Figure 1-5.**   Installation screen

```
                    T E X T   P R I N T E R (S)

     Anadex
     C. Itoh
     Canon                                 Select the brand of your text
     DEC                                   printer from the list to the
     Diablo                                left.  (The list takes up two
  ▶ Epson                                  screens.)  If you have more
     GE/Genicom                            than one text printer, you can
     HP                                    return to this list to select
     IBM                                   another.  To cancel a
     IDS                                   selection, highlight it and
     Inforunner                            press [DELETE].
     Infoscribe
     MPI
     NEC
     Okidata
 Use ↓ to see more selections below.

   ↓  and  ↑  move menu pointer.        [F1] displays a Help screen.
 [RETURN] selects highlighted choice.   [F9] takes you to main menu.
 [ESCAPE] takes you to previous screen. [F10] shows current selections.
```

**Figure 1-6.**   Installation screen

An Introduction to 1-2-3                                              **15**

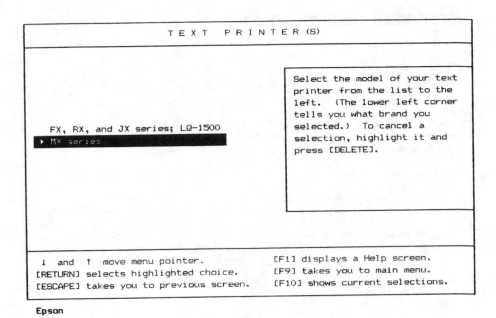

```
          T E X T   P R I N T E R (S)
 ┌────────────────────────────────────────────────────────────┐
 │                              ┌───────────────────────────┐  │
 │                              │ Select the model of your text │
 │                              │ printer from the list to the  │
 │                              │ left.  (The lower left corner │
 │                              │ tells you what brand you      │
 │  FX, RX, and JX series; LQ-1500 │ selected.)  To cancel a    │
 │ ▶ MX series                  │ selection, highlight it and   │
 │                              │ press [DELETE].               │
 │                              │                               │
 │                              └───────────────────────────┘  │
 │                                                             │
 ├─────────────────────────────────┬──────────────────────────┤
 │ ↓ and ↑ move menu pointer.      │ [F1] displays a Help screen. │
 │ [RETURN] selects highlighted choice. │ [F9] takes you to main menu. │
 │ [ESCAPE] takes you to previous screen. │ [F10] shows current selections. │
 └─────────────────────────────────┴──────────────────────────┘
```

Epson

**Figure 1-7.**    Installation screen

you plan to create two or more sets, you can start over with the first-time installation option for each driver. It is important that you use a different name for each driver. After proceeding to the end of the installation process and saving your choices on the System Disk, the PrintGraph Disk, and A View of 1-2-3, you will be back at the main installation menu (Figure 1-4).

At this time you may want to press F10 to view your current selections (you will see something like Figure 1-8), or you may want to alter some of the advanced options such as sort sequences that will control the order that 1-2-3 uses for resequencing information in its data management environment. The only way to access the advanced options is to select

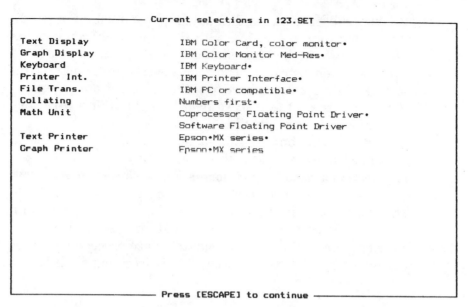

```
 ┌──────────── Current selections in 123.SET ────────────┐
 │                                                        │
 │ Text Display         IBM Color Card, color monitor·    │
 │ Graph Display        IBM Color Monitor Med-Res·        │
 │ Keyboard             IBM Keyboard·                     │
 │ Printer Int.         IBM Printer Interface·            │
 │ File Trans.          IBM PC or compatible·             │
 │ Collating            Numbers first·                    │
 │ Math Unit            Coprocessor Floating Point Driver·│
 │                      Software Floating Point Driver    │
 │ Text Printer         Epson·MX series·                  │
 │ Graph Printer        Epson·MX series                   │
 │                                                        │
 │                                                        │
 │                                                        │
 │                                                        │
 │                                                        │
 │                                                        │
 └──────────── Press [ESCAPE] to continue ───────────────┘
```

**Figure 1-8.**     Current installation selections

Modify Current Driver Set from the Advanced Options menu. This will be covered in the "Modifying the Current Driver" section later in the chapter. You have the option of placing numbers first or last in the sort sequence with one of the advanced installation options.

## Installing With a Hard Disk

Installing with a hard disk is actually a little easier than installation with a floppy disk system. You will not have to make separate backup copies of the Lotus disks because you will be copying them to your hard disk and can therefore use your original diskettes as backups. This eliminates the formatting step to prepare the diskettes and expedites the installation program, since you will not have to interchange disks in your drives. Everything that Install needs will already be on your hard drive.

You will have one additional step, establishing a subdirectory for your 1-2-3 files, with this approach. Subdirectories provide a method for establishing different categories of information on your disk. They can save a significant amount of time, since 1-2-3 will have to search through only a section of the entries on the disk rather than through a directory with an entry for every file.

Our instructions for this section assume that DOS is on your hard drive and that you are using release 2 of 1-2-3. This section also contains information on the optional removal of the System Disk from the startup procedure for 1-2-3. This disk must normally be inserted in drive A even though you have copied the data to your hard disk. 1-2-3 checks the authorization code from the diskette before proceeding unless you take a special step to prevent this from happening.

### Establishing a Subdirectory

The preliminary steps for a hard disk installation will proceed quickly. You need only set up your 1-2-3 subdirectory and copy the files to the hard disk.

1. Start DOS in your system by booting with the door to drive A open. This will force your system to boot from the copy of DOS stored on your hard disk, drive C.

2. Enter the date if you do not have a clock card. The format you should use is 12-15-86 for a date of December 15, 1986. Press ENTER after supplying the date.

3. Enter the time in the form HH:MM. If the time is 1:30 P.M., for example, type **13:30** and press ENTER. If there is a clock card in your system, you do not have to enter the time.

Now establish the subdirectory that will contain all your 1-2-3 files. For our example we will use a subdirectory name of 123, but the choice of a name is up to you.

1. At C>, the DOS prompt, type **MD \123** to make a subdirectory called 123. This directory will be immediately below the root directory for your disk.

2. Make 123 the current directory by typing **CD \123.**

You now have a directory to which you can copy all your 1-2-3 files. This is a real convenience, since it will save you from having to swap disks as you transfer from 1-2 3 to PrintGraph to Translate.

1. Place your 1-2-3 System Disk in drive A and close the door.

2. Type **COPY A:*.* C:.** This will copy every file except the hidden protection to the hard disk. Remove the System Disk from drive A.

3. Repeat this with every disk except the Backup System Disk. When you have completed the process, every file from every disk will reside in the 123 subdirectory.

### Running Install
### With a Hard Disk System

With the DOS C> prompt on your screen, type **Install** and press ENTER. The rest is easy, since all of the installation files you will need are now on your hard disk. With the information from Figure 1-2 handy, type in the information that Install needs.

1. Since this is a first-time installation, select that option from the menu screen presented to you (see Figure 1-4). 1-2-3 will then take you on a guided tour through the entire installation process. Refer to the earlier section on the keyboard if you wish to make selections described at the bottom of the screen and are uncertain of the location of keys on your keyboard.

2. You will be asked to select the monitor and the text and graphics printers in your configuration. Figures 1-5 through 1-7 show several of the selection screens that will be presented to you during installation. Refer to the equipment configuration you listed on your worksheet to supply the correct selections.

3. If you are creating only one set of installation parameters, you will want to save your selections as 123.SET. If you are creating two or more sets, each must have a different name. After proceeding to the end of installation and saving your choices on the System Disk, the Print-Graph Disk, and A View of 1-2-3, you will be back at the main installation menu (Figure 1-4).

At this time you may want to press F10 to view your current selections (you will see something like Figure 1-8), or you may want to alter some of the advanced options such as sort sequences. The only way to access the advanced options is to select Modify Current Driver Set from the Advanced Options menu. This will be covered in the "Modifying the Current Driver" section later in the chapter. You have the option of placing numbers first or last in the sort sequence with one of the advanced installation options.

With Install completed, you are now ready to use 1-2-3. You can display graphs and interface with your printer or plotter. Changing between 1-2-3 programs will be easy, since all the Lotus files are stored on your disk. Since the System Disk contains a key to unlock 1-2-3's features, however, you will still need to insert that disk in drive A every time you load 1-2-3 into your system. Once 1-2-3 is started, you can remove this key disk and use the files on your hard disk. If you would like to eliminate this step, Lotus has provided routines with release 2 to place the key information on your hard disk. There are two separate processes for doing this, depending on whether you are using the AT or another system. The next two sections will provide instructions for completing this task for an IBM AT or other machine.

## Copyon and Copyoff

Copyon and Copyoff are optional programs for adding the key information to your hard disk and taking it off again when working with release 2. This information allows you to start 1-2-3 from your hard disk without having to place the System Disk in drive A. These two programs are not designed to work with the IBM AT. To transfer the key information on that system, use the two programs described in the next section.

The Copyon program takes the key information recorded on the System Disk and places it on your hard drive. You can use Copyon with only one hard disk system at a time. If you wish to use it with another system, you must first use Copyoff to remove the information from the first hard disk. After this process is complete, you can use Copyon with the second system.

You will want to take precautions to ensure that the key information is not damaged once it is placed on your hard disk. Use the DOS command RESTORE /P for file restoration. The /P option causes DOS to prompt you before restoring files that were changed since the last backup and to wait for your confirmation before restoring a file. When you restore files from a backup, you must tell DOS that you do not wish to restore read-only files. Since this key information is in a read-only file, it will remain unaffected. Also, if you ever need to reformat your hard disk, remove the key information first with either Copyoff or Copyhard /U. Note that Copyon and Copyhard cannot be used if your device is a server in a local area network.

Copyon and Copyoff expect your hard disk to be drive C. Start with the C> prompt on your screen.


1. Make 123 the current directory by typing **CD \123** and pressing ENTER. Of course, if you used a different directory name for your 1-2-3 files, you will want to make that directory current instead.

2. Remove the write protect tabs from the PrintGraph Disk and the System Disk.

3. Place PrintGraph in drive A.

4. Type **A:** and press ENTER. Drive A will now be the current drive.

5. Type **Copyon** and press ENTER. Review the screen message as a reminder that your disk should be drive C.

6. You can press any key to continue or CTRL-C to stop.

7. Remove PrintGraph from drive A at the prompt.

8. Place the System Disk in drive A, close the drive door, and press ENTER. A message will ask you if you wish to copy the protected information to the hard disk, and you can respond with **Y** for yes. Messages will appear, indicating that both the key information and the serial number have been copied to your hard disk. If you had typed **N**, Copyon would have stopped and a DOS prompt would have appeared on your screen.

Copyoff allows you to remove the key information from your hard disk temporarily or permanently. The procedure for removing this key information is as follows:

1. Start with the C> prompt on your screen.

2. Make 123 your current directory with CD \123. If you used a different directory for 123, use the name of the other directory.

3. Remove the write protect tabs from the System Disk and the PrintGraph Disk.

4. Place the PrintGraph Disk in drive A.

5. Make drive A the current drive by typing **A:** and pressing ENTER.

6. Type **Copyoff** and press ENTER.

7. Press any key to continue or CTRL-C to stop.

8. If you chose to continue, remove PrintGraph when prompted. Insert the System Disk in drive A and press ENTER.

9. Type **Y** and press ENTER to continue or **N** and ENTER to stop.

When Copyoff finishes, a message on your screen will inform you that the key information has been removed from your hard disk. You can now use Copyon to place the information on a new hard disk.

## Copyhard and Copyhard /U

Copyhard is used for systems where the hard drive has a designation other than drive C. If you use Copyhard on your IBM AT, you will want to run it from your low-capacity disk drive (360K). If you remove the key information with Copyhard /U using the 1.2MB high-density drive, you will not be able to access that information later from a low-capacity drive.

The steps required for adding the key information to a hard disk with Copyhard are as follows:

1. Make sure your hard disk prompt (D>, for example) is on the screen.

2. Make your 1-2-3 directory the current directory; that is, type **CD \123** and press ENTER if your directory name is 123.

3. Remove the write protect tabs from PrintGraph and the System Disk and place the PrintGraph Disk in drive A.

4. Type **A:** as the current drive unless you are using an AT and B is your low-capacity drive. In the latter case, type **B:**. Press ENTER after your entry.

5. Type **Copyhard** and press ENTER to access the program.

6. Type the same disk drive letter that you used in step 4.

7. Type the letter for your hard disk drive, for example, **D:**.

8. Remove the PrintGraph Disk from the drive specified in step 6, insert the System Disk, and press ENTER.

9. Type **Y** and press ENTER to proceed. If you want to stop, type **N** and ENTER.

The Copyhard program will now have copied the key code to your hard disk. You will not need to insert the diskette when starting 1-2-3 as long as the code remains on your hard disk.

Before you can use Copyhard on a second hard disk, you must remove the key code from the first hard disk with the Copyhard /U option. In addition to removing the code from the hard disk, this program flags your disks so they can be used to place the key code on another hard disk. Here are the steps required for this program:

1. Ensure that your hard disk prompt (D>, for example) is on the screen.

2. Type **CD \123** and press ENTER to change the current directory.

3. Remove the write protect tabs from your System Disk and PrintGraph Disk, then insert PrintGraph in drive A (or drive B, the low-density drive, on an AT).

4. Type the drive letter and a colon, then press ENTER. Use the same drive as in step 3.

5. Type **Copyhard /U** and press ENTER.

6. Enter the drive letter used in step 4 and press ENTER.

7. Type the drive letter for your hard disk (for example, D) and press ENTER.

8. Remove PrintGraph at the prompt and insert the System Disk in the same drive, then press ENTER.

9. Type **Y** and press ENTER to continue. To abort the process, leaving the key information intact, type **N** and press ENTER.

When this step completes, the key information will be removed from your hard disk. This will allow you to use Copy-hard to place it on a new hard disk if you wish.

## Creating More Than One Driver Set

If you are using your Lotus software on more than one computer, or if you frequently alter the configuration of your system, you will want more than one driver set. This will allow you to use 1-2-3 with both your home system and the one at the office, for example, without having to change the installation parameters each time.

If you use more than one driver set, pick a meaningful driver name for each, such as 2MONITOR.SET, PLOTTER.SET, or HOME.SET. You can use up to eight characters for the first part of the name. You must avoid the following symbols: , . ; : / ? * ^ + = < > [ ] \'. You also must use SET as the extension for the file name after the dot (.)—for example, COLOR.SET.

Use the first-time installation option to create each driver set. Save each driver set under a different name. You may want to store these multiple drivers on a separate disk, as there will not be room on your Lotus disks for more than one or two driver sets. In this case, when you are prompted to insert your System Disk to save the newly created driver set, insert a blank disk instead. Then return to the Installation menu rather than inserting PrintGraph and the other disks.

To use one of your other driver sets, copy it to the 1-2-3 disk before starting the program. Another option is to specify the pathname of the driver set: 123 B:\HOME.SET, for example. The pathname is the drive designation followed by the directory and file name. On a floppy disk without subdirectories, simply give the drive designation and the file name separated by a backslash ( \ ), for example, B:\HOME.SET.

## Modifying the Current Driver

Install has two kinds of options for modifying the 1-2-3 driver files. They are the Modify option and the Advanced options. Modify allows you to change the hardware configuration for your existing driver set. It is the option to use if you have upgraded your hardware with a new printer or a plotter, for example, and wish to make a permanent change in your driver set.

The Advanced options allow you to change the collating sequence for the existing driver set. With earlier releases you had no choice about the collating sequence, since standard ASCII sequence was used for sorting. However, release 2 provides three options: Numbers First, Numbers Last, and the standard ASCII sequence. If you are not familiar with sorting sequences, look at the 1-2-3 help screen shown in Figure 1-9 for a sample of the three options. The Advanced options also offer choices such as making another driver set current and adding new drivers. To make a change to a feature like the collating sequence, select Advanced Options from the menu and then select Modify Current Set from the second-level menu.

## Changing Other Configuration Parameters

Most of the hardware configuration options are specified in the installation process. However, two additional options that could require frequent change can be changed directly from 1-2-3. One is the disk drive assignment for data files, and the other is the printer settings. The disk drive assignment can be changed from the default drive of B to A or C. The command to do this within 1-2-3 is /Worksheet Global Default Disk. Printer options can be changed with /Worksheet Global Default Printer.

```
┌─────────────────────── Help Screen ───────────────────────┐
│                                                            │
│  The collating sequence determines the order in which 1-2-3 sorts entries  │
│  that include both numbers and letters.  Here are the results of a sort in  │
│  ascending order, depending on which collating sequence you choose:  │
│                                                            │
│                                                            │
│    Numbers first          Numbers last          ASCII      │
│    -------------          ------------          -----      │
│                                                            │
│    22 Rye Road            One emerald city      22 Rye Road │
│    23 Chestnut Avenue     One Emerson Place      23 Chestnut Avenue │
│    39 Columbus Street     Parkway Towers         39 Columbus Street │
│    One emerald city       Three Center Plaza     One Emerson Place │
│    One Emerson Place      22 Rye Road            One emerald city │
│    Parkway Towers         23 Chestnut Avenue     Parkway Towers │
│    Three Center Plaza     39 Columbus Street     Three Center Plaza │
│                                                            │
│  Note that ASCII is identical to Numbers first, except that uppercase letters │
│  come before lowercase.  Earlier releases of 1-2-3 use the ASCII collating  │
│  sequence.                                                  │
│                                                            │
└─────────────────── Press [ESCAPE] to leave Help ──────────┘
```

**Figure 1-9.**    1-2-3 help screen for collating sequences

## Preparing Data Disks

Whether you have Lotus on a hard or a floppy disk system, you can use diskettes for data storage. They will need to be prepared before you can store data on them. Use the formatting process described in your DOS manual under FORMAT before storing data on new diskettes. Since you already have an extra diskette prepared, you can wait to prepare additional data diskettes if you choose.

# The Access System, Display, And Keyboard

**The Lotus Access System**
**The Display**
**The Keyboard**

This chapter will cover the Lotus Access System, your entry into everything 1-2-3 has to offer. It will also take a look at the screen display and the keyboard in some detail. Although this chapter will not require you to type any 1-2-3 commands, you should become comfortable with the keyboard and the information provided by 1-2-3's display as soon as possible. They are designed to assist you in your work with the package.

The Lotus Access System is found on the System Disk. It ties together all the different programs in the 1-2-3 system. The main menu for the Access System is shown in Figure 2-1.

Since you cannot copy DOS to any of the 1-2-3 disks with release 2, you will have to load DOS before accessing any of the 1-2-3 programs. You can then access any program directly, or you can key in **Lotus** to load the Access System. From the Access System you can select 1-2-3, PrintGraph, Translate, Install, View, or Exit. If you wish to use a driver set other than 123.SET, you will need to specify the set name. If you wanted to use a driver set called OFFICE.SET, for example, you would type **Lotus Office** and then press ENTER. Using the Access System makes it easy to transfer from program to program, since you will be returned to the

```
┌──────────────────────────────────────────────────────────────────────┐
│ 1-2-3  PrintGraph  Translate  Install  View  Exit                      │
│ Enter 1-2-3 -- Lotus Worksheet/Graphics/Database program               │
└──────────────────────────────────────────────────────────────────────┘

┌──────────────────────────────────────────────────────────────────────┐
│                       1-2-3 Access System                              │
│                  Lotus Development Corporation                         │
│                        Copyright 1985                                  │
│                       All Rights Reserved                              │
│                          Release 2                                     │
│                                                                        │
│ The Access System lets you choose 1-2-3, PrintGraph, the Translate     │
│ utility, the Install program, and A View of 1-2-3 from the menu at     │
│ the top of this screen.  If you're using a diskette system, the        │
│ Access System may prompt you to change disks.  Follow the              │
│ instructions below to start a program.                                 │
│                                                                        │
│ o  Use [RIGHT] or [LEFT] to move the menu pointer (the highlight bar   │
│    at the top of the screen) to the program you want to use.           │
│                                                                        │
│ o  Press [RETURN] to start the program.                                │
│                                                                        │
│ You can also start a program by typing the first letter of the menu    │
│ choice.  Press [HELP] for more information.                            │
└──────────────────────────────────────────────────────────────────────┘
```

**Figure 2-1.**     Access menu

Access System after working with each program. On a floppy disk system you will have to place the proper diskette in the drive to access each of the various programs, but on a hard disk you can copy all the programs to the hard disk, as explained in Chapter 1.

Now let's review briefly each of the choices on the Access System menu. Most of the attention in this book will focus on the 1-2-3 option, since that is the main part of the package, but the PrintGraph and Translate programs will also receive additional coverage later in the book.

## 1-2-3

1-2-3 is the main option on the Access System menu for all releases of the package. You can enter it from that menu or by typing 123 from DOS. This latter approach will save a little memory, since the Access System routines will not then have to be loaded into memory.

However you elect to load 1-2-3 into memory, you will have to have DOS active in the system before you begin. To fully utilize the power of the package you will want to respond to the DOS date and time prompts with the correct information, unless you have a clock card in your system. With release 2, you can both date and time stamp your worksheet with the @NOW function, described in Chapter 7. Earlier releases allow you to date stamp the worksheet with @TODAY.

You can use the menu and features of 1-2-3 to build spreadsheet models, construct databases, and display graphs on your screen through a series of nested menus. Most of the work you do with the package will be done through the 1-2-3 program. The other Access System features are designed to handle more specialized needs, such as data translation and graphics printing.

Returning to the Access System after working with 1-2-3 is easy. Simply type /Q from 1-2-3's main menu to quit. If you initially entered 1-2-3 from the Access System, you will be returned to the Access System menu. If you entered 1-2-3 directly from DOS and have copied the COMMAND.COM file to your 1-2-3 disk or are running 1-2-3 from a hard disk, the DOS prompt, either A> or C>, will appear on your screen.

## Translate

The Translate program permits data interchange between 1-2-3 and other programs by translating files from other programs into a form 1-2-3 can handle. This program is located on the Utility Disk, so if you are working with diskettes, you will have to insert this disk after requesting Translate from the Access System menu. The Access System will provide a prompt message requesting you to insert the proper disk. If you want to access Translate directly from either a floppy or a hard disk, type **TRANS**. On a floppy disk system, insert the Utility Disk before pressing ENTER.

Once Translate is loaded, you will be presented with the menu shown in Figure 2-2. This menu will allow you to

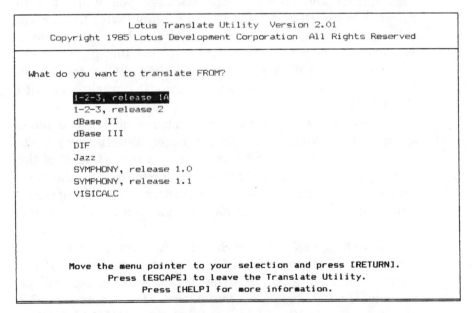

```
                  Lotus Translate Utility  Version 2.01
      Copyright 1985 Lotus Development Corporation  All Rights Reserved

  What do you want to translate FROM?

          1-2-3, release 1A
          1-2-3, release 2
          dBase II
          dBase III
          DIF
          Jazz
          SYMPHONY, release 1.0
          SYMPHONY, release 1.1
          VISICALC




          Move the menu pointer to your selection and press [RETURN].
              Press [ESCAPE] to leave the Translate Utility.
                  Press [HELP] for more information.
```

**Figure 2-2.**    Translate menu

translate from one of the Lotus formats to such formats as DIF, Symphony, or dBASE III or to translate from one of the other formats to a specific Lotus format.

The process has been made very simple with the release 2 version of Translate. If you select DIF (Data Interchange Format) from the first menu, for example, the menu shown in Figure 2-3 will appear. Select the format you wish the DIF file converted to, and the program will take the information in the DIF file and create a second copy of it in the form you specified. This option is useful if you have data from other programs like VisiCalc that occur in DIF or other formats that 1-2-3 can translate. Translate is discussed further in Chapter 8.

## PrintGraph

The PrintGraph program provides a comprehensive range of options for printing or plotting your graphs. Its many menu

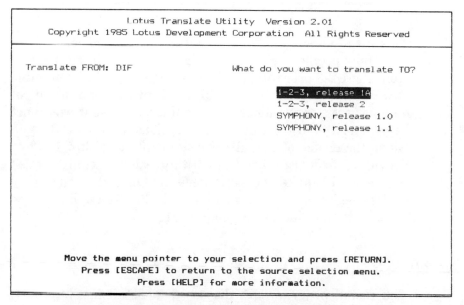

**Figure 2-3.**    Selecting a conversion format

selections provide a tremendous amount of flexibility in the final printing.

You can access PrintGraph from the Access System menu by pointing to that selection and pressing ENTER. On a floppy disk system you will be prompted to place the PrintGraph Disk in the drive. You can also access PrintGraph directly from a hard or floppy disk by typing **PGRAPH** and pressing ENTER. With a floppy disk system you should place the PrintGraph Disk in the drive before pressing ENTER.

Like other components of 1-2-3, PrintGraph has a nested menu structure. The first menu looks like this:

If you select Settings from this menu, you will then be presented with a menu like this:

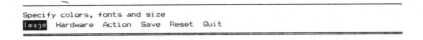

This menu allows you to further refine your choice.

Many people wish that graphs could be printed directly from the 1-2-3 program. Such convenience would be possible only at the expense of flexibility. Providing an array of options uses a tremendous amount of memory, so it would not be practical to provide all of these options within 1-2-3 itself. Given the choice of including basic printing within 1-2-3 or providing a separate program with greater flexibility, most people would make the same decision Lotus did, once they understood the trade-offs involved. PrintGraph will be covered in more detail in Chapter 11.

## Install

The Install program was discussed in detail in Chapter 1. You can enter the program from the Access System menu by selecting Install. Since the Install program is located on the Utility Disk, you will be requested to insert this disk if you are using a floppy drive system. If you wish, you can enter Install without the Access System by typing **Install**, but with a floppy drive system you should place the Utility Disk in your drive first.

## View

A View of 1-2-3 is new with release 2. It replaces the Tutorial Disk from release 1A and provides a much more comprehensive introduction to the package. You can access this on-screen tutorial through the Access System by selecting View, or you ^an enter View directly. The View programs are on the disk A View of 1-2-3, which must be inserted on a floppy drive system.

View's main menu is shown in Figure 2-4. This tutorial has three sections. Two are oriented toward new 1-2-3 users,

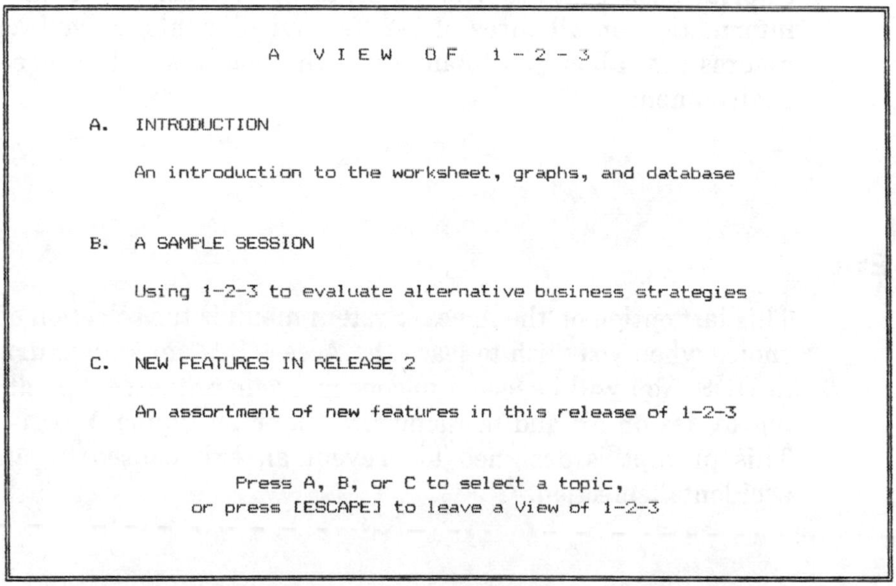

```
                    A   VIEW   OF   1 - 2 - 3


   A.   INTRODUCTION

        An introduction to the worksheet, graphs, and database


   B.   A SAMPLE SESSION

        Using 1-2-3 to evaluate alternative business strategies


   C.   NEW FEATURES IN RELEASE 2

        An assortment of new features in this release of 1-2-3


              Press A, B, or C to select a topic,
        or press [ESCAPE] to leave a View of 1-2-3
```

**Figure 2-4.**    A View of 1-2-3 selections

and the third, for experienced users, highlights the differences between release 1A and release 2.

Both sections for new users provide information on all three of 1-2-3's environments. The first section, a general introduction to the package features, requires from 45 minutes to an hour to complete. The second section provides a business application and introduces the new user to some of 1-2-3's features by establishing business strategies for a fictitious company called Better Mousetraps. It takes approximately an hour to complete. The last option in A View of 1-2-3 provides a transition from release 1A to release 2 and highlights some of the new applications for release 2.

A View of 1-2-3 can be accessed by placing the disk in the drive or on your hard drive, typing **View**, and pressing ENTER. Later in this chapter you will see that it can be accessed in another way as well.

With release 1A of 1-2-3, the tutorial was a disk containing a number of lessons on 1-2-3's features. As noted, this is handled by A View of 1-2-3 with release 2. Release 2 also has a tutorial in book form. It is designed to be used after you have mastered the basic concepts on the View disk. The tutorial book contains over 20 separate lessons. It provides information on all three of 1-2-3's environments as well as macros that allow you to automate the features of the three environments.

## Exit

This last option on the Access System menu is the selection of choice when you wish to leave the Access System and return to DOS. You will be asked to confirm your request by pointing to Yes or No and pressing ENTER or by typing **Y** or **N**. This prompt is designed to prevent an exit caused by an accidental selection.

1-2-3's display is divided into three areas: a control panel at the top of the screen, a worksheet area in the middle, and an area at the bottom that displays error messages and descriptions. Under release 2, this bottom area also displays the date and time. A border containing the column names separates the control panel from the worksheet portion of the display, and the date area appears at the bottom of the screen below the display of the last row number. Figure 2-5 shows a screen display with all three of the areas labeled.

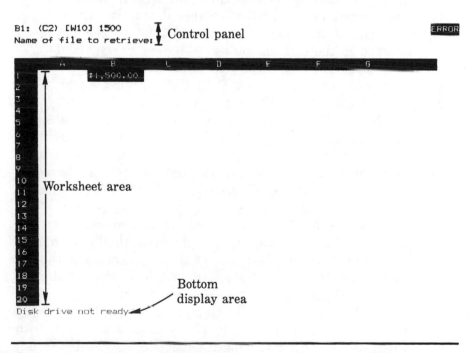

**Figure 2-5.**    Screen display

## The Control Panel

Each of the three lines in the control panel area has a specific purpose. The second and third lines will be discussed under "The Menu," later in this chapter. The top line provides the greatest number of individual pieces of information. At the far left corner you will find the current location of the cursor, that is, the highlighted bar visible on the worksheet. In Figure 2-5 the cursor is in cell B1 or the intersection of column B and row 1, so this location reads B1.

Immediately to the right of the cursor location, in parentheses, you will see any special display attributes assigned to the cell. 1-2-3 allows you to display numbers as currency, percents, and other special formats. Each assigned format has a special code representing the format, such as C for currency, and this code will appear in the control panel for a cell that has had a special format assigned to it. In our example, a format of currency with two decimal places has been assigned to the cell, so you see (C2). The C represents currency and the 2 shows the number of decimal places. Other commonly used formats are F for fixed, P for percent, G for general, T for text, and , for comma.

Release 2 also provides information on the protection status of a cell and the cell width if a width different from the default has been assigned to the column the cell is in. These features are also represented by special character codes, which will be discussed in Chapter 4. The codes appear in brackets.

To the right of the format code is the content of the cell as it was entered. Suppose, for example, that you entered 514.76. If you are displaying the entry as currency with zero decimal places, you will see $515 on the worksheet, but in this location you will see your original entry.

On the top line at the far right, in a highlighted area, you will find the mode indicator. This indicator tells you both what 1-2-3 is doing and what it expects from you. It can tell you to wait, correct an error, point to a worksheet location, or tell 1-2-3 what to do next.

Table 2-1 lists the indicators and their meanings. For example, as soon as you begin a cell entry by typing a

| Indicator | Meaning |
|---|---|
| EDIT | Cell entry is being edited. EDIT can be generated by 1-2-3 when your entry contains an error and 1-2-3 wants you to edit it. It can also be generated by pressing the F2 (EDIT) key to change a cell entry. |
| ERROR | 1-2-3 has encountered an error. The problem will be noted in the lower left corner of the screen. Press ESC to clear the error message and correct the problem specified in the error message at the bottom of the screen. |
| FILES | 1-2-3 wants you to select a file name to proceed. This message is also shown when you request a list of files on your disk with /File List. |
| FIND | The /Data Query command is active. |
| HELP | A help display is active. |
| LABEL | 1-2-3 has decided that you are making a label entry. |
| MENU | 1-2-3 is waiting for you to make a menu selection. |
| NAMES | 1-2-3 is displaying a menu of range or graph names. |
| POINT | 1-2-3 is waiting for you to point to a cell or range. As soon as you begin to type, POINT mode will change to EDIT mode. |
| READY | 1-2-3 is currently idle and is waiting for you to make a new request. |
| STAT | Worksheet status information is being displayed. |
| VALUE | 1-2-3 has decided that you are making a value entry. |
| WAIT | 1-2-3 is processing your last command and cannot begin a new task until the flashing WAIT indicator changes to READY. |

Table 2-1.    Mode Indicators

number, 1-2-3's mode indicator changes from READY to VALUE. Once 1-2-3 is in a certain mode, you have to either follow along with its plans or find a way to change the indicator. Many of a new user's frustrations come from not understanding and watching the mode indicator. In order to maintain a smooth working relationship with 1-2-3, you must stay in sync with 1-2-3's mode indicators.

## The Worksheet

The worksheet occupies most of your display screen. This display serves as a window to your overall worksheet and allows you to look at any section you choose.

The worksheet has an orderly arrangement of rows and columns. The row numbers and column letters appear on the display in Figure 2-6. Later you will learn about an option that eliminates the headings and gridlines from the display if they are not appropriate for your application.

Every entry you make on the worksheet will be in a specific cell address. These entries will be numbers, labels, and formulas. You will learn more about the specific worksheet options in Chapter 3.

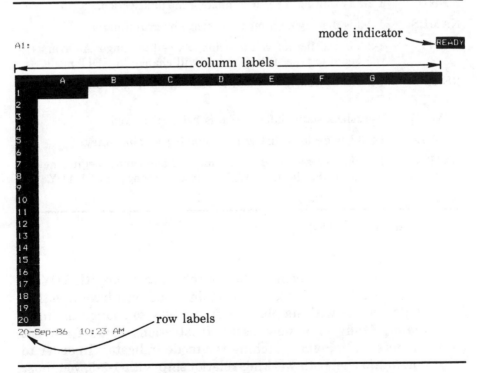

**Figure 2-6.** Worksheet display

## The Bottom Display Area

The date and time display at the bottom of your screen is constantly updated as your screen is refreshed. This display is temporarily suppressed to display error messages such as Disk Full, Printer Not Ready, or Disk Not Ready. Whenever an error message is displayed at the bottom of your screen, the Mode Indicator at the top right corner will also say ERROR. To proceed, you will have to hit ESC to eliminate the error message and the ERROR indicator.

Descriptions in this bottom area also let you know when certain keys have been depressed or certain other settings for the package are in use. The five key indicators and their meanings are

CAPS     This indicator will light up at the bottom when the CAPS LOCK key is depressed. When the CAPS indicator is on, the alphabetic keys will produce capital letters.

END     This indicates that the END key was pressed and 1-2-3 is waiting for you to press a direction arrow key.

NUM     This indicates the NUM LOCK was pressed. This key allows you to enter a number from the numeric keypad.

SCROLL     This indicator means that the SCROLL LOCK key was pressed, which affects the way information scrolls off your screen. SCROLL LOCK toggles the effect of the arrow keys between moving one row or column in any direction and shifting the entire screen one row or column in the direction of the arrow. When the SCROLL indicator is on, the entire window will shift when the arrow keys are pressed.

STEP     This indicates that the step mode is in effect for macro execution. This mode is activated by pressing ALT+F2. STEP is discussed further in Chapter 12.

Four additional indicators have a broader meaning than one key being pressed. These indicators and their meanings are as follows:

CALC      This indicates that the worksheet needs to be recalculated. In other words, changes have been made to the data that are not yet recalculated in the screen display. You will see this indicator only when recalculation is set to manual. In the automatic mode, the entire worksheet is recalculated as soon as a change is made.

CIRC      This indicates that the worksheet contains a circular reference, that is, a cell that refers back to itself. Release 2 provides special help to locate the defective entry with the /Worksheet Status command.

CMD      This indicator appears during the execution of a macro.

SST      This is the macro indicator that appears during single-step execution for a macro. The STEP indicator will change to SST when the execution of a macro begins. SST is discussed further in Chapter 12.

## Help Features

You can change your screen to an on-line reference source at will. All you have to do is press the F1 (HELP) key. 1-2-3 will guess at what your question might be and supply information based on your current task. If you want additional help or help with a different area than what was displayed, you can use the help index or ask for one of the other topics listed at the bottom of the help screen. If you are using a floppy based system and have removed the System Disk after loading 1-2-3, you will not have access to the help features.

Figure 2-7 presents the help that 1-2-3 provides for

```
C4:                                                              [HELP]
+C2-
```

---

VALUE Mode

You can enter either a number or a formula. These keys have special meanings:

```
[ESCAPE]      Cancels entry and returns to READY mode.
[BACKSPACE]   Erases character preceding cursor.
[DELETE]      Erases character at cursor.
[RETURN]      Completes the entry. 1-2-3 stores the number or formula
              in the current cell, recalculates all formulas (if the
              Recalculation setting is Automatic), and returns to READY mode.
[EDIT]        Switches to EDIT mode. Pressing it again returns you to VALUE mode.
[ABS]         Switches an address among Absolute, Mixed, and Relative.  Use only
              when highlighting to a cell or range while writing a formula.
[CALC]        Converts a formula to its current value.
Pointer-Movement Keys    Complete the entry and move the pointer.
```

---

Erasing Entries              Pointing to Ranges
Formulas                     Help Index


20-Sep-86  10:37 AM

---

**Figure 2-7.**    Help screen


entering a formula in a cell. Figure 2-8 shows the comprehensive list of topics that 1-2-3 can provide help with.


## The Menu

Lines 2 and 3 of the control panel can be transformed into a
menu of command selections by pressing the slash key (/).
Figure 2-9 shows the main menu that this produces. Menus
are the backbone of the 1-2-3 program and are your way of
accessing all the features 1-2-3 provides. You can make them
available at will with the slash key, but they will not clutter
the screen when you do not need them.

    1-2-3's menus offer an advantage over some earlier
spreadsheet programs in that they are self-documenting. The

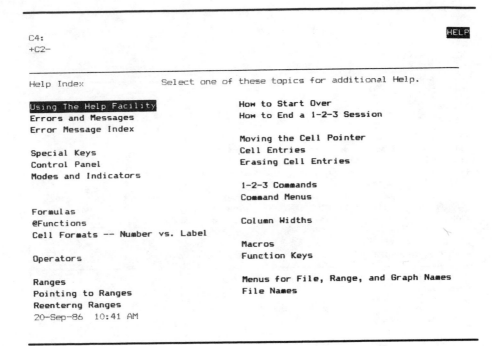

```
C4:                                                         HELP
+C2-

Help Index          Select one of these topics for additional Help.

Using The Help Facility          How to Start Over
Errors and Messages              How to End a 1-2-3 Session
Error Message Index
                                 Moving the Cell Pointer
Special Keys                     Cell Entries
Control Panel                    Erasing Cell Entries
Modes and Indicators
                                 1-2-3 Commands
                                 Command Menus
Formulas
@Functions                       Column Widths
Cell Formats -- Number vs. Label
                                 Macros
Operators                        Function Keys

Ranges                           Menus for File, Range, and Graph Names
Pointing to Ranges               File Names
Reenterng Ranges
20-Sep-86   10:41 AM
```

**Figure 2-8.**    Help topics

line beneath the individual menu options is used for a description of the current menu selection. You can point to different menu items with the cursor movement keys on the keypad. As you move from item to item, the description line will change accordingly. For instance, when you point to the Worksheet option in the menu, the second line will list all the specific worksheet options: Global, Insert, Delete, Column, Erase, Titles, Window, Status, and Page. These are not completely descriptive of the functions provided, but they will serve as reminders once you are exposed to the commands.

To select a menu item you can either type the first letter of the menu item (for example, W for Worksheet) or point to the item with your cursor and press ENTER. Either way will invoke the selected command or present a menu for further selections.

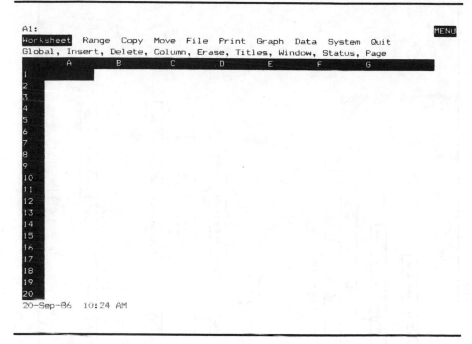

**Figure 2-9.**     Main 1-2-3 menu

Figure 2-10 presents a map of the menu selections available after pressing /**W** (for Worksheet). Each menu level down is selected in the same manner as the first selection, with each level refining your choice further. If you choose a menu item in error, you can back out to the previous level by pressing ESC once. Each time you press ESC, you will back up to the next highest menu level until you are eventually back at READY mode.

## The Keyboard

You will begin using the keyboard in the next chapter as you make entries in spreadsheet cells. This section focuses on the

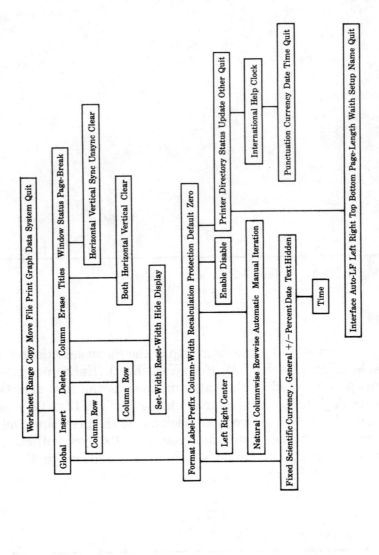

**Figure 2-10.** Map of 1-2-3 commands

® Lotus Development Corporation 1986. Used with permission.

keyboard for the IBM PC. The same keyboard configuration is used for the IBM PC/XT, IBM Portable, and Compaq computers. There are some differences between these and keyboards of other popular systems that work with 1-2-3, as Appendix B shows. These differences will not require changes in the installation of 1-2-3 or limit your use of the program, but they may affect the keys you use to access 1-2-3's features.

All keys will be covered in this chapter in order to provide a single reference source for all keyboard functions. Individual features will be pointed out again in later chapters where they will be helpful, so you do not have to worry about absorbing all of this information now.

The IBM PC keyboard has three basic sections, as shown in Figure 2-11. The highlighted keys to the far left are the function keys. These keys are made available to software developers for whatever purpose they wish to use them, so

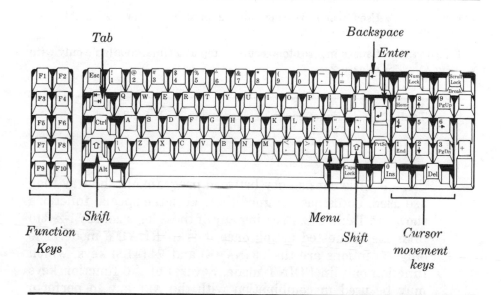

**Figure 2-11.**    Keyboard

| | |
|---|---|
| F1 (HELP) | Provides context-sensitive help. |
| F2 (EDIT) | Allows you to alter the contents of the current cell without reentering all the information. You can add or delete just a few characters if you wish. |
| F3 (NAME) | Displays a list of your range names when you are in POINT mode. When pressed a second time, this key provides a full-screen display of the range name information. |
| F4 (ABS) | Like F3, functions only when you are in POINT mode. Allows you to toggle from a relative address to an absolute or mixed address. |
| F5 (GOTO) | Moves your cursor to the range or address you enter after pressing the key. |
| F6 (WINDOW) | Functions as a toggle switch, moving you into the other window when there are two windows. |
| F7 (QUERY) | Causes 1-2-3 to repeat the last query operation. |
| F8 (TABLE) | Repeats the most recent table operation from the Data menu option. |
| F9 (CALC) | Causes the entire worksheet to be recalculated. Useful when recalculation of the worksheet is set at manual. |
| F10 (GRAPH) | Redraws the most recent graph. |
| ALT+F1 (COMPOSE) | Used when creating international characters. Available only with release 2. |
| ALT+F2 (STEP) | Causes macros to execute a step at a time. Available only with release 2. |

**Table 2-2.**  Function Key Assignments With 1-2-3

there is little consistency between programs in the way they are used. Lotus has assigned these keys the special functions shown in Table 2-2. Pressing any of these keys causes 1-2-3 to take the requested action once it is in READY mode. The only exceptions are the F3 (NAME) and F4 (ABS) keys, which function only in POINT mode. Several of the function keys may be used in combination with the ALT key to perform additional tasks.

The highlighted keys to the far right make up the numeric keypad. Table 2-3 explains where each of these keys will move the cursor. You will notice that keys also have direction arrows and other writing on them. This shows their normal function in 1-2-3 when they are used for cursor movement. If you depress the NUM LOCK key, you can also use these keys for numeric entries. Be careful to press this key only once, though. Like the CAPS LOCK key, it toggles each time it is pressed.

Let's look at a brief example to show the use of these keys. A screen display from 1-2-3 is shown in Figure 2-12. The cursor or highlighted area is found in location C3. The location can be determined by the row and column designators at the side and top of the display or by looking at the left

| | |
|---|---|
| HOME | Moves the cursor to the home position or upper leftmost corner of the spreadsheet. |
| | When in EDIT mode, moves the cursor to the beginning of the entry. |
| Up arrow | Moves the cursor up one cell on the worksheet. |
| Down arrow | Moves the cursor down one cell on the worksheet. |
| Right arrow | Moves the cursor one cell to the right. |
| Left arrow | Moves the cursor one cell to the left. |
| PGUP | Moves the cursor up 20 rows. |
| PGDN | Moves the cursor down 20 rows. |
| END followed by one of the arrow keys | Moves the cursor to the end of your entries in the direction indicated by the arrow key when the cursor is on a cell containing an entry. |
| | When the cursor is on a blank cell, takes the cursor to the next cell in that direction that has an entry. |
| CTRL+right or left arrow | Moves your window into the spreadsheet a full screen to the right or left. |

Table 2-3.    Numeric Keypad Functions

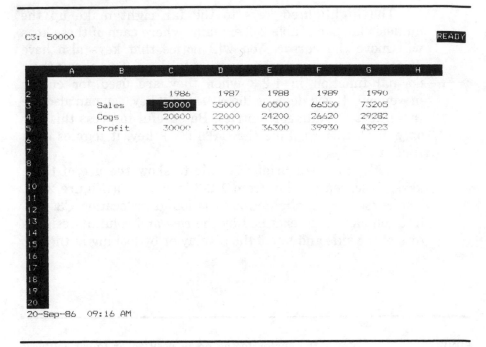

**Figure 2-12.** Screen display

of the control panel. Using the keypad keys will cause the cursor to shift to new locations. The following table shows the new location of the cursor after the listed keys are pressed, assuming the cursor is returned to C3 before each new entry.

| Key Sequence | New Cursor Location |
| --- | --- |
| Left arrow | B3 |
| Right arrow | D3 |
| Up arrow | C2 |
| Down arrow | C4 |
| END followed by down arrow | C5 |
| END followed by up arrow | C2 |
| END followed by right arrow | G3 |
| END followed by left arrow | B3 |

| Key Sequence | New Cursor Location |
|---|---|
| PGUP | C1 (cursor cannot move up 20 rows from its present location) |
| PGDN | C23 |
| HOME | A1 |
| CTRL+right arrow | I3 |
| CTRL+left arrow | Beeps since it cannot scroll screen to the left |

The function of these keys will become clearer in Chapter 3 when we put them to work in a spreadsheet example.

The keys in the center are in most cases identical to the key assignments on a regular typewriter. Table 2-4 lists some of the special keys and additional uses for the regular keys.

| | |
|---|---|
| ESC | Cancels the last request. |
| TAB | Moves the pointer right. SHIFT + TAB moves the pointer left. |
| CTRL | Used only in combination with other keys. |
| CAPS | Causes letter keys to produce capitals. Also called the SHIFT key. |
| ALT | Used only in combination with other keys. |
| BACKSPACE | Deletes the last character entered (destructive backspace). |
| ENTER | Finalizes the last entry made. |
| PRTSC | Used with the CAPS key (SHIFT key) to print current screen. |
| CAPS LOCK | Produces all capitals. Toggles each time it is pressed. This key does not affect the number keys at the top of the keyboard or any of the special symbols at the tops of keys. CAPS must be used to access them. |
| INS | Toggles between insert and overstrike in EDIT mode. |
| NUM LOCK | Toggles numeric keypad between cursor movement and numeric entries. |
| SCROLL LOCK | Toggles scroll display between rolling a line of the display every time an arrow key is pressed and just moving the pointer on a stationary display. |

Table 2-4.    Special Keys

# THREE

# Entering Data
# In 1-2-3's Spreadsheet

**The Spreadsheet**
**Types of Entries**
**Correcting Errors in Entries**
**Ranges**
**Storage Capacity**

**T
H
R
E
E**

Learning how to make entries on 1-2-3's spreadsheet is one of the most important steps in gaining full use of the package's features. Everything you do with 1-2-3 will be dependent upon the entries you make in spreadsheet cells. These entries will be the basis for financial models and projections. They will also be the basis for files used in the data management environment, since data records are nothing more than a special organization of data entered into spreadsheet cells. Furthermore, these entries will be the basis for the graphs you create, because graphs are created by referencing entries in your spreadsheet.

Chapter 2's discussion of the spreadsheet display referred only to the upper left corner of the spreadsheet. The 7 columns and 20 rows you saw there are a very small part of the whole sheet. In its entirety the release 2 worksheet has 256 columns and 8,192 rows. The entire spreadsheet is organized just like the small section you examined.

Since the spreadsheet is a replacement for green-bar columnar pads, it may be interesting to make a size comparison. The space for one entry on a green-bar sheet is about 1 1/8 inches by 1/4 inch. If you multiply this area by the number of cells in the 1-2-3 worksheet, you would find that the equivalent of your electronic sheet would require a piece of green-bar paper over 23 feet wide and 170 feet long! The electronic version is certainly more practical in the space it requires for storage, and it offers the added advantage of automatic recalculation.

1-2-3's spreadsheet has not always been this large. Release 1A had only 2,048 rows. Even if you are using release 1A, however, you still have a sizable area for performing calculations or storing data.

Figure 3-1 shows the layout of the electronic worksheet. You can use the screen as a window into any part of the worksheet you wish to see. You can make entries in any of the cells, within the memory limitations of your system. Each cell can only contain one entry at a time, however. If you make a second entry in a cell that already contains information, the existing information will be replaced by the new information.

## Types of Entries

1-2-3 categorizes entries as either label entries or value entries. *Label entries* contain at least one text character. Examples include Accounting, Sales, John Smith, 111 Simmons Lane, and 456T78. Even the last example, which is

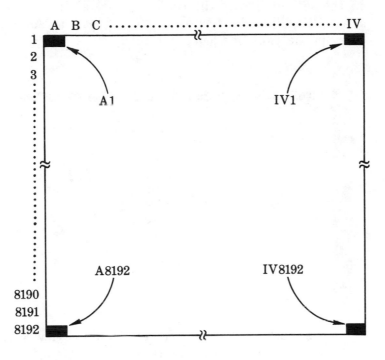

**Figure 3-1.** Spreadsheet layout

mostly composed of numbers, has one character and there-fore would be categorized as a label entry. Label entries cannot be used in arithmetic operations. *Value entries*, on the other hand, are either numbers or formulas. Most value entries can be used in arithmetic operations.

1-2-3 determines the type of entry for a particular cell by reading the first character you type in the cell. Once 1-2-3 determines the entry type, the only way you can change its mind is by either pressing ESC and starting a new entry in the cell or editing the cell to remove or add a label indicator. A *label indicator* is a single character that appears at the front of each label entry and tells 1-2-3 how to display the entry in the cell. You can enter a label indicator or have 1-2-3 generate one for you.

As you make an entry into a cell, 1-2-3 displays the entry on the second line of the control panel at the top of your screen. This line is referred to as the Edit line. An example entry in the Edit line looks like this.

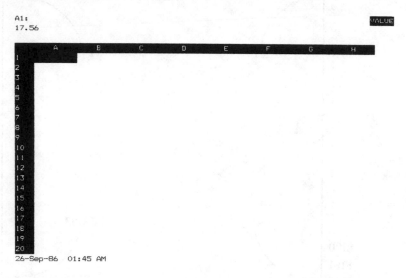

Once you have finished your entry and reviewed its contents in the Edit line, you can finalize it by pressing ENTER or by moving to a new cell with one of the cursor movement keys. This causes the entry to appear in the worksheet cell, as shown here.

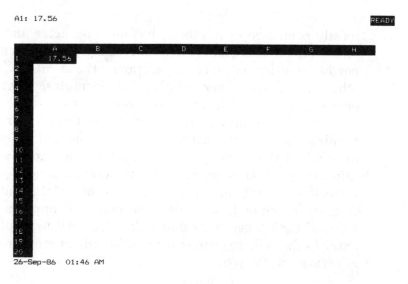

When the entry is a formula, the results of the formula's calculation will appear on the worksheet. For example, if cell A1 contains 10 and A2 contains 5, entering the formula +A1/A2 in cell A3 will cause a 2 to appear in A3 on the worksheet. Otherwise, the entry will appear as entered, except that the current format option will be applied. For example, if you enter .4 and the format is Percent, your entry will display as 40% in the cell. The entry will appear in the top line of the control panel exactly as you typed it, however.

## Label Entries

You will use label entries whenever you want to enter text or character data into a spreadsheet cell. They can contain descriptive information as well as character data. Some of the key rules concerning label entries are summarized in the box called "Rules for Labels."

Labels can be up to 240 characters in length. 1-2-3 will display as much of the label as possible in the cell you use for

---

### Rules for Labels

Labels cannot be longer than 240 characters.

An entry is automatically recognized as a label if the first character is an alphabetic character or any character other than 0 through 9 or any of the following: ./+ − $ ( @ #.

Any entry that contains alphabet letters or editing characters is considered a label, even if it also contains numbers. When a label begins with a numeric digit or symbol, a label indicator must be typed before the label.

Labels longer than the cell width will borrow display space from cells to the right if those cells are empty.

---

the entry. If the label is longer than your cell width and the cells to the right are empty, 1-2-3 will borrow space from them to permit the complete display of the label. If the adjacent cell is not empty, 1-2-3 will truncate the display at the number of characters that will fit. The extra characters are not lost; they are stored internally and will be displayed if the cell is widened or the contents of cells to the right are erased.

As descriptive information, a label might be a report heading containing the company name placed in a cell near the top of the spreadsheet. Labels can also be column headings indicating the months of the year, row headings indicating account names, or descriptors placed anywhere on the worksheet.

Label entries can also record text data anywhere on the worksheet. Part numbers, employee names, sales territories, and warehouse locations are all examples of data containing text characters. A worksheet to project salaries might contain employee names as label entries. Worksheets that deal with suppliers, inventory items, product sales projections, and client accounts are all likely to have some label entries.

If a label begins with a number, you must enter a label indicator before you type the first number in the label entry, since 1-2-3 determines the type of an entry by the first character entered in a cell. If you type a text character in the cell, 1-2-3 will automatically generate a label indicator for the entry. However it is generated, the label indicator will appear in the top line of the control panel but will not show in the worksheet cell. Only the effects of the indicator appear on the worksheet.

You can also use label indicators to control placement of an entry in a cell. 1-2-3 provides three label indicators for this purpose, as the box called "Label Indicators" shows. The single quotation mark is the default label indicator, that is, the one 1-2-3 generates for you when you enter character data. It causes an entry to be left justified within the cell. You must type a single quotation mark yourself if your entry

## Label Indicators

1-2-3 provides a default label indicator of ', which will left justify a label. This default can be changed with a menu command (see Chapter 6) or by typing a different indicator at the beginning of the label entry. The label indicators and their effects are as follows:

'   Left justified—the default setting

"   Right justified

^   Center justified

\   Repeat the character that follows until the cell is filled

begins with a number but contains text—for example, '134 Tenth Street or '213-78-6751. (The hyphens in this latter entry count as text.) If you do not enter the label indicator, 1-2-3 will not let you make such an entry in the cell.

The other two label indicators that can be used for entry placement are the double quotation mark (") and the caret (^). The double quotation mark causes label entries to be right justified, while the caret causes entries to be centered within the cell.

Let's look at a few examples of label entries to clarify the differences.

1. The word Sales was entered in B1. As soon as the first character was entered, 1-2-3 changed the READY mode indicator to LABEL. When the entry was completed, the top line of the control panel showed 'Sales, since 1-2-3 generated a single quotation mark. The entry was left justified in the cell and appeared without the quotation mark.

2. ^Sales was typed in B2. The caret (^) caused the entry to be centered in the cell.

3. "Sales was typed in B3. This caused the entry to be right  justified.

In Chapter 6 you will learn how to alter the default label indicator with /Worksheet Global Default Label-Prefix. For now, though, if you want something other than left justification, enter the appropriate label indicator before you start typing your entry.

One additional label indicator, the backslash (\), has the special function of causing the character that follows it to be repeated until the entire cell is filled with this character. For example, entering \- will fill the cell with -'s. Figure 3-2 shows how \* has been used to enter asterisks in all the cells

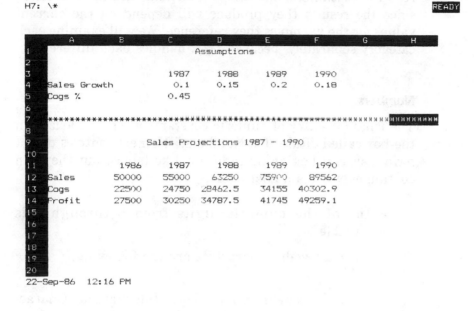

H7: \*                                                          READY

|   | A | B | C | D | E | F | G | H |
|---|---|---|---|---|---|---|---|---|
| 1 | | | | Assumptions | | | | |
| 2 | | | | | | | | |
| 3 | | | 1987 | 1988 | 1989 | 1990 | | |
| 4 | Sales Growth | | 0.1 | 0.15 | 0.2 | 0.18 | | |
| 5 | Cogs % | | 0.45 | | | | | |
| 6 | | | | | | | | |
| 7 | ****************************************************************** | | | | | | | |
| 8 | | | | | | | | |
| 9 | | | Sales Projections 1987 - 1990 | | | | | |
| 10 | | | | | | | | |
| 11 | | 1986 | 1987 | 1988 | 1989 | 1990 | | |
| 12 | Sales | 50000 | 55000 | 63250 | 75900 | 89562 | | |
| 13 | Cogs | 22500 | 24750 | 28462.5 | 34155 | 40302.9 | | |
| 14 | Profit | 27500 | 30250 | 34787.5 | 41745 | 49259.1 | | |
| 15 | | | | | | | | |
| 16 | | | | | | | | |
| 17 | | | | | | | | |
| 18 | | | | | | | | |
| 19 | | | | | | | | |
| 20 | | | | | | | | |

22-Sep-86   12:16 PM

**Figure 3-2.**    Repeating label entry

in one row of the worksheet to serve as a dividing line
between the worksheet assumptions and the calculation section. (You can use any character to create dividing lines.) You
can also use the \ to make multiple characters repeat: \abc
would result in abc being repeated for the width of the cell.

Labels provide readability to a spreadsheet and allow
you to enter text data. Since a spreadsheet is primarily
involved in projections and calculations, however, you clearly
also need a way to deal with numeric entries.

## Value Entries

Value entries are treated as numeric entries by 1-2-3. They
must follow much more rigid rules than label entries. There
are two basic types of value entries: *numbers* and *formulas*.

Like labels, numbers are constants; they do not change as the result of arithmetic operations. Formulas are not constants, since the results they produce will depend on the current values for the variables they reference. We will examine each category separately, because 1-2-3 handles each differently.

## Numbers

The rules for entry of numeric constants are summarized in the box called "Rules for Numbers." Numeric entries do not have a special beginning indicator like labels, but they can contain only certain characters.

- Any of the numeric digits from 0 through 9 is acceptable.

- Other allowable characters are the following: ^ . + − @ $ ( )

- Other characters from the Lotus International Character Set that represent foreign monetary units such as yen, pounds, and guilders can be substituted for the $. The LICS codes for these other currency symbols are found in Appendix C.

- A % can be used to indicate a percentage but cannot begin a numeric entry. It must be placed at the end of the entry.

- Spaces, commas, and other characters cannot be added to a numeric entry, except for the letter E when it is part of a scientific notation entry.

- Alphabetic characters with similar appearance cannot be substituted for numeric digits as they can on a typewriter. Using the lower-case l for a numeric 1 or a lower-case o for a numeric 0 will cause an invalid entry for a value.

**Size**    Numbers can be as large as $10^{99}$ or as small as $10^{-99}$, where the caret symbol (^) represents exponentiation (that is, 10 raised to the 99th power or 10 raised to the

−99th power). Up to 240 characters can be used to represent the numbers.

If you wish, you can use scientific notation to enter large numbers. Scientific notation is just a method of entering a number along with the power of ten that it will be multiplied by. In this format, the letter E (either E or e may be used) separates the number from the positive or negative power of 10 that will be used. This kind of notation offers the advantage of representing very large or very small numbers in a minimum of space. The following examples should help clarify scientific notation:

$9.76E+4 = 97,600$
$6.543e+5 = 654,300$
$6.71E-02 = .0671$
$3.86e-5 = .0000386$

The number that follows E must be between −99 and 99 to conform with the entry size that 1-2-3 allows. Although you cannot exceed this limitation for entries, 1-2-3 can store calculated numbers that are much larger and smaller. The storage limitations are numbers between $10^{-308}$ and $10^{308}$ when the number is the result of calculations.

**Entry**     In one sense, entering numbers is easier than entering labels, since all you do is make your entry using the allowable characters and then press either ENTER or an arrow key. You do not need a special character at the beginning of a numeric entry.

As soon as you type any of the allowable characters, the mode indicator will change from READY to VALUE. Once 1-2-3 has determined that you are entering a value, you must continue entering only allowable characters. If you attempt to finalize an entry containing unallowed characters, 1-2-3 will place you in EDIT mode so that you can make necessary corrections. If you realize your error before trying to finalize the original entry, you can use BACKSPACE to remove the incorrect characters or press ESC to eliminate the entire entry.

Looking at a few numeric entries may clarify the entry process and the way 1-2-3 displays such entries in a cell.

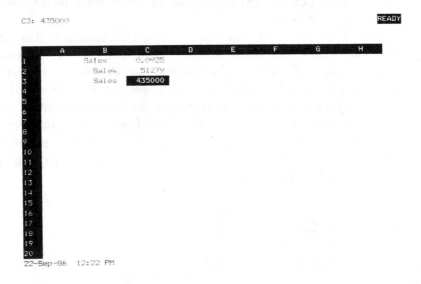

1. With the cursor on C1, .0925 was entered, and the cursor was moved to C2 to finalize the entry.

2. 51279 was entered in C2.

3. 4.35E+05 was entered in C3.

Notice that 1-2-3 converted the third entry to 435000, since the number was not too large for decimal display. The first two entries were displayed just as entered, except that a zero was added in front of the decimal in C1. There is no consistency in the number of decimal places displayed because the General format is in effect. General format is the default format for all new worksheets. In Chapter 4 you will learn how to change the format to cause entries to display as currency, percentages, or with a consistent number of decimal places. In the next section of this chapter you will get a closer look at the display with the General format in effect.

**Display**   The numbers you enter are shown both in the control panel and in the worksheet. They are also stored internally. The form of the numbers may be slightly different in each case. Internally 1-2-3 can store up to 12 decimal digits for an entry. The control panel will display up to 9 of these decimal digits. The display on the worksheet will depend on the format for the cell.

If the General format is in effect, 1-2-3 will display the number as you have entered it if at all possible. If the number is too large, space is not borrowed in the cell to the right for the additional digits, as happened with labels. Instead, 1-2-3 converts the display to scientific notation and displays it that way. If General format were not in effect, 1-2-3 would display the number as a series of asterisks (*********). The default cell width is nine positions, so you can see that long numbers will not fit unless you expand the width of the column. You will learn how to perform that feat in Chapter 4.

The following example shows how 1-2-3 reacts to long numeric entries.

1. .000000000134 was entered in cell C4. The worksheet display changed this to scientific notation and displayed it as 1.3E−10.

2. 9578000000 was entered in C5. 1-2-3 performed another conversion and shows the entry as 9.6E+09 in the cell. The entry appears in its original form in the Contents line.

You have no control over format in the control panel or the internal storage of a number. In both cases 1-2-3 will retain as much accuracy as possible (9 decimal digits maximum for the control panel and 15 for internal storage). You control the accuracy of the number that appears on the worksheet by selecting a format. You will learn how to do this in Chapter 4.


## Formulas

Formulas are the second type of value entry. Unlike number and label entries, they produce variable results depending on the numbers they reference. This ability makes formulas the backbone of spreadsheet features. They allow you to make what-if projections and to look at the impact of changing

1-2-3: The Complete Reference

### Formula Types

1-2-3 provides three types of formulas for your use: arithmetic formulas, logic formulas, and string formulas.

Arithmetic formulas involve constants, cell references, and the arithmetic operators (+ − * / ^). Arithmetic formulas calculate the formula entered and return its result. Examples are +A2*A3 or +Sales−Cogs (where Sales and Cogs are names of cells that contain numerical data).

Logical formulas involve cell references, constants, and comparison operators (<> = <= >= < >). These formulas evaluate the condition listed to determine whether it is true or false. If the condition is false, the formula returns 0; if true, a 1 is returned. An example of a logical formula is +C2<=500.

String formulas are new to release 2. They permit the joining of two or more character strings. The concatenation character (&) can be used to join string variables or constants—for example, +"Sales for the "&"Midwest "&"Region".

Functions provide predefined formulas for a variety of calculations, including mathematical formulas, financial calculations, logical evaluations, statistical computations, and string manipulation. Functions have a unique appearance: They begin with an at sign (@) and contain a list of specific values for arguments within parentheses.

variable values. To produce an updated result with a formula, you do not need to change the formula. Simply change one of the values the formula references, and the entire formula can be recalculated for you.

Early releases of 1-2-3 provided only two types of formulas, arithmetic formulas and logical formulas. Release 2 added string formulas. These formulas are summarized in the box called "Formula Types."

A few rules pertain to all formulas:

• Formulas cannot contain spaces, except for the spaces in range names or string variables.

• The first character of a formula must be one of the following:

+ − ( @ # $ . 0 1 2 3 4 5 6 7 8 9

• Formulas contain special operators to define the operation you wish performed. Operators are assigned priorities in 1-2-3, as shown in the box called "Operation Priorities."

• Formulas can also contain numeric constants or string constants (such as 77 or "sales total"), cell references (such as F4 or Z3), special built-in functions (such as @MIN), or range names (such as total).

**Arithmetic Formulas**     Arithmetic formulas calculate numeric values. These formulas are built with arithmetic operators and references to values in other cells on the worksheet. The value references are either the cell address (such as A1 or Z10) or a name that has been assigned to the cell or cells (such as Cash or Interest). You will learn how to assign range names in Chapter 6. For now, all your formulas will be built with cell addresses.

The arithmetic operators used in 1-2-3 are + for addition, − for subtraction, / for division, * for multiplication, and ^ for exponentiation. An instruction to multiply 3 by 4 would be written as 3*4. These operators are listed in the "Operation Priorities" box. There are some things to keep in mind when entering cell references. If you want to multiply the current contents of C1 by the contents of C2, entering C1*C2 would seem logical. This will not work, however. The problem here is the initial C. As soon as 1-2-3 realizes a C has been entered, it flags the cell as a label entry. It will show the entry as a label on the worksheet rather than giving the result of the formula calculation. To avoid this problem, you

## Operation Priorities

1-2-3 has a variety of operators for arithmetic, logical, and string formulas. Often more than one operator is used in a formula. In this situation it is important to know which operation 1-2-3 will evaluate first. This table provides the priority order for each operation within 1-2-3, with the highest number being the highest priority. If several operators in a formula have the same priority, they will be evaluated from left to right.

| Priority | Operator | Operation Performed |
|----------|----------|---------------------|
| 8 | ( | Parenthesis for grouping |
| 7 | ^ | Exponentiation |
| 6 | + − | Positive and negative indicators |
| 5 | / * | Division and multiplication |
| 4 | + − | Addition and subtraction |
| 3 | = <> < > <br> <= >= | Logical operators |
| 2 | #NOT# | Complex not indicator |
| 1 | #AND# <br> #OR# & | Complex and, complex or, and string operator |

must start the formula with a character that 1-2-3 recognizes as a value entry. The + is the logical choice, since it requires only one additional keystroke and does not alter the formula. Therefore, place a + at the front of all formulas that begin with a cell address. The formula just discussed can be entered as +C1*C2, for example. The example here shows this formula entered in cell D1 on the worksheet.

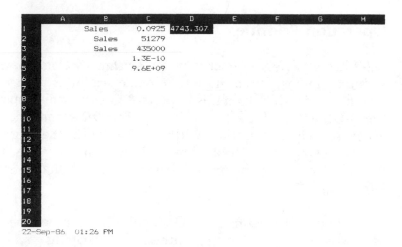

The result of the formula appears on the worksheet, while the formula itself is displayed in the top line of the control panel. Formula results will be displayed on the worksheet automatically unless you change the worksheet format to Text.

Parentheses in arithmetic expressions change the order of operations. For example, 3+4*5 equals 23, but (3+4)*5 equals 35. Otherwise, operators in formulas will be evaluated according to the priority list, proceeding from left to right within the expression if there is more than one operator at the same level. In the first expression, multiplication has a higher priority than addition, so it will be carried out first. This makes the expression 3+20, which is equal to 23. In the second expression, the parentheses take priority. Therefore, 3 will be added to 4 first, making the expression 7*5 or 35.

1-2-3 allows up to 32 sets of parentheses in one expression, so you can use them liberally to override the natural priority order. With nested parentheses, the priority sequence will apply within each set of parentheses. Here is an example of priority order within nested parentheses.

$$4*((1+2)*2)/2+3$$

| | | | | |
|---|---|---|---|---|
| 3rd | | 2nd | | 5th |
| | 1st | | 4th | |

You have learned how to build a formula by typing cell addresses and arithmetic operators. This method will work fine if you are good at remembering the cell addresses you want to use and do not make mistakes in typing. If this is not the case, a second method of formula construction can alleviate both potential problems. This new method lets you point to the cell references you wish to include in the formula and type only the arithmetic operators. After you type an operator, simply move your cursor to the cell whose value you wish included in the formula. The mode indicator changes from VALUE to POINT as you move your cursor. To finalize the selection of the cell reference, either type the next operator or, if you have reached the end of the formula, press ENTER. If you type another operator, the cursor returns to the formula's entry cell and 1-2-3 then waits for you to move your cursor to a new location.

Here is a sample worksheet that was developed using this method:

To produce this example, .0925 was entered in C1, and 51279 was entered in C2. The cursor was then moved to D1 and a + was typed. After the operator was typed, the cursor was moved to C1, putting 1-2-3 in POINT mode. An asterisk for multiplication was then typed, causing the cursor to return to D1. With 1-2-3 still in POINT mode, the left and down arrow keys were used to move to C2. Finally, pressing ENTER caused the formula to appear in cell D1, as shown in our example.

This may seem like a lot of work compared to typing in cell references. Once your worksheet becomes large, however, the pointing method can save considerable time. It speeds up the testing and verification process for your model because it forces you to visually verify cell references and therefore eliminates many formula errors.

**Logical Formulas**     Logical formulas use the logical operators to compare two or more values. Such formulas can be used to evaluate a series of complex decisions or to influence results in other areas of the worksheet. As noted in the "Operation Priorities" box, the logical operators are = for equal, <> for not equal, < for less than, > for greater than, <= for less than or equal to, and >= for greater than or equal to. The logical operators all have the same priority and will be evaluated from left to right in an expression. All the logical operators are lower in priority than the arithmetic operators.

Logical formulas do not calculate numeric results like arithmetic formulas. They produce a result of either zero or one, depending on whether the condition that was evaluated is true or false. If it is a true condition, 1 will be returned; if the condition is false, 0 will be returned. For example, if C1 contains .0925, the logical expression +C1>=500 will return 0, since the condition is false.

1-2-3 also has a few compound operators. These operators are used either to negate a logical expression or to join two logical expressions. The negation operator #NOT# has priority over the other two compound operators, #AND# and #OR#. These latter operators can join two expressions, as in C1>=500#AND#C2=50. In this example the expression will return a 1 for true only if both conditions are true.

The function of #NOT# is to negate an expression. For instance, the formula #NOT#(A1=2#AND#D2=1) will return a 1 for true only if the contents of cell A1 are not equal to 2 and those of cell D1 are not equal to 1. (If #OR# replaced #AND# in this formula, the formula would be true if either cell A1 were not equal to 2 or cell D2 were not equal to 1.) For practical purposes, you are more likely to use the not equal logical operator, <>, than the more cumbersome #NOT# operator. The formula A1<>2#AND#D2<>1 is easier to read than is #NOT(A1=2#AND#D2=1), and its meaning is identical.

One application of logical operators in a spreadsheet might be the calculation of a commission bonus. Figure 3-3 shows a calculation worksheet to determine the quarterly

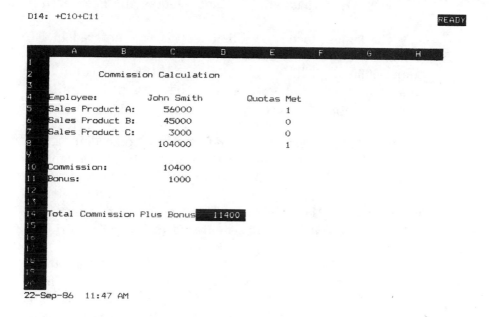

```
D14:  +C10+C11                                                    READY

        A       B        C         D        E       F      G       H
1
2               Commission Calculation
3
4  Employee:              John Smith       Quotas Met
5  Sales Product A:          56000              1
6  Sales Product B:          45000              0
7  Sales Product C:           3000              0
8                           104000              1
9
10 Commission:               10400
11 Bonus:                     1000
12
13
14 Total Commission Plus Bonus      11400
15
16
17
18
19
20

22-Sep-86   11:47 AM
```

**Figure 3-3.**    Total pay calculation

check that should be prepared for salesman John Smith. The calculation has two components: the regular commission and a bonus for meeting sales quotas.

The regular commission is 10% of total sales. The bonus is calculated by product. Each salesperson has a $50,000 quota for each of three products. A bonus of $1,000 is given for each product for which the sales quota is met. A salesperson could thus gain $3,000 by meeting the quota for all three products.

Let's look at the steps taken to build the model shown in the figure. First a number of labels are entered in B2 through A7. Next John Smith is entered in C4, and 56000, 45000, and 3000 are entered in C5 through C7. These numbers are totaled in C8 by entering the formula +C5+C6+C7 in that cell. The label Quotas Met is entered in E4.

The logical formula +C5>50000 is now entered in E5. When ENTER is pressed, if sales of product A are greater than 50000, a 1 will be returned, but if they are equal to or less than this number, a 0 will be returned. Similarly, +C6>50000 is entered in E6, and +C7>50000 is entered in E7. Pressing ENTER produces the result of the logical formula in both cases. The total formula is placed in E8 as +E5+E6+E7 to determine the number of bonus categories.

Additional labels of Commission: and Bonus: are entered in A10 and A11. +C8*.1 is then entered in C10, and +E8*1000 is entered in C11. A label for total commission is placed in A14, and the final formula is entered in D14 as +C10+C11.

**String Formulas**    String or text formulas are new to release 2. They allow you to join or concatenate two or more groups of characters. This in turn allows you to access and manipulate character data to build headings, correct errors, and convert text formats to a satisfactory format for reporting. There is only one operator for string formulas, the ampersand (&). If you want to join the string John with the string Smith, you could enter the string formula "John"&"Smith" to produce JohnSmith or "John"&" "&"Smith" to produce John Smith.

String formulas let you alter data previously entered in a worksheet, so you can use them to correct errors or change formats. For example, if names have been entered in a spreadsheet with the last name first and you wish to reverse the sequence, you can combine string functions such as @RIGHT, @LEFT, and @MID to produce that result. (String functions are explained in Chapter 7.) String formulas also offer a creative approach to producing new reports by providing an opportunity to join data from two or more locations on your worksheet. They can be used in combination with cell references to produce flexible report headings, for instance.

Figure 3-4 shows a report heading created by combining string constants and string variables. There are three string

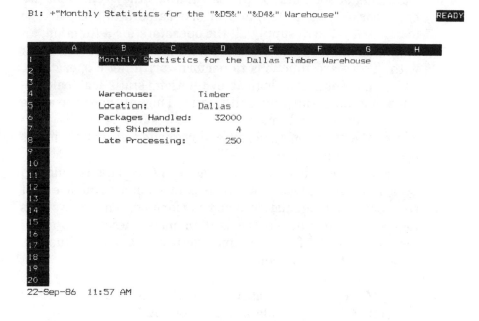

```
        A        B       C        D       E      F      G      H
1                 Monthly Statistics for the Dallas Timber Warehouse
2
3
4                 Warehouse:          Timber
5                 Location:           Dallas
6                 Packages Handled:    32000
7                 Lost Shipments:          4
8                 Late Processing:       250
9
10
11
12
13
14
15
16
17
18
19
20
```

22-Sep-86   11:57 AM

**Figure 3-4.**    A string formula

constants in this formula: "Monthly Statistics for the ", " ", and " Warehouse". The constants were enclosed in quotation marks and entered into the formula. The variables are references to cell addresses that contain text data. The two variables here are D5 and D4, which contain Dallas and Timber, respectively.

The string concatenation operator, along with #AND# and #OR#, has the lowest priority of all the operators. This does not diminish the usefulness of these operators; it just means that they are the last operators to be evaluated in an expression.

**Functions**     1-2-3's built-in functions are a special category of formulas. They can be used alone or as part of a formula you create. Functions have the advantage that the entire algorithm or formula for the calculations they represent has been worked out, tested, and incorporated into the package features. 1-2-3 will supply all the operators for a function; all you need to supply are the values that the operators work with. There are functions to perform arithmetic operations, string manipulation, logical evaluation, statistical calculations, and date and time arithmetic. They all have the same general format and must abide by the same rules. Regardless of the function type, all are regarded as value entries because they are formulas.

Functions all start with an at sign (@). This is followed by a function keyword, which is a character sequence that represents the calculation being performed. The keyword is followed by arguments enclosed in parentheses. The arguments define the function's specific use in a given situation. A few of 1-2-3's functions are

| | |
|---|---|
| @MAX | Calculates the maximum value |
| @SUM | Calculates a sum or total |
| @ROUND | Rounds a number to a certain number of decimal places |
| @NPV | Calculates the net present value |

Release 2 of 1-2-3 has nearly 100 of these built-in functions, spanning calculations in financial, mathematical, logical, statistical, string, and other areas. Functions will be covered thoroughly in Chapter 7.

Figure 3-5 shows an example of the use of the @SUM function to produce a total. After entering appropriate numbers and labels, the sum formula was entered in E6 by typing **@SUM(**. The cursor was then moved to C6, the beginning of the range to be summed, and this reference was locked in place as the beginning of the range by typing a period. The cursor was next moved to the right to include the value in D6. As a last step, the closing parenthesis ) was entered and ENTER was pressed to produce the sum shown in the figure. The remaining two sum formulas could be added in the same way.

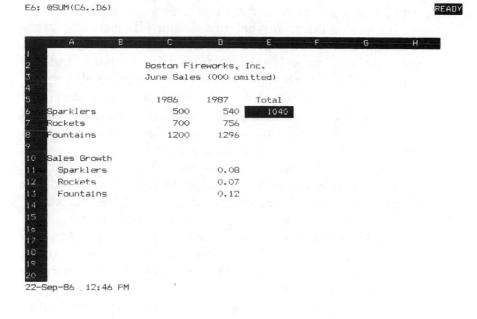

**Figure 3-5.**    Using @SUM

**How 1-2-3 Treats Formulas**    You will need to know some facts about formulas beyond the procedure for their entry. 1-2-3 offers a number of recalculation options that affect the timeliness of recalculation and the order of formula evaluation. You will probably begin your use of the 1-2-3 package with the default settings, but you should be aware that other alternatives can enhance your use of the package when you begin to build models with greater sophistication.

   With the default settings, 1-2-3 recalculates the entire worksheet every time you change a variable on the sheet. Unless your worksheet is very large, you will hardly notice the amount of time required to perform these calculations. 1-2-3 is one of the fastest spreadsheet packages marketed, due to the fact that it is written in assembly language. The use of assembler means that the initial development of the package may have taken longer, but the results provide benefits every time a user recalculates a spreadsheet.

Release 2 offers further processing efficiency for users who have an 8087 or 80287 math coprocessor chip installed in their systems, since it can automatically recognize and use this chip. The math coprocessor provides noticeable speed improvements for iterative calculations, including the /Data Table features explained in Chapter 10, and reduces the time involved for recalculation when a worksheet contains numerous trigonometric or mathematical functions.

In addition to fast recalculation, 1-2-3's speed in format changes, cursor movement, window switching, and copying functions sets standards for the other spreadsheet packages. This is not to say that you will never become impatient with the package, since most users want no delay at all. At these times you can take comfort from knowing that 1-2-3 is using the features of your computer to the fullest. Furthermore, as you will learn in Chapter 6, there is a method to temporarily turn off recalculation when you have data entry tasks to perform.

Early spreadsheet packages had a fixed recalculation order. You had a choice of calculating by row or column. If you chose row, every formula in row 1 would be calculated, then every formula in row 2, and so on down the worksheet. Similarly, if you chose column sequence, column 1 was calculated, then column 2, and so on.

Great care had to be taken in worksheet design with this method, since a formula in column 1 could not refer to a calculated value in column 3 under column recalculation order without creating a backward reference (reference to a value that had not yet been calculated). Undetected backward references could cause people to make decisions from projection printouts that were not in sync.

Fortunately, this problem can be resolved with 1-2-3's default setting of Natural Recalculation Order. In this setting, 1-2-3 bears the burden of determining the appropriate order for evaluating formulas. Backward references do not occur.

## Reference Types

1-2-3 has three different reference types. These types do not affect the original formula but do affect copy operation. You can type the $'s where required or add them with the F4 (ABS) key when you are in POINT mode.

Relative references: A2, B10, Z43

Absolute references: $A$2, $B$10, $Z$43

Mixed references: A$2, $A2, B$10, $B10

**Reference Types**    The cell references in 1-2-3's formulas can be relative, absolute, or mixed. These three reference types will be covered in detail in Chapter 6 in connection with the /Copy command. They must be mentioned here as well, however, because references must be entered in one of the three formats when you type in your original formulas, even though the reference type does not have any effect on the original calculation. The "Reference Types" box provides examples of the three reference type formats. It is important to know that the way you enter cell references in your original formula can have long-term and widespread consequences if the formula is copied.

## Correcting Errors in Entries

1-2-3 offers a variety of error correction techniques. They are summarized in the "Error Correction Methods" box. The method you use will depend mostly on whether the entry to

**1**
**2**
**3**

## Error Correction Methods

If data is in the control panel but not yet entered in the cell:

Use the ESC key to erase the entire entry.

Use the BACKSPACE key to delete one character at a time until the erroneous character has been eliminated.

Press F2 (EDIT), then use HOME, END, right arrow, and left arrow to move within the entry. Use BACKSPACE to delete the character in front of the cursor and DEL to erase the character above the cursor. INS can be used to toggle between INSERT and REPLACE modes.

If data has already been entered in the cell:

Retype the entry; the new entry will replace the old.

Press F2 (EDIT), then use HOME, END, right arrow, and left arrow to move within the entry. Use BACKSPACE to delete the character in front of the cursor and DEL to erase the character above the cursor. INS can be used to toggle between INSERT and REPLACE modes.

be corrected has been finalized (by pressing ENTER or one of the arrow keys).

When an entry is short and has been finalized, retyping is a good correction method. It will replace the existing contents of the cell with your new entry. A quick option for an unfinalized entry is pressing ESC, which will make your entire entry disappear.

If you have not finalized an entry, the most common error correction technique is to use the BACKSPACE key as a destructive backspace, deleting the previous character each time you press it. This approach is ideal when you realize that the last character you typed was incorrect.

Placing yourself in EDIT mode by pressing the F2 (EDIT) key is a good way to correct errors in entries that have been finalized. When this key is pressed, a small cursor will appear at the end of the entry in the Edit line of the control panel. This small cursor marks your place in the entry as you move within it and make changes. EDIT mode is also a good solution for long, incomplete entries where the error is near the beginning of the entry.

The cursor movement keys take on new functions in EDIT mode, as follows:

- The HOME key will move you not to cell A1 but to the first character in your entry.

- The END key will move you to the last character in your entry.

- The right and left arrow keys move you one character at a time in your entry.

- The BACKSPACE key still performs its destructive function.

- DEL also eliminates characters from entries. Rather than deleting the previous character, DEL removes the character above the edit cursor.

If you have left out a character in an entry, you can move to the character that follows the desired location and type the character you wish to add. It will be inserted, as long as you have not changed the default setting of INSERT mode. If you should want to change this setting so that what you type will overlay an existing character rather than adding a character, release 2 provides the option of pressing INS. To change the setting back again, just press INS a second time, since the key functions as a toggle switch.

Let's look at a brief example using EDIT mode to make a correction. In this situation, sales has been entered in B1 and finalized. To change the first letter to a capital, you would follow these steps:

1. Move the cursor back to the cell containing the error, B1.

2. Press F2 (EDIT) to place 1-2-3 in EDIT mode.

3. Use the HOME key to move to the beginning of the entry and then use the right arrow to move under the s (the extra character at the front of the entry is the label indicator.

4. Press the DEL key to remove the s, leaving the cursor under the a.

5. Type S, then press ENTER to finalize your corrected entry.

Errors can be frustrating, but having several options makes the correction process as painless as possible. You can use the same error correction techniques to change the justification of a label entry by altering the label indicator that appears at the beginning of the entry. Simply press F2 (EDIT), then HOME to move to the front of the entry. Press DEL to remove the label indicator, then type a caret (^). When ENTER is pressed, this entry will be center justified.

## Ranges

Most of the formulas discussed in this chapter have operated on individual cells—for example, C1*C2, where the value in one cell was multiplied by the value in another cell. The one exception was the use of a range of cells with the @SUM function example. When using 1-2-3's built-in functions and other commands, however, you will often work with more than one cell at a time. There is no problem with this as long as the cells form a contiguous rectangle. Figure 3-6 presents examples of valid and invalid ranges. The examples on the left are invalid because the cell groups do not form one contiguous rectangle. Ranges can be large rectangles of cells, or they can be as small as a single cell.

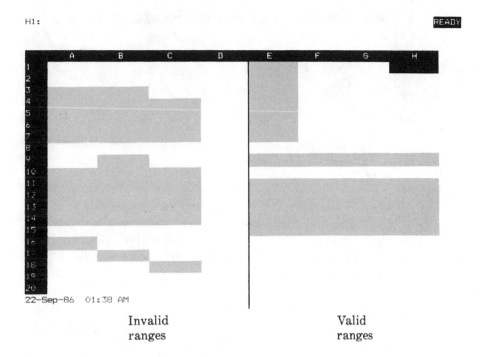

**Figure 3-6.**    Valid and invalid ranges

Cell ranges can be typed in just like a single address, highlighted with your cursor, or specified with a range name (covered in Chapter 6). To specify a range, type the cell names of two diagonally opposite corners of the rectangle separated by one or two periods. For example, the range of cells shown here can be specified as B4.C8, B4..C8, B8..C4, B8.C4, C8..B4, C8.B4, C4..B8, or C4.B8. The most common way to represent a range is by specifying the left upper-most cell first and the right lower-most cell last, however. Also, since 1-2-3 will supply the second period, you might as well save a keystroke and just type B4.C8.

```
C8: 33                                                       POINT
Enter range to erase: B4..C8

        A       B       C       D       E       F       G       H
  1
  2
  3
  4               10      13
  5               13      22
  6                2      31
  7               45      12
  8               24      33
  9
 10
```

## Storage Capacity

Although you can place your entries anywhere you wish on the 1-2-3 worksheet, there are a few limitations you should be aware of. They relate to the way the different releases of 1-2-3 use the computer's memory.

1. Release 1 and release 1A utilize memory inefficiently if you make entries that are not in adjacent areas of the worksheet. In other words, blank spaces between entry areas use memory. This problem has been solved with release 2, where memory is used much more efficiently.

2. 1-2-3 can use up to 640K of RAM and can be extended with 4MB of additional memory if you are using release 2. The amount of data that can be entered in a worksheet or data file with 1-2-3 will depend on a number of factors, including whether the entries are constants or formulas, whether numbers are decimal numbers or integers, and what range options (formatting, justification, and so on) have been used. With 640K you can make tens of thousands of entries in the spreadsheet, as long as the length of the average entry is not excessive. In Chapter 6 you will learn how to monitor utilization of existing memory.

# Changing the Appearance
# Of the Worksheet Display

**FOUR**

**Global and Range Changes**
**Worksheet Changes**
**Format Options**
**Advanced Features**
**COMMAND REFERENCE: Worksheet Display**
**/Range Format**
**/Range Justify**
**/Worksheet Column**
**/Worksheet Global Column-Width**
**/Worksheet Global Default Other Clock**
**/Worksheet Global Default Other International**
**/Worksheet Global Default Update**
**/Worksheet Global Format**
**/Worksheet Global Zero**

Using what you have learned up to now, you can make entries on the worksheet that convey useful information. The format of the numeric portion of this information, however, probably is not as attractive as you would like. It has no dollar signs, commas, or aligned decimal points. 1-2-3 can, and indeed must, provide these special edit characters for you; you should never enter them yourself.

This chapter will describe the features 1-2-3 provides for formatting your worksheet. It will demonstrate global and range formatting options, which give you a choice of making changes to all or just a portion of your worksheet. It will teach you commands to change the width of your spreadsheet columns if the formats you have chosen require additional display space. It will also describe some advanced ways to change 1-2-3's default display options. For an overview of the commands covered in this chapter, see the command map at the start of the command reference section on page 121.

## Global and Range Changes

1-2-3 has several menu commands for improving the appearance of your worksheet. These commands can work their magic globally, changing the entire worksheet at once, or they can affect only a single range of cells. The /Worksheet Global Format command changes the appearance of the entire worksheet from the global setting of General to another display format. The /Range Format command changes the appearance of just the cells within the specified range.

The range format option has priority over the worksheet format option. This means you can select a worksheet option that matches your needs for most of the worksheet cells and

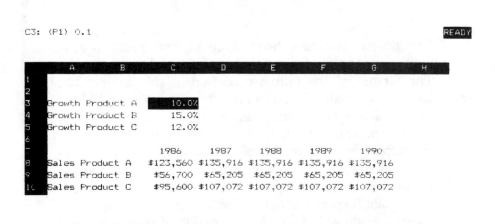

**Figure 4-1.**    Worksheet with range and global formats

still tailor individual cells to have a different appearance. In Figure 4-1 the /Worksheet Global Format command was used to set the overall format to Currency, and then the /Range Format option was used to change C3..C5 to Percent format. Changing the global format again would change every numeric worksheet cell except C3..C5. Those cells would not be affected by a worksheet format change because a range format instruction was previously used to change them, and the range format has priority.

Before making a change to your worksheet, you should always determine the extent of the change you wish to make. You can then select the command that makes just the amount of change you need. This chapter will look separately at global changes and range changes and will then take an in-depth look at each format option that 1-2-3 provides, whether globally or for ranges.

## Worksheet Changes

All the worksheet commands are accessed through the Worksheet option on the main menu, which looks like this:

Worksheet is selected either by pressing ENTER while the command is highlighted or by typing **W**. This chapter will discuss only the Worksheet menu options that are found under Column and Global on the submenu presented after you choose Worksheet on the main menu.

## Column Commands

Every column on a new worksheet is the same width. Unless you change the default width, each column is 9 positions wide. This means that labels with 9 characters or numeric entries with 8 digits can be entered in the cell. (Numeric entries are always restricted to one digit less than the cell width.)

If you enter labels that are too long for this width, they will be truncated for display if the cells to their right are not empty. If the cells are empty, 1-2-3 will borrow space from them to show the complete label entry. If you enter numbers that are too long, they either will be rounded to fit the cell width or will display as asterisks, depending on the format in effect for the cell. If you are using the General format, the numbers will be cut off without rounding.

### Set-Width

The /Worksheet Column menu looks like this:

The first two options, Set-Width and Reset-Width, change the width of the column where the cursor is located. You will therefore want to position your cursor before requesting the command.

The following display shows account names that were entered in column A but are too long to display in that column's default width of 9.

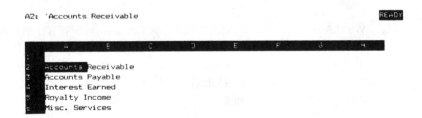

The entries could be allowed to borrow space from adjacent columns, or column A's width could be changed with the Set-Width command so that the entire entries could be shown in that column. This option is especially useful if you already have entries in column B and the account names in column A therefore are being truncated. First, make sure your cursor is in column A. Then invoke the command by entering /Worksheet Column Set-Width. Next, either you can enter the desired number of characters and press ENTER, or you can move with the right and left arrow until the column is the desired width and press ENTER. The latter method is preferred, since guessing wrong about the desired number of characters means that you have to start over with /Worksheet Column Set-Width. In the following example, the width was set at 19.

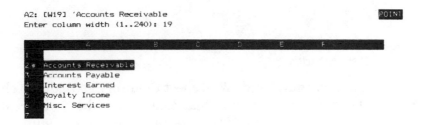

```
A2: [W19] 'Accounts Receivable                                    POINT
Enter column width (1..240): 19

        A            B        C        D        E        F
1
2 # Accounts Receivable
3   Accounts Payable
4   Interest Earned
5   Royalty Income
6   Misc. Services
7
```

This width could have been set either by typing the entire entry, /Worksheet Column Set-Width 19, and pressing ENTER or by using the right arrow key to widen the column one position at a time.

The Set-Width command can also be used when numbers are too large to display in the default column width. In Figure 4-2, numeric entries were made for the account balances. These cells were formatted as currency with two decimal places, meaning that 1-2-3 added a $ and a comma after the thousands position. (To produce this format, type /**Range Format Currency**, press ENTER, type **B2..B6**, and press ENTER again.) These cells display as asterisks because the value they contained became too large for the cell width once the dollar sign and comma were added to the existing digits. This column can be widened sufficiently by typing /**Worksheet Column Set-Width** and moving the right arrow three times before pressing ENTER. Figure 4-3 shows the display after the cells were changed to a width of 12.

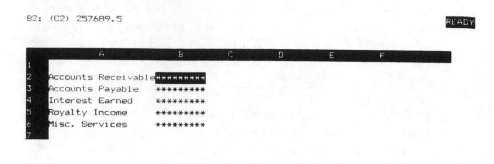

B2: (C2) 257689.5                                                    READY

| | A | B | C | D | E | F |
|---|---|---|---|---|---|---|
| 1 | | | | | | |
| 2 | Accounts Receivable | ********* | | | | |
| 3 | Accounts Payable | ********* | | | | |
| 4 | Interest Earned | ********* | | | | |
| 5 | Royalty Income | ********* | | | | |
| 6 | Misc. Services | ********* | | | | |
| 7 | | | | | | |

**Figure 4-2.**    Currency format with entries that will not fit in cell

### Reset-Width

Once you have used /Worksheet Column Set-Width to change
the width of a column, that column will be a different size
from its neighbors. If that width ceases to be useful, you can
return the column to the Global column width with the
Reset-Width command. In the situation shown in Figure 4-3,
placing the cursor in column C and entering /Worksheet
Column Reset-Width will return the column to a width of 9,
causing the asterisks to reappear.

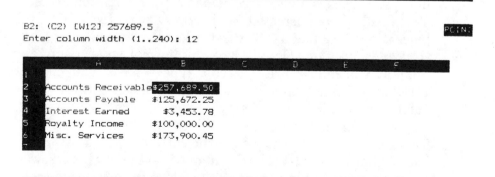

B2: (C2) [W12] 257689.5                                              POINT
Enter column width (1..240): 12

| | A | B | C | D | E | F |
|---|---|---|---|---|---|---|
| 1 | | | | | | |
| 2 | Accounts Receivable | $257,689.50 | | | | |
| 3 | Accounts Payable | $125,672.25 | | | | |
| 4 | Interest Earned | $3,453.78 | | | | |
| 5 | Royalty Income | $100,000.00 | | | | |
| 6 | Misc. Services | $173,900.45 | | | | |
| 7 | | | | | | |

**Figure 4-3.**    Column widened to 12 to show numbers

When the width of a column is changed with /Worksheet Column Set-Width, the column width assigned will be displayed for each cell in that column under release 2. In other words, if you place your cursor on any cell in a column where a special width has been used, you will see the width on the command line (that is, the top line) in the control panel of the display. The indicator is shown in brackets. Thus, for example, [W8] means width 8, [W4] means width 4, and [W25] means width 25. This display feature can prove useful in identifying the exact width you have established for worksheet columns. Widths from 1 to 240 with release 2 and 1 to 72 with release 1A can be assigned to any column.

## Hidden Columns

Release 2 introduced the hidden column feature to 1-2-3. This option allows you to eliminate individual columns from the display. In effect, it cuts a section from the worksheet temporarily. You can restore the display at any time, since the data has not been erased. The /Worksheet Column Hide command eliminates a column or columns from view. If you press ENTER after typing this command, the column where the cursor was located will be hidden. Alternately, you can use the right and left arrow keys or specify a range of columns before pressing ENTER. Following is a worksheet before Hide is invoked.

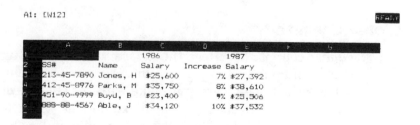

After columns C and D are hidden by placing the cursor in column C and typing /**Worksheet Column Hide** followed by right arrow and ENTER, the worksheet will look like this:

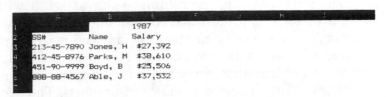

The /Worksheet Column Display command redisplays hidden columns. The command displays the letters of the formerly hidden columns with asterisks next to them, as can be seen here.

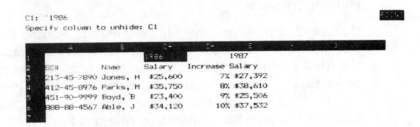

After typing the command, you can move the cell pointer to the column you want to redisplay and press ENTER, or you can select a range if you want to redisplay adjacent columns.

## Global Commands

Global commands affect the entire worksheet. Every row, every column, and every cell in each row and column are affected by the changes you make with the Global command options, although most of the Global options will affect only numeric cell entries. The options available under the Global menu are shown as follows:

Format Label-Prefix Column-Width Recalculation Protection Default Zero

In this chapter you will have the opportunity to use Column-Width, Format, Zero, and Default. The first three commands will be covered next, while the more advanced options offered under Default will be discussed at the end of the chapter. Additional Global options will be described in Chapter 5.

## Column-Width

Changing the column width for the entire spreadsheet with the Worksheet Column option would take much too long. 1-2-3 therefore allows you to change the width of every column on the worksheet with one command. This command is /Worksheet Global Column-Width. With this option you can make all the columns on your worksheet any width from 1 to 240 instead of the default setting of 9 positions.

Since this command will affect the entire spreadsheet, there is no need to position your cursor before invoking it. The following example shows columns of numbers, none of which come close to the default setting of 9.

A1:                                                                    READY

|  | A | B | C | D | E | F | G | H |
|---|---|---|---|---|---|---|---|---|
| 1 | | | | | | | | |
| 2 | Projected Staff Levels 1987 | | | | | | | |
| 3 | | | | | | | | |
| 4 | Dept | 1/87 | 2/87 | 3/87 | 4/87 | 5/87 | 6/87 | 7/87 |
| 5 | 100 | 35 | 35 | 34 | 34 | 34 | 33 | 33 |
| 6 | 110 | 15 | 15 | 15 | 15 | 15 | 15 | 15 |
| 7 | 125 | 12 | 12 | 13 | 13 | 13 | 14 | 14 |
| 8 | 135 | 56 | 55 | 55 | 55 | 54 | 54 | 54 |
| 9 | 159 | 65 | 65 | 65 | 65 | 63 | 63 | 63 |
| 10 | 160 | 41 | 39 | 38 | 37 | 36 | 35 | 35 |
| 11 | 175 | 4 | 4 | 4 | 4 | 4 | 4 | 4 |
| 12 | | | | | | | | |

Shrinking the size of the columns would allow you to display more information on the sheet. By typing /Worksheet Global Column-Width 5 and pressing ENTER, you could change the display to match the one shown here.

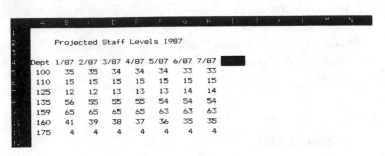

```
I4:                                                          READY

    A    B     C    D     E    F     G    H    I    J   K   M   N
1
2         Projected Staff Levels 1987
3
4  Dept  1/87  2/87  3/87  4/87  5/87  6/87  7/87
5   100   35    35   34    34    34    33    33
6   110   15    15   15    15    15    15    15
7   125   12    12   13    13    13    14    14
8   135   56    55   55    55    54    54    54
9   159   65    65   65    65    63    63    63
10  160   41    39   38    37    36    35    35
11  175    4     4    4     4     4     4     4
12
```

The /Worksheet Column command will take precedence over this command. You could use both commands if you had a spreadsheet where all but one column could be narrow. You would use /Worksheet Global Column-Width to set the narrow width for the entire worksheet. You would then move your cursor to the column requiring the wider width, type **/Worksheet Column Set-Width**, and specify the wider width needed for that column.

## Format

Format can also be changed on a global basis. The default setting is General format, but if you want all your entries to be in Currency, Percent, Scientific Notation, or any of the other available formats, every worksheet cell can be reformatted with the /Worksheet Global Format command and the format specification of your choice. Here is a worksheet created with the General format setting.

```
A1:                                                          READY

    A        B        C        D        E       F        H
1
2
3             Budget   Actual   Diff.
4  Salaries   120678   125690   -5012
5  Supplies   34578.5  34250    328.5
6  Rent        6789    6955.5   -166.5
7  Postage      325     400.2   -75.2
8  Ins.        1235     1350    -115
9  Legal       4500     5000    -500
10
```

The appearance of this worksheet can be markedly improved by use of a single command, /Worksheet Global Format Currency. After the initial command sequence, 0 was typed to indicate zero decimal places and ENTER was pressed. The newly formatted worksheet looks like this:

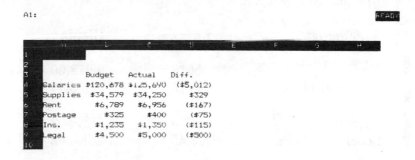

Any one of the format options listed in the Format Options box can be used. Some formats require more space than others, however. If the display turns to *'s when you change your format, you will have to widen your columns if you want to see your data under the new format. As you will learn later in the chapter, a Range Format command always takes precedence over a Global Format change.

## Zero Suppression

A new feature of release 2 is the ability to choose whether zero values will be displayed on the worksheet. In the past, a zero value always resulted in a cell containing a 0. If you choose the Zero Suppression option, it will cause zero values in every location on the worksheet to be hidden. They will not be lost, as they can be referenced for calculations, but any cell with a zero value will appear as a blank. To suppress the display of zeros on the worksheet, type /**Worksheet Global Zero Yes**. To restore the display, type /**Worksheet Global Zero No**.

The one problem with zero suppression is that 1-2-3 feels free to write over a zero-suppressed cell if you type a new entry there because the cell appears blank. A solution for

# Format Options

This table provides a quick reference to the formatting features offered by 1-2-3.

| Format | Entry | Display |
|---|---|---|
| Fixed 2 decimal places | 5678 −123.45 | 5678.00 −123.45 |
| Scientific 2 decimal places | 5678 −123.45 | 5.68E+03 11.23E+02 |
| Currency 2 decimal places | 5678 −123.45 | $5,678.00 ($123.45) |
| , (comma) 2 decimal places | 5678 −123.45 | 5,678.00 (123.45) |
| General | 5678 −123.45 | 5678 −123.45 |
| +/− | 4 −3 0 | ++++ − − − . |
| Percent 0 decimal places | 5 .1 | 500% 10% |
| Date (D1) | 31679 | 24-Sep-86 |
| Time (T1) | .5 | 12:00:00 PM |
| Text | +A2*A3 | +A2*A3 |

this problem is discussed under Protection in Chapter 5. The first illustration following shows a worksheet with Zero set at No, and the second illustration shows the same worksheet with the Zero option set at Yes.

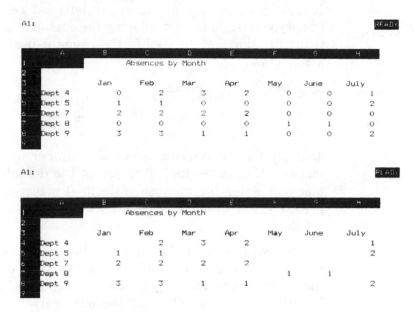

## Range Format Commands

Range format changes to just what their name implies: they change the format for a specified range of cells on the worksheet. Any of the valid ranges described in Chapter 2 can be affected. The range can be as small as one cell, or it can be a row, column, or rectangle of cells.

Let's look at an example of the /Range Format command in action. The worksheet shown here has three different types of entries.

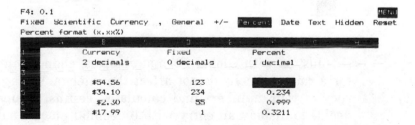

Two of these worksheet entries have already been formatted, and one is in the process of being changed. To change the format of these cells, you would follow these steps:

1. Move your cursor to the upper leftmost cell in the range you wish to format. Placing the cursor in this location will allow you to specify the range using only the arrow keys.

2. Type /**Range Format**.

3. Select the Percent format from the menu either by typing **P** or by pointing and pressing ENTER.

4. If the format requires a certain number of decimal places, either press ENTER to accept the default of two places or enter the number of decimal places and then press ENTER. In our example, 1 was entered to replace the default.

5. 1-2-3 will request the range to format. Specify the range by using the right and down arrow keys to move to the right lowermost cell you wish to format. If you are formatting just one cell, do not move the cursor. After all the cells to be formatted are highlighted, press ENTER, and they will be displayed with the new format. The worksheet will then look like this:

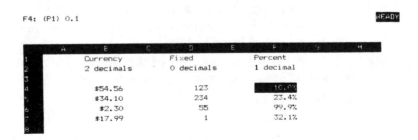

Just as with Global Format changes, changes in format for a range of cells do not affect the internal storage accuracy of your numbers and calculated results. Suppose you decide to display an entry with 0 decimal places, but internally six or more places are stored. When that cell is used in a calculation, the full internal accuracy will be applied. Later, in Chapter 7, you will learn a way to change the internal accuracy as well.

Range Format commands always take priority over Global Format commands. You can use this fact to your advantage. Before constructing a new worksheet, plan its design. Determine which format will be used more than any other, and use /Worksheet Global Format to establish this format. Then, where necessary, use /Range Format commands to alter the format of individual cells or ranges.

The Range Format commands have a feature not found in Global Format commands. Once a cell has been formatted with a Range command, the top line in the control panel will show the format for the cell. (F2) means Fixed with two decimal places, (C0) means Currency with zero decimal places, and so on.

## Format Options

Each of the format options in this section, with the exception of Reset, can be used with either the /Worksheet Global Format or the /Range Format command. Since Reset is used to undo a Range Format command by changing the cells back to the Worksheet setting, this option is not needed on the Worksheet Format menu. The format options are summarized for you in the Format Options box shown earlier in the chapter.

## Fixed

The Fixed format lets you choose the number of places to the right of the decimal point that you wish to display. Like General format, it does not display dollar signs or commas.

If you use the Fixed Format option and the numbers you enter or calculate with formulas do not contain a sufficient number of decimal places, zeros will be added. For example, if you enter 5.67 in a cell that you formatted as Fixed with 4 decimal places, your entry will display as 5.6700. The zeros used for padding are always added to the right.

If, conversely, you enter or calculate numbers with more decimal places than have been specified, they will be rounded to the appropriate number of decimal places. Any number of 5 or above will be rounded upwards by 1-2-3. The following table may help you remember the action 1-2-3 will take in various circumstances.

| Entry | Fixed 0 | Fixed 2 | Fixed 4 |
|-------|---------|---------|---------|
| 7.23 | 7 | 7.23 | 7.2300 |
| 8.54 | 9 | 8.54 | 8.5400 |
| 3.5674 | 4 | 3.57 | 3.5674 |
| .98 | 1 | .98 | .9800 |

After you apply a Fixed format to a range of cells, the command line of the control panel will show something like (F0), (F2), or (F4). The number following the F for Fixed is the number of decimal places that you specified for your display.

The Fixed format option presents an appealing display whenever you have many decimal numbers. This format is particularly useful when these decimal numbers are the result of formulas, since it permits numbers to be displayed with the decimals aligned, which General format does not.

With Fixed format you may select from 0 to 15 decimal places. If the column is not wide enough, asterisks will appear. Leading zero integers are always added for decimal numbers.

## Scientific

This format displays numbers in exponential notation. You can choose from 0 to 15 decimal places in the first or multiplier portion of the expression, which makes the Scientific option different from the Scientific Notation display generated by the General Format option. With General, if scientific notation is required for a very large or very small number, the package will determine the number of decimals in the multiplier. With Scientific you make the determination when you establish the format.

The following table shows entries as they are made in a worksheet cell and the display that results when each of several Scientific decimal settings is established for the multiplier.

| Entry | Scientific 0 | Scientific 2 | Scientific 4 |
|---|---|---|---|
| 100550000 | 1E+08 | 1.01E+08 | 1.0055E+08 |
| 7896543 | 8E+06 | 7.90E+06 | 7.8965E+06 |
| .00005678 | 6E−05 | 5.68E−05 | 5.6780E−05 |

The indicator for Scientific when the Range Format command is used is an S combined with the number of decimals. It is displayed within parentheses in the command line of the control panel in the same way Fixed format was. Thus, you will see (S0), (S2), (S4), and so on.

Scientific notation is useful when you need to display very large or very small numbers in a limited cell width. It is used primarily in scientific and engineering applications and would not be acceptable on most business reports.

## Currency

This format places a dollar sign ($) in front of each entry. It also adds a comma separator between thousands and hundreds and between millions and thousands. This format shows negative numbers in parentheses.

From 0 to 15 decimal places can be specified for this format, although the most common settings are 0 for whole dollars and 2 to show both dollars and cents. Since the default setting is 2, you will only have to press ENTER after typing Currency in either the /Worksheet Format Currency or /Range Format Currency option if you want to show dollars and cents. With the Range command you will then need to specify the size of the range to be formatted.

In release 2, the /Worksheet Global Default Other International command can change the way the Currency option works. In the "Advanced Features" section near the end of this chapter, you will learn to use symbols for other currencies such as pounds and guilders and place the symbol either in front of or behind the currency amount. In addition, the symbols used for the comma separator and the decimal point can be changed to meet your needs in working with international currencies.

Let's look at the impact on several numeric entries of using different Currency formats.

| Entry | Currency 0 | Currency 2 | Currency 4 |
|---|---|---|---|
| 34.78 | $35 | $34.78 | $34.7800 |
| −123 | ($123) | ($123.00) | ($123.0000) |
| 1234.56 | $1,235 | $1,234.56 | $1,234.5600 |

To display these entries the column width would have to be widened to 10 for the middle column and to 12 for the column on the far right.

The indicator for the Currency format is a C followed by the number of decimal places. Like the other format indicators, this will appear in front of the cell entry on the command line in the control panel.

The Currency format is used frequently in business reports because of the many dollar figures shown in such reports. If you want to conserve space when printing your reports, remember that you can use a format of (C0) and an appropriate column width without losing the additional decimal accuracy.

## Comma

The Comma format is just like the Currency format except that the dollar sign is not used in the Comma format. Just as with the Currency format, negative numbers are shown in parentheses and commas are added as separators.

From 0 to 15 decimal places can be shown with this format. Enter the number of decimal places when prompted with the default. If you wish to accept the default, just press ENTER.

A sample of the displays created with the Comma format follows.

| Entry | , 0 | , 2 | , 4 |
|---|---|---|---|
| 34.78 | 35 | 34.78 | 34.7800 |
| −123 | (123) | (123.00) | (123.0000) |
| 1234.56 | 1,235 | 1,234.56 | 1,234.5600 |

You will notice that the same entries were used for this example as were used for the Currency format. This allows you to compare their use.

A comma and the number of decimal places are used as the indicator for this format. Thus, (,0), (,2), and (,4) in the command line represent this format with zero, two, and four decimal places, respectively.

The Comma format is frequently combined with the Currency format for financial statements. As in the following example, the top and bottom line of a financial statement typically have the $ added, whereas the other numbers are shown in Comma format.

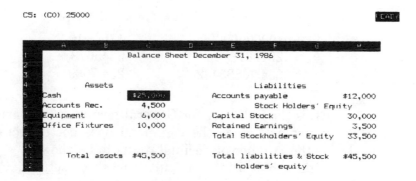

The best strategy for producing this layout is to use /Worksheet Global Format , followed by /Range Format Currency for the top and bottom line of the display.

## General

Since General is the default format, it is the one you have seen in the entries made on your worksheet until now. This format does not provide consistent displays the way that the other formats do, since it depends on the size of the number you enter. As you saw in Chapter 3, very large and very small numbers will display in Scientific format when General format is in effect. Some numbers will display as they are entered, while others will be altered to have a leading zero indicator added or to be rounded to a number of decimal digits that will fit in the cell width you have selected. This format also suppresses trailing zeros after the decimal point, so if you have used them, they will not appear in the display.

General format does not provide a choice of the number of zeros for the display, and it often results in a display that has varying numbers of decimal places in the entries. There is also no way to establish the number of digits for the multiplier when the Scientific Format option is used for very small and very large numbers.

Looking at the way various entries appear in General format will help you decide when it is an appropriate format for your needs.

| Entry | General Display |
|-------|-----------------|
| 10000000000 | 1.0E+10 |
| 2345678 | 2345678 |
| 234.76895432 | 234.7689 |

(G) is the indicator for General format. A numeric digit is not present, since the command does not expect you to decide the number of decimal digits to be shown.

Although it is the default worksheet setting, General format is seldom selected as the display of choice. For most applications you will want a more dependable display, even if it does require more room on the worksheet. This format would be particularly useful, however, if you were really short of space, since it automatically converts to Scientific Notation when the entry becomes too large or small to fit in the cell width.

# +/−

This is one of the most unusual formats available in 1-2-3. It creates a series of + or − signs as a representation of the size of the number in the cell, producing a sort of bar graph. These signs will change to asterisks if the size of the bar exceeds the column width. When the value of the cell is zero, a period (.) will display on the left side of the cell.

The +/− format will create the following horizontal displays from the entries shown:

| Entry+ | /− Display |
|--------|-----------|
| 0 | . |
| 5 | +++++ |
| −4 | − − − − |
| −3.85 | − − − |

The indicator (+ or −) will appear in the command line when the cursor is on any cell that has been formatted with the +/− format using the Range command.

The +/− format can be used to create a series of small bars to show, for example, growth or decline in sales over a period of time. In this situation you may want to divide the sales figure by 100 or some other appropriate number so that the result can be shown in a reasonable cell width. This approach has been used to create the bar graph shown here.

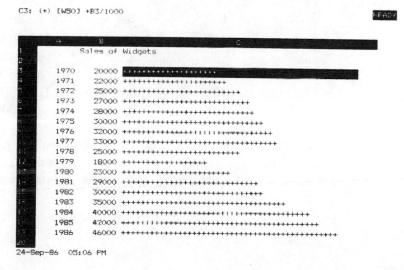

This format can also be used to highlight plus and minus values on your worksheet. You could add a column for the $+$ and $-$ displays and place a formula in each cell within the column that is simply a reference to the corresponding value in the column being monitored. You could then scan this second column quickly to see which values were $+$ and which were $-$ values.

## Percent

With the Percent format you can display percentages attractively and have the % symbol added to the end of each cell. You can choose any number of decimal places between 0 and 15.

Entries to be formatted as percentages should be entered as decimal fractions. This means that ten percent should be entered as .1, for example. When the Percent format is applied, the number you have entered is multiplied by 100 before the % symbol is added. Thus, an entry of .1 would become 10%, and an entry of 10 would become 1000%. You can see why it is important to enter the correct decimal fraction for the percent you want.

In the Percent format the following entries will display as shown, depending on how many decimal places you specify:

| Entry | 0 | 2 | 4 |
|-------|-----|--------|----------|
| 5 | 500% | 500.00% | 500.0000% |
| $-.089635$ | $-9\%$ | $-8.96\%$ | $-8.9635\%$ |
| .45 | 45% | 45.00% | 45.0000% |
| $-1$ | $-100\%$ | $-100.00\%$ | $-100.0000\%$ |
| .12 | 12% | 12.00% | 12.0000% |

The Percent format is used in many areas of business reports. Percentage growth rates, interest on loans, and sales increases all can be computed and formatted as percents.

## Date/Time

This format is used for date and time entries. Time could not be entered or computed in earlier releases of 1-2-3, but release 2 provides a single serial number that represents both the date and the time. The whole number portion of the entry represents the date, and the fractional portion of the entry represents the time.

A number of built-in functions of the package allow you to enter dates and times in worksheet cells. There are also package functions that allow you to access the system date and time. These functions will all be covered in Chapter 7, and two will also be considered here. These are the @TODAY function, used in release 1 and release 1A to access the current system date, and the @NOW function, used in release 2 to access both the current system date and time (release 2 will accept @TODAY and convert it to @NOW). Neither @NOW nor @TODAY requires function arguments; they are entered into worksheet cells simply as either @NOW or @TODAY.

Using either of these functions requires that you respond with the proper date and time to the DOS prompts during the booting process. If you do not respond to the date and time prompts and your system does not have a clock card to keep track of date and time for you, the date will appear as Jan 1 1980. If you respond to the DOS prompt, the value you give will be stored internally in your system for later reference and can be accessed with the @NOW and @TODAY functions.

1-2-3 shows dates as serial numbers representing the number of days from December 31, 1899, to the current day. The serial number for September 24, 1986, is 31679, for example. Without formatting, that is exactly the way the number will appear on your worksheet. Fortunately, Date formats provide a number of other options. You can display the date as 24-Sep-86, 24-Sep, or Sep-86. With release 2 you also have such options as 09/24/86 and 09/86. Any of these present a much more understandable version of the date than the serial date that displays in a cell under General format.

Assuming that @NOW was entered in each of several cells and generated the serial number shown in the Entry column, here are the displays you would see with different Date formats.

| Entry | DD-MMM-YY | DD-MM |
|-------|-----------|-------|
| 31679 | 24-Sep-86 | 24-Sep |

| MMM-YY | Long Int | Short Int |
|--------|----------|-----------|
| Sep-86 | 09/24/86 | 09/24 |

The indicators for dates vary depending on which Date format you select. The following table lists the Date formats found in release 2 and the indicators that will appear in the control panel for cells that have these formats added with a Range command.

| Indicator | Format |
|-----------|--------|
| D1 | (DD-MMM-YY) |
| D2 | (DD-MMM) |
| D3 | (MMM-YY) |
| D4 | (MM/DD/YY) |
| D5 | (MM/DD) |

For each cell you will have to decide whether to apply a Date or a Time format, since both formats cannot be applied to the same cell. This means that although the @NOW function places both a time and a date in a cell, you will be able to see only one at a time. The one you see depends on the format you choose.

The whole number 1 makes up one day. To represent time, therefore, 1-2-3 uses decimal fractions of the number 1. Twelve hours is .5 and six hours is .25, for example. As you can see, the fractions are based on a 24-hour clock. As with dates, you will probably want to use the special Time formats to make the time easier to read. The Time format options are just as varied as the Date formats. A time of 10 PM can be represented as 10:00:00 PM, 10:00 PM, 22:00:00, or 22:00.

Time formats are accessed through the Date Format option by selecting Time. There are four Time formats. Two use the AM and PM designation, and the other two are international formats that use a 24-hour day like military time.

The effect of format selection on the display of time in worksheet cells can be seen in the table that follows.

| Entry | T1 | T2 | Long Int | Short Int |
|-------|----|----|----------|-----------|
| .25 | 06:00:00 AM | 06:00 AM | 06:00:00 | 06:00 |
| .5 | 12:00:00 PM | 12:00 PM | 12:00:00 | 12:00 |
| .75 | 06:00:00 PM | 06:00 PM | 18:00:00 | 18:00 |

Date and time entries are used in a variety of applications. They can be used to represent shipment receipts or line processing time, for instance. They can also be used to represent loan due dates, appointment dates, or order dates.

## Text

Text format allows you to display actual formulas on the worksheet, rather than displaying the results of formula calculations as will happen with any of the other formats. Using Text format causes a cell to display exactly what you enter. If your entry was a formula, 1-2-3 also remembers the result of the formula, and the results can be accessed with a reference to the cell.

The following table shows how different entries appear when a cell is formatted as text.

| Entry | Text Display |
|-------|--------------|
| +A1+A2 | +A1+A2 |
| +A3*A4/A5 | +A3*A4/A5 |
| Sales | Sales |
| 23.56 | 23.56 |

When the cursor is on a cell formatted as text with a Range command, the indicator (T) will appear in the upper

T4: (C2) [W13] ((R4-1)*(Q4/12))+((12-(R4-1))*(1+S4)*(Q4/12))          `READY`

```
              P              Q        R    S           T
1
2  Name          Base Salary    Inc. Mo. % INC    1985 Salary
3
4  Jones, Ray         $25,000.00        2    5.00%    $26,145.93
5  Larkin, Mary       $29,000.00        3    7.00%    $30,691.67
6  Harris, John       $15,000.00        6    5.00%    $15,437.50
7  Parson, Mary       $18,000.00        9    4.00%    $18,240.00
8  Smith, Jim         $23,000.00        4    7.00%    $24,207.50
9  Harker, Pat        $35,000.00       10    4.00%    $35,350.00
10 Jenkins, Paul      $45,000.00        2    9.00%    $48,712.50
11 Jacobs, Norman     $12,000.00        1    4.00%    $12,480.00
12 Merriman, Angela   $36,900.00        4    7.00%    $38,837.25
13 Campbell, David    $40,000.00        1   10.00%    $44,000.00
14 Campbell Keith     $32,000.00        1    9.00%    $34,880.00
15 Stevenson, Mary    $18,900.00       11    7.50%    $19,136.25
16
17
18
19
20
```
24-Sep-86   05:34 PM

---

**Figure 4-4.**     Worksheet displaying results

line of the control panel.

The Text format can be used to create a documentation copy of a worksheet. The documentation copy will contain the actual formulas used in worksheet calculations. For example, to create the documentation copy of the worksheet shown in Figure 4-4, you would follow these steps.

1. Use /Worksheet Global Format Text to set the global format to Text. This will not completely change the display because some of the entries have been formatted with Range commands, which always override Global settings.

2. Use /Range Format Reset P1..X15 and ENTER to reset all the Range formats back to Global settings.

3. Move your cursor to column T. Use /Worksheet Column Set-Width and press the right arrow until column T is 51 characters across. Press ENTER to select 51 as the column width. Now you have a copy of the worksheet with all the formulas documented. It should look like Figure 4-5.

After you learn about saving files in Chapter 8, you will want to make sure that you never save a documentation file under the same file name you used for your original file. If you do, you will lose all the formats and column widths that you worked so hard to establish for it. In the next chapter you will learn how to print a documentation copy of your worksheet so you will have a paper to file away and refer to if your disk copies are ever damaged or destroyed.

R1:                                                                                    READY

```
         R       S                           T
1
2  Inc. Mo. % INC     1985 Salary
3
4          2      0.05  ((R4-1)*(Q4/12))+((12-(R4-1))*(1+S4)*(Q4/12))
5          3      0.07  ((R5-1)*(Q5/12))+((12-(R5-1))*(1+S5)*(Q5/12))
6          6      0.05  ((R6-1)*(Q6/12))+((12-(R6-1))*(1+S6)*(Q6/12))
7          9      0.04  ((R7-1)*(Q7/12))+((12-(R7-1))*(1+S7)*(Q7/12))
8          4      0.07  ((R8-1)*(Q8/12))+((12-(R8-1))*(1+S8)*(Q8/12))
9         10      0.04  ((R9-1)*(Q9/12))+((12-(R9-1))*(1+S9)*(Q9/12))
10         2      0.09  ((R10-1)*(Q10/12))+((12-(R10-1))*(1+S10)*(Q10/12))
11         1      0.04  ((R11-1)*(Q11/12))+((12-(R11-1))*(1+S11)*(Q11/12))
12         4      0.07  ((R12-1)*(Q12/12))+((12-(R12-1))*(1+S12)*(Q12/12))
13         1       0.1  ((R13-1)*(Q13/12))+((12-(R13-1))*(1+S13)*(Q13/12))
14         1      0.09  ((R14-1)*(Q14/12))+((12-(R14-1))*(1+S14)*(Q14/12))
15        11     0.075  ((R15-1)*(Q15/12))+((12-(R15-1))*(1+S15)*(Q15/12))
16
17
18
19
20
24-Sep-86   05:32 PM
```

**Figure 4-5.**    Documentation copy displaying formulas

## Hidden

Hidden format causes a cell to display as a blank; that is, 1-2-3 will suppress the display of the cell. The cell's contents have not been lost, even though they do not appear on the worksheet. They are still stored internally and are accessed when you reference the cell in a formula. In fact, the contents of the cell will display in the control panel when you move your cursor to the cell.

With the Hidden format, all entries regardless of type will appear as blanks. The indicator for a Hidden cell when the format is applied with a Range command is (H) in the control panel. Here you see the cursor pointing to a hidden cell and the contents displayed in the control panel.

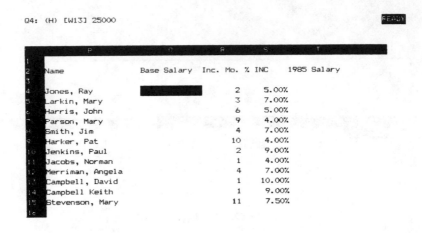

The main use of hidden cells is in macro applications. If the application is kept completely under macro control, the Hidden format could provide a measure of security. For more about macros, see Chapters 10 and 11.

The two features discussed in this section are not things you would want to change every day, like the other formatting options, but it is nice to know that they exist. One is the /Worksheet Global Default Other International option, which changes the way 1-2-3 handles punctuation, currency, date, and time displays. A related command alters the clock display format on your screen. The second feature is the justification options available under /Range Justify. This command manipulates a column of text-type entries in your worksheet. Let's look at each of these options in more detail.

## Other International Format Options

The /Worksheet Global Default Other International command is the longest command sequence discussed so far. This command allows you to customize the display for numeric punctuation, currency, date, and time.

### Punctuation

The numeric punctuation indicators you can control are the point separator (that is, the decimal indicator in a number like 55.98), the thousands separator for numbers, and the argument separator in functions. The initial point separator is a period (.), but you have the option of changing it to a comma (,). The initial thousands separator is a comma and can be changed to a period (.) or a space. The argument separator is initially set as a comma and can be changed to a period (.) or a semicolon (;). The options are not chosen individually but rather in a threesome once you select Punctuation. The option selections you have follow next.

| Option | Point | Argument | Thousands |
|--------|-------|----------|-----------|
| A (default) | . | , | , |
| B | , | . | . |
| C | . | ; | , |
| D | , | ; | . |
| E | . | , | space |
| F | , | . | space |
| G | . | ; | space |
| H | , | ; | space |

The following table shows how each choice affects the display of numbers and the arguments for functions like @SUM.

| Punctuation Option | Numeric Entry Currency | Function Arguments |
|--------------------|------------------------|--------------------|
| A (default) | $1,200.50 | @SUM(D2,A8..A10) |
| B | $1.200,50 | @SUM(D2.A8..A10) |
| C | $1,200.50 | @SUM(D2;A8..A10) |
| D | $1.200,50 | @SUM(D2;A8..A10) |
| E | $1 200.50 | @SUM(D2,A8..A10) |
| F | $1 200,50 | @SUM(D2.A8..A10) |
| G | $1 200.50 | @SUM(D2;A8..A10) |
| H | $1 200,50 | @SUM(D2;A8..A10) |

## Currency

This option allows you to change the currency symbol from the standard $ to one of the international currency symbols found in the LICS codes. You can also use any of the other LICS codes if the currency symbol you want is not in the table. In addition, you have the choice of placing the symbol at the end of your entry rather than at the beginning as in the initial setting.

Examples of currency symbols you may wish to use are those for Dutch Guilders, Pounds, Yen, and Pesetas. The LICS codes for these entries are as follows:

| Currency | LICS Code | Symbol |
|----------|-----------|--------|
| Dutch guilders | ff | ƒ 67,893.00 |
| Pounds | L= | £ 67,893.00 |
| Yen | Y= | ¥ 67,893.00 |
| Pesetas | PT | ₧ 67,893.00 |

To change from $ to one of these symbols, invoke /Worksheet Global Default Other International Currency and then use the Compose sequence to type the appropriate LICS code sequence followed by ENTER. The Compose sequence allows you to enter more than one character in a single position. To access it, hold down the ALT key while you press F1, then type the characters specified. For pounds you would type an **L** followed by =, for example. When this option is combined with the numeric punctuation options, you have an effective way to display international currency amounts.

## Date

The international date formats—Date formats D4 and D5—can be altered with the Date option from the /Worksheet Global Default Other International command. The initial setting for the international date is MM/DD/YY. This can be changed to three other forms. The choices for this setting are as follows:

| | |
|---|---|
| A | MM/DD/YY |
| B | DD/MM/YY |
| C | DD.MM.YY |
| D | YY-MM-DD |

The application of these formats to D4 and D5 are shown in the following table for the entry of September 24, 1986.

| | D4 | D5 |
|---|------|------|
| A | 09/24/86 | 09/24 |
| B | 24/09/86 | 24/09 |
| C | 24.09.86 | 24.09 |
| D | 86-09-24 | 09-24 |

## Time

The appearance of the international time formats can be changed with this option. Format D8 shows hours, minutes, and seconds, while format D9 shows only hours and minutes. The initial international time setting is HH:MM:SS. Each of the four options is indicated by a letter, as follows:

| | |
|---|---|
| A | HH:MM:SS |
| B | HH.MM.SS |
| C | HH,MM,SS |
| D | HHhMMmSSs |

Using these settings to display the time for 12:30:25 PM would result in the following:

| | D8 | D9 |
|---|---|---|
| A | 12:30:25 | 12:30 |
| B | 12.30.25 | 12.30 |
| C | 12,30,25 | 12,30 |
| D | 12h30m25s | 12h30m |

## Update

Any changes made with /Worksheet Global Default Other International commands are in effect only for the current session. Next time you load 1-2-3, the original values will be in effect. If you wish to make such changes permanent, invoke the /Worksheet Global Default Update command to save your changes. This will make your changes the new default values, and they will be in effect the next time 1-2-3 is loaded into memory.

# Clock Display

The clock that displays on your screen under release 2 can have its format changed. The command to do this is /Worksheet Global Default Other Clock. The options available under this command are Standard, International, and None.

Standard is the default display for the clock. It causes the date to display in the long format as DD-MMM-YY. The time displays as HH:MM AM/PM.

Selecting International changes the display of both date and time. Time becomes the short international format, D9. Date displays in the long international format, D4. The clock display with International chosen looks like this:

Choosing None eliminates the time display from the screen. This is useful for applications where you do not wish to have part of the screen dedicated to a time and date display.

## Range Justify

The /Range Justify command is as close as 1-2-3 comes to providing word processing features. It adjusts the length of a line of text to fit within margin limitations.

With this command, you can enter one or more long labels in a column and then, after the entry is complete, decide how many characters wide the display of this information should be. The width of the display is determined by selecting a justify range. If that range is two cells wide, for example, the long labels will be redistributed so that they take up more rows but display only in two columns.

This feature does not provide full word processing support, but it does allow you to write readable documentation on the screen or to write a short memo that references worksheet data. It frees you from having to concentrate on the length of your entry as you type. When all your data is typed in, 1-2-3 can adjust the line length according to your specifications.

Here is an example of long labels entered into A1..A6 of the worksheet.

```
A1: 'To test the /Range Justify command, we will type a series          READY

       A        B        C        D        E        F        G        H
1   To test the /Range Justify command, we will type a series
2   of long labels in Column A. Then we will attempt to confine the
3   display of these long labels to the first three columns.
4   To do this we will use /Range Justify and specify our justify range
5   as A1..C1. The labels will be shortened to use only the allotted
6   spaces and will require additional spreadsheet rows for the display.
7
```

The labels all have different lengths. Suppose you entered these labels and then decided that the display should be confined to columns A through C. (The labels are entered in column A and will remain in that location; what you are changing is the space they borrow for display purposes.) To make the change, you would use the following sequence of instructions.

1. Move your cursor to the beginning of the range you will use for display—A1 in the example.

2. Type /**Range Justify**.

3. Highlight the cells in the range A1..C1 with the right arrow key.

**4.** Press ENTER. Your transformed data should look like this:

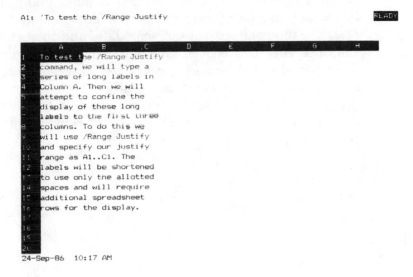

```
A1:  'To test the /Range Justify                                      READY

         A       B       C       D       E       F       G       H
 1  To test the /Range Justify
 2  command, we will type a
 3  series of long labels in
 4  Column A. Then we will
 5  attempt to confine the
 6  display of these long
 7  labels to the first three
 8  columns. To do this we
 9  will use /Range Justify
10  and specify our justify
11  range as A1..C1. The
12  labels will be shortened
13  to use only the allotted
14  spaces and will require
15  additional spreadsheet
16  rows for the display.
17
18
19
20
24-Sep-86  10:17 AM
```

If you decided to make the display wider again, you could move your cursor to A1 and start the process over. For example, you might want to specify A1..F1 as the justify range. The first six columns would then be used for the display.

If there is information in column A under the justify range, the /Range Justify command will displace it as it expands the long label down the worksheet. Since the label was originally entered in column A, *only* the cell entries in column A will be displaced, even if the justify range includes columns A..C. If there is information in cells to the right of column A, it will not be displaced. For instance, a table in cells B10..C14 would be unaffected by the paragraph rearrangement shown in the illustration. Instead, the label display in column A would be truncated in rows 10 through 14, just as it is when an entry to the right of any long label causes the label display to be truncated.

## Conclusion

In this chapter you have learned how to make many changes in the appearance of your worksheet. These changes do not alter the internal accuracy of your data, and they can make the difference between an amateur and a professional presentation of the information contained in a worksheet. You should now feel confident in using either Worksheet or Range commands to change the worksheet format. In the next chapter you will learn how to create a printed copy of your worksheet information.

# WORKSHEET DISPLAY

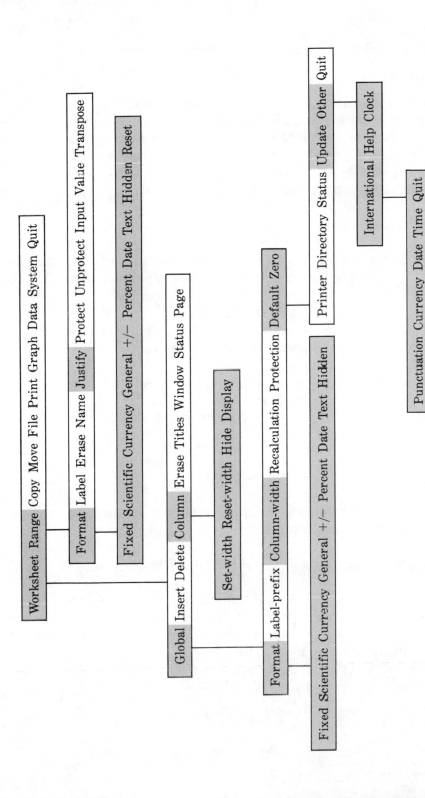

Worksheet Range Copy Move File Print Graph Data System Quit

Format Label Erase Name Justify Protect Unprotect Input Value Transpose

Fixed Scientific Currency General +/− Percent Date Text Hidden Reset

Global Insert Delete Column Erase Titles Window Status Page

Set-width Reset-width Hide Display

Format Label-prefix Column-width Recalculation Protection Default Zero

Fixed Scientific Currency General +/− Percent Date Text Hidden

Printer Directory Status Update Other Quit

International Help Clock

Punctuation Currency Date Time Quit

# /Range Format

## Description

The /Range Format command allows you to determine the appearance of numeric entries on your worksheet. With this command you can change the specific display format for one or many cells in a contiguous range on the worksheet. You will be able to choose the number of decimal places displayed (0 to 15) for most formats and determine whether the numeric information is displayed as currency, scientific notation, a date, a time (release 2 only), or one of several other options.

The display format you select will not affect the internal storage of numbers. You can elect to display a number with seven decimal places as a whole number, for example, but all seven places will be maintained internally.

Regardless of the format you choose, the column must be wide enough to display your selection. If the column is not wide enough, *'s will appear. Using a column width of 3 and attempting to format a number as currency with two decimal places would result in a display of asterisks, for example, because the $ and the decimal point also take up space.

## Options

1-2-3 provides a menu to allow you to define your format. You may choose from the following:

Fixed Scientific Currency , General +/− Percent Date Text Hidden Reset

To employ the /Range Format command, enter /Range Format and select the option you wish to use. Then respond to 1-2-3's prompts concerning the number of decimal places (or the Date format) you desire. Finally, select the range of cells to be formatted by entering either the address or a range name or by highlighting the cells with your cursor.

**Fixed**     Fixed format allows you to display all entries with a specific number of decimal places. Two places are the default, but you may select any number between 0 and 15. Examples with three decimal places are .007, 9.000, and 4.156.

**Scientific**     Scientific format displays numbers in exponential form, showing the power of 10 that the number must be multiplied by. This format allows you to concisely represent very large or very small numbers. From 0 to 15 places can be specified for the multiplier. Some examples with two decimal places are 6.78E−20, 4.11E+5, and 0.78E+8.

**Currency**     Currency format will cause your entry to be preceded by a dollar sign ($). It will also insert a separator such as a comma between the thousands and hundreds positions. You may specify from 0 to 15 decimal places for this format; 2 is the default. Negative amounts will appear in parentheses. Examples with two decimal places are $3.40, $1,400.98, and ($89.95).

**, (Comma)**     Comma format is identical to the Currency format except that Comma lacks the dollar sign ($). Comma format uses the thousands separator and allows you to specify any number of decimal places you want between 0 and 15. Two decimal places is the default. Negative numbers are displayed in parentheses. Examples with two decimal places are 1,200.00, (5,678.00), and 45.00.

**General**     General is the default format for 1-2-3. With it the leading zero integer will always appear, as in 0.78, but trailing zeros will be suppressed. If the number is very large or very small, it will appear in scientific notation. Examples of numeric displays with the General format are 15.674, 2.7E+12, and 0.67543.

**+/−**     +/− format produces a horizontal bar graph showing the relative size of numbers. Each integer is represented by a symbol. For example, $-3$ would be $---$, and 5 would be $+++++$. A . is used to represent 0.

**Percent**     Percent format displays your entries as percentages. Each entry will be multiplied by 100, and a % symbol will be added to the end. Because of this multiplication, you must enter percents as their decimal equivalents. For example, you must enter .05 for 5%. If you enter 5 and format the cell as Percent, it will display as 500%. You may specify from 0 to 15 decimal places; 2 is the default. Examples with two decimal places are 4.00%, 3.15%, and 1200.00%.

**Date**     The Date option is the only format choice that provides a second menu of possibilities. From this second menu you can select specific formats for the date. The formats accessible through the date option are as follows:

| | | |
|---|---|---|
| D1 | (DD-MMM-YY) | 08-Sep-86 |
| D2 | (DD-MMM) | 08-Sep |
| D3 | (MMM-YY) | Sep-86 |
| D4 | (MM/DD/YY) | 09/08/86 |
| D5 | (MM/DD) | 09/08 |

In release 2, Time formats are accessed through the Date format. When you select Time from the Date options, a menu of four time formats will be presented. Two of the formats use the AM and PM designation, and the other two are international formats that use a 24-hour day like military time. The formats available for the display of time in your worksheet cells can be seen in the following table.

| | | |
|---|---|---|
| (D6) T1 | HH:MM:SS AM/PM | 06:00:00 AM |
| (D7) T2 | HH:MM | 06:00 AM |
| D8) T3 | Long International | 06:00:00 * |
| (D9) T4 | Short International | 06:00 * |

*This format can be changed to a number of options with the /Worksheet Global Default Other International command.

**Text**     Text format displays the cells selected exactly as you have entered them. In the case of formulas, the formula rather than the result will be displayed.

**Hidden**     Hidden format causes the selected cells to appear blank on the screen. If you move your cursor to one of these cells, the control panel will display the entry you made in the cell.

**Reset**     This option returns the range of cells you select to the default format setting.

# /Range Justify

## Description

The /Range Justify command allows to change the way a label is displayed. Once a label is entered (for instance, a long label entered in cell A1), you use Range Justify to redistribute the label so that it is displayed differently. For instance, the long label in cell A1 might be displayed in the range A1..C3. The width of the display is determined by selecting a justify range, which may be one to several cells wide (the maximum is 240 characters) and one to several rows long.

If you use Range Justify to redistribute a label in cell A1 to the single-row justify range A1..C1, the label will be reformatted to display in the first three columns of however many rows it takes to display the full label. The label will be contained only in the cells of column A, however.

Information in cells to the right of a justify range is not displaced when you use Range Justify. Instead, the display of a label in the justify range is truncated—even though the contents of the cells containing the label are not affected.

## Options

You have the option of specifying one or more rows for the justify range. If you specify one row, 1-2-3 will include all labels from that row down to either the bottom of the worksheet or the first row that does not contain a label. Cells containing nonlabel entries below the justify range may be shifted up or down depending on the space requirements for the justified labels.

If you specify more than one row with /Range Justify, you assume the burden of allowing sufficient space for the justification. If there is not enough space in the range you choose, you will see the error message "Justify range is full or line is too long." With a selection of more than one row for the range, only the labels in the range down to the first nonlabel entry will be justified. In addition, when you specify more than one row, cells outside of the justify range will not be affected.

### Note

Do not use this command for cells that have been assigned range names. Although the contents of the cell may be displaced, the range name will still be assigned to the same cell.

## /Worksheet Column

### Description

The /Worksheet Column command allows you to change the characteristics of the worksheet columns. You can use the command to change the column width and to hide and display columns.

### Options

After entering /Worksheet Column, you will be presented with the following options:

Set-Width Reset-Width Hide Display

**Set-Width**    After choosing this option, either use the right and left arrow keys to change the column width of the current column or type in the exact width desired for that column. With release 1A, any width between 1 and 72 can be chosen. With release 2, any width between 1 and 240 is acceptable. If you choose a column width narrower than the width of your data, the data will display as asterisks.

**Reset-Width**    This option returns the width setting for the current column to the default setting—that is, either the initial setting of nine characters or the setting established with /Worksheet Global Column-Width if that command has been used.

**Hide**    This option affects the display and printing of worksheet data. You can hide one or many columns, depending on the range you specify for this command. The hidden columns will not appear on your display. They also will not be printed, even if the print range spans cells on both sides of them.
   This command will not affect the data in the cells. At any time you can bring the data back into view with the Display command.

**Display**    This command allows you to redisplay one or more hidden columns. Each hidden column will have an asterisk next to the column number. The columns can be redisplayed either by highlighting a cell within each column you wish to redisplay or by entering a range that includes the hidden columns you wish to redisplay.

## /Worksheet Global Column-Width

### Description

The /Worksheet Global Column-Width command allows you to change the default column width for every column on the worksheet.

### Options

After entering /Worksheet Global Column-Width, either use the right and left arrow keys to change the column width or type in the exact width desired. With release 1A, any width between 1 and 72 can be chosen. With release 2, any width between 1 and 240 is acceptable.

## /Worksheet Global Default Other Clock

### Description

This command allows you to display the format for the date and time in the left corner of your screen if you are using release 2.

### Options

This command provides the following three options:

Standard International None

**Standard**    This is the default setting. It displays the date in the format DD-MMM-YY and the time as HH:MM AM/PM.

**International**    This option displays the date in whichever long international format is in effect (month, day, and year will be shown) and the time in whichever short international format is in effect (hours and minutes based on a 24-hour clock). The international format options are discussed in more detail under /Worksheet Global Default Other International.

**None**    This option suppresses the date and time display in the lower left corner of the screen.

## Description

The /Worksheet Global Default Other International command allows you to customize the display for numeric punctuation, currency, date, and time.

## Options

The command has the following four options:

*Punctuation Currency Date Time*

**Punctuation**    The numeric punctuation indicators you can control are the point separator (the decimal indicator in numbers like 55.98), the thousands separator for numbers, and the argument separator used in functions. The initial point separator is a period (.), but you have the option of changing it to a comma (,). The initial thousands separator is a comma. It can be changed to a period (.) or a space. The argument separator is initially set as a comma. It can be changed to a period (.) or a semicolon (;). The options are not chosen individually but in a threesome once you select Punctuation. The options available are shown in the following table:

| Option | Point | Argument | Thousands |
|--------|-------|----------|-----------|
| A | . | , | , |
| B | , | . | . |
| C | . | ; | , |
| D | , | ; | . |
| E | . | , | space |
| F | , | . | space |
| G | . | ; | space |
| H | , | ; | space |

**Currency**    This option allows you to change the currency symbol from the standard $ to one of the international currency symbols found in the LICS codes. You can also use any of the other LICS codes if the currency symbol you want is not in the table. You have the further choice of placing the symbol at the end of your entry rather than at the beginning as in the initial setting.

To change the currency indicator, invoke /Worksheet Global Default International Currency and then use the Compose sequence to type the LICS code sequence followed by ENTER. The Compose sequence allows you to enter more than one character in a single position. To access it, hold down the ALTERNATE key (ALT) while you press F1, then type the characters specified. For pounds you would type L followed by an equal sign, for example.

**Date**     The international date formats (Date formats D4 and D5) can be altered with the Date option under the /Worksheet Global Default Other International command. The initial setting for the international date (option A) is MM/DD/YY. This can be changed to three other options, as follows:

| | |
|---|---|
| B | DD/MM/YY |
| C | DD.MM.YY |
| D | YY-MM-DD |

**Time**     The appearance of the international time formats can be changed with this option. Format D8 shows hours, minutes, and seconds, while format D9 shows only hours and minutes. The initial international time setting (option A) is HH:MM:SS. The three options to which this setting can be changed are shown in the following table.

| | |
|---|---|
| B | HH.MM.SS |
| C | HH,MM,SS |
| D | HHhMMmSSs |

As an example, using these settings to display the time for 12:30:25 PM. would result in the following:

|   | **D8** | **D9** |
|---|--------|--------|
| A | 12:30:25 | 12:30 |
| B | 12.30.25 | 12.30 |
| C | 12,30,25 | 12,30 |
| D | 12h30m25s | 12h30m |

## /Worksheet Global Default Update

### Description

The /Worksheet Global Default Update command allows you to save changes made to 1-2-3's default settings with the /Worksheet Global Default commands so that the new settings will be available the next time you work with 1-2-3. The settings will be saved in the 123.CNF file on your 1-2-3 disk.

### Options

There are no options for this command.

## /Worksheet Global Format

### Description

The /Worksheet Global Format command allows you to change the default display format for the entire worksheet. All numeric entries on the worksheet will use the format chosen with this command unless they have been formatted with the /Range Format command, which has priority over /Worksheet Global Format.

### Options

To define your format selection you have the following menu options:

**Fixed**     Fixed format allows you to display all entries with a specific number of decimal places. Two places are the default, but you may select any number between 0 and 15. Examples with three decimal places are .007, 9.000, and 4.156.

**Scientific**     Scientific format displays numbers in exponential form, showing the power of 10 that the number must be multiplied by. This format allows you to concisely represent very large or very small numbers. From 0 to 15 places can be specified for the multiplier. Some examples with two decimal places are 6.78E−20, 4.11E+5, and 0.78E+8.

**Currency**     Currency format will cause your entries to be preceded by a dollar sign ($). It will also insert a separator such as a comma between the thousands and hundreds positions. You may specify from 0 to 15 decimal places for the Currency format; 2 is the default. Negative amounts will appear in parentheses. Examples with two decimal places are $3.40, $1,400.98, and ($89.95).

**, (Comma)**     Comma format is identical to the Currency format except that Comma lacks the dollar sign ($). Comma format uses the thousands separator and allows you to specify the number of decimal places you want between 0 and 15. Two decimal places is the default. Negative numbers are displayed in parentheses. Examples with two decimal places are 1,200.00, (5,678.00), and 45.00.

**General**     General is the default format for 1-2-3. With it the leading zero integer will always appear, as in 0.78, but trailing zeros will be suppressed. If the number is very large or very small, it will appear in scientific notation. Examples of numeric displays with the General format are 15.674, 2.7E+12, and 0.67543.

**+/−**     +/− format produces a horizontal bar graph showing the relative size of numbers. Each integer is represented by a symbol. For example $-3$ would be $---$, and 5 would be $+++++$. A . is used to represent 0.

**Percent**     Percent format displays your entries as percentages. Each entry will be multiplied by 100, and a % symbol will be added to the end. Because of this multiplication, you must enter percents as their decimal equivalents. For example, you must enter .05 for 5%. If you enter 5 and format the cell as Percent, it will display as 500%. You may specify from 0 to 15 decimal places; 2 is the default. Examples with two decimal places are 4.00%, 3.15%, and 1200.00%.

**Date**     The Date option is the only format choice that provides a second menu of possibilities. From this second menu you can select specific formats for the date. The formats accessible through the date option are as follows:

| D1 | (DD-MMM-YY) | 08-Sep-86 |
|----|-------------|-----------|
| D2 | (DD-MMM) | 08-Sep |
| D3 | (MMM-YY) | Sep-86 |
| D4 | (MM/DD/YY) | 09/08/86 |
| D5 | (MM/DD) | 09/08 |

In release 2, Time formats are accessed through the Date format. When you select Time from the Date format options, a menu of four time formats will be presented. Two of the formats use the AM and PM designation, and the other two are international formats that use a 24-hour day like military time. The formats available for the display of time in your worksheet cells can be seen in the following table.

| (D6) T1 | HH:MM:SS AM/PM | 06:00:00 AM |
|---------|----------------|-------------|
| (D7) T2 | HH:MM | 06:00 AM |
| (D8) T3 | Long International | 06:00:00 * |
| (D9) T4 | Short International | 06:00 * |

*This format can be changed to a number of options with the /Worksheet Global Default Other International command.

**Text**     Text format displays the cells selected exactly as you have entered them. In the case of formulas, the formula rather than the result will be displayed.

**Hidden**     Hidden format causes the selected cells to appear blank on the screen. If you move your cursor to one of these cells, the control panel will display the entry you made in the cell.

## /Worksheet Global Zero

### Description

This command allows you to suppress the display of cells that have a value equal to zero. It is available only under release 2.

### Options

The /Worksheet Global Zero command presents only two options: Yes and No. The default is No, which allows zero values to display. Choosing the Yes option will suppress the display of zero values.

# Printing

Working with your models on the screen is great if you want to make changes and see their immediate impact. But when you have to go to a meeting and reference these same numbers, the screen in your office is no help. Fortunately 1-2-3 has extensive print features that allow you to create anything from a quick hard copy of important figures to a formal multipage report.

Preparation for using the print features of 1-2-3 begins before you build your first model. With release 2, you must install your package before you can print any model. The installation process creates a driver set that can speak the correct language for your particular printer. If you have not yet installed your package, go back to Chapter 1 for detailed directions on completing this vital step.

In this chapter you will have an opportunity to work with all of 1-2-3's commands related to printing, which are shown in the command map on page 175, preceding the reference section for this chapter. In addition to Print menu commands, you will explore the Global Default Printer options and the other commands in the Worksheet menu that deal with printing. With these commands you will be able to set up parameters such as margins and page length as defaults that will be used every time you work with 1-2-3. By the time you finish this chapter you should have mastered simple printing tasks and should also be familiar with the more advanced print options that 1-2-3 provides.

## Print Destination

The first choice you must make when selecting Print from the main menu is the destination of your print output. You must decide whether you want the information sent directly to your printer or written to a disk file for later printing. Often other factors make this decision for you. If you do not have a printer attached to your system, for example, a disk file will be your only choice. Likewise, if your printer is broken or if you need to further manipulate your output with a print utility, you will want to choose File. Sideways is one popular print utility. It allows you to print your 1-2-3 output to a disk file and then have this utility print from the disk to your printer. Among other things, Sideways can turn the output so that it prints sideways across the paper, allowing you to print a report as wide as you want.

When 1-2-3 writes your print file to disk, it will assign the suffix .PRN to the file name to distinguish the file from the worksheet files on your disk, which will have suffixes of .WKS or .WK1 depending on which release of 1-2-3 you are using. If you want to review the contents of your print file, you can use DOS commands like TYPE to scroll through the output on your screen. You can also use your word processor to view the print file.

Once you select Printer or File, you will need to tell 1-2-3 such things as what part of the worksheet you want printed and what left and right margins you want. All the Print command options can be used with both File and Printer. Review the options, then make your selections from 1-2-3's Print menus. As you do this, be aware that several of 1-2-3's Print menus do not disappear like other menus after you have made your selection. They tend to stick around in case you want to select other options. To eliminate these menus from your screen, select Quit.

## Print Range

Whether you are printing to your printer or a disk file, you will have to decide what worksheet cells you want to print. You can print every cell that contains entries, or just a few. In either case you will need to specify the range of cells to 1-2-3. You do this through the Range option in the main Print menu shown in Figure 5-1. To see how this works, assume you want to print the model shown in Figure 5-2. If you have never printed this worksheet before, 1-2-3 will assume that the starting location for printing is the current cursor location. Therefore you will probably want to position your cursor on A1 before pressing /PP to tell 1-2-3 to print to the printer.

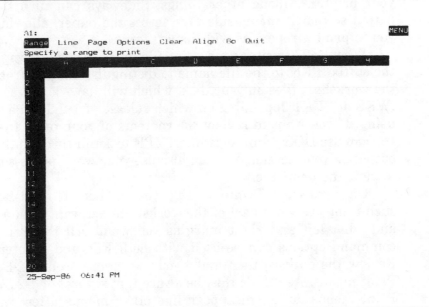

**Figure 5-1.** Range option on the main Print menu

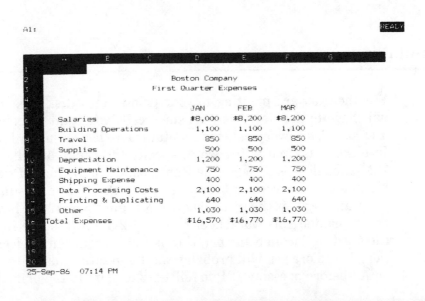

**Figure 5-2.** Worksheet example for specifying print range

To tell 1-2-3 what range to print, follow these steps:

1. Press R to select the range option.

2. Lock the beginning of the range in place at A1 by typing a period.

3. Move to the end of the model by pressing the special sequence of END followed by HOME.

4. Press ENTER to tell 1-2-3 that the range has been selected.

5. Assuming that all the default settings are acceptable, check to make sure the printer is turned on and the paper is aligned properly, then select Go from the Print menu. You should get the printout shown in Figure 5-3.

The default margins and page length used in producing 1-2-3 printouts are illustrated in Figure 5-4. Other options to change the appearance of your printed output will be covered later in the chapter. Some of these options allow you to change the default margins, page size, and other print characteristics. Changes in the default setting would be made

```
                        Boston Company
                    First Quarter Expenses

                            JAN        FEB        MAR
        Salaries           $8,000     $8,200     $8,200
        Building Operations 1,100      1,100      1,100
        Travel               850        850        850
        Supplies             500        500        500
        Depreciation       1,200      1,200      1,200
        Equipment Maintenance 750        750        750
        Shipping Expense     400        400        400
        Data Processing Costs 2,100     2,100      2,100
        Printing & Duplicating 640       640        640
        Other              1,030      1,030      1,030
Total Expenses            $16,570    $16,770    $16,770
```

**Figure 5-3.**    Printed output from worksheet example

| Name | Base Salary | Inc. Mo | % INC | 1985 Salary | Benefits |
|------|------------|---------|-------|-------------|----------|
| Alpen, Pat | $35,000.00 | 10 | 4.00% | $35,350.00 | $4,949.00 |
| Arbor, Jim | $23,000.00 | 4 | 7.00% | $24,207.50 | $3,389.05 |
| Bunde, Norman | $12,000.00 | 1 | 4.00% | $12,480.00 | $1,747.20 |
| Campbell Keith | $32,000.00 | 1 | 9.00% | $34,880.00 | $4,883.20 |
| Campbell, David | $40,000.00 | 1 | 10.00% | $44,000.00 | $6,160.00 |
| Denmore, Mary | $18,900.00 | 11 | 7.50% | $19,136.25 | $2,679.08 |
| Farper, David | $40,000.00 | 1 | 10.00% | $44,000.00 | $6,160.00 |
| Fork, Angela | $36,900.00 | 4 | 7.00% | $38,837.25 | $5,437.22 |
| Guest, Norman | $12,000.00 | 1 | 4.00% | $12,480.00 | $1,747.20 |
| Guest, Paul | $45,000.00 | 2 | 9.00% | $48,712.50 | $6,819.75 |
| Guiness, Pat | $35,000.00 | 10 | 4.00% | $35,350.00 | $4,949.00 |
| Harker, Pat | $35,000.00 | 10 | 4.00% | $35,350.00 | $4,949.00 |
| Harper, Angela | $36,900.00 | 4 | 7.00% | $38,837.25 | $5,437.22 |
| Harper, David | $40,000.00 | 1 | 10.00% | $44,000.00 | $6,160.00 |
| Harris, Jim | $23,000.00 | 4 | 7.00% | $24,207.50 | $3,389.05 |
| Harris, John | $15,000.00 | 6 | 5.00% | $15,437.50 | $2,161.25 |
| Harvey, Jim | $23,000.00 | 4 | 7.00% | $24,207.50 | $3,389.05 |
| Hitt, Mary | $18,000.00 | 9 | 4.00% | $18,240.00 | $2,553.60 |
| Jacobs, Norman | $12,000.00 | 1 | 4.00% | $12,480.00 | $1,747.20 |
| Jenkins, Paul | $45,000.00 | 2 | 9.00% | $48,712.50 | $6,819.75 |
| Jones, Ray | $25,000.00 | 2 | 5.00% | $26,145.83 | $3,660.42 |
| Just, Ray | $25,000.00 | 2 | 5.00% | $26,145.83 | $3,660.42 |
| Kaylor, Angela | $36,900.00 | 4 | 7.00% | $38,837.25 | $5,437.22 |
| Kiger, Keith | $32,000.00 | 1 | 9.00% | $34,880.00 | $4,883.20 |
| Kommer, John | $15,000.00 | 6 | 5.00% | $15,437.50 | $2,161.25 |
| Korn, Pat | $35,000.00 | 10 | 4.00% | $35,350.00 | $4,949.00 |
| Larkin, Mary | $29,000.00 | 3 | 7.00% | $30,691.67 | $4,296.83 |
| Litt, Norman | $12,000.00 | 1 | 4.00% | $12,480.00 | $1,747.20 |
| Merriman, Angela | $36,900.00 | 4 | 7.00% | $38,837.25 | $5,437.22 |
| Morn, Pat | $35,000.00 | 10 | 4.00% | $35,350.00 | $4,949.00 |
| Nest, Paul | $45,000.00 | 2 | 9.00% | $48,712.50 | $6,819.75 |
| Parden, Mary | $29,000.00 | 3 | 7.00% | $30,691.67 | $4,296.83 |
| Parker, Mary | $29,000.00 | 3 | 7.00% | $30,691.67 | $4,296.83 |
| Parson, Mary | $18,000.00 | 9 | 4.00% | $18,240.00 | $2,553.60 |
| Piltman, Mary | $18,000.00 | 9 | 4.00% | $18,240.00 | $2,553.60 |
| Polk, Mary | $18,900.00 | 11 | 7.50% | $19,136.25 | $2,679.08 |
| Rensler, Jane | $12,000.00 | 1 | 4.00% | $12,480.00 | $1,747.20 |
| Rolf, John | $15,000.00 | 6 | 5.00% | $15,437.50 | $2,161.25 |
| Rolf, Mary | $18,000.00 | 9 | 4.00% | $18,240.00 | $2,553.60 |
| Sarper, Angela | $36,900.00 | 4 | 7.00% | $38,837.25 | $5,437.22 |
| Smith, Jim | $23,000.00 | 4 | 7.00% | $24,207.50 | $3,389.05 |
| Stanbor, Jim | $23,000.00 | 4 | 7.00% | $24,207.50 | $3,389.05 |
| Stark, Nancy | $18,900.00 | 11 | 7.50% | $19,136.25 | $2,679.08 |
| Stedman, David | $40,000.00 | 1 | 10.00% | $44,000.00 | $6,160.00 |
| Stephens, Paul | $45,000.00 | 2 | 9.00% | $48,712.50 | $6,819.75 |
| Stevenson, Mary | $18,900.00 | 11 | 7.50% | $19,136.25 | $2,679.08 |
| Stone, Mary | $29,000.00 | 3 | 7.00% | $30,691.67 | $4,296.83 |
| Stone, Ray | $25,000.00 | 2 | 5.00% | $26,145.83 | $3,660.42 |
| Tolf, John | $15,000.00 | 6 | 5.00% | $15,437.50 | $2,161.25 |
| Tolf, Mary | $18,000.00 | 9 | 4.00% | $18,240.00 | $2,553.60 |
| Tone, Mary | $29,000.00 | 3 | 7.00% | $30,691.67 | $4,296.83 |
| Trundle, John | $15,000.00 | 6 | 5.00% | $15,437.50 | $2,161.25 |
| Umber, Paul | $45,000.00 | 2 | 9.00% | $48,712.50 | $6,819.75 |

**Figure 5-4.**   Default margins and page length

between steps 4 and 5 in the print procedure previously described.

There may be one additional step in the printing procedure if you have already printed a worksheet before and want to print a new area of it. This is done by reissuing the /Print Printer Range command. If you have chosen File rather than Printer, selecting Go will start the process for writing your information to the disk.

## Controlling the Printer From the Keyboard

1-2-3 provides several commands that allow you to control the paper in your printer from the keyboard so you can leave some blank space if you want to. The three menu options to be explored in this context are Line, Page, and Align.

## Advancing Printer Paper
## A Line at a Time

The /Print Printer Line command spaces the paper in the printer up by one line. It acts just as if you turned your printer off line and pressed the line feed button, with one important exception. Pressing line feed does not alter the internal line count that 1-2-3 maintains to determine when a new page is needed. The Line command, however, will add one to 1-2-3's internal line count so it will stay in sync with the paper. Line assumes that you have positioned your paper at the top of a form before turning your printer on. If you did not, all pages will start at the same place on the form as your first page did, since 1-2-3's line count will not change. The Align command, discussed later in this section, can remedy this problem.

## Advancing Printer Paper
## A Page at a Time

The /Print Printer Page command moves the paper in your printer to the top of the next form. When you select this command, 1-2-3 checks its internal line count to determine how many lines must be spaced to complete a full page and reach the top of the next page. The result is similar to pressing form feed with your printer off line except that the Page command will print a footer (if you have defined one), for the bottom of your page, while form feed will not. Like Line, Page assumes that you started printing at the top of a form.

## Using Align to Reset
## The Printer Line Count

The /Print Printer Align command is another page adjustment command. Rather than moving the paper in the printer, it resets the line count to zero to represent the top of a page. Every time you position your paper at the top of a new form with /Print Printer Page or the printer control buttons, you should also use Align to tell 1-2-3 to start the line count of a new page from that point. If you do not remember to use Align, your new page will not be filled completely, since 1-2-3 will continue to use its existing line count even though it does not match the page currently in the printer.

## Exiting the Print Menu

The /Print Printer Quit command is the selection to make when you are finished with the Print menu. All "sticky" menus in 1-2-3 (that is, menus that do not automatically disappear when you select a command) provide the Quit option as a means of exiting the menu. Pressing ESC will also allow you to exit the menu.

You have had an opportunity to explore the default settings for printing and how they can be permanently changed. In this section you will learn how to tailor printing to the task at hand, making changes that affect only the current session or worksheet. Thus you can set the default to reflect what you need most of the time and still make temporary changes by using the Print Printer Options menu, shown here.

## Headers and Footers

Headers and footers are lines printed at the top and bottom, respectively, of every page of your report. Except for page numbers, they are usually the same for each page. A header or footer may be, for example, a date, company name, report name, department, page number, or some combination of these. Since 1-2-3 allows you to use a total header or footer width equal to the maximum printed report width of 240 characters and permits you to divide both headers and footers into separate segments for the right, left, and center portions of each line, you can place more than one piece of information in a header or footer. Rules for setting up headers and footers are summarized in the box called "Header and Footer Rules."

Headers and footers in 1-2-3 are specified through the /Print Printer Options Header and Footer commands. To separate the information you are entering into each section of the header or footer, use the vertical bar character (¦). Any

# 1
# 2
# 3

## Header and Footer Rules

Several characters are essential to creating headers and footers: the vertical bar (¦), the at sign (@), and the pound sign (#).

¦   This character is used to divide the three sections of a header or footer (right, left, and center). For example, entering the header Accounting Department¦Texas Company¦Rpt: 8976 would place the department name at the left, the company name in the center, and the report identification at the right. The heading ¦¦Rpt 4356 would place the report identifier on the far right; the left and center portions of the header are empty, as indicated by the two vertical bars.

@   This character can be used anywhere in a header or footer to incorporate the current system date. It can be combined with a character string such as Today's Date: to provide additional description.

#   This character can be placed anywhere in a header or footer to incorporate the current page number. It, too, can be combined with character strings for additional description, such as Page Number:.

spaces included between the vertical bars will be counted as characters to be included in the heading and will affect the alignment of the heading sections. To place the company name of Adams & Associates on the left and the report number 1234 on the right of a heading, for example, you would enter

Adams & Associates¦¦Rpt. No. 1234

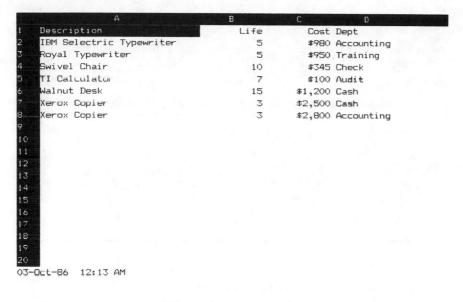

```
A1: [W28] 'Description                                    EDIT
Enter Header Line: Adams & Associates!!Rpt. No. 1234

               A                    B        C        D
1    Description                   Life     Cost Dept
2    IBM Selectric Typewriter        5      $980 Accounting
3    Royal Typewriter                5      $950 Training
4    Swivel Chair                   10      $345 Check
5    TI Calculator                   7      $100 Audit
6    Walnut Desk                    15    $1,200 Cash
7    Xerox Copier                    3    $2,500 Cash
8    Xerox Copier                    3    $2,800 Accounting
9
10
11
12
13
14
15
16
17
18
19
20
03-Oct-86   12:13 AM
```

**Figure 5-5.**     Entering a header

in response to the prompt, as shown in Figure 5-5. This
would display on your report as shown in Figure 5-6. To
place a heading only at the right of each page, you would
precede the header information with two vertical bars (‖).

Two special characters can be used in headers and footers to have 1-2-3 add the page number and date. Use # to
represent the location where you want 1-2-3 to add a page
number. 1-2-3 will begin with 1 and automatically increment
the number for each page. If you use page numbers on a
report, you will need to Clear and reset the Printer options
before printing again. Otherwise, the second report's paging
sequence will continue from the first.

Use @ to represent the location where you would like
1-2-3 to place the current date. 1-2-3 will obtain this date

```
Adams & Associates                                    Rpt. No. 1234

Description              Life    Cost Dept       Type         Inv Code
IBM Selectric Typewriter   5    $980 Accounting  Office         54301
Royal Typewriter           5    $950 Training    Office         54455
Swivel Chair              10    $345 Check       Furniture      54789
TI Calculator              7    $100 Audit       Office         54177
Walnut Desk               15  $1,200 Cash        Furniture      54138
Xerox Copier               3  $2,500 Cash        Processing     54392
Xerox Copier               3  $2,800 Accounting  Processing     54999
```

**Figure 5-6.**   Print output with a header

```
A1: [W24] 'Description                                              EDIT
Enter Header Line: Today's Date: @¦Page #¦Rpt. No. 1234
```

| | A | B | C | D | E | F |
|---|---|---|---|---|---|---|
| 1 | Description | Life | Cost | Dept | Type | Inv Code |
| 2 | IBM Selectric Typewriter | 5 | $980 | Accounting | Office | 54301 |
| 3 | Royal Typewriter | 5 | $950 | Training | Office | 54455 |
| 4 | Swivel Chair | 10 | $345 | Check | Furniture | 54789 |
| 5 | TI Calculator | 7 | $100 | Audit | Office | 54177 |
| 6 | Walnut Desk | 15 | $1,200 | Cash | Furniture | 54138 |
| 7 | Xerox Copier | 3 | $2,500 | Cash | Processing | 54392 |
| 8 | Xerox Copier | 3 | $2,800 | Accounting | Processing | 54999 |
| 9 | | | | | | |
| 10 | | | | | | |
| 11 | | | | | | |
| 12 | | | | | | |
| 13 | | | | | | |
| 14 | | | | | | |
| 15 | | | | | | |
| 16 | | | | | | |
| 17 | | | | | | |
| 18 | | | | | | |
| 19 | | | | | | |
| 20 | | | | | | |

```
25-Sep-86   08:17 PM
```

**Figure 5-7.**   Using date and page number in a header

from the system date, which is stored in your computer's memory. The only way to change this date is to access the DOS DATE command through the /System menu option (see Chapter 8), enter a new date, and then EXIT to return to 1-2-3.

These special characters can be entered in any header or footer segment and can be combined with other text, such as Page No: or Today's Date:. Figure 5-7 shows the construction of a header, while the finished product appears at the top of the report in Figure 5-8.

## Margins

The /Print Printer Options Margins command controls the amount of white space at the top, bottom, and sides of your printed document. A graphic representation of the page layout, including margins, can be seen in Figure 5-9. If you are printing a narrow range of cells, for example, you might want to increase the side margin settings to center the output on the paper, as shown in Figure 5-10. On the other hand, if you want to spread a great deal of data across a page, you might want to use very small side margin settings, like those in Figure 5-11.

```
Today's Date: 25-Sep-86        Page 1                  Rpt. No. 1234


Description              Life    Cost Dept       Type        Inv Code
IBM Selectric Typewriter    5    $980 Accounting  Office        54301
Royal Typewriter            5    $950 Training    Office        54455
Swivel Chair               10    $345 Check       Furniture     54789
TI Calculator               7    $100 Audit       Office        54177
Walnut Desk                15  $1,200 Cash        Furniture     54138
Xerox Copier                3  $2,500 Cash        Processing    54392
Xerox Copier                3  $2,800 Accounting  Processing    54999
```

**Figure 5-8.**    Printed output with the date and page number

Today's Date: 01-Oct-86                                    Rpt: 8901          header

| Name | Base Salary | Inc. Mo% | INC | 1985 Salary |
|------|-------------|----------|-----|-------------|
| Alpen, Pat | $35,000.00 | 10 | 4.00% | $35,350.00 |
| Arbor, Jim | $23,000.00 | 4 | 7.00% | $24,207.50 |
| Bunde, Norman | $12,000.00 | 1 | 4.00% | $12,480.00 |
| Campbell Keith | $32,000.00 | 1 | 9.00% | $34,880.00 |
| Campbell, David | $40,000.00 | 1 | 10.00% | $44,000.00 |
| Denmore, Mary | $18,900.00 | 11 | 7.50% | $19,136.25 |
| Farper, David | $40,000.00 | 1 | 10.00% | $44,000.00 |
| Fork, Angela | $36,900.00 | 4 | 7.00% | $38,837.25 |
| Guest, Norman | $12,000.00 | 1 | 4.00% | $12,480.00 |
| Guest, Paul | $45,000.00 | 2 | 9.00% | $48,712.50 |
| Guiness, Pat | $35,000.00 | 10 | 4.00% | $35,350.00 |
| Harker, Pat | $35,000.00 | 10 | 4.00% | $35,350.00 |
| Harper, Angela | $36,900.00 | 4 | 7.00% | $38,837.25 |
| Harper, David | $40,000.00 | 1 | 10.00% | $44,000.00 |
| Harris, Jim | $23,000.00 | 4 | 7.00% | $24,207.50 |
| Harris, John | $15,000.00 | 6 | 5.00% | $15,437.50 |
| Harvey, Jim | $23,000.00 | 4 | 7.00% | $24,207.50 |
| Hitt, Mary | $18,000.00 | 9 | 4.00% | $18,240.00 |
| Jacobs, Norman | $12,000.00 | 1 | 4.00% | $12,480.00 |
| Jenkins, Paul | $45,000.00 | 2 | 9.00% | $48,712.50 |
| Jones, Ray | $25,000.00 | 2 | 5.00% | $26,145.83 |
| Just, Ray | $25,000.00 | 2 | 5.00% | $26,145.83 |
| Kaylor, Angela | $36,900.00 | 4 | 7.00% | $38,837.25 |
| Kiger, Keith | $32,000.00 | 1 | 9.00% | $34,880.00 |
| Kommer, John | $15,000.00 | 6 | 5.00% | $15,437.50 |
| Korn, Pat | $35,000.00 | 10 | 4.00% | $35,350.00 |
| Larkin, Mary | $29,000.00 | 3 | 7.00% | $30,691.67 |
| Litt, Norman | $12,000.00 | 1 | 4.00% | $12,480.00 |
| Merriman, Angela | $36,900.00 | 4 | 7.00% | $38,837.25 |
| Morn, Pat | $35,000.00 | 10 | 4.00% | $35,350.00 |
| Nest, Paul | $45,000.00 | 2 | 9.00% | $48,712.50 |
| Parden, Mary | $29,000.00 | 3 | 7.00% | $30,691.67 |
| Parker, Mary | $29,000.00 | 3 | 7.00% | $30,691.67 |
| Parson, Mary | $18,000.00 | 9 | 4.00% | $18,240.00 |
| Piltman, Mary | $18,000.00 | 9 | 4.00% | $18,240.00 |
| Polk, Mary | $18,900.00 | 11 | 7.50% | $19,136.25 |
| Rensler, Jane | $12,000.00 | 1 | 4.00% | $12,480.00 |
| Rolf, John | $15,000.00 | 6 | 5.00% | $15,437.50 |
| Rolf, Mary | $18,000.00 | 9 | 4.00% | $18,240.00 |
| Sarper, Angela | $36,900.00 | 4 | 7.00% | $38,837.25 |
| Smith, Jim | $23,000.00 | 4 | 7.00% | $24,207.50 |
| Stanbor, Jim | $23,000.00 | 4 | 7.00% | $24,207.50 |
| Stark, Nancy | $18,900.00 | 11 | 7.50% | $19,136.25 |
| Stedman, David | $40,000.00 | 1 | 10.00% | $44,000.00 |
| Stephens, Paul | $45,000.00 | 2 | 9.00% | $48,712.50 |
| Stevenson, Mary | $18,900.00 | 11 | 7.50% | $19,136.25 |
| Stone, Mary | $29,000.00 | 3 | 7.00% | $30,691.67 |
| Stone, Ray | $25,000.00 | 2 | 5.00% | $26,145.83 |
| Tolf, John | $15,000.00 | 6 | 5.00% | $15,437.50 |
| Tolf, Mary | $18,000.00 | 9 | 4.00% | $18,240.00 |
| Tone, Mary | $29,000.00 | 3 | 7.00% | $30,691.67 |
| Trundle, John | $15,000.00 | 6 | 5.00% | $15,437.50 |
| Umber, Paul | $45,000.00 | 2 | 9.00% | $48,712.50 |

← left
margin →                                                    ← right
                                                              margin →

Page 1        footer

↑

bottom
margin

↓

**Figure 5-9.**    Page layout

```
                                        JAN
          Salaries                     $8,000
          Building Operations           1,100
          Travel                          850
          Supplies                        500
          Depreciation                  1,200
          Equipment Maintenance           750
          Shipping Expense                400
          Data Processing Costs         2,100
          Printing & Duplicating          640
          Other                         1,030
    Total Expenses                     $16,570
```

**Figure 5-10.**    Wide margins

The four options under the Margins command are Left,
Right, Top, and Bottom, corresponding to the four margins.
These options get their default values from settings specified
with /Worksheet Global Default Printer.

The default setting for the left margin is 4, but you can
change it to any number between 0 and 240. The default for
the right margin is 76, indicating 76 characters from the left
edge of the paper. You can assign it any value from 0 to 240.

```
                                    Boston Company


                        JAN      FEB      MAR      APR      MAY
     Salaries          $8,000   $8,200   $8,200   $8,700   $8,700
     Building Operations 1,100   1,100    1,100    1,100    1,100
     Travel               850     850      850      850      850
     Supplies             500     500      500      500      500
     Depreciation       1,200   1,200    1,200    1,200    1,200
     Equipment Maintenance 750    750      750      750      750
     Shipping Expense     400     400      400      400      400
     Data Processing Costs 2,100 2,100    2,100    2,100    2,100
     Printing & Duplicating 640   640      640      640      640
     Other              1,030   1,030    1,030    1,030    1,030
Total Expenses         $16,570  $16,770  $16,770  $17,270  $17,270
```

**Figure 5-11.**    Narrow margins

To use values greater than 80, you will either need to use compressed print when the worksheet is printed (specified through /Print Printer Options Setup) or have a wide-carriage printer that allows you to use paper wider than eight inches across. The top margin is initially set at 2 but can be revised to any number from 0 to 32 (0 to 10 for release 1A). The bottom margin is just the same.

To change any margin setting, simply type the new number after specifying the appropriate Margins option. The changes you make to the margin setting will be saved with the document if you save it to disk again after updating the Print options.

## Borders

The /Print Printer Options Borders command allows you to print identifying information found at the top of columns or along the left side of rows in your worksheet on every page of a report. This feature is useful if you have the months of the year across the worksheet, for example, and have more data than will fit on one page. You can print the worksheet with the months at the top of each page if the row containing the months is specified as a border.

Similarly, if your report is wider than it is long, you can print the information found at the far left of your worksheet on every page of your report. This information could be account names or other identifying descriptions. The range of worksheet cells you specify for printing will be printed either to the right of or below the border information. Do not select the border rows or columns as part of this print range, or you will have duplicate information on the first page of your output. Rules for borders are summarized in the box called "Border Options."

### Column Borders

The /Print Printer Options Borders Columns command is used when you have more columns of data than will fit across one page and have labels or other information in a column or columns on the left side of the worksheet that will help iden-

## Borders Options

The Borders option allows you to carry over descriptive information on multipage reports. The descriptive information may be in columns, rows, or both. Avoid the common mistake of including border rows or columns in your print range, since this will produce duplicate information in the printout.

tify data printed on subsequent pages of your report. Selecting these columns as borders will cause the columns to print on each page of the report.

The expense worksheet containing monthly figures, shown in Figure 5-12, serves as an example. If more than one range

```
C1:                                                          POINT
Enter Border Columns: A1..C1
```

|     | A | B | C | D | E | F | G |
|-----|---|---|---|---|---|---|---|
| 1   |   |   |   |   |   |   |   |
| 2   |   |   |   |   |   |   |   |
| 3   |   |   |   |   |   |   |   |
| 4   |   |   |   |   |   |   |   |
| 5   |   |   |   | JAN | FEB | MAR | APR |
| 6   | Salaries |   |   | $8,000 | $8,200 | $8,200 | $8,700 |
| 7   | Building Operations |   |   | 1,100 | 1,100 | 1,100 | 1,100 |
| 8   | Travel |   |   | 850 | 850 | 850 | 850 |
| 9   | Supplies |   |   | 500 | 500 | 500 | 500 |
| 10  | Depreciation |   |   | 1,200 | 1,200 | 1,200 | 1,200 |
| 11  | Equipment Maintenance |   |   | 750 | 750 | 750 | 750 |
| 12  | Shipping Expense |   |   | 400 | 400 | 400 | 400 |
| 13  | Data Processing Costs |   |   | 2,100 | 2,100 | 2,100 | 2,100 |
| 14  | Printing & Duplicating |   |   | 640 | 640 | 640 | 640 |
| 15  | Other |   |   | 1,030 | 1,030 | 1,030 | 1,030 |
| 16  | Total Expenses |   |   | $16,570 | $16,770 | $16,770 | $17,270 |
| 17  |   |   |   |   |   |   |   |
| 18  |   |   |   |   |   |   |   |
| 19  |   |   |   |   |   |   |   |
| 20  |   |   |   |   |   |   |   |

25-Sep-86   08:23 PM

**Figure 5-12.**   Entering the border columns

```
                                                           JAN
        Salaries               Salaries              $8,000
        Building Operations    Building Operations    1,100
        Travel                 Travel                   850
        Supplies               Supplies                 500
        Depreciation           Depreciation           1,200
        Equipment Maintenance  Equipment Maintenance    750
        Shipping Expense       Shipping Expense         400
        Data Processing Costs  Data Processing Costs  2,100
        Printing & Duplicating Printing & Duplicating   640
        Other                  Other                  1,030
  Total Expenses         Total Expenses         $16,570
```

**Figure 5-13.**    Columns printed twice

is used, the second range prints without the descriptive account name information. Setting these account names as column borders will allow you to print them on each page. To do this, select /Print Printer Options Borders Columns. In response to the request for columns, enter the range A1..C1. Begin your print range with D1. (If you begin it with A1, account name column information will be duplicated, as shown in Figure 5-13.) The correct multipage printout should look like Figure 5-14.

### Row Borders

The /Print Printer Options Borders Rows command is used when the identifying data you want repeated on each page is located in rows at the top of your worksheet. Use this option if there are more rows of data to print than will fit on one page. To use this option, enter the command. Then highlight a cell at the top of the border range, anchor it with a period (.), and highlight the cell on the far side of the border range. Once you have defined the borders, Quit the Options menu and select a print range that does not include the border cells. (If you include them, they will be printed twice.)

The example shown in Figure 5-15 has a set of column headings in row 1 and seven lines of data below it. On a nor-

```
                           JAN       FEB       MAR       APR
    Salaries              $8,000    $8,200    $8,200    $8,700
    Building Operations    1,100     1,100     1,100     1,100
    Travel                   850       850       850       850
    Supplies                 500       500       500       500
    Depreciation           1,200     1,200     1,200     1,200
    Equipment Maintenance    750       750       750       750
    Shipping Expense         400       400       400       400
    Data Processing Costs  2,100     2,100     2,100     2,100
    Printing & Duplicating   640       640       640       640
    Other                  1,030     1,030     1,030     1,030
Total Expenses           $16,570   $16,770   $16,770   $17,270
```

```
                           MAY      JUNE      JULY       AUG      SEPT
    Salaries              $8,700    $7,500    $7,500   $10,000   $10,000
    Building Operations    1,100     1,100     1,100     1,100     1,300
    Travel                   850       850       850       850       850
    Supplies                 500       500       500       500       500
    Depreciation           1,200     1,200     1,200     1,200     1,200
    Equipment Maintenance    750       750       750       750       750
    Shipping Expense         400       400       400       400       400
    Data Processing Costs  2,100     2,100     2,100     2,100     2,100
    Printing & Duplicating   640       640       640       640       640
    Other                  1,030     1,030     1,030     1,030     1,030
Total Expenses           $17,270   $16,070   $16,070   $18,570   $18,770
```

```
                           OCT       NOV       DEC
    Salaries             $10,000   $10,000   $10,000
    Building Operations    1,300     1,300     1,300
    Travel                   850       850       850
    Supplies                 500       500       500
    Depreciation           1,200     1,200     1,200
    Equipment Maintenance    750       750       750
    Shipping Expense         400       400       400
    Data Processing Costs  2,100     2,100     2,100
    Printing & Duplicating   640       640       640
    Other                  1,030     1,030     1,030
Total Expenses           $18,770   $18,770   $18,770
```

**Figure 5-14.** Three pages of print using border columns

```
         A                    B        C    D            E           F
1  Description              Life    Cost Dept         Type        Inv Code
2  IBM Selectric Typewriter   5    $980 Accounting   Office         54301
3  Royal Typewriter           5    $950 Training     Office         54455
4  Swivel Chair              10    $345 Check        Furniture      54789
5  TI Calculator              7    $100 Audit        Office         54177
6  Walnut Desk               15  $1,200 Cash         Furniture      54138
7  Xerox Copier               3  $2,500 Cash         Processing     54392
8  Xerox Copier               3  $2,800 Accounting   Processing     54999
9
10
11
12
13
14
15
16
17
18
19
20
```

25-Sep-86   05:18 PM

**Figure 5-15.**     Purchases worksheet for multipage printout

mal-size page, this information could fit on one sheet. If you selected very large top and bottom margins so that only the heading and the first four lines would fit on page 1, however, you would also want the descriptive information from row 1 placed at the top of page 2. To do this you must select this row as a border row. The steps involved in the selection are as follows:

1. Before beginning, move your cursor to A1.

2. Select /Print Printer Options Borders Rows.

3. You need to select only one cell in the row you want 1-2-3 to use as a border before pressing ENTER. (If you want to use more than one row in your border, select a range that includes the first cell in each border row.)

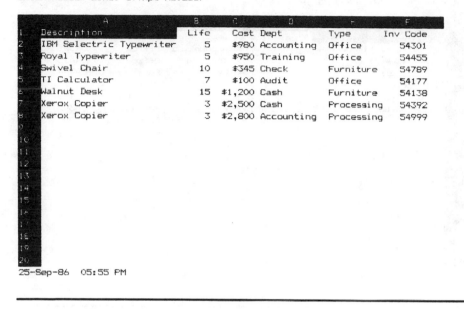

```
A1: [W24] 'Description                                              [DIT]
Enter Header Line: @||Rpt No:2657

            A               B      C        D          E          F
 1  Description            Life   Cost   Dept        Type      Inv Code
 2  IBM Selectric Typewriter  5  $980   Accounting  Office      54301
 3  Royal Typewriter          5  $950   Training    Office      54455
 4  Swivel Chair             10  $345   Check       Furniture   54789
 5  TI Calculator             7  $100   Audit       Office      54177
 6  Walnut Desk              15  $1,200 Cash        Furniture   54138
 7  Xerox Copier              3  $2,500 Cash        Processing  54392
 8  Xerox Copier              3  $2,800 Accounting  Processing  54999
 9
10
11
12
13
14
15
16
17
18
19
20
25-Sep-86  05:55 PM
```

**Figure 5-16.**    Entering a header

4. If you elect to enter both a header and footer for the report, select Header next and enter a header such as @||Rpt No:2657, as shown in Figure 5-16. This example entry will place the date at the left of the header and the report number on the right.

5. Footer would be your next selection. To center the page number, enter ¦ Page No: as shown in Figure 5-17.

6. The remaining two entries needed are Margins Top and Margins Bottom. In our example, the top margin was set at 25 and the bottom margin at 30, leaving only five print lines on a 66-line page once the header, footer, and other blank lines at the top and bottom are included.

7. Finally, press Q to quit the Options menu and select Range to tell 1-2-3 what range to print. In this case you

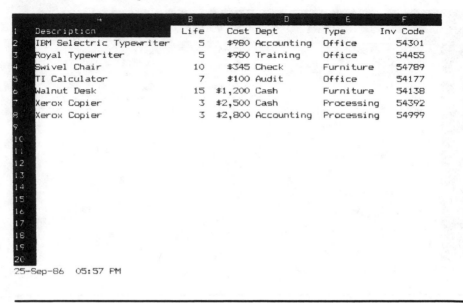

```
A1: [W24] 'Description                                              EDIT
Enter Footer Line: !Page No: #

                A           B      C      D         E          F
 1  Description            Life    Cost Dept       Type      Inv Code
 2  IBM Selectric Typewriter  5    $980 Accounting  Office     54301
 3  Royal Typewriter          5    $950 Training    Office     54455
 4  Swivel Chair             10    $345 Check       Furniture  54789
 5  TI Calculator             7    $100 Audit       Office     54177
 6  Walnut Desk              15  $1,200 Cash        Furniture  54138
 7  Xerox Copier              3  $2,500 Cash        Processing 54392
 8  Xerox Copier              3  $2,800 Accounting  Processing 54999
 9
10
11
12
13
14
15
16
17
18
19
20
25-Sep-86   05:57 PM
```

**Figure 5-17.**    Entering a footer

would select the range A2 to F8, carefully excluding the
border row so it will not print twice. Then select Go from
the Print menu.

The product of this process should be the two report
pages shown in Figure 5-18. If you had extended the top and
bottom margins a little further, you could have produced a
report with only one data line per page.

## Talking to Your Printer
## With Setup Strings

Most printers have a variety of special features that you can
access if you can "speak the language" of the printer. 1-2-3
has the ability to speak the language of most printers if you
supply it with the correct words.

```
25-Sep-86                                                Rpt No:2657


Description              Life    Cost Dept         Type      Inv Code
IBM Selectric Typewriter   5    $980 Accounting    Office     54301
Royal Typewriter           5    $950 Training      Office     54455
Swivel Chair              10    $345 Check         Furniture  54789
TI Calculator              7    $100 Audit         Office     54177


                         Page No. 1
```

```
25-Sep-86                                                Rpt No:2657


Description              Life    Cost Dept         Type      Inv Code
Walnut Desk               15  $1,200 Cash          Furniture  54138
Xerox Copier               3  $2,500 Cash          Processing 54392
Xerox Copier               3  $2,800 Accounting    Processing 54999


                         Page No: 2
```

**Figure 5-18.**   Printout using border rows

Your printer may have such features as compressed print, six or eight lines to the inch, boldface printing, and enlarged print. Unfortunately, there is no single set of codes to access these features in all printers that have them; each printer has its own "language." You will have to look in your printer manual for the decimal codes assigned to that printer's features. The "Setup String Chart" box provides a handy form for making a reference list of these printer codes once you have found them.

## 1 2 3 Setup String Chart

Setup strings allow you to utilize the full features of your printer. You must use a setup string customized for your printer to access the features your printer supports. This chart can serve as a convenient reference for your printer's setup codes once you have looked them up in your printer manual. Add other features to this list as needed so you can have all your codes in one place.

Begin Boldface                _____
End Boldface                  _____
Begin Compressed              _____
End Compressed                _____
Begin Enlarged                _____
End Enlarged                  _____
Begin Emphasized              _____
End Emphasized                _____
Begin Auto Underline          _____
End Auto Underline            _____
Print 6 lines per inch        _____
Print 8 lines per inch        _____

To enter the desired printer code or codes as a setup string, you first enter the command sequence /Print Printer Options Setup and press ENTER. If another setup string is already displayed, press ESC before entering a new string. Next enter the printer code or codes you want, preceding each decimal code with a backslash (\) and a zero. This will produce entries such as \027, \018, or \015. After the complete setup string is entered, press ENTER again. Then select Quit from the Options menu and Go from the main print menu to obtain your printout.

Setup strings can include more than one feature. For instance, you may want both compressed print and boldface characters. You can have up to 39 characters in a setup string. The feature your setup string requests will remain in effect, in most cases, until you send another setup string that turns off the feature you selected. For example, the setup string for compressed print on the Epson 100 printer is \015. This compressed or smaller-sized print will remain in effect until the Epson setup string \018 is transmitted to turn off the compressed print feature or the printer is turned off to erase its print buffer. Figure 5-19 shows the setup string for compressed print on the Epson, and Figure 5-20 shows a report printed with this feature.

It is also possible to include setup strings in worksheet cells with release 2. The advantage of this approach is that it allows you to change print characteristics more than once while printing a worksheet. Place these entries in blank rows, since the entire row is ignored after the setup string is processed. Setup strings in a worksheet cell must be preceded by two vertical bars (‖). Placing \015 in a cell would mean entering ‖\015 in the cell, for example.

Let's look at an example in detail. Suppose you have a small worksheet on which you would like to print the company name in boldface. Since the printing will be done on an Epson MX100 printer, you need to use Epson print codes. You will place the print code for boldface, ‖027G, on the line above the company name. (Notice that this print code looks a little different from those presented earlier in that it includes a letter. A number of print codes do use letters; you will have to check your manual for the right code for your printer.) On

```
        A         B           C         D        E        F        G
1
2
3
4
5                                          JAN      FEB      MAR      APR
6       Salaries                          $8,000   $8,200   $8,200   $8,700
7       Building Operations                1,100    1,100    1,100    1,100
8       Travel                               850      850      850      850
9       Supplies                             500      500      500      500
10      Depreciation                       1,200    1,200    1,200    1,200
11      Equipment Maintenance                750      750      750      750
12      Shipping Expense                     400      400      400      400
13      Data Processing Costs              2,100    2,100    2,100    2,100
14      Printing & Duplicating               640      640      640      640
15      Other                              1,030    1,030    1,030    1,030
16 Total Expenses                        $16,570  $16,770  $16,770  $17,270
17
18
19
20
25-Sep-86   08:29 PM
```

**Figure 5-19.**    Entering a setup string

| | JAN | FEB | MAR | APR | MAY | JUNE | JULY | AUG | SEPT | OCT | NOV |
|---|---|---|---|---|---|---|---|---|---|---|---|
| Salaries | $8,000 | $8,200 | $8,200 | $8,700 | $8,700 | $7,500 | $7,500 | $10,000 | $10,000 | $10,000 | $10,000 |
| Building Operations | 1,100 | 1,100 | 1,100 | 1,100 | 1,100 | 1,100 | 1,100 | 1,100 | 1,300 | 1,300 | 1,300 |
| Travel | 850 | 850 | 850 | 850 | 850 | 850 | 850 | 850 | 850 | 850 | 850 |
| Supplies | 500 | 500 | 500 | 500 | 500 | 500 | 500 | 500 | 500 | 500 | 500 |
| Depreciation | 1,200 | 1,200 | 1,200 | 1,200 | 1,200 | 1,200 | 1,200 | 1,200 | 1,200 | 1,200 | 1,200 |
| Equipment Maintenance | 750 | 750 | 750 | 750 | 750 | 750 | 750 | 750 | 750 | 750 | 750 |
| Shipping Expense | 400 | 400 | 400 | 400 | 400 | 400 | 400 | 400 | 400 | 400 | 400 |
| Data Processing Costs | 2,100 | 2,100 | 2,100 | 2,100 | 2,100 | 2,100 | 2,100 | 2,100 | 2,100 | 2,100 | 2,100 |
| Printing & Duplicating | 640 | 640 | 640 | 640 | 640 | 640 | 640 | 640 | 640 | 640 | 640 |
| Other | 1,030 | 1,030 | 1,030 | 1,030 | 1,030 | 1,030 | 1,030 | 1,030 | 1,030 | 1,030 | 1,030 |
| Total Expenses | $16,570 | $16,770 | $16,770 | $17,270 | $17,270 | $16,070 | $16,070 | $18,570 | $18,770 | $18,770 | $18,770 |

**Figure 5-20.**    Worksheet printed with compressed print

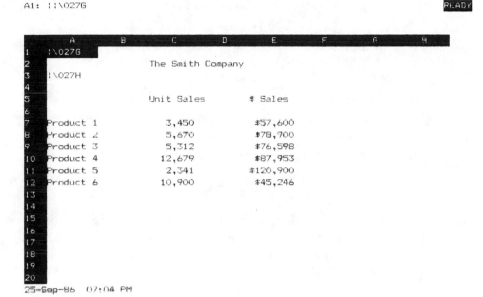

A1:  ||\027G                                                                    READY

```
         A          B          C          D          E          F          G          H
1   |\027G
2                         The Smith Company
3   |\027H
4
5                        Unit Sales       $ Sales
6
7   Product 1              3,450         $57,600
8   Product 2              5,670         $78,700
9   Product 3              5,312         $76,598
10  Product 4             12,679         $87,953
11  Product 5              2,341        $120,900
12  Product 6             10,900         $45,246
13
14
15
16
17
18
19
20
```

25-Sep-86   07:04 PM

**Figure 5-21.**    Entering setup strings on the worksheet

the line below the company name you will enter the code to
stop boldface, ‖\027H, as shown in Figure 5-21. (Only one
vertical bar displays in the cell.) If you then enter the range
A1..E12, quit Options, and select Go from the Print menu,
the report shown in Figure 5-22 should be produced. Notice
that the lines containing the print codes do not print on the
report. It is as if these lines do not exist except for their
effect on print characteristics.

## Page Length

Page length is the number of lines that could be printed on a
sheet of paper, assuming every line was used. With the

```
                        The Smith Company

                        Unit Sales        $ Sales
        Product 1          3,450          $57,600
        Product 2          5,670          $78,900
        Product 3          5,312          $76,598
        Product 4         12,679          $87,953
        Product 5          2,341         $120,900
        Product 6         10,900          $45,246
```

**Figure 5-22.**    Heading printed in boldface

default options in effect and print at 6 lines per inch, only 56 lines will be printed for a page length of 66. This is because lines 1, 2, 65, and 66 are reserved for top and bottom margins. Line 3 is left blank for a header, and lines 4 and 5 are blank to make space between header and text. Similarly, line 64 is left blank for a footer and lines 62 and 63 for space. This leaves lines 6 through 61 for printing your worksheet data. Of course, if you elect to print at 8 lines per inch by supplying the proper setup code, you can increase the page length to 88 on the same 11-inch sheet of paper. You can reset the default page length with the /Print Printer Options Pg-Length command sequence.

## Other Options

The /Print Printer Options Other command allows you to decide whether information will be printed with or without formatting that has been added to the text. It also allows you to print formulas rather than the information displayed on your screen.

### Printing What You See on the Screen

The default setting, As-Displayed, will cause your report to contain the same information you see on the screen. This means that the results of formulas will be printed just as they are displayed on the screen. The formats in effect on your screen display will be used for the printout, as will the column width for the current active window. In short, you will have an exact duplicate of the worksheet portion of the screen display, except that you are not restricted to screen size for your printout. You will be restricted to the limitations of the established page size, however. If you want to change the printout relative to your normal worksheet display, you could set up a second window (see Chapter 5), make formatting changes to this window, and print from there.

### Printing Cell Formulas

In the last chapter you learned how to display formulas in cells by using the /Range Format Text command. To print a Text format worksheet like the one described in Chapter 4, you could use the As-Displayed option, since the formulas are already displayed. Alternatively, you could use 1-2-3's built-in formula printing option. With this option you do not have to change the format and width of cells as you did in Chapter 4, because the package does not print the formulas in the shape of the spreadsheet. Instead, it prints the formulas one per line down the page. The documentation produced by this approach thus can be quite a long list if an entire large spreadsheet is involved. This is an excellent way to print the formulas for a smaller range of cells, however, because it involves so little work on your part. All you have to do is select your print range and then choose Options Other Cell-Formulas. Quitting the Options menu and selecting Go from the Print menu will produce a formula listing like the one in Figure 5-23. With release 2 the formulas print according to the row they are in, with the order being A1, B1, C1, A2, B2, and so on. With release 1A the print order is by column.

### Using Format Options for Printing

Like As-Displayed, Formatted is another default setting in the Other menu. It will use page breaks, headers, footers,

```
T2:  [W13] '1985 Salary
U2:  'Benefits
T4:  (C2) [W13] ((R4-1)*(Q4/12))+((12-(R4-1))*(1+S4)*(Q4/12))
U4:  +T4*0.14
T5:  (C2) [W13] ((R5-1)*(Q5/12))+((12-(R5-1))*(1+S5)*(Q5/12))
U5:  +T5*0.14
T6:  (C2) [W13] ((R6-1)*(Q6/12))+((12-(R6-1))*(1+S6)*(Q6/12))
U6:  +T6*0.14
T7:  (C2) [W13] ((R7-1)*(Q7/12))+((12-(R7-1))*(1+S7)*(Q7/12))
U7:  +T7*0.14
T8:  (C2) [W13] ((R8-1)*(Q8/12))+((12-(R8-1))*(1+S8)*(Q8/12))
U8:  +T8*0.14
T9:  (C2) [W13] ((R9-1)*(Q9/12))+((12-(R9-1))*(1+S9)*(Q9/12))
U9:  +T9*0.14
T10: (C2) [W13] ((R10-1)*(Q10/12))+((12-(R10-1))*(1+S10)*(Q10/12))
U10: +T10*0.14
```

**Figure 5-23.**     Cell-Formulas printout

and any other formatting you have done to create a professional report. Formatting is used almost every time a report
is printed on a printer.

### Eliminating Formatting From Output

When you write files to disk for use with another program,
you often do not want formatting characters added. The
other program may not know what to do with them and may
try to process them as data. Choosing the Unformatted option
alleviates this problem by causing the files to be written
without formatting. This means that 1-2-3 will ignore page
breaks, headers, footers, and any other formatting you have
added to the text. Usually use of this option is confined to
printing to disk. It might also be used when you print a list
that barely runs over to the next page. You might prefer to
keep such a list together even if it prints over the page perfo-
ration. You could do this by choosing /Print Printer Options
Other Unformatted.

## Saving Print Settings

When a worksheet file is saved, the print settings associated with this file are also saved. This means that saving a worksheet after setting margins, setup strings, and other options will ensure that you will not have to reenter these settings next time you use this file.

## Clearing Print Settings

The Clear options let you eliminate some or all of the special print settings you have used for a report and return to the default settings. The four options presented from the Clear menu are All, Range, Borders, and Format.

### Clearing All Settings

The All option restores the default for all of your print settings, including print range, borders, setup strings, and margins. If you want to be more selective, you can use one of the other three options.

### Clearing Range Settings

The Range option eliminates only a range specification made earlier for the worksheet. Other print options are not affected.

### Clearing Border Settings

The Borders option cancels the specification of any rows or columns as borders. Other print options are not affected.

### Clearing Format Settings

The Format command returns margins, setup strings, and page length to their default values but does not affect range or borders.

It takes little effort to get a printed copy of your worksheet because 1-2-3 does much of the preliminary work for you by setting up default values for many of the print options. These default values are available whenever you load 1-2-3. Sometimes, however, you may wish to change the default values. This section shows how you can make permanent changes to these options, and the next section shows how to make changes that apply to just one particular worksheet.

The command you will need to change the default values is not found in the Print menu. It is /Worksheet Global Default Printer. It presents the following menu.

By changing these options to values that meet your particular needs, you can save time by not having to change print options every time you load 1-2-3. Notice the Quit option at the end of this menu, which indicates that it is another menu that will stick around until you eliminate it with Quit.

### Printer Interface

The /Worksheet Global Default Printer Interface option allows you to specify the default printer interface. The default setting is 1 for a parallel interface. This is the appropriate setting for a parallel printer adapter. Seven other settings are possible. The first three are as follows:

(2) Serial 1 for a serial printer with an RS-232 interface

(3) Parallel 2 for a second parallel printer

(4) Serial 2 for a second serial printer

The remaining four options are DOS devices for use when your computer is part of a local area network. They are available only under release 2. Here is a list of them.

    5 LPT1

    6 LPT2

    7 LPT3

    8 LPT4

You will need to specify additional information concerning your network configuration, such as baud rate, when selecting any of these last four settings.

## Automatic Line Feed

The /Worksheet Global Default Printer Auto-LF command determines whether 1-2-3 needs to generate a line feed after every carriage return. Its two options are No, indicating that your printer does not generate line feeds, and Yes, indicating that it does. If your printed output looks the way you want it to, you do not have to worry about this setting. If extra line feeds are being generated, you will want to change this setting to Yes. If line feeds are missing, you will want to change this setting to No.

## Left Margin

The /Worksheet Global Default Printer Left command establishes a default left margin of 4. You can use this option to change the default to any number from 0 to 240.

## Right Margin

The /Worksheet Global Default Printer Right command establishes a default right margin of 76, four spaces in from the right edge of a paper that holds 80 characters across. As with the left margin setting, you can use any setting for this option from 0 to 240.

## Top Margin

The /Worksheet Global Default Printer Top command is set at 2 for a top margin. You can change this option to allow a default of 0 to 32 lines with release 2 and 0 to 10 with release 1A.

## Bottom Margin

The default for the bottom margin is also set at 2. You can change it to any number from 0 to 32 for release 2 and 0 to 10 for release 1A with the /Worksheet Global Default Printer Bottom command.

## Page Length

The default setting for page length is 66. This is the correct setting for 8 1/2- by 11-inch paper, assuming printing at 6 lines per inch. You can change the default to any number from 10 to 100 for version 2 and 20 to 100 for version 1A with the /Worksheet Global Default Printer Pg-Length command.

## Paper Feeding

The /Worksheet Global Default Printer Wait option indicates whether you wish to wait for a paper change at the end of each sheet. The default setting is No, which is appropriate for continuous-feed paper. Changing the setting to Yes is appropriate when single sheets are used.

## Printer Setup

As you saw earlier in this chapter, setup strings are special codes you can transmit to your printer to access its special features. The default setting is no setup string, but if you have features you wish to use on a regular basis, such as double strike or compressed print, you should add the setup string to the default settings with the /Worksheet Global Default Printer Setup command.

There is no menu under this option because of the wide variations in setup strings from model to model. Your printer manual supplies the decimal codes that represent the options you wish to use. In most printer manuals you will find a two-digit decimal code. Precede this code by a backslash ( \ ) and a zero to transform it into a 1-2-3 setting. For instance, \015 is the 1-2-3 form of the code that tells the Epson printer to use its compressed print feature.

## Choosing Your Printer

The /Worksheet Global Default Printer Name option allows you to specify the name of the printer you wish to use if you have more than one. The menu is customized during installation to include the names of your existing printers.

## Exiting the Default Printer Menu

The /Worksheet Global Default Printer Quit option is the last menu choice. Aside from repeatedly pressing ESC, it is the only way out of the Worksheet Global Default Printer menu.

## Saving Global Default Settings

Changing the Default Printer options does not produce a permanent modification unless you quit the Worksheet Global Default Printer menu and choose Update from the prior menu. This command stores the default options in a file called 123.CNF. This file will be on your hard drive if you have one. With a two-drive system, 1-2-3 will write your configuration file on your 1-2-3 diskette. In this case you will want to temporarily remove the write protect tab and place the disk in drive A before selecting Update so 1-2-3 can write the configuration file on the disk.

## Other Worksheet Commands for Printing

Most of the commands that affect printed output are found under the Print option on the main menu. You have seen that some of the default settings are located under the /Worksheet Global Default Printer option. There are two additional commands under the Worksheet menu that affect printing. The /Worksheet Column Hide command affects the worksheet display and also excludes hidden columns from the printed output. The /Worksheet Page command will insert a page break anywhere you wish in your document.

```
                              Boston Company
                           First Quarter Expenses

                                   JAN       FEB       MAR
           Salaries             $8,000    $8,200    $8,200
           Building Operations   1,100     1,100     1,100
           Travel                  850       850       850
           Supplies                500       500       500
           Depreciation          1,200     1,200     1,200
           Equipment Maintenance   750       750       750
           Shipping Expense        400       400       400
           Data Processing Costs 2,100     2,100     2,100
           Printing & Duplicating  640       640       640
           Other                 1,030     1,030     1,030
     Total Expenses            $16,570   $16,770   $16,770


           Second Quarter Expenses

      APR       MAY      JUNE
   $8,700    $8,700    $7,500
    1,100     1,100     1,100
      850       850       850
      500       500       500
    1,200     1,200     1,200
      750       750       750
      400       400       400
    2,100     2,100     2,100
      640       640       640
    1,030     1,030     1,030
  $17,270   $17,270   $16,070
```

**Figure 5-24.**    Two print ranges printed consecutively

## Using Hidden Columns
## To Affect Print Range

If you want to print more than one range from a worksheet, you could select one range, print it, and then select and print a second one. The second range would print immediately after the first range, as shown in Figure 5-24, where two ranges from the worksheet were printed separately without a page break between them. You will notice that the second range does not have descriptive information preceding it.

In many instances it is not possible to fit all the information in your worksheet across one printed page. You can use the /Worksheet Column Hide feature, discussed in Chapter 3, to choose which columns to print, effectively extending the print features. Figure 5-25 presents part of a worksheet, the

A1:                                                                          READY

|   | A | B | C | G | H | I | J | K |
|---|---|---|---|---|---|---|---|---|
| 1 | | | | | | | | |
| 2 | | | | | | | | |
| 3 | | | | Second Quarter Expenses | | | | |
| 4 | | | | | | | | |
| 5 | | | | APR | MAY | JUNE | | |
| 6 | Salaries | | | $8,700 | $8,700 | $7,500 | | |
| 7 | Building Operations | | | 1,100 | 1,100 | 1,100 | | |
| 8 | Travel | | | 850 | 850 | 850 | | |
| 9 | Supplies | | | 500 | 500 | 500 | | |
| 10 | Depreciation | | | 1,200 | 1,200 | 1,200 | | |
| 11 | Equipment Maintenance | | | 750 | 750 | 750 | | |
| 12 | Shipping Expense | | | 400 | 400 | 400 | | |
| 13 | Data Processing Costs | | | 2,100 | 2,100 | 2,100 | | |
| 14 | Printing & Duplicating | | | 640 | 640 | 640 | | |
| 15 | Other | | | 1,030 | 1,030 | 1,030 | | |
| 16 | Total Expenses | | | $17,270 | $17,270 | $16,070 | | |
| 17 | | | | | | | | |
| 18 | | | | | | | | |
| 19 | | | | | | | | |
| 20 | | | | | | | | |

25-Sep-86   07:50 PM

**Figure 5-25.**    Worksheet with hidden columns

```
                                    Second Quarter Expenses

                              APR        MAY       JUNE
        Salaries              $8,700     $8,700    $7,500
        Building Operations    1,100      1,100     1,100
        Travel                   850        850       850
        Supplies                 500        500       500
        Depreciation           1,200      1,200     1,200
        Equipment Maintenance    750        750       750
        Shipping Expense         400        400       400
        Data Processing Costs  2,100      2,100     2,100
        Printing & Duplicating   640        640       640
        Other                  1,030      1,030     1,030
  Total Expenses             $17,270    $17,270   $16,070
```

**Figure 5-26.**    Printed output with hidden columns

result of using /Worksheet Column Hide to eliminate columns D through F. Entering Print Printer Range A1..I16 and then using Go will create the printed report shown in Figure 5-26.

Using hidden columns is one way to print a second range with descriptive information. It is also useful when some columns contain data you really do not need in your report.

## Inserting a Page Break
## In the Printed Worksheet

A worksheet with many separate sections was a printing nightmare in the past. You had two options: you could sit at the printer and request each section separately and hope that you remembered to Page and Align during print requests, or you could set up a print macro to do the remembering for you. Neither way was easy.

Release 2's introduction of the /Worksheet Page command makes it possible to split the printing of your reports wherever you want. Entering /Worksheet Page causes 1-2-3

```
         A      B       C        D        E        F        G       H
1  ***********************************************************
2  *              ASSUMPTIONS                            *
3  *  Sales Growth                                       *
4  *     Product A     10.0%                             *
5  *     Product B     12.0%                             *
6  *     Product C      9.0%                             *
7  ***********************************************************
8  ::
9
10                     1986     1987     1988     1989     1990
11 Sales
12     Product A    100,000  110,000  121,000  133,100  146,410
13     Product B     50,000   56,000   62,720   70,246   78,676
14     Product C     45,000   49,050   53,465   58,276   63,521
15 Cost of Goods Sold 87,750  96,773  106,733  117,730  129,873
16 Profit           107,250  118,278  130,451  143,892  158,734
17
18
19
20
```
26-Sep-86   05:09 AM

---

**Figure 5-27.**    Worksheet showing page break

to insert a blank line, adding a page indicator (::) at the cursor location. (The /Range Erase command can be used to erase an unwanted page break.)

Figure 5-27 presents a worksheet with a page break inserted. When A1..G16 is selected as the print range, the output shown on the two pages in Figure 5-28 is produced, since the page break indicator causes the page break to be inserted before the first page is filled.

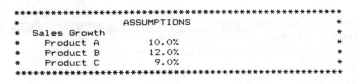

```
****************************************************
*              ASSUMPTIONS                          *
*   Sales Growth                                    *
*      Product A       10.0%                         *
*      Product B       12.0%                         *
*      Product C        9.0%                         *
****************************************************
```

|                    | 1986    | 1987    | 1988    | 1989    | 1990    |
|--------------------|---------|---------|---------|---------|---------|
| Sales              |         |         |         |         |         |
| Product A          | 100,000 | 110,000 | 121,000 | 133,100 | 146,410 |
| Product B          | 50,000  | 56,000  | 62,720  | 70,246  | 78,676  |
| Product C          | 45,000  | 49,050  | 53,465  | 58,276  | 63,521  |
| Cost of Goods Sold | 87,750  | 96,773  | 106,733 | 117,730 | 129,873 |
| Profit             | 107,250 | 118,278 | 130,451 | 143,892 | 158,734 |

**Figure 5-28.**    Printout using /Worksheet Page

# PRINTING

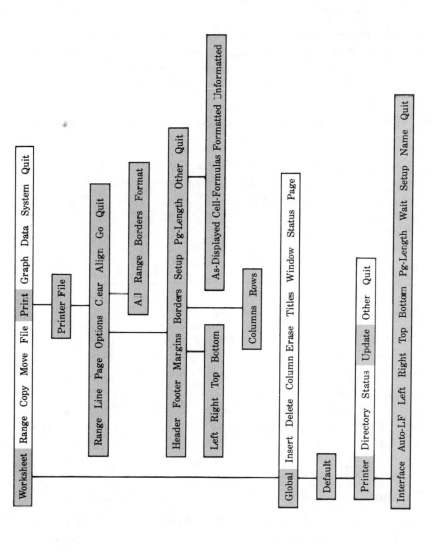

© Lotus Development Corporation 1986. Used with permission.

# /Print File

### Description

The /Print File command allows you to print a report to a disk file. This command is useful at times when your printer is not available. It can also be used to prepare data for other programs that manipulate 1-2-3's print output.

### Options

All of the /Print Printer options are also valid when you choose /Print File. You will be able to select print ranges and apply any of the other options to them.

# /Print Printer

### Description

This command is used whenever you wish to print information from a worksheet file on your printer. Since the package contains default values for most of the Print parameters, printing can be as simple as specifying a print range. When you need greater sophistication or would like to tailor a report to your exact needs, you have a realm of options to work with.

### Options

The Printer command has the same options as the File command. You can make simple selections like specifying the range of worksheet cells to print, or you can make more sophisticated selections like specifying a set of printer control codes to meet your exact needs. You can change margins, select rows or columns to print on all pages of a report, print the worksheet cells as they display, or print the formulas behind them.

# /Print Printer Align

## Description

This command will set 1-2-3's internal line count to zero. 1-2-3 then assumes that the printer is aligned at the top of a page. Any entries after this point will begin to add to the new line count.

## Options

There are no options for this command. Your only real concern is that the printer carriage be stationed at the top of a form before you enter the command sequence.

# /Print Printer Clear

## Description

This command can be used to eliminate some or all of the special print settings. It returns the specified print settings to the defaults. If you have added a setup string, header, footer, and borders when printing a report and want to print it again without these special features, the Clear option saves you time by eliminating these entries. Without it you would have to reexecute each of the commands for the special settings and delete the entries you had made.

## Options

The options for /Print Printer Clear let you decide whether you want to clear all or some print settings.

**All**     This option eliminates all the special entries made through the print menus. The current print range is canceled. Borders, headers, and footers are all eliminated. Margins, page length, and setup strings are returned to their default settings.

**Range**  This option cancels only the current print range.

**Borders**  This option clears both row and column borders.

**Format**  This option resets the margin, page length, and setup string to the default setting found under /Worksheet Global Default Printer.

## /Print Printer Go

### Description

This command tells 1-2-3 to begin transmitting the print range to the printer (if Printer was selected) or to your disk drive (if File was selected).

### Options

There are no options for this command.

## /Print Printer Line

### Description

This command is used to generate a line feed. It allows you to print two ranges with only one line between them by selecting Line after printing the first range and then selecting the second range and printing it. It adds one to 1-2-3's internal line count.

### Options

There are no options for this command.

**Note**

This command offers an advantage over using the printer's line feed button, since the command increments 1-2-3's internal line count by one, keeping the printing of a page in sync with the page's physical length.

## /Print Printer Options

### Description

This command provides access to all the bells and whistles 1-2-3 offers for printing. Through the submenu this option presents you can make many modifications to the appearance of a report.

### Options

The Options menu includes choices for Header, Footer, Margins, Borders, Setup, Pg-Length, Other, and Quit. These options will be covered individually in the sections that follow.

## /Print Printer Options Borders

### Description

The Borders option allows you to print specified rows or columns on every page. You select the option you wish (either rows or columns) and specify the range of cells you wish to have duplicated on each page. Be careful not to include the border rows or columns in your print range; otherwise they will be printed twice.

### Options

With this command you have the choice of using either rows or columns as borders.

**Rows** This is the option to use when you have a report that is too long for one page. Select the border rows you wish to print again on the second and subsequent pages to provide descriptive information on each page.

**Columns** Use this option when your report is too wide for one sheet of paper and there is identifying information at the far left of your worksheet. The command will duplicate the selected column information at the left side of each page.

### Note

If you accidentally select this command, the current row or column will become a border, depending on whether you choose Rows or Columns. The way to undo the damage is to select /Print Printer Clear Borders.

## /Print Printer Options Footer

### Description

This command allows you to add one line of up to 240 characters at the bottom of each page of a report. Typical contents for the line are date, report name or number, company name or department, and page number. 1-2-3 allows you to have three different entries for the footer line.

### Options

The three Footer options allow an entry to be placed at the left, center, or right section of the footer. Entries are separated by the vertical bar character. Use a bar to end each of the sections, even if they are not used (in other words, a single footer at the right should be preceded by two bars).

You also have the option of using @ or # in your footer. The # represents the current page number, and the @ represents the current date.

## Note

If you include the page number in your footer, you will have to clear the Print options and respecify them before printing a second time. Otherwise, 1-2-3 will pick up with the next page number for the second printing of the report rather than beginning again with page 1.

# /Print Printer Options Header

### Description

This command allows you to add one line of up to 240 characters at the top of each page of a report. Typical contents for the line are date, report name or number, company name or department, and page number. 1-2-3 allows you to have three different entries for the header line.

### Options

Header options allow an entry to be placed at the left, center, or right section of the header. Entries are separated by the vertical bar character. Use a bar to end each of the sections, even if they are not used. (In other words, a single header at the right should be preceded by two bars.)

You also have the option of using @ or # in your header. The # represents the current page number, and the @ represents the current date.

### Note

If you include the page number in your header, you will have to clear the print options and respecify them before printing a second time. Otherwise, 1-2-3 will pick up with the next page number for the second printing of the report rather than beginning again with page 1.

## /Print Printer Options Margins

### Description

This command allows you to control the amount of blank space at the top, bottom, and sides of a printed page. If you do not make an entry for Margins, the default values will be used.

### Options

There is a Margins option for each of the four areas where you can control the amount of blank space on a printed page.

**Left**     The default setting for the left margin is 4 spaces. You can enter any number from 0 to 240 to establish a new setting. You will want to make sure that the value you enter for the left margin is less than the value entered for the right margin, since it is the difference between these two values that determines how many characters will print in a line of your report.

**Right**     The default setting for the right margin is 76. You can enter any number between 0 and 240 to change this margin setting. You will want to make sure that the value you enter for the right margin is greater than the value entered for the left margin, since it is the difference between these two values that determines how many characters will print in a line of your report.

**Top**    The default setting for the top margin is 2. You can enter any number from 0 to 32 (release 2) to change the value for this setting.

**Bottom**    The default setting for the bottom margin is 2. You can enter any number from 0 to 32 (release 2) to change the value for this setting.

## /Print Printer Options Other

### Description

This is an unusual command in that it provides two very different sets of features. First, it lets you decide whether output should be the information displayed in worksheet cells or the formulas behind the display. Second, this command lets you determine whether print or file output should be formatted or unformatted. The Unformatted option is especially useful if you are attempting to take 1-2-3 data into another program, since it will strip off headers and other special formats.

### Options

The Other command has four options: As-Displayed, Cell-Formulas, Formatted, and Unformatted. The options form two pairs, with each member of a pair having an effect opposite to that of the other.

**As-Displayed**    This is the default option. It causes your printout to match the screen display in the active window in terms of cell values, format, and width. If you want to change the display from your normal worksheet display, you could set up a second window (see Chapter 5), make width and formatting changes to this window, and print from there. After printing, the window could be cleared.

**Cell-Formulas**    This option causes the formulas for cells rather than their results to be displayed. The formulas are shown one per line down the page.

**Formatted**    This option prints the output with all of your formatting options, such as headers, footers, and page breaks. This is normally the way you want your output to appear when you send it to a printer.

**Unformatted**    This option strips all the formatting from your data. In other words, information is written to the output device without page breaks, headers, or footers. This option is useful when you are writing the output to a file for use by another program or when you want the printer to ignore page breaks.

## /Print Printer Options Pg-Length

### Description

This option determines the number of lines in a page of output. The default is 66, but 1-2-3 (release 2) will accept entries from 10 to 100. (There are not actually 66 lines of printed output on a default page because top and bottom margins, headers, footers, and the two blank lines below the header and above the footer must be subtracted from the page length to determine the number of print lines.)

### Options

The only options for this command are to enter a page length between 10 and 100 for release 2 and between 20 and 100 for release 1A.

## /Print Printer Options Quit

### Description

This command allows you to exit from the Options menu. Since this menu stays around for you to make a series of selections, you need Quit to make an exit when you have completed your selections.

### Options

There are no options for this command.


## /Print Printer Options Setup

### Description

This command allows you to transmit control codes to your printer. These control codes let you use the special features the printer offers. These special features may include enlarged, compressed, emphasized, or boldface printing as well as different numbers of lines to be printed per inch.

### Options

The options available for this command are dictated by the features your printer supports. A few of the options for the Epson MX100 printer and their respective setup strings are as follows:

\015 Set compressed print

\018 Stop compressed print

\027G Start boldface print

\027H Stop boldface print

The decimal codes you will need for setup strings can be found in your printer manual. When entering them into 1-2-3, precede each code with a backslash and a zero, as in the example.

## /Print Printer Page

### Description

This command advances the paper to the top of the next form. This is done right from the keyboard as the command is entered; there is no need to touch the printer. It prints a footer if one has been specified.

### Options

There are no options for this command.

## /Print Printer Quit

### Description

This command is used to exit the Print menu and place you back in READY mode. Since the Print menu stays around while you make selections, you will need to use Quit to leave it. Even after printing, you will not return to READY mode until you have chosen Quit. Pressing the ESC key produces the same result.

### Options

There are no options for this command.

# /Print Printer Range

### Description

This command determines how much of the worksheet will be printed. Any valid range of cells can be specified, from one cell to the entire worksheet. 1-2-3 will decide how much of the range can be placed on one page, based on the margin and page length settings, and will carry the remainder of the range over to additional pages.

### Options

The only option for this command is to specify a range. The format used for ranges is cell address..cell address, where the cell addresses specified are at opposite corners of the range of cells to be printed. For example, if you wanted to print cells A1 through D10, you could specify the range as A1..D10, D10..A1, D1..A10, or A10..D1.

# /Worksheet Global Default Printer

### Description

This command allows you to change the default printer settings. These settings determine the way a document prints if you have not made particular specifications for it through the Print menu. They also determine the default interface between 1-2-3 and your printer. Changes made with this command are not permanent unless you save them with /Worksheet Global Default Update.

### Options

The following options are the ones presented with release 2. The Interface options will be more limited if you are using an earlier release of 1-2-3. The last four Interface options, for local area network support, are available only in release 2.

**Interface**     This option determines the type of connection between your printer and 1-2-3. There are three basic options with several choices: parallel connection, serial connection, or connection through a local area network. The available options are as follows:

(1) Parallel (default setting)

(2) Serial 1

(3) Parallel 2

(4) Serial 2

(5) DOS device LPT1

(6) DOS device LPT2

(7) DOS device LPT3

(8) DOS device LPT4

**Note**

If you select one of the serial interface options, 1-2-3 will also ask you to specify a baud rate (the transmission speed it supports). For 110 baud you will have to set your printer at 2 stop bits, 8 bits, and no parity. For speeds other than 110, 1 stop bit will be sufficient.

**Auto-LF**     This option specifies whether your printer automatically issues line feeds after carriage returns. Installation sets this to correspond with your printer, although the initial setting is No, indicating that the printer does not automatically print line feeds. If you are getting double spacing on everything you print, you will want to set Auto-LF to Yes. If your paper is not advancing as it should, you will want to change this setting to No.

**Left**     This setting has a default value of 4, but you can change it to any number between 0 and 240.

**Right**     This setting has a default value of 76, but you can change it to any number between 0 and 240.

**Top**     This option has a default value of 2 but will accept values between 0 and 32.

**Bottom**     This option has a default setting of 2 but will accept values between 0 and 32.

**Pg-Length**     The default page length is 66, but in release 2 it can be changed to any value between 10 and 100.

**Wait**     This option allows you to set the default for continuous or single-sheet-feed paper. The initial value is No, indicating continuous paper. If you change it to Yes for single sheets, it will cause 1-2-3 to wait after each page is printed.

**Setup**     This option specifies a string of control characters to be sent to your printer before every print request. The default is blank, indicating no print control codes. You may supply any valid control codes up to 39 characters in length. The control codes can be obtained from your printer manual. Precede each code with a backslash ( \ ) and a zero.

**Name**     If you installed more than one text printer for 1-2-3, this option allows you to specify the printer to use. The initial value is the first printer selected during installation.

**Quit**     This option allows you to exit the Worksheet Global Default menu.

## /Worksheet Global Default Update

### Description

This command saves entries made with the /Worksheet Global Default Printer command to a file called 123.CNF. This file will be loaded every time you bring up the 1-2-3 package.

**Options**

This command has no options. It will save all changes that have been made with the /Worksheet Global Default Printer command.

# SIX

# Basic Worksheet
# Commands

Working With Ranges
Protecting Worksheet Cells
Cutting and Pasting
Duplicating Existing Entries
Making Other Worksheet Changes
Recalculating the Worksheet
Modifying the Screen Display
Displaying the Status of Worksheet Options
COMMAND REFERENCE: Basic Worksheet
/Copy
/Move
/Range Erase
/Range Input
/Range Label
/Range Name Create
/Range Name Delete
/Range Name Labels
/Range Name Reset
/Range Name Table
/Range Protect
/Range Transpose
/Range Unprotect
/Range Value
/Worksheet Delete
/Worksheet Erase
/Worksheet Global Label-Prefix
/Worksheet Global Protection
/Worksheet Global Recalculation
/Worksheet Insert
/Worksheet Status
/Worksheet Titles
/Worksheet Window

This chapter focuses on menu commands that will extend your productivity in using the worksheet. During the chapter you will use commands on the Worksheet menus. You will also use Range commands to name worksheet cells, transpose data, and establish a restricted input area. You will use the /Copy command and the /Move command to speed the development of new spreadsheets. By the time you have finished reading this chapter, you will have experience with all the worksheet commands except for those that have a very specialized purpose. A complete list of the commands you will work with in this chapter is shown on the command map at the beginning of the Reference Section for this chapter.

## Working With Ranges

In Chapter 4 you learned to use some of the Range commands to change the appearance of your worksheet. In this chapter you will expand your range options with commands that allow you to access cells through names rather than cell addresses. You will also learn Range commands that have the ability to change a column of worksheet entries into entries in a row of the worksheet. You will learn how to freeze formulas at their existing values for a large or small range of cells. Finally, you will learn additional commands that alter the worksheet format, either erasing all entries for a range or changing the justification for labels stored in the range.

## Methods of Specifying Cell Ranges

You can communicate the range you wish to work with to 1-2-3 in a variety of ways. The easiest method is using the arrow keys to point to the desired range. This method works only with commands that suggest a complete range. Here is an example using the /Range Format command from Chapter 4.

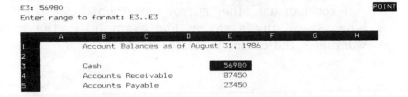

If your cursor is positioned at the beginning of the range before you invoke the menu with a slash (/), you need only move with the arrow keys to complete the range, as shown.

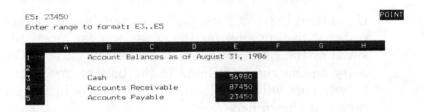

Notice that 1-2-3 highlights the range when you use this method.

If you forget to position your cursor properly before invoking one of the Range commands, you will have to unlock the beginning of the range before you can change it. To do this, press ESC and move the cursor to the desired location. You must lock the beginning of the range again by entering a period before you try to expand the range with the cursor movement keys. If the beginning of a range is not locked into place, 1-2-3 will display only the beginning of the range, like this:

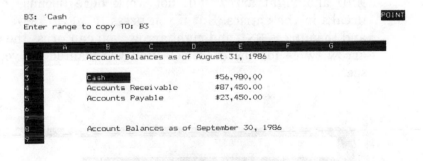

You can use other cursor movement keys to save time when specifying a range. For example, in the following worksheet the cursor is located in A1.

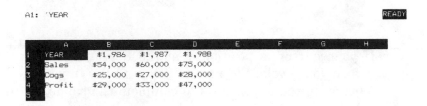

If you want to select the complete rectangle of cells shown, in response to a prompt for the range you can press END followed by the right arrow key to move your cursor to the last entry on the right. To move to the bottom, press END and DOWN. This will include all the filled cells in the selected range, as shown here.

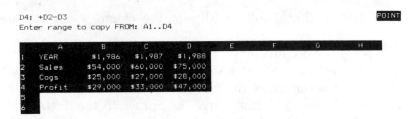

The END key can be used in other situations with a little planning. Let's say you want to format all the cells in row 3. You could move to the beginning of row 3, that is, cell A3, and then enter /**Range Format Fixed** and press ENTER. END and right arrow will not work here because of the breaks in the entries. But if you press HOME to move to A1 and then press END and right arrow, you can press the down arrow twice for the exact selection you wanted, as you can see.

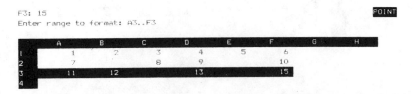

It is preferable to have 1-2-3 generate the cell addresses in a range whenever possible, but you always have the option of typing a reference in response to one of the range prompts. When you type a single period in a reference (D4.D10), 1-2-3 will duplicate it so that two periods display (D4..D10). You can enter any two opposite corners of a rectangle of cells to specify a range, but normally the upper left and the lower right corner are used.

## Naming Cell Ranges

In some respects, all worksheet cells automatically have names, since they have unique cell addresses by which they can be referenced, such as A2, U7, or AX89. It is clear exactly what cell you mean when you use these addresses. However, it is not clear what A2, U7, or AX89 contains. Is it the interest rate, the number of employees, or the Los Angeles Dodgers' batting average? It can take quite a bit of time to move your cursor to the appropriate location every time you are uncertain of a particular cell's contents.

The /Range Name commands provide a solution for this dilemma. With these commands you can assign names to ranges consisting of one or many cells, using these names to provide meaningful information about the contents of the groups of cells they reference. If cell A10 contains sales for 1986, for example, you might assign it the name SALES__86. If cells B3..B25 contain all the expenses for a certain department, you might assign this range a name like TOTAL__EXPENSES. 1-2-3 will allow you to assign any name to any range of cells, provided that the name does not exceed fifteen characters. The box called "A Few Pointers for Creating Range Names" provides some additional tips on range names. Once you have assigned a name to a range, you can use the name the same way that you use a cell address. For example, you could create a formula for profit using assigned range names: +SALES__86 −TOTAL__EXPENSES.

# A Few Pointers for Creating Range Names

1-2-3 has few restrictions in range names, but it is helpful to add a few for the sake of clarity.

- 1-2-3 does not prevent you from using spaces in range names, but it is preferable to avoid these characters. The name TOTAL SALES could be mistaken for two range names by someone glancing at a formula, but TOTAL_SALES is clearly one name.

- You are also allowed to use arithmetic operators in range names, but they, too, can cause problems. TOTAL* SALES could be confusing as a range name because someone could interpret it as a request for an arithmetic operation that would multiply TOTAL by SALES.

- Another permitted type of name to avoid is a name that could be confused with a cell address, such as A3 or D4.

- Remember that numbers cannot be used as range names unless they are used in combination with letters. For example, SALES86 is acceptable but 56 is not acceptable as a range name.

## Assigning Range Names

There are two basic methods for assigning range names. Usually you will use the /Range Name Create command to enter your range names. In specialized cases where the name you want to use will be assigned to a single cell and already appears in an adjacent worksheet cell, you can use the /Range Name Labels command.

**Creating New Names**     The easiest way to name a range of cells is to move your cursor to the upper left corner of the range, type /**Range Name Create**, type your range name, and press ENTER. If you want to name just one cell, simply press ENTER again. If the desired range for the name is larger than one cell, move your cursor to the lower right cell in the range and then press ENTER. Alternatively, you can leave your cursor on any worksheet cell, type /**Range Name Create**, type the range name, and press ENTER. You then type the cell coordinates corresponding to the range and press ENTER. For example, you might type /**Range Name Create SALES A1** or /**Range Name Create EXPENSES B2..B6**.

1-2-3 allows you to assign more than one name to a range. For example, suppose you have data in cells F4..F25 that represents expenses for 1986. You might wish to name this range EXPENSES—86. Now suppose you also wish to use these expenses to project next year's budget. You might want to assign this same range of cells the name PREVIOUS—YR— EXP for use in your budget calculations. 1-2-3 would permit you to assign both names.

The following worksheet offers several opportunities to use the /Range Name Create command.

Suppose you want to name the cells containing Sales and Cost of Goods Sold. To do this, place the cursor in B3 on the figure for sales and enter /**Range Name Create**. In response to the request for a name, enter SALES—86, like this.

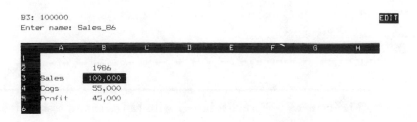

Basic Worksheet Commands

Then press ENTER. The next prompt wants the range to assign the name to. Since the name is for just this one cell, simply press ENTER again.

Now move the cursor to B4 and repeat the process, using the name COGS_86. You can see from the formula for profit shown in Figure 6-1 that 1-2-3 will use range names in a formula display once you have assigned them. You can also reference cells by their assigned range names when you construct new formulas. Once a name has been assigned to a cell or a range of cells, you can use this name anywhere you could use a cell reference.

1-2-3 has a special feature for accessing names once they have been assigned: the F3 (NAME) key. When you are using Range commands, you can press this key to access the list of names you have assigned. You can then select a name from the list for use with the Range command you entered.

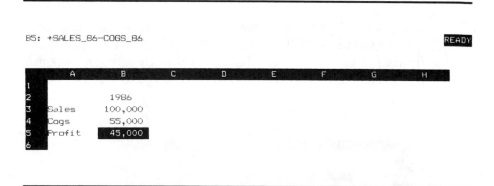

**Figure 6-1.** Formula display with range names assigned

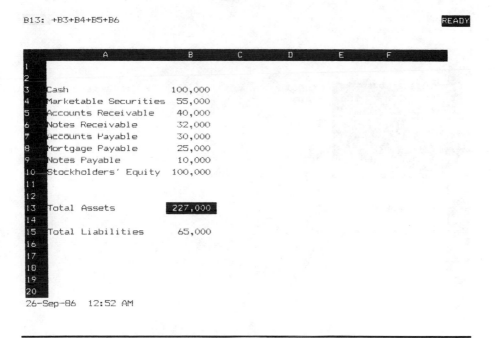

```
B13:  +B3+B4+B5+B6                                              READY
```

|   | A | B | C | D | E | F |
|---|---|---|---|---|---|---|
| 1 | | | | | | |
| 2 | | | | | | |
| 3 | Cash | 100,000 | | | | |
| 4 | Marketable Securities | 55,000 | | | | |
| 5 | Accounts Receivable | 40,000 | | | | |
| 6 | Notes Receivable | 32,000 | | | | |
| 7 | Accounts Payable | 30,000 | | | | |
| 8 | Mortgage Payable | 25,000 | | | | |
| 9 | Notes Payable | 10,000 | | | | |
| 10 | Stockholders' Equity | 100,000 | | | | |
| 11 | | | | | | |
| 12 | | | | | | |
| 13 | Total Assets | 227,000 | | | | |
| 14 | | | | | | |
| 15 | Total Liabilities | 65,000 | | | | |
| 16 | | | | | | |
| 17 | | | | | | |
| 18 | | | | | | |
| 19 | | | | | | |
| 20 | | | | | | |

26-Sep-86   12:52 AM

**Figure 6-2.**    A range suitable for /Range Name Labels

**Using Existing Worksheet Labels**    The /Range Name Labels command can save you data entry time when assigning range names if conditions are right. First, the name you plan to use must already exist on the worksheet. It must also be in a cell adjacent to the cell you plan to name. With this command you can assign a name only to a single cell, so if you want more than one cell in a range, you must use the /Range Name Create command. An advantage of /Range Name Labels is that you can use it to assign several range names at once.

The cells in B3..B10 in Figure 6-2 can all have range names assigned with one execution of the /Range Name Labels command. To do this, you would position the cursor in A3 and enter **/Range Name Labels**. Since the names are located to the left of the cells to which the names will be

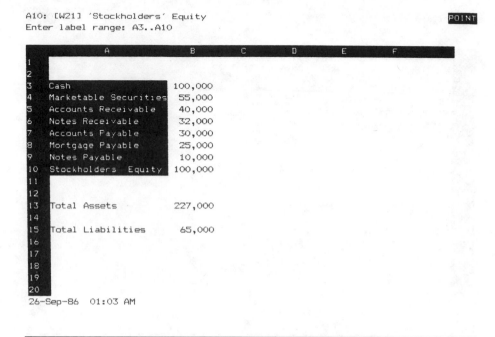

```
A10: [W21] 'Stockholders' Equity                                      POINT
Enter label range: A3..A10

              A              B         C         D         E         F
 1
 2
 3   Cash                100,000
 4   Marketable Securities 55,000
 5   Accounts Receivable  40,000
 6   Notes Receivable     32,000
 7   Accounts Payable     30,000
 8   Mortgage Payable     25,000
 9   Notes Payable        10,000
10   Stockholders Equity 100,000
11
12
13   Total Assets        227,000
14
15   Total Liabilities    65,000
16
17
18
19
20
26-Sep-86   01:03 AM
```

**Figure 6-3.**     Specifying the label range

assigned, choose Right next. As a final step, move the cursor
to A10, as shown in Figure 6-3, and press ENTER.

In Figure 6-2, you will note that cell addresses appear in
the formula shown in the control panel. In Figure 6-4, by
contrast, the names of some of the cells just named with the
/Range Name Labels command have been substituted in the
formula. Notice that some of the labels have been truncated,
since 1-2-3 enforces a 15-character limit on range names.

### Deleting Range Names

Assigned range names use a small amount of 1-2-3's internal
memory. If you are not using some of your old range names,
consider deleting them to free up the memory space that they
use. It is best to delete a range name as soon as you know it is

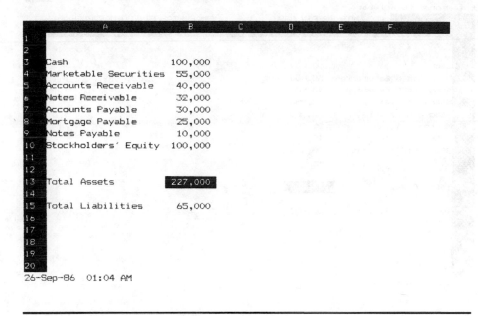

B13: +CASH+MARKETABLE SECU+ACCOUNTS RECEIV+NOTES RECEIVABL    READY

```
            A               B      C      D      E      F
1
2
3  Cash                 100,000
4  Marketable Securities  55,000
5  Accounts Receivable    40,000
6  Notes Receivable       32,000
7  Accounts Payable       30,000
8  Mortgage Payable       25,000
9  Notes Payable          10,000
10 Stockholders' Equity  100,000
11
12
13 Total Assets          227,000
14
15 Total Liabilities      65,000
16
17
18
19
20
26-Sep-86  01:04 AM
```

**Figure 6-4.**    Formula with range names substituted for cell addresses

no longer required, since later on you may forget whether you need it or not.

To delete a range name, enter /**Range Name Delete**. 1-2-3 will then present a list of all the assigned range names at the top of your screen, as shown in the example in Figures 6-5 and 6-6. You have the option of typing in the name to delete or using the cursor to point to the name to delete. In either case, press ENTER after making your selection. This action causes the selected range name to disappear permanently.

### Resetting Range Names

The /Range Name Delete option is ideal when you have only a few names to delete. If you have many names to delete,

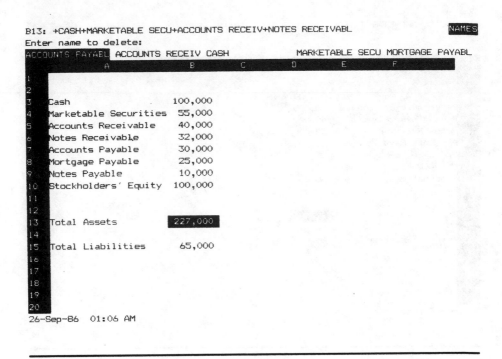

```
B13: +CASH+MARKETABLE SECU+ACCOUNTS RECEIV+NOTES RECEIVABL          NAMES
Enter name to delete:
ACCOUNTS PAYABL ACCOUNTS RECEIV CASH          MARKETABLE SECU MORTGAGE PAYABL
             A              B        C        D        E        F
 1
 2
 3    Cash                100,000
 4    Marketable Securities  55,000
 5    Accounts Receivable   40,000
 6    Notes Receivable      32,000
 7    Accounts Payable      30,000
 8    Mortgage Payable      25,000
 9    Notes Payable         10,000
10    Stockholders' Equity 100,000
11
12
13    Total Assets         227,000
14
15    Total Liabilities     65,000
16
17
18
19
20
26-Sep-86  01:06 AM
```

**Figure 6-5.**     Partial list of names to delete

however, this option is slow. The /Range Name Reset command can speed up the process when you are deleting most or all of your range names. Since this command deletes all range names, it is perfect for situations when you want all the names deleted. When you have a large number of names and want most of them deleted, it may be quicker to delete them all and use /Range Name Create to enter the essential names again than to delete the names one by one with /Range Name Delete. Figure 6-7 shows the options presented with /Range Name Delete after /Range Name Reset has been used. Since all range names have been deleted by /Range Name Reset, there are no remaining names to delete.

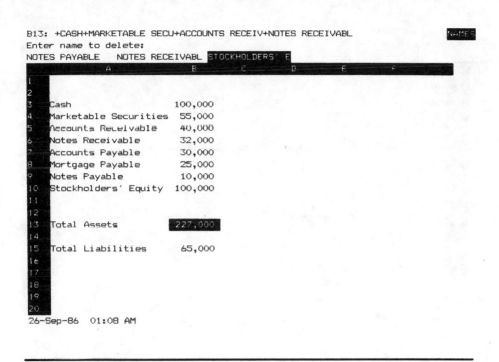

B13: +CASH+MARKETABLE SECU+ACCOUNTS RECEIV+NOTES RECEIVABL        NAMES
Enter name to delete:
NOTES PAYABLE    NOTES RECEIVABL STOCKHOLDERS' E

```
         A              B         C      D      E      F
1
2
3   Cash              100,000
4   Marketable Securities  55,000
5   Accounts Receivable   40,000
6   Notes Receivable      32,000
7   Accounts Payable      30,000
8   Mortgage Payable      25,000
9   Notes Payable         10,000
10  Stockholders' Equity  100,000
11
12
13  Total Assets       227,000
14
15  Total Liabilities     65,000
16
17
18
19
20
```

26-Sep-86  01:08 AM

**Figure 6-6.**     End of alphabetized list to delete

## Creating a Table of Range Names

With releases 1 and 1A of 1-2-3, the only method of determining what range names were assigned and the ranges to
which they were assigned was using the /Range Name
Create command to bring the list of names to the screen.
Once the names were listed, you could select the one you were
interested in, and the range it was assigned to would be highlighted. Pressing ENTER ensured that the assignment was
not changed, but if you wanted to know the location of other
range assignments, you had to go through the same sequence
for each range name.

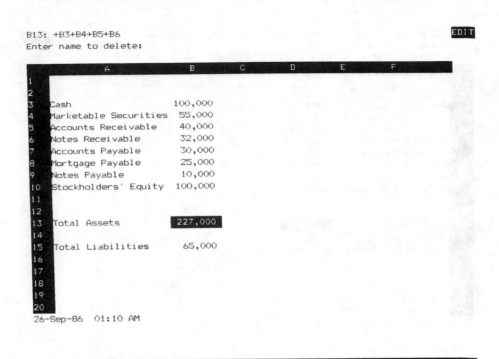

```
                        A              B        C        D        E        F
 1
 2
 3   Cash                        100,000
 4   Marketable Securities        55,000
 5   Accounts Receivable          40,000
 6   Notes Receivable             32,000
 7   Accounts Payable             30,000
 8   Mortgage Payable             25,000
 9   Notes Payable                10,000
10   Stockholders' Equity        100,000
11
12
13   Total Assets                227,000
14
15   Total Liabilities            65,000
16
17
18
19
20
26-Sep-86  01:10 AM
```

**Figure 6-7.**      List after /Range Name Reset was used

The situation has improved considerably in release 2. This version has a new command that allows you to build a table of range names and the cell addresses they reference, using any empty area of the worksheet. This table can serve as documentation for all the range names used in your worksheet.

Before executing the required command sequence, choose a good table location—one where the table cannot overwrite data or important formulas if it is longer than you expect. When you are ready to create the table, enter /**Range Name Table** and respond to 1-2-3's prompt by typing in the table location. 1-2-3 will permit you to supply just the upper left corner of the table range and will then use as much space as it needs for the table. Figure 6-8 presents a table created

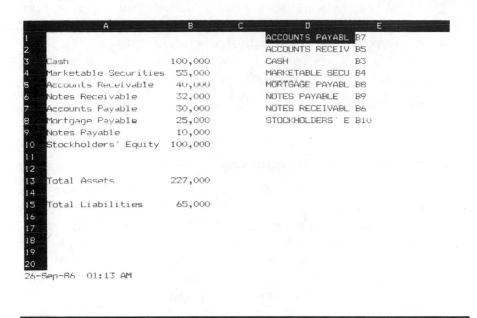

Figure 6-8.    Output of /Range Name Table

with the /Range Name Table command. Note that the range names are listed in alphabetical order.

## Practical Applications for Range Names

Assigning range names may seem like so much extra work that you may wonder why you should bother using them. For very small models they may not be worthwhile, but for larger models they can offer a significant payback. They make formulas much more readable, for one thing. They also help prevent incorrect formula references, since you will see a descriptive name rather than a cryptic cell address. As data becomes farther removed from the formula location, the payback becomes greater, since you cannot see the data at the same time as the formula to verify the correctness of the cell addresses used.

When range names are used, you will find that rows and columns can be inserted in the middle of a range and the range reference will be adjusted automatically. The references will also be updated if you delete rows or columns from the middle of a range. If you want to see the updated references in a table, however, you will need to execute /Range Name Table again.

## Transposing Rows and Columns

Sometimes you will want to rearrange a range of entries that you have made in a worksheet. You may have changed your mind about the best presentation method, or you may want to use an existing worksheet as the basis for a new worksheet but must reorganize the presentation to make this possible.

1-2-3 provides the /Range Transpose command to permit you to change data entered horizontally across a row to a vertical column organization or vice versa. The command will operate on single or multiple rows or columns. To use this command, enter /**Range Transpose** and press ENTER. Select a From range (the original location of your data) in response to 1-2-3's prompt message and press ENTER. When asked to specify a To range (the new location), enter a range that has the opposite orientation but the same number of entries as the From range. In other words, when the From range is a row, the To range should be a column, and vice versa. For example, if your From range was A2..B10, your To range might be D2..M3, the same number of cells but with a row rather than a column orientation. Alternatively, you can just enter the upper left cell in the To range and 1-2-3 will determine the end boundary for the range.

If some of the cells in the To range already contain data, their contents will be replaced as a result of the transposition operation. Formulas that referred to these former values will now refer to the results of the transposition. If the cells to be transposed contain formulas with relative addresses, you will not want to use this command, because 1-2-3 will not adjust the relative references as part of the transposing operation.

Here is an example of the transposing operation. The original worksheet entries are shown in cells A3..B5.

The results of using /Range Transpose are shown horizontally in D1..F2.

## Converting Formulas to Values

At times during the model creation process, you may want to change some of your projections to fixed values rather than allowing them to be recalculated each time the worksheet is recalculated. One example would be the budgeting process. As you prepare a budget, you want to look at various possibilities. Once the budget is submitted, however, the projections you made are recorded and will serve as the target for your operation throughout the budget period. You may thus wish to freeze some of the formulas used to make the budget projection. Release 2 of 1-2-3 provides the perfect way to do this in the form of the /Range Values command. (With release 1A your only option is to use the F2 (EDIT) F9 (CALC) sequence for each individual cell you want to change.)

The /Range Values command copies the values produced by formulas to a new location. It copies only the values displayed in worksheet cells, not the formulas used to produce these values. Thus the original entry can still change as new values are entered for assumptions, but the copy will not be affected by changes in the assumptions. If you want to use this command to freeze formula values, you can use the same range for From and To. This will replace the original formulas with the values they currently display.

As an example, the entry in B3 in the following worksheet displays in the worksheet cell as a number but displays as a formula in the control panel.

The same cell after /Range Values was used with B3 as a From and a To range is now a value in both places.

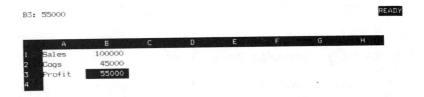

You will notice that the worksheet display is the same, but the control panel now shows the cell as containing a value, not a formula.

## Changing the Justification of Labels

As a default, 1-2-3 begins labels at the left side of cells. You have already learned that you can change the alignment of an individual label by preceding it with a caret (^) for center justification or a double quotation mark (") for right justification. Using these options can be very time consuming when you want to change the alignment of a whole range of cells, however. The /Range Label command can handle this situation much more efficiently. You simply specify the range you want to change the label prefix for and then execute the command. 1-2-3 ensures that existing label entries in the specified cells receive the correct label indicator. Neither entries made after /Range Label is entered nor nonlabel entries in the specified cells will be affected. New label entries will receive the default label prefix.

With this command you can select left, right, or center justification for an existing range of labels. Labels originally entered using the label default prefix of a single quotation mark (') are left justified, as shown here.

When /Range Label is entered and Right is selected to change the orientation of the labels to the right side of each cell, the results look like this.

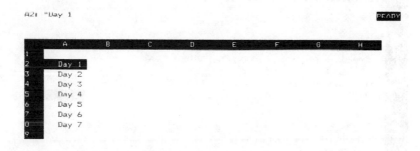

Entering the command again and choosing Center causes each label to display in the center of the cell.

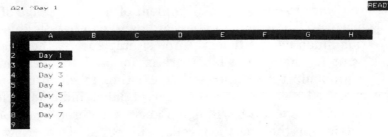

The Left option could be used to change either of these results back to the original display format.

## Erasing Cell Ranges

The /Range Erase command will eliminate the entries in a range of cells. It does not matter whether the entries are numbers, labels, or formulas. Using this command will not affect the numeric format assigned to the cell, its width, or its protection status. Figure 6-9 shows a worksheet contain-

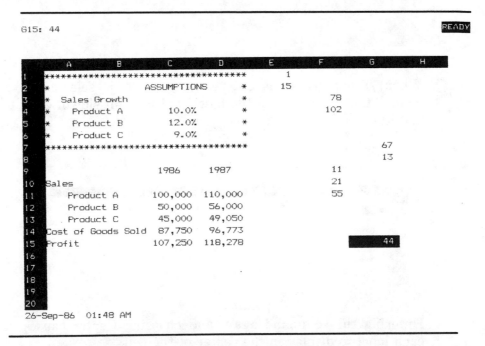

**Figure 6-9.**    Extraneous worksheet entries

ing miscellaneous entries in E1 through G15 that are no longer required. To remove these entries, you would move the cursor to E1 and type /**Range Erase**. Then move the cursor to G15 to extend the range and press ENTER to achieve the results shown in Figure 6-10. Note that if worksheet protection has been enabled so that cells are protected, the /Range Erase command will not be able to erase the contents of these cells.

## Protecting Worksheet Cells

A completed worksheet often represents hours or days of work in planning, formula entry, and testing. Once you have created a well-planned and tested worksheet application, you will want to protect it from accidental damage that could

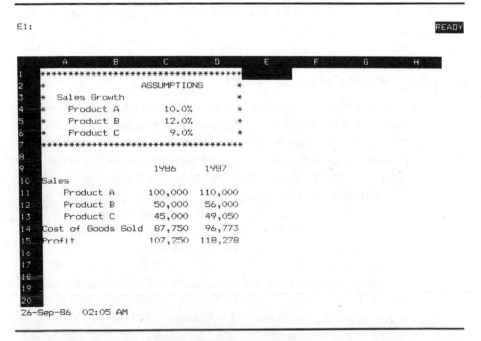

**Figure 6-10.** Results of /Range Erase

cause you to overwrite formulas or other vital data. 1-2-3 provides features that will prevent accidental writeovers or erasures of important cells. These features can also make other users more comfortable in using models that you create for them, since they know that they will not be able to make mistakes that will destroy the models.

The protection features of 1-2-3 allow you to determine which cells will be protected and which ones will allow entries. They also offer an easy way to temporarily disable the protection mechanism without changing a cell's basic definition as a protected or unprotected cell. Finally, 1-2-3 provides a command that is used in conjunction with protection to restrict the cursor to a single input range on the worksheet.

1-2-3's protection process requires that you first decide which worksheet cells you wish to have protected. All cells are protected as an initial default. If you wish to allow entries in certain cells, you can unprotect them with /Range Unprotect. You can then turn on the protection features of the package, and these cells will still permit entries. Protection is turned on with a Global option under the Worksheet menu.

## Deciding What Cells to Protect

1-2-3 establishes a default status of Protected for every worksheet cell. This might sound strange, since you can make an entry anywhere on a new worksheet. You can do that because the protection features of the package are initially turned off. If you turn on the protection features, the Protected status of each cell will be energized, and 1-2-3 will reject any additional entries you attempt to make in worksheet cells. It is therefore important to decide what cells should allow entries before you turn on the protection features.

You might find it useful to think of 1-2-3's protection as a fence placed around every worksheet cell. The fences do not protect the contents of cells in a new worksheet, since none of the fence gates are closed. The /Worksheet Global Protection Enable command will close all the gates, thereby protecting the contents of the cells. Cells that you do not wish to have protected should have their fences torn down. Then, when the gates are closed with /Worksheet Global Protection Enable, you will still be able to change these cells because a gate without a fence does not offer effective protection. You can tear down the fences with the /Range Unprotect command.

The /Range Unprotect command strips cell protection from a range of one or many cells. To unprotect a range, enter **/Range Unprotect** and either point to the limiting cells or enter the range. If you change your mind and decide that a cell previously unprotected should be protected again, you can use the /Range Protect command to restore protection for the cell. Unprotecting a cell makes the cell become highlighted on a monochrome display or green on a color display. It has no other apparent effect on a cell unless the Global Protection (discussed in the following section) features are turned on. The only other indication that a cell is no longer protected that can be seen before protection is enabled is the U that appears in the top line of the control panel after the cell address when the cursor is on the cell (see Figure 6-11).

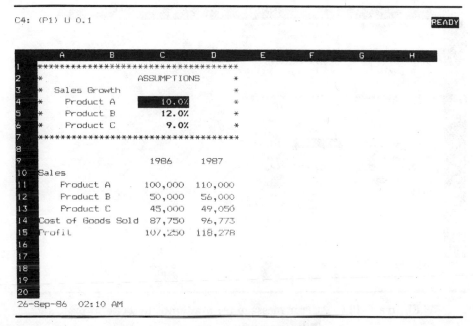

**Figure 6-11.** Unprotected cell highlighted

## Turning on Worksheet Protection

As noted in the analogy established previously, the /Worksheet Global Protection Enable command "closes the gate" on every protected worksheet cell, ensuring that protected cells cannot be altered. It also places the entry PR in the control panel for every protected cell if you are using release 2.

If you have not altered the default cell protection, you will not be able to make entries in any worksheet cell once protection is enabled with this command. You can enter characters from the keyboard while pointing to one of these cells, but when you attempt to finalize the entry, the error message shown in Figure 6-12 will appear, alerting you to the protected status of the cell. If you have used the /Range Unprotect command to strip away protection from some of

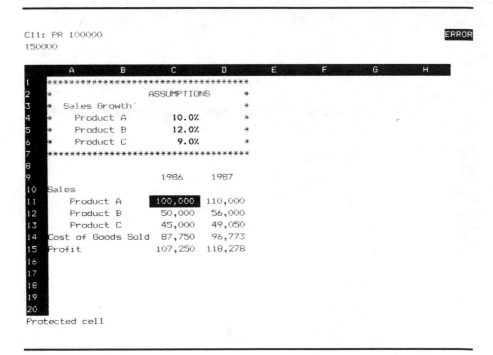

**Figure 6-12.** Error message from attempt to write in protected cell

the cells, you will still be able to make entries in these cells.

If you decide to turn protection off after enabling it, you can enter /**Worksheet Global Protection Disable**. This command allows you to temporarily suspend protection to make a change to a formula, for example.

## Specifying an Input Range

The /Range Input command is used in conjunction with the protection features. Once a worksheet is protected, using /Range Input will allow you to restrict cursor movement to unprotected cells within the input range. It is useful for focusing attention on the cells available for entry during data input. The steps for using this command are as follows:

1. The worksheet should be set up and all labels and formulas entered. In other words, design your worksheet before restricting the cursor.

2. The cells requiring data entry should be unprotected with /Range Unprotect.

3. The protection features should be enabled with /Worksheet Global Protection Enable.

4. Enter /**Range Input** and select the range of cells in which you want to allow input.

Your screen will display the input range in the upper left corner. You will be able to edit cells in the specified range or complete new entries in them. You will also be able to use ESC, HOME, END, ENTER, F1 (HELP), F2 (EDIT), BACKSPACE, or any of the arrow keys in completing your entries. Your cursor will always remain within the input range, since that is the only area where entries can be made. Pressing either the ESC or the ENTER key without making an entry cancels the /Range Input command. While this command is in effect, the END and HOME keys will move you to the end or the beginning of the input range. This command is used in the macro environment to assist with automating applications (see Chapter 13).

Cutting and pasting can extend your productivity with 1-2-3 by allowing you to move or copy existing entries to new locations. You can thus restructure a worksheet to meet new needs without reentering data. 1-2-3 also provides commands that let you cut the worksheet to add new rows and to eliminate rows and columns that are no longer required.

## Moving Information

Creating a worksheet can sometimes be a trial and error process, during which you attempt to obtain the most effective placement of data. 1-2-3 provides a /Move command that permits you to move a range of cells to another location on the worksheet. The command requires that you specify both a From and a To range. The From range marks the original location of the data to be moved, and the To range is the new location you have selected. 1-2-3 will prompt you for these ranges when it is time to enter them. You can use any of the normal methods for specifying a range location, including range names, cell addresses, and pointing.

It is easier to specify the From range for the /Move command if you place your cursor on the upper left cell in the range to be moved before invoking the command. That is because 1-2-3 assumes that the current cell is the range you wish to move. To expand this range, you simply move the cursor in the direction you want; the beginning cell remains anchored in place.

If you do not like the beginning of the range which 1-2-3 suggests, you will have to press ESC to unlock the beginning of the range and move your cursor to the upper left cell in the range you wish to move, type a period, and move to the end of the range. Alternatively, you can just type a new range when presented with 1-2-3's suggestion. Unless you are typing the range reference, you will have to move your cursor for the To range even if you position your cursor prior to executing the command, since 1-2-3 will suggest the same range for To as it suggested for From. Since the suggestion for To is a single cell, you will not need to press ESC to unlock the beginning of the range. Just move to whatever beginning cell you wish for the To range or enter the range from the keyboard. Only the beginning cell needs to be specified for To, even if many cells are being moved.

The /Move command can be used to move one or many worksheet cells. The example in Figure 6-13 shows a long label that is not in the center of the worksheet. To enter the label in a more central location would be time consuming. It is much quicker to move it with /Move. To do this, you would place the cursor in A3 and enter /**Move**. Since the From range is the cursor location, you would press ENTER to accept the current cell address for the From range. You would then move the cursor to C3 and press ENTER to accept C3 as the To range. Figure 6-14 presents the worksheet after the move is complete. Although the label displays in multiple cells, the complete entry was in one cell and was therefore moved by specifying one cell each for the From and To ranges.

As another example, suppose that in the worksheet shown in Figure 6-15 you wanted to move the entries in cells A2..C15 to the right. These cells contain numbers, labels, and formulas. (The formulas are shown in Figure 6-16.) You could use the /Move command to move these entries by enter-

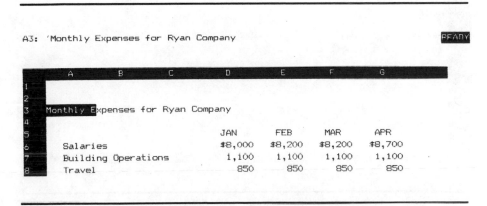

**Figure 6-13.** Long label to be moved

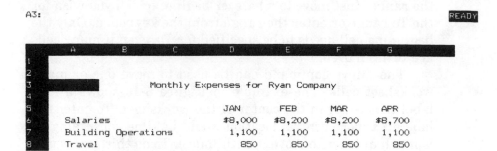

Figure 6-14.    Result of moving label

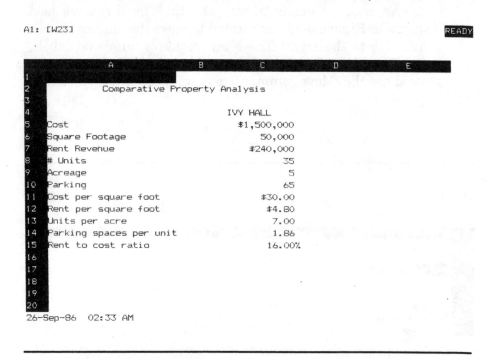

**Figure 6-15.**    Entries in A2..C15

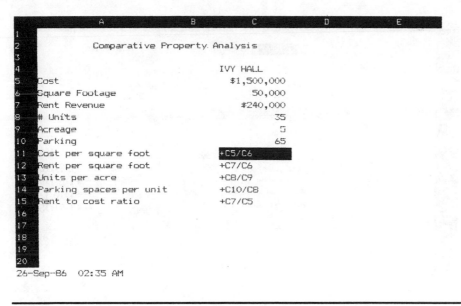

**Figure 6-16.**     Display of formulas

ing /**Move** and the range A2..C15. When the To range is requested, enter B2. Only one cell is needed to tell 1-2-3 where to begin the To range; it will automatically use B2..D15 as the complete To range. Figure 6-17 shows the worksheet after the move, including the way in which the formulas have been adjusted to reflect their new locations. You will also notice that there is an overlap between the From and To ranges. 1-2-3 is able to handle this.

## Adding Rows or Columns

The /Worksheet Insert command will add blank rows or columns to a worksheet. You can use them to add a heading for a report, include new or unexpected information, or other-

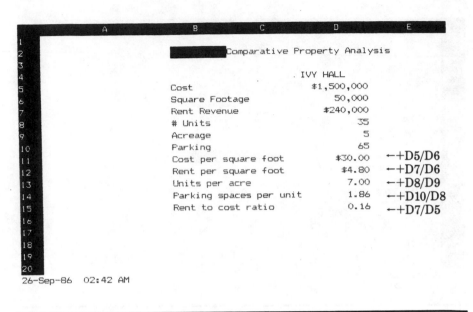

**Figure 6-17.**     Result of move

wise restructure your worksheet. Adding blank rows and columns can also improve your worksheet design by making it more readable.

The /Worksheet Insert command is position dependent in that rows and columns can be added at the cursor location if you position it before entering the command. Position your cursor in the column to the right of where you wish to insert or in the row below where you wish to insert, because 1-2-3 always inserts columns to the left of the cursor and rows above the cursor. After you enter /**Worksheet Insert**, 1-2-3 will ask whether you want to add rows or columns. Make the appropriate selection. 1-2-3 will then ask for the range you wish to insert. You can expand your cursor across columns or down rows, covering the number of rows or columns you wish to insert. If you forget to position your cursor prior to enter-

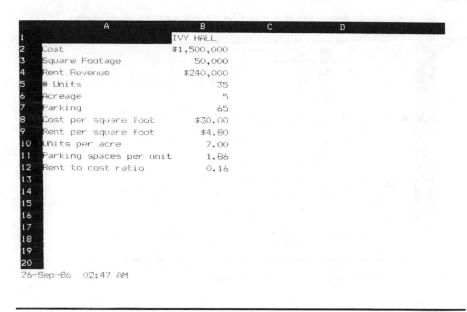

|    | A                      | B          | C | D |
|----|------------------------|------------|---|---|
| 1  |                        | IVY HALL   |   |   |
| 2  | Cost                   | $1,500,000 |   |   |
| 3  | Square Footage         | 50,000     |   |   |
| 4  | Rent Revenue           | $240,000   |   |   |
| 5  | # Units                | 35         |   |   |
| 6  | Acreage                | 5          |   |   |
| 7  | Parking                | 65         |   |   |
| 8  | Cost per square foot   | $30.00     |   |   |
| 9  | Rent per square foot   | $4.80      |   |   |
| 10 | Units per acre         | 7.00       |   |   |
| 11 | Parking spaces per unit| 1.86       |   |   |
| 12 | Rent to cost ratio     | 0.16       |   |   |
| 13 |                        |            |   |   |
| 14 |                        |            |   |   |
| 15 |                        |            |   |   |
| 16 |                        |            |   |   |
| 17 |                        |            |   |   |
| 18 |                        |            |   |   |
| 19 |                        |            |   |   |
| 20 |                        |            |   |   |

26-Sep-86   02:47 AM

**Figure 6-18.**   Worksheet before insertions

ing the command, you can always type in the range or use
ESC to free the beginning of the range so you can move it.

Figure 6-18 presents a worksheet before insertions are
made to improve the appearance with additional blank
spaces. To make the insertions, you would move the cursor to
A1 to insert blank columns to the left, enter /**Worksheet
Insert Column**, and move the cursor to expand the range to
B1. When you press ENTER, two columns will be inserted to
the left of column A, causing the worksheet to appear as
shown in Figure 6-19. Next, place the cursor in A1 to insert
blank rows above the cursor and enter /**Worksheet Insert
Row**. Move the cursor down three rows to A3 and press
ENTER to add three rows. The final version of the worksheet,
after the insertion of both rows and columns, is shown in
Figure 6-20.

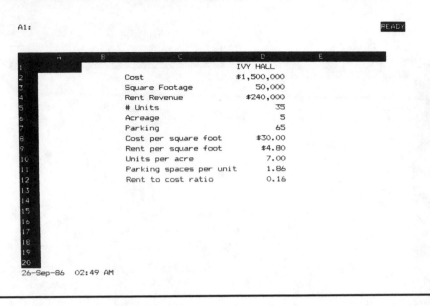

**Figure 6-19.**    Two columns inserted

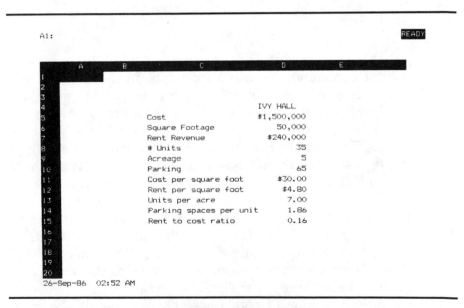

**Figure 6-20.**    Rows and columns inserted

```
        A       B       C        D        E       F       G
1
2
3
4            Expenses - Jan 87
5
6        Salaries                 $8,000
7        Building Operations       1,100
8        Travel                      850
9        Supplies                    500
10       Depreciation              1,200
11       Equipment Maintenance       750
12       Shipping Expense            400
13       Data Processing Costs     2,100
14       Printing & Duplicating      640
15       Other                     1,030
16  Total Expenses               $16,570
17
18
19
20
26-Sep-86   02:57 AM
```

**Figure 6-21.**    Original worksheet formula

When rows or columns are inserted in the middle of a range, the range is automatically expanded to allow for the insertions. This applies to range names that have been assigned and to ranges used in formulas. For example, Figure 6-21 shows a sum formula for departmental expenses. When two additional rows are inserted in the middle of the range, the sum formula is automatically adjusted to include two extra cells, as shown in Figure 6-22. If entries were made in these rows, a new total would display, as shown in Figure 6-23.

When rows or columns are inserted before the first entry or after the last entry, no adjustment is made to the range. Whenever you wish to expand a range, therefore, pick a spot somewhere in the middle for your insertion.

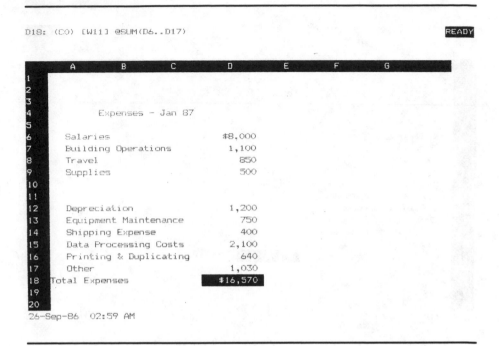

```
        A         B          C          D         E       F        G
1
2
3
4           Expenses - Jan 87
5
6      Salaries                      $8,000
7      Building Operations            1,100
8      Travel                           850
9      Supplies                         500
10
11
12     Depreciation                   1,200
13     Equipment Maintenance            750
14     Shipping Expense                 400
15     Data Processing Costs          2,100
16     Printing & Duplicating           640
17     Other                          1,030
18   Total Expenses                 $16,570
19
20
26-Sep-86  02:59 AM
```

**Figure 6-22.**     Sum formula adjusted

## Deleting Rows or Columns

1-2-3 also provides a command that will delete one or many complete rows or columns. Just as with the insertion command, it is easiest to use this command when you position your cursor prior to execution. If you are deleting rows, place your cursor in the uppermost row to be deleted. If you are deleting columns, your cursor should be in the leftmost column to be deleted. Note that cells that are protected cannot be deleted when worksheet protection is enabled.

The rows or columns deleted can be blank, or they can contain worksheet data, including formulas. When deleting rows or columns, be sure that the formulas and data in them are not referenced by other worksheet cells. If such references exist, incorrect data may be referenced after the deletion, or an error condition may occur if the new cells are no longer numeric. Figure 6-24 shows the error message that resulted

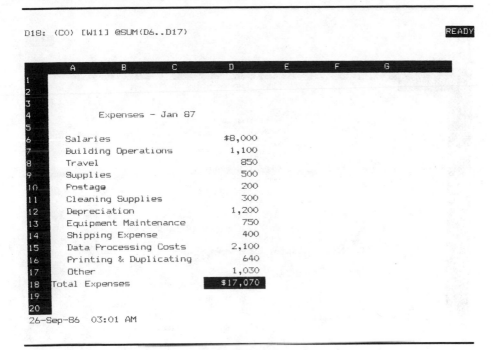

Figure 6-23.    New total after entries

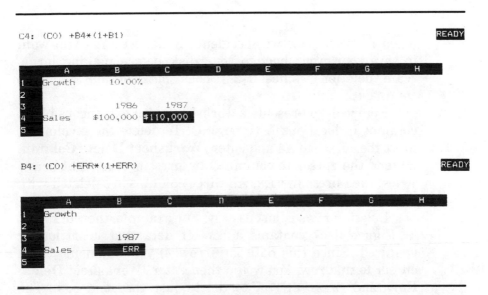

Figure 6-24.    Result of accidental deletion

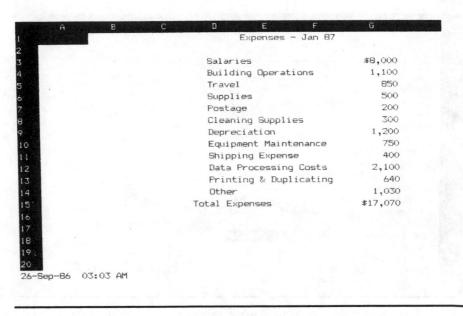

READY

| | A | B | C | D | E | F | G |
|---|---|---|---|---|---|---|---|

Expenses - Jan 87

Salaries                    $8,000
Building Operations          1,100
Travel                         850
Supplies                       500
Postage                        200
Cleaning Supplies              300
Depreciation                 1,200
Equipment Maintenance          750
Shipping Expense               400
Data Processing Costs        2,100
Printing & Duplicating         640
Other                        1,030
Total Expenses             $17,070

26-Sep-86   03:03 AM

**Figure 6-25.**    Worksheet with three extra columns

when a critical row was accidentally deleted. You will want to save your worksheet to your disk before making large-scale deletions, since 1-2-3 does not contain an undo command.

Figure 6-25 presents a worksheet with extraneous blank columns in locations A through C. To delete these columns, move the cursor to A1 and enter /**Worksheet Delete Column**. Extend the cursor to column C by pressing the right arrow twice, then press ENTER. All three columns are deleted with this one command, producing the display in Figure 6-26.

Deleting rows is just as easy. For example, the worksheet in Figure 6-27 contains a row of data that is no longer required. Since this data is in row 4, you would move the cursor to that row. You would then enter /**Worksheet Delete Row** and press ENTER to delete just that one row. The

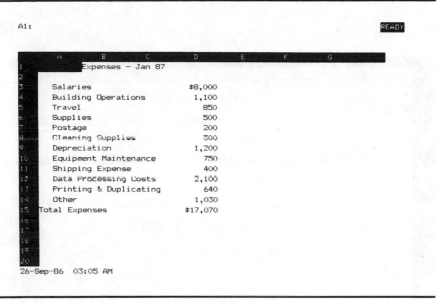

```
        A       B       C       D       E       F       G
1               Expenses - Jan 87
2
3       Salaries                        $8,000
4       Building Operations              1,100
5       Travel                             850
6       Supplies                           500
7       Postage                            200
8       Cleaning Supplies                  300
9       Depreciation                     1,200
10      Equipment Maintenance              750
11      Shipping Expense                   400
12      Data Processing Costs            2,100
13      Printing & Duplicating             640
14      Other                            1,030
15      Total Expenses                 $17,070
16
17
18
19
20
        26-Sep-86  03:05 AM
```

**Figure 6-26.**    Three columns deleted

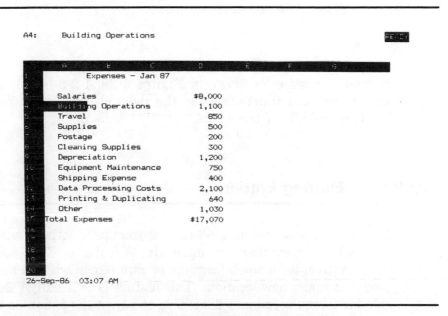

A4:     Building Operations                                            READY

```
        A       B       C       D       E       F       G
1               Expenses - Jan 87
2
3       Salaries                        $8,000
4       Building Operations              1,100
5       Travel                             850
6       Supplies                           500
7       Postage                            200
8       Cleaning Supplies                  300
9       Depreciation                     1,200
10      Equipment Maintenance              750
11      Shipping Expense                   400
12      Data Processing Costs            2,100
13      Printing & Duplicating             640
14      Other                            1,030
15      Total Expenses                 $17,070
16
17
18
19
20
        26-Sep-86  03:07 AM
```

**Figure 6-27.**    Row of unneeded data in row 4

Basic Worksheet Commands                                            **227**

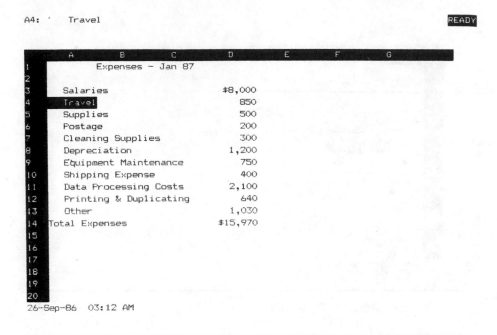

```
        A      B       C         D        E       F       G
1              Expenses - Jan 87
2
3      Salaries              $8,000
4      Travel                   850
5      Supplies                 500
6      Postage                  200
7      Cleaning Supplies        300
8      Depreciation           1,200
9      Equipment Maintenance    750
10     Shipping Expense         400
11     Data Processing Costs  2,100
12     Printing & Duplicating   640
13     Other                  1,030
14    Total Expenses        $15,970
15
16
17
18
19
20
26-Sep-86   03:12 AM
```

**Figure 6-28.**    Worksheet after deletion

altered worksheet is shown in Figure 6-28. 1-2-3 is able to adjust the sum function, since the deleted row was taken from the middle of the range.

## Duplicating Existing Entries

The copying features of 1-2-3 extend your productivity with the package more than any other single feature. /Copy permits you to enter a label, formula, or number in one cell and copy it to many new locations. This feature is especially valuable for formulas, since 1-2-3 is able to adjust the formulas to conform with their new locations.

## Copy Options

The /Copy command will perform its task in a variety of situations. You can use /Copy to copy the contents of one cell to another cell. /Copy will also copy one cell to a range of many cells. You can speed up the copying process by copying a range of cells to a second range of the same size. Lastly, the /Copy command can copy a range of cells to a second range whose size is a multiple of the original range. Let's look at an example for each of these uses.

Suppose a label entry is placed in cell A1, like this:

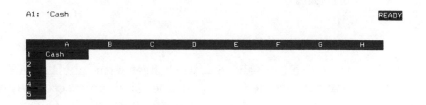

To copy this label to another cell, the easiest approach is to place your cursor on A1 before beginning. When you enter /**Copy**, 1-2-3 asks what you want to copy from. Since your cursor is already positioned on A1, just press ENTER. If the cursor had not been positioned first, you would have had to press ESC before moving the cursor to the correct location. After the From location is specified, 1-2-3's next prompt requests the To range. To copy the entry to B3, move the cursor to B3 in response to this prompt and press ENTER. The completed copy operation generates a second label in B3, as shown below:

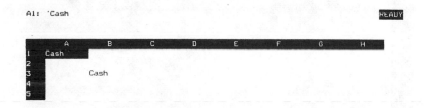

The next example will start with the entry of Cash in A1 again, but this time the entry will be copied to many cells.

The beginning of the operation is the same: place the cursor on A1 and enter /**Copy**. Press ENTER in response to the From range prompt. The entry is to be copied to D1..D51; therefore, when the To range prompt is presented, move the cursor to D1. Enter a period to lock the beginning of the range in place. Move the cursor down to D51 and then press ENTER. The result should have the label copied into every specified cell from D1 down, like this.

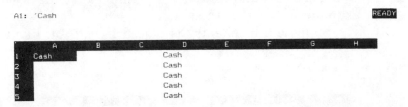

Figure 6-29 shows a worksheet with labels in A3..A15. /Copy can be used to copy these labels to a second range of the same size and shape as the original. The best way to

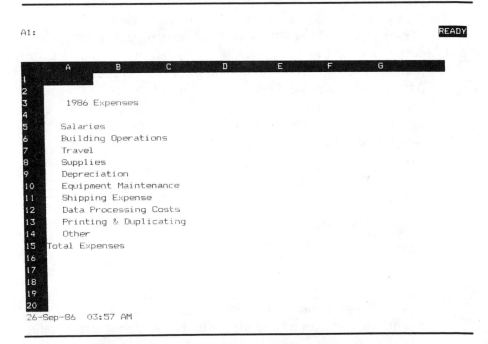

**Figure 6-29.** Label entries to be copied

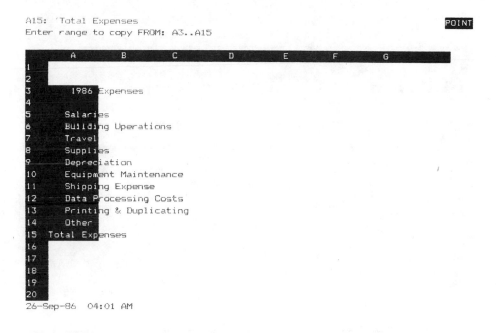

```
              A         B         C         D         E         F         G
1
2
3        1986 Expenses
4
5        Salaries
6        Building Operations
7        Travel
8        Supplies
9        Depreciation
10       Equipment Maintenance
11       Shipping Expense
12       Data Processing Costs
13       Printing & Duplicating
14       Other
15   Total Expenses
16
17
18
19
20
26-Sep-86   04:01 AM
```

**Figure 6-30.**    From range

begin is to place the cursor in the upper left cell in the range, which would be A3 in this example. Type /**Copy**. Then, instead of pressing ENTER, move the cursor to the bottom of the From range as shown in Figure 6-30 (the entries are all long labels within column A). 1-2-3 requests the To range after ENTER is pressed. At this point the cursor should be moved to the top cell in the To range. For the present example this will be E3. Since 1-2-3 knows that the To range must match the From range in size and shape, you need specify only the upper left corner of the To range. You then press ENTER, producing the results shown in Figure 6-31. With just a few keystrokes an entire range of label entries can be duplicated much faster than anyone could enter them.

The last use of /Copy is even more powerful, since it copies one row or column of entries to many rows or columns in one operation. For an example, let's use the labels found in

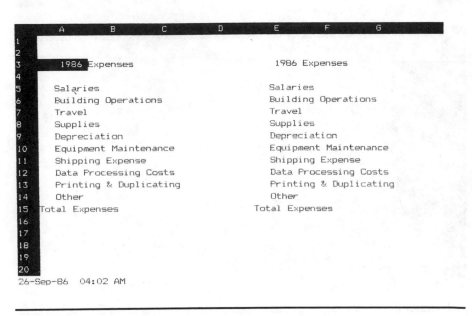

| | A | B | C | D | E | F | G |
|---|---|---|---|---|---|---|---|
1
2
3 1986 Expenses                              1986 Expenses
4
5 Salaries                                   Salaries
6 Building Operations                        Building Operations
7 Travel                                     Travel
8 Supplies                                   Supplies
9 Depreciation                               Depreciation
10 Equipment Maintenance                     Equipment Maintenance
11 Shipping Expense                          Shipping Expense
12 Data Processing Costs                     Data Processing Costs
13 Printing & Duplicating                    Printing & Duplicating
14 Other                                     Other
15 Total Expenses                            Total Expenses
16
17
18
19
20

26-Sep-86  04:02 AM

**Figure 6-31.**    Result of copying

Figure 6-32. To copy them, place the cursor in A3 and enter
/**Copy**. Move the cursor to A15 in response to a request for
the From range and press ENTER. This time the labels are to
be copied into B3..B15, C3..C15, D3..D15, and E3..E15.
When 1-2-3 requests the To range, therefore, move the cursor
to the top of the first column where the labels will be copied,
B3, and enter a period to lock the beginning of the range in
place. Since 1-2-3 knows it is copying a partial column of labels that will extend down to row 15, it needs to be told only
how far across the worksheet this partial column should be
copied. To do this, move the cursor to E3 and press ENTER.
The display in Figure 6-33 should be produced with this
operation.

Copying numbers will work the same way as copying
labels. Copying formulas can be even more valuable. Although

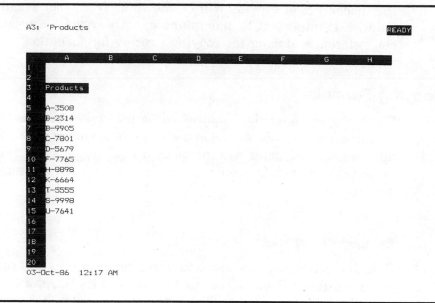

**Figure 6-32.**    Column of label entries

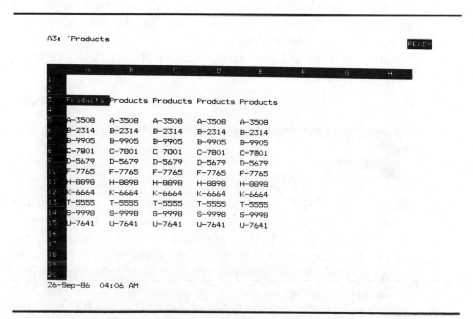

**Figure 6-33.**    Result of copying to many locations

the mechanics of copying will be the same from your stand-point, it is important to understand exactly how 1-2-3 treats cell references during the copying process for formulas.

## Copying Formulas

Since copying formulas requires adjusting cell references, it is important to have a complete understanding of cell addressing. This topic was introduced in Chapter 4 but will be expanded in this section to cover the three addressing options completely.

### Relative References

Relative references are the addresses generated when you enter regular cell addresses into formulas. A19, D2, and X15 are all relative references. This is the normal reference style used with formulas in 1-2-3. When a formula is created with this reference style, 1-2-3 records the cell addresses for the formula and also translates the formula cell references into the relative distance and direction that each of these addresses is from the cell containing the formula. For example, when you enter the formula +A1+A2 in A3, 1-2-3 remembers facts that are not shown in the worksheet.

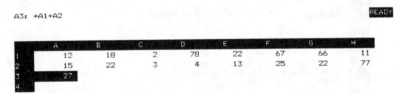

Specifically, 1-2-3 remembers the distance and direction that must be traveled to obtain each of the references in the formula. For A1, the reference is in the same column as the formula result but is two rows above it. A2 is in the same column but is one row above the result. This ability adds great power to the /Copy command. Let's say that you wanted the same type of formula in B3 but you wanted it to add the values in B1 and B2 together. /Copy can handle this, since it remembers the directions for the data.

To make this transfer, place the cursor on A3, enter /**Copy**, and press ENTER. Then move the cursor to B3 as the To location and press ENTER again. The formula is replicated into B3 and, in addition, adjustments are made that make the formula appropriate for B3. You will notice here that the formula has been adjusted for column B.

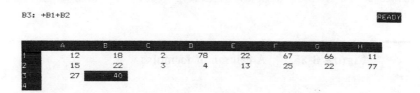

Suppose you want to try this again but this time copy from B3 across the remainder of the row. Enter /**Copy** with the cursor on B3 and press ENTER. Move the cursor to C3 as the beginning of the To range, enter a period, and move the cursor to H3 before pressing ENTER again. Figure 6-34 shows

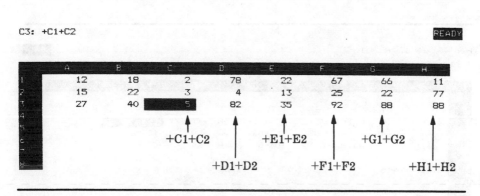

**Figure 6-34.** Result of formula copying across a row

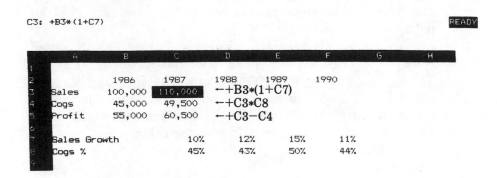

**Figure 6-35.**　　A column of formulas

that the appropriate formulas were copied across the row.

Relative references can be used in formulas anytime you want the formula adjusted during the copying process. Figure 6-35 shows another worksheet with a column of formulas. To copy the formulas, position the cursor on C3 and enter /**Copy**. Then move the cursor to C5, which expands the highlighting, and press ENTER. Move the cursor to D3, type a period, and move the cursor across to F3 before pressing ENTER to finalize the To range. Figure 6-36, which contains

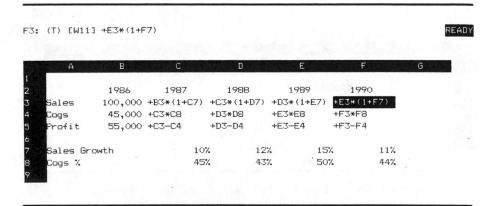

**Figure 6-36.**　　Result of copying of formulas, displayed as text

the results of the copying process, has been changed to a text format so that you can review 1-2-3's work in copying the formulas.

### Absolute References

Absolute references are references that you want held constant. In other words, you do not want these references to change when they are copied to a different location. This is the kind of reference you want for, say, a single interest rate, a specific value in an assumption block, or a table that is in a fixed location.

Entering absolute cell references in formulas requires a little more work in that absolute references must have a $ in front of both the column and the row portion of the address. $A$4, $F$87, and $X$1 are all absolute references. 1-2-3 does not remember the relative direction and distance that must be traveled to obtain these values when they are used in a formula. Instead, it remembers the absolute cell address.

There are two ways to enter the $s during formula entry. You can type them wherever they are required, or you can have 1-2-3 enter them for you. To get 1-2-3 to do the work, you must enter your formulas with the pointing method. For example, the worksheet in Figure 6-37 will require formulas

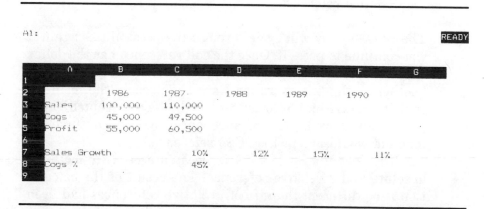

**Figure 6-37.** Model requiring relative and absolute references

that use both relative and absolute references, since there are varying sales growth rates but one fixed Cogs (cost of goods sold) percent that will apply to all years. The formulas that were already entered for the 1987 sales used only relative references. The formula for Cost of Goods Sold (row 4) will require both a relative reference to Sales for the current year and an absolute reference to the Cost of Goods Sold % (cell C8). An absolute reference is required because the same Cost of Goods Sold % will be used for all years. The formula will be +C3*$C$8 for 1987, +D3*$C$8 for 1988, and so forth.

To enter this formula in cell C4 (it will later be copied to other cells in row 4), place the cursor in C4 and enter a +. The first cell reference needed in the formula is the 1987 Sales figure in C3, so use the up arrow to point to C3. Since you want to multiply this figure by the Cost of Goods Sold %, enter a * representing multiplication, next. Then move the cursor to C8 to reference the Cost of Goods Sold %. If a relative reference were wanted, you would press ENTER now, but since you want an absolute reference to this cell, $s are needed first. 1-2-3 will enter them for you from the POINT mode if you press F4 (ABS). The first time this key is pressed, the reference becomes $C$8. You could continue to press it to cycle through all the possibilities:

| | |
|---|---|
| Absolute reference | $C$8—first time |
| Mixed address | C$8—second time |
| Mixed address | $C8—third time |
| Relative reference | C8—fourth time |

The F4 (ABS) key will cycle through the possibilities again if you continue to press it. Once the cell reference has the dollar signs added in both positions, press ENTER to accept it. If another arithmetic operation were required in the formula, typing the arithmetic operator would have accepted the $ placement as well. (For instance, entering + to continue the formula would accept the $C$8 reference.)

The formula +C3*$C$8 is now entered with both an absolute and a relative reference. The result of the calculation is no different than if both relative references had been

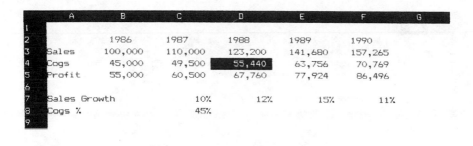

|   | A | B | C | D | E | F | G |
|---|---|---|---|---|---|---|---|
| 1 | | | | | | | |
| 2 | | 1986 | 1987 | 1988 | 1989 | 1990 | |
| 3 | Sales | 100,000 | 110,000 | 123,200 | 141,680 | 157,265 | |
| 4 | Cogs | 45,000 | 49,500 | 55,440 | 63,756 | 70,769 | |
| 5 | Profit | 55,000 | 60,500 | 67,760 | 77,924 | 86,496 | |
| 6 | | | | | | | |
| 7 | Sales Growth | | 10% | 12% | 15% | 11% | |
| 8 | Cogs % | | 45% | | | | |
| 9 | | | | | | | |

**Figure 6-38.**    Result of copying

used. Only when the formula is copied to new locations will the difference become apparent. Before this is demonstrated, let's examine one more formula in this example, the one needed to calculate the profit for 1987. This formula is simply +C3−C4, with both references relative. All three formulas will be copied at once for subsequent years. To do this, move the cursor to the top cell in the range to be copied, C3, and enter /**Copy**. Move the cursor down twice to highlight the entire From range. Move the cursor to D3 as the first location in the To range and then enter a period before moving the cursor across to F3 and pressing ENTER. Figure 6-38 shows the results of the copying process.

The formulas in the different cells are shown in Figure 6-39. If an absolute reference had not been used for the Cost of Goods Sold %, 1-2-3 would have attempted to increment the cell reference for each new formula, and blank cells would have been referenced for years beyond 1987.

As you can see from this example, you can combine relative and absolute references to create formulas that meet your exact needs. 1-2-3 has one more reference type that extends the package features still further. This reference type is a mixed address, which combines relative and absolute features in one cell reference.

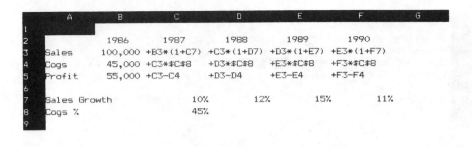

**Figure 6-39.**   Formula display

## Mixed Addresses

Since a cell address is composed of a row and a column reference, it is possible to make one component absolute while leaving the other relative. This gives you the flexibility, for example, to have the column portion of an address updated when a formula is copied across the page but to keep the row portion of the same address constant when the formula is copied down the worksheet.

Figure 6-40 presents an application where the mixed addressing feature is useful. In this worksheet the 1986 figures are historic numbers, and all of the projections for subsequent years use these figures as base numbers. Sales projections for each product will use the appropriate growth factor from C4..C6. For Product A, for example, the sales figure from 1986 will be multiplied by 110%. This could be written in cell D11 as +C11*(1+C4). This formula would work fine for this one year, but it would cause a problem when it was copied across to subsequent years, since C4 would be updated to D4, E4, and so on.

Using $C$4 in this formula would present another problem, since the Product A formulas could not be copied down for Product B and Product C. If an absolute reference were used for C4, the copied formulas would not be able to refer-

D11: +C11*(1+$C4)                                                        READY

```
         A        B         C         D         E         F         G         H
1  *****************************************************************
2  *             ASSUMPTIONS                            *
3  *   Sales Growth                                     *
4  *      Product A      10.0%                          *
5  *      Product B      12.0%                          *
6  *      Product C       9.0%                          *
7  *****************************************************************
8
9                       1986      1987      1988      1989      1990
10 Sales
11     Product A     100,000   110,000   121,000   133,100   146,410
12     Product B      50,000    56,000    62,720    70,246    78,676
13     Product C      45,000    49,050    53,465    58,276    63,521
14 Cost of Goods Sold  87,750    96,773   106,733   117,730   129,873
15 Profit            107,250   118,278   130,451   143,892   158,734
16
17
18
19
20
```
26-Sep-86  04:46 AM

**Figure 6-40.**   An application of mixed addressing

ence C5 and C6. The ideal situation would be to freeze the column portion of the address but allow the row portion to vary. Mixed addressing can provide this capability. If the formula reference is written as $C4, only the column portion of the address will be absolute; the row portion will be allowed to vary during the copy process.

A little thought and planning is required to decide how to construct the address type you need. Many people would just use a different formula for each of the product types. That is all right, but if there were twenty-five products rather than three, the mixed addressing feature would really save significant time, since it would allow you to devise one formula that would work for all situations.

The formula devised for D11 is +C11*(1+$C4). Mixed addressing allows this formula to be used for all the sales projections. You would first copy it down column C to C12

Basic Worksheet Commands                                                241 and C13. Then you would copy the range C11..C13 across to column D through column G. The formulas automatically created in E11..G13 are as follows:

    E11:  +D11*(1+$C4)
    F11:  +E11*(1+$C4)
    G11:  +F11*(1+$C4)
    E12:  +D12*(1+$C5)
    F12:  +E12*(1+$C5)
    G12:  +F12*(1+$C5)
    E13:  +D13*(1+$C6)
    F13:  +E13*(1+$C6)
    G13:  +F13*(1+$C6)

Using mixed addressing, you could enter one formula and have 1-2-3 generate the other 11 formulas for you. Although it is not useful in all models, its payback under appropriate circumstances is significant enough to make mixed addressing a desirable part of your model building toolkit.

## Making Other Worksheet Changes

Several additional features bring advanced capabilities to worksheet preparation. In this section you will look at options that allow you to change label justification for the entire worksheet and erase the complete worksheet with one command. An additional capability, for embedding page breaks in a worksheet, is discussed in Chapter 5.

## Changing Label Justification for the Worksheet

The default worksheet setting for labels provides left justification for every label entry. This means that a single quotation mark will be generated as the first character of every label entry. As you learned in Chapter 3, you always have the option of center justifying a label entry by typing the center justification character yourself. For example, entering ^Sales would center justify Sales in the cell where it was entered. You can also right justify a single entry by beginning your label entry with a double quotation mark (").

1-2-3 offers further flexibility with the /Range Label command, which allows you to change the justification of label entries that are already in cells. But if you want all of your labels to be, say, center justified, neither the single entry nor the range option is exactly right. For such circumstances, 1-2-3 provides the /Worksheet Global Label-Prefix command to change the default label prefix for every worksheet entry. To make the change, enter /Worksheet Global Label-Prefix and select the justification you want for the worksheet from the menu, as shown in this example.

With the Worksheet option, existing entries are unaffected, while new entries will have the new label prefix. Just the opposite is true with /Range Label. With both options you should remember that numeric and formula entries are unaffected by changes made to the label prefix.

## Erasing the Worksheet

1-2-3 provides a command to erase the entire worksheet. This feature is useful when you have made so many mistakes that you would prefer to wipe the slate clean and start over again or when you have saved a completed worksheet on disk and want to begin a new worksheet.

When you enter /Worksheet Erase to request this feature, 1-2-3 presents the following screen:

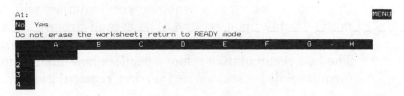

You can confirm your selection from this menu or abandon the operation. This confirmation step is provided because there is no undo command for Erase. In other words, once you have erased a worksheet, there is no way to bring it back unless you have saved a copy of it on disk. You will notice that the cursor is positioned over the No option on the confirmation screen initially, so if you just press ENTER without looking, you will not lose your worksheet. To erase the worksheet you will have to take an action, either typing **Y** or pointing to the Yes option before pressing ENTER.

## Recalculating the Worksheet

1-2-3's recalculation abilities provide the power behind its formula features, since 1-2-3 will recalculate each worksheet formula every time you change a single cell entry on the worksheet. All the recalculation options are accessed through the /Worksheet Global Recalculation command.

## Default Recalculation Settings

1-2-3's recalculation features have three different setting categories, all selected from the following menu.

One group determines whether recalculation will be automatic or only upon request. The second group relates to the order in which the worksheet formulas will be reevaluated. The last recalculation option specifies how many times each formula will be reevaluated during recalculation.

## Timing of Recalculation

The default setting for a new worksheet is Automatic recalculation. This means that any new number, changed number, or new formula will automatically cause 1-2-3 to recalculate all worksheet formulas. The time needed for this recalculation depends on the number and complexity of the worksheet formulas. It may show as anything from a slight flicker of the screen to the appearance of a WAIT mode indicator, signifying 1-2-3's preoccupation with the current task, for 10 or more seconds.

## Order of Recalculation

The default setting for recalculation order is Natural. This means that 1-2-3 will examine each worksheet formula for dependencies on other formulas and determine which formulas must be calculated first to provide the results needed by the formulas to be reevaluated next. This Natural recalculation order set a new standard for other spreadsheets when it was first introduced. Before then the only options were rowwise or columnwise recalculation.

Rowwise recalculation evaluates all the formulas in row 1, then all the formulas in row 2, and so on. The problem with this method is that if a formula in row 1 references a value in a row further down the worksheet, the formula will end up referencing the value from a prior recalculation. The same type of problem occurs with columnwise recalculation when early columns reference values further to the right that have not yet been recalculated. These deficiencies in the existing methods made 1-2-3's Natural recalculation order a welcome addition to the recalculation features of the package.

## Iterations of Recalculation

The default setting for the number of iterations for one recalculation is once. This means that each formula will be reevaluated one time each time the worksheet is recalculated.

## Changing the Recalculation Settings

If you don't want the default settings, each of the three categories of recalculation options can be changed. In some cases you have several options to choose from. The various recalculation options and appropriate circumstances for their use are summarized in the box called "Recalculation Options and Potential Pitfalls."

## Recalculation Options And Potential Pitfalls

The recalculation options span three different features of recalculation. Here are the specific options, along with a few tips for their use:

**Automatic**     This option, which causes the worksheet to recalculate automatically after every worksheet entry, is the default setting. You can stop the automatic recalculation by invoking /Worksheet Global Recalculation Manual.

**Manual**     This option turns off the automatic recalculation feature. The worksheet will not recalculate with this option in effect unless you use F9 (CALC). You can restore automatic recalculation with /Worksheet Global Recalculation Automatic.

**Natural**     This option affects the order in which formulas are recalculated. This is the default setting, and makes 1-2-3 responsible for determining which formula to evaluate first. You can change to either Rowwise or Columnwise recalculation.

**Rowwise**     This option disables the natural recalculation sequence and switches to recalculation by rows. Row 1 is calculated from left to right, then row 2, and so on from top to bottom of the worksheet. The potential problem with this approach is backward references that refer to values not yet recalculated.

**Columnwise**　　This option disables the natural recalculation sequence and switches to recalculation by columns. Column 1 is calculated from top to bottom, then column 2, and so on from left to right on the worksheet. Again, the potential problem with this approach is backward references that refer to values not yet recalculated.

**Iterations**　　The normal setting for this option is 1, meaning that each formula is recalculated once during every recalculation. Circular references and other applications requiring iterative calculations to refine approximations would require the iteration count to be set higher. The highest number 1-2-3 will accept is 50.

### Timing of Recalculation

If you find that Automatic recalculation slows down data entry too much, you may want to turn this option off by entering **/Worksheet Global Recalculation Manual**. When the Manual option is in force, the worksheet will not recalculate unless you turn Automatic recalculation back on or press the F9 (CALC) key. The Manual option can speed up your data entry, since you can enter everything before requesting a recalculation.

### Order of Recalculation

If you want recalculation to be done in row order or column order rather than natural order, you can obtain these options by entering **/Worksheet Global Recalculation Rowwise** or

**/Worksheet Recalculation Columnwise**, respectively. One time you might want to use these other recalculation orders is when you import data from another worksheet package. If you bring a model created with a package like VisiCalc into 1-2-3, you might want to retain the recalculation order used with the original model.

### Iterations of Recalculation

In calculations that involve a circular calculation pattern, one iteration is not sufficient. This is because each calculation depends on the result of some other calculation, with the final result referring back to one of the earlier calculations. In situations like this 1-2-3 is not able to identify a clear recalculation sequence for the formulas. Multiple calculations are required so that each will approximate the correct answer a little more closely.

Increasing 1-2-3's iterative count can solve the problem with circular references. This increase means that 1-2-3 will recalculate more than once each time the worksheet is calculated automatically or the F9 (CALC) key is pressed.

An example of a circular reference requiring iteration for resolution is shown in the following worksheet.

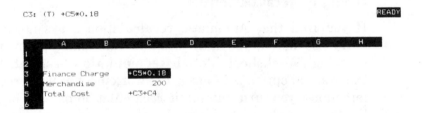

When the formulas are first entered, C3 displays as zero and C5 displays as 200. Since these two formulas are dependent on each other, each recalculation refines the accuracy of the result. The results after several recalculations with the F9 (CALC) key appear in the worksheet as follows.

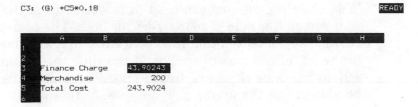

C3: (G) +C5*0.18                                    READY

Slight changes continue to occur over the next several recalculations, until a final approximation is reached. All of these calculations could have been performed the first time the worksheet was calculated if the iteration count had been set higher.

## Modifying the Screen Display

1-2-3 has several screen display options that are especially useful for large worksheets. One option allows you to lock the titles or descriptive labels at the side or top of your screen so that you can look at data in remote parts of the worksheet and still have these labels in view. The second lets you split the screen vertically or horizontally and use each section as a window into a different part of the worksheet.

## Freezing Titles

The /Worksheet Titles command presents the following menu:

With these options you can elect to freeze titles at the top of your screen, the side of your screen, or both. The command is position dependent in that it freezes titles that are above and to the left of the cursor location at the time the command is requested. Once titles are frozen on the screen, you will not be able to use the arrow keys to move to these cells. If you need to move there to make spelling corrections or other changes, you can use the F5 (GOTO) key. Pressing this key temporarily brings two copies of the titles to the screen, as shown:

This double title will disappear when you scroll away from the title area.

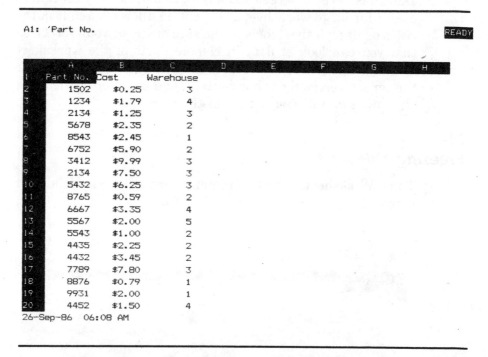

**Figure 6-41.**    Section of large worksheet

| | A | B | C | D | E | F | G | H |
|---|---|---|---|---|---|---|---|---|
| 3 | 1234 | $1.79 | 4 | | | | | |
| 4 | 2134 | $1.25 | 3 | | | | | |
| 5 | 5678 | $2.35 | 2 | | | | | |
| 6 | 8543 | $2.45 | 1 | | | | | |
| 7 | 6752 | $5.90 | 2 | | | | | |
| 8 | 3412 | $9.99 | 3 | | | | | |
| 9 | 2134 | $7.50 | 3 | | | | | |
| 10 | 5432 | $6.25 | 3 | | | | | |
| 11 | 8765 | $0.59 | 2 | | | | | |
| 12 | 6667 | $3.35 | 4 | | | | | |
| 13 | 5567 | $2.00 | 5 | | | | | |
| 14 | 5543 | $1.00 | 2 | | | | | |
| 15 | 4435 | $2.25 | 2 | | | | | |
| 16 | 4432 | $3.45 | 2 | | | | | |
| 17 | 7789 | $7.80 | 3 | | | | | |
| 18 | 8876 | $0.79 | 1 | | | | | |
| 19 | 9931 | $2.00 | 1 | | | | | |
| 20 | 4452 | $1.50 | 4 | | | | | |
| 21 | 3311 | $1.75 | 5 | | | | | |
| 22 | 1133 | $1.00 | 2 | | | | | |

26-Sep-86   06:10 AM

**Figure 6-42.**     Titles lost with scrolling

### Freezing Horizontal Titles

If you choose /Worksheet Titles Horizontal, the titles above
the cursor will be frozen. Figure 6-41 presents a section
from a worksheet with many entries. If you move your cursor
toward the bottom of the entries, the top lines will scroll off.
Figure 6-42 shows the worksheet with the two top lines,
including the identifying labels, scrolled off. The remaining
numbers are difficult to interpret without the labels. To
freeze the labels on the original top line, you could move the
cursor to A2 on the original screen and select /**Worksheet
Global Titles Horizontal**. Now, when the cursor is moved
down the worksheet, the titles will still be visible, as shown
in Figure 6-43. You will notice that the figure starts with
row 1, which displays the horizontal titles, but the data displayed is from row 4 to 22.

Basic Worksheet Commands           

| | A | B | C | D | E | F | G | H |
|---|---|---|---|---|---|---|---|---|
| 1 | Part No. | Cost | Warehouse | | | | | |
| 4 | 2134 | $1.25 | 3 | | | | | |
| 5 | 5678 | $2.35 | 2 | | | | | |
| 6 | 8543 | $2.45 | 1 | | | | | |
| 7 | 6752 | $5.90 | 2 | | | | | |
| 8 | 3412 | $9.99 | 3 | | | | | |
| 9 | 2134 | $7.50 | 3 | | | | | |
| 10 | 5432 | $6.25 | 3 | | | | | |
| 11 | 8765 | $0.59 | 2 | | | | | |
| 12 | 6667 | $3.35 | 4 | | | | | |
| 13 | 5567 | $2.00 | 5 | | | | | |
| 14 | 5543 | $1.00 | 2 | | | | | |
| 15 | 4435 | $2.25 | 2 | | | | | |
| 16 | 4432 | $3.45 | 2 | | | | | |
| 17 | 7789 | $7.80 | 3 | | | | | |
| 18 | 8876 | $0.79 | 1 | | | | | |
| 19 | 9931 | $2.00 | 1 | | | | | |
| 20 | 4452 | $1.50 | 4 | | | | | |
| 21 | 3311 | $1.75 | 5 | | | | | |
| 22 | 1133 | $1.00 | 2 | | | | | |

26-Sep-86  06:12 AM

**Figure 6-43.**    Titles visible with scrolling after freezing

### Freezing Vertical Titles

Worksheets that are wider than the screen are candidates for freezing titles vertically. Doing so will allow you to move to the right across the screen and still have identifying labels visible on the left side of the screen. You freeze titles vertically simply by moving your cursor to the right of the titles you want frozen and entering /**Worksheet Titles Vertical**.

### Freezing Titles in Both Directions

You may want to freeze in both directions when the worksheet is both longer and wider than the screen and has descriptive titles at both the top and the left side of the screen.

| | A | B | C | D | E | F | G | H |
|---|---|---|---|---|---|---|---|---|
| 1 | | | New Employees By Department | | | | | |
| 2 | | | | | | | | |
| 3 | DEPT. | 1975 | 1976 | 1977 | 1978 | 1979 | 1980 | 1981 |
| 4 | 100 | 51 | 66 | 83 | 82 | 73 | 53 | 43 |
| 5 | 120 | 33 | 93 | 31 | 38 | 29 | 12 | 71 |
| 6 | 130 | 20 | 28 | 95 | 25 | 39 | 78 | 35 |
| 7 | 140 | 88 | 59 | 0 | 33 | 52 | 73 | 56 |
| 8 | 145 | 23 | 31 | 32 | 7 | 22 | 39 | 27 |
| 9 | 150 | 84 | 18 | 72 | 59 | 47 | 76 | 78 |
| 10 | 160 | 64 | 89 | 62 | 55 | 26 | 21 | 54 |
| 11 | 175 | 85 | 22 | 27 | 93 | 46 | 37 | 17 |
| 12 | 180 | 5 | 92 | 17 | 8 | 60 | 73 | 98 |
| 13 | 190 | 21 | 36 | 41 | 76 | 6 | 9 | 57 |
| 14 | 195 | 5 | 65 | 14 | 91 | 83 | 5 | 39 |
| 15 | 200 | 0 | 85 | 43 | 48 | 87 | 13 | 32 |
| 16 | 210 | 62 | 45 | 11 | 60 | 61 | 19 | 52 |
| 17 | 220 | 31 | 23 | 39 | 66 | 31 | 20 | 30 |
| 18 | 225 | 61 | 5 | 38 | 42 | 18 | 74 | 64 |
| 19 | 228 | 50 | 47 | 85 | 1 | 49 | 49 | 57 |
| 20 | 230 | 33 | 96 | 73 | 46 | 9 | 78 | 70 |

03-Oct-86   01:30 AM

**Figure 6-44.**    Worksheet with extra width and depth

Figure 6-44 presents a worksheet like this. To freeze the titles in both directions, you would move the cursor to cell B4, which is to the right of the side titles and below the top titles, and then enter /**Worksheet Titles Both**. When the cursor is moved to M25, causing information to scroll off the top and left of the screen, both sets of titles are still visible, as you can see in Figure 6-45.

### Unfreezing Titles

/Worksheet Titles Clear eliminates any titles that you have set. This command is not position dependent. It will remove the titles regardless of your cursor location.

| | A | D | E | F | G | H | I | J |
|---|---|---|---|---|---|---|---|---|
| 1 | | yees By Department | | | | | | |
| 2 | | | | | | | | |
| 3 | DEPT. | 1977 | 1978 | 1979 | 1980 | 1981 | 1982 | 1983 |
| 10 | 160 | 62 | 55 | 26 | 21 | 54 | 59 | 36 |
| 11 | 175 | 27 | 93 | 46 | 37 | 17 | 43 | 80 |
| 12 | 180 | 17 | 8 | 60 | 73 | 98 | 42 | 92 |
| 13 | 190 | 41 | 76 | 6 | 9 | 57 | 50 | 45 |
| 14 | 195 | 14 | 91 | 83 | 5 | 39 | 15 | 87 |
| 15 | 200 | 43 | 48 | 87 | 13 | 32 | 94 | 16 |
| 16 | 210 | 11 | 60 | 61 | 19 | 52 | 23 | 87 |
| 17 | 220 | 39 | 66 | 31 | 20 | 30 | 94 | 44 |
| 18 | 225 | 38 | 42 | 18 | 74 | 64 | 19 | 28 |
| 19 | 228 | 85 | 1 | 49 | 49 | 57 | 100 | 23 |
| 20 | 230 | 73 | 46 | 9 | 78 | 70 | 6 | 9 |
| 21 | 235 | 70 | 73 | 82 | 4 | 2 | 57 | 62 |
| 22 | 240 | 9 | 7 | 88 | 34 | 36 | 18 | 43 |
| 23 | 245 | 5 | 28 | 1 | 9 | 76 | 51 | 28 |
| 24 | | | | | | | | |
| 25 | TOTAL | 845 | 937 | 910 | 775 | 994 | 820 | 902 |
| 26 | | | | | | | | |

03-Oct-86   01:34 AM

**Figure 6-45.**    Titles frozen in both directions

## Adding a Second Window

Having two windows in your screen display will allow you to look at information in two completely different areas of the worksheet at the same time. You can split the screen into two vertical or horizontal sections and then move your cursor within either window to bring whichever cells you choose into view.

The size of each window will be dependent on the cursor location at the time the split is requested. The split is placed to the left of or above the cursor location, depending on whether the split is vertical or horizontal. The command to split the worksheet is /Worksheet Window. This command produces the following menu:

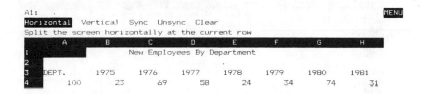

You will notice that there is not an option for splitting the screen in both directions at once. This is due to 1-2-3's two-window limitation. In addition to the Horizontal and Vertical options, the /Worksheet Window command has options that decide whether movement in one window will cause a corresponding shift of information in the second window. These options are Sync and Unsync.


## Splitting the Screen Horizontally

A horizontal screen split is appropriate when you need the entire screen width to show two different sections of a worksheet report. To split the screen horizontally, move the cursor to a location within the row immediately below the desired split location. For example, Figure 6-46 shows the cursor positioned in A12. Then enter /Worksheet Window Horizontal, and the screen will be split into two different windows, with the size of the two windows being dictated by the cursor location at the time of the request. Figure 6-47 shows the result of the split in our example after F6 (WINDOW) is pressed and the cursor is moved to the Total line.

Once the screen is split, you can move the cursor around in the current window or use the F6 (WINDOW) key to move the cursor into the other window. After the cursor is in the second window, the arrow keys can move it to the desired location within that window.

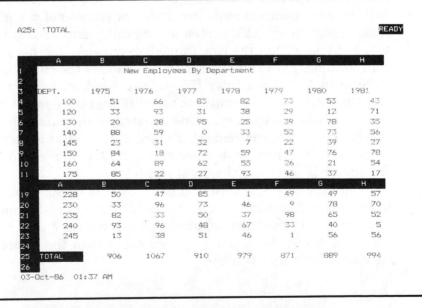

A12: 180                                                                    READY

```
         A        B        C        D        E        F        G        H
                        New Employees By Department
1
2
3  DEPT.       1975     1976     1977     1978     1979     1980     1981
4       100      23       69       58       24       34      ·74       31
5       120      40       53       25       61       15       51       76
6       130      72       66       41       52       82       24       30
7       140      17        5       67       13       84       46       64
8       145      59       55       32       67        3       18       60
9       150      55       81       14       61        6       97       54
10      160       3       88       93       35       81        0       67
11      175      12        7       82       61       93       43       78
12      180      65       84       36       19        7       78       14
13      190      87       46       82       12       23       64       32
14      195      81       93       68       51       23       70       19
15      200      56       20       94       12       72       30        5
16      210       6       92       49       96       73       43       94
17      220      61        9       24       54       56        0       66
18      225      40       22       97       52       46       58       62
19      228      97       28       30       39       97       62       84
20      230       2       47       46       77       16       45       22
26-Sep-86  06:32 AM
```

**Figure 6-46.**    Cursor positioned for horizontal window split

A25:  'TOTAL                                                                 READY

```
         A        B        C        D        E        F        G        H
                        New Employees By Department
1
2
3  DEPT.       1975     1976     1977     1978     1979     1980     1981
4       100      51       66       83       82       73       53       43
5       120      33       93       31       38       29       12       71
6       130      20       28       95       25       39       78       35
7       140      88       59        0       33       52       73       56
8       145      23       31       32        7       22       39       27
9       150      84       18       72       59       47       76       78
10      160      64       89       62       55       26       21       54
11      175      85       22       27       93       46       37       17
         A        B        C        D        E        F        G        H
19      228      50       47       85        1       49       49       57
20      230      33       96       73       46        9       78       70
21      235      82       33       50       37       98       65       52
22      240      93       96       48       67       33       40        5
23      245      13       38       51       46        1       56       56
24
25  TOTAL       906     1067      910      979      871      889      994
26
03-Oct-86  01:37 AM
```

**Figure 6-47.**    Horizontally split screen

|   | A | B | C | D | E | F | G | H |
|---|---|---|---|---|---|---|---|---|
| 1 | | | | New Employees By Department | | | | |
| 2 | | | | | | | | |
| 3 | DEPT. | 1975 | 1976 | 1977 | 1978 | 1979 | 1980 | 1981 |
| 4 | 100 | 23 | 69 | 58 | 24 | 34 | 74 | 31 |
| 5 | 120 | 40 | 53 | 25 | 61 | 15 | 51 | 76 |
| 6 | 130 | 72 | 66 | 41 | 52 | 82 | 24 | 30 |
| 7 | 140 | 17 | 3 | 67 | 13 | 84 | 46 | 64 |
| 8 | 145 | 59 | 55 | 32 | 67 | 3 | 18 | 60 |
| 9 | 150 | 55 | 81 | 14 | 61 | 6 | 97 | 54 |
| 10 | 160 | 3 | 88 | 93 | 35 | 81 | 0 | 67 |
| 11 | 175 | 12 | 7 | 82 | 61 | 93 | 43 | 78 |
| 12 | 180 | 65 | 84 | 36 | 19 | 7 | 78 | 14 |
| 13 | 190 | 87 | 46 | 82 | 12 | 23 | 64 | 32 |
| 14 | 195 | 81 | 93 | 68 | 51 | 23 | 70 | 19 |
| 15 | 200 | 56 | 20 | 94 | 12 | 72 | 30 | 5 |
| 16 | 210 | 6 | 92 | 49 | 96 | 73 | 43 | 94 |
| 17 | 220 | 61 | 9 | 24 | 54 | 56 | 0 | 66 |
| 18 | 225 | 40 | 22 | 97 | 52 | 46 | 58 | 62 |
| 19 | 228 | 97 | 28 | 30 | 39 | 97 | 62 | 84 |
| 20 | 230 | 2 | 47 | 46 | 77 | 16 | 45 | 22 |

26-Sep-86   06:37 AM

**Figure 6-48.**     Worksheet ready for vertical split

## Splitting the Screen Vertically

A vertical screen split is appropriate when you would like the full length of the screen to show sections of the worksheet but do not require the full width. Cursor position at the time of the request will again determine the size of the two windows. The split will occur to the left of the column in which the cursor is located.

Figure 6-48 presents a worksheet in which the screen will be split vertically at the cursor location. To produce this split, you would position the cursor in column E and enter **/Worksheet Window Vertical**. If you then press the F6 (WINDOW) key and move the cursor to column I, the display shown in Figure 6-49 should be produced. Note that just as with the Horizontal option, the cursor was moved into the second window with F6 (WINDOW). Each time F6 (WINDOW) is pressed, the cursor will move into the opposite window.

New Employees By D...

| DEPT. | 1975 | 1976 | 1977 | | 1983 | 1984 | 1985 | 1986 |
|---|---|---|---|---|---|---|---|---|
| 100 | 23 | 69 | 58 | | 47 | 73 | 50 | 42 |
| 120 | 40 | 53 | 25 | | 81 | 46 | 17 | 69 |
| 130 | 72 | 66 | 41 | | 58 | 71 | 87 | 23 |
| 140 | 17 | 5 | 67 | | 38 | 74 | 15 | 27 |
| 145 | 59 | 55 | 32 | | 44 | 29 | 99 | 90 |
| 150 | 55 | 81 | 14 | | 39 | 76 | 29 | 98 |
| 160 | 3 | 88 | 93 | | 1 | 61 | 76 | 73 |
| 175 | 12 | 7 | 82 | | 41 | 23 | 90 | 29 |
| 180 | 65 | 84 | 36 | | 62 | 33 | 26 | 5 |
| 190 | 87 | 46 | 82 | | 8 | 4 | 13 | 5 |
| 195 | 81 | 93 | 68 | | 70 | 62 | 41 | 80 |
| 200 | 56 | 20 | 94 | | 18 | 9 | 23 | 68 |
| 210 | 6 | 92 | 49 | | 69 | 6 | 2 | 58 |
| 220 | 61 | 9 | 24 | | 95 | 74 | 19 | 20 |
| 225 | 40 | 22 | 97 | | 91 | 2 | 36 | 32 |
| 228 | 97 | 28 | 30 | | 4 | 37 | 62 | 95 |
| 230 | 2 | 47 | 46 | | 22 | 71 | 79 | 69 |

26-Sep-86   06:42 AM

**Figure 6-49.**   Vertical split

### Moving in Both Windows at Once

1-2-3's default setting has its two windows synchronized. This means that if you move in one window, the other window will automatically scroll to match it. With horizontal windows, if you move from column A to column Z in one window, the other window will automatically be scrolled to match the window in which you moved the cursor. With vertical windows, moving from row 1 to row 120 in one window automatically updates the other window to display row 120 as well.

### Moving in One Window at a Time

Sometimes you will want information, such as a table, to remain stationary while you scroll in the other window. You can make this change from either window by **entering /Worksheet Window Unsync**. With Unsync, the contents of the two windows are totally independent. If you choose, you can show the same information in both windows. If you want to return to a synchronized mode, simply enter **/Worksheet Window Sync**. This will cause the two windows to move in tandem again.

### Clearing the Second Window

When you decide to return to a single-window display, enter **/Worksheet Window Clear**. If the screen was split horizontally, the single window will obtain its default settings from the top window. If the screen was split vertically, returning to one window means that the settings for the left window will be used.

## Displaying the Status of Worksheet Options

When you go back to a worksheet you used earlier, you may not remember all the options you chose for it. Conveniently, 1-2-3 lets you see the settings for all the worksheet options on one screen.

Entering **/Worksheet Status** displays the status of the options listed in Figure 6-50. With this command you can monitor the available memory, the existence of a math coprocessor to speed numeric calculations, the recalculation options, the default options for cell display, the global protection status, and any cell causing a circular reference in the worksheet (see Chapter 4). The box called "A Closer Look at the Status Settings" provides a detailed look at the various status items listed. The full status reference is only available in release 2; release 1A does not monitor circular references, expanded memory, or the existence of a math coprocessor, since it does not support these last two hardware enhancements. In neither release can you make changes through the status display.

```
Available Memory:
  Conventional..... 420368 of 420368 Bytes (100%)
  Expanded......... (None)

Math Co-processor: (None)

Recalculation:
  Method.......... Automatic
  Order........... Natural
  Iterations....... 1

Circular Reference: (None)

Cell Display:
  Format.......... (G)
  Label-Prefix.....  '
  Column-Width..... 9
  Zero Suppression. Off

Global Protection: Off

26-Sep-86  06:45 AM
```

**Figure 6-50.**　　Status display

## 1 2 3 A Closer Look at the Status Settings

There is a variety of information to monitor from the status screen. Even though these settings are not individually selectable because they relate to different features of the worksheet, we will regard them as options and discuss each separately.

**Available Memory**　　This portion of the display reports the amount of available memory you have used. Conventional and expanded memory are shown separately. This information helps you plan the remainder of your worksheet entries.

When memory is almost full, you may have to split your worksheet in two.

**Math Coprocessor**     Release 2 supports the use of a math coprocessor chip. This section reports whether one of the supported chips is installed on your system.

**Recalculation**     This section reports on all the recalculation options. You can tell whether recalculation is set at Automatic or Manual. You can also monitor the current recalculation order to see whether it is set at Natural, Row-wise, or Columnwise. The current number of iterations set to occur during recalculation is also displayed. To change any of the recalculation options use /Worksheet Global Recalculation.

**Circular Reference**     Anyone who has struggled to find a circular reference in earlier releases of 1-2-3 will appreciate this display. It shows you the address of the cell that is causing the CIRC indicator to appear at the bottom of your screen.

**Cell Display**     This section of the status screen provides four different pieces of information: the global format settings, the label-prefix, the column-width, and whether zero suppression is on or off. Format changes can be made with /Worksheet Global Format. The label-prefix is changed with /Worksheet Global Label-Prefix. Changes to column-width are made with /Worksheet Global Column-Width. Changes to zero suppression are made with /Worksheet Global Zero.

**Global Protection**     The last area of the status screen shows whether global protection is enabled or disabled. Changes to this setting can be made with /Worksheet Global Protection.

Worksheet Range Copy Move File Print Graph Data System Quit

Format Label Erase Name Justify Protect Unprotect Input Value Transpose

Global Insert Delete Column Erase Titles Window Status Page

### Description

The /Copy command is the most powerful command 1-2-3 has to offer. It copies numbers, labels, and formulas to new locations on the worksheet. It can copy one cell or many cells in a range to either a cell or a range.

Copying is a simple process that requires telling 1-2-3 only two things. First, it wants to know where to copy from. The From range can be one cell or many. Multiple cells to be copied can be arranged in a row, column, or rectangle. The From range can be typed, referenced with a range name, or highlighted with the cursor.

The second piece of information you must tell 1-2-3 is the To range. This defines whether you are making one or several copies and specifies the exact location where you would like them placed. Each duplication of the From information requires only that the top left cell in the To range be included. For example, if you were copying A1..A15 to B1..E15, the To range would be specified as B1..E1, since only the top cell in each copy is included.

### Options

The /Copy command supports four copying procedures:

- One cell to one cell.
- One cell to many cells.
- A range of cells to a range the same size as the original range.
- A range of cells to a range whose size is a multiple of the original range, for example, a column of five cells can be duplicated in several additional columns of five cells.

The specification of the From and To range determines what

type of copying will take place.

## Note

The /Copy command provides a quick solution for recalculating a range of cells. When you have recalculation set at Manual, or when your the worksheet is so large that it takes a minute or two for the entire worksheet to be recalculated, you may be interested in recalculating just a few formulas. If you copy the cells containing the formula to be recalculated to themselves—that is, make the From and To ranges the same—these cells will be recalculated.

# /Move

## Description

The /Move command allows you to move a range of worksheet entries to any location on the worksheet. This command will adjust the formulas within the range to correspond to their new location if relative references (references like A3 or D4) are used. Absolute references within formulas (references like $A$2) will not be updated by the moving process.

## Options

This command permits you to move one or many cells to a new location. For example, you can move A2 to B3 by entering /**Move A2**, pressing ENTER, then entering **B3** and pressing ENTER. To move a range of cells to a new location, you might enter /**Move A2..B6** and press ENTER, then enter a new destination like D2 and press ENTER. 1-2-3 will move the entire range, locating the contents of its left uppermost cell (A2) in the designated To cell. You can use any of the options for specifying ranges, such as pressing F3 (NAME), pointing to the range, or typing the complete range address.

## /Range Erase

### Description

The /Range Erase command eliminates entries you have made in worksheet cells. Without this command your only options for removing a cell entry would be to make a new entry in the cell, edit the cell's contents, or use the space bar to replace the entry with blanks. None of these approaches leaves a label cell completely blank, however, since at minimum the cell would still contain a label indicator.

### Options

There are no special options for this command. Your only choices are whether to specify a single cell or many cells in the range and whether to type the range reference or highlight the included cells by pointing.

### Note

The /Range Erase command does not affect cell formats. A cell formatted as currency will still be formatted as currency after /Range Erase is used. To eliminate a format you can use /Range Format and a new format option or use /Range Format Reset to return the range to the default setting. The /Range Erase command also does not affect protection or cell width. Protected cells cannot be erased when worksheet protection is enabled. In this situation 1-2-3 will present you with an error message instead of erasing the protected cells.

## /Range Input

### Description

This command is used to restrict cursor movement to unprotected cells. To use the command, first construct a worksheet and make sure the desired input cells are unprotected with /Range Unprotect. Then enable worksheet protection with /Worksheet Global Protection Enable. Next, enter **/Range Input** and select a range of unprotected cells for the input area. Remember that ranges must be rectangular; this command will not work on input cells scattered across the entire worksheet.

### Options

While in the /Range Input command you can use many of the cursor movement keys to move among the unprotected cells in the selected area. HOME moves to the first unprotected cell, and END moves to the last cell. The arrow keys will move you within the selected range. ESC can be used to cancel an entry, but if you have not made an entry, it will cancel /Range Input. ENTER can be used to finalize entries, but if no entries have been made, it will cancel /Range Input. Selections cannot be made from the command menus, although some of the function keys are operational. These are F1 (HELP), F2 (EDIT), and F9 (CALC).

### Note

This command is especially useful in the macro environment where you are attempting to automate applications for inexperienced 1-2-3 users. See Chapter 13 for more details.

# /Range Label

### Description

The /Range Label command changes the justification (placement) of existing worksheet labels. Cells within the range that are blank will not save the label indicator entered with /Range Label and apply it to later entries, however. Later entries will use the default worksheet setting.

### Options

/Range Label has three options: Left, Center, and Right. These selections dictate the label indicator that will be used for existing cell entries. Using Left changes the label indicator to ' for all entries in the range and causes all the entries to be left justified in the cell. Using Center places a ^ at the front of each label and causes the existing labels to appear in the center of the cells. The last option, Right, places " at the beginning of each entry and causes cell entries in the specified range to be right justified in the cells.

# /Range Name Create

### Description

The /Range Name Create command allows you to assign names to cell ranges. Using names rather than cell addresses makes formulas easier to understand and helps you develop worksheet models that are self-documenting. Range names can be used anywhere cell addresses can be used.

### Options

After entering /**Range Name Create,** you have two options: working with an existing range name or entering a new one. If you choose to work with an existing range name, you can select one of the names from the list of existing range names in the menu and have 1-2-3 highlight the cells that are currently assigned this name. At this point you can hit ESC to undo the existing range name assignment and specify a new range name.

To establish a new range name, after entering /**Range Name Create** you type a new range name of up to 15 characters and press ENTER. Next, respond to 1-2-3's prompt for the range by pointing to or entering a range and then pressing ENTER. The range name you choose should be as meaningful as possible.

1-2-3 does not restrict you to a single name for a given range of cells. If a range is used for more than one purpose, you can assign multiple names to it by using /Range Name Create a second time.

## /Range Name Delete

### Description

The /Range Name Delete command allows you to delete range names that are no longer needed. Each execution of this command can remove a single range name. To delete a range name, enter **/Range Name Delete**, point to the appropriate name in the list 1-2-3 provides, and press ENTER. Alternatively, type the name that you wish to delete after entering the command sequence.

### Options

There are no options for this command.

## /Range Name Labels

### Description

The /Range Name Labels command allows you to use label entries on the worksheet for range names in certain situations. With this command, each label can be assigned as a name only to a single cell. Furthermore, the name must be in a cell adjacent to the cell you wish to assign the name to. If you choose a label that exceeds the fifteen-character limit for range names, the label will be truncated. The /Range Name

Labels command is most useful when you have a column or row of labels and wish to assign each one to the adjacent cell as a range name. One execution of this command can assign all of the range names.

### Options

The /Range Name Labels command has four options that are selected from a submenu. They tell 1-2-3 the direction to go to find the cell to apply the label to. The choices are Right, Down, Up, and Left.

## /Range Name Reset

### Description

The /Range Name Reset command is equivalent to a "delete all" option. Rather than using /Range Name Delete to eliminate range names one by one, you can use this command to eliminate all range names with one command.

### Options

There are no options for this command.

## /Range Name Table

### Description

The very useful /Range Name Table command is new under release 2 of 1-2-3. With it you can obtain a list of all your range names and the range to which each name has been assigned. Decide what area of your worksheet will be used to store the table of range names and assignments before executing the command. After you enter /**Range Name Table**, all you have to do is specify the table location. 1-2-3 will do the rest.

### Options

The only options you have with this command are whether to specify the entire area for the table or just the upper left cell in the table range. If you specify the entire range, 1-2-3 will not use additional space if the range is not large enough to contain all the entries. If you specify only the upper left corner, 1-2-3 will use as much space as required and will overwrite entries if cells that it uses contain other entries.

# /Range Protect

### Description

The /Range Protect command is used for reprotecting cells that you have unprotected with the /Range Unprotect command. It allows you to change your mind and reestablish the protection features that are initially provided by 1-2-3 for every worksheet cell. Using the /Range Protect command has no apparent effect on a cell while the worksheet protection features are turned off. Once protection is turned on, cells that are protected will not accept entries of any type.

Since this command must be used in combination with /Worksheet Global Protection, you will also want to read the entry for this command.

### Options

The only options for this command are the variety of ways for entering the range once you have requested the command. You can type the range, use POINT mode to expand the cursor to include the entire range, or type the range name that you wish to use.

## /Range Transpose

### Description

The /Range Transpose command is new in release 2. It provides additional flexibility in restructuring a worksheet in that it will copy data from either a row or column orientation to the opposite orientation; that is, data stored in rows can be copied to columns, and vice versa. Note, however, that formulas in a transpose range may not be copied correctly, since 1-2-3 will not adjust relative cell references based on the new locations. You may want to consider freezing formulas to values with /Range Values before using this command or, alternatively, editing the formulas to change all the relative address references (such as T5 or A3) to absolute addresses ($T$5 or $A$3).

### Options

The two options built into the command are selecting a From range with either a row or a column orientation. The choice is not made with a menu selection but rather with the entry of a cell range. 1-2-3 interprets this range as having either a row or a column orientation and produces a To range with the opposite orientation.

## /Range Unprotect

### Description

The /Range Unprotect command is used to change the cell protection characteristics of a range of cells. Using this command will allow entries in the selected cells after worksheet protection features are enabled.

Unless the /Range Unprotect option is used, all worksheet cells have a status of Protected. This means that entries cannot be made in the cells once the worksheet protection features are enabled. To remove the protected status from a group of cells, simply enter **/Range Unprotect** and the range to unprotect.

### Options

The only options for this command are the variety of ways for entering the range once you have requested the command. You can type the range, use POINT mode to expand the cursor to include the entire range, or type the range name that you wish to use.

## /Range Value

### Description

The /Range Value command is used to copy the values displayed by formula cells without copying the formulas. The cells containing the values can be copied to a different range on the worksheet or to the location containing the original formulas. In both cases the cells copied to will not contain formulas, only the value result of the original formula.

### Options

This command provides two options. When you enter **/Range Value** and specify the From range, you can specify a different To range to retain the original formulas and just make a copy of the values they contain, or you can specify the same range for To, thus eliminating the original formulas and retaining just the values.

# /Worksheet Delete

### Description

The /Worksheet Delete command allows you to delete unneeded rows and columns. These rows or columns may be blank, or they may contain data. You can use this command to delete single or multiple rows and columns. Deletions from the middle of a range cause 1-2-3 to automatically adjust the range to compensate for the deletions.

### Options

The /Range Delete command provides two options, Row and Column. You also have the option of deleting one or many rows or columns with one execution of the command. The best approach is to place your cursor on the top row or left column to be deleted, enter **/Worksheet Delete Row** or **/Worksheet Delete Column**, and then expand your cursor to include all the rows or columns you wish to have deleted.

### Note

A complete row or column must be deleted, since 1-2-3 does not provide an option for deleting part of a row or column.


# /Worksheet Erase

### Description

The /Worksheet Erase command can be equivalent to a destroy instruction. It erases the working copy of your model from memory. Unless you have another copy of the worksheet stored on disk, you will not be able to retrieve the worksheet after using the /Worksheet Erase Yes option.

### Options

The command presents a submenu with two options. One is Yes, indicating you want to proceed with the erasure of memory. The other, the default selection, is No. The No option abandons the erase operation.

# /Worksheet Global Label-Prefix

### Description

The /Worksheet Global Label-Prefix command allows you to change the default prefix, and therefore the justification (placement in the cell), for all label entries on the worksheet. Entries made prior to the use of this command will retain their original label indicators and their existing justification. Entries made in any cell after the command is used will have the new label indicator at the front of the entry.

### Options

This command has three options: Left, Right, and Center. Left generates a " as the label prefix; Right generates a '; and Center generates a ^ at the beginning of each label entry.

### Note

This command takes a different approach from that of the /Range Label command, which changes the label indicator and justification for existing entries but does not affect entries into cells within the range that have not yet been made. Entries made after the employment of /Range Label will use the default label prefix.

### Description

The /Worksheet Global Protection command allows you to turn the protection features on for all worksheet cells that are protected. This command is also used to disable protection for the entire worksheet. The command works with the /Range Protect feature to determine which worksheet cells are protected and which are unprotected. If this command is used to enable protection for a new worksheet, you will not be able to make entries in any worksheet cells, since all the cells have a default status of Protected.

Once protection has been enabled, you will see a PR in the control panel when your cursor is in cells that are protected. The color and highlighting created with the /Range Unprotect command is maintained. With a color monitor, unprotected cells are highlighted in green, providing a "green light" signal that you can proceed with entries for that cell. Other cells remain their normal color. With a monochrome display, the unprotected cells are highlighted to indicate that you can make entries in these cells.

### Options

This command has two options. The Enable option turns protection on for the entire worksheet. Entering /**Worksheet Global Protection Enable** will prevent entries to cells that have a Protected status and allow entries only to those cells that have a status of Unprotected.

The second option is Disable. This option turns off protection for the entire worksheet and permits entries to all cells. This command can be used to temporarily turn off protection so that you can modify a formula, erase or delete worksheet entries, or unprotect some of the worksheet cells.

**Note**

It is necessary to use the /Range Unprotect command before you enable protection. Otherwise, you will be locked out of all worksheet cells.

## /Worksheet Global Recalculation

### Description

This command provides access to all the recalculation options. With the use of /Worksheet Global Recalculation you can affect the number of recalculations for a worksheet, determine whether the recalculation is automatic, and specify the order in which formulas are recalculated.

### Options

The options for this command affect three different features of recalculation.

**Automatic**    This option causes the worksheet to recalculate automatically after every worksheet entry.

**Manual**    This option turns off the automatic recalculation feature.

**Natural**    This option places the responsibility for determining which formula to evaluate first with 1-2-3.

**Rowwise**    This option disables the natural recalculation sequence and switches to recalculation by rows.

**Columnwise**    This option disables the natural recalculation sequence and switches to recalculation by columns.

**Iterations**    The normal setting for this option is 1, meaning that every formula is recalculated once during every recalculation. It can be reset by typing in the number of iterations you want.

## /Worksheet Insert

### Description

The /Worksheet Insert command can be used to add blank rows and columns to your worksheet. These blank areas can be used to improve readability or to allow for the addition of new information to your worksheet.

Inserts made to the middle of a range of cells will automatically expand the reference for a range name applied to those cells. The same is true for formulas that reference this range; they will automatically be expanded to allow for the additional rows or columns.

### Options

This command provides two options, Rows and Columns, which are selectable from a menu. Columns are always added to the left of the cursor location or the range you specify. Rows are always added above the cursor or the range you specify.

## /Worksheet Status

### Description

This command provides a screen snapshot of your current worksheet environment. It allows you to monitor available memory as well as many of the default worksheet settings. No changes to any of the settings can be made from this screen.

### Options

In one sense there are no options for this command, since /Worksheet Status has no submenu. A variety of information is presented on the status screen, however. Even though the different items are not individually selectable, they can be regarded as options.

**Available Memory**     This portion of the display reports on the amount of available memory that you have used. Conventional and expanded memory are shown separately. This information helps you plan the remainder of your worksheet entries. If memory is almost fully used, you may have to split your worksheet in two.

**Math Coprocessor**     Release 2 supports the use of a math coprocessor chip. This item on the status screen reports whether one of the supported chips is installed in your system.

**Recalculation**     This section reports all the recalculation options. You can tell whether recalculation is set at Automatic or Manual. You can also see whether the current recalculation order is set at Natural, Rowwise, or Columnwise. The current number of iterations of recalculation is also displayed. To make changes to any of the recalculation options, you must use /Worksheet Global Recalculation.

**Circular Reference**     Anyone who has struggled to find a circular reference in earlier releases of 1-2-3 will appreciate this display. It shows you the address of the cell causing the CIRC indicator to appear at the bottom of your screen.

**Cell Display**     This section of the status screen provides four different pieces of information: the global format settings, the current default label prefix, the current default column width, and whether zero suppression is turned on or off. Changes to format can be made with /Worksheet Global Format. The label prefix is changed with /Worksheet Global Label-Prefix. Changes to column width are made with /Worksheet Global Column-Width. Changes to zero suppression are made with /Worksheet Global Zero.

**Global Protection**  The last area of the status screen shows whether global protection is enabled or disabled. Changes to the protection status can be made with /Worksheet Global Protection.

## /Worksheet Titles

### Description

The /Worksheet Titles command allows you to freeze label information at the top or left side of the screen. This is useful when you have a worksheet that is either wider or longer than the screen. Without the titles frozen on the screen you would not have any descriptive information. The cursor movement keys will not move your cursor to the titles area once it is frozen on the screen. If you want to move there, you will have to use the F5 (GOTO) key, which will cause the title area to be shown on the screen twice. When you scroll away from this area, the double view of the titles will disappear from the screen.

### Options

The options for this command are Both, Horizontal, Vertical, and Clear.

**Both**  This command freezes information above and to the left of the cursor on your screen.

**Horizontal**  This command freezes information above the cursor on your screen.

**Vertical**     This option freezes information to the left of the cursor on your screen.

**Clear**     This option eliminates freezing of titles.


# /Worksheet Window

### Description

The /Worksheet Window command allows you to create two separate windows on your screen. This has advantages for large worksheets where you cannot view the entire worksheet on one screen. You can view two different sections of the worksheet through the two windows created by this command. The windows' sizes are controlled by the location of your cursor at the time you request the screen split. When the screen is split vertically, a dividing line will replace one of the worksheet columns, and when it is split horizontally, the dividing line will replace one of the rows. You can move easily between windows with the F6 (WINDOW) key. The F6 key always moves you to the window opposite the one you are located in.


### Options

There are five options for the Window command: Horizontal, Vertical, Sync, Unsync, and Clear. One clears (removes) the extra window, two control the type of window, and two control data movement within the windows.

**Horizontal**     This option splits the screen into two horizontal windows. The dividing line is inserted immediately above the cursor.

**Vertical**     This option splits the screen into two vertical windows. The dividing line is inserted immediately to the left of the cursor.

**Sync**    This option causes scrolling in the two windows to be synchronized. That is, when you scroll in one window, the other window will automatically scroll along with it. This is the default setting when you create a second window.

**Unsync**    This option allows you to scroll in one window while the other window remains stationary.

**Clear**    This option removes the second window from the screen. The window that remains will be the top window when the split was horizontal and the left window when the split was vertical.

You have learned a great number of worksheet commands in this chapter. You will want to practice on important commands like /Copy and /Move before continuing on. Although all the commands presented in this chapter are important, those two commands are the workhorses that can help you create professional quality worksheets.

# SEVEN

# 1-2-3's Built-in Functions

Date and Time Functions
Financial Functions
Mathematical Functions
Logical Functions
Special Functions
Statistical Functions
String Functions

1-2-3's built-in functions provide ready-made formulas for a wide variety of specialized calculations. Since the formulas are already designed and tested, you can have instant reliability when you include them in your models. The built-in functions also allow you to perform calculations like square root and cosine, extending your range of formulas beyond those you can create with the formula operators covered in Chapter 3.

The 90 functions in release 2 of 1-2-3 are grouped into eight categories. The categories are database statistical, date and time, financial, mathematical, logical, special, statistical, and string. Each of these groups except the first will be covered in this chapter. Since the database functions require a knowledge of 1-2-3's data management features, they will be covered in Chapter 9. The remaining functions will be covered by category. If you are using release 1A, you may want to skip the section on string functions, since they are not available in release 1A. Table 7-1 provides a list of 1-2-3's built-in functions and the cate-

| Function | Type | Available Only in Release 2 |
|---|---|---|
| @@(cell) | Special | * |
| @ABS(number) | Math | |
| @ACOS(number) | Math | |
| @ASIN(number) | Math | |
| @ATAN(number) | Math | |
| @ATAN2(number) | Math | |
| @AVG(list) | Statistical | |
| @CELL(attribute string,range) | Special | * |
| @CELLPOINTER(attribute string) | Special | * |
| @CHAR(code) | String | * |
| @CHOOSE(number,list) | Special | |
| @CLEAN(string) | String | * |
| @CODE(string) | String | * |
| @COLS(range) | Special | * |
| @COS(number) | Math | |
| @COUNT(list) | Statistical | |
| @CTERM(interest,future value,present value) | Financial | * |
| @DATE(year,month,day) | Date & Time | |
| @DATEVALUE(date string) | Date & Time | * |
| @DAVG(input range,offset column,criteria range) | Database | |
| @DAY(serial date number) | Date & Time | |
| @DCOUNT(input range,offset column,criteria range) | Database | |
| @DDB(cost,salvage,life,period) | Financial | * |
| @DMAX(input range,offset column,criteria range) | Database | |
| @DMIN(input range,offset column,criteria range) | Database | |
| @DSTD(input range,offset column,criteria range) | Database | |
| @DVAR(input range,offset column,criteria range) | Database | |
| @ERR | Special | |
| @EXACT(string1,string2) | String | * |
| @EXP(number) | Math | |
| @FALSE | Logical | |
| @FIND(search string,entire string,starting location) | String | * |
| @FV(payment,interest,term) | Financial | |
| @HLOOKUP(code to be looked up,table location, offset) | Special | |
| @HOUR(serial time number) | Date & Time | |

Table 7-1.    1-2-3's Built-in Functions

| Function | Type | Available Only in Release 2 |
|---|---|---|
| @IF(condition to be tested,value if true,value if false) | Logical | |
| @INDEX(table location,column number,row number) | Special | |
| @INT(number) | Math | |
| @IRR(guess,range) | Financial | |
| @ISERR(value) | Logical | |
| @ISNA(value) | Logical | |
| @ISNUMBER(value) | Logical | |
| @ISSTRING(number) | Logical | * |
| @LEFT(string,number of characters to be extracted) | String | * |
| @LENGTH(string) | String | * |
| @LN(number) | Math | |
| @LOG(number) | Math | |
| @LOWER(string) | String | * |
| @MAX(list) | Statistical | |
| @MID(string,start number,number of characters) | String | * |
| @MIN(list) | Statistical | |
| @MINUTE(serial time number) | Date & Time | * |
| @MOD(number,divisor) | Math | |
| @MONTH(serial date number) | Date & Time | |
| @N(range) | String | * |
| @NA | Special | |
| @NOW | Date & Time | * |
| @NPV(discount rate,range) | Financial | |
| @PI | Math | |
| @PMT(principal,interest,term of loan) | Financial | |
| @PROPER(string) | String | * |
| @PV(payment,periodic interest rate,number of periods) | Financial | |
| @RAND | Math | |
| @RATE(future value,present value,number of periods) | Financial | * |
| @REPEAT(string,number of times) | String | * |
| @REPLACE(original string,start location,# characters, new string) | String | * |
| @RIGHT(string,number of characters to be extracted) | String | * |

**Table 7-1.**     1-2-3's Built-in Functions (*continued*)

| Function | Type | Available Only in Release 2 |
|---|---|---|
| @ROUND(number to be rounded,place of rounding) | Math | |
| @ROWS(range) | Special | * |
| @S(range) | String | * |
| @SECOND(serial time number) | Date & Time | * |
| @SIN(number) | Math | |
| @SLN(cost,salvage value,life of the asset) | Financial | * |
| @SQRT(number) | Math | |
| @STD(list) | Statistical | |
| @STRING(number,number of decimal places) | String | * |
| @SUM(list) | Statistical | |
| @SYD(cost,salvage value,life,period) | Financial | * |
| @TAN(number) | Math | |
| @TERM(payment,interest,future value) | Financial | * |
| @TIME(hour,minute,second) | Date & Time | * |
| @TIMEVALUE(time string) | Date & Time | * |
| @TRIM(string) | String | * |
| @TRUE | Logical | |
| @UPPER(string) | String | * |
| @VALUE(string) | String | * |
| @VAR(list) | Statistical | |
| @VLOOKUP(code to be looked up,table location, offset) | Special | |
| @YEAR(serial date number) | Date & Time | |

*in the Release 2 column indicates the function is only available under release 2

**Table 7-1.** 1-2-3's Built-in Functions (*continued*)

gory to which each belongs for quick reference.

All the built-in functions follow the same basic format. Each has a special keyword or name that tells 1-2-3 which function you wish to use. Most also require arguments that define your exact requirements for the function in a particular situation. The basic format rules for functions are as follows:

• Every function begins with an at sign (@).

• The at sign is followed by a function name or keyword. When entering this name, you must match 1-2-3's spelling exactly. Either upper or lower case can be used, although function names will be shown in upper case throughout this chapter.

• Never use spaces within a function. Always write @SUM(A5,A15..A17), not @SUM (A5, A15..A17) or @SUM(A5, A15..17).

There are also a few general rules that apply to all function arguments. They are as follows:

• A set of parentheses must be used to encase all function arguments.

• Functions that require no arguments do not require parentheses. One example is @RAND, which generates a random number between 0 and 1. The other six functions that do not require arguments are @PI, @TRUE, @FALSE, @ERR, @NA, and @NOW.

• When a function is used as an argument for another function, you must use a second set of parentheses, because each function must have its arguments enclosed within parentheses. To use the result of @SUM in an @ROUND function, for example, enter the functions like this:

@ROUND(@SUM(A2..A10),2)

• In most cases functions will require arguments to be separated by commas (the separator character can be changed with /Worksheet Global Default International Punctuation, as described in Chapter 4). These arguments can be numeric values, cell addresses, string values, or special codes. The exact requirements for each function will be covered in the expanded description of the function in this chapter.

Different functions require different types of arguments and use them in different ways. Here are some of the format rules that pertain to different function types and uses:

• Some functions such as @SUM expect a list of arguments that can be entered in any order. @SUM will add together all the entries in its argument list to produce a sum, for example. If you wanted to sum the values in B1..B10, D4, and D7, you could enter the function as @SUM(B1..B10,D4,D7), @SUM(D7,B1..B10,D4), or any other order of the three entries within the parentheses.

• Arguments that must be provided in a specific order cannot be reordered without causing erroneous results. The @ROUND function is one example. It requires two arguments, the number to be rounded and the position. The latter argument tells 1-2-3 how many places from the decimal to round the number. The function must always be written as @ROUND(number,position), with the numbers or references substituted in the function. If you enter the function as @ROUND(position,number), you will cause an error.

• Arguments that require a specific argument type cannot have another type substituted without causing an error. For example, the @TRIM function removes leading, trailing, and consecutive spaces from a string and requires a string as an argument. An error will result if any argument other than a string is provided.

• For arguments requiring string values, enclose the actual values in double quotation marks—for example, "this is a string". For string arguments you can also enter a cell address (C3), a range name (SALES), or a string formula (+B3&"Company Report"). If you need to review string arithmetic, reread the String Formulas section in Chapter 3.

• If a function requires a range as an argument, you can specify the range with a range address (A2..A10), a range name (SALES), or a combination (SALES,A2..A10).

• Functions requiring numeric values will accept them in many formats. You can use actual values (876.54), cell addresses (A2), range names (SINGLE_CELL), formulas (2*A3), functions (@PI), and combinations of the other options (@PI*3+SUM(D2..D4)+NUMBER).

You will see examples of these various kinds of functions and arguments in use as you proceed through the examples in this chapter. You may want to read through the descriptions of all the function groups, or you may prefer to concentrate on particular categories that meet an immediate need. The descriptive paragraphs at the beginning of the section on each function category provide an overview of the types of formulas offered by the functions in the group. The description of each individual function will cover its format, its arguments if any, and its use. The functions in each category are covered in alphabetical order.

## Date and Time Functions

Release 2 has added time functions to the date functions that were present in earlier releases of 1-2-3. With these functions you can access, create, and manipulate the serial numbers 1-2-3 uses to represent dates and times. For example, you can use date and time arithmetic in your models to determine elapsed time for a production process, to learn whether a loan is overdue, or to age your accounts receivable.

1-2-3 can handle dates between January 1, 1900, and December 31, 2099. A unique serial number is assigned to each of these days, with the number for January 1, 1900, being 1 and December 31, 2099, being 73050. The serial date number represents the number of days since December 31, 1899. Although this may seem a little strange, representing every date in terms of its distance from this date in the past is what provides the date arithmetic features of the package. If all dates have the same comparison point, you can subtract one date from another to determine how many days apart they are. This provides an effective solution for the overdue loan determination, for example, in that the loan due date can be compared to the current date. If the loan due date is less than the current date, the loan is overdue.

Time of day is represented by fractional serial numbers. Midnight is 0.000, 6 a.m. is .25, noon is .5, 6 p.m. is .75, 11:59:59 p.m. is .99999, and so on. Serial time numbers can be entered in either decimal (.75) or fraction (3/4) format.

Serial date and time numbers will always be used in calculations, but you can use the Format commands to create a more understandable display. Either /Worksheet Global Format or /Range Format can be used to select one of the date or time displays. Since one cell can contain both a whole and a fractional serial number, representing the date and time respectively, you will have to decide which component you would like displayed, since one cell cannot show both a date and a time format. Release 2 provides five date formats, with the last two offering additional options through the /Worksheet Global Default Other International Date command. There are four time formats. The first two are permanent, and the latter two can be altered with the /Worksheet Global Default Other International Date command. As an example, the serial number 31681.75 represents 6 p.m. on September 26, 1986. When the cell containing the entry is formatted with date format 1, it will display as 26-Sep-86. When it is formatted with D6, or time format 1, it will display as 06:00:00 PM. Review the date and time formats in Chapter 4 if you are not familiar with these options.

Some of the date and time functions generate serial numbers (@DATE, @NOW), while others expect them as arguments (@DAY, @YEAR). For those functions that expect serial numbers as arguments, entering both an integer and fractional serial number for a function expecting a date will cause 1-2-3 to ignore the fractional part of the entry. The integer number portion would be ignored if a serial time number was expected. If only the integer portion is entered, .0, representing midnight, will be used for the time.

## @DATE

The @DATE function allows you to create a serial date number when you supply the date components.

### Format

@DATE(*year,month,day*)

### Arguments

*year*   a number between 0 and 199. 1900 is represented by 0, 1986 by 86, and 2099 by 199.

*month*  a number from 1 through 12.

*day*    a number from 1 through 31. The number must be valid for the month chosen. Since month 9 or September has only 30 days, for example, 31 would be an invalid value for the day when 9 was used for the month.

The arguments must be supplied in the order shown. Selecting an invalid number for any of the arguments will cause 1-2-3 to return ERR.

### Use

The @DATE function can be used anywhere you wish to enter a serial date number on a worksheet. Any date used in arithmetic calculations must be in serial form. Figure 7-1 shows an application for the @DATE function. In this example, the charge for each video rental is determined by the number of days a patron has had the video. The date the video was checked out is entered in column C, and the date it was returned is entered in column D. The two serial dates are subtracted, and the result is multiplied by the daily charge of $2.25 to determine the amount the patron should

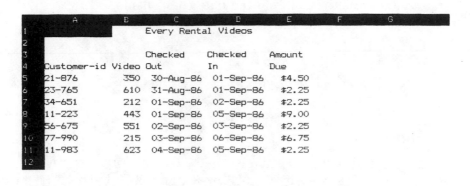

**Figure 7-1.**  Worksheet using @DATE entries

pay—for example, (+D5−C5)*2.25. These formulas are stored in column E. A date format is applied to the range of entries in columns C and D, and currency format is applied to the range of entries in column E. The formulas for this model are shown in Figure 7-2.

E5: (T) [W15] (D5−C5)*2.25                                        READY

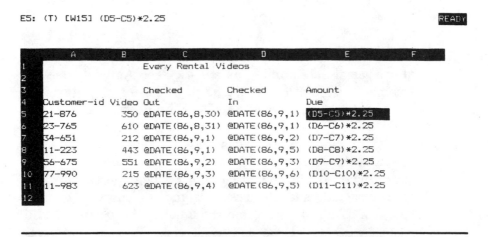

**Figure 7-2.**  Formulas for @DATE

## Note

1-2-3 assigns a serial number to February 29, 1900, even though 1900 was not a leap year. This will cause problems only when you are using dates between January 1, 1900, and March 1, 1900.

## @DATEVALUE (Release 2)

The @DATEVALUE function returns a serial date number when you supply a date string in one of the five date formats.

### Format

@DATEVALUE(*date string*)

### Arguments

*date string*    a string argument that is in one of the five acceptable date formats and is enclosed in double quotation marks.

Three of the acceptable date formats are fixed, and two are dependent on the format chosen with /Worksheet Global Default Other International Date. Acceptable date string formats for September 29, 1986, are "29-Sep-86", "2-Sep", "Sep-86", "29.09.86" if D4 (Date Format 4) is set at DD.MM.YY, "9/29/86" if D4 is set at MM/DD/YY, "29/09/86" if D4 is set at DD/MM/YY, and "86-09-29" if D4 is set at YY-MM-DD. Acceptable D5 (Date Format 5) options are similar except that only the month and day are shown, for example, "09-29".

### Use

The @DATEVALUE function can be used when you want to perform arithmetic with dates that have been entered in string format. For example, if you were to enter @DATE-VALUE("23-Oct-86") in a cell, 31708 would be returned. You

```
            A         B       C         D          E        F       G
  1                          Every Rental Videos
  2
  3                         Checked   Checked   Amount
  4    Customer-id Video    Out       In        Due
  5    21-876        350    30-Aug-86 01-Sep-86   $4.50
  6    23-765        610    31-Aug-86 01-Sep-86   $2.25
  7    34-651        212    01-Sep-86 02-Sep-86   $2.25
  8    11-223        443    01-Sep-86 05-Sep-86   $9.00
  9    56-675        551    02-Sep-86 03-Sep-86   $2.25
 10    77-990        215    03-Sep-86 06-Sep-86   $6.75
 11    11-983        623    04-Sep-86 05-Sep-86   $2.25
 12
```

**Figure 7-3.**   Using @DATEVALUE to work with label (string) dates

could then use this value in a formula. Figure 7-3 provides an example of a model using the @DATEVALUE function. It solves the same problem as the model for video charges in Figure 7-1 except that it uses the @DATEVALUE function and string date formats in the function arguments. The formulas to subtract the two dates are located in column E and follow the format of (@DATEVALUE(C3)-@DATEVALUE (A3))*1.5, as shown in Figure 7-4.

## @DAY

The @DAY function extracts the day number from a serial date number.

### Format

@DAY(*serial date number*)

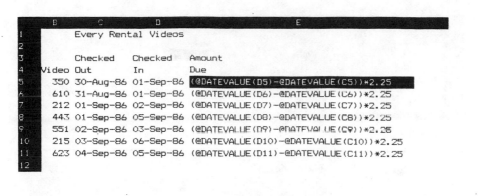

|   | B | C | D | E |
|---|---|---|---|---|
| 1 |   | Every Rental Videos | | |
| 2 |   |   |   |   |
| 3 |   | Checked | Checked | Amount |
| 4 | Video | Out | In | Due |
| 5 |   | 350 | 30-Aug-86 | 01-Sep-86 | (@DATEVALUE(D5)-@DATEVALUE(C5))*2.25 |
| 6 |   | 610 | 31-Aug-86 | 01-Sep-86 | (@DATEVALUE(D6)-@DATEVALUE(C6))*2.25 |
| 7 |   | 212 | 01-Sep-86 | 02-Sep-86 | (@DATEVALUE(D7)-@DATEVALUE(C7))*2.25 |
| 8 |   | 443 | 01-Sep-86 | 05-Sep-86 | (@DATEVALUE(D8)-@DATEVALUE(C8))*2.25 |
| 9 |   | 551 | 02-Sep-86 | 03-Sep-86 | (@DATEVALUE(D9)-@DATEVALUE(C9))*2.25 |
| 10 |   | 215 | 03-Sep-86 | 06-Sep-86 | (@DATEVALUE(D10)-@DATEVALUE(C10))*2.25 |
| 11 |   | 623 | 04-Sep-86 | 05-Sep-86 | (@DATEVALUE(D11)-@DATEVALUE(C11))*2.25 |
| 12 |   |   |   |   |

**Figure 7-4.**    Formulas for @DATEVALUE

### Arguments

*serial date number*    the serial date number of the de-sired date, which must be between 1 and 73050 to stay within the acceptable range of January 1, 1900, to December 31, 2099. The serial date number can be generated by another function such as @NOW, @DATEVALUE, or @DATE.

### Use

This function is used whenever you are interested in only the day portion of a date. Used with @DATE, the function would be recorded as @DAY(@DATE(86,12,14)) and would return 14. Used with @DATEVALUE, it might be @DAY(@DATE-VALUE("24-Dec-86")) and would return a value of 24.

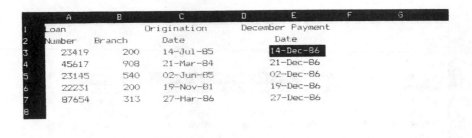

**Figure 7-5.** Using @DAY

As a sample use for this function, suppose you want to extract the day from a loan origination date so you can use it to generate payment due dates. @DAY can do this. The dates in Figure 7-5 are generated with @DATE, using a day generated with @DAY. The cell must be formatted with one of the date formats or the serial date number will display. The advantage of this approach is that the same date formulas could be used for all loans, as only the day numbers will vary. Naturally you would have to make some allowance for February and days 29 through 31. This could be handled with the @IF function, covered later in this chapter.

## @HOUR (Release 2)

The @HOUR function extracts the hour from a serial time number, using a military time representation. For example, @HOUR(.75) will equal 6:00 p.m.

### Format

@HOUR(*serial time number*)

## Arguments

*serial time number*     a decimal fraction between 0.000 and 0.9999. Serial time number can be entered as a fraction or a decimal number. It can be generated by @TIME, @TIMEVALUE, or @NOW.

## Use

This function is used whenever you wish to work with only the hour portion of a time entry. The function will always return a value between 0 and 23. Used with @TIME, which creates a serial time number when provided with arguments of hour, minute, and second, the function might read @HOUR (@TIME(10,15,25)) and would return 10.

If you were interested in recording the delivery hour for packages received, you might capture the time at receipt and use the @HOUR function to access the specific hour. Figure 7-6 provides an example of using the @HOUR function for this purpose.

---

D3: @HOUR(A3)                                                              READY

|   | A | B | C | D | E | F |
|---|---|---|---|---|---|---|
| 1 | Time | Package | | | | |
| 2 | Received | Number | Recipient | Hour | | |
| 3 | 08:04:06 AM | 1761 | B. Jones | 8 | | |
| 4 | 09:11:00 AM | 3421 | R. Gaff | 9 | | |
| 5 | 09:30:00 AM | 2280 | J. Bowyer | 9 | | |
| 6 | 09:45:00 AM | 7891 | J. Kiger | 9 | | |
| 7 | 10:30:00 AM | 1975 | M. Williams | 10 | | |
| 8 | 11:05:00 AM | 3411 | B. Jobes | 11 | | |
| 9 | 11:15:00 AM | 5412 | R. Gaff | 11 | | |
| 10 | 11:55:00 AM | 1562 | K. Larson | 11 | | |
| 11 | | | | | | |

---

**Figure 7-6.**    Using @HOUR

## @MINUTE (Release 2)

The @MINUTE function extracts the minute from a serial time number.

### Format

@MINUTE(*serial time number*)

### Arguments

*serial time number*     a decimal fraction between 0.000 and 0.9999. Serial time number can be entered as a fraction or a decimal number. It can be generated by @TIME, @TIMEVALUE, or @NOW.

### Use

This function is used whenever you wish to work with only the minute portion of a time entry. The function will always return a value between 0 and 59. Used with @TIME, which creates a serial time number when provided with arguments of hour, minute, and second, the function might read @MINUTE(@TIME(10,15,25)) and would return 15.

If you were managing a radio station and were interested in recording the minutes of which you received calls for hourly radio contests, you could use the @MINUTE function to handle the task. Certain types of contests might generate many calls and immediate winners, whereas other types might be able to be announced throughout the hour before a winner called in with the correct answer. You might decide to capture the time of receipt of the calls and record whether the caller was the contest winner. Figure 7-7 shows the use of the @MINUTE function for this purpose.

| | A | B | C | D | E | F |
|---|---|---|---|---|---|---|
| 1 | Contest | | Time | | Minutes | |
| 2 | Type | Prize | Of Call | Winner | After Hour | |
| 3 | Mystery Guest | $50.00 | 09:30:00 AM | D. Black | 30 | |
| 4 | Golden Oldies | record | 10:05:00 AM | P. Silver | 5 | |
| 5 | Wacky DJ Quiz | $125.00 | 09:08:00 AM | B. Brown | 8 | |
| 6 | Mystery Guest | $75.00 | 01:05:00 PM | J. Lyson | 5 | |
| 7 | Unknown Music | dinner | 02:13:00 AM | F. Pitts | 13 | |
| 8 | Golden Oldies | record | 04:20:00 AM | C. Vernier | 20 | |
| 9 | Wacky DJ Quiz | $150.00 | 02:18:00 AM | D. Gleason | 18 | |
| 10 | Mystery Guest | $300.00 | 09:45:00 AM | S. Moore | 45 | |
| 11 | Golden Oldies | record | 10:02:00 AM | W. Koone | 2 | |
| 12 | Unknown Music | dinner | 12:06:00 PM | R. Stork | 6 | |
| 13 | | | | | | |

**Figure 7-7.**　　Using @MINUTE

## @MONTH

The @MONTH function extracts the month number from a
serial date number.

### Format

@MONTH(*serial date number*)

### Arguments

*serial date number*　　the serial date number of the desired date, which must be between
1 and 73050 to stay within the
acceptable range of January 1, 1900,
and December 31, 2099. The serial
date number can be generated by
another function such as @NOW,
@DATEVALUE, or @DATE.

**Use**

This function is used whenever you are interested in only the month portion of a date. Used with @DATE, the function would be recorded as @MONTH(@DATE(86,12,14)) and would return 12. Used with @DATEVALUE, it might be @MONTH(@DATEVALUE("24-Dec-86") and return a value of 12.

One sample use for this function would be to learn the vacation months of employees from historic data so you could monitor vacation schedules to plan for temporary help. You could use this function to extract the month from the vacation start date. The dates in Figure 7-8 are generated with @DATE and used to extract the month number. The advantage of this approach is that the same date formulas can be used for all vacations, as only the month numbers will vary.

F4: @MONTH(D4)                                                                    READY

| | A | B | C | D | E | F |
|---|---|---|---|---|---|---|
| 1 | | | 1985 Vacation Schedule | | | |
| 2 | | YEARS | | VACATION | VACATION | VACATION |
| 3 | EMPLOYEE | SERVICE | DEPT. | START | STOP | MONTH |
| 4 | G. Brown | 5 | 100 | 15-Jun-85 | 29-Jun-85 | 6 |
| 5 | M. Wilson | 2 | 200 | 03-Jul-85 | 10-Jul-85 | 7 |
| 6 | N. Staunton | 10 | 100 | 02-Jun-85 | 23-Jun-85 | 6 |
| 7 | H. Mailer | 3 | 100 | 21-Jul-86 | 28-Jul-86 | 7 |
| 8 | B. Wyler | 25 | 200 | 03-Aug-86 | 31-Aug-86 | 8 |
| 9 | K. Wilmer | 2 | 100 | 22-Jun-85 | 29-Jun-85 | 6 |
| 10 | D. Jason | 5 | 200 | 01-Apr-85 | 15-Apr-85 | 4 |
| 11 | | | | | | |

**Figure 7-8.**    Using @MONTH

## @NOW (Release 2)

The @NOW function is used to stamp a worksheet cell with the current system date and time. The function does not require any arguments and is simply entered as @NOW.

### Use

The @NOW function can be used whenever you wish to place the current date or time in a worksheet cell. The integer portion of the serial number generated will be the current date, and the decimal fraction will be the time.

@NOW will appear as a date if formatted with one of the date format options and will display as time if formatted with one of the time formats. @NOW will be recalculated when the worksheet containing it is loaded into memory and every time the worksheet is recalculated thereafter. This feature can prevent the problem of having multiple printed reports and not being able to tell which one is the most current. If the @NOW function is entered somewhere in every worksheet and always included in your print range, you will always be able to identify the most recent copy of a report. Figure 7-9 shows a worksheet where two cells, G1 and G2, have @NOW entered in them. One is formatted as a date and the other as a time. Including these cells in the print range when a report is printed will date and time stamp the report. Since the value of @NOW is calculated only when it is entered and when the worksheet is recalculated, the time display at the bottom of the screen may show a more recent time if the worksheet has not been recalculated recently.

Using F2 (EDIT) followed by F9 (CALC), then pressing ENTER, will freeze the serial date and time number placed in a cell by @NOW, changing it to a fixed value.

### Note

This function can be used in conjunction with the @MOD function, covered later in the chapter, to determine the day of the week. @MOD(@NOW,7) will return a value between 0

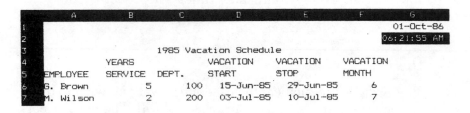

```
         A          B          C          D          E          F          G
1                                                                    01-Oct-86
2                                                                    06:21:55 AM
3                            1985 Vacation Schedule
4                  YEARS                 VACATION   VACATION   VACATION
5    EMPLOYEE      SERVICE   DEPT.        START      STOP       MONTH
6    G. Brown            5      100       15-Jun-85  29-Jun-85       6
7    M. Wilson           2      200       03-Jul-85  10-Jul-85       7
```

**Figure 7-9.**     Using @NOW as a date and time stamp

and 6, since the @MOD function returns the remainder from a division. If the result is 0, the day is Saturday, and if the result is 6, the day is Friday. Each of the other days is represented by one of the other numbers between 0 and 6.

## @SECOND (Release 2)

The @SECOND function extracts the second from a serial time number.

### Format

@SECOND(*serial time number*)

### Arguments

*serial time number*   a decimal fraction between 0.000 and .9999. Serial time number can be entered as a fraction or a decimal number. It can be generated by @TIME, @TIMEVALUE, or @NOW.

## Use

This function is used whenever you wish to work with only the second portion of a time entry. The function will always return a value between 0 and 59. If cell A3 contains a serial time number representing 11:08:19, @SECOND(A3) will equal 19. Used with @TIME, the function might read @SECOND(@TIME(10,15,25)) and would return 25.

## @TIME (Release 2)

The @TIME function allows you to create a serial time number when you supply the time components.

### Format

@TIME(*hour,minute,second*)

### Arguments

| | |
|---|---|
| *hour* | must be a number between 0 and 23. Midnight is represented by 0 and 11 p.m. by 23. |
| *minute* | must be a number between 0 and 59. |
| *second* | must be a number between 0 and 59. |

If an invalid number is entered for any of these arguments, a value of ERR is returned by the @TIME function.

### Use

This function is used anywhere you want to enter time on a worksheet. When time is entered with this function, you will be able to perform arithmetic operations with it, since it will be stored as a serial time number.

Figure 7-10 presents a worksheet that uses the @TIME function to record the time vehicles are brought in for repair

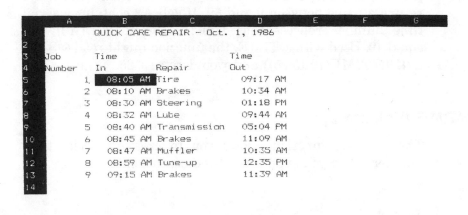

**Figure 7-10.**     Recording time in a worksheet cell

and the time at which the work on each is completed. Entering both sets of numbers makes it easy to perform calculations with the time values, and the /Range Format Date Time command allows you to choose a suitable time display format. Figure 7-11 shows the worksheet with formulas added in column E to represent the difference between the time each car was brought in for repair and the time it was completed, for example, +D5−B5. Using the Short International format under /Range Format Date Time allows you to show just the hours and minutes (represented by the decimal fraction) for the difference between the two time values.

## @TIMEVALUE (Release 2)

The @TIMEVALUE function returns the serial time number, given the string value of the time.

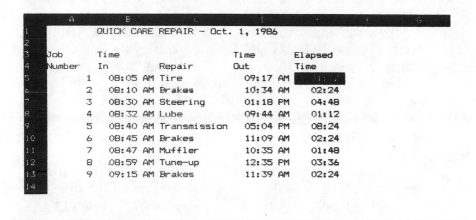

|   | A | B | C | D | E | F | G |
|---|---|---|---|---|---|---|---|
| 1 |   | QUICK CARE REPAIR — Oct. 1, 1986 |   |   |   |   |   |
| 2 |   |   |   |   |   |   |   |
| 3 | Job | Time |   | Time |   | Elapsed |   |
| 4 | Number | In |   | Repair | Out |   | Time |
| 5 |   | 1 | 08:05 AM | Tire | 09:17 AM | 01:12 |   |
| 6 |   | 2 | 08:10 AM | Brakes | 10:34 AM | 02:24 |   |
| 7 |   | 3 | 08:30 AM | Steering | 01:18 PM | 04:48 |   |
| 8 |   | 4 | 08:32 AM | Lube | 09:44 AM | 01:12 |   |
| 9 |   | 5 | 08:40 AM | Transmission | 05:04 PM | 08:24 |   |
| 10 |   | 6 | 08:45 AM | Brakes | 11:09 AM | 02:24 |   |
| 11 |   | 7 | 08:47 AM | Muffler | 10:35 AM | 01:48 |   |
| 12 |   | 8 | 08:59 AM | Tune-up | 12:35 PM | 03:36 |   |
| 13 |   | 9 | 09:15 AM | Brakes | 11:39 AM | 02:24 |   |
| 14 |   |   |   |   |   |   |   |

**Figure 7-11.**     Time arithmetic

## Format

@TIMEVALUE(*time string*)

## Arguments

*time string*        a single string value conforming to one of
the acceptable time formats and enclosed
in double quotation marks.

"HH:MM:SS AM/PM" is acceptable, since it conforms to
the D6 (Date Format 6) format, which is the first time format option; "HH:MM AM/PM" is acceptable, since it conforms to the D7 format, which is the second time format
option. Formats D8 and D9 have more than one option and
are changeable through the /Worksheet Global Default International Time command. The acceptable formats for D8 and
D9 will depend on which format is in effect. Chapter 4 provides additional information about time formats.

## Use

This function is used whenever you wish to generate a serial time number from a string value. For example, suppose entry in your worksheet was originally entered as a string, but you decide you want to use it in a calculation of elapsed time. The @TIMEVALUE function can make this possible. It has the same ability as the @TIME function but accepts a string for input rather than three separate numeric values for hour, minute, and second. As an example, you might enter @TIMEVALUE("2:14:14 PM"), which gives the value 0.5932175926. This value could then be used in a time formula.

The same worksheet used in Figure 7-10 is reproduced for the @TIMEVALUE example except that all the times are entered as labels. For example, the entry in D5 is '09:17 AM. This means that the formula in column E will have to be changed, since two label values cannot be used to determine a difference. The formula is changed to use @TIMEVALUE, as shown in cell E5 of Figure 7-12. The entry in this cell is

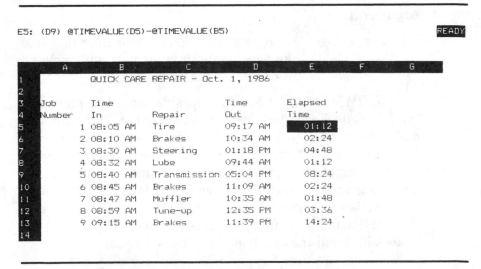

Figure 7-12.   Working with time labels

@TIMEVALUE(D5)−@TIMEVALUE(B5), and the cell is formatted in the short international time format.

## @YEAR

The @YEAR function extracts the year number from a serial date number.

### Format

@YEAR(*serial date number*)

### Arguments

*serial date number*     the serial date number of the desired date, which must be between 1 and 73050 to stay within the acceptable range of January 1, 1900, to December 31, 2099. The serial date number can be generated by another function such as @NOW, @DATEVALUE, or @DATE.

### Use

This function is used whenever you are interested in only the year portion of a date. Used with @DATE, the function would be recorded as @YEAR(@DATE(86,12,14)) and would return 86. Used with @DATEVALUE, it might be @YEAR(@DATEVALUE("24-Dec-86") and return a value of 86.

One sample use for this function would be to determine the start year for each of a group of employees. You can reference the date of hire and just extract the year for an easy reference to the anniversary year, shown in Figure 7-13.

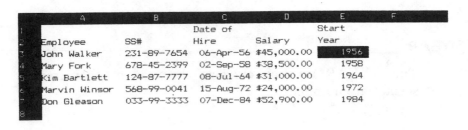

|  | A | B | C | D | E | F |
|---|---|---|---|---|---|---|
| 1 |  |  | Date of |  | Start |  |
| 2 | Employee | SS# | Hire | Salary | Year |  |
| 3 | John Walker | 231-89-7654 | 06-Apr-56 | $45,000.00 | 1956 |  |
| 4 | Mary Fork | 678-45-2399 | 02-Sep-58 | $38,500.00 | 1958 |  |
| 5 | Kim Bartlett | 124-87-7777 | 08-Jul-64 | $31,000.00 | 1964 |  |
| 6 | Marvin Winsor | 568-99-0041 | 15-Aug-72 | $24,000.00 | 1972 |  |
| 7 | Don Gleason | 033-99-3333 | 07-Dec-84 | $52,900.00 | 1984 |  |
| 8 |  |  |  |  |  |  |

**Figure 7-13.**    Using @YEAR

## Financial Functions

The primary use of 1-2-3's financial functions is in investment calculations and other calculations concerned with the time value of money. For example, you can use them to monitor loans, annuities, and cash flows over a period of time. Several new depreciation functions have been added to this category with release 2. With these new functions you can quickly compare the impact of the double declining balance depreciation method with those of the sum of the years digits and straight line depreciation.

Since many of these functions deal with interest rate calculations, you will want to be aware of the two acceptable ways of entering interest rates for these calculations. You can always enter a percent as a decimal, for example, .15 for 15%. Your other option is to enter the percent with the percentage indicator and have 1-2-3 convert it to a decimal for internal storage. For example, you might enter 15% and 1-2-3 would store it as .15.

Many of the financial functions require a term and a rate as arguments. It is important that the same unit of time be used for both arguments. If a term is expressed in years, an annual interest rate should be used. If a term is expressed in months, a monthly interest rate should be used.

## @CTERM (Release 2)

Given a present and a future value for an investment as well as a fixed interest rate, this function will compute the number of time periods it will take to reach the future value.

### Format

@CTERM(*interest,future value,present value*)

### Arguments

| | |
|---|---|
| *interest* | the fixed interest rate per compounding period. It can be expressed as a percent or a decimal fraction within the function, or it can be stored in a cell and referenced with the cell address or a range name. It can also be computed with a formula from within the function. |
| *future value* | the value the investment will grow to at some point in the future. The objective of the @CTERM function is to determine the point at which an investment will reach a specified future value. This argument must be a value or a reference to a cell containing a value. |
| *present value* | the current value of the investment. This argument must be a value or a reference to a cell containing a value. |

### Use

The @CTERM function can provide a quick answer when you want to know how long it will take an investment to grow to a certain value. The formula used by the function is as follows:

$$\frac{\text{natural log(future value/present value)}}{\text{natural log(1 + periodic interest rate)}}$$

As an example, if you have $5,000 to invest today and feel you can get an 11% return on your money, you might want to know how long it would take to triple your money at that rate. @CTERM(11%/12,15000,5000) will provide the answer, assuming the compounding occurs monthly. The result is shown in the example worksheet.

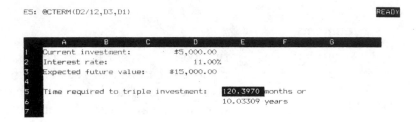

## @DDB (Release 2)

The @DDB function calculates depreciation expense for a specific period using the double declining balance method.

### Format

@DDB(*cost,salvage,life,period*)

### Arguments

cost the amount you paid for the asset. This argument must be a value or a reference to a cell containing a value.

salvage the value of the asset at the end of its useful life. Like the cost, this argument must be a value or a reference to a cell containing a value.

| life | the expected useful life of the asset; that is, the number of years needed to depreciate the asset from its cost to its salvage value. Normally expressed in years, this argument too must be a value or a reference to one. |
| period | the specific time period for which you are attempting to determine the depreciation expense. Normally the number of the year for which you are calculating depreciation expense, this argument must be a value or a reference to one. |

## Use

The @DDB function gives you a figure for depreciation expense, using an accelerated depreciation method (one that allows you to write off more depreciation expense in the early years of an asset's life). The asset will no longer be depreciated when its book value (that is, cost minus total depreciation to date) equals its salvage value.

The formula used in the calculation of double declining balance depreciation is as follows:

$$\frac{\text{book value for the period times 2}}{\text{life of the asset}}$$

1-2-3 will make adjustments in the calculations to ensure that total depreciation is exactly equal to the asset cost minus the salvage value.

Figure 7-14 shows the use of this function to determine the proper depreciation expense to charge for each year in an asset's five-year life. The cost of the asset was $11,000, and its salvage value is $1,000.

## @FV

The @FV function computes the future value of an investment based on the assumption that equal payments will be generated at a specific rate over a period of time.

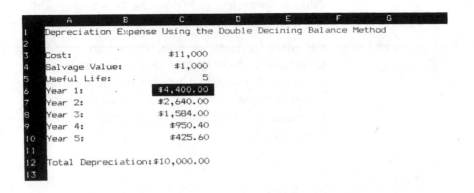

|    | A | B | C | D | E | F | G |
|----|---|---|---|---|---|---|---|
| 1  | Depreciation Expense Using the Double Decining Balance Method |||||||
| 2  |   |   |   |   |   |   |   |
| 3  | Cost: | | $11,000 | | | | |
| 4  | Salvage Value: | | $1,000 | | | | |
| 5  | Useful Life: | | 5 | | | | |
| 6  | Year 1: | | $4,400.00 | | | | |
| 7  | Year 2: | | $2,640.00 | | | | |
| 8  | Year 3: | | $1,584.00 | | | | |
| 9  | Year 4: | | $950.40 | | | | |
| 10 | Year 5: | | $425.60 | | | | |
| 11 |   |   |   |   |   |   |   |
| 12 | Total Depreciation: | | $10,000.00 | | | | |
| 13 |   |   |   |   |   |   |   |

**Figure 7-14.**    Double declining balance depreciation

## Format

@FV(*payment,interest,term*)

## Arguments

*payment*    the amount of the equal payments for the investment. This argument must be a value or a reference to a value.

*interest*    the periodic interest rate earned by the investment. This argument must be a value or a reference to a value.

*term*    the number of periods for the investment. This argument must be a value or a reference to a value.

## Use

This function is designed to perform calculations for an ordinary annuity. It uses the following formula:

$$\text{payment} * \left( \frac{(1 + \text{periodic interest rate}) \text{ raised to the n power}}{\text{periodic interest rate}} \right) -1$$

where n is the number of periods.

This worksheet shows an example of the @FV function used to calculate the value for an ordinary annuity. We will assume that you plan to deposit $500 a month for each of the next 36 months and will continue to receive interest on this money at a constant rate of 12% compounded monthly. The formula used is @FV(500,1%,36).

```
C5: (C0) @FV(C1,C2/12,C3)                                      READY

        A         B         C         D      E      F      G      H
1   Monthly Deposit:       $500
2   Interest Rate:          12%
3   # Deposits:              36
4
5   Future Value:       $21,538
6
```

This example is based on the premises that interest is paid at the end of the year and that your next contribution is always made on the last day of the year.

### Note

This function can be adapted to work with an annuity due, which uses this formula:

@FV(*payment,interest,term*)*(1 + *periodic interest rate*)

This is appropriate for a situation where you must make contributions on the first day of the year. Assuming you made annual payments of $5000 at the beginning of each year and they earned interest at a rate of 10%, the value at the end of 10 years would be represented by

@FV(5000,10%,10)*(1+10%)

This formula would return $87,655.83, the value of your annuity after 10 years.

## @IRR

The @IRR function calculates the internal rate of return on investments.

### Format

@IRR(*guess,range*)

### Arguments

*guess*      an estimate of the internal rate of return. Although any number between 0% and 100% will probably work, you will encounter examples where the correct internal rate of return cannot be closely approximated. If you think the internal rate of return for an investment is between 15% and 25%, 20% would be a good guess to start with. A series of cash flows that alternates between positive and negative will result in more than one internal rate of return. The guess you make will affect which of the values is returned.

        Twenty iterations are the default for this function. If 1-2-3 cannot approximate the result to within 0.0000001 after these 20 attempts, ERR will result. When this happens, you can use /Worksheet Global Recalculation Iteration to increase the iteration count to, say, 50.

*range*      the range of cells containing the cash flows to be analyzed. Negative numbers in this range are considered outflows, and positive numbers are inflows. The first number in the range is expected to be negative, since it is the cost of the investment opportunity.

### Use

The @IRR function is used whenever you wish to find the rate that will equate the initial investment with the expected future cash flows generated by the investment. Cash flows must be at equal intervals. 1-2-3 can deal with uneven cash flows, but it cannot handle a mixture of positive and negative cash flows because two different internal rate of return calculations could result from this situation.

The following illustration shows the @IRR function being used to analyze the stream of projected cash flows shown in A2..A7. As required, the first number in the range is negative, signifying the cost of the investment opportunity. A guess of 12% was placed in D2. The /Range Format Percent command was used to obtain the percent in D2 and E2. The formula for the internal rate of return is placed in E2 as @IRR(D2,A2..A7). In this example, the function returns 19.58%.

## @NPV

The @NPV function computes what you should be willing to pay for a projected stream of cash flows, given your desired rate of return.

### Format

@NPV(*discount rate,range*)

### Arguments

*discount rate*     a fixed periodic interest rate used to discount the expected cash flows in order to project their worth in today's dollars.

*range*   the series of cash flows to be discounted. These cash flows do not have to be equal, but they must be evenly spaced over a period of time (monthly, quarterly, or whatever) and are assumed to occur at the end of a period. The first cash flow will be received at the end of the first period.

## Use

This is one of the most frequently used functions in 1-2-3, since it deals with the time value of money.

Figure 7-15 presents a sample use of @NPV. The expected cash flows are shown in B2..G2. You will notice from the column headings that these are to be received monthly. The interest rate in D4 is expressed as an annual rate. You will want to make a note of this discrepancy between the time periods of the interest and the payments. The difference can be resolved by changing the interest rate to a monthly figure in the function argument. The formula for the calculation is @NPV(D4/12,B2..G2). It produces a result of $57,636.93, indicating that if the discount rate is 15%, you should be willing to pay $57,396.93 for this investment.

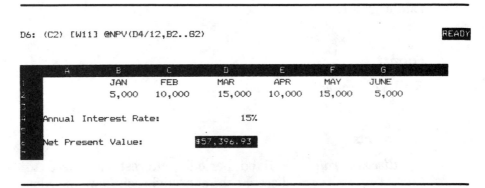

D6: (C2) [W11] @NPV(D4/12,B2..G2)      READY

|   | A | B | C | D | E | F | G |
|---|---|---|---|---|---|---|---|
| 1 |   | JAN | FEB | MAR | APR | MAY | JUNE |
| 2 |   | 5,000 | 10,000 | 15,000 | 10,000 | 15,000 | 5,000 |
| 3 |   |   |   |   |   |   |   |
| 4 | Annual Interest Rate: |   |   | 15% |   |   |   |
| 5 |   |   |   |   |   |   |   |
| 6 | Net Present Value: |   |   | $57,396.93 |   |   |   |

**Figure 7-15.**   Net present value calculations

### Note

This function is not designed to handle situations where you make an immediate or up-front payment, although you could easily construct a formula to do this. Since the initial payment is already in today's dollars, there is no need to discount it. Your initial outflow can be added to the result of the @NPV function.

As an example, let's say that you must pay $5,000 today for an investment that will return $4,000, $3,000, $2,000, and $1,500 respectively at the end of each of the next four years. The formula would be $-5000+@NPV(.13,B2..B5)$, where .13 is the discount rate and the cash flows are stored in B2..B5.

## @PMT

The @PMT function will calculate the appropriate payment amount for a loan when given the principal, interest rate, and term.

### Format

@PMT(*principal,interest,term of loan*)

### Arguments

*principal*    a numeric value representing the amount borrowed. It can be provided as a number or as a cell address, formula, range name, or other function.

*interest*    a numeric value representing the interest rate. It can be provided as a numeric constant in the formula or as a cell reference, formula, or range name. If you elect to enter it in the formula or a cell, you may enter it as a decimal fraction or followed by a %. To specify 9%, for example, you can enter .09 or 9%.

*term*    the number of payments in the loan term. If monthly payments will be made on a loan spanning several years, multiply the years of the term by 12 and use the product for this argument. It can be expressed as a fraction, a formula, a range name, or a cell address.

It is extremely important that the same unit of time be used for both the term and the interest rate. An annual interest rate means a term of a number of years, whereas a monthly interest rate should be indicative of a term consisting of a number of months.

## Use

This function can be used wherever you want to calculate the amount of a loan payment. The ease of calculation with this function makes it simple to produce your own personal loan tables. Given a specific range for the principal and interest rate, you can look at a range of options and see which are possible given your current monthly income.

Figure 7-16 provides an example of a payment table. Interest rates are entered across row three. Nine percent is the first rate and is placed in B3. The numbers in C3..G3 are generated with a formula entered in C3 to add .005 to B3. This formula is copied across. The entire row is formatted as percent.

Cells A4..A20 are used for hypothetical principal amounts. The starting point is 100,000, with a 5,000 increment. The last number in A20 is 180,000. These principal amounts are formatted as currency with 0 decimal places.

Only one payment formula must be entered; the rest can be copied. @PMT($A4,B$3/12,240) is the formula used. The $s are required to keep part of the references from changing as the formula is copied. $A4 indicates that the column for the reference is absolute, although the row can change. The reverse is true of B$3: the row can change, but the column is constant. B$3 is divided by 12 to convert the annual interest

B4: @PMT($A4,B$3/12,240)                                              READY

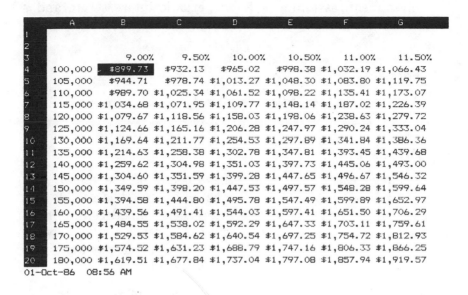

|       | A       | B         | C         | D         | E         | F         | G         |
|-------|---------|-----------|-----------|-----------|-----------|-----------|-----------|
| 1     |         |           |           |           |           |           |           |
| 2     |         |           |           |           |           |           |           |
| 3     |         | 9.00%     | 9.50%     | 10.00%    | 10.50%    | 11.00%    | 11.50%    |
| 4     | 100,000 | $899.73   | $932.13   | $965.02   | $998.38   | $1,032.19 | $1,066.43 |
| 5     | 105,000 | $944.71   | $978.74   | $1,013.27 | $1,048.30 | $1,083.80 | $1,119.75 |
| 6     | 110,000 | $989.70   | $1,025.34 | $1,061.52 | $1,098.22 | $1,135.41 | $1,173.07 |
| 7     | 115,000 | $1,034.68 | $1,071.95 | $1,109.77 | $1,148.14 | $1,187.02 | $1,226.39 |
| 8     | 120,000 | $1,079.67 | $1,118.56 | $1,158.03 | $1,198.06 | $1,238.63 | $1,279.72 |
| 9     | 125,000 | $1,124.66 | $1,165.16 | $1,206.28 | $1,247.97 | $1,290.24 | $1,333.04 |
| 10    | 130,000 | $1,169.64 | $1,211.77 | $1,254.53 | $1,297.89 | $1,341.84 | $1,386.36 |
| 11    | 135,000 | $1,214.63 | $1,258.38 | $1,302.78 | $1,347.81 | $1,393.45 | $1,439.68 |
| 12    | 140,000 | $1,259.62 | $1,304.98 | $1,351.03 | $1,397.73 | $1,445.06 | $1,493.00 |
| 13    | 145,000 | $1,304.60 | $1,351.59 | $1,399.28 | $1,447.65 | $1,496.67 | $1,546.32 |
| 14    | 150,000 | $1,349.59 | $1,398.20 | $1,447.53 | $1,497.57 | $1,548.28 | $1,599.64 |
| 15    | 155,000 | $1,394.58 | $1,444.80 | $1,495.78 | $1,547.49 | $1,599.89 | $1,652.97 |
| 16    | 160,000 | $1,439.56 | $1,491.41 | $1,544.03 | $1,597.41 | $1,651.50 | $1,706.29 |
| 17    | 165,000 | $1,484.55 | $1,538.02 | $1,592.29 | $1,647.33 | $1,703.11 | $1,759.61 |
| 18    | 170,000 | $1,529.53 | $1,584.62 | $1,640.54 | $1,697.25 | $1,754.72 | $1,812.93 |
| 19    | 175,000 | $1,574.52 | $1,631.23 | $1,688.79 | $1,747.16 | $1,806.33 | $1,866.25 |
| 20    | 180,000 | $1,619.51 | $1,677.84 | $1,737.04 | $1,797.08 | $1,857.94 | $1,919.57 |

01-Oct-86   08:56 AM

**Figure 7-16.**   Creating a payment table

into a monthly interest. The term is 20 years, which equates
to 240 monthly periods, so 240 will be entered. After this cell
is formatted as currency with two decimal places, it can be
copied to the remaining places in the table. You will need to
widen some of the columns in order to fit the currency display in the cells.

### Note

Financial institutions calculate payment amounts in a number
of ways. The formula used by the @PMT function is as follows:

*principal*\*(*interest*/(1−(1+*interest*) raised to the −*n* power))

where n is the number of payments.

## @PV

The @PV function determines the present value of an investment, assuming a fixed periodic interest rate and a series of equal payments over a period of time.

### Format

@PV(*payment,periodic interest rate,number of periods*)

### Arguments

*payment*  the amount of the equal payments, expressed as a value or a reference to a cell containing a value. Only one value may be referenced, since payments are assumed to be equal.

*periodic interest rate*  the periodic interest rate that will be used to discount the cash flows. This argument must be a value or a reference to a cell containing a value.

*number of periods*  the term over which the payments will be generated. This argument must be a value or a reference to a cell containing a value.

### Use

This function is used whenever you wish to determine the value to you today of money to be received in the future. You can use the function to assess what you should be willing to pay for an investment today, given that it will return a certain amount of money in future periods. You can also use the function to evaluate a lump sum payment as compared to future periodic payments if you have this option on the sale of a property or the receipt of prize money.

Let's say you have the option of taking a one-time cash payment of $500,000 versus monthly payments of $5,000 for the next 20 years. To compare the two options you must look at the present value of the future cash flows. This means you must make an assessment of the rate of return you would receive for investing the $500,000 lump sum payment today. We will assume that you could gct 12%, compounded monthly. The present value becomes @PV(5000,1%,240). The worksheet shows this same formula, except that the numbers are stored in cells to provide easy update capabilities. The result indicates that the best decision, if you are attempting to maximize return, is to choose the lump sum payment.

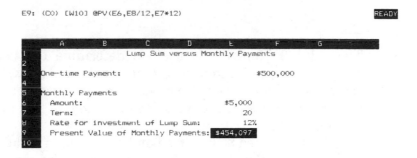

### Note

This comparison of the value of a lump sum payment and periodic payments does not take tax effects into consideration.

# @RATE (Release 2)

The @RATE function determines the periodic interest rate that must be earned to increase a specified present value to a future value over a specific term.

### Format

@RATE(*future value,present value,number of periods*)

## Arguments

*future value*    the value of the investment at the end of a specified growth period. This argument must be a value or a reference to a value.

*present value*    the current value of an investment. This argument can contain a numeric value, a formula, or a reference to one of those two options.

*number of periods*    the compounding periods over which the investment will grow. This argument must be a value or a reference to a value.

## Use

The @RATE function is used to determine the periodic interest rate that is required to realize a desired growth rate. If you give the number of periods in months, you will get a monthly rate. You can convert this to an annual rate by multiplying by 12.

If you invested $5,000 in a bond maturing in eight years, you could use the @RATE function to calculate the rate of return. For this example we will assume that the maturity value is $10,000 and that interest is compounded monthly. The required formula is as follows:

@RATE(10000,5000,8*12)

This is shown in the worksheet through references to cells that store the arguments. The rate of return is .72%, a monthly rate. To annualize it, multiply by 12 to obtain 8.7%.

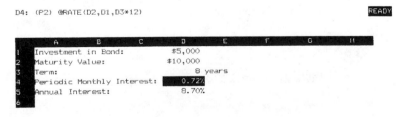

D4: (P2) @RATE(D2,D1,D3*12)                                                     READY

| | A | B | C | D | E | F | G | H |
|---|---|---|---|---|---|---|---|---|
| 1 | Investment in Bond: | | | $5,000 | | | | |
| 2 | Maturity Value: | | | $10,000 | | | | |
| 3 | Term: | | | 8 years | | | | |
| 4 | Periodic Monthly Interest: | | | 0.72% | | | | |
| 5 | Annual Interest: | | | 8.70% | | | | |
| 6 | | | | | | | | |

## @SLN (Release 2)

The @SLN function computes the straight line depreciation for one period in an asset's life.

### Format

@SLN(*cost,salvage value,life of the asset*)

### Arguments

*cost*   the amount paid for the asset. This number can be included in the function or stored in a cell and referenced with an address or range name.

*salvage value*  the remaining value of the asset at the end of its useful life. This number can be included in the function or stored in a cell and referenced with an address or range name.

*life*   the number of years of useful life, or the time required to depreciate the asset to its salvage value. This number can be included in the function or stored in a cell and referenced with an address or range name.

### Use

The @SLN function can be used whenever you wish to depreciate an asset evenly over its useful life, since the depreciation expense will be the same for all years. The formula used by the function is as follows:

$$\frac{cost - salvage\ value}{life}$$

As an example, if you purchase a $12,000 machine and estimate its salvage value to be $2,000 at the end of its five-year life, you can use @SLN to calculate its depreciation expense. The formula is shown in the following worksheet.

```
D6:  (CO) @SLN(D3,D4,D5)                                          READY
```

|   | A | B | C | D | E | F | G | H |
|---|---|---|---|---|---|---|---|---|
| 1 | | STRAIGHT LINE DEPRECIATION | | | | | | |
| 2 | | | | | | | | |
| 3 | Cost: | | | $12,000 | | | | |
| 4 | Salvage Value: | | | $2,000 | | | | |
| 5 | Useful Life: | | | 5 | | | | |
| 6 | Depreciation Expense: | | | $2,000 | | | | |
| 7 | | | | | | | | |

## @SYD (Release 2)

The @SYD function computes depreciation expense for an asset using an accelerated depreciation method—that is, one that will depreciate an asset more in the early years of its life.

### Format

@SYD(*cost, salvage value, life, period*)

### Arguments

*cost*          the amount paid for the asset. This number can be included in the function or stored in a cell and referenced with an address or range name.

*salvage value*   the remaining value of the asset at the end of its useful life. This number can be included in the function or stored in a cell and referenced with an address or range name.

*life*          the number of years of useful life, or the time required to depreciate the asset to its salvage value. This number can be included in the function or stored in a cell and referenced with an address or range name.

| *period* | the year within the useful life of the asset for which you wish the depreciation expense calculated. This number can be included in the function or stored in a cell and referenced with an address or range name. It should not be greater than the life of the asset. |
|---|---|

## Use

The @SYD function will permit you to calculate the sum of the years digits depreciation expense for any period in the life of an asset. The formula used by the function is as follows:

$$\frac{(cost-salvage)*(life-period\ for\ depreciation\ expense+1)}{(life*(life+1)/2)}$$

The following worksheet shows the sum of the years digits depreciation expense for an asset that was purchased for $12,000 and has a $2,000 salvage value. The cursor points to the formula for the depreciation expense for the first year. This calculation uses the formula @SYD(12000,2000,5,1). The worksheet shows the depreciation expense for the other four years as well. The only difference in the remaining formulas is in the last argument, which indicates the period for which depreciation expense is being calculated.

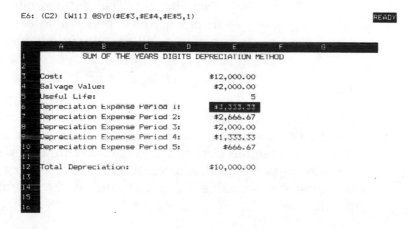

E6: (C2) [W11] @SYD($E$3,$E$4,$E$5,1)        READY

|   | A | B | C | D | E | F | G |
|---|---|---|---|---|---|---|---|
| 1 | | SUM OF THE YEARS DIGITS DEPRECIATION METHOD | | | | | |
| 2 | | | | | | | |
| 3 | Cost: | | | | $12,000.00 | | |
| 4 | Salvage Value: | | | | $2,000.00 | | |
| 5 | Useful Life: | | | | 5 | | |
| 6 | Depreciation Expense Period 1: | | | | $3,333.33 | | |
| 7 | Depreciation Expense Period 2: | | | | $2,666.67 | | |
| 8 | Depreciation Expense Period 3: | | | | $2,000.00 | | |
| 9 | Depreciation Expense Period 4: | | | | $1,333.33 | | |
| 10 | Depreciation Expense Period 5: | | | | $666.67 | | |
| 11 | | | | | | | |
| 12 | Total Depreciation: | | | | $10,000.00 | | |
| 13 | | | | | | | |
| 14 | | | | | | | |
| 15 | | | | | | | |
| 16 | | | | | | | |

## @TERM (Release 2)

The @TERM function returns the number of payment periods required to accumulate a given future value if the payment amount remains fixed.

### Format

@TERM(*payment, interest, future value*)

### Arguments

*payment*    a fixed periodic payment, stored as a number in the function or in a cell that can be referenced by the function.

*interest*    the fixed interest rate per compounding period. It can be expressed as a percent or decimal fraction within the function, or it can be stored in a cell and referenced with the cell address or a range name. It can also be computed with a formula from within the function.

*future value*    the value the investment will grow to at some point in the future. The objective of the @TERM function is to determine the point at which the investment will reach its specified future value. This argument must be a value or a reference to a cell containing a value.

### Use

The @TERM function is used to calculate the number of periods required for an ordinary annuity to reach a given value. For example, it permits you to determine how long it will take to save for a dream vacation home or luxury yacht, assuming you set aside a fixed amount at the end of each month.

The formula behind 1-2-3's calculations is as follows:

$$\frac{\text{natural } \log(1+(\text{future value} * \text{interest}/\text{payment}))}{\text{natural } \log(1+\text{interest})}$$

The worksheet shows an example where $350 is set aside at the end of each month for the purpose of accumulating a $25,000 down payment on a vacation home. If the funds are placed in a money market fund paying 10.25%, @TERM will calculate the time required to accumulate the down payment. The formula is @TERM(350,.1025,25000).

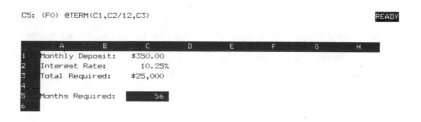

## Note

This function differs from the @CTERM function in that you must provide the payment amount, not the present value. @CTERM focuses on the number of growth periods required for an investment to reach a specific value, while @TERM is concerned with the number of payment periods for an ordinary annuity. To calculate the term of an annuity due, you would need to use @TERM(payment,interest,future value/(1+interest)).

## Mathematical Functions

1-2-3's mathematical functions perform trigonometric and other numeric calculations. Their primary use is in engineering, manufacturing, and scientific applications.

The angles the functions work with are all expressed in

radians, a unit of measure that equates the radius and arc length. If you prefer to work with angles in degrees, multiplying radians by 180/@PI will produce the conversion. All angles that you enter for the @SIN, @COS, and @TAN functions should be expressed in radians. If they are in degrees, you can multiply by the inverse of the conversion factor (that is, @PI/180) to change degrees into radians. If you are working with @ASIN, @ACOS, @ATAN, or @ATAN2, you will want to remember that these functions return angles in radians. To convert them to degrees, multiply by 180/@PI.

## @ABS

The @ABS function returns the positive or absolute value of a number.

### Format

@ABS(*number*)

### Arguments

*number*    any value, including references to a cell containing a value. If a string is used for number, an error will result.

### Use

The @ABS function is used whenever you are interested in the relative size of a number and do not care whether it is positive or negative. A good example might be the need to monitor cash overages and shortages in the registers of a retail establishment. Consistent cash overages and shortages indicate a cash control problem that should be corrected. If you monitored both overages and shortages, adding their + and − signs, they might cancel each other out. Looking at the absolute value of the overages and shortages, however, provides a look at the total amount of the differences.

```
        A      B        C          D       E        F        G        H
  1                         Hot Dog House Register
  2                      Week of September 15, 1986
  3
  4                        Over/Under         Absolute Value
  5   Monday               $42.00               $42.00
  6   Tuesday             ($35.00)               $35.00
  7   Wednesday            $22.78               $22.78
  8   Thursday            ($57.00)               $57.00
  9   Friday               $12.58               $12.58
 10   Saturday             $0.58                $0.58
 11   Sunday              ($2.10)                $2.10
 12
 13   TOTAL DIFFERENCE FOR THE WEEK:          $172.04
 14
```

**Figure 7-17.**    Adding absolute values

Figure 7-17 provides a look at a restaurant's cash overages and shortages by adding absolute values. If @ABS had
not been used, the positive and negative numbers would have
partially canceled each other, making the cash differences
seem like less of a problem.

## @ACOS

The @ACOS function returns the inverse cosine (arccosine)
when you provide the cosine of an angle.

### Format

@ACOS(*number*)

### Arguments

*number*  the cosine of an angle, which can be in the
      range of −1 to 1. This numeric value can be
      provided within the function or through a

reference to a cell or range. If you provide a number outside the allowable limits, ERR will be returned.

## Use

The function is used when you know the cosine of an angle but want to know the angle in radians. If you would prefer the angle measurement in degrees, you can multiply the result of this function by 180/@PI.

Suppose you were in a lighthouse at the top of a 100-foot cliff and wanted to know the angle you would have to use to make a projectile reach a boat approximately 200 feet away (see Figure 7-18). You could find the cosine of the angle by performing the following calculation:

cos of angle = 100/200
cos of angle = .5
@ACOS(.5)*180/@PI = 60 degrees.

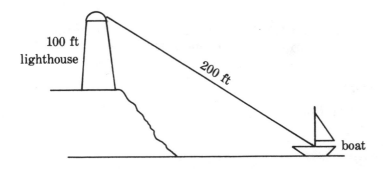

**Figure 7-18.**     Angle from the lighthouse to the boat

# @ASIN

The @ASIN function is used to determine the arcsine or inverse sine of an angle.

## Format

@ASIN(*number*)

## Arguments

*number*  the sine of an angle, which can be in the range of −1 to 1. This numeric value can be provided within the function or through a reference to a cell or range. If you provide a number outside the allowable limits, ERR will be returned.

## Use

The @ASIN function returns an arcsine between @PI/2 and −@PI/2 and represents an angle in quadrant 1 or 2.

As an example, you can use the @ASIN function to determine the angle of a platform that will be used to roll a barrel into a truck. A diagram of the truck bed and platform is shown in Figure 7-19. The bed of the truck is 3 feet from the ground, and the platform used to roll the barrel is 6 feet long. The sine of the angle between the board and the ground is equal to 3/6 or .5. @ASIN(.5)*180/@PI equals 30 degrees, as shown in the worksheet.

A1: @ASIN(0.5)*180/@PI

# @ATAN

The @ATAN function calculates the arctangent or inverse tangent of an angle for use in trigonometric problems.

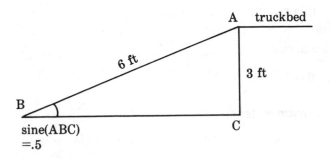

**Figure 7-19.**    Using a ramp to get merchandise into a truck

## Format

@ATAN(*number*)

## Arguments

*number*    the tangent of an angle, which can be in the range of −1 to 1. This numeric value can be provided within the function or through a reference to a cell or range. If you provide a number outside the allowable limits, ERR will be returned.

## Use

The @ATAN function returns an arctangent between @PI/2 and −@PI/2 and represents an angle in quadrant 1 or 4.

This function can be used to solve many trigonometric problems. For example, suppose you are playing a championship game of pool and need to pass a ball from point A through point B in the diagram shown in Figure 7-20. The

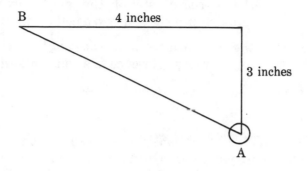

B       4 inches

3 inches

A

**Figure 7-20.**     Making the pool shot

@ATAN function can determine the angle at which you should hit the ball.

The location of the ball is three inches from the bumper, and the location of the pocket in relationship to the bumper is 4 inches. The tangent between the pocket and the bumper is equal to 4/3 or 1.333333. @ATAN(1.333333) is .927295 radians. When this is multiplied by 180/@PI, it will provide the number of degrees, as shown in the worksheet.

```
A1: @ATAN(1.333333)*(180/@PI)                              READY
```

```
        A        B       C       D       E       F       G       H
1   53.13009
2
```

## @ATAN2

The @ATAN2 function returns the 4 quadrant arctangent or the angle in radians whose tangent is y/x.

### Format

@ATAN2($x,y$)

## Arguments

> $x$    the x coordinate of the angle, expressed as a number or a reference to a cell containing a number.

> $y$    the y coordinate of the angle, expressed as a number or a reference to a cell containing a number.

## Use

The @ATAN2 function is used to solve trigonometric problems where you want to differentiate angles found in the first and third quadrants from those found in the second and fourth quadrants. The chart shows the values of @ATAN2 for the different quadrants. @ATAN2(1,.5) returns .463647 radians.

Quadrants

| 2<br>@PI/2 to @PI | 1<br>0 to @PI/2 |
|---|---|
| 3<br>−@PI to<br>−@PI/2 | 4<br>−@PI/2<br>to 0 |

Values of @ATAN2

# @COS

The @COS function returns the cosine of an angle.

## Format

@COS(*number*)

## Arguments

> *number*    a number representing the radians in an angle.

## Use

The @COS function is used when you have an angle in radians and want to determine the cosine of that angle. This number can assist you in making other determinations, such as distances and other angles. As an example, a surveyor can use the @COS function to determine the length of a side of a plot of land in the shape of a right triangle (see Figure 7-21). The longest side of the plot of land is 50 feet. There is a 60-degree angle at the point of the lot where the surveyor is standing. He would like to know the length of the side on his left (the adjacent side, in mathematics terminology). He constructs the formula @COS 60 = x/50. The @COS(60*@PI/180) function returns .5, which can be used to solve for x of 25. @PI/180 was needed because the angle was supplied in radians, as shown in the worksheet.

A1: @COS(60*@PI/180)                                                                READY

| | A | B | C | D | E | F | G | H |
|---|---|---|---|---|---|---|---|---|
| 1 | 0.5 | | | | | | | |
| 2 | | | | | | | | |
| 3 | | | | | | | | |

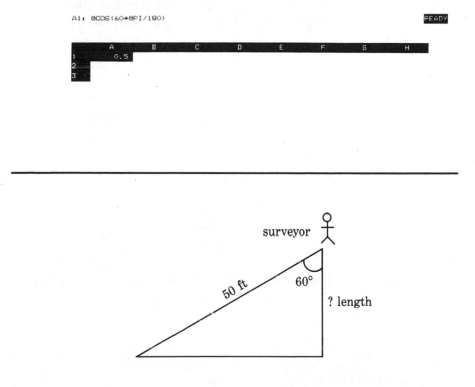

**Figure 7-21.**  Determining the length of the side of a plot of land

## @EXP

The @EXP function raises the constant e (2.718281) to a specific power.

### Format

@EXP(*number*)

### Arguments

*number*    the power to which you want to raise e. This argument must be a numeric value or a reference to one. The number cannot exceed 230 if you wish to display the number, although it can be as high as 709 if you just plan to store the number for later calculations.

### Use

@EXP is the inverse of @LN and is used whenever you wish to raise e to a specific power. Here are several examples:

@EXP(1) equals 2.718281

@EXP(10) equals 22026.46

@EXP(@LN(5)) equals 5

## @INT

The @INT function allows you to truncate the decimal places in a number to produce a whole number.

### Format

@INT(*number*)

## Arguments

*number*      any value that you wish to use the integer portion of. Any digits to the right of the decimal point in the number will be truncated.

## Use

This function is used whenever you wish to eliminate the decimal portion of a number. It could be used to determine the number of complete batches finished by a production line, for example. In this situation, partly completed batches may not be of interest, since they would not be ready for shipment. Similarly, if you needed to calculate the number of items that could be produced from a given amount of raw materials, partial items would be of no interest. In both examples, you would not want the number rounded; you would simply want to truncate the decimal portion of the number to look at the number of units. This can be handled with @INT.

The worksheet shows the use of @INT in calculating the number of wallets that can be created from different sized pieces of cowhide. Partial wallets are not of interest, since one hide will not necessarily match another.

```
D4: @INT(A4/$E$1)                                          READY

         A        B        C        D        E        F        G        H
1  Cowhide needed for 1 wallet =        0.6789 sq. ft.
2
3  Available sizes              Wallets Produced
4         1                          1
5         5                          7
6        10                         14
7        15                         22
8        20                         29
9        25                         36
10
```

## Note

The @INT function can be used with @NOW to eliminate the time portion of the serial date and time number. @INT (@NOW) will return only the serial date number, since the time portion of the entry will be truncated.

## @LN

The @LN function returns the natural log of a number.

### Format

@LN(*number*)

### Arguments

| | |
|---|---|
| *number* | Any value greater than zero. If number is less than 0, ERR will be returned. |

### Use

Natural logarithms are logarithms to the base e, where e is approximately 2.718282. @LN is the inverse of @EXP, which means that you can incorporate e in any calculation with @EXP(1). @LN(@EXP(4)) equals 4, and @EXP(@LN(8)) equals 8. The primary use of logarithms is to make complex calculations less complex. A few examples follow:

@LN(9) equals 2.197224

@LN(1.5) equals 0.405465

## @LOG

The @LOG function computes the base 10 logarithm of a number.

### Format

@LOG(*number*)

### Arguments

*number*     Any value greater than zero. If number is less than 0, ERR will be returned.

### Use

Like natural logs, base 10 logs are primarily used in scientific or other complex calculations where the rules of logarithms can be used to simplify the math involved. The results returned by 1-2-3 from a few examples of @LOG are as follows:

@LOG(10) equals 1

@LOG(100) equals 2

@LOG(190) equals 2.278753

## @MOD

The @MOD function returns the modulus or remainder when a number is divided by a divisor number.

### Format

@MOD(*number,divisor*)

### Arguments

*number*     any positive or negative number or a reference to one.

*divisor*    any number other than zero used to divide number, as in number/divisor.

### Use

The @MOD function, which provides the remainder from dividing number by divisor, is useful in a variety of situations, although creativity is often required to see the applications. For example, as the following worksheet shows, you can use @MOD to determine how many parts will be left over after building the maximum number of complete items from the parts in an inventory. If you are building windmills that each require 12 blades and you have 750 blades on hand, @MOD(750,12) will let you know that you will have 6 blades left over. To determine how many complete windmills can be built, you can use @INT(750/12).

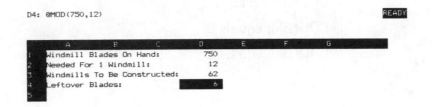

### Note

This function can be used in conjunction with the date functions covered earlier in the chapter to determine the day of the week. @MOD(@NOW,7) will return a value between 0 and 6, since the @MOD function returns the remainder from a division. If the result is 0, the day is Saturday, and if the result is 6, the day is Friday. Each of the other days is represented by one of the other numbers between 0 and 6.

## @PI

The @PI function returns an approximation of the constant $\pi$ or 3.14159265. The format of the function is simply @PI, since the function does not require any arguments.

## Use

@PI is used frequently in geometric problems involving circumference and area. The circumference of (distance around) a circle is 2*@PI*radius. Given a circle with a radius of 5", you could find the circumference of 31.4 using this formula, as shown here.

```
A1: 2*@PI*5                                                    READY

        A        B      C      D      E      F      G      H
1   31.41592
2
```

## @RAND

The @RAND function generates random numbers between 0 and 1. The format of the function is just @RAND, since it has no arguments.

### Use

This function is useful for generating test data for simulations. Each time the worksheet is recalculated, the @RAND function will take on a new value. You can create rows and columns of a worksheet with this function to generate data for queueing theory problems or other applications. Each @RAND will be a different number, since 1-2-3 uses 15 decimal digits for these numbers.

The worksheet shows numbers generated with the @RAND function. You can control the range of the random number by multiplying the result by a number or adding a number to it. Multiplying @RAND by a factor will raise the upper limit to the number you are multiplying by. @RAND*100 will provide random numbers between 0 and 100. Adding a fixed number to @RAND raises the lower limit. @RAND*100+50 generates random numbers between 50 and 150.

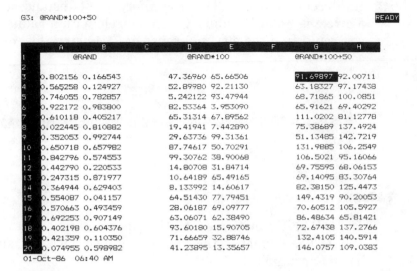

```
G3:  @RAND*100+50                                            READY

        A        B        C        D        E        F        G        H
1            @RAND                    @RAND*100              @RAND*100+50
2
3    0.802156 0.166543          47.36960 65.66506       91.69897 92.00711
4    0.565258 0.124927          52.89980 92.21130       63.18327 97.17438
5    0.746055 0.782857          5.242122 93.47944       68.71865 100.0851
6    0.922172 0.983800          82.53364 3.953090       65.91621 69.40292
7    0.610118 0.405217          65.31314 67.89562       111.0202 81.12778
8    0.022445 0.810882          19.41941 7.442890       75.38689 137.4924
9    0.352053 0.992744          29.63736 99.31361       51.13485 142.7219
10   0.650718 0.657982          87.74617 50.70291       131.9885 106.2549
11   0.842796 0.574553          99.30762 38.90068       106.5021 95.16066
12   0.442790 0.220533          14.80708 31.84714       69.75595 68.06153
13   0.247315 0.871977          10.64189 65.49165       69.14095 83.30764
14   0.364944 0.629403          8.133992 14.60617       82.38150 125.4473
15   0.554087 0.041157          64.51430 77.79451       149.4319 90.20053
16   0.570663 0.493459          28.06187 69.09777       70.60512 105.5927
17   0.692253 0.907149          63.06071 62.38490       86.48634 65.81421
18   0.402198 0.604376          93.60180 15.90705       72.67438 137.2766
19   0.421359 0.110350          71.66659 32.88746       132.4105 140.5914
20   0.074955 0.598982          41.23895 13.35657       146.0757 109.0383
01-Oct-86   06:40 AM
```

## @ROUND

The @ROUND function is used to round a number in internal storage to a specified number of decimal places.

### Format

@ROUND(*number to be rounded,place of rounding*)

### Arguments

*number to be rounded*      any value or reference to a value that you want rounded to a specified number of places.

*place of rounding*      the number of places to the right or left of the decimal point where rounding should occur. A digit of five or higher in this location will cause the number

**342**                                                       1-2-3: The Complete Reference to the left to be increased by one. Using 0 for the place of rounding indicates that you want to round to the nearest whole number. Positive numbers indicate rounding to the right of the decimal point, with each higher number moving further to the right. Negative numbers start at the tens position and move further to the left in identifying the place of rounding. For example, Figure 7-22 shows the number 12345.678123 rounded to varying numbers of decimal places in column B, using the formulas in column C.

## Use

1-2-3 will allow you to display numbers in rounded form by specifying the number of decimal places you wish to see with

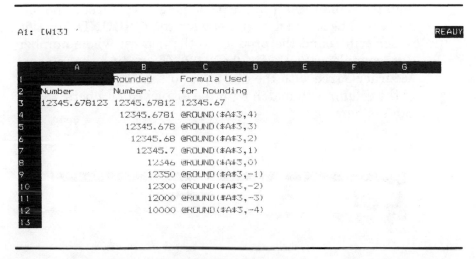

**Figure 7-22.**     Using @ROUND

the Format options (/Worksheet Global Format or /Range Format), but the full accuracy of the original number, with all its decimal places, is maintained internally. This can cause totals at the bottom of a column seemingly to not agree with the display, since the numbers in the column are displayed as rounded but the internal number has greater decimal accuracy. When all this additional accuracy is summed, it can make the total disagree with the display you see.

The following worksheet shows this discrepancy in column E.

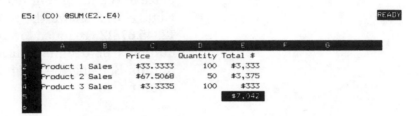

The figures in column E are a product of column C and column D but are displayed as currency with zero decimal places. The column E figures alone suggest that the total should be $7,041, not the $7,042 that is shown. The difference of 1 is due to the rounding discrepancy. To solve this problem, more than just a product formula is required. The formula will become an argument for the @ROUND function which will round the product to the nearest whole number (for example, @ROUND(C2*D2,0)). This makes the internal accuracy agree with the display, and the sum at the bottom of the column will match with the displayed numbers, as you can see here.

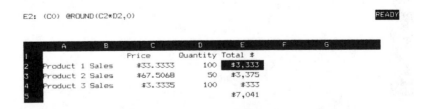

Often a complex worksheet model will require that the

@ROUND function be used with many of the formulas in the worksheet. To use it, follow the same procedure as shown in the preceding example, making each formula an argument for the @ROUND function.

## @SIN

The @SIN function returns the sine of an angle.

### Format

@SIN(*number*)

### Arguments

    *number*    a number representing the radians in an angle.

### Use

The @SIN function is used when you have the measurement of an angle in radians and want to determine the sine of the angle. You can use this information to help you make other determinations regarding physical aspects of a problem, such as length or other angles. The example that follows provides one potential application.

The diagram in Figure 7-23 shows a terrain containing a large swampy area that blocks a road crew from traversing the path from point C to point B. They know that the distance from A to C is 100 meters. If they can determine the distance from B to C, they will be able to use that number in the Pythagorean theorem to determine the distance from point A to point B. Their entire distance traveled to avoid the swamp would be C to A, then A to B. The angle ACB is 30 degrees.

To calculate the distance from C to B, the crew could use the formula SIN(30)=100/x. Using the @SIN function to determine the sine of 30, they would get .5 if it is recorded as

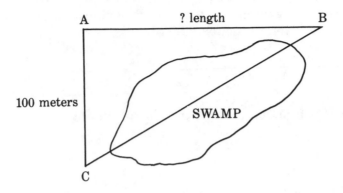

A ? length B

100 meters

SWAMP

C

**Figure 7-23.** Going around the swamp

@SIN(30*@PI/180). The @PI/180 converts 30 degrees to the appropriate number of radians. The distance then is 100/.5 or 200 meters. Using the Pythagorean theorem, $a^2=b^2+c^2$, they get $200^2=100^2+s^2$. This means that 40,000 equals 10,000 plus the unknown side squared. The side is thus equal to the square root of 30,000, which they can find with @SQRT(30,000). This function returns 173.2, so the distance from A to B is 173.2 meters.

## @SQRT

The @SQRT function will determine the square root of any positive number.

**Format**

@SQRT(*number*)

## Arguments

*number*      any positive integer included in the function or stored in a cell and referenced with a cell address or range name. If number is negative, ERR will be returned.

## Use

A number of statistical calculations, the Pythagorean theorem, and economic order quantity all require square root calculations. Here are a few examples of the way the square root function operates:

@SQRT(9) equals 3

@SQRT(64) equals 8

@SQRT(100) equals 10

# @TAN

The @TAN function returns the tangent of an angle.

## Format

@TAN(*number*)

## Arguments

*number*      a number representing the radians in an angle.

## Use

The @TAN function returns the tangent, a value useful in solving trigonometric problems. The diagram in Figure 7-24

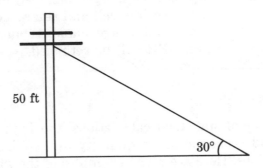

**Figure 7-24.** Guide wires for high tension power lines

shows the use of the function to determine the distance of guide wires for high tension electric wires. The electric company has high tension wires at the top of a pole 50 feet high and wants to install guide wires from the top of the pole at a 30-degree angle with the ground. The tangent function can be used to determine the distance away from the high tension wires that the guide wires should be attached. The tangent of 30 must be calculated, and, since the angle was measured in degrees, it must also be converted to radians. The formula thus becomes @TAN(30*@PI/180). The height of 50 feet is divided by the result of .5774 to provide a distance of 87 feet, as you can see here.

## The Simple Logical Operators

Simple logical operators are used to compare two or more values. The basic conditions you can check for with these operators are equal to, greater than, and less than. The latter two conditions can also be used in combination with the first condition. The simple logical operators and their meanings are as follows:

| | |
|---|---|
| = | equal to |
| > | greater than |
| < | less than |
| >= | greater than or equal to |
| <= | less than or equal to |
| <> | not equal to |

All the simple logical operators have the same evaluation priority. They will be evaluated from left to right in an expression.

## Logical Functions

1-2-3's logical functions allow you to build conditional features into your models. These functions return logical (true or false) values as the result of condition tests that they perform. A value of 0 means False, and a value of 1 means True.

Some of the logical functions work with ERR (error) and NA (not available). Both of these values are regarded as

## The Compound Logical Operators

Compound logical operators can be used to join two logical expressions or to negate an expression. The compound logical operators and a sample use for each one follow.

#AND#    C1=2#AND#D1=7 Both condition C1=2 and condition D1=7 must be true for this expression to evaluate as true.

#OR#    C1=2#OR#D1=7 If either condition is true, the statement evaluates as true.

#NOT#    #NOT#C1=3 This statement negates C1=3. The #NOT# operator has priority over the other two compound operators.

---

numeric and can be tested. This is a particularly important feature because of the ability of NA and ERR to ripple through all the formulas on a worksheet. As an example, if NA is used to flag a missing grade for a student, that student's average will be shown as NA, and when statistics for all students are combined, these total values will also take on the value NA. @ISERR, @ISNA, @ISNUMBER, and @ISSTRING allow you to check for ERR and NA values and stop their effect on the remainder of the worksheet cells by substituting a value of zero for them.

The logical functions frequently use logical operators. For example, @IF(A2<>5,3,6) uses a simple operator, and @IF(A1=1#AND#B3=7,5,2) uses a complex operator. These operators were covered in Chapter 3 in detail and are summarized here in the boxes called "The Simple Logical Operators" and "The Complex Logical Operators."

# @FALSE

The @FALSE function always returns the logical value 0, permitting you to use it to avoid ambiguity in formulas. @FALSE does not use any arguments.

## Use

The @FALSE function is a substitute for the number 0 in formulas. It may seem a lot quicker to type 0 than to type the function, but the function is self-documenting and indicates that you want to set up a logical false condition. As an example, @IF(A3=10,"A3 is equal to 10",@FALSE). If A3 is equal to 10, the string "A3 is equal to 10" will be stored in the cell. If A3 is not equal to 10, a 0 will be stored in the cell.

The following worksheet shows @FALSE and its counterpart @TRUE used to determine whether the number of items ordered and the number billed are equal. The formula in D3 checks the numbers ordered and billed for equality and places @TRUE or @FALSE as the value in the cell accordingly. @FALSE will display as 0 and @TRUE as 1. You can then use these 0s and 1s to determine how many discrepancies were in the orders. The @COUNT function is used to get an item count for the number of entries in C3..C6, which is 4. This function is placed in C7 as @COUNT(C3..C6). @SUM is then used to total the 0s and 1s, returning 3, in D7. Lastly, G9 contains a formula that subtracts D7 from C7 (+C7−D7), producing a value of 1— that is, a discrepancy between number ordered and number billed exists for one product.

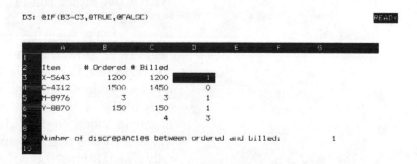

D3: @IF(B3=C3,@TRUE,@FALSE)        READY

| | A | B | C | D | E | F | G |
|---|---|---|---|---|---|---|---|
| 1 | | | | | | | |
| 2 | Item | # Ordered | # Billed | | | | |
| 3 | X-5643 | 1200 | 1200 | 1 | | | |
| 4 | C-4312 | 1500 | 1450 | 0 | | | |
| 5 | M-8976 | 3 | 3 | 1 | | | |
| 6 | Y-8870 | 150 | 150 | 1 | | | |
| 7 | | | 4 | 3 | | | |
| 8 | | | | | | | |
| 9 | Number of discrepancies between ordered and billed: | | | | | | 1 |
| 10 | | | | | | | |

## @IF

The @IF function permits you to test a logical condition to determine the appropriate value for a cell.

### Format

@IF(*condition to be tested,value if true,value if false*)

### Arguments

*condition to be tested*   any logical expression that can be evaluated as true or false. Examples are A1>=4, D2=H3, and A2+D3<85. The first expression will return a value of true only if A4 contains a value greater than or equal to 4. When this condition is met, the cell containing the @IF will take on the value for true conditions (1); otherwise, it will take on the value for false (0).

The logical IF statement can also work with compound conditions joined by #OR# and #AND#. With #AND#, both conditions must be true in order for the True value to be used for the cell. With #OR#, either condition may be true to produce the True value. #NOT# can be used to negate a condition. For example, #NOT#(Sales>100000) is equivalent to Sales<=100000. D1>8 #AND#H3=4 means that the numeric value in D1 must be greater than 8 and the numeric value in H3 must be equal to 4 in order for the function to return a value of True.

*value if true*    the value the cell containing the @IF statement will assume if the condition is true. This can be either a value or a label. When labels are included in the @IF statement, they must be enclosed in double quotation marks. If they are stored in a cell, they can be referenced with a cell address or range name. String formulas are also acceptable as labels. Value entries can be numbers, formulas, or references to cells containing numbers or formulas.

*value if false*   the value the cell containing the @IF statement will assume if the condition is false. All the conditions listed under value if true also apply here. Release 2 allows strings to be used with the logical IF condition. Numbers and blanks in cells involved in the condition test can cause error, however. For example, the statement @IF(A1="TEN", "TRUE","FALSE") will result in TRUE if A1 contains the label TEN, FALSE if A1 contains any other label entry, and ERR if A1 contains either a blank or a numeric value. Changing the condition to @IF(A1=10,"TRUE", "FALSE") will result in TRUE if A1 contains the value 10, FALSE if A1 contains any other

number or is blank, and ERR if
A1 contains a label.

**Use**

@IF is one of the most powerful built-in functions because it
allows you to get around the limitation of having to have only
one entry in a cell. Now you can set up two different values for
a cell and determine which one to use, based on other conditions in your worksheet. You can use this function to establish
two discount levels, commission structures, payroll deductions,
or anything else requiring more than one alternative.

1-2-3 allows you to nest conditions several levels deep,
that is, use a second @IF statement for the true and/or false
value in the original @IF. As an example, you might want to
determine whether a purchase is made by cash or credit and
have a code of 1 for cash, making the assumption that entries
without a 1 are credit sales. Once the type of sale is determined, you might want to check the amount of the sale to see
if it is over the minimum for a discount. The statement
might be coded as

@IF(TYPE=1,@IF(SALE>1000,.05,.02),@IF(SALE>2500,
.04,.01))

if TYPE and SALE were named ranges. Regardless of the
value for TYPE or SALE, the cell will contain a discount
amount, but the amount will depend on the value of both variables. The following chart shows the appropriate discounts.

| Type = 1 | Discount |
|---|---|
| Sale > 1000 | .05 |
| Sale <= 1000 | .02 |
| Type <> 1 | |
| Sale > 2500 | .04 |
| Sale <= 2500 | .01 |

As another example, let's look at a projection for total
salary expenses that uses the logical @IF function to deter-

mine allowances for FICA and FUTA taxes. The first part of the model, which does not involve functions, is shown in Figure 7-25. Except for column T, where the salary computation is entered, all the entries in this section of the model are label or value entries. The formula in T4 is as follows:

$$((R4-1)*(Q4/12))+((12-(R4-1))*(1+S4)*(Q4/12))$$

The purpose of this rather cumbersome formula is to compute next year's salary expense for the individual, based on the month of increase and the percentage increase that has been given. The essence of the formula is to multiply the months at the old salary times the old monthly salary and add to that the months at the new salary times the new monthly salary.

The @IF function becomes important in the second section of the model, which is shown in Figure 7-26. The values for benefits in column U are calculated by a simple formula that multiplies the projected salary by a flat percentage for

---

T4:  (C2) [W13]  ((R4−1)*(Q4/12))+((12−(R4−1))*(1+S4)*(Q4/12))                   READY

| | P | Q | R | S | T |
|---|---|---|---|---|---|
| 1 | | | | | |
| 2 | Name | Base Salary | Inc. Mo. | % INC | 1985 Salary |
| 3 | | | | | |
| 4 | Jones, Ray | $25,000.00 | 2 | 5.00% | $26,145.83 |
| 5 | Larkin, Mary | $29,000.00 | 3 | 7.00% | $30,691.67 |
| 6 | Harris, John | $15,000.00 | 6 | 5.00% | $15,437.50 |
| 7 | Parson, Mary | $18,000.00 | 9 | 4.00% | $18,240.00 |
| 8 | Smith, Jim | $23,000.00 | 4 | 7.00% | $24,207.50 |
| 9 | Harker, Pat | $35,000.00 | 10 | 4.00% | $35,350.00 |
| 10 | Jenkins, Paul | $45,000.00 | 2 | 9.00% | $48,712.50 |
| 11 | Jacobs, Norman | $12,000.00 | 1 | 4.00% | $12,480.00 |
| 12 | Merriman, Angela | $36,900.00 | 4 | 7.00% | $38,837.25 |
| 13 | Campbell, David | $40,000.00 | 1 | 10.00% | $44,000.00 |
| 14 | Campbell Keith | $32,000.00 | 1 | 9.00% | $34,880.00 |
| 15 | Stevenson, Mary | $18,900.00 | 11 | 7.50% | $19,136.25 |

**Figure 7-25.**   Projecting next year's salaries

V4: (C2) [W10] @IF(T4<42600,T4*0.0715,42600*0.0715)                    READY

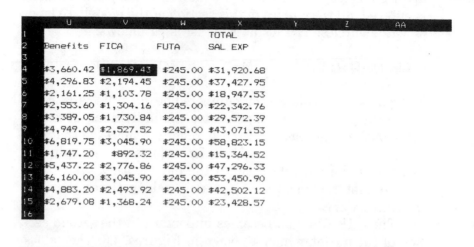

**Figure 7-26.**    Calculating FICA with the logical IF

benefits. The FICA formula in column V is the first one that puts the @IF function to work. It was a condition that compares the projected salary to a FICA cap amount (that is, the highest amount of salary on which an employer would pay FICA tax) of $42,600. If the projected salary is less than the cap amount, FICA tax will be calculated as the salary times 7.15%, but if the salary is equal to or greater than the cap amount, FICA tax will be paid on $42,600 at the rate of 7.15%.

The FUTA calculation, for unemployment tax, follows a similar pattern. The formula in W4 is

$$@IF(T4<7000,T4*.0305,7000*.0305)$$

This states that the FUTA tax will be 3.05% of salary if the salary is less than $7,000 but will be paid on the cap amount of $7,000 if the salary exceeds that amount.

# @ISERR

The @ISERR function checks for a value of ERR in a cell. It returns 1 if the cell contains an error and 0 if it does not.

## Format

@ISERR(*value*)

## Arguments

*value*      normally this is a reference to a cell value, although it may be a formula or a numeric value.

## Use

This function is seldom used by itself, although there is nothing to prevent you from doing so. It is normally used in conjunction with the @IF function to prevent values of ERR from rippling through a worksheet. The rippling occurs because any formula that references a cell with ERR will have a result of ERR.

The following worksheet shows ERR in column A for one of the prices. This ERR entry could have been generated by placing @ERR in the cell, or it could be the result of an incorrect formula. When this cell is referenced to supply the unit cost for multiplication, it causes ERR to appear in column C. Again, when the sum is taken in C8, ERR will be the result, since one of the cells in the sum range contains ERR.

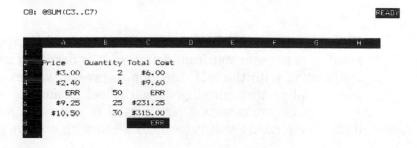

If you do not want ERR to ripple through the worksheet like this, use the @ISERR function in conjunction with @IF, as shown in the following worksheet. This allows you to confine ERR to one location.

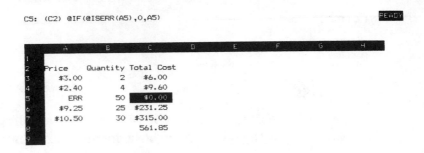

C5: (C2) @IF(@ISERR(A5),0,A5)                                    READY

|   | A | B | C | D | E | F | G | H |
|---|---|---|---|---|---|---|---|---|
| 1 | | | | | | | | |
| 2 | Price | Quantity | Total Cost | | | | | |
| 3 | $3.00 | 2 | $6.00 | | | | | |
| 4 | $2.40 | 4 | $9.60 | | | | | |
| 5 | ERR | 50 | $0.00 | | | | | |
| 6 | $9.25 | 25 | $231.25 | | | | | |
| 7 | $10.50 | 30 | $315.00 | | | | | |
| 8 | | | 561.85 | | | | | |
| 9 | | | | | | | | |

## @ISNA

The @ISNA function allows you to check for a value of NA in a cell. It returns 1 if the cell contains NA and zero if it does not.

### Format

@ISNA(*value*)

### Arguments

*value*    normally this is a reference to a cell value, although it may be a formula or a numeric value.

### Use

This function is seldom used by itself, although there is nothing to prevent you from doing so. It is normally used in conjunction with the @IF function to prevent values of NA from rippling through all your worksheet formulas.

In some worksheets @NA is used to represent missing data. Any formula that references a cell with a value of NA

E3: (C2) @IF(@ISNA(D3),"Missing Unit Price",C3*D3)    READY

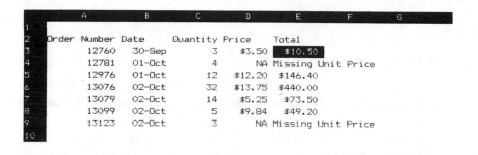

|   | A | B | C | D | E | F | G |
|---|---|---|---|---|---|---|---|
| 1 | | | | | | | |
| 2 | Order Number | Date | Quantity | Price | Total | | |
| 3 | 12760 | 30-Sep | 3 | $3.50 | $10.50 | | |
| 4 | 12781 | 01-Oct | 4 | NA | Missing Unit Price | | |
| 5 | 12976 | 01-Oct | 12 | $12.20 | $146.40 | | |
| 6 | 13076 | 02-Oct | 32 | $13.75 | $440.00 | | |
| 7 | 13079 | 02-Oct | 14 | $5.25 | $73.50 | | |
| 8 | 13099 | 02-Oct | 5 | $9.84 | $49.20 | | |
| 9 | 13123 | 02-Oct | 3 | NA | Missing Unit Price | | |
| 10 | | | | | | | |

**Figure 7-27.** Checking for missing data

will produce a result of NA. If you would like to prevent the NA value from carrying forward in this way, you can check for the value NA and substitute a zero or some other value, or you can display an error message to show that the value is missing.

Figure 7-27 presents a sample use of the @ISNA function combined with @IF. The @IF function checks the condition @ISNA(D3). If D3 is equal to NA, the condition will be considered true because @ISNA will evaluate as 1. On a true condition, the error message "Missing Unit Price" will display. If D3 is not equal to NA, column E will contain the result of column C times column D.

## @ISNUMBER

The @ISNUMBER function allows you to check for a numeric value in a cell. It returns 1 if the cell contains a number and 0 if it does not.

### Format

@ISNUMBER(*value*)

## Arguments

*value*  normally this is a reference to a cell value, although it may be a formula or a numeric value.

## Use

This function is seldom used by itself, although there is nothing to prevent you from doing so. As an example, an entry of @ISNUMBER(56) in a worksheet cell would return 1, whereas @ISNUMBER("56") would return 0. Formulas are regarded as numeric entries and will therefore return 1 with this function. @ISNUMBER is normally used in conjunction with the @IF function to check whether data entries are of the proper type.

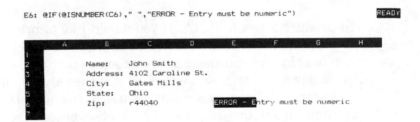

The worksheet shows name and address information entered in column C. If you want to check C6 to ensure that the zip code was entered as a numeric value, you could use the formula @IF(@ISNUMBER(C6)," ","ERROR - Entry must be numeric"). This formula states that if the entry in C6 is numeric, a blank will be placed in E6, where the formula is located. If the cell contains a nonnumeric value, as it does in the worksheet, an error message will appear. This type of error check allows the data entry operator to glance at column E to check quickly for error flags rather than having to study entries individually.

## @ISSTRING

The @ISSTRING function allows you to check for a string value in a cell. It returns 1 if the cell contains a string and 0 if it does not.

### Format

@ISSTRING(*value*)

### Arguments

*value*    normally this is a reference to a cell value, although it may be a formula or a string.

### Use

This function is seldom used by itself, although there is nothing to prevent you from doing so. It is normally used in conjunction with @IF to test for a string entry during data entry. @ISSTRING("John") will return 1, whereas @ISSTRING(56) will return 0. Since ERR and NA are regarded as numeric values, @ISSTRING(ERR) or @ISSTRING(NA) will return 0.

The worksheet shows name and address information entered in column C. If you would like to check C2..C5 to ensure that the data was entered as strings, formulas like the one in E2 will handle the task. E2 contains @IF(@ISSTRING(C2)," ","Entry is invalid - it is numeric"). This formula states that if the entry in C2 is a string, a blank will be placed in E2, where the formula is located. If the cell contains something other than a string value, as shown in the worksheet, an error message will appear. This type of error check can allow the data entry operator to glance at column E to check quickly for error flags rather than having to study entries individually.

E2: @IF(@ISSTRING(C2)," ","Entry is invalid — it is numeric")          READY

```
              A       B        C         D       E       F       G       H
1
2             Name:            3                 Entry is invalid — it is numeric
3             Address: 4102 Caroline St.
4             City:    Gates Mills
5             State:   Ohio
6             Zip:        44040
7
```

## @TRUE

The @TRUE function always returns the logical value 1, permitting you to use it to avoid ambiguity in formulas. The format of the function is @TRUE; it does not use any arguments.

### Use

The @TRUE function is a substitute for the number 1 in formulas. It may seem a lot quicker to type a 1 than to type the function, but the function is self-documenting and indicates that you want to set up a logical true condition. Here is an example:

@IF(A3=10,@TRUE,"A3 is not equal to 10")

The following worksheet shows @TRUE and its counterpart @FALSE used to determine whether the number of items ordered and the number billed are equal. The formula in D3 checks the numbers ordered and billed for equality and places @TRUE or @FALSE as the value in the cell accordingly. @TRUE will display as 1, @FALSE as 0. You can then use these 0s and 1s to determine how many discrepancies were in the orders. The @COUNT function is used to get an item count for the number of entries in C3..C6, which is 4. @SUM is then used to total the 0s and 1s, returning 3 in D7. Lastly, G9 contains a formula that subtracts D7 from C7 (+C7−D7). The value produced is 1, indicating a discrepancy in one of the orders.

```
D3: @IF(B3=C3,@TRUE,@FALSE)                                    READY
```

|    | A      | B        | C        | D   | E | F | G |
|----|--------|----------|----------|-----|---|---|---|
| 1  |        |          |          |     |   |   |   |
| 2  | Item   | # Ordered | # Billed |     |   |   |   |
| 3  | X-5643 | 1200     | 1200     | 1   |   |   |   |
| 4  | C-4312 | 1500     | 1450     | 0   |   |   |   |
| 5  | M-8976 | 3        | 3        | 1   |   |   |   |
| 6  | Y-8870 | 150      | 150      | 1   |   |   |   |
| 7  |        |          | 4        | 3   |   |   |   |
| 8  |        |          |          |     |   |   |   |
| 9  | Number of discrepancies between ordered and billed: | | | | 1 | | |
| 10 |        |          |          |     |   |   |   |

## Special Functions

1-2-3's special functions perform advanced calculations that do not fit neatly into any of the other categories. Some of them extend the logical features of the package by providing a table lookup feature and the ability to choose a value from a list of options. Others can be used to trap errors or determine the number of rows or columns in a range of cells. Still others are able to examine the contents of worksheet cells closely, providing information about the cell value or other attributes. This category should be thought of as a smorgasbord of sophisticated features that can add power to your models. You will want to examine the functions in this category one by one, gradually adding each of them to your repertoire of skills with the 1-2-3 package.

### @@

The @@ function provides an indirect addressing capability that lets you reference the value in a cell pointed to by the cell referenced in the argument of @@.

**Format**

@@(*cell*)

## Arguments

*cell*    an address of a cell containing a string value that looks like a cell address, such as R10, Z2, or B3; a range name, such as SALES or PROFIT; or a string formula that will create a string that looks like an address, such as "A"&"A"&"1"&"3", which creates AA13.

## Use

The indirect referencing capabilities this function provides can permit you to set up various values for key variables and easily change the one you wish to use.

The worksheet shows the annual sales and commissions for a sales staff. The base commission rate for the company is set at 7%, but if it has a profitable year, the company wants the ability to change the commission to a higher percentage. The @@ function provides an easy way to do this. You will notice that the formula in C2 is @@($A$10)*B2. A10 in turn contains a reference to one of the commissions in E1..E5. The entry should be a string variable in the form of a cell address. It is currently E4, so the commission is calculated using an 11% rate. Changing the commission to another rate merely requires a change to A10.

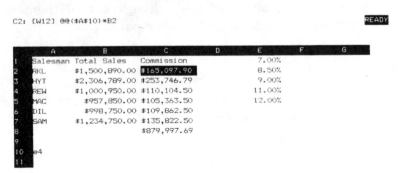

C2: [W12] @@($A$10)*B2                 READY

| | A | B | C | D | E | F | G |
|---|---|---|---|---|---|---|---|
| 1 | Salesman | Total Sales | Commission | | 7.00% | | |
| 2 | RKL | $1,500,890.00 | $165,097.90 | | 8.50% | | |
| 3 | HYT | $2,306,789.00 | $253,746.79 | | 9.00% | | |
| 4 | REW | $1,000,950.00 | $110,104.50 | | 11.00% | | |
| 5 | MAC | $957,850.00 | $105,363.50 | | 12.00% | | |
| 6 | DIL | $998,750.00 | $109,862.50 | | | | |
| 7 | SAM | $1,234,750.00 | $135,822.50 | | | | |
| 8 | | | $879,997.69 | | | | |
| 9 | | | | | | | |
| 10 | e4 | | | | | | |
| 11 | | | | | | | |

You can see in this second worksheet that when the entry in A10 is changed to E2, all the commissions are recalculated. Note that a lower-case e can be used to reference the cell address.

```
C2: [W12] @@($A$10)*B2                                          READY
```

```
        A         B           C          D        E        F       G
 1   Salesman  Total Sales  Commission            7.00%
 2   RKL       $1,500,890.00 $127,575.65           8.50%
 3   HYT       $2,306,789.00 $196,077.07           9.00%
 4   REW       $1,000,950.00  $85,080.75          11.00%
 5   MAC         $957,850.00  $81,417.25          12.00%
 6   DIL         $998,750.00  $84,893.75
 7   SAM       $1,234,750.00 $104,953.75
 8                           $679,998.22
 9
10   e2
11
```

## @CELL

The @CELL function allows you to examine characteristics of any worksheet cell, including the format, content, address, and other detail settings.

### Format

@CELL(*attribute string,range*)

### Arguments

*attribute string*    a character string corresponding to one of the attributes the @CELL function can check or a reference to a cell containing one. If the characters are entered in the function, they must be enclosed in double quotation marks. Acceptable attribute strings and the values they return are as follows:

| String Attribute | Result |
| --- | --- |
| address | the address of the current cell—for example, $K$3 |
| row | a number between 1 and 8192, representing the row number |
| col | a number between 1 and 256, representing the column number |

|  |  |
|---|---|
| **String Attribute** | **Result** (*continued*) |
| contents | the contents of the cell |
| format | the current format of the cell. The representation used for each of the formats follows:<br>C0-C15 for currency with 0 to 15 decimal places<br>D1 for DD-MM-YY<br>D2 for DD-MM<br>D3 for MM-YY<br>D4 for MM/DD/YY, DD/MM/YY, DD.MM.YY, or YY-MM-DD<br>D5 for MM.DD, DD/MM, DD.MM, or MM-DD<br>D6 for HH:MM:SS AM/PM<br>D7 for HH:MM AM/PM<br>D8 for HH:MM:SS, HH.MM.SS, HH,MM,SS, or HHhMMmSSs, with all formats using a 24-hour representation<br>D9 for HH:MM, HH.MM, HH,MM, or HHhMMm, with all formats using a 24-hour representation<br>F0-F15 for fixed with 0 to 15 decimal places<br>G for general<br>H for hidden<br>P0-P15 for percent with 0 to 15 decimal places<br>T for text<br>S0-S15 for scientific with 0 to 15 decimal places<br>blank if the cell is empty |
| prefix | label prefix for the cell unless the cell is blank or contains a value when a blank will appear. The label prefix ^ will appear for centered entries, ' for left justified entries, and " for right justified entries. |
| protect | protection status of the cell, with 1 representing Protected and 0 representing Unprotected |

| String<br>Attribute | Result (*continued*) |
|---|---|
| type | the type of data in the cell. The value types are b for blank, v for a numeric value, and l for a label. |
| width | a number between 1 and 240, representing the current cell width |
| *range* | a single or multiple cell range, such as A3..A3 or A2..D10. You must express the argument as a range. If the range refers to multiple cells, only the upper left cell will be used. Another way to express a single cell range is to precede the address with an exclamation point. For example, !A3 is equivalent to A3..A3. |

## Use

This function is primarily used in macros, although you may use it any time you wish to examine the contents of a cell closely. It can be combined with the @IF function to test for certain situations and take appropriate actions.

Figure 7-28 provides a look at all the @CELL options. The main entry for examination is in A1. @CELL functions are stored in column C and are shown again in column E as formulas so you can compare the entry and the results. The formula in C1 reads @CELL("contents",A1..A1) and returns the contents of 123.45, the exact number entered without the addition of formatting characters.

The entry in A11 allows you to check the prefix of a label entry. C11 contains the formula @CELL("prefix",A11..A11) and returns a ^, indicating center justification for the entry.

## @CELLPOINTER

The @CELLPOINTER function allows you to examine attributes of the cell where the cursor is located. If you move the cursor and recalculate, new results will be computed.

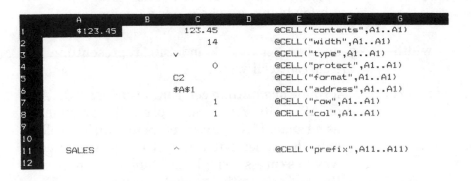

A1:  (C2) U [W14] 123.45                                                    READY

|    | A        | B | C       | D | E | F       | G                           |
|----|----------|---|---------|---|---|---------|-----------------------------|
| 1  | $123.45  |   | 123.45  |   |   | @CELL("contents",A1..A1)    |
| 2  |          |   | 14      |   |   | @CELL("width",A1..A1)       |
| 3  |          |   | v       |   |   | @CELL("type",A1..A1)        |
| 4  |          |   |      0  |   |   | @CELL("protect",A1..A1)     |
| 5  |          |   | C2      |   |   | @CELL("format",A1..A1)      |
| 6  |          |   | $A$1    |   |   | @CELL("address",A1..A1)     |
| 7  |          |   |      1  |   |   | @CELL("row",A1..A1)         |
| 8  |          |   |      1  |   |   | @CELL("col",A1..A1)         |
| 9  |          |   |         |   |   |                             |
| 10 |          |   |         |   |   |                             |
| 11 | SALES    |   | ^       |   |   | @CELL("prefix",A11..A11)    |
| 12 |          |   |         |   |   |                             |

**Figure 7-28.**    Using @CELL for a close-up look at a cell

**Format**

@CELLPOINTER(*attribute string*)

**Arguments**

*attribute string*    a character string corresponding to one of the attributes the @CELL-POINTER can check or a reference to a cell containing one. If characters are entered in the function, they must be enclosed in double quotation marks. Acceptable attribute strings and the values they return are as follows:

| String Attribute | Result (*continued*) |
|---|---|
| address | the address of the current cell—for example, $K$3 |
| row | a number between 1 and 8192, representing the row number |

| String Attribute | Result (*continued*) |
|---|---|

**col**     a number between 1 and 256, representing the column number

**contents**     the contents of the cell

**format**     the current format of the cell. The representation used for each of the formats follows:
C0-C15 for currency with 0 to 15 decimal places
D1 for DD-MMM-YY
D2 for DD-MMM
D3 for MMM-YY
D4 for MM/DD/YY, DD/MM/YY, DD.MM.YY, or YY-MM-DD
D5 for MM.DD, DD/MM, DD.MM, or MM-DD
D6 for HH:MM:SS AM/PM
D7 for HH:MM AM/PM
D8 for HH:MM:SS, HH.MM.SS, HH,MM,SS, or HHhMMmSSs, with all formats using a 24-hour representation
D9 for HH:MM, HH.MM, HH,MM, or HHhMMm, with all formats using a 24-hour representation
F0-F15 for fixed with 0 to 15 decimal places
G for general
H for hidden
P0-P15 for percent with 0 to 15 decimal places
T for text
S0-S15 for scientific with 0 to 15 decimal places
blank if the cell is empty

**prefix**     label prefix for the cell unless the cell is blank or contains a value when a blank will appear. The label prefix ^ will appear for centered entries, ' for left justified entries, and " for right justified entries.

| String Attribute | Result (*continued*) |
|---|---|
| protect | protection status of the cell, with 1 representing Protected and 0 representing Unprotected |
| type | the type of data in the cell. The value types are b for blank, v for a numeric value, and l for a label. |
| width | a number between 1 and 240, representing the current cell width |

## Use

This function is primarily used in macros, although you may use it any time you wish to examine the contents of a cell closely. It can be combined with the @IF function to test for certain situations and take appropriate actions.

Figure 7-29 provides a look at most of the @CELL-POINTER options. Since the cursor is located in A1, the results of the @CELLPOINTER function will provide information about A1. If you were to move the cursor to a new location and recalculate the worksheet with F9 (CALC),

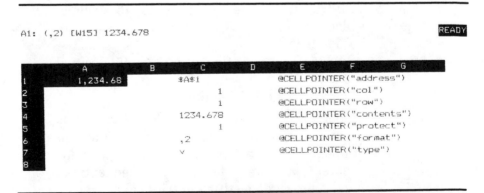

**Figure 7-29.**    Examining the current cell with @CELLPOINTER

you would get updated results. @CELLPOINTER functions are stored in column C and are shown again in column E as formulas so you can compare the entry and the results. For example, the formula in C1 reads @CELLPOINTER("address") and returns $A$1, the address of the current cell.

## @CHOOSE

The @CHOOSE function allows you to select a suitable value from a list of values.

### Format

@CHOOSE(*number,list*)

### Arguments

| | |
|---|---|
| *number* | the position number of the value from the list that you wish to use. The first value in the list has a position number of 0. This argument can be a number, formula, or a reference to either. Number cannot be greater than the number of values in the list. If number is not a whole number, 1-2-3 will use only the whole number portion for the argument. |
| *list* | a group of numeric or string values that are not limited in number, except that the @CHOOSE function must be able to be recorded in 240 characters. 1-2-3 will allow you to mix string and numeric values in one list. |

### Use

The @CHOOSE function is ideal when you have a set of codes in your data that are limited in number and consecutive. Since every number used to look up a number in the list must have a value in the list, the number of values in the list must range from 0 to the largest number used to find a value in the list. If you had codes of 1, 20, 300, and 750, @CHOOSE could not be used; you would have to turn to @VLOOKUP or @HLOOKUP. With consecutive and limited codes, however, @CHOOSE can provide a quick solution for supplying varying values.

A few examples of the @CHOOSE function and the values returned follow:

@CHOOSE(0,"Bill","Sally","Tom") equals Bill

@CHOOSE(1,"Bill","Sally","Tom") equals Sally

@CHOOSE(2,B10,A3,C2/4,A3*B4) equals the value C2/4

@CHOOSE(INTEREST,.09,.15,.08,.11) equals .15 when INTEREST equals 1.

The worksheet in Figure 7-30 shows the @CHOOSE function being used to determine a shipping cost from a warehouse location. Warehouse 1 adds $5.00 shipping charges, warehouse 3 adds $15.00, warehouse 4 adds $3.00, and warehouse 5 adds $20.00.

E2:  (C2)  @CHOOSE(A2,0,5,10,15,3,20)                                    READY

|   | A | B | C | D | E | F | G |
|---|---|---|---|---|---|---|---|
| 1 | Warehouse | Item | Quantity | Unit Price | Shipping | Total Cost | |
| 2 | 1 | 2302 | 3 | $50.00 | $5.00 | $155.00 | |
| 3 | 4 | 1710 | 2 | $20.00 | $3.00 | $43.00 | |
| 4 | 5 | 2350 | 15 | $15.00 | $20.00 | $245.00 | |
| 5 | 3 | 3125 | 13 | $3.00 | $15.00 | $54.00 | |
| 6 | 1 | 1245 | 4 | $120.00 | $5.00 | $485.00 | |
| 7 | 4 | 1111 | 12 | $75.00 | $3.00 | $903.00 | |
| 8 | 5 | 2302 | 4 | $50.00 | $20.00 | $220.00 | |
| 9 | 5 | 5562 | 2 | $100.00 | $20.00 | $220.00 | |
| 10 | | | | | | | |

**Figure 7-30.**    Choosing the correct value

The warehouse codes are in column A. The item numbers are in column B. The quantity and unit prices are in columns C and D respectively. The calculation for shipping cost requires the @CHOOSE formula. A dummy value must be used for warehouse 0, since all @CHOOSE lists start with 0. A $0 shipping charge will therefore be included in the list. The function is recorded in E2 as @CHOOSE(A2,0,5,10,15,3,20). The cell is formatted as currency, and the formula is copied down column E. Total cost in the model, shown in column F, is simply the entry in column C times the entry in column D with the addition of the shipping cost from column E.

## @COLS (Release 2)

The @COLS function is used to determine the number of columns within a specified range.

### Format

@COLS(*range*)

### Arguments

*range*  a cell range in the format A2..F7 or a range name

### Use

This function is used primarily with range names. For example, you may have a range of cells containing employee information across the columns. By knowing how many columns there were in the range, you could tell how many employees were listed. A few more examples may help you understand this function.

@COLS(A2..H3) equals 8

@COLS(EMPLOYEES) equals 26 when EMPLOYEES refers to the range A3..Z10

Figure 7-31 shows sales figures for a number of months. The range name SALES—STATS is used to refer to the data for all the months. You could tell how many months of data are in the range by using @COLS(SALES—STATS), as shown in D10.

## @ERR

The @ERR function is used to return the value ERR in a cell and any other cells that reference the cell. The format of the function is @ERR; it has no arguments.

### Use

This function is used to flag error conditions. You can use it to verify that two totals are equal, for example, if you combine it with @IF. If the two values are not equal, the cell containing the formula can be flagged with ERR. Such a formula might look like this:

@IF(A1=D2,0,@ERR)

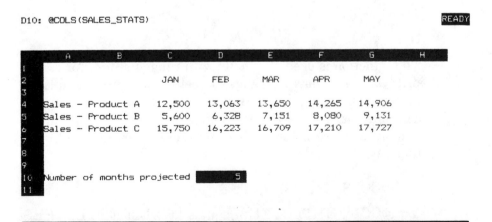

Figure 7-31.    Determining the number of columns

Another situation where @ERR would be useful might involve the verification of data input. An appropriate formula here might be written as @IF(A6<500,0,@ERR). ERR will appear if A6 is greater than or equal to 500. Any cells that reference the cell containing @ERR will also be given a value of ERR.

### Note

1-2-3 generates ERR on its own when errors are made in the entry or one of the arithmetic operations in a formula. The effect of both ERR conditions is the same, even though they are generated in different ways.

## @HLOOKUP

The @HLOOKUP function allows you to search a table for an appropriate value to use in your worksheet. The distinction between this function and the @VLOOKUP function is that @HLOOKUP stores its table across the worksheet in a horizontal orientation, whereas @VLOOKUP uses a vertical orientation for table values.

### Format

@HLOOKUP(*code to be looked up,table location,offset*)

### Arguments

*code to be looked up* — the entry in your worksheet that will be compared against the table entry. When numeric values are used, 1-2-3 looks for the largest value in the table that is not greater than the code. When string values are used (permissible with release 2), the search is for an exact match.

<table>
<tr><td>*table location*</td><td>a range containing at least two partial rows on the worksheet. A table is composed of a set of codes and one or more sets of return values in adjacent cells. It can be placed in any area of your worksheet. The top row in the range will contain the codes, and the subsequent rows will contain return values.</td></tr>
<tr><td>*offset*</td><td>a number that determines which row should be consulted for the return value when a matching code is found. The first row beneath the row of codes has an offset of 1, the second an offset of 2, and so on. Negative offset numbers will cause ERR to be returned, as will offset numbers that exceed the range established in table location. If desired, you may use an offset of zero to return the comparison code.</td></tr>
</table>

The following worksheet shows a table in A2..H3. The codes are in A2..H2, and the return values are in A3..H3.

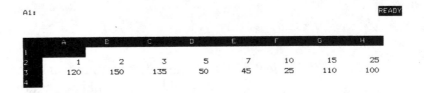

The process 1-2-3 uses for determining the value to be returned is as follows:

- The specified code is compared against the values in the top row of the table.

- The largest value in the top row of the table that is not greater than the code is considered a match.

- Offset is used to determine which value in the column that contains the matching table cell will be returned. If offset is zero, the matching code value itself is returned. If offset is one, the value below the matching value is returned, and so on.

- A code with a value less than the first value in the top row of the table will return ERR.

- A code value greater than the last value in the first row of the table will be considered to match the last value.

- If you are using label entries for codes and have label entries in the top row of the table, only exact matches will return table values. If the code to be looked up in the table is 3.5, the value adjacent to the 3 would be returned.

Building a table with numeric codes requires that they be in ascending sequence. They are not required to be consecutive numbers, however, nor do the gaps between numbers have to be of a consistent size. With label entries, the codes do not have to be in any special sequence within the table.

### Use

Tables are a powerful feature that can be used for everything from tax withholding amounts to shipping rates. They are especially valuable because they can allow you to look at potential changes in discount or commission structures with only a few changes to table values and no alterations in your worksheet formulas.

This worksheet shows a table located in cells C3..F7.

| | A | B | C | D | E | F | G | H |
|---|---|---|---|---|---|---|---|---|
| 1 | | | | | | | | |
| 2 | | | 0 | 4.5 | 15 | 99 | | |
| 3 | | | 11 | 22 | 33 | 44 | | |
| 4 | | | 1 | 2 | 3 | 4 | | |
| 5 | | | 55 | 66 | 77 | 88 | | |
| 6 | | | 0.05 | 0.09 | 0.04 | 0.1 | | |
| 7 | | | 9 | 8 | 7 | 6 | | |
| 8 | | | | | | | | |

The codes that follow would return the values shown from the table, assuming the offsets listed were provided:

| Code | Offset | Return Value |
|---|---|---|
| 4.5 | 1 | 22 |
| 11 | 2 | 2 |
| 15 | 3 | 77 |
| 0 | 1 | 11 |
| 99 | 1 | 44 |
| 4.5 | 0 | 4.5 |
| 11 | 1 | 22 |
| 15 | 2 | 3 |
| 102 | 1 | 44 |
| −1 | 1 | ERR |

Figure 7-32 provides an example of a purchase discount model for a wholesale store that has a minimum $100 order amount. The model relies on @HLOOKUP to compute the purchase discount. The table is placed in B11..F14, with the comparison codes in B11..F11. The discount rates are dependent on both the amount of the purchase and the purchase type. Purchase type 1 corresponds to cash and carry, which requires the lowest overhead and provides the highest discount structure. Purchase type 2 is cash but requires delivery and uses a lower discount structure. The lowest discount structure of all is for credit sales. The purchase type will be used as the offset code to access the proper row of the table. The comparison code in the table will be chosen based on the purchase amount in column C.

The formula required to look up the first discount is @HLOOKUP(C3,$B$11..$F$14,B3)*C3. This formula looks

D3: (C2) @HLOOKUP(C3,$B$11..$F$14,B3)*C3                    READY

| | A | B | C | D | E | F | G |
|---|---|---|---|---|---|---|---|
| 1 | Customer | Purchase | Purchase | | Net | | |
| 2 | ID Number | Type | Amount | Discount | Due | | |
| 3 | 23-789 | 3 | $500.00 | $15.00 | $485.00 | | |
| 4 | 12-987 | 2 | $100.00 | $3.00 | $97.00 | | |
| 5 | 56 435 | 2 | $175.00 | $5.25 | $169.75 | | |
| 6 | 54-345 | 3 | $980.00 | $29.40 | $950.60 | | |
| 7 | 23-567 | 1 | $1,200.00 | $96.00 | $1,104.00 | | |
| 8 | 12-333 | 1 | $6,000.00 | $540.00 | $5,460.00 | | |
| 9 | 21-999 | 3 | $10,000.00 | $500.00 | $9,500.00 | | |
| 10 | | | | | | | |
| 11 | | 100 | 500 | 1000 | 5000 | 10000 | |
| 12 | 1 | 5.00% | 7.00% | 8.00% | 9.00% | 10.00% | |
| 13 | 2 | 3.00% | 4.00% | 5.00% | 5.00% | 6.00% | |
| 14 | 3 | 3.00% | 3.00% | 3.00% | 5.00% | 5.00% | |
| 15 | | | | | | | |

**Figure 7-32.**    Horizontal table lookup

up the code in C3 in a table located in B11 through F14. The
$s indicate the absolute addresses for the table range and
thus permit the formula to be copied down the page for calculation of the remaining discounts. The offset for the table is
B3, the purchase type. The value returned is multiplied by
the purchase amount to compute the discount. For this first
entry this is 3% times $500, or $15. The net due is obtained by
subtracting the discount (D3) from the purchase amount
(C3). The remaining entries are obtained by copying from
D3..E3 to D4..D9.

## @INDEX (Release 2)

The @INDEX function allows you to retrieve a value from a
table of codes by specifying the row and column number of
the entry you wish to access.

**Format**

@INDEX(*table location,column number,row number*)

**Arguments**

| | |
|---|---|
| *table location* | the location of the table of codes to be accessed by this function. Unlike the lookup functions, @INDEX does not use a comparison value to access the codes. You must specify a row and column address to obtain the code of your choice. |
| *column number* | the number of the column in the table from which you want to obtain a code. The leftmost column in the table range is column 0, with the numbers increasing by 1 for each column to the right that you move. The column that you specify must be within the valid range established for the table. If the number you supply is not a whole number, the decimal portion will be truncated. |
| *row number* | the number of the row in the table from which you wish to obtain a code. The upper row in the table is considered to be row zero. The row number specified must be in the relevant range for the table. If it is not a whole number, the decimal portion of the number will be truncated. The code returned will be the one at the intersection of the row and column you have specified. |

**Use**

The @INDEX function can be used whenever your data values can be used to access the proper row and column of a table. This type of function would work fine for quoting insurance rates, shipping charges, and any other calculation where you could specify the exact code from the table you wished to access.

Figure 7-33 provides an example of a commission application that uses total sales and region values to index the proper commission percentage. The table is located in A1..G3. The row from which the return value will be selected will be the sales region minus 1, since tables begin with row 0, not row 1. The column from which the return value will be selected is calculated as (Total Sales Amount divided by $10,000) minus 1. The percent obtained from this function will be multiplied by the sales figure to determine commissions.

## @NA

This function causes NA, meaning "not available," to appear in the cell where this function is entered as well as in all cells that reference it. The format for the function is @NA; it has no arguments.

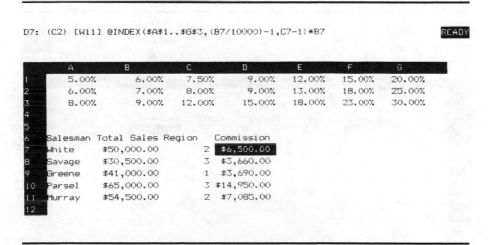

Figure 7-33.    Finding the appropriate value with @INDEX

## Use

The @NA function is used when data is not available for entry in a cell. It serves as a flag for data that must be entered before correct model results can be computed. @NA entered in óne worksheet cell can ripple through a worksheet, since every cell that references a cell containing @NA will also turn to NA.

The @NA function would be useful for an instructor recording student grades, to give one example. All students who missed an exam would have @NA rather than a score recorded. Figure 7-34 shows the effect on the grade point average for students with missing grades. At the end of the semester, the instructor may change all grades that are still NA to 0.

## Note

The label NA entered in a cell is not equivalent to entering @NA, which produces a numeric rather than a label entry.

---

F4:  (F1)  @AVG(B4..E4)                                                    READY

| | A | B | C | D | E | F | G |
|---|---|---|---|---|---|---|---|
| 1 | | | Fall Semester -- 1986 | | | | |
| 2 | | | | | | | |
| 3 | Student | Exam 1 | Exam 2 | Exam 3 | Final | Average | |
| 4 | B. Black | 75 | NA | 82 | 88 | NA | |
| 5 | S. Conners | 67 | 78 | 72 | 81 | 74.5 | |
| 6 | F. Dalton | 78 | 90 | 89 | 92 | 87.3 | |
| 7 | G. Limmer | 88 | 81 | 93 | 87 | 87.3 | |
| 8 | S. Melton | 67 | 55 | 40 | 60 | 55.5 | |
| 9 | P. Stock | 67 | 89 | NA | 78 | NA | |
| 10 | J. Zimmer | 91 | 82 | 75 | 89 | 84.3 | |
| 11 | | | | | | | |

---

**Figure 7-34.**    The impact of NA on formulas

## @ROWS (Release 2)

The @ROWS function is used to determine the number of rows within a specified range.

### Format

@ROWS(*range*)

### Arguments

*range*    a cell range in the format A2..F7 or a range name

### Use

This function is used primarily with range names. You may have a range of cells containing order information with the orders listed down the worksheet, for example. If all the order information was included in one range named ORDERS, you could tell how many orders there were with @ROWS (ORDERS). A few other examples may help to show how this function works.

@ROWS(A2..H3) equals 2
@ROWS(EMPLOYEES) equals 8 when EMPLOYEES refers to the range A3..Z10

The example worksheet shows the use of the @ROWS function to determine the number of orders. The range name ORDERS is assigned to A3..C6. Since the number of orders will be the same as the number of rows in the range, @ROWS (ORDERS) will provide the correct answer, as shown in B9.

B9: [W10] @ROWS(ORDERS)                                                                READY

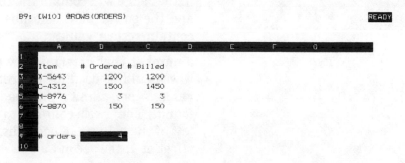

1-2-3 Built-in Functions

## @VLOOKUP

The @VLOOKUP function allows you to search a table for an appropriate value to use in your worksheet. The distinction between this function and the @HLOOKUP function is that @VLOOKUP stores its table down the worksheet in a vertical orientation, whereas @HLOOKUP uses a horizontal orientation for table values.

### Format

@VLOOKUP(*code to be looked up,table location,offset*)

### Arguments

| | |
|---|---|
| *code to be looked up* | the entry in your worksheet that will be compared against the table entry. When numeric values are used, 1-2-3 looks for the largest value in the table that is not greater than the code. When string values are used (permissible with release 2), the search is for an exact match. |
| *table location* | a range containing at least two partial columns on the worksheet. A table is composed of a set of codes and one or more sets of return values in adjacent cells and can be placed in any area of your worksheet. The left column in the range will contain the codes, and the subsequent columns will contain return values. |
| *offset* | a number that determines which row should be used for the return value when a matching code is found. The first column to the left of the column of codes has an offset of 1, the second an offset of |

2, and so on. Negative offset numbers will cause ERR to be returned, as will offset numbers that exceed the range established in table location. If desired, you may use an offset of zero to return the comparison code from the first column of the table.

The following worksheet shows a table in A2..D8.

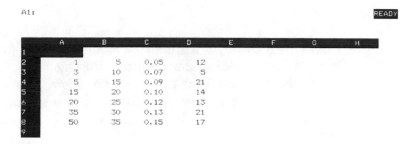

The codes are in A2..A8, and the return values are in B2..D8. The process 1-2-3 uses for determining the value to be returned is as follows:

• The specified code is compared against the values in the left column of the table.

• The largest value in the left column of the table that is not greater than the code is considered a match.

• Offset is used to determine which value in the row that contains the matching table cell will be returned. If offset is zero, the matching code value itself is returned. If offset is one, the value to the right of the matching value is returned, and so on.

• A code with a value less than the first value in the left column of the table will return ERR.

• A code value greater than the last value in the first column of the table will be considered to match the last value.

• If you are using label entries for codes and have label entries in the left column, only exact matches will return table values. If the code to be looked up in the table is 3.5, the value adjacent to the 3 would be returned.

Building a table with numeric codes requires that they be in ascending sequence. They are not required to be consecutive numbers, however, nor do the gaps between numbers have to be of a consistent size. With label entries, the codes do not have to be in any special sequence within the table.

## Use

Tables are a powerful feature that can be used for everything from tax withholding amounts to shipping rates. They are especially valuable because they can allow you to look at potential changes in discount or commission structures with only a few changes to table values and no alterations in your worksheet formulas.

Figure 7-35 provides an example of a portion of a model

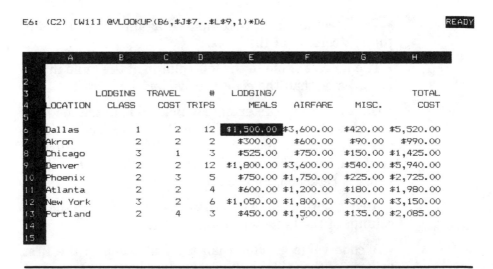

E6: (C2) [W11] @VLOOKUP(B6,$J$7..$L$9,1)*D6          READY

| LOCATION | LODGING CLASS | TRAVEL COST | # TRIPS | LODGING/ MEALS | AIRFARE | MISC. | TOTAL COST |
|---|---|---|---|---|---|---|---|
| Dallas | 1 | 2 | 12 | $1,500.00 | $3,600.00 | $420.00 | $5,520.00 |
| Akron | 2 | 2 | 2 | $300.00 | $600.00 | $90.00 | $990.00 |
| Chicago | 3 | 1 | 3 | $525.00 | $750.00 | $150.00 | $1,425.00 |
| Denver | 2 | 2 | 12 | $1,800.00 | $3,600.00 | $540.00 | $5,940.00 |
| Phoenix | 2 | 3 | 5 | $750.00 | $1,750.00 | $225.00 | $2,725.00 |
| Atlanta | 2 | 2 | 4 | $600.00 | $1,200.00 | $180.00 | $1,980.00 |
| New York | 3 | 2 | 6 | $1,050.00 | $1,800.00 | $300.00 | $3,150.00 |
| Portland | 2 | 4 | 3 | $450.00 | $1,500.00 | $135.00 | $2,085.00 |

**Figure 7-35.** An application for a vertical table

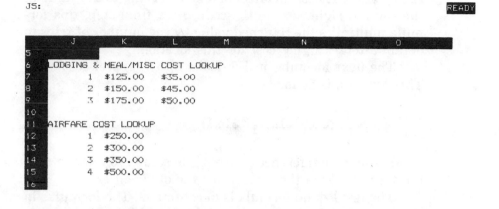

```
J5:                                                              READY

     J         K         L         M         N         O
5
6    LODGING & MEAL/MISC COST LOOKUP
7           1  $125.00   $35.00
8           2  $150.00   $45.00
9           3  $175.00   $50.00
10
11   AIRFARE COST LOOKUP
12          1  $250.00
13          2  $300.00
14          3  $350.00
15          4  $500.00
16
```

**Figure 7-36.** Vertical tables for the travel cost model

to project travel costs. The tables for this model are located in J7..L9 and J12..K15 (see Figure 7-36). The first table is designed to allow you to assign a code to a projected travel location that will provide an estimate of one night's meal and lodging costs for that location, as well as miscellaneous costs such as taxis, phone calls, and so on. The second table allows you to assign a second code to a location that will provide an estimate of the airfare costs for reaching that destination. Two tables are needed because the lodging and meal estimates and the travel cost estimates are based on different criteria.

The model in Figure 7-35 contains city names in column A. Column B contains a numeric code for lodging class that categorizes cities according to their relative living costs. Column C contains the numeric code for travel cost, which is assigned on the basis of distance from the origination point. Column D contains the number of trips to the location. This model assumes that all trips are for one night, but you could easily insert another column here to show variable numbers of nights.

The next column contains the first lookup formula. From the three arguments in the function you can see that it

looks up B6 in the table with the absolute address of $J$7..$L$9. It uses an offset of one, referring to the value in the column right next to the code. As a final step, this formula multiplies the returned value by the number of trips to obtain a total lodging cost for this location.

The next formula, in F6, looks up the travel cost code. This formula is as follows:

@VLOOKUP(C6,$J$12..$K$15,1)

Again the table reference address is absolute, so you can copy the formula down the column for the other cities.

The last lookup formula is in column G. The formulas in this column follow the pattern of the formula in G6, which is as follows:

@VLOOKUP(C6,$J$7..$L$9,2)

The difference between this formula and the first vertical lookup formula is that here the offset is two, indicating that the value two columns away from the code should be returned. Total travel costs for a location are obtained with @SUM(E6..G6).

All the formulas described for this model are valid for the other city entries. They will be adjusted automatically if /Copy is used to place them in the other locations.

## Statistical Functions

1-2-3's statistical functions perform their magic on lists of values. Frequently these lists are a contiguous range of cells on the worksheet. They can also be a series of individual values or a combination of range and individual values. Blank ranges can be included within the list, but all the values in the blank range will count as zeros. When a range has multiple cells, 1-2-3 will ignore cells containing blanks. If a single blank cell is used in the list, 1-2-3 will assign a 0 to the cell.

The majority of the statistical functions work only with numeric values. @COUNT is the exception, since it counts the number of nonblank cells in a list and will also accept string values.

## @AVG

The @AVG function finds the average of a list of values.

### Format

@AVG(*list*)

### Arguments

*list*    any set of numeric values. They can be individual cell references, individual values, or a range of cells. You can also combine the options in one list. Examples are @AVG(A2..A9,D4,L2) and @AVG (D4..D15). Note that the components in the list are separated by commas.

### Use

This worksheet uses @AVG to calculate the average bid received from vendors. The vendor bids are shown in B4..B11, and the formula is entered in B13 as @AVG(B4..B11).

```
B13: (C2) [W10] @AVG(B4..B11)                          READY
```

|  | A | B | C | D | E | F | G |
|---|---|---|---|---|---|---|---|
| 1 |  |  |  |  |  |  |  |
| 2 | VENDOR | BID |  |  |  |  |  |
| 3 |  |  |  |  |  |  |  |
| 4 | Saunders | $5,178.00 |  |  |  |  |  |
| 5 | Jacobs | $6,500.00 |  |  |  |  |  |
| 6 | Harris & Sons | $8,700.00 |  |  |  |  |  |
| 7 | Brownlowe | $4,100.00 |  |  |  |  |  |
| 8 | Wiggins | $3,900.00 |  |  |  |  |  |
| 9 | Stauffer | $8,100.00 |  |  |  |  |  |
| 10 | Trever & Co. | $5,600.00 |  |  |  |  |  |
| 11 | Bristol | $4,300.00 |  |  |  |  |  |
| 12 |  |  |  |  |  |  |  |
| 13 | ** AVERAGE ** | $5,097.25 |  |  |  |  |  |
| 14 | BID |  |  |  |  |  |  |
| 15 |  |  |  |  |  |  |  |

# @COUNT

The @COUNT function determines the number of nonblank entries in a list. A cell that contains a label prefix will still count as a nonblank, even though the cell displays as a blank.

## Format

@COUNT(*list*)

## Arguments

*list*    any set of numeric values. They can be individual cell references or a range of cells. You can also combine the two in one list. Examples are @COUNT(A2..A9,D4,L2) and @COUNT(D4..D15). Note that the components in the list are separated by commas.

## Use

The @COUNT function does not require numeric data. It will count all the nonblank entries in a list regardless of whether they are values or characters. The worksheet shows @COUNT used to count the number of employees. The name field is referenced for the count, using the following formula:

@COUNT(A4..A15)

B17: [W12] @COUNT(A4..A15)                                             READY

|   | A | B | C | D | E | F |
|---|---|---|---|---|---|---|
| 1 |  |  |  |  |  |  |
| 2 | Name | Base Salary | Inc. Mo. | % INC | 1985 Salary |  |
| 3 |  |  |  |  |  |  |
| 4 | Jones, Ray | $25,000.00 | 2 | 5.00% | $26,145.83 |  |
| 5 | Larkin, Mary | $29,000.00 | 3 | 7.00% | $30,691.67 |  |
| 6 | Harris, John | $15,000.00 | 6 | 5.00% | $15,437.50 |  |
| 7 | Parson, Mary | $18,000.00 | 9 | 4.00% | $18,240.00 |  |
| 8 | Smith, Jim | $23,000.00 | 4 | 7.00% | $24,207.50 |  |
| 9 | Harker, Pat | $35,000.00 | 10 | 4.00% | $35,350.00 |  |
| 10 | Jenkins, Paul | $45,000.00 | 2 | 9.00% | $48,712.50 |  |
| 11 | Jacobs, Norman | $12,000.00 | 1 | 4.00% | $12,480.00 |  |
| 12 | Merriman, Angela | $36,900.00 | 4 | 7.00% | $38,837.25 |  |
| 13 | Campbell, David | $40,000.00 | 1 | 10.00% | $44,000.00 |  |
| 14 | Campbell Keith | $32,000.00 | 1 | 9.00% | $34,880.00 |  |
| 15 | Stevenson, Mary | $18,900.00 | 11 | 7.50% | $19,136.25 |  |
| 16 |  |  |  |  |  |  |
| 17 | NUMBER OF EMPLOYEES: | 12 |  |  |  |  |
| 18 |  |  |  |  |  |  |
| 19 |  |  |  |  |  |  |
| 20 |  |  |  |  |  |  |

01-Oct-86   07:07 AM

# @MAX

The @MAX function searches a list of values and displays the largest value in the list.

## Format

@MAX(*list*)

## Arguments

*list*    any set of numeric values. They can be individual cell references, individual values, or a range of cells. You can also combine the options in one list. Examples are @MAX(A2..A9,D4,L2) and @MAX (D4..D15). Note that the components in the list are separated by commas.

## Use

The worksheet shows the @MAX function used to obtain the highest bid in a group of vendor bids. The bids are entered in B4..B11, with the corresponding vendor names in column A. The @MAX function is placed in B13 as @MAX(B4..B11). The maximum bid of $8,700.00 is returned by the function.

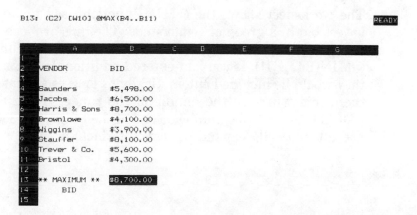

If you entered additional vendor bids, they would be included automatically as long as you inserted them somewhere in the middle of the range. If you added your entries at the beginning or end of the range, 1-2-3 would not automatically expand the range to include them.

## @MIN

The @MIN function searches a list of values and displays the smallest value in the list.

### Format

@MIN(*list*)

### Arguments

*list*    any set of numeric values. They can be individual cell references, individual values, or a range of cells. You can also combine the options in one list. Examples are @MIN(A2..A9,D4,L2) and @MIN (D4..D15). Note that the components in the list are separated by commas.

### Use

The worksheet shows the @MIN function used to find the lowest bid in a group of vendor bids. The bids are located in B4..B11, and the minimum is found with the function @MIN(B4..B11). If you had entered additional vendor bids, they would be included automatically as long as you inserted them somewhere in the middle of the range. If you added your entries at the beginning or end of the range, 1-2-3 would not automatically expand the range to include them.

B13: (C2) [W10] @MIN(B4..B11)

|    | A            | B          | C | D | E | F | G |
|----|--------------|------------|---|---|---|---|---|
| 1  |              |            |   |   |   |   |   |
| 2  | VENDOR       | BID        |   |   |   |   |   |
| 3  |              |            |   |   |   |   |   |
| 4  | Saunders     | $5,498.00  |   |   |   |   |   |
| 5  | Jacobs       | $6,500.00  |   |   |   |   |   |
| 6  | Harris & Sons| $8,700.00  |   |   |   |   |   |
| 7  | Brownlowe    | $4,100.00  |   |   |   |   |   |
| 8  | Wiggins      | $3,900.00  |   |   |   |   |   |
| 9  | Stauffer     | $8,100.00  |   |   |   |   |   |
| 10 | Trever & Co. | $5,600.00  |   |   |   |   |   |
| 11 | Bristol      | $4,300.00  |   |   |   |   |   |
| 12 |              |            |   |   |   |   |   |
| 13 | ** MINIMUM **| $3,900.00  |   |   |   |   |   |
| 14 |      BID     |            |   |   |   |   |   |
| 15 |              |            |   |   |   |   |   |

## @STD

The @STD function is used to determine the standard deviation of a set of values, or how much variation there is from the average of the values. It is the square root of the variance.

### Format

@STD(*list*)

### Arguments

*list*   any set of numeric values. They can be individual cell references or a range of cells. You can also combine the two in one list. Examples are @STD (A2..A9,15,L2) and @STD(D4..D15). Note that the components in the list are separated by commas. Blank cells within the list will be ignored, but label entries will be assigned a value of 0. The inclusion of label entries in this list can cause a problem, since @STD uses a count of the entries as part of its calculation.

## Use

The @STD function will determine the standard deviation when you have access to the values for the entire population — that is, all the values for the entire group you are studying. If you are measuring the deviation in the weight of packages filled in a plant, population would refer to *all* packages filled, not just a sample. If you are working with only a sample of the population, use the formula in the note that follows this discussion of the population standard deviation.

The purpose of the standard deviation calculation is to determine the amount of variation between individual values and the mean. Suppose, for example, that you look at the ages of your employees and determine that their average age is 40. This could mean that half of your employees were 39 and the other half 41, or it could mean that you had employees whose ages ranged from 18 to 65. The latter case would show a greater standard deviation because of the greater variance from the mean.

The @STD function is biased, since it uses a count as part of its calculations. Specifically, it uses the following formula:

$$\sqrt{\frac{\sum (x_i - \text{AVG})^2}{n}}$$

where $x_i$ is the ith item in the list and $n$ is the number of items in the list.

As an example, suppose that the Commemorative Bronze Company has made 50 replicas of antique bronze cash registers and wants to determine the standard deviation in the weight of these products. The worksheet shows the list of weights and the formula for the standard deviation.

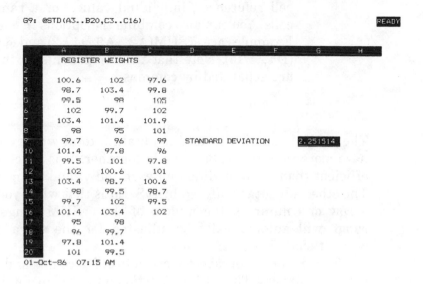

```
G9: @STD(A3..B20,C3..C16)                                          READY

        A          B         C         D         E       F       G       H
 1    REGISTER WEIGHTS
 2
 3    100.6        102       97.6
 4     98.7      103.4       99.8
 5     99.5         98        105
 6      102       99.7        102
 7    103.4      101.4      101.9
 8       98         95        101
 9     99.7         96         99    STANDARD DEVIATION     2.251514
10    101.4       97.8         96
11     99.5        101       97.8
12      102      100.6        101
13    103.4       98.7      100.6
14       98       99.5       98.7
15     99.7        102       99.5
16    101.4      103.4        102
17       95         98
18       96       99.7
19     97.8      101.4
20      101       99.5
01-Oct-86  07:15 AM
```

### Note

The @STD function is designed to calculate population standard deviation. If you want to calculate the sample standard deviation, you can create your own formula, as follows:

$$\frac{@SQRT(@COUNT(list)}{(@COUNT(list)-1))*@STD(list)}$$

## @SUM

The @SUM function totals a list of numeric values.

### Format

@SUM(*list*)

### Arguments

*list*      any set of numeric values. They can be individual cell references, individual values, or a range of cells. You can also combine the options in one list. Examples are @SUM(A2..A9,D4,L2) and @SUM (D4..D15). Note that the components in the list are separated by commas.

### Use

The @SUM function is used to obtain a total wherever you have more than two values to add together. It is much more efficient than using addition on each individual component. The other advantage offered by @SUM is that when you add a row or column in the middle of the @SUM range, the range will automatically be adjusted for the extra entry without changing the formula.

    The example worksheet shows a list of accounts and their current balances. The @SUM function was used to obtain the total, rather than a formula like +B4+B5+B6+B7..... @SUM(B4..B11) was entered in B13.

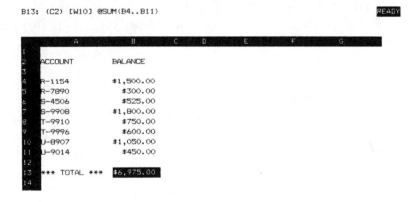

### @VAR

The @VAR function computes the variance of values in a population, or the amount the individual population values vary from the average.

**Format**

@VAR(*list*)


**Arguments**

*list*  any set of numeric values. They can be individual
        cell references or a range of cells. You can also
        combine the two in one list. Examples are
        @VAR(A2..A9,15,L2) and @VAR(D4..D15). Note
        that the components in the list are separated by
        commas. Blank cells within the list will be
        ignored, but label entries will be assigned a value
        of 0. The inclusion of label entries in this list can
        cause a problem because @VAR uses a count of
        the entries as part of its calculation.


**Use**

The @VAR function will determine the variance when you
have access to the values for the entire population—that is,
all the values for the entire group you are studying. If you
are measuring the deviation in the weight of packages filled
in a plant, population would refer to *all* packages filled, not
just a sample. If you are working with only a sample of the
population, use the formula in the note that follows this discussion of population variance.

The purpose of the variance calculation is to determine
the amount of variation between individual values and the
mean. Suppose, for example, that you look at the ages of your
employees and determine that their average age is 40. This
could mean that half of your employees were 39 and the other
half 41, or it could mean that their ages ranged from 18 to 65.
The latter case would show a greater variance because of the
greater dispersion from the mean. The variance is equal to
the standard deviation squared.

The @VAR function is biased, since it uses a count as
part of its calculation. Specifically, it uses the following
formula:

$$\frac{\sum (x_i - \text{AVG})^2}{n}$$

where $x_i$ is the ith item in the list and $n$ is the number of items in the list.

As an example, suppose that the Commemorative Bronze Company has made 50 replicas of antique bronze cash registers and wants to determine the variance in the weight of these products. The worksheet shows the list of weights and the formula for the variance.

```
F9: @VAR(A3..B20,C3..C16)                                          READY
```

```
         A         B         C         D        E        F        G        H
1            REGISTER WEIGHTS
2
3      100.6       102      97.6
4       98.7     103.4      99.8
5       99.5        98       105
6        102      99.7       102
7      103.4     101.4     101.9
8         98        95       101
9       99.7        96        99     VARIANCE      5.069316
10     101.4      97.8        96
11      99.5       101      97.8
12       102     100.6       101
13     103.4      98.7     100.6
14        98      99.5      98.7
15      99.7       102      99.5
16     101.4     103.4       102
17        95        98
18        96      99.7
19      97.8     101.4
20       101      99.5
01-Oct-86   07:18 AM
```

**Note**

The @VAR function is designed to calculate population variance. If you wish to calculate the sample variance, you can create your own formula, as follows:

$$\frac{@COUNT(list)}{(@COUNT(list)-1))*@VAR(list)}$$

String functions are new with release 2. They provide a variety of character manipulation formulas that give you flexibility in rearranging text entries. You can work with an entire entry and change its order, or you can use just a piece of a cell entry.

1-2-3's string functions often work with the individual characters in a text string. The numbering system that 1-2-3 uses for the characters in a string may not be what you expect. The character at the far left of a string is regarded as character 0, not character 1. The numbering proceeds with 1, 2, and so on, moving to the right in the character string. Understanding these positions within a string is very important, since you will want to be sure you are working with the characters you expect. String position numbers can range from 0 through 239, since a 240-character string is the largest that 1-2-3 can work with.

String position numbers must always be expressed as positive integers. A negative integer will cause 1-2-3 to return ERR. Using a number with a decimal will cause 1-2-3 to drop the decimal and use only the whole number portion of the value. No rounding will occur; for example, 1-2-3 will truncate a value of 5.6 to 5 when it is used as a position number in a string. The following shows the positions for entries within a label.

```
T h i s   i s   a   s t r i n g
0 1 2 3 4 5 6 7 8 9 | | | | | |
                    0 1 2 3 4 5
```

It is also important to note that the label indicator that begins a string is not assigned a position number. An empty or null string has a length of zero. A cell with a null string contains no entry except a label indicator. It is not the same as a blank cell without a label indicator.

When you use string values as arguments in a string function, you must enclose them in double quotation marks. These same entries referenced by a cell address will not require quotation marks, however. For example, if you want to use the character string "This is a string" in the @RIGHT string function to remove the last 6 characters on the right, and the entry is stored in D10, you could use @RIGHT(D10,6), but if you put the string itself in the function, it would have to be written as @RIGHT("This is a string",6).

Some string functions will produce numeric results equating to a position in a string, while others will produce a string value. You will want to become familiar with the workings of string functions before you indiscriminately combine the results of two string functions. Many of the examples in this section will combine several string functions, however, since this is the way string functions are most commonly used.

## @CHAR (Release 2)

The @CHAR function is used to return a character that corresponds to an ASCII/LICS code number.

### Format

@CHAR(*code*)

### Arguments

*code*    any numeric value from 1 to 255. Decimal fractions will be truncated; only the whole number portion of the entry will be used. Numbers less than 1 or greater than 255 will return ERR.

### Use

This function will convert an ASCII/LICS code to a displayable and printable character. ASCII/LICS codes above 127 produce foreign currency symbols, accent marks, and other special characters that your monitor will not be able to display. If the character represented by the code number you specify cannot be displayed on your monitor, a blank or a character resembling the desired character will be substituted. Codes below 32, which are nonprintable, will also be returned as blanks. Here are a few examples:

@CHAR(40) equals (

@CHAR(49) equals 1

The primary use for this function is to compose characters from within a macro.

## @CLEAN (Release 2)

The @CLEAN function strips nonprintable ASCII codes from a string.

### Format

@CLEAN(*string*)

### Arguments

*string* any character sequence up to 240 characters. If the characters are entered in the function, they must be enclosed in double quotation marks. They can also be stored in a cell and referenced with a cell address or range name. A range address is not acceptable, since this function will work with only one string at a time. Numeric characters can be used as long as they are preceded by a label prefix.

### Use

This function can be used whenever you have ASCII codes from 0 to 32 in a character string. This might occur with data from another program or data transmitted to you from a remote location. The maximum number of characters that can be in the cell is 240.

## @CODE (Release 2)

The @CODE function will return the ASCII/LICS code number of the first character in the function argument.

### Format

@CODE(*string*)

### Arguments

*string*    any character sequence up to 240 characters. If the characters are entered in the function, they must be enclosed in double quotation marks. They can also be stored in a cell and referenced with a cell address or range name. Numeric characters can be used as long as they are preceded by a label prefix.

### Use

This function finds its primary application in macros in working with composed characters. The purpose of the function is to convert characters to their ASCII/LICS code. A few examples of @CODE are as follows:

@CODE("$") equals 36

@CODE("V") equals 86

@CODE("@") equals 64

## Note

Upper-case and lower-case characters have different codes. For example, an upper-case A is code 65, but a lower-case a is code 97.

## @EXACT (Release 2)

The @EXACT function allows you to determine whether two string values are exactly equal.

### Format

@EXACT(*string1,string2*)

### Arguments

*string1*    any character sequence that does not exceed 240 characters. If the string is placed in the function, the total length of the formula will not be able to exceed 240 characters, so the string will be restricted to a size that fits within this limitation. If it is used in the function, it must also be enclosed in double quotation marks.

*string2*    any character sequence that does not exceed 240 characters. If the string is placed in the function, the total length of the formula will not be able to exceed 240 characters, so the string will be restricted to a size that fits within this limitation. If it is used in the function, it must also be enclosed in double quotation marks.

### Use

The @EXACT function will return 1 when the two strings match exactly and 0 when they do not. Everything about the two strings must be the same, including blank spaces and capitalization, or 0 will be returned. Although this function can be used by itself, it is usually used with condition tests (that is, with @IF).

Several examples of @EXACT follow:

@EXACT("Mary Brown","MARY BROWN") equals 0

@EXACT("2144","2144") equals 1

@EXACT(2144,"2144") equals ERR, since string1 is a numeric value

@EXACT(A10,"MARY BROWN") equals 1 if A10 contains MARY BROWN

### Note

Use @IF and the equal operator (=) if you do not want to consider case difference. For example, @IF("Tom Jones"= "tom jones","True","False") will return True, since the case difference is not considered.

## @FIND (Release 2)

The @FIND function permits you to search a character string to find out if a substring (search string) appears within it. If the search string is found, the function returns the starting location of this string.

### Format

@FIND(*search string,entire string,starting location*)

## Arguments

*search string*    a character sequence or a reference to a cell containing one. When the characters are entered directly in the function, they must be enclosed in quotation marks. The maximum length of the search string must be at least one character less than the entire string to be searched. Since @FIND is case sensitive, the search string must match a portion of the entire string exactly if the search string is to be found.

*entire string*    a character sequence or a reference to a cell containing one. When the characters are entered directly in the function, they must be enclosed in quotation marks. The maximum length of this string is 240 characters.

*starting location*    The position in the entire string where you wish to begin your search. Remember that the leftmost character in the string is character 0. The maximum starting location can be one less than the number of characters in the string because of the zero start location.

## Use

The @FIND function is used whenever you wish to locate a string within a string. It can be used to identify the location of the blank space between a first and last name, for example. This information, when combined with other string functions, can permit you to reverse the name entry so that the last name appears first in the cell. ERR is returned when your start number is not valid (that is, it is negative or is greater than the last position of the entire string) or when the search string is not found.

Several examples of @FIND are as follows:

@FIND("-","ABF-6785",0) equals 3

@FIND("-","213-46-2389",4) equals 6

@FIND("-""ABF-6785",8) equals ERR

The worksheet provides an example of the use of @FIND to locate the space between first and last names. The formula in C2 is the pattern for the other formulas in column C: @FIND(" ",A2,0). Because of the 0 start location for strings, the location of the space is equivalent to the number of characters in the first name.

### Note

@MID can be used with @FIND to extract the search string. For example, to extract Smith from John Smith you could use @MID(A10,@FIND(A1,A10,0),@LENGTH(A1)), where A1 contains Smith and A10 contains John Smith.

## @LEFT (Release 2)

The @LEFT function allows you to extract a specified number of characters from the left side of a string.

### Format

@LEFT(*string,number of characters to extract*)

## Arguments

*string*

a sequence of characters included in the function either by enclosing them in double quotation marks or by a reference to a cell address or range name containing the characters.

*number of characters to extract*

a number representing the characters to be extracted from the string. If you want to extract the first three characters, for example, this number would be 3. ERR will result if this number is greater than the number of characters in the string.

## Use

The @LEFT function will allow you to extract one or many characters from a string. It can be used alone or in combination with other string functions. Some examples of the function follow:

@LEFT("Lotus 1-2-3",5) equals Lotus

@LEFT("12:30:59",4) equals 12:3

@LEFT("    ABC COMPANY",7) equals ABC with four leading blanks

The worksheet shows the @LEFT function coupled with @FIND to extract the first name from worksheet entries. C2 contains the pattern for column C formulas: @LEFT(A2, @FIND(" ",A2,0)). This formula finds the location of the blank space between first and last name and uses it as the number of characters to extract from the string.

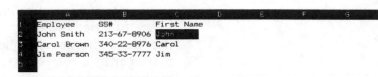

|   | A | B | C | D | E | F | G |
|---|---|---|---|---|---|---|---|
| 1 | Employee | SS# | First Name | | | | |
| 2 | John Smith | 213-67-8906 | John | | | | |
| 3 | Carol Brown | 340-22-8976 | Carol | | | | |
| 4 | Jim Pearson | 345-33-7777 | Jim | | | | |
| 5 | | | | | | | |

## @LENGTH (Release 2)

The @LENGTH function returns the number of characters in a string.

### Format

@LENGTH(*string*)

### Arguments

*string*    a group of characters that can be included in the function (if they are enclosed in double quotation marks) or placed in a cell and referenced. You can also use a string formula as the string. Numeric entries are not allowed and will return ERR.

### Use

This function can be used to determine the length of an entry you wish to manipulate, to verify input data, or to determine the length of a line. The following examples should clarify the results produced by @LENGTH:

| Function | Length |
|---|---|
| @LENGTH("sales") | 5 |
| @LENGTH("profit "&"and loss") | 15 |
| @LENGTH(A2) where A2 contains abc | 3 |

The worksheet shows an example of the @LENGTH function used to determine the number of characters in names. The formula @LENGTH(A2) is copied down column C to return the length of all the entries in column A.

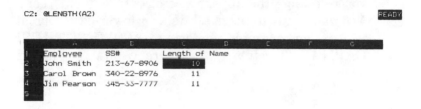

C2: @LENGTH(A2)                                           READY

|   | A | B | C |
|---|---|---|---|
| 1 | Employee | SS# | Length of Name |
| 2 | John Smith | 213-67-8906 | 10 |
| 3 | Carol Brown | 340-22-8976 | 11 |
| 4 | Jim Pearson | 345-55-7777 | 11 |
| 5 |  |  |  |

### Note

This function is frequently used in combination with other string functions such as @MID, @RIGHT, @LEFT, and @FIND when restructuring label entries.

## @LOWER (Release 2)

The @LOWER function will convert strings to lower case.

### Format

@LOWER(*string*)

### Arguments

*string*    a group of characters that can be in any case, such as upper, lower, or mixed upper and lower case. The characters can be included in the function if they are enclosed in double quotation marks, or they can be placed in a cell and referenced. You can also use a string formula as the string. Numeric entries are not allowed and will return ERR.

### Use

This function is valuable when data from several sources must be combined and data entry was not done in a consistent manner. @LOWER is one of the functions that permit you to change the appearance of data without reentering it. You can use it to place all data in lower-case format.

As an example, entering @LOWER("THESE ARE CAPITALS") returns "these are capitals". The worksheet shows that changing proper case is just as easy: @LOWER ("This Is Proper Case") returns "this is proper case".

### Note

To use this function to change text data entered with incorrect capitalization, first enter the function in an empty area of the worksheet, referencing the data to be corrected. You will need to restructure the data in a different location before copying it back, and you will want to be sure you do not overlay important data in the process of doing so. After the formulas are entered, you can freeze the values in the cells with F2 (EDIT) followed by F9 (CALC). You can then transfer them with /Move. Alternatively, you can use /Range Value to freeze the formulas as values and copy them all in one step. After verifying the correctness of the data, you can erase the work area that originally contained the formula.

## @MID (Release 2)

The @MID function will extract characters from the middle of a string when you specify the number of characters to extract and the starting location.

## Format

@MID(*string,start number,number of characters*)

## Arguments

| | |
|---|---|
| *string* | a group of characters that can be included in the function (if they are enclosed in double quotation marks) or placed in a cell and referenced. You can also use a string formula as the string. Numeric entries are not allowed and will return ERR. |
| *start number* | a number representing the first character position you wish to extract from the string. When you choose this number, remember that the leftmost position in the string is position 0. Start number should not be negative. If start number is greater than the number of positions in the string, an empty string will be returned. @MID("ABC",0,1) returns 1 character from the 0 position in the string or "A". |
| *number of characters* | a number representing the number of characters you wish to extract from the string. This number can be stored in a cell and referenced by the function through a cell address or range name. When this argument is 0, an empty string is the result. You can set this number at 240 if you do not know how many characters are in the string and you want to extract all of them. |

**Use**

The @MID function can be used whenever you wish to extract a portion of a string. The function offers complete flexibility: you can start anywhere in the string and extract as few or as many characters as you wish. A few examples follow:

@MID("abcdefghi",3,3) equals def

@MID("123"&"456",1,240) equals 23456

The worksheet in Figure 7-37 shows @MID used with @LENGTH and @FIND to reverse a name entry. The formula uses the location of the "," plus 2 to identify the beginning of the first name. The number of characters in the first name is the length of the entire entry less the location of the "," . This is concatenated with a space and the last name. The last name is made up of the characters on the left up to the "," . Creating the correct formula may require a little trial and error if you are not familiar with string functions, but once you have worked out the correct formula, you can copy it down the column to reverse all the name entries.

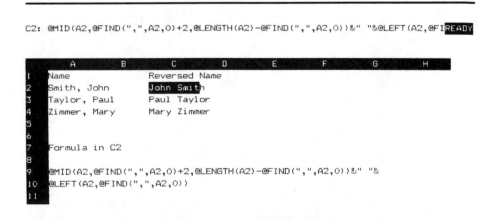

**Figure 7-37.**   Reversing name entries with @MID and other string functions

### Note

The @RIGHT and @LEFT functions are actually special versions of @MID that extract from the right or left edge of a string, respectively. When 0 is used for the start number, @MID is functionally equivalent to @LEFT, since it begins extracting with the leftmost character in the string.

@MID can be used with @FIND to extract a search string. For example, to extract Smith from John Smith you could use @MID(A10,@FIND(A1,A10,0),@LENGTH(A1)) where A1 contains Smith and A10 contains John Smith.

## @N (Release 2)

The @N function returns the numeric value of a single cell.

### Format

@N(*range*)

### Arguments

*range*   a reference to a range, using either the cell addresses (for example, R2..U20) or a range name. Even though this function uses only the upper left cell of the range, the argument must still be in range format, that is, A2..A2.

### Use

The function is used to return the value of the upper left cell in a range. If the cell contains a label, a zero will be returned.

The @N function is useful in macro applications to examine data in a cell. It is also a quick way of excluding label data from your calculations.

The worksheet shows an example of @N. In this particular example, the range is a single cell.

```
      A         B         C         D         E         F         G         H
1    85
2
3              85
4
```

## @PROPER (Release 2)

The @PROPER function converts strings to proper case (a format where the first letter of each word is capitalized).

### Format

@PROPER(*string*)

### Arguments

*string*    a group of characters that can be in upper, lower, or mixed upper and lower case. The characters can be included in the function (if they are enclosed in double quotation marks), or they can be placed in a cell and referenced. You can also use a string formula as the string.

### Use

This function is valuable when data from several sources must be combined and data entry was not done in a consistent manner. @PROPER is one of the functions that permit you to change the appearance of data without reentering it. @PROPER(A2&" "&B3), where A2 contains JOBBARD MILLING COMPANY and B3 contains east dallas division, would return Jobbard Milling Company East Dallas Division. Every word in each string was converted to proper case (lower case with initial capital). The worksheet shows several additional conversions. Entries are made in column A, and @PROPER formulas are used to obtain the remainder of the display.

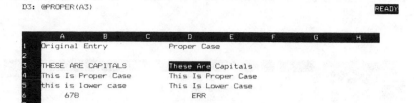

D3: @PROPER(A3)
READY

## @REPEAT (Release 2)

The @REPEAT function is used to duplicate a character string a specified number of times.

### Format

@REPEAT(*string,number of times*)

### Arguments

| | |
|---|---|
| *string* | a series of characters enclosed in quotation marks or a reference to a cell containing a string. The string can be one character or many. |
| *number of times* | a numeric value indicating the number of times to repeat the string. |

### Use

The primary use for the @REPEAT function is to improve the appearance of a worksheet. @REPEAT can create dividing lines between a report's assumptions and the final result, for example, or between assumptions and the finished model. @REPEAT is in one sense similar to the backslash ( \ ) character, since it repeats characters. It differs in the sense that \ is restricted to filling a single cell, whereas @REPEAT can extend across many worksheet cells.

Figure 7-38 provides an example of the @REPEAT function. In this example it is used to create dividing lines on

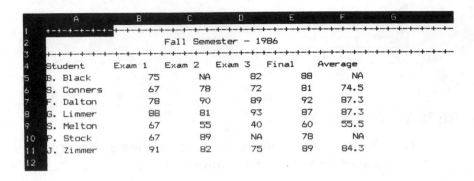

A1: [W12] @REPEAT("+-",36)                                                READY

```
        A           B         C         D         E         F         G
1  +-+-+-+-+-+-+-+-+-+-+-+-+-+-+-+-+-+-+-+-+-+-+-+-+-+-+-+-+-+-+-+-+-+-+-+-
2                       Fall Semester - 1986
3  +-+-+-+-+-+-+-+-+-+-+-+-+-+-+-+-+-+-+-+-+-+-#-+-+-+-+-+-+-+-+-+-+-+-+-+-
4  Student    Exam 1    Exam 2    Exam 3   Final     Average
5  B. Black       75        NA        82       88        NA
6  S. Conners     67        78        72       81       74.5
7  F. Dalton      78        90        89       92       87.3
8  G. Limmer      88        81        93       87       87.3
9  S. Melton      67        55        40       60       55.5
10 P. Stock       67        89        NA       78        NA
11 J. Zimmer      91        82        75       89       84.3
12
```

**Figure 7-38.**    Using @REPEAT to duplicate a label

a cumulative grade report. The formula is placed in A1 as @REPEAT("+−",36). This means that +− will be repeated across the screen, since the screen will display 72 characters.

**Note**

The string returned from this function should not exceed 240 characters. The maximum number of times you can repeat a 12-character string is 20, for example.

## @REPLACE (Release 2)

The @REPLACE function replaces characters in a string with other characters.

**Format**

@REPLACE(*original string,start location,# characters,new string*)

## Arguments

*original string*  a series of characters enclosed in quotation marks or a reference to a cell containing a string. The string can be one character or many. It must specify the complete string entry you wish to work with.

*start location*  the position number in the original string where you want the replacement to begin. Remember that the first character in the original string is position zero. If start location is greater than the length of the original string, the new string will be added at the end.

*# characters*  the number of characters to remove from the original string. When # characters equals zero, the new string is inserted without removal of any part of the original string. When # characters is the same as the number of characters in the original string, the entire string will be replaced.

*new string*  a series of characters enclosed in quotation marks or a reference to a cell containing a string. The string can be one character or many. When new string is an empty string, that is, " ", @REPLACE will simply delete characters from the original string.

## Use

The @REPLACE function enables you to make changes to a string without retyping the original string. You can use this function to manipulate a part number into a warehouse location or an account code into a department number, for instance. Sample uses include the following:

@REPLACE("Department 100",11,3,"200") equals Department 200

@REPLACE("Commissions for: ",17,10,"Mary Brown") equals Commissions for: Mary Brown

@REPLACE("AX/1265",2,1,"-") equals AX-1265

@REPLACE("AX/1265",0,7,"-") equals -

The worksheet shows a whole list of part numbers that were changed with the @REPLACE function.

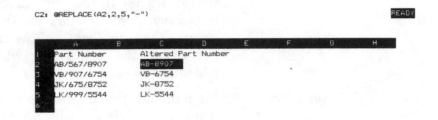

## Note

To use this function to change text data entered incorrectly, first enter the function in an empty area of the worksheet, referencing the data to be corrected. You will need to re-structure the data in a different location before copying it back, and you will want to be sure you do not overlay important data in the process of doing so. After the formulas are entered, you can freeze the values in the cells with F2 (EDIT) followed by F9 (CALC). You can then transfer them with /Move. Alternatively, you can use /Range Value to freeze the formulas as values and copy them all in one step. After verifying the correctness of the data, you can erase the work area that originally contained the formula.

## @RIGHT (Release 2)

The @RIGHT function allows you to extract a specified number of characters from the right side of a string.

**Format**

@RIGHT(*string,number of characters to extract*)

**Arguments**

*string*                          a sequence of characters included
                                  in the function by enclosing them
                                  in double quotation marks or by
                                  referencing a cell address or
                                  range name containing the
                                  characters.

*number of characters*
*to extract*                      a number representing the char-
                                  acters to be extracted from the
                                  string. If this number is greater
                                  than the number of characters
                                  in the string, the entire string
                                  will be extracted.

**Use**

The @RIGHT function will allow you to extract one or many
characters from the right side of a string. It can be used
alone or in combination with other string functions. Some
examples of the function follow:

@RIGHT("Lotus 1-2-3",5) equals 1-2-3

@RIGHT("1:30:59",5) equals 30:59

@RIGHT("ABC COMPANY        ",8) equals Y with
seven trailing blanks

The worksheet in Figure 7-39 shows the @RIGHT function coupled with @FIND and @LENGTH to extract the last
name from worksheet entries. C2 contains the pattern for
column C formulas: @RIGHT(A2,@LENGTH(A2)−@FIND
(" ",A2,0)−1). This formula finds the location of the blank
space between first and last name and subtracts that number

C2: @RIGHT(A2,@LENGTH(A2)-@FIND(" ",A2,0)-1)

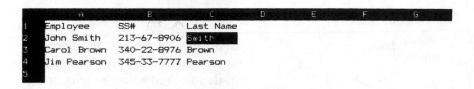

**Figure 7-39.**　The @RIGHT function

plus 1 from the length of the string. The result of this calculation is the number of characters to be extracted from the right side of the string.

## @S (Release 2)

The @S function returns a value as a string.

### Format

@S(*range*)

### Arguments

*range*　　a reference to a range using either cell addresses (such as R2..U20) or a range name. Even though this function uses only the upper left cell of the range, the argument must still be in range format (A2..A2).

### Use

The function is used to return the value of the upper left cell in a range. If the cell contains a number, a zero will be returned. This action can prevent the error condition that occurs if strings and numbers are mixed in one formula. If you have any doubt about the contents of a cell you are combining with a string, you can use @S, which will convert it to an empty string entry if it contains a number.

Given the following worksheet, @S(A3) equals SALES, @S(A4) equals COGS, and @S(B3) equals a blank. To correct potential errors you might use @LENGTH(@S(B2)), since this will return a zero, whereas @LENGTH(B2) equals ERR.

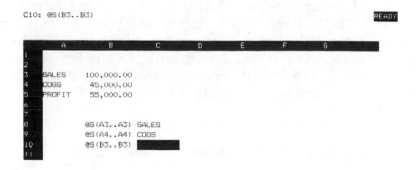

## @STRING (Release 2)

The @STRING function converts numeric values to strings and allows you to specify the number of decimal places to be used for a string.

### Format

@STRING(*number,number of decimal places*)

### Arguments

| | |
|---|---|
| *number* | a numeric value or reference to a numeric value |
| *number of decimal places* | the number of places that should be used when the |

string is created from the number. If the number is longer than the specified number of places, rounding will occur. If the number is shorter, zeros will be used for padding.

**Use**

The primary use of this function is to permit the combination of numeric values with strings in a string formula. If @ STRING is not used to convert numbers first, ERR will be returned by any such string formula. The @STRING function uses the Fixed format with the number of places you specify to dictate the appearance of the resulting string. Several examples of @STRING follow:

@STRING(1.6,0) equals the string 2

@STRING(12,4) equals the string 12.0000

The worksheet shows the @STRING function used in a string formula to obtain some numeric information and include it in the formula. Without the @STRING function, this numeric information could not have been combined with the string data. Although it may appear easier to simply type the 400 in the heading, the string formula approach allows a manager to set up templates for use by all the departments in the organization and minimizes the entries each group has to make. It also eliminates the possibility that someone will forget to update the heading.

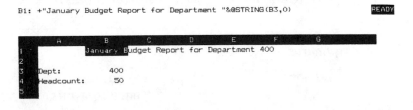

B1: +"January Budget Report for Department "&@STRING(B3,0)                    READY

## @TRIM (Release 2)

The @TRIM function allows you to strip away extraneous blanks from a string entry.

### Format

@TRIM(*string*)

### Arguments

*string*    a sequence of characters included in the function by enclosing them in double quotation marks or by referencing a cell address or range name containing the characters.

### Use

This function is used to remove trailing, preceding, and multiple internal blanks from a string. It can allow you to clean up existing entries on a worksheet and to establish a consistent format for data storage. @TRIM can be used with string formulas as well as strings. The examples that follow include both types of entries.

@TRIM("    Sales") equals Sales

@TRIM("January "&" Fuel Allowance") equals January Fuel Allowance. Note that @TRIM retains one space between strings separated by an ampersand (&).

### Note

This command can be used in conjunction with some of the long labels transferred from ASCII files. See Chapter 8 for more information.

## @UPPER (Release 2)

The @UPPER function will convert lower-case, proper-case, and mixed upper- and lower-case character strings to all upper case.

### Format

@UPPER(*string*)

### Arguments

*string*    a group of characters that can be in proper, lower, or mixed upper and lower case. The characters can be included in the function (if they are enclosed in double quotation marks), or they can be placed in a cell and referenced. You can also use a string formula as the string.

### Use

This function is valuable when data from several sources must be combined and data entry was not done in a consistent manner. @UPPER is one of the functions that permit you to change the appearance of data without reentering it. @UPPER(A2&" "&B3), where A2 contains Jobbard Milling Company and B3 contains east dallas division, would return JOBBARD MILLING COMPANY EAST DALLAS DIVISION. All of every word in each string is converted to upper case. The worksheet shows several additional conversions. Entries are made in column A, and @UPPER formulas are used to obtain the remainder of the display.

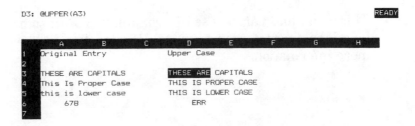

## @VALUE (Release 2)

The @VALUE function is designed to convert a string that looks like a number into an actual numeric value.

### Format

@VALUE(*string*)

### Arguments

*string*      a sequence of characters included in the function by enclosing them in double quotation marks or by referencing a cell address or range name containing the characters. The sequence of characters must look like a number. Acceptable examples would be 345.674, 345.1E8, 7, and 7/8 (a fraction). If string references an empty string, 0 will be returned.

### Use

This function converts strings that look like numbers into actual numeric values so they can be used in calculations. The function will remove any leading or trailing blanks from the string as it converts it to a number. Here are a few examples:

@VALUE("      23.98") returns the number 23.98

@VALUE(Z10) returns 0 if Z10 is blank and ERR if Z10 contains a label such as abc.

The worksheet shows part numbers in column A that have the weight of the product as the last character in the part number. This last character can be extracted with a formula like @RIGHT(A2,1), but it cannot be used to calculate shipping costs, since a numeric value is required. The use of @VALUE solves this problem, as shown in the formulas in column E. The formula for E2 is +C2*(@VALUE

(@RIGHT(A2,1)))*B2, since the shipping cost for each unit ordered is stored in column B and is multiplied by the weight of the item.

```
E2: (C2) +C2*(@VALUE(@RIGHT(A2,1)))*B2                          READY
```

| | A | B | C | D | E | F | G |
|---|---|---|---|---|---|---|---|
| 1 | Part # | Shipping per lb. | Quantity | Customer | Shipping | | |
| 2 | AC-789-1 | 0.75 | 3 | J. Brown | $2.25 | | |
| 3 | AX-456-8 | 0.85 | 10 | M. Smith | $68.00 | | |
| 4 | BD-666-5 | 0.95 | 7 | L. Jones | $33.25 | | |
| 5 | | | | | | | |

# Working With Files

The worksheets discussed so far have all been stored in part of your computer's memory (RAM). RAM offers an advantage in the instant availability of information stored in it. Changes, additions, and deletions to information stored in RAM can be accomplished very quickly. The disadvantage of RAM storage is that it is very volatile. Losing the power to your computer for even a brief instant causes everything stored in RAM to be permanently lost. A more permanent means of storage is clearly required. This normally takes the form of disk files. The 1-2-3 program itself is a file. That is why it is permanently available on your disk. If the program is lost from memory, you can restore it by reloading it from your disk. This chapter will focus on the data files that contain information on the applications you have created on 1-2-3. You will learn how to save, retrieve, and delete files. You will also learn to combine files and perform other operations on them.

## Naming and Using Files

1-2-3 uses disk files for the permanent storage of all information. These files can be stored on either hard or floppy diskettes. They can be transferred from one disk to another by using either Access System commands or commands in the DOS operating system. Because 1-2-3 runs under DOS, the conventions established by DOS for the naming of files must be followed. A comprehensive discussion of rules for file names and storage can be found in your DOS manual.

## File Names and File Types

The 1-2-3 program creates three types of data files: worksheet files, graph files, and print files. 1-2-3 automatically appends a suffix to each file name that allows you to distinguish one file type from another. In addition, 1-2-3 has many files of its own that are part of the program and its various features.

DOS imposes an eight-character limit on file names and

a three-character limit on file name extensions. A period (.) is used to separate the file name from the extension.

Under release 1A of 1-2-3 your file names can be composed of only the letters of the alphabet (A-Z), the numeric digits (0-9), and the underscore character (_). 1-2-3 automatically changes lower-case characters to upper-case. Other special characters are permitted only if your specific release of the operating system allows them. Release 2 will accept any LICS character except the space as long as your operating system supports the use of the character. Examples of valid file names are SALES, REGION_1, EMPLOYEE, and 85_SALES.

If you enter more than eight characters for a file name, 1-2-3 will truncate the file name after the eighth character. SALES_REGION_1 thus becomes SALES_RE, which would be indistinguishable from SALES_REGION_2, and SALES_REGION_#, or anything similar.

1-2-3 distinguishes file types by the extension added to the file. The box called "1-2-3 File Types" lists all the extensions for data files and special file types used by 1-2-3. The three most common types of files and their extensions are as follows:

| File Type | Extension |
|---|---|
| Worksheet | WK1 (release 2) |
| | WKS (release 1A) |
| Print | PRN |
| Graph | PIC |

Worksheet files are the only files for which the extensions for releases 1A and 2 differ. For release 2, you also have the option of supplying your own extension for any file type. If you supply this extension when you create a file, you will need to supply it every time you access that file. If you use 1-2-3's default extensions, the package will supply them for you at all times.

# 1-2-3 File Types

| File Type | Extension |
|---|---|
| Worksheet | WK1 (release 2) |
| | WKS (release 1A) |
| Print | PRN |
| Graph | PIC |
| Configuration | CNF |
| Program | COM (release 2) |
| | EXE (release 1A) |
| Help | HLP |
| Drivers | SET (release 2) |
| | DRV (release 1A) |
| Driver Library | LBR (release 2 only) |
| DOS | BAT |
| Tutorial | TUT |

## Subdirectories

On a hard disk system, you can create subdirectories for the storage of files. Using subdirectories lessens the time required for file retrieval because 1-2-3 does not have to search the directory for the entire hard disk to determine the file's location. Since release 2 of 1-2-3 requires that you use at least version 2 of DOS, subdirectories are always allowed with release 2. Since release 1A may be used with releases of DOS that do not support the use of subdirectories, the use of them with release 1A will depend on which release of DOS you are using.

If you are using subdirectories, 1-2-3 must know the drive and the pathname in order to find a file. The drive designation is the drive letter followed by a colon, for example, A:, B:, or C:. The pathname tells 1-2-3 what directory the file is located in. Higher-level directories are always listed first. \SALES indicates that the file is in the first-level directory SALES, whereas \SALES\REGION\ONE indicates that the file is several levels down from the top directory in a subdirectory called ONE.

Although both release 1A and release 2 support subdirectories, there are differences in their use in certain /File commands. In general, release 2 allows more flexibility in changing directories than release 1A. These differences will be covered in the discussions of the individual commands. If you are not familiar with the ins and outs of subdirectories, review your DOS manual for more information on this subject.

## The File Menu Options

File is one of the options on 1-2-3's main menu. Most of the commands that manipulate files are options on the File submenu, which is shown in the following illustration. Let's look at each of these menu options in detail.

```
A1:                                                              MENU
Retrieve  Save  Combine  Xtract  Erase  List  Import  Directory
Erase the current worksheet and display the selected worksheet
```

## Saving a File to Disk

Any worksheet model in RAM must be saved to a disk file if it is to be available in later 1-2-3 sessions. You will use the /File Save option to place a copy of the current worksheet on your disk.

If the file name you plan to use is not currently on the disk, enter the name in response to 1-2-3's prompt and then press ENTER. If the file has already been saved in the current session, 1-2-3 will suggest that it be saved again under the same name. If you agree, press ENTER. When prompted to confirm this decision, select Replace if you would like the existing file replaced with the current worksheet. If you decide not to replace the file, select Cancel to return to READY mode.

1-2-3 will automatically append .WK1 to the file name if you are using release 2 and .WKS if you are using release 1A. If you are using release 2, you can choose any file suffix you wish, although you must be prepared to reenter this suffix every time you wish to access the file.

If you wish to use an existing file name, you can point to it in the list and press ENTER.

1-2-3 will then provide a confirmation prompt like the following, which asks if you wish to Cancel the request or Replace the file on the disk with the current contents of memory.

This prompt is needed because each disk or subdirectory can have only one file with a particular name. If you reuse a name, only the last data you saved will be in the file when you attempt to retrieve it.

Under release 2 you can decide to save a file to a different drive or directory by specifying the drive and directory designation along with the file name, for example, C:\SALES\REGION\FILE1. Under release 1A, saving to a different directory requires changing the drive or directory designation with /File Directory before executing the /File Save command.

1-2-3 makes it so easy to save files that you will want to save frequently. If your system goes down, you will have to retrieve the most recently saved version of the file, and it will be easier to reconstruct what was lost if it has not been too long since the last save.

### Retrieving a File From Disk

The /File Retrieve command permits you to retrieve a file from your disk. When 1-2-3 loads this worksheet file into memory, the information previously in memory will be erased. If you have not saved that information, there will be no way to bring it back.

When you enter this command, 1-2-3 searches the current disk or subdirectory and lists all the files with a .WK1 (release 2) or .WKS (release 1A) suffix. As shown here, release 2 displays up to five names across the third line of the display screen (eight for release 1A). You can use the right arrow key to move across the display. Continuing to use the right arrow will scroll across to additional file names until you finally cycle through all of them and move back to the beginning of the file.

Using the left arrow key moves you back toward the beginning of the list. Other options available with the cursor control keys are as follows:

HOME  Moves the cursor to the beginning of the list

END   Moves the cursor to the end of the list

DOWN  Presents the next five options in the list

UP    Presents the previous five options from the list

If you wish to see all the file names at once, press F3 (NAME). You will see a list like that in Figure 8-1. Moving your cursor to a particular file name supplies additional information concerning the date that file was saved and its size. You can choose a file by pressing RETURN or cancel the full display by pressing F3 (NAME) a second time.

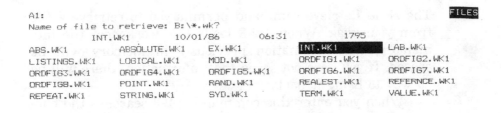

```
Name of file to retrieve: B:\*.wk?
          INT.WK1        10/01/86       06:31          1795
ABS.WK1        ABSOLUTE.WK1   EX.WK1         INT.WK1        LAB.WK1
LISTINGS.WK1   LOGICAL.WK1    MOD.WK1        ORDFIG1.WK1    ORDFIG2.WK1
ORDFIG3.WK1    ORDFIG4.WK1    ORDFIG5.WK1    ORDFIG6.WK1    ORDFIG7.WK1
ORDFIG8.WK1    POINT.WK1      RAND.WK1       REALEST.WK1    REFERNCE.WK1
REPEAT.WK1     STRING.WK1     SYD.WK1        TERM.WK1       VALUE.WK1
```

```
02-Oct-86  12:55 AM
```

**Figure 8-1.**    Complete file name display generated with F3 (NAME)

With release 2 you can access a file in another directory by typing the complete pathname for the file. You can also access a file with a suffix other than .WK1 or .WKS under release 2 by specifying the suffix along with the file name. Release 1A does not provide either option. Under release 1A, if you want to access a file in another directory, you must first change the directory with /File Directory.

### Using Passwords With Files

Passwords are a form of protection for your files. They are available only under release 2. When they are in effect, a person will not be allowed to retrieve a file unless he or she can supply the correct password.

Passwords are added to a file when it is saved. If you want to specify a password after entering the file name, type a space and a **p** before pressing ENTER.

```
A1:                                                          EDIT
Enter save file name: B:\sales p
```

1-2-3 then prompts for the password, which can be up to 15 characters. When you type in the password, it will not be displayed; each character is instead represented by a square in the control panel, like this:

```
A1:                                                          EDIT
Enter password: ■■■■■■■■■■■■
```

Your use of upper- and lower-case will be recorded and will need to be duplicated to access the file later. When you press ENTER, you will be prompted to enter the password again for verification.

```
A1:                                                          ERROR
Enter password: ■■■■■■■■■■■■         Verify password: ■
```

If the passwords entered on both occasions are not an exact match, 1-2-3 provides an error message to that effect. This second prompt also offers a way to stop the addition of the password: simply press ESC. Once you have pressed ENTER for the final time, the password will be added to the disk, and you will need to use it when you retrieve the file.

To access a file with a password, enter the command you wish to use in working with the file, such as /File Retrieve. 1-2-3 will then generate a prompt for the password and wait for you to enter it. If you cannot reproduce the password exactly as it was originally entered, including the correct use of upper- and lower-case, 1-2-3 will not retrieve the file and will show an error message.

## Combining Information From Two Files

The /File Combine options allow you to bring information from worksheet files into your current worksheet. With this capability you can produce budget consolidations or build a new worksheet using components of several existing worksheet files. Unlike /File Retrieve, the Combine options do not erase all of memory. The three Combine options are Copy, Add, and Subtract. All three depend on the location of the cursor in the current worksheet for the actions they take.

### Copying Information From a File
### To a Worksheet

The /File Combine Copy command allows you to replace the contents of some of your current worksheet cells with the contents of cells in a disk file. The replacement begins at the cursor location in the current worksheet, and its extent will depend on how many cells are being copied from the disk. Values, labels, and formulas can all be copied from the file on disk.

You have two options for determining the extent of the replacement. First, you can choose an entire file. This will take each cell in the file that contains a value, label, or formula and replace one of the current worksheet cells with its contents. The location of the cell replaced is determined by the location of the cursor at the time of the request and the amount of the displacement of the particular cell within the file. The same displacement will be used to determine the replacement cell, with the base point being the cursor location.

As an example, suppose you have a file named HEADING that is stored on disk and looks like this:

Your current worksheet file is the following:

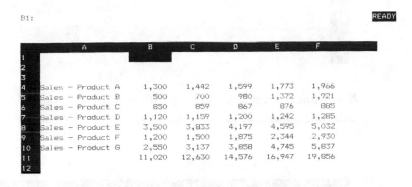

B1:                                                                    READY

| | A | B | C | D | E | F |
|---|---|---|---|---|---|---|
| 1 | | | | | | |
| 2 | | | | | | |
| 3 | | | | | | |
| 4 | Sales – Product A | 1,300 | 1,442 | 1,599 | 1,773 | 1,966 |
| 5 | Sales – Product B | 500 | 700 | 980 | 1,372 | 1,921 |
| 6 | Sales – Product C | 850 | 859 | 867 | 876 | 885 |
| 7 | Sales – Product D | 1,120 | 1,159 | 1,200 | 1,242 | 1,285 |
| 8 | Sales – Product E | 3,500 | 3,833 | 4,197 | 4,595 | 5,032 |
| 9 | Sales – Product F | 1,200 | 1,500 | 1,875 | 2,344 | 2,930 |
| 10 | Sales – Product G | 2,550 | 3,137 | 3,858 | 4,745 | 5,837 |
| 11 | | 11,020 | 12,630 | 14,576 | 16,947 | 19,856 |
| 12 | | | | | | |

Position your cursor in B1 and choose **/File Combine Copy**. Specify the file name and enter **Enter-File**. The results should look like this:

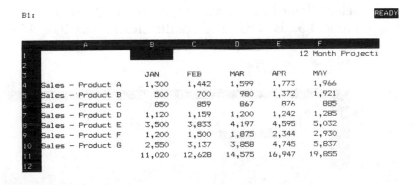

B1:                                                                    READY

| | A | B | C | D | E | F |
|---|---|---|---|---|---|---|
| 1 | | | | | | 12 Month Projecti |
| 2 | | | | | | |
| 3 | | JAN | FEB | MAR | APR | MAY |
| 4 | Sales – Product A | 1,300 | 1,442 | 1,599 | 1,773 | 1,966 |
| 5 | Sales – Product B | 500 | 700 | 980 | 1,372 | 1,921 |
| 6 | Sales – Product C | 850 | 859 | 867 | 876 | 885 |
| 7 | Sales – Product D | 1,120 | 1,159 | 1,200 | 1,242 | 1,285 |
| 8 | Sales – Product E | 3,500 | 3,833 | 4,197 | 4,595 | 5,032 |
| 9 | Sales – Product F | 1,200 | 1,500 | 1,875 | 2,344 | 2,930 |
| 10 | Sales – Product G | 2,550 | 3,137 | 3,858 | 4,745 | 5,837 |
| 11 | | 11,020 | 12,628 | 14,575 | 16,947 | 19,855 |
| 12 | | | | | | |

The /File Combine Copy command will overwrite the existing contents of cells.

If you do not wish to copy the enter file and the disk file has named ranges, you can use /File Combine Copy's second option, Named-Range. This option will copy only the range of values that you specify. For example, suppose this highlighted range of cells, named 85—TOT, is saved in a worksheet file called 85—BUDG.

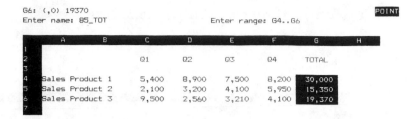

You want to copy 85—TOT to the column headed 85 Sales on this worksheet.

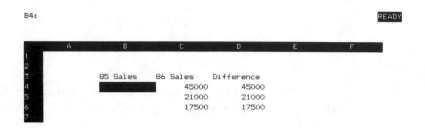

Place the cursor in B5 and select /File Combine Copy. Then select Named-Range and enter **85—TOT**, followed by the file name, **85—BUDG**. The results should look like this:

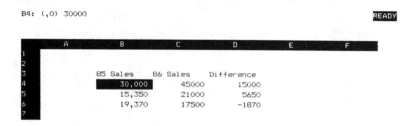

## Adding Information From a File
## To a Worksheet

The /File Combine Add command allows you to add the values of cells in a disk file to some of the current worksheet cells. The addition begins at the cursor location in the current worksheet, and its extent will depend on how many cells are being added from the disk. Only values are involved in the addition process. Labels and formulas are ignored, and the values in the current worksheet are retained for those cells. Unlike the Copy option, both /File Combine Add and /File Combine Subtract do not overlay the contents of existing worksheet cells.

You have two options for determining the extent of the addition. First, you can choose Entire-File. This will add each cell in the disk file that contains a value to one of the current worksheet cells. The location of the cell to which the disk cell value is added is determined by the location of the cursor at the time of the request and the amount of the displacement of the particular cell within the file. The same displacement will be used to determine the cell to be added to, with the base point being the cursor location. The second option is to choose Named-Range. In this case, only the cells in the named range will be added.

Addition is the perfect solution for budget consolidations. If you have files containing individual department or subsidiary budgets, the /File Combine Add command will permit you to add all the figures into one consolidated budget. Figure 8-2 shows a portion of the budgets for each department

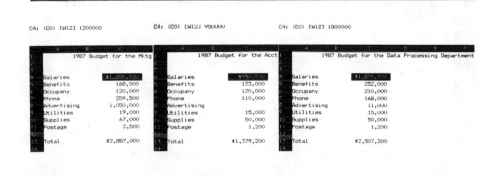

**Figure 8-2.**    Department budgets

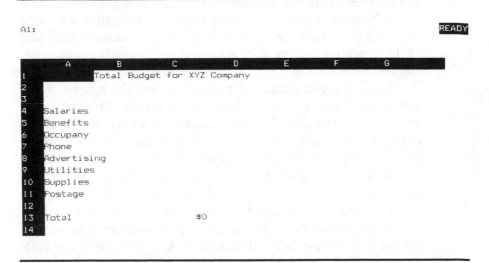

**Figure 8-3.** Total budget worksheet

in a company. Notice that the format for all three is identical: this is required if you want to combine entire files. Add the three files one by one to the total worksheet, as shown in Figure 8-3. Since the entire file is being added in each case,

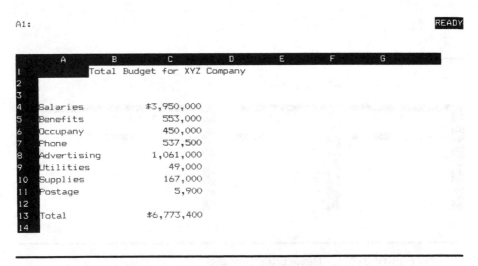

**Figure 8-4.** Result of /File Combine Add

place your cursor in A1 before invoking the /File Combine Add command. The final results are shown in Figure 8-4.

### Subtracting Information in a File
### From a Worksheet

The /File Combine Subtract command allows you to subtract the values of cells in a disk file from some of the current worksheet cells. The subtraction begins at the cursor location in the current worksheet, and its extent will depend on how many cells from the disk are being subtracted from the worksheet cells. Only values are involved in the subtraction process. Labels and formulas are ignored and the values in the current worksheet are retained for those cells.

You have two options for determining the extent of the subtraction. First, you can choose Entire-File. This subtracts each cell in the disk file that contains a value from one of the current worksheet cells. The location of the cell from which the disk cell value is subtracted is determined by the cursor location at the time of the request and by the displacement of the particular cell within the file. The same displacement will be used to determine the cell to be subtracted from, using the cursor location as the base point. If you choose Named Range, only the cells in the named range will be subtracted. This will begin at the location of the cursor in the worksheet.

The subtraction feature is useful after you have completed file consolidation with the /File Combine Add command. /File Combine Subtract can allow you to see the effect of taking the budget figures for one department or subsidiary away from the total, thereby simulating the effect of closing it.

## Saving Part of a Worksheet

The /File Xtract command permits you to save part of a worksheet. The specified section of the worksheet is saved as a .WK1 or .WKS file, depending on the release of 1-2-3 you are using. This feature is useful when you wish to save sections of a worksheet for use in constructing new models or when you have a file that is too large to save on one disk and need to split it into more than one file. Settings established for the current worksheet are saved in the new file.

1-2-3 allows you to save these worksheet sections as either Formulas or Values. If you choose Values, 1-2-3 will save the current values of the selected cells. If you choose Formulas, 1-2-3 will save formulas as they were entered, but the value(s) a formula references will not be saved unless they are in the range selected. When labels are extracted, the result will be the same whether you select Formulas or Values, since labels will not reference other cells.

If you use the Formula option, you should be aware of the way 1-2-3 handles formula references. Absolute cell references (cell references containing $s such as A$2, $A2, or $A$2) will be adjusted in the new file, just as if they were relative references. For example, a cell that referred to a value four rows away will still refer to a cell four rows away. Absolute references will contain the $s after the adjustment, so they will remain absolute in the new worksheet. Relative references will retain their same relative directions.

Extracting formulas that reference cells outside the extract range has the biggest potential for error. For instance, if you were to extract E1..H12 and there was a formula in E2 that referred to A1, when this reference was adjusted for the new file it would refer to cell IS1, since the reference would be computed from A1 of the new worksheet. This cell would probably not contain what you expected. Similar problems can result from combining extracted formulas with an existing worksheet by using the /Copy command: some of the formulas may reference inappropriate cells in the new worksheet and thereby cause errors.

If you select Values, only calculated results and labels will be retained in the new file. All formulas will be replaced by the result of the formula calculations.

The procedure for using either option is to enter /**File Xtract** and choose either Formulas or Values. You will be prompted for the file name to use for storage and can either type a name or choose one from the list of worksheet files on the disk. If you choose an existing file name, you will have to

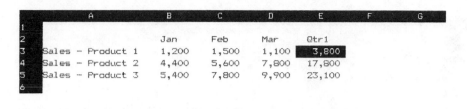

**Figure 8-5.**    Worksheet containing formulas

confirm your choice with Replace. The other option, Cancel, returns you to READY mode without saving the extract file. The last prompt asks you to supply the range to extract by highlighting or typing the address.

Figure 8-5 shows a worksheet that contains formulas in column E. Suppose you extract the entries in column E and save them as Values. You then add this extract to another worksheet with /File Combine Copy. The result is shown in Figure 8-6, where all the formula entries appear as the calculated values from the previous worksheet. If you were to do

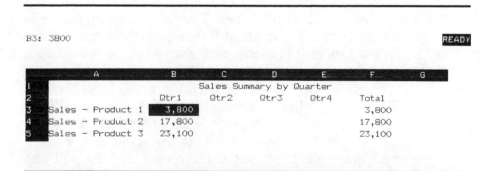

**Figure 8-6.**    Result of /File Combine Copy with values produced by Xtract

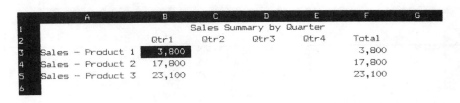

**Figure 8-7.**     Result of /File Combine Copy with formulas produced
by Xtract

this again with /Xtract Formulas, you would obtain the
results shown in Figure 8-7, since the formulas are copied
into a new location without the references they used in the
original worksheet. Although the results still look the same,
this is a dangerous situation. The formula in B3 now reads
@SUM(IU3..A3), since the formula was adjusted but retains
the relative references of the old worksheet.

## Erasing Files From the Disk

From time to time you will have files that you no longer
require. You can remove them from your disk with the file
DEL command under DOS, or you can eliminate them from
within 1-2-3 with /File Erase. The advantage of the /File
Erase option is that you are still in 1-2-3, so you can retrieve
a file and look at it to make sure that you really want to get
rid of it, rather than just blindly deleting it.

The /File Erase command permits you to choose the type
of file you would like to erase. You will choose from Worksheet, Print, Graph, or Other (release 2 only), and 1-2-3 will
then list all the files of that type that are on the disk or in the
current directory. If you are using release 2, 1-2-3 will also
list the subdirectory names (if any) for the current directory.
You can then use the cursor to change directories if you wish.

Release 1A requires that you use /File Directory to make the change.

If you choose Worksheet, all .WKS and .WK1 file names will be displayed. With Print as your selection, all files having a .PRN suffix will be displayed. Choosing Graph will display .PIC files. A choice of Other under release 2 will cause 1-2-3 to display all the file names on the current disk or in the current directory.

After selecting the type of file, you can pick a file name from the display or enter a name yourself. Once the name is entered, 1-2-3 will ask you to confirm your choice by responding with Yes. If you elect not to proceed, select No at the confirmation prompt.

The /File Erase command offers wildcard features, just as DOS does. A ? can replace any single character in the file name, and an asterisk will specify that any characters will be accepted from that point to the end of the file name. As an example, J?N would match with JAN, JUN, JON, JEN, and so on. J* would match with all of the previous options as well as names like JUNE, JANUARY, JOLLY, and JOINT.

## Determining What Files Are On Your Disk

As your list of worksheet models and other 1-2-3 files grows longer, you may have trouble remembering all the files you have on a disk. You can always use the DOS DIR command to see a list of them, but you also have the option of using /File List from the 1-2-3 menu.

When you enter /**File List**, you are presented with a menu of options to determine the file type you are interested in. You can choose from Worksheet, Print, Graph, or Other (release 2 only), and 1-2-3 will then list all the files of that type on the disk or in the current directory. If you are using release 2, 1-2-3 will also list the subdirectory names (if any) for the current directory. You can then use the cursor to change directories if you wish. Release 1A requires that you use /File Directory to make the change.

If you choose Worksheet, all .WKS and .WK1 file names will be displayed, as shown in Figure 8-8. With Print as your selection, all files having a .PRN suffix will be displayed. Choosing Graph will display .PIC files. A choice of Other under release 2 will cause 1-2-3 to display all the file names on the current disk or in the current directory. Regardless of the file type selected, you will be able to point to a file name in the list and see its size and the date it was last saved to disk.

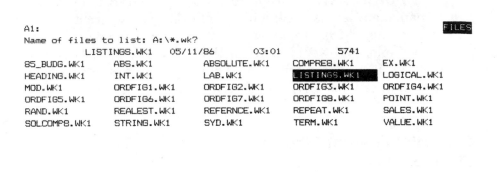

## Adding Text Files to the Worksheet

The /File Import command allows you to transfer data from a word processing program or other package that generates standard ASCII text input to your worksheet. You must be sure that the word processor does not include special characters in the file. (Most word processors have an option to eliminate special characters from the text file.) A standard ASCII text file is created by 1-2-3 every time you use the /Print File command.

The file name that will be imported must have the extension .PRN. If it does not, you have several options for renaming the file so it includes the proper suffix. If you have not yet entered 1-2-3, you can use the DOS RENAME command directly. The format of the command is RENAME OLD-NAME NEWNAME. With release 1A, you can use 1-2-3's File-Manager to handle the renaming operation. Finally, if you are using release 2, you can exit 1-2-3 temporarily with the /System command. You can then access RENAME and later EXIT back to 1-2-3.

1-2-3 imposes a limit on the size of the imported file of 8192 lines for release 2 and 2048 lines for release 1A. The maximum number of characters in a line for both releases is 240.

There are two basic options for importing text data into a 1-2-3 worksheet: Text and Numbers. These options determine how the data will be placed in the worksheet. Use the Text option when you want to import the entire file. Numbers is useful when you want to strip away everything but numeric values.

When you import data as Text, each line of the word processor document will become one long left justified label. You will thus end up with a column of long labels. If you are working with release 2, you can use /Data Parse to split the labels into individual pieces. You can also use /Range Justify if you wish to change the placement of the long labels on the worksheet.

If you elect to use the Numbers option, characters enclosed in double quotation marks as well as all numbers will be imported. Characters not in quotation marks, as well as blanks, will be eliminated in the import process. Each number in a line of the text file will generate a numeric cell entry, and each quote-enclosed label will create a left justified label cell. Entries from the same line of a text file will produce entries in the same row of the worksheet, proceeding from the left to the right of the row with each new entry. Blank spaces and punctuation marks will be used to separate the end of one label from the beginning of the next label.

Figure 8-9 shows text entered into a WordStar file. Suppose this file is saved and the DOS RENAME option is used

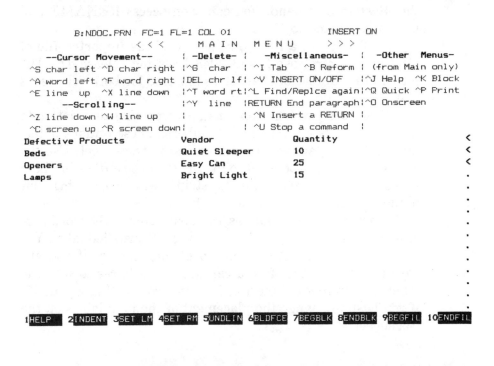

**Figure 8-9.** WordStar text

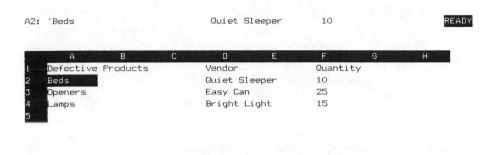

**Figure 8-10.** /File Import with Text

to change its suffix to .PRN. You now have two choices for importing the information into 1-2-3. If you place your cursor in A1 and use the /File Import Text option, the results in Figure 8-10 will be produced. You will notice from the display of A2 that each of the entries is a long label with the entire WordStar line in the one label. If you were to choose Numbers, the output in Figure 8-11 would result. In this instance only the numbers are transferred, since the label entries were not enclosed in quotes.

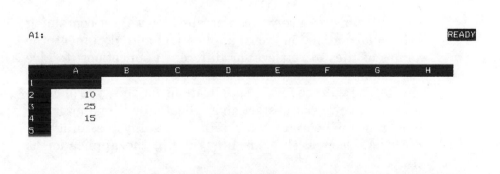

**Figure 8-11.** /File Import with Numbers

## Changing the Current Directory

The /File Directory command permits you to change the disk drive or directory for your current 1-2-3 session. This command is particularly useful in release 1A, since you do not have the ability to change directories from within the other File commands as you do under release 2.

When you enter /File Directory, 1-2-3 will display the existing directory. You can press ENTER to accept it or type a new directory or pathname. If you just want to reach a lower-level directory, you can add a new level onto the existing directory listing.

## Other Ways to Work With Files

1-2-3 provides several commands and features in addition to those on the File menu that are useful in working with files. They will be discussed in this section.

## Creating an Automatically Loaded Worksheet File

1-2-3 provides the ability to automatically load a particular worksheet every time you bring 1-2-3 up in your machine. The only requirement to create this special worksheet is that you must name it AUTO123.

With this feature you can create a worksheet containing help information for your application and document the names of files to retrieve for different applications, to give one example. When you learn about macros in Chapters 12 and 13, you will see further applications for this type of capability. It allows you to start an application with no intervention from the operator, which eliminates any possibility for error. As soon as 1-2-3 is brought up, the application is started.

## Changing the Default Permanently

The /File Directory command is used to change the disk or directory for the current 1-2-3 session. To change the default directory permanently, use /Worksheet Global Default Directory followed by /Worksheet Global Default Update to save your changes in the file 123.CNF.

The /Worksheet Global Default Directory command allows you to change the default disk drive or directory that 1-2-3 uses when saving or retrieving data files. If you do not change the default directory, it is set as the root directory for drive A under release 2 and the root directory for drive B under release 1A.

To change the directory, enter /**Worksheet Global Default Directory** and then enter the directory you want to use. After you press ENTER, this directory will be in effect for the remainder of your 1-2-3 session.

To make the change to the default directory permanent, enter /**Worksheet Global Default Update** after temporarily removing the write protect tabs from your floppy disk. This saves any changes that have been made through the Default options and ensures that they will be available for your next 1-2-3 session. The changes are saved onto 1-2-3's configuration file, which is called 123.CNF.

## Using Operating System Commands

Release 2 allows you to access DOS commands from within 1-2-3. Release 1A provided different ways of accessing DOS.

### Release 2

The /System command is a new addition to release 2. It allows you to access DOS commands while still retaining your worksheet in memory. The only requirement for using it is that COMMAND.COM be on your System Disk or in the 1-2-3 root directory on your hard disk.

If you plan to import a file to the worksheet but forgot to assign it a suffix of .PRN, for example, you could leave 1-2-3 temporarily and use the DOS RENAME command. Likewise, if you attempt to save a file and the disk is full, you could use /System to access DOS and format a disk while keeping your current worksheet in memory.

To access DOS commands, enter /**System**. At the A> prompt you can then enter the DOS command of your choice, though you should keep in mind that options like PRINT that cause DOS to overlay memory will cause your worksheet data to be lost. Any memory-resident DOS command, such as DIR or COPY, can be used with no problem. DOS commands such as GRAPHICS and MODE that require that a program be permanently loaded in memory can cause problems, however. FORMAT is an externally stored program, but it will not remain permanently resident and thus can be used without problems.

When you wish to work with DOS temporarily and invoke /System, the DOS header shown in Figure 8-12 will be presented. You can enter your DOS commands as usual, inserting the DOS disk if you are using floppy drives and wish to access an external DOS program like FORMAT. When you are finished with DOS, enter **EXIT** and return to your 1-2-3 worksheet exactly where you left off.

---

```
(Type EXIT and press [RETURN] to return to 1-2-3)


The IBM Personal Computer DOS
Version 2.00 (C)Copyright IBM Corp 1981, 1982, 1983

A>
```

---

**Figure 8-12.**    DOS header

### Release 1A

Since the /System command was not available under release 1A of 1-2-3, another method was needed to work with files. The File-Manager and Disk-Manager options from the Access menu shown here were the two methods provided. File-Manager deals with individual files, and Disk-Manager works with a disk full of files at once. Translate is available under release 2 as well. It assists in the conversion of information between 1-2-3 and other popular programs. Let's take a brief look at each of these Access System options.

```
Lotus Access System  V.1A  (C)1983 Lotus Development Corp.        MENU
------------------------------------------------------------------------
1-2-3  File-Manager  Disk-Manager  PrintGraph  Translate  Exit
Enter Lotus File Management system
========================================================================
```

**Disk-Manager**      The Disk-Manager program is part of the Lotus Access System and is available on the Utility Disk. It can be accessed directly from DOS or through the Access System menu. Disk-Manager provides four disk handling functions: disk formatting (Prepare), disk copy (Disk-Copy), comparison of two disks (Compare), and a status of the disk directory (Status). The function of each is explained in more detail in the following list.

Prepare
: This option formats disks, preparing them for data storage. Prepare is equivalent to the DOS FORMAT command.

Disk-Copy
: This option creates a complete duplicate of a disk. Disk-Copy is the equivalent of the DOS DISKCOPY command.

Compare
: This option checks to determine whether the contents of two disks are exactly equal. Compare is functionally equivalent to the DOS DISKCOMP command.

Status
: This command checks for inconsistencies in a disk directory. It is equivalent to the DOS CHKDSK command.

**File-Manager**   The File-Manager program is part of the Lotus Access System and resides on the Utility Disk. It provides six different file-handling functions. It can be accessed directly from DOS or through the Access System. Its options are as follows:

Disk-Drive     This option permits you to select the source drive for the File-Manager functions.

Copy          This option copies files from the source disk to a target disk. Copy is equivalent to the DOS COPY command. Use the space bar as a toggle switch to select file and undo your selection if you change your mind. The remaining commands will use the same procedure for selection.

Erase         This option erases files from a disk. It is equivalent to the DOS DEL command.

Rename        This option permits you to change a file name or add a suffix. It is equivalent to the DOS RENAME command.

Archive       This option creates a copy of a file on the current disk under a new name.

Sort          This option arranges file names in alphabetic sequence, using either ascending or descending order and either one or two of the four directory entries that files have. The command operates the same as /Data Sort. Refer to Chapter 9 if you are not familiar with 1-2-3's sorting features.

## Translating Files From Other Programs

The Translate program is part of the Lotus Access System. It provides the ability to translate 1-2-3 files to other formats and files from other programs to the 1-2-3 format. The pro-

```
                    Lotus Translate Utility   Version 2.01
          Copyright 1985 Lotus Development Corporation  All Rights Reserved

What do you want to translate FROM?

            1-2-3, release 1A
            1-2-3, release 2
            dBase II
            dBase III
            DIF
            Jazz
            SYMPHONY, release 1.0
            SYMPHONY, release 1.1
            VISICALC




          Move the menu pointer to your selection and press [RETURN].
              Press [ESCAPE] to leave the Translate Utility.
                   Press [HELP] for more information.
```

**Figure 8-13.**   From options for Translate

```
                    Lotus Translate Utility   Version 2.01
          Copyright 1985 Lotus Development Corporation  All Rights Reserved

Translate FROM: 1-2-3, release 1A     What do you want to translate TO?

                                      1-2-3, release 2
                                      dBase II
                                      dBase III
                                      DIF
                                      SYMPHONY, release 1.0
                                      SYMPHONY, release 1.1








          Move the menu pointer to your selection and press [RETURN].
           Press [ESCAPE] to return to the source selection menu.
                   Press [HELP] for more information.
```

**Figure 8-14.**   To options for Translate

gram for Translate is on the Utility Disk in both release 1A and release 2. It can be accessed directly from DOS or through the Access System. To use it you must quit 1-2-3 with /Quit Yes. If you are not working with a hard disk system, you will be prompted to place the Utility Disk in the drive.

When you are working with Translate, you will first have to select the format to translate from. A list of the release 2 From Format options is shown in Figure 8-13. After making this selection, you will be prompted to choose from the list of To formats shown in Figure 8-14. Translate provides a message if the formats you choose do not need translation. As shown in Figure 8-15, you do not need to translate release 1A files to use them under release 2. You also will not need to translate Symphony files for use with release 2 of 1-2-3 nor release 2 files for use with Symphony 1.1. However, release 2 files may not fit in release 1A of 1-2-3 or release 1 of Symphony, since these packages utilize memory less effectively than release 2 of 1-2-3.

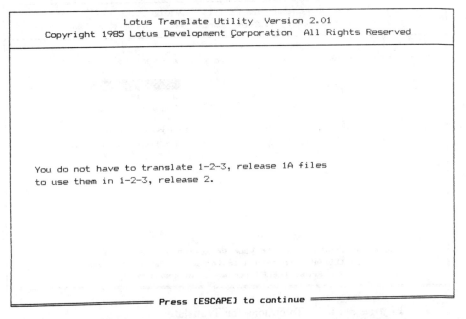

**Figure 8-15.** Message that translation is not required

# FILES

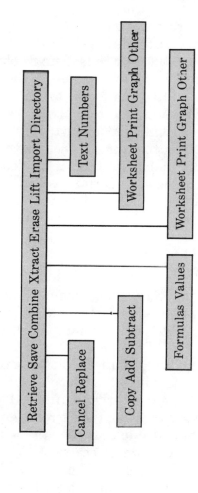

© Lotus Development Corporation, 1986. Used with permission.

### Description

The /File Combine Add command permits you to add some or all of the values from a worksheet file to current worksheet values. The addition process uses the cursor location in the current worksheet as the left uppermost cell to be combined with the first cell in the worksheet or range you are adding to it. Only cells that are blank or contain values will be affected by this process. Cells that contain formulas or labels will be unaffected by this addition.

The Add feature is useful when you are performing a budget consolidation. You can begin with a total budget worksheet that contains nothing more than labels and a few total formulas. As long as all departmental budgets are in exactly the same format as the total worksheet, you will be able to use /File Combine Add once for each worksheet file to produce a budget consolidation.

### Options

Like the other /File Combine commands, Add permits you to combine an entire file or a named range. In either case, it begins the combination at the cursor location.

**Entire-File** With this option, every value cell in the worksheet file will be added to a cell in the current worksheet. Cell A1 in the worksheet file will be added to the cell where the cursor rests in the current worksheet. Remaining values will be added to the cell with the proper displacement from the current cursor location.

When you select Entire-File, the names of the worksheet files on the current disk (in the current directory if you are using a hard disk) will be presented. You can either point to one of the entries in the list of file names or enter the file name you wish to use. Since release 2 allows you to create file names that have a suffix different from the regular release 2 suffix of .WK1, you can type the name of a file that has a suffix other than .WK1 as long as you supply the proper suffix. Likewise, you can access files on a different drive or in a different directory if you supply the complete pathname.

**Named-Range**    With this option, 1-2-3 will ask you to specify a range name and then the file that contains this range name. The range name you specify must be a valid name for the file name specified. The rules for entering the file name are the same as for Entire-File.

## /File Combine Copy

### Description

The /File Combine Copy command permits you to replace some or all of the values from the current worksheet with values (including formulas and labels) from a worksheet file. The copying process uses the cursor location in the current worksheet as the upper leftmost cell you wish to replace with the first cell in the worksheet or range you are copying to it. Unlike the case with Add, even current worksheet cells containing formulas and labels are affected by /File Combine Copy. They will be overwritten by the copied information.

The Copy feature is useful when you would like to copy headings and values from an existing worksheet to one you are currently creating. Although formulas can be copied, you must be sure that the values they will require are also copied, or an error could result.

### Options

Like the other /File Combine commands, Copy permits you to combine an entire file or a named range. In either case, it begins the replacement at the cursor location.

**Entire-File**    With this option, every value cell in the worksheet file will be added to a cell in the current worksheet. Cell A1 in the worksheet file will be added to the cell where the cursor rests in the current worksheet. Remaining values will be added to the cell with the proper displacement from the current cursor location.

When you select Entire-File, the names of the worksheet files on the current disk (in the current directory if you are using a hard disk) will be presented. You can either point to one of the entries in the list of file names or enter the file name you wish to use. Since release 2 allows you to create file names that have a suffix different from the regular release 2 suffix of .WK1, you can type the name of a file that has a suffix other than .WK1 as long as you supply the proper suffix. Likewise, you can access files on a different drive or different directory if you supply the complete pathname.

**Named-Range**    With this option, 1-2-3 will ask you to specify a range name and then the file that contains this range name. The range name you specify must be a valid name for the file name specified. The rules for entering the file name are the same as for Entire-File.

## /File Combine Subtract

### Description

The /File Combine Subtract command permits you to subtract some or all of the values from a worksheet file from the current worksheet values. The subtraction process uses the cursor location in the current worksheet as the upper left-most cell to be combined with the first cell in the worksheet or range you are subtracting from it. Only cells that are blank or contain values will be affected by this process. Cells that contain formulas or labels will be unaffected by this subtraction operation.

The Subtract feature is useful when you are performing a budget consolidation. You can begin with a total budget worksheet. Then, to see the effect of closing one of a company's departments or subsidiaries, you can subtract the file containing its budget projections from the total. All subsid-

iary budgets must be in exactly the same format as the total
worksheet, however.

## Options

Like the other /File Combine commands, Subtract permits
you to combine an entire file or a named range. In either
case, it begins the combination at the cursor location.

**Entire-File**   With this option, every value cell in the worksheet file will be subtracted from a cell in the current worksheet. Cell A1 in the worksheet file will be subtracted from
the cell where the cursor rests in the current worksheet.
Remaining values will be subtracted from the cell with the
proper displacement from the current cursor location.

When you select Entire-File, the names of the worksheet
files on the current disk (in the current directory if you are
using a hard disk) will be presented. You can either point to
one of the entries in the list of file names or enter the file
name you wish to use. Since release 2 allows you to create file
names that have a suffix different from the regular release 2
suffix of .WK1, you can type the name of a file that has a
suffix other than .WK1 as long as you supply the proper suffix. Likewise, you can access files on a different drive or different directory if you supply the complete pathname.

**Named-Range**   With this option, 1-2-3 will ask you to
specify a range name and then the file that contains this
range name. The range name you specify must be a valid
name for the file name specified. The rules for entering the
file name are the same as for Entire-File.

# /File Directory

## Description

The /File Directory command allows you to check or change
the current root directory that 1-2-3 is using for file storage

and retrieval. Under release 2, the default directory is drive A; under release 1A, it is drive B. This original default is stored in the file 123.CNF, which 1-2-3 checks every time you load 1-2-3 into your system. The /File Directory command allows you to make a change only for the current session. If you wish to change the default directory permanently, use /Worksheet Global Default Directory followed by /Worksheet Global Default Update to save your change.

## Options

With this command, you have the choice of reviewing the current directory setting or making a change to it. To review the setting, simply press ENTER in response to the display you see when you type /**File Directory**.

To make a change to the directory, you must first decide whether you want to change the complete directory designated or whether you want to stay in the same directory and just change the lower-level subdirectory you are working in. You can change the drive, the directory, and the subdirectory with this command.

**Drive**     To change the drive, type the drive designator followed by a backslash, for example, **B:\**. To change the path as well, type the pathname at the same time, for example, **B:\123\SALES**.

**Current Directory**     If the current directory is ACCT and you want to change it to MKTG, enter **MKTG\**.

**A Lower Level in the Current Directory**     This allows you to maintain the current directory setting but use a specific subdirectory within it. If your current directory is C:123\SALES and you wish to be in the subdirectory MICHIGAN within SALES, enter **\MICHIGAN** or **C:123\SALES\MICHIGAN**.

**A Higher Level in the Current Directory**     To change the directory to one level higher, enter .. (this is the DOS symbol for a directory one level higher). If your current directory level is C:123\SALES\MICHIGAN and you want to be at the level of SALES, you can enter either **C:123\SALES** or **..** (the latter is clearly much quicker).

## Note

When you use release 1A with release 1.1 of DOS, subdirectories are not allowed.

# /File Erase

## Description

The /File Erase command is used to remove one or more files from the disk.

## Options

You must first choose the type of the file or files you wish to remove from the disk. With release 2, your options are the following:

| | |
|---|---|
| Worksheet | Files with the suffix .WK1 |
| Print | Files with the suffix .PRN |
| Graph | Files with the suffix .PIC |
| Other | Files with a suffix other than .WK1, .PRN, or .PIC |

With release 1A, only the first three options are possible. Also with release 1A, worksheet files have the suffix .WKS.

Once you have specified the file type you wish to delete, 1-2-3 will list all the files of that type on the current drive or directory. You can point to the file you wish to delete or type in the file name. If the file you wish to delete is on a different file or in a different directory, you will have to type the drive designator and pathname in addition to the file name (release 2 only; with release 1A you will need to use /File Directory first).

You can use wildcard characters when specifying the file names you wish to delete. The special characters used in creating wildcard file names are as follows:

?     Will match any single character in the file name. For example, ?CCT would match ACCT, TCCT, and LCCT.

*     Matches all remaining characters in the file name. For example, S* matches SALES, SALES1, and SALARY.

## /File Import

### Description

The /File Import command lets you load information in a Print file into the current worksheet at the cursor location. Standard ASCII files not exceeding 240 characters in width and 8192 characters in length (2048 lines for release 1A) can be imported, as long as each file has a suffix of .PRN.

### Options

The /File Import command provides two options, allowing you to bring either a column of long labels or a combination of numbers and labels into the worksheet.

**Text**     This option will bring each line of the imported text file into the worksheet as a single long label. /Data Parse can split files imported as text into separate entries rather than one long label (see Chapter 10 for more information).

**Numbers**     This option searches the imported file for numbers and for text entries enclosed in quotes. Each number will be placed in a worksheet cell as a value, and each entry in quotes will be placed in the worksheet cell as a left justified label. If more than one number or quote enclosed entry is found in a line of the text file, more than one column of the worksheet will be used. When the next line of the imported file is processed, entries will again begin in the same column as the cursor.

## Note

Special characters added by some word processors can cause problems. Most word processors have an option that excludes these special characters to produce a standard ASCII file.

## /File List

### Description

The /File List command lists all the files of the specified type in the current directory.

### Options

With release 2, you have four choices:

| | |
|---|---|
| Worksheet | Files with the suffix .WK1 |
| Print | Files with the suffix .PRN |
| Graph | Files with the suffix .PIC |
| Other | Files with a suffix other than .WK1, .PRN, or .PIC. |

With release 1A, only the first three options are possible. Also with release 1A, worksheet files have the suffix .WKS.

# /File Retrieve

### Description

The /File Retrieve command loads a file from disk into the memory of your computer system. Any information in memory before the file is retrieved is erased by the loading of the new file.

### Options

You can retrieve a file from the current disk or directory, or you can retrieve from a different one if you specify the pathname (release 2 only; with release 1A, you must change directories with /File Directory first). With release 2, you can retrieve password-protected files by supplying the password when 1-2-3 prompts you.

# /File Save

### Description

The /File Save command allows you to save the current worksheet and any settings you have created for it to a worksheet file.

### Options

You can save the worksheet file to the current disk by entering the file name and pressing ENTER if the file has never been saved to the disk. Under release 2, if you wish to use a different disk or directory than the current one, you can do so by specifying the complete pathname. With release 1A, you must use /File Directory.

If the file is already saved on the disk, 1-2-3 will prompt you with the existing file name. Press ENTER to accept it.

The next prompt is Cancel or Replace. Cancel stops the /File Save command and returns you to READY mode. Replace places the current contents of memory on the disk under the existing file name, replacing what was stored in the file previously.

This command also allows you to add a password to a file when it is saved. Once a file is saved with a password, you will not be able to retrieve the file unless you can supply the password. After typing the name of the file to be saved, press the space bar and type **p**. This causes 1-2-3 to prompt you for a password up to 15 characters long. After you enter one, a verify prompt will ask for you to type the password again. If you wish to abort the procedure instead of responding to the verify prompt, you can press ESC several times to return to READY mode without saving the file and adding a password.

### Note

If you save a file with the name AUTO123, the file will be retrieved every time you load 1-2-3 as long as it is in the same directory as 1-2-3.

# /File Xtract

### Description

The /File Xtract command allows you to save a portion of the current worksheet in a worksheet file. Settings established for the current worksheet, such as graph and print settings and range names, are saved in the new file.

### Options

The /File Xtract command allows you to save either values or formulas from the range specified.

**Formulas**     This option saves current worksheet formulas as well as labels and values in the worksheet file.

**Values**     This option saves numbers and labels in the worksheet files. Formulas are evaluated to determine the numbers for saving, but the formulas are not saved.

After entering the /File Xtract command and choosing Formulas or Values, select a file name for saving from the menu or enter a new name. Next, enter a range of cell addresses or a range name. If the file name is new, pressing ENTER will complete the process. If you are using an existing file name, 1-2-3 will present you with a prompt asking if you wish to Cancel the request or Replace the existing file with the contents of the range selected.

### Note

You can use /File Combine to add this extracted information to a worksheet file in memory.

## /System

### Description

The /System command allows you to use the operating system commands without quitting 1-2-3. This means you can access some of the DOS commands while your 1-2-3 worksheet remains in memory. In order for you to use this command, COMMAND.COM must be copied from your DOS disk to your 1-2-3 disk. The /System command is available only under release 2.

### Options

Any DOS command that does not overlay memory can be used with /System. EXIT returns you to your worksheet.

# /Worksheet Global Default Directory

### Description

This command permits you to specify the directory that 1-2-3 will automatically search for your files when it is loaded. Unless you change it, the default is drive A for release 2 and drive B for release 1A.

### Options

Normally, when you enter /Worksheet Global Default Directory, you will enter a new default directory. A second option is to clear the existing entry without entering a new one. In this case 1-2-3 will use the directory that was current when 1-2-3 was loaded as the default for file storage and retrieval.

### Note

To make this directory change permanent, use /Worksheet Global Default Update to save the change to the file 123.CNF.

# /Worksheet Global Default Update

### Description

This command allows you to save any changes that you have made to the Worksheet Global Default settings to the file 123.CNF. The disk containing 1-2-3 must be in the current drive at the time this command is executed.

### Options

There are no options for this command.

## Disk-Manager

### Description

The Disk-Manager program is part of the Lotus Access System under release 1A. It can be accessed directly from DOS or through the Access System menu.

### Options

Disk-Manager provides four disk-handling functions. These are disk formatting (Prepare), disk copy (Disk-Copy), comparison of two disks (Compare), and a status check of the disk directory (Status).

## File-Manager

### Description

The File-Manager program is part of the Lotus Access System under release 1A. It provides six different file-handling functions. It can be accessed directly from DOS or through the Access System.

### Options

The options for File-Manager are as follows:

| | |
|---|---|
| Disk-Drive | Selects the source drive |
| Copy | Copies files from the source disk to a target disk |
| Erase | Erases files from a disk |
| Rename | Changes a file name |
| Archive | Creates a copy of a file on the current disk under a new name |
| Sort | Arranges file names in alphabetic sequence |

# Translate

## Description

The Translate option allows you to exchange data files between 1-2-3 and other popular programs. It is available from the main Access System menu. You must quit 1-2-3 with /Quit Yes to use Translate. The program for Translate is stored on the Utility Disk, so if you are not working with a hard disk system, you will be prompted to place the Utility Disk in the drive.

## Options

You have two types of options for the Translate program. You can select from a list of file formats to translate from and a list of file formats to translate to.

The From options are as follows:

1-2-3 release 1A
1-2-3 release 2
dBASE II
dBASE III
DIF
Jazz
Symphony release 1.0
Symphony release 1.1
VisiCalc

The To options are as follows:

1-2-3 release 2
dBASE II
dBASE III
DIF
Symphony release 1.0
Symphony release 1.1

**Note**

You will not need to translate Symphony files for use with release 2 of 1-2-3 nor release 2 files for use with Symphony 1.1. Release 2 files may not fit in release 1A of 1-2-3 or release 1 of Symphony, however, since these packages utilize memory less effectively than release 2 of 1-2-3.

# Data Management, Graphics, and Macros

# Data Management

**N
I
N
E**

In one sense, all the work you have done with 1-2-3 up to this point can be considered data management, because it has all involved the management of information recorded on the worksheet. But data management, as 1-2-3 uses it, is a special term that refers to the more formalized process of design, entry, and retrieval of information from a database.

The world of data management has its own terminology. A *database*, for example, is a collection of all the information you have about a set of things. These things can be customers, orders, parts in inventory, employees, or anything else. If you created a database of employee information, for example, you would want to place information about each of your employees in the database. All the information about one employee would be one *record* in the database. A record is composed of all the pieces of information you are interested in recording about one thing in the set, such as one employee. These individual pieces of information in a record are referred to as *fields*. Fields you might want to put in each record in an employee database might include name, address, job classification, date of hire, social security number, department, benefits, and salary. When you design a new database, you will need to decide what fields will be included in each record.

This chapter will examine the /Data commands that permit organization and retrieval of information from 1-2-3's worksheet. The next chapter will examine the /Data commands that add power to the calculations you do on the worksheet. Some of the commands covered in this chapter serve a dual purpose. They will work when information management is your only requirement, but they can also lend assistance when your objective is the more traditional use of the worksheet for calculations. In the next chapter you will find some hints on using these data management techniques with traditional spreadsheet applications.

A 1-2-3 database is a range of cells on a worksheet. It can be in any area of the worksheet you want, but the field names, that is, the names you use to categorize data, must run across the top row of the range. The records in the database that contain data for each field are placed in the rows immediately following the row of field names. Figure 9-1 presents a section of an employee database in A1..F20. The field names are located in A1..F1, and the first database record is located in A2..F2.

As a database, 1-2-3 has both strengths and weaknesses compared to other packages. You may find it helpful to look

| | A | B | C | D | E | F |
|---|---|---|---|---|---|---|
| 1 | Last Name | First Name | SS# | Job Code | Salary | Location |
| 2 | Larson | Mary | 543-98-9876 | 23 | $12,000 | 2 |
| 3 | Campbell | David | 213-76-9874 | 23 | $23,000 | 10 |
| 4 | Campbell | Keith | 569-89-7654 | 12 | $32,000 | 2 |
| 5 | Stephens | Tom | 219-78-8954 | 15 | $17,800 | 2 |
| 6 | Caldor | Larry | 459-34-0921 | 23 | $32,500 | 4 |
| 7 | Lightnor | Peggy | 560-55-4311 | 14 | $23,500 | 10 |
| 8 | McCartin | John | 817-66-1212 | 15 | $54,600 | 2 |
| 9 | Justof | Jack | 431-78-9963 | 17 | $41,200 | 4 |
| 10 | Patterson | Lyle | 212-11-9090 | 12 | $21,500 | 10 |
| 11 | Miller | Lisa | 214-89-6756 | 23 | $18,700 | 2 |
| 12 | Hawkins | Mark | 215-67-8973 | 21 | $19,500 | 2 |
| 13 | Hartwick | Eileen | 313-78-9090 | 15 | $31,450 | 4 |
| 14 | Smythe | George | 560-90-8645 | 15 | $65,000 | 4 |
| 15 | Wilkes | Caitlin | 124-67-7432 | 17 | $15,500 | 2 |
| 16 | Deaver | Ken | 198-98-6750 | 23 | $24,600 | 10 |
| 17 | Kaylor | Sally | 312-45-9862 | 12 | $32,900 | 10 |
| 18 | Parker | Dee | 659-11-3452 | 14 | $19,800 | 4 |
| 19 | Preverson | Gary | 670-90-1121 | 21 | $27,600 | 4 |
| 20 | Samuelson | Paul | 219-89-7080 | 23 | $28,900 | 2 |

03-Oct-86   06:35 AM

**Figure 9-1.**    Employee database

at some ways in which 1-2-3's features differ from those of its competitors.

• The data in your 1-2-3 database is all stored in memory while you are working with the database. Unlike other packages that must read data from the disk when you need it, 1-2-3 can provide unprecedentedly quick responses to requests for resequencing records and finding those that match specific criteria. This feature does require that you have sufficient memory to fit your entire database in memory at once, however. This means you will need a large memory capacity, a fairly small database, or both.

• 1-2-3's data management commands are similar to its worksheet commands, which makes them easy for a user of the package's worksheet features to learn. By contrast, other packages may require a significant time investment to master their command structure.

• Most data management packages allow the creation of a formatted screen to enter or review one record at a time. Symphony and dBASE are among the packages that offer this formatting feature.

• Release 2 permits the entry of up to 8192 records in one database, while release 1A places the limit at 2048. As noted, both releases are also restricted by the amount of memory available, since the entire file resides in memory. These limits are sufficient for many applications, but some other products allow an unlimited number of records.

• 1-2-3 permits you to have up to 256 fields in one database. Some packages allow more and others less.

## Setting Up a Database

The first step in designing a 1-2-3 database should be to create a list of fields you want your database to contain. Once you have all the field names recorded, estimate the number of characters that each field will require for storage and the number of records in your database. Add the number of characters for each field to get a record total and then multiply by the number of records. If the potential number of records exceeds 1-2-3's limits, you will have to find another alternative, such as splitting your file into two sections. Similarly, if the number of records times the length of one record exceeds the available memory in your system, you will not want to proceed with the design process unless you can use multiple subfiles in your application.

## Choosing a Location for the Database

The next step is to select an area of the worksheet for storing the database. Here are some considerations to keep in mind as you select a location for your database.

• To allow your database to expand with additional records, choose an area below calculations and other fixed information in your worksheet.

• If you plan to place more than one database on the worksheet, place them side by side so each can expand downward.

• If you have sufficient memory and have two databases in one worksheet, you might want to start one in A1 and the other to the right but beneath the last record in the first database. This wastes some memory but allows you to use the /Worksheet Delete and /Worksheet Insert commands and delete and insert records in either database without affecting the other.

## Entering Field Names

Record your selected field names across the top row of your database area. Following these rules for field names will help you create a workable database.

• Make sure you record field names in the same order in which they appear in the form you plan to use for data entry. This will minimize the time required for entry.

• Each field name should be placed in one cell.

• The names you choose for your fields will be used with some of the other database features. Therefore, choose meaningful names, but do not choose names so long that reentry in other places will lead to misspellings.

• Do not enter spaces at the ends of field names. It will not be apparent that you included them, and the names will not match with later entries for other data management features that do not include trailing spaces.

A layout of field names for an employee database might look like this.

## Entering Information

The first database record should begin immediately beneath the row of field names. Do not leave blank lines or use special symbols as divider lines.

All entries in each field of the database should be of the same type. For example, if a field contains numeric data, the value for that field in every record should be numeric. Mixing numeric values and labels in a single field will cause the two groups to be separated when records are sorted and when you attempt to select a subset of the records. It is acceptable to leave a field within a particular record blank if you lack data. Figure 9-2 presents an employee database after the first ten records have been entered.

As your database grows longer, the field names at the top of your screen will disappear from view. You can prevent this by using the /Worksheet Titles Horizontal command to lock the field names in place on your screen. If you have forgotten how this command works, go back to Chapter 5 for a quick review.

## Making Changes

Entries in a database can be changed with any of the techniques you have used on regular worksheets. An entry can be retyped to replace its current value. The F2 (EDIT) key can be used to insert, delete, and replace characters within an entry.

|  | A | B | C | D | E | F |
|---|---|---|---|---|---|---|
| 1 | Last Name | First Name | SS# | Job Code | Salary | Location |
| 2 | Larson | Mary | 543-98-9876 | 23 | $12,000 | 2 |
| 3 | Campbell | David | 213-76-9874 | 23 | $23,000 | 10 |
| 4 | Campbell | Keith | 569-89-7654 | 12 | $32,000 | 2 |
| 5 | Stephens | Tom | 219-78-8954 | 15 | $17,800 | 2 |
| 6 | Caldor | Larry | 459-34-0921 | 23 | $32,500 | 4 |
| 7 | Lightnor | Peggy | 560-55-4311 | 14 | $23,500 | 10 |
| 8 | McCartlin | John | 817-66-1212 | 15 | $54,600 | 2 |
| 9 | Justof | Jack | 431-78-9963 | 17 | $41,200 | 4 |
| 10 | Patterson | Lyle | 212-11-9090 | 12 | $21,500 | 10 |
| 11 | Miller | Lisa | 214-89-6756 | 23 | $18,700 | 2 |
| 12 |  |  |  |  |  |  |

**Figure 9-2.** Employee database

You can use /Worksheet Insert to add a blank row for a new record or add a blank column for another field. The /Worksheet Delete command can be used to remove records or fields. Bear in mind, though, that the entire worksheet is affected by both of these commands, so it is important to assess potential damage to areas outside the database. One good strategy would be to save the file before using insertion or deletion commands. Then, if you had a problem, you could restore the file from disk. The /Copy command can be used to copy field values from other database records as well.

## Sorting Your Data

1-2-3 provides extremely fast sort features because of the storage of the database in RAM. Any change in sequence can take place at the speed of transfer within RAM, which is considerably faster than sorting records from disk.

All the commands that you will need to specify the records to be sorted, specify the sort sequence, and tell 1-2-3 to begin the sort are located under the /Data Sort option. The submenu for this command looks like this.

The steps for resequencing your data using the various Sort commands are summarized in the box called "Steps for Sorting Your Data."

## Determining What Data to Sort

You can sort all the records in your database or just some of them, depending on the range you specify. Always be sure to include all the fields in the sort, since excluding some fields would mean that those fields would remain stationary while the remainder of a record was resequenced. If you ever plan to return your records to their original entry sequence after a sort, you will need to include a field for record number in the record. A sequential number can be placed in this field at the time of entry.

To set the range for the database, enter /**Data Sort Data-Range**. Then specify the range for the database as shown. Be sure you *do not* include the field names.

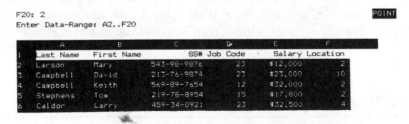

If you include them, they will be sorted along with the record values.

## Steps for Sorting Your Data

Sorting is a quick and easy process, but it requires a sequence of commands from the /Data Sort menu. The steps and commands to use are as follows:

1. Enter /**Data Sort** and choose Data-Range.

2. Highlight (specify) all database records and fields, but do not include the field names within the range.

3. Select Primary-Key from the Sort menu.

4. Highlight any data value within the column you wish to use to control the sort sequence.

5. If you expect duplicate primary keys within your database, choose Secondary-Key.

6. Highlight any data value within the column that you wish to use as the tie breaker if there are duplicate primary keys.

7. Select Go from the Sort menu to have 1-2-3 resequence your data.

**1**
**2**
**3**

## Specifying the Sort Sequence

1-2-3 permits you to specify either one or two sort keys. In all cases the primary key will control the sequence of the records. The secondary key will be ignored, even when you specify one, except where duplicate examples of the primary key occur. In this situation, the secondary key will be used to break the tie.

In release 2, another setting also affects the sort order. This is the collating sequence, which can be selected in the Install program. As mentioned in Chapter 1, there are three options for collating sequence: Numbers First, Numbers Last, and ASCII. Release 1A uses the ASCII sequence. The "Effect of Collating Sequence on Sorting" box describes these options in further detail. To make a change, you will need to go back to Install and make a different selection for collating sequence.

**1 2 3**

## Effect of Collating Sequence On Sorting (release 2 only)

The order of your data after a sort is partly dependent on the collating sequence in release 2. This sequence is specified during the Install program. Sort order in the three possibilities for ascending sequence is as follows:

- Numbers last: Blank cells, label entries with letters in alphabetical order, label entries beginning with numbers in numeric sequence, labels beginning with special characters, then values.

- Numbers first: values, blank cells, labels beginning with numbers in numeric sequence, labels beginning with letters in alphabetical order, then labels beginning with special characters.

- ASCII: blank cells, followed by labels and values in ASCII order. Capitalization will affect the sort order with this choice.

## Choosing a Primary Sort Key

To specify a primary key, simply enter /**Data Sort Primary-Key** and point to a cell containing data for a particular field within the database. This field (column) will become your primary sort key. If you prefer, you can type the cell address instead of pointing. In either case you will next be prompted to choose the sort order. The two choices are A for ascending order and D for descending order. When you choose A, the collating sequence you chose with Install will be used. When you choose D, the sequence will be reversed. Enter the letter for the choice you want, as shown:

```
A1: [W12] 'Last Name                                    EDIT
Primary sort key: D2         Sort order (A or D): A
```

You will note that a default sort order may already be present on your screen. It will be the order you chose for your last previous sort. To keep this default, press ENTER in response to the prompt.

Setting the sort sequence does not automatically resequence your data. You also have to specify the data range and then select Go from the Sort menu.

## Choosing a Secondary Sort Key

The secondary sort key serves as a tie breaker. For example, in the case of an employee file where last name has been specified as the primary sort key, you may wish to use first name as the secondary key to handle instances where more than one employee has the same last name. Within the group of duplicate last names, records will then be sorted by first name.

You can set the secondary key by entering /**Data Sort Secondary-Key** and either pointing to a cell containing a data value for the field you want to sort on or by typing the cell address. You will then need to specify A for ascending or D for descending sort order, as you did with the primary key.

```
A1: [W12] 'Last Name                                              EDIT
Secondary sort key: E2              Sort order (A or D): A
```

Again, the default sequence will be the last order you selected. (Thus, if you selected A last time, the default will be A.) If you wish to keep the current setting, press ENTER in response to this prompt.

## Starting and Stopping the Sort

With the data range and (at a minimum) a primary key selected, you are ready to resequence your data. Simply select Go from the Sort menu after completing these other steps, and your data will be sorted in the specified sequence. The sort will be complete as soon as you lift your finger after selecting Go.

Figure 9-3 presents an employee database with the records in random sequence. Suppose the data range is selected as A2..H20, using /Data Sort Data-Range. Next the Last Name field (A2) is selected as the primary key, and A for ascending sort order is chosen. A secondary key of First Name (B2) is then chosen, and A for ascending sort order is again entered. Once Go is selected from the /Data Sort menu, the records will be placed in the new sequence shown in Figure 9-4. Notice that the two records with a last name of Campbell are sequenced by first name.

When you are through sorting, you will need to use another command to get rid of the "sticky" Sort menu. The command is /Data Sort Quit.

## Starting Over

Once you have made choices for a sort, 1-2-3 will use these settings as a default. Making a new selection for data range

A1: [W12] 'Last Name READY

| | A | B | C | D | E | F |
|---|---|---|---|---|---|---|
| 1 | Last Name | First Name | SS# | Job Code | Salary | Location |
| 2 | Larson | Mary | 543-98-9876 | 23 | $12,000 | 2 |
| 3 | Campbell | David | 213-76-9874 | 23 | $23,000 | 10 |
| 4 | Campbell | Keith | 569-89-7654 | 12 | $32,000 | 2 |
| 5 | Stephens | Tom | 219-78-8954 | 15 | $17,800 | 2 |
| 6 | Caldor | Larry | 459-34-0921 | 23 | $32,500 | 4 |
| 7 | Lightnor | Peggy | 560-55-4311 | 14 | $23,500 | 10 |
| 8 | McCartin | John | 817-66-1212 | 15 | $54,600 | 2 |
| 9 | Justof | Jack | 431-78-9963 | 17 | $41,200 | 4 |
| 10 | Patterson | Lyle | 212-11-9090 | 12 | $21,500 | 10 |

**Figure 9-3.** Employee records in random sequence

A3: [W12] 'Campbell READY

| | A | B | C | D | E | F |
|---|---|---|---|---|---|---|
| 1 | Last Name | First Name | SS# | Job Code | Salary | Location |
| 2 | Caldor | Larry | 459-34-0921 | 23 | $32,500 | 4 |
| 3 | Campbell | David | 213-76-9874 | 23 | $23,000 | 10 |
| 4 | Campbell | Keith | 569-89-7654 | 12 | $32,000 | 2 |
| 5 | Deaver | Ken | 198-98-6750 | 23 | $24,600 | 10 |
| 6 | Hartwick | Eileen | 313-78-9090 | 15 | $31,450 | 4 |
| 7 | Hawkins | Mark | 215-67-8973 | 21 | $19,500 | 2 |
| 8 | Justof | Jack | 431-78-9963 | 17 | $41,200 | 4 |
| 9 | Kaylor | Sally | 312-45-9862 | 12 | $32,900 | 10 |
| 10 | Larson | Mary | 543-98-9876 | 23 | $12,000 | 2 |
| 11 | Lightnor | Peggy | 560-55-4311 | 14 | $23,500 | 10 |
| 12 | McCartin | John | 817-66-1212 | 15 | $54,600 | 2 |
| 13 | Miller | Lisa | 214-89-6756 | 23 | $18,700 | 2 |
| 14 | Parker | Dee | 659-11-3452 | 14 | $19,800 | 4 |
| 15 | Patterson | Lyle | 212-11-9090 | 12 | $21,500 | 10 |
| 16 | Preverson | Gary | 670-90-1121 | 21 | $27,600 | 4 |
| 17 | Samuelson | Paul | 219-89-7080 | 23 | $28,900 | 2 |
| 18 | Smythe | George | 560-90-8645 | 15 | $65,000 | 4 |
| 19 | Stephens | Tom | 219-78-8954 | 15 | $17,800 | 2 |
| 20 | Wilkes | Caitlin | 124-67-7432 | 17 | $15,500 | 2 |

03-Oct-86 04:49 AM

**Figure 9-4.** Resequenced records

or either of the sort keys will replace your existing selection. If you want to eliminate your settings to make sure that you have to enter a new data range and primary key before sorting again, you can use /Data Sort Reset. This option eliminates default settings for data range, primary sort key, and secondary sort key.

## Adding Record Numbers

1-2-3 does not have an "unsort" feature. Once you have changed the sequence of your records, there is no command that will automatically restore them to their original sequence. There is a solution to this dilemma, however, if you plan ahead. You can add a field for record number to each record and assign a sequential number to the field when the records are added to the database. To return sorted records to their entry sort order, you could then simply re-sort on record number.

You can get 1-2-3 to do the work of sequential number assignment by using the /Data Fill command. With this command, you can have 1-2-3 generate any series of numbers that have even increments by specifying the start, stop, and increment numbers you wish to use.

A look at the command in action will clarify the steps required for its use. A blank column has been inserted at the left of the employee database for sequence numbers, and Sequence was entered in A1. These numbers will be used to keep track of the original entry order for records. To make /Data Fill supply the numbers, you would follow these steps:

1. Move the cursor to A2, the left uppermost cell in the range where the numbers will be generated.

2. Enter /**Data Fill** and specify the fill range as A2..A20, either by pointing or by typing the range reference.

3. Enter **1** for the start value at the prompt, as shown:

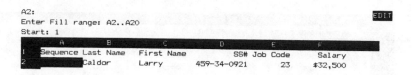

4. The next prompt is for the step or increment (that is, the amount to add to each value to generate the next number). Enter another **1**.

5. The last piece of information you are prompted for is the *stop value*—the highest number that can be in the series. You could enter a 19, since this will be the last value in the range, but as long as the default value is not less than the stop value you want, you can let 1-2-3 generate the stop value from the range and increment you have supplied. To do this, accept the default of 8191 by pressing ENTER, as shown. You can use this approach when 8191 is greater than the last value in your series. 1-2-3 will stop when it reaches your last value.

The result of the data fill operation is shown in Figure 9-5.

## Using More Than Two Sort Keys

Although 1-2-3's Sort command supplies only a primary and secondary sort key, release 2 lets you effectively sort on more than two fields. You can do this by adding a field to your

| | A | B | C | D | E | F |
|---|---|---|---|---|---|---|
| 1 | Sequence | Last Name | First Name | SS# | Job Code | Salary |
| 2 | 1 | Larson | Mary | 543-98-9876 | 23 | $12,000 |
| 3 | 2 | Campbell | David | 213-76-9874 | 23 | $23,000 |
| 4 | 3 | Campbell | Keith | 569-89-7654 | 12 | $32,000 |
| 5 | 4 | Stephens | Tom | 219-78-8954 | 15 | $17,800 |
| 6 | 5 | Caldor | Larry | 459-34-0921 | 23 | $32,500 |
| 7 | 6 | Lightnor | Peggy | 560-55-4311 | 14 | $23,500 |
| 8 | 7 | McCartin | John | 817-66-1212 | 15 | $54,600 |
| 9 | 8 | Justof | Jack | 431-78-9963 | 17 | $41,200 |
| 10 | 9 | Patterson | Lyle | 212-11-9090 | 12 | $21,500 |
| 11 | 10 | Miller | Lisa | 214-89-6756 | 23 | $18,700 |
| 12 | 11 | Hawkins | Mark | 215-67-8973 | 21 | $19,500 |
| 13 | 12 | Hartwick | Eileen | 313-78-9090 | 15 | $31,450 |
| 14 | 13 | Smythe | George | 560-90-8645 | 15 | $65,000 |
| 15 | 14 | Wilkes | Caitlin | 124-67-7432 | 17 | $15,500 |
| 16 | 15 | Deaver | Ken | 198-98-6750 | 23 | $24,600 |
| 17 | 16 | Kaylor | Sally | 312-45-9862 | 12 | $32,900 |
| 18 | 17 | Parker | Dee | 659-11-3452 | 14 | $19,800 |
| 19 | 18 | Preverson | Gary | 670-90-1121 | 21 | $27,600 |
| 20 | 19 | Samuelson | Paul | 219-89-7080 | 23 | $28,900 |

03-Oct-86   05:03 AM

**Figure 9-5.**    Result of /Data Fill

database. You then create a string formula for this field that combines two or more of the database fields into one field. Although the usefulness of this approach is dependent on fields having the same number of characters or digits in each entry, it does present a solution to the need for more than two sort keys in some situations.

As an example, suppose you need to sort expense data that is coded by division, region, branch, and expense code. The data for this example is shown in Figure 9-6. The string formula will need to convert numeric entries to strings with @STRING so they can be combined. The formula to be

| | A | B | C | D | E | F | G |
|---|---|---|---|---|---|---|---|
| 1 | Expense Code | Division | Region | Branch | Amount | | |
| 2 | RX-1254 | 3 | 1 | 100 | $1,208.90 | | |
| 3 | ST-8978 | 2 | 1 | 110 | $2,341.00 | | |
| 4 | RF-1265 | 1 | 2 | 200 | $6,785.00 | | |
| 5 | ST-1100 | 2 | 2 | 500 | $7,500.00 | | |
| 6 | RX-1254 | 2 | 1 | 110 | $1,200.00 | | |
| 7 | ST-1100 | 3 | 1 | 110 | $560.00 | | |
| 8 | RT-1000 | 1 | 1 | 300 | $998.00 | | |
| 9 | ST-8978 | 1 | 2 | 200 | $1,050.00 | | |
| 10 | RF-1265 | 3 | 2 | 610 | $2,341.00 | | |
| 11 | | | | | | | |

**Figure 9-6.**  Expense data

placed in F2 is @STRING(B2,0)&@STRING(C2,0)&@
STRING(D2,0)&A2. The most important field for sorting is
listed first in the string formula, continuing across to the
least important field in the sort. This formula is copied for
the remaining entries in column F.

  To make your sort, you would enter /Data Sort Data-
Range as A2..F20, specify a primary key of F2, select
ascending sort order, and then select Go. The sorted records
are shown in Figure 9-7. As you can see, you have used just
one of 1-2-3's sort keys but have effectively done a four-key
sort.

## Searching the Database

As your database grows large, it becomes increasingly
important that you be able to review the information it con-

```
F2: [W13] @STRING(B2,0)&@STRING(C2,0)&@STRING(D2,0)&A2                  READY

        A          B        C         D       E            F              G
1   Expense Code Division Region   Branch   Amount      Sort-Key
2   RF-1265          1        2       200 $6,785.00 12200RF-1265
3   ST-1100          2        2       500 $7,500.00 22500ST-1100
4   RX-1254          2        1       110 $1,200.00 21110RX-1254
5   ST-1100          3        1       110   $560.00 31110ST-1100
6   RT-1000          1        1       300   $998.00 11300RT-1000
7   ST-8978          1        2       200 $1,050.00 12200ST-8978
8   RF-1265          3        2       610 $2,341.00 32610RF-1265
9   RX-1254          3        1       100 $1,208.90 31100RX-1254
10  ST-8978          2        1       110 $2,341.00 21110ST-8978
11
```

**Figure 9-7.** Sorted records

tains selectively. The ability to work selectively with information in your database provides an exception reporting capability; that is, information can be brought to your attention if it is considered to be outside an established norm. You can also use the selective review feature to clean up your database or to create reports in response to unexpected requests.

All the commands required to review information selectively are found in the /Data Query menu shown here.

```
A1: [W12] 'Last Name                                                MENU
Input  Criterion  Output  Find  Extract  Unique  Delete  Reset  Quit
Set the range containing data records
```

You will need to use at least three of the /Data Query commands to make a selection. Your database must be specified with /Data Query Input and your selection criteria identified with /Data Query Criterion before you can select a specific action for the Query command to perform. In addition, your database records and selection criteria must be entered on the worksheet before you enter a Query command. The steps required for using Query commands are summarized in the "Steps for Using Query Commands" box. Let's now examine each of the /Data Query options in detail.

---

## Steps for Using Query Commands

The /Data Query commands allow you to access selected records in your database. Obtaining the results you desire involves some preliminary work as well as a number of /Data Query options. The required steps are as follows:

1. Enter the query criteria on your worksheet.

2. If you plan to use either Extract or Unique, enter the field names you will want to copy in the output area of your worksheets.

3. Enter /Data Query Input and specify the range for your database, including field names.

4. Choose Criteria from the Query menu and specify the location of your criteria.

5. If you plan to use Extract or Unique, choose Output and specify the location of your output area.

6. Select the option you wish to use: Find, Delete, Extract, or Unique.

7. If you choose Find, press ESC after you have finished browsing in your file and then select Quit to exit Query.

---

## Telling 1-2-3 Where Your Data Is Located

When you use the Query options, 1-2-3 must know where your field names and data records are located. Contrary to the case with /Data Sort, you *must* use field names here. These field names will be matched against the field names in the selection criteria area to ensure that selections are matched against the correct data.

The command by which you specify the location of the database is /Data Query Input. After you enter this command, you can point to your data range or type the required cell references. In both cases you should be sure to include the field names, as shown in the selection in Figure 9-8.

---

F20: 2                                                                POINT
Enter Input range: A1..F20

| | A | B | C | D | E | F |
|---|---|---|---|---|---|---|
| 1 | Last Name | First Name | SS# | Job Code | Salary | Location |
| 2 | Larson | Mary | 543-98-9876 | 23 | $12,000 | 2 |
| 3 | Campbell | David | 213-76-9874 | 23 | $23,000 | 10 |
| 4 | Campbell | Keith | 569-89-7654 | 12 | $32,000 | 2 |
| 5 | Stephens | Tom | 219-78-8954 | 15 | $17,800 | 2 |
| 6 | Caldor | Larry | 459-34-0921 | 23 | $32,500 | 4 |
| 7 | Lightnor | Peggy | 560-55-4311 | 14 | $23,500 | 10 |
| 8 | McCartin | John | 817-66-1212 | 15 | $54,600 | 2 |
| 9 | Justof | Jack | 431-78-9963 | 17 | $41,200 | 4 |
| 10 | Patterson | Lyle | 212-11-9090 | 12 | $21,500 | 10 |
| 11 | Miller | Lisa | 214-89-6756 | 23 | $18,700 | 2 |
| 12 | Hawkins | Mark | 215-67-8973 | 21 | $19,500 | 2 |
| 13 | Hartwick | Eileen | 313-78-9090 | 15 | $31,450 | 4 |
| 14 | Smythe | George | 560-90-8645 | 15 | $65,000 | 4 |
| 15 | Wilkes | Caitlin | 124-67-7432 | 17 | $15,500 | 2 |
| 16 | Deaver | Ken | 198-98-6750 | 23 | $24,600 | 10 |
| 17 | Kaylor | Sally | 312-45-9862 | 12 | $32,900 | 10 |
| 18 | Parker | Dee | 659-11-3452 | 14 | $19,800 | 4 |
| 19 | Preverson | Gary | 670-90-1121 | 21 | $27,600 | 4 |
| 20 | Samuelson | Paul | 219-89-7080 | 23 | $28,900 | 2 |

03-Oct-86   05:37 AM

---

**Figure 9-8.**      Selecting an input range

## Specifying the Desired Records

1-2-3 uses criteria to determine what records from the database will be used to fill your request. The criteria you specify will be checked against each record in the database range, and records that do not meet the criteria will not be used.

When entering criteria, keep in mind two things. First, criteria must be entered on the worksheet in an out-of-the-way location that will not interfere with the expansion of the database. This action must be taken from READY mode, not from within /Data Query, since once you select /Data Query, you cannot make entries on the worksheet. Second, 1-2-3 will need to be told where the criteria have been stored by means of the /Data Query Criterion command.

### Location of Criteria

You can choose any location you desire for your criteria. A popular location is to the right of the database, since this allows for the expansion of the criteria area to the right and does not interfere with the expansion of your database. If your database occupies columns A through M, for example, you may wish to begin your criteria in column R. This would allow for the expansion of the database by four new fields before the criteria would have to be moved.

### Types of Criteria

You can use a variety of different ways to specify which records in the database you wish to use. You can use values that match your database entries exactly; you can use 1-2-3's wildcard features to specify only a portion of the entry you are looking for; or you can specify formulas. For matches other than formulas, the field name for the field in the database you are searching must appear above the specific entry you are searching for. For formula matches you can use any name, although for documentation purposes it is best to use the name of the field reference in the formula. If you wanted to search the last name field in an employee database for all records with a last name of Smith, for example, your criteria area might look like this:

Note that the criteria area is J2..J3. The entry in J1 is documentation. The search value is placed immediately underneath the field name in the criteria area. The field name in the criteria area must be an exact match with the field name in your database. A space at the end of one or the other or a difference in label alignment within the cells can cause a problem. The safest approach is to copy the field name from its location above the data to the criteria area where you wish to use it.

**Values**     To search for numeric values in your records, you would record the desired field name in the criteria area. Underneath this field name you would enter the value you were searching for. Placing the field name in the criteria area but not placing a value beneath it will cause 1-2-3 to regard the entry as a wildcard, and it will count all records as matches. Assuming the following criteria area, only records for Job Code 23 would match.

**Labels**     If you want to match label entries, you can enter them exactly as they appear in your database under the field name for the field you wish to search. Entering Last Name in the criteria area and placing Jones beneath will cause

1-2-3 to select those records that contain Jones in the last name field, for example. Placing the field name in the criteria area but not placing a label beneath it will cause 1-2-3 to regard the entry as a wildcard and assume everything to be a match with the criterion.

1-2-3 has two special characters that are useful when specifying criteria for fields that contain labels. These characters are * and ?.

The asterisk is placed at the end of a criteria entry to indicate that if the first part of the entry matches with a database record, any characters from the location of the asterisk (*) to the end of the database entry should be accepted. Using the following criteria would search the Last Name field for all records beginning with Sm, for example.

Smith would match, as would Smithfield, Smothers, and Smeltman.

The ? replaces any one character in an entry. When you use the question mark, you are saying that you do not care what character comes at that location in the data entry as long as all the other characters match exactly. Using the following criteria tells 1-2-3 that you do not care what character is located in the second position of the Last Name field as long as "B" is the first character and "tman" are the third through the sixth characters of the entry.

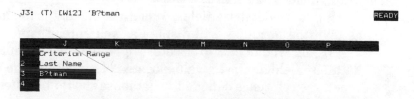

Bitman, Butman, Batman, Botman, and Betman would be among the matching entries if records containing these names were in the database. All entries longer than six characters would be rejected. Bitmanson would not match with the criteria, for example.

**Formulas**     The ability to create formulas to serve as criteria offers additional power. You can use formula comparisons to check for records that contain values with a specific range, and, if you are using release 2, you can even use string formulas in your criteria. When you enter a formula as criteria, it will display as 0 or 1, depending on whether it evaluates to True or False for the first database record. You may want to format the cell as Text so it will display as the formula you entered.

When you create formulas as criteria, it is not important that the field name used in the criteria area match with the field referenced in the formula, although for clarity it is always best to use the proper field name. As you construct your formulas to compare values in the database against a specific value, you will always reference the first value for the field in the database. As an example, to find all values in the salary field located in column E that are greater than $25,000, you might use criteria like this.

The cell referenced is E2, since that is the first value in the salary field. Note that a relative reference is used when referring to all database fields. When you format criteria cells as text, the formulas will display as you enter them.

If you would like to create a formula that compares a database field against a value located elsewhere in the worksheet, the reference outside the database should be entered as an absolute reference. Let's say you want to compare the salaries in Figure 9-9 against the average salary stored in

| | A | B | C | D | E | F |
|---|---|---|---|---|---|---|
| 1 | Last Name | First Name | SS# | Job Code | Salary | Location |
| 2 | Larson | Mary | 543-98-9876 | 23 | $12,000 | 2 |
| 3 | Campbell | David | 213-76-9874 | 23 | $23,000 | 10 |
| 4 | Campbell | Keith | 569-89-7654 | 12 | $32,000 | 2 |
| 5 | Stephens | Tom | 219-78-8954 | 15 | $17,800 | 2 |
| 6 | Caldor | Larry | 459-34-0921 | 23 | $32,500 | 4 |
| 7 | Lightnor | Peggy | 560-55-4311 | 14 | $23,500 | 10 |
| 8 | McCartin | John | 817-66-1212 | 15 | $54,600 | 2 |
| 9 | Justof | Jack | 431-78-9963 | 17 | $41,200 | 4 |
| 10 | Patterson | Lyle | 212-11-9090 | 12 | $21,500 | 10 |
| 11 | Miller | Lisa | 214-89-6756 | 23 | $18,700 | 2 |
| 12 | Hawkins | Mark | 215-67-8973 | 21 | $19,500 | 2 |
| 13 | Hartwick | Eileen | 313-78-9090 | 15 | $31,450 | 4 |
| 14 | Smythe | George | 560-90-8645 | 15 | $65,000 | 4 |
| 15 | Wilkes | Caitlin | 124-67-7432 | 17 | $15,500 | 2 |
| 16 | Deaver | Ken | 198-98-6750 | 23 | $24,600 | 10 |
| 17 | Kaylor | Sally | 312-45-9862 | 12 | $32,900 | 10 |
| 18 | Parker | Dee | 659-11-3452 | 14 | $19,800 | 4 |
| 19 | Preverson | Gary | 670-90-1121 | 21 | $27,600 | 4 |
| 20 | Samuelson | Paul | 219-89-7080 | 23 | $28,900 | 2 |

03-Oct-86   05:59 AM

**Figure 9-9.** Salary data

J10. The following criteria could be used to identify all records where the salary exceeded the average by $3,000.

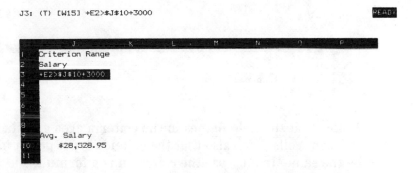

The complex operators #AND#, #OR#, and #NOT# can be used in formula criteria. You may wish to check to see if a salary is less than or equal to $25,000 or greater than or equal to $50,000, for example. The proper formula to use is shown in these criteria.

If you use the #AND# operator, the condition on both sides of the operator must be true for the record to be selected. If you use #OR#, either condition may be true for the record to be selected. #NOT# negates the condition that follows it.

**Compound Criteria**    Whenever you use more than one field in the criteria area, you are using compound criteria. 1-2-3 allows up to 32 fields to be used for search criteria at one time. These criteria will be joined by implied "ands" and "ors."

If two criteria values are placed on the same line beneath their separate field names, they are joined by an implied "and." The following criteria, for example, will select records where the job code is equal to 23 and the salary is less than $16,000.

Notice that the field names in the criteria area are placed in adjacent cells. Note also that the criteria types do not have to be the same. In one case the criterion is a formula and in the other a value. A record must meet both criteria in order to be selected.

If the entry for one of the fields is placed one row below the other, the two criteria are joined by an implied "or." Perhaps you want records with a job code of 23 or a salary of less than $16,000. The criteria shown would select records where either of these conditions was met.

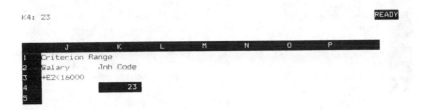

When you use one of the /Data Query commands that requires the use of criteria, you must use the /Data Query Criterion command to tell 1-2-3 the location of the criteria. (Remember that the criteria themselves must be entered before you select /Data Query.) Entering criteria and telling 1-2-3 where they are located with /Data Query Criterion will not show you the matching records, however. A number of other commands can display the matching records, copy them to a new area, or delete them from your database.

## Highlighting Selected Records

1-2-3's /Data Query Find command will highlight records that match the criteria you have defined. The records are highlighted one at a time, beginning at the top of the database. The down arrow key will move you to the next matching record that meets your criteria. If you want to move to a previously highlighted record, use the up arrow key. In databases where the number of fields exceeds the width of the screen, you can use the right and left arrow keys to move within the highlighted record.

Finding records requires a few preliminary steps. You must have defined your database, including the field names, with /Data Query Input. You must also have entered your criteria on the worksheet before requesting the Query commands and then defined the criteria to 1-2-3 with /Data

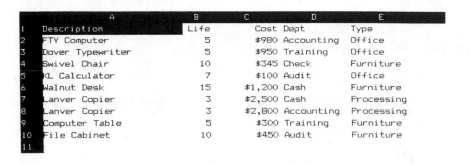

|   | A | B | C | D | E |
|---|---|---|---|---|---|
| 1 | Description | Life | Cost | Dept | Type |
| 2 | FTY Computer | 5 | $980 | Accounting | Office |
| 3 | Dover Typewriter | 5 | $950 | Training | Office |
| 4 | Swivel Chair | 10 | $345 | Check | Furniture |
| 5 | KL Calculator | 7 | $100 | Audit | Office |
| 6 | Walnut Desk | 15 | $1,200 | Cash | Furniture |
| 7 | Lanver Copier | 3 | $2,500 | Cash | Processing |
| 8 | Lanver Copier | 3 | $2,800 | Accounting | Processing |
| 9 | Computer Table | 5 | $300 | Training | Furniture |
| 10 | File Cabinet | 10 | $450 | Audit | Furniture |
| 11 | | | | | |

**Figure 9-10.**    Asset records

Query Criterion. Figure 9-10 shows a database that has been defined with /Data Query Input as A1..E10. The following criteria are used to locate records for the Accounting Department.

Figure 9-11 shows the first record matching the criteria highlighted on the screen.

     The /Data Query Find option is a good one if you need a quick answer to a question concerning data you have stored in your database. The difficulty with it is that all the matching records are not listed at once and cannot be printed out. If you need either of these things, you will want to use the /Data Query Extract and /Data Query Unique commands.

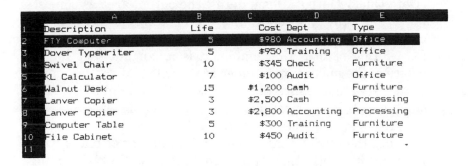

| | A | B | C | D | E |
|---|---|---|---|---|---|
| 1 | Description | Life | Cost | Dept | Type |
| 2 | FTY Computer | 5 | $980 | Accounting | Office |
| 3 | Dover Typewriter | 5 | $950 | Training | Office |
| 4 | Swivel Chair | 10 | $345 | Check | Furniture |
| 5 | KL Calculator | 7 | $100 | Audit | Office |
| 6 | Walnut Desk | 15 | $1,200 | Cash | Furniture |
| 7 | Lanver Copier | 3 | $2,500 | Cash | Processing |
| 8 | Lanver Copier | 3 | $2,800 | Accounting | Processing |
| 9 | Computer Table | 5 | $300 | Training | Furniture |
| 10 | File Cabinet | 10 | $450 | Audit | Furniture |
| 11 | | | | | |

**Figure 9-11.**     Finding records for a specific department

## Writing Selected Records
## On the Worksheet

1-2-3 provides two commands that make a copy of selected records and fields from your database to another area of the worksheet. You can add a heading to these new areas to create an instant report that can be shared with others. Before you can have 1-2-3 copy database information, however, you must prepare an output location.

### Defining an Output Area

You must decide on a location and prepare it to receive data. The bottom of your existing database is a commonly selected location. Just make sure you leave some blank rows at the bottom of the database to allow for expansion, or you will find yourself moving the output area all the time. With the location selected, enter the names of the fields you wish to copy from matching records. They do not need to be in the same sequence as the fields in your database, and you do not need to include every field.

Once the field names are placed in the output area, you are ready to define its location to 1-2-3. This is done with /Data Query Output. If you define the output area as consisting of only the row containing the headings, 1-2-3 will use cells from the heading area to the bottom of the worksheet for writing records that match. It is important that you be aware of the maximum number of records that can be copied to this area and ensure that data is not located in these cells, since it will be overwritten.

You can also specify a range for the output area that includes the row of field names and a number of blank rows beneath it. With this approach, 1-2-3 will stop copying matching database records when the output area becomes full.

### Extracting All Matches

To extract matching records, simply enter /**Data Query Extract** once you have set up the criteria and output areas on your worksheet and defined the database, criteria, and output to 1-2-3. Every time you select the Extract command, 1-2-3 will erase the output area before writing the newly selected records to it. Since so many preliminary steps are required before using this command, let's review them in order, using the database in Figure 9-12 as an example.

1. Add selection criteria to the worksheet, as shown:

2. Set up the output area on the worksheet to look like this:

|   | A | B | C | D | E |
|---|---|---|---|---|---|
| 1 | Description | Life | Cost | Dept | Type |
| 2 | FTY Computer | 5 | $980 | Accounting | Office |
| 3 | Dover Typewriter | 5 | $950 | Training | Office |
| 4 | Swivel Chair | 10 | $345 | Check | Furniture |
| 5 | XL Calculator | 7 | $100 | Audit | Office |
| 6 | Walnut Desk | 15 | $1,200 | Cash | Furniture |
| 7 | Lanver Copier | 3 | $2,500 | Cash | Processing |
| 8 | Lanver Copier | 3 | $2,800 | Accounting | Processing |
| 9 | Computer Table | 5 | $300 | Training | Furniture |
| 10 | File Cabinet | 10 | $450 | Audit | Furniture |
| 11 | | | | | |

**Figure 9-12.**     Database for selection

3. Use the /Data Query Input command to define the database as located in A1..E10.

4. Since the Data Query menu is a sticky menu, all you have to enter is **Criterion** in order to define the criteria location as J2..K3.

5. Define the output area next by entering **Output** and its location of A21..C21 at the prompt.

6. Enter **Extract**, and the following output will be produced.

|   | A | B | C | D | E |
|---|---|---|---|---|---|
| 21 | Description | Cost | Dept | | |
| 22 | Dover Typewriter | $950 | Training | | |
| 23 | | | | | |

If you want to turn extracted records into a report, you need only add a report title at the top of the extract area and print the worksheet range containing the heading and the extract area.

## Writing Only Unique Records

The Unique option is very similar to Extract in that it writes records to the output area. Its difference is that it writes only unique records to this area, so if two entries to be written to output are an exact match, only one will be written. Uniqueness of records is determined by the fields written to the output area.

Every time you use the Unique command, the output area is erased so that the newly selected records can be written to it. The number of records written to the output area can be affected by the number of fields you plan to write there. If two records are alike in five of the six fields you plan to write to the output area, they are still unique, but if you select fewer fields, the records may well match.

Using the following criteria

and the database records shown in Figure 9-13, 1-2-3 produced the following in the output area when Unique was selected from the /Data Query menu. You will note that Tower College appears only once, even though several qualifying records for it exist in the database.

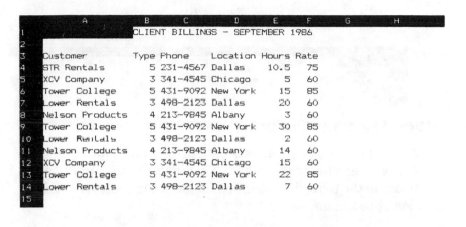

**Figure 9-13.**    Database used with Unique

## Deleting Selected Records

/Data Query Delete is a powerful yet dangerous command. In one easy process it can purge outdated records from your database — but if you make a mistake in entering your criteria, it can also purge records you still need. You would be wise to test your criteria with Find or Extract before selecting the Delete option.

If you specified the criteria shown

J3: (T) [W12] +E2>18000                                                  READY

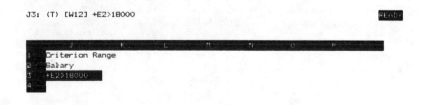

and the database in Figure 9-14 and then chose the Delete option, only these records would remain in the database:

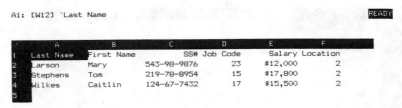

## Resetting Selection Options

All of the Query specifications can be eliminated with the /Data Query Reset command. This includes the Input specification, the Criterion specification, and the Output specification if you made one.

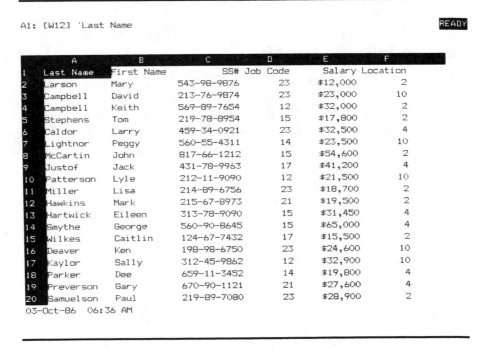

**Figure 9-14.**    Database before deletion

1-2-3: The Complete Reference

## Quitting the Query Menu

When you want to leave the query operation, choose Quit from the Query menu to return to READY mode. This will allow you to make new entries for criteria and perform other tasks. If you would like to return to /Data Query after making changes, you can reenter through the menu. Alternatively, if you want to use the same choices for Data-Range and Criterion and would like to perform the same query operation as the last one you performed (Find, Unique, Delete, or Extract), you have an easier option. Simply press F8 (QUERY), and another query will be executed.

## Adding a Second Database

More than one database can be entered on the same worksheet, but because of the availability of only one set of parameters for Query and Sort, only one can be in active use at a time. When you wish to use the second one, you will have to redefine the data range and possibly the criteria and output areas.

Deciding where to place the second database on the worksheet can be difficult. If you place it at the end of the first database, you limit the growth of the top database. If you place the databases side by side, the use of /Worksheet Insert and /Worksheet Delete in one database will cause unexpected changes in the other. There is no one correct answer for proper placement; you will just have to consider the tradeoffs in making your decision.

## The Database Statistical Functions

1-2-3's database statistical functions are a special category of functions designed to coordinate with the other data management features. Using criteria you enter on your worksheet, they can perform a statistical analysis on selected records in your database. Each of the database statistical functions has a D immediately following the @ in the function to show that it is a database function. The characters that follow the D indicate the exact task the function performs and also correspond to the name of one of the statistical functions covered in Chapter 7.

## @DAVG

The @DAVG function allows you to obtain an average of a selected group of database records.

### Format

@DAVG(input records,offset in database,criteria location)

### Arguments

input records    The location of your database, including field names and all the database records and fields. This argument can be supplied as a range (A1..F67) or as a range name assigned to the database (RECORDS). This argument can also refer to just a section of the database, as long as the field names for the included fields are within the specified range.

offset in database    The position number of the field in the database you wish to use in the average calculation. This field should contain numeric values. The first column of the database has an offset of zero. As you move successively to each field to the right of the first, 1 will be added to the offset. This argument can be supplied as a number or a reference to a cell containing a number.

criteria location    The location of the criteria to be used in selecting records. This can be specified as a range or a range name. It should include the field names that appear at the top of the criteria area.

**Use**

The @DAVG function is used whenever you wish to obtain an average of the values in a field in a selected group of records in the database. The database and criteria in Figure 9-15 are used with the @DAVG function to calculate an average salary for employees in job code 23 of $21,550. You will notice that the database was defined as being located in A1..F12. The offset for the salary field is 4, and the criteria used in the selection are located in A15..A16.

## @DCOUNT

The @DCOUNT function allows you to obtain a count of a selected group of database records.

---

F16: (C0) [W9] @DAVG(A1..F12,4,A15..A16)                    READY

|    | A | B | C | D | E | F |
|----|---|---|---|---|---|---|
| 1 | Last Name | First Name | SS# | Job Code | Salary | Location |
| 2 | Larson | Mary | 543-98-9876 | 23 | $12,000 | 2 |
| 3 | Campbell | David | 213-76-9874 | 23 | $23,000 | 10 |
| 4 | Campbell | Keith | 569-89-7654 | 12 | $32,000 | 2 |
| 5 | Stephens | Tom | 219-78-8954 | 15 | $17,800 | 2 |
| 6 | Caldor | Larry | 459-34-0921 | 23 | $32,500 | 4 |
| 7 | Lightnor | Peggy | 560-55-4311 | 14 | $23,500 | 10 |
| 8 | McCartin | John | 817-66-1212 | 15 | $54,600 | 2 |
| 9 | Justof | Jack | 431-78-9963 | 17 | $41,200 | 4 |
| 10 | Patterson | Lyle | 212-11-9090 | 12 | $21,500 | 10 |
| 11 | Miller | Lisa | 214-89-6756 | 23 | $18,700 | 2 |
| 12 | Hawkins | Mark | 215-67-8973 | 21 | $19,500 | 2 |
| 13 |  |  |  |  |  |  |
| 14 | Criteria Range |  |  |  |  |  |
| 15 | Job Code |  |  |  |  |  |
| 16 | 23 |  | Average Salary for Job Code 23: | | $21,550 | |
| 17 |  |  |  |  |  |  |

**Figure 9-15.    Using @DAVG**

**Format**

@DCOUNT(input records,offset in database,criteria location)

**Arguments**

input records    The location of your database, including field names and all the database records and fields. This argument can be supplied as a range (A1..F67) or as a range name assigned to the database (RECORDS). This argument can also refer to just a section of the database, as long as the field names for the included fields are within the specified range.

offset in database    The position number of the field in the database you wish to use in the count calculation. This field does not need to contain numeric values. The first column of the database has an offset of zero. As you move successively to each field to the right of the first, 1 will be added to the offset. This argument can be supplied as a number or a reference to a cell containing a number.

criteria location    The location of the criteria used in selecting records. This can be specified as a range or a range name. It should include the field names that appear at the top of the criteria area.

**Use**

The @DCOUNT function is used whenever you wish to obtain a count of the records in the database that match your selection criteria. The database and criteria in Figure 9-16 are used with the @DCOUNT function to count the last names for records with a job code of 23. You will notice that the database was defined as being located in A1..F12. The offset to refer to the last name field is 0, and the criteria used in the selection are located in A15..A16. Since @DCOUNT counts only records with a nonblank entry in the specified field, you will want to choose the field that you count carefully. While some records may not have a location assign-

|    | A | B | C | D | E | F |
|----|---|---|---|---|---|---|
| 1 | Last Name | First Name | SS# Job | Code | Salary | Location |
| 2 | Larson | Mary | 543-98-9876 | 23 | $12,000 | 2 |
| 3 | Campbell | David | 213-76-9874 | 23 | $23,000 | 10 |
| 4 | Campbell | Keith | 569-89-7654 | 12 | $32,000 | 2 |
| 5 | Stephens | Tom | 219-78-8954 | 15 | $17,800 | 2 |
| 6 | Caldor | Larry | 459-34-0921 | 23 | $32,500 | 4 |
| 7 | Lightnor | Peggy | 560-55-4311 | 14 | $23,500 | 10 |
| 8 | McCartin | John | 817-66-1212 | 15 | $54,600 | 2 |
| 9 | Justof | Jack | 431-78-9963 | 17 | $41,200 | 4 |
| 10 | Patterson | Lyle | 212-11-9090 | 12 | $21,500 | 10 |
| 11 | Miller | Lisa | 214-89-6756 | 23 | $18,700 | 2 |
| 12 | Hawkins | Mark | 215-67-8973 | 21 | $19,500 | 2 |
| 13 | | | | | | |
| 14 | Criteria Range | | | | | |
| 15 | Job Code | | | | | |
| 16 | 23 | | Number of Employees in Job Code 23: | | | 4 |
| 17 | | | | | | |

**Figure 9-16.**    Using @COUNT

ment, for example, all records should have a last name.

## @DMAX

The @DMAX function allows you to obtain the maximum value in a field within a selected group of database records.

### Format

@DMAX(input records,offset in database,criteria location)

### Arguments

input records    The location of your database, including field names and all the database records and fields. This argument can be supplied as a range (A1..F67) or as a range name assigned to the database (RECORDS). This argument can also refer to just a section of the database, as long as the field names for the included fields are within the specified range.

offset in database    The position number of the field in the database you wish to use in the maximum calculation. This field should contain numeric values. The first column of the database has an offset of zero. As you move successively to each field to the right of the first, 1 will be added to the offset. This argument can be supplied as a number or a reference to a cell containing a number.

criteria location    The location of the criteria used in selecting records. This can be specified as a range or a range name. It should include the field names that appear at the top of the criteria area.

### Use

The @DMAX function is used whenever you wish to obtain the maximum value in a field for records in the database that match your selection criteria. The database and criteria in Figure 9-17 are used with the @DMAX function to determine the maximum salary for employees with a job code of 23. You will notice that the database was defined as being located in A1..F12. The offset to refer to the salary field is 4, and the criteria used in the selection are located in A15..A16.

## @DMIN

The @DMIN function allows you to obtain the minimum value in a field within a selected group of database records.

### Format

@DMIN(input records,offset in database,criteria location)

```
F16:  (CO)  [W9]  @DMAX(A1..F12,4,A15..A16)                        READY
```

|    | A          | B          | C          | D         | E         | F        |
|----|------------|------------|------------|-----------|-----------|----------|
| 1  | Last Name  | First Name |        SS# | Job Code  |    Salary | Location |
| 2  | Larson     | Mary       | 543-98-9876 | 23       | $12,000   | 2        |
| 3  | Campbell   | David      | 213-76-9874 | 23       | $23,000   | 10       |
| 4  | Campbell   | Keith      | 569-89-7654 | 12       | $32,000   | 2        |
| 5  | Stephens   | Tom        | 219-78-8954 | 15       | $17,800   | 2        |
| 6  | Caldor     | Larry      | 459-34-0921 | 23       | $32,500   | 4        |
| 7  | Lightnor   | Peggy      | 560-55-4311 | 14       | $23,500   | 10       |
| 8  | McCartin   | John       | 817-66-1212 | 15       | $54,600   | 2        |
| 9  | Justof     | Jack       | 431-78-9983 | 17       | $41,700   | 4        |
| 10 | Patterson  | Lyle       | 212-11-9090 | 12       | $21,500   | 10       |
| 11 | Miller     | Lisa       | 214-89-6756 | 23       | $18,700   | 2        |
| 12 | Hawkins    | Mark       | 215-67-8973 | 21       | $19,500   | 2        |
| 13 |            |            |            |           |           |          |
| 14 | Criteria Range |        |            |           |           |          |
| 15 | Job Code   |            |            |           |           |          |
| 16 |        23  |            | Maximum Salary in Job Code 23: | | $32,500 | |
| 17 |            |            |            |           |           |          |

**Figure 9-17.**     Using @DMAX

## Arguments

input records     The location of your database, including field names and all the database records and fields. This argument can be supplied as a range (A1..F67) or as a range name assigned to the database (RECORDS). This argument can also refer to just a section of the database, as long as the field names for the included fields are within the specified range.

offset in database     The position number of the field in the database you wish to use in the minimum calculation. This field should contain numeric values. The first column of the database has an offset of zero. As you move successively to each field to the right of the first, 1 will be added to the offset. This argument can be supplied as a number or a reference to a cell containing a number.

criteria location    The location of the criteria used in selecting records. This can be specified as a range or a range name. It should include the field names that appear at the top of the criteria area.

## Use

The @DMIN function is used whenever you wish to obtain the minimum value in a field for records in the database that match your selection criteria. The database and criteria in Figure 9-18 are used with the @DMIN function to determine the minimum salary for employees with a job code of 23. You will notice that the database was defined as being located in A1..F12. The offset to refer to the salary field is 4, and the criteria used in the selection are located in A15..A16.

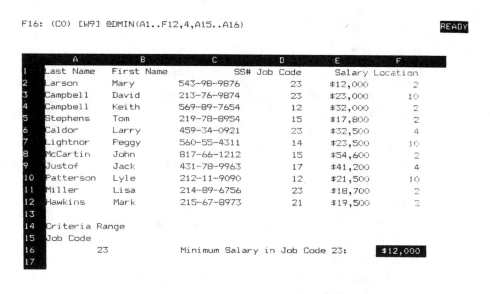

**Figure 9-18.**    Using @DMIN

# @DSTD

The @DSTD function is used to determine the standard deviation of a set of values, or how much variation there is from the average of the values. The values used in this calculation will be from selected records in the database. The standard deviation is the square root of the variance.

## Format

@DSTD(input records,offset in database,criteria location)

## Arguments

input records     The location of your database, including field names and all the database records and fields. This argument can be supplied as a range (A1..F67) or as a range name assigned to the database (RECORDS). This argument can also refer to just a section of the database, as long as the field names for the included fields are within the specified range.

offset in database     The position number of the field in the database you wish to use in the standard deviation calculation. This field should contain numeric values. The first column of the database has an offset of zero. As you move successively to each field to the right of the first, 1 will be added to the offset. This argument can be supplied as a number or a reference to a cell containing a number.

criteria location     The location of the criteria used in selecting records. This can be specified as a range or a range name. It should include the field names that appear at the top of the criteria area.

## Use

The @DSTD function will determine the standard deviation when the selected records comprise the entire population you are measuring. If you are working with only a sample of the population, use the formula in the note that follows the discussion of the population standard deviation.

The purpose of the standard deviation is to determine the amount of variation between individual values and the mean. If you determine that the average age of your employees is 40, this could mean that half of your employees were 39 and the other half 41, or it could mean that you had employees whose ages ranged from 18 to 65. The latter case would show a greater standard deviation due to the greater variance from the mean.

The @DSTD function is biased, since it uses a count as part of the standard deviation calculation. The following formula is used:

$$\sqrt{\frac{\sum (X_i - AVG)^2}{n}}$$

where $X_i$ is the ith item in the list and n is the number of items in the list.

The database in Figure 9-19 shows the @DSTD function being used to determine the standard deviation of salaries for employees in job code 15. The criteria are located in A15..A16.

**Note**

The @DSTD function is designed to calculate population standard deviation. If you are interested in the sample standard deviation, you can create your own formula, as follows:

$$\frac{@SQRT(@DCOUNT(list)}{(@DCOUNT(list)-1))*@DSTD(list)}$$

## @DSUM

The @DSUM function allows you to obtain the total of values in a field within a selected group of database records.

| | A | B | C | D | E | F |
|---|---|---|---|---|---|---|
| | Last Name | First Name | SS# | Job Code | Salary | Location |
| 1 | | | | | | |
| 2 | Larson | Mary | 543-98-9876 | 23 | $12,000 | 2 |
| 3 | Campbell | David | 213-76-9874 | 23 | $23,000 | 10 |
| 4 | Campbell | Keith | 569-89-7654 | 15 | $17,700 | 2 |
| 5 | Stephens | Tom | 219-78-8954 | 15 | $17,800 | 2 |
| 6 | Caldor | Larry | 454-34-0921 | 23 | $32,500 | 4 |
| 7 | Lightnor | Peggy | 560-55-4311 | 14 | $23,500 | 10 |
| 8 | McCartin | John | 817-66-1212 | 15 | $17,750 | 2 |
| 9 | Jusluf | Jack | 431-78-9763 | 17 | $41,200 | 4 |
| 10 | Patterson | Lyle | 212-11-9090 | 12 | $21,500 | 10 |
| 11 | Miller | Lisa | 214-89-6756 | 23 | $18,700 | 2 |
| 12 | Hawkins | Mark | 215-67-8973 | 21 | $19,500 | 2 |
| 13 | | | | | | |
| 14 | Criteria Range | | | | | |
| 15 | Job Code | | | | | |
| 16 | 15 | | Standard Deviation for Salaries | | | 40.82482 |
| 17 | | | in Job Code 15 | | | |
| 18 | | | | | | |
| 19 | | | | | | |
| 20 | | | | | | |

03-Oct-86　07:07 AM

**Figure 9-19.**　Using @DSTD

## Format

@DSUM(input records,offset in database,criteria location

## Arguments

input records　　The location of your database, including field names and all the database records and fields. This argument can be supplied as a range (A1..F67) or as a range name assigned to the database (RECORDS). This argument can also refer to just a section of the database, as long as the field names for the included fields are within the specified range.

offset in database    The position number of the field in the database you wish to use in the sum calculation. This field should contain numeric values. The first column of the database has an offset of zero. As you move successively to each field to the right of the first, 1 will be added to the offset. This argument can be supplied as a number or a reference to a cell containing a number.

criteria location    The location of the criteria used in selecting records. This can be specified as a range or a range name. It should include the field names that appear at the top of the criteria area.

### Use

The @DSUM function is used whenever you wish to obtain the total of values in a field for records in the database that match your selection criteria. The database and criteria in Figure 9-20 are used with the @DSUM function to determine the total of salaries for employees with a job code of 23. You will notice that the database was defined as being located in A1..F12. The offset to refer to the salary field is 4, and the criteria used in the selection are located in A15..A16.

## @DVAR

The @DVAR function computes the variance of values in a population, or the amount that the individual population values vary from the average. The records used in the computation are selected from the database with your criteria.

### Format

@DVAR(input records,offset in database,criteria location)

### Arguments

input records    The location of your database, including field names and all the database records and fields. This

|   | A | B | C | D | E | F |
|---|---|---|---|---|---|---|
| 1 | Last Name | First Name | SS# | Job Code | Salary | Location |
| 2 | Larson | Mary | 543-98-9876 | 23 | $12,000 | 2 |
| 3 | Campbell | David | 213-76-9874 | 23 | $23,000 | 10 |
| 4 | Campbell | Keith | 569-89-7654 | 12 | $32,000 | 2 |
| 5 | Stephens | Tom | 219-78-8954 | 15 | $17,800 | 2 |
| 6 | Caldor | Larry | 459-34-0921 | 23 | $32,500 | 4 |
| 7 | Lightnor | Peggy | 560-55-4311 | 14 | $23,500 | 10 |
| 8 | McCartin | John | 817-66-1212 | 15 | $54,600 | 2 |
| 9 | Justof | Jack | 431-78-9963 | 17 | $41,200 | 4 |
| 10 | Patterson | Lyle | 212-11-9090 | 12 | $21,500 | 10 |
| 11 | Miller | Lisa | 214-89-6756 | 23 | $18,700 | 2 |
| 12 | Hawkins | Mark | 215-67-8973 | 21 | $19,500 | 2 |
| 13 | | | | | | |
| 14 | Criteria Range | | | | | |
| 15 | Job Code | | | | | |
| 16 | 23 | | Total Salaries for Job Code 23: | | $86,200 | |
| 17 | | | | | | |

**Figure 9-20.**    Using @DSUM

argument can be supplied as a range (A1..F67) or as a range name assigned to the database (RECORDS). This argument can also refer to just a section of the database, as long as the field names for the included fields are within the specified range.

offset in database     The position number of the field in the database you wish to use in the variance calculation. This field should contain numeric values. The first column of the database has an offset of zero. As you move successively to each field to the right of the first, 1 will be added to the offset. This argument can be supplied as a number or a reference to a cell containing a number.

criteria location     The location of the criteria used in selecting records. This can be specified as a range or a range name. It should include the field names that appear at the top of the criteria area.

Data Management                                                            **521**

## Use

The @DVAR function will determine the variance when the selected records comprise the entire population you are measuring. If you are working with only a sample of the population, use the formula in the note that follows the discussion of the population variance.

The purpose of the variance is to determine the amount of variation between individual values and the mean. If you determine that the average age of your employees is 40, this could mean that half of your employees were 39 and the other half 41, or it could mean that you had employees whose ages ranged from 18 to 65. The latter case would show a greater variance due to the greater dispersion from the mean.

The @DVAR function is biased, since it uses a count as part of the variance calculation. The following formula is used:

$$\frac{\sum (X_i - AVG)^2}{n}$$

where $X_i$ is the ith item in the list and n is the number of items in the list.

The worksheet in Figure 9-21 shows the @DVAR function used with criteria located in A15..A16 to determine the variance for salaries of employees with a job code of 15.

## Note

The @DVAR function is designed to calculate population variance. If you are interested in the sample variance, you can create your own formula, as follows:

$$\frac{@DCOUNT(list)}{(@DCOUNT(list)-1)) * @DVAR(list)}$$

F16: (G) [W9] @DVAR(A1..F12,4,A15..A16)                                    READY

|    | A          | B          | C            | D        | E        | F        |
|----|------------|------------|--------------|----------|----------|----------|
| 1  | Last Name  | First Name | SS#          | Job Code | Salary   | Location |
| 2  | Larson     | Mary       | 543-98-9876  | 23       | $12,000  | 2        |
| 3  | Campbell   | David      | 213-76-9874  | 23       | $23,000  | 10       |
| 4  | Campbell   | Keith      | 569-89-7654  | 15       | $17,700  | 2        |
| 5  | Stephens   | Tom        | 219-70 0754  | 15       | $17,800  | 7        |
| 6  | Caldor     | Larry      | 459-34-0921  | 23       | $32,500  | 4        |
| 7  | Lightnor   | Peggy      | 560-55-4311  | 14       | $23,500  | 10       |
| 8  | McCartin   | John       | 817-66-1212  | 15       | $17,750  | 2        |
| 9  | Justof     | Jack       | 431-78-9963  | 17       | $41,200  | 4        |
| 10 | Patterson  | Lyle       | 212-11-9090  | 12       | $21,500  | 10       |
| 11 | Miller     | Lisa       | 214-89-6756  | 23       | $18,700  | 2        |
| 12 | Hawkins    | Mark       | 215-67-8973  | 21       | $19,500  | 2        |
| 13 |            |            |              |          |          |          |
| 14 | Criteria Range |        |              |          |          |          |
| 15 | Job Code   |            |              |          |          |          |
| 16 |    15      |            | Salary Variance for Job Code 15: | | 1666.666 | |
| 17 |            |            |              |          |          |          |

**Figure 9-21.**    Using @DVAR

# DATA MANAGEMENT

Worksheet Range Copy Move File Print Graph Data System Quit

Fill Table Sort | Query Distribution Matrix Regression Parse

Data-Range Primary-Key Secondary-Key Reset Go Quit

Input Criterion Output Find Extract Unique Delete Reset Quit

Cancel Delete

© Lotus Development Corporation 1986. Used with permission.

## /Data Fill

### Description

The /Data Fill command allows you to produce an ascending or descending list of numbers. The numbers in the list must be separated by the same interval. The following series can all be generated with /Data Fill:

1 2 3 4 5 6 7 8 9 10 11 12 13 14 15 16
5001 5006 5011 5016 5021 5026 5031 5036
90 88 86 84 82 80 78 76 74 72 70 68 66

When you use the /Data Fill command, you will first need to tell 1-2-3 the range of cells that you wish to have filled with a numeric series. After this you will be prompted for the three variables that provide flexibility in series generation.

### Options

When you use /Data Fill, you will be asked to supply a start value, a stop value, and an increment or step value. The start value is the beginning number in your sequence and has a default of 0. The stop value is the last value in your sequence. The default is 8191 or the last number that will fit within the range selected. The increment (step) is the distance between each pair of numbers in the series. It has a default value of 1. It can be either positive or negative.

## /Data Query Criterion

### Description

The /Data Query Criterion command permits you to specify the location of the criteria you have entered on the worksheet for database record selection. Criteria must already be entered on the worksheet when you issue this command.

### Options

The only option you have with this command is the method you use to specify the criteria range. Pointing, keying the cell addresses, and using a range name are all acceptable methods of specifying the range.

## /Data Query Delete

### Description

The /Data Query Delete command searches database records for specified criteria and deletes all the records in the input area that match the criteria. The database records must first be specified with /Data Query Input, and the criteria must be entered on the worksheet and specified with /Data Query Criterion.

### Options

There are no options for this command.

### Note

Since the deletion process is permanent, you will want to save your file before deleting records. This way you can always retrieve the file if you make a mistake in specifying your criteria and delete too many records. Another protective strategy is to use your criteria to extract records before using the same criteria for a deletion.

## /Data Query Extract

### Description

The /Data Query Extract command searches database records for specified criteria and writes all the records from the input area that match the criteria to an output area on the worksheet. Preliminary steps that must be completed before using this command are as follows:

- The database records to be searched must first be specified with /Data Query Input.

- The criteria for extraction must be entered on the worksheet and specified with /Data Query Criterion.

- An output area must be specified with /Data Query Output. This area must be large enough to hold all the extracted records and must be out of the way of your other data.

## Options

There are no options for this command.

# /Data Query Find

## Description

The /Data Query Find command searches database records for specified criteria and individually highlights all the records from the input area that match those criteria. Before using this command you must specify the database records to be searched with /Data Query Input. You must also enter the search criteria on the worksheet and specify them with /Data Query Criterion.

## Options

There are no options for this command.

# /Data Query Input

### Description

The /Data Query Input command permits you to specify the location of the database you have entered on the worksheet. Database records should already be entered on the worksheet when you issue this command.

### Options

The only option you have with this command is the method you use to specify the input range. Pointing, keying the cell addresses, and using a range name are all acceptable methods of specifying the range.

### Note

The input range should always include the field names at the top of your database.

# /Data Query Output

### Description

The /Data Query Output command permits you to specify the location of the extract area you plan to use when pulling information from a database. The field names for the data you wish to extract should already be entered on the worksheet when you issue this command.

### Options

You have two options with this command: specifying the entire output area or just the top row. You also have a number of options for specifying the range for the output area.

If you specify a one-row output range that includes only the field names, 1-2-3 will use as many rows as required for writing data in the columns selected for the output range. If you specify a multiple-row output range, 1-2-3 will stop extracting records when your output range is full. Options for specifying the range are pointing, keying the cell addresses, and using a range name.

## /Data Query Quit

### Description

This command permits you to exit the sticky Data Query menu.

### Options

This command has no options.

## /Data Query Reset

### Description

This command will clear the range specifications for Input, Criterion, and Output.

### Options

There are no options for this command.

# /Data Query Unique

## Description

The /Data Query Unique command searches database records for specified criteria and writes all the nonduplicate records from the input area that match the criteria to an output area on the worksheet. Preliminary steps that must be completed before using this command are as follows:

• The database records to be searched must first be specified with /Data Query Input.

• The criteria for search must be entered on the worksheet and specified with /Data Query Criterion.

• An output area must be specified with /Data Query Output. This area must be large enough to hold all the selected records and must be out of the way of your other data.

## Options

There are no options for this command.

# /Data Sort Data-Range

## Description

The /Data Sort Data-Range command permits you to specify the location of the records you plan to sort. Database records should already be entered on the worksheet when you issue this command.

## Options

The only option you have with this command is the method you use to specify the input range. Pointing, keying the cell addresses, and using a range name are all acceptable methods of specifying the range.

## Note

The sort range should not include the field names at the top of the database. If you accidentally include the field names, they will be sorted.

# /Data Sort Go

## Description

The /Data Sort Go command tells 1-2-3 it is time to sort the records. Before this command is executed, the database should be defined with the /Data Sort Data-Range command. The primary and potentially the secondary key should also be specified.

## Options

There are no options for this command.

# /Data Sort Primary-Key

## Description

The /Data Sort Primary-Key command permits you to specify a new sequence for your database records by selecting a field to control the resequencing. Enter the address of a data-containing cell within the field that you wish to use for controlling the sort sequence.

### Options

The command permits you to specify either ascending or descending sort order.

## /Data Sort Quit

### Description

The /Data Sort Quit option is used to exit the sticky Sort menu.

### Options

There are no options for this command.

## /Data Sort Reset

### Description

The /Data Sort Reset command cancels the current settings for the primary and secondary keys and the data range.

### Options

There are no options for this command.

## /Data Sort Secondary-Key

### Description

The /Data Sort Secondary-Key command permits you to select a field within the database to serve as a tie breaker in the event that there is more than one primary key with the same value. When this situation occurs, Sort uses the secondary key to provide a sequence for the records containing the duplicate entries. As an example, you may have an employee file with the last name field selected as the primary key. When you encounter three employees with the last name of Smith and have selected first name as the secondary key, the three Smiths will appear in a sequence determined by their first names.

A secondary key is selected in the same manner as a primary key. Any data-containing cell within a field can be specified as the secondary key.

## Options

You have two options for this command, A for ascending and D for descending sort order.

# Using Data Management Features in the Spreadsheet Environment

**T**
**E**
**N**

In Chapter 9 you learned how to use the data management features of 1-2-3 to build your own database of information. In this chapter you will learn ways that data management commands can assist you with calculations and other spreadsheet tasks. You will see some of the same commands used in Chapter 9, such as /Data Sort' and /Data Fill, but they will be presented in a new light. You will also explore more sophisticated features that allow you to handle tasks like regression and sensitivity analysis. These features will introduce new commands, such as /Data Table and /Data Regression.

The /Data Fill command can save you considerable time when you are preparing a spreadsheet model. You can use this command to generate a series of dates, invoice numbers, purchase order numbers, new account numbers, or i.d. numbers for new employees, for example. Whenever you need to enter a data series with evenly spaced values in either ascending or descending sequence, /Data Fill can handle the task for you.

To use /Data Fill, place your cursor in the upper left cell of the row or column in which you want the series generated and enter **/Data Fill**. Next, enter the range you wish to use for the series. 1-2-3 will prompt you for the first number in the series and suggest the default value of 0. You can press ENTER to accept this value or enter whatever number you want to begin with. The prompt for the increment is next. To accept the default of 1, press ENTER again. Alternatively, enter any positive or negative number for the increment before pressing ENTER. 1-2-3's last prompt is for a stop value. As long as the default value of 8191 is greater than or equal to your planned stop value, you can press ENTER and allow 1-2-3 to determine a stop value based on the size of your range and the other values you have supplied. If 8191 is not large enough, enter a new stop value before pressing ENTER.

For example, suppose you needed to enter a series of dates that were each seven days apart. As a preliminary step you would need to determine the serial date number of the first date. You could enter the @DATE function to determine the serial number. If the first date you needed was January 3, 1987, you could enter **@DATE(87,1,3)** and get a serial date number of 31780. Assuming you wanted to enter the dates in cells A2..A20 of your worksheet, you would place your cursor in A2 to begin and enter **/Data Fill**. For the start value you would enter **31780**, for the increment you would enter 7, and for the stop value you could enter **45000**, since you could be sure this number will be larger than the last number required to fill the range. The results are shown in Figure

10-1. If you entered 31800 as the stop value, your results would have been quite different, since the stop value would have been reached before the end of the range.

You will find /Data Fill useful in conjunction with some of the commands covered later in this chapter. In particular, keep its features in mind as you read the instructions for the /Data Distribution and /Data Table commands, since both of these commands frequently utilize a numeric series with regular intervals.

## Performing Statistical Analyses With Data Commands

The statistical commands that are part of the Data options allow you to perform sophisticated analyses of your data. You

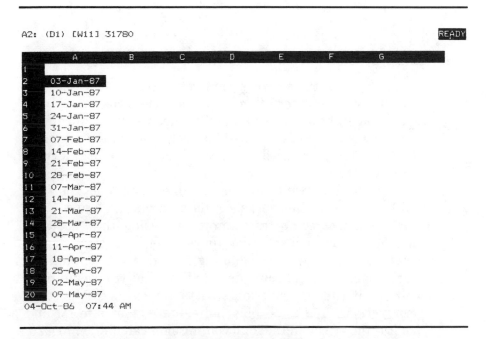

Figure 10-1.    Output from /Data Fill

can perform a regression analysis, create a frequency distribution, or prepare a sensitivity analysis.

## Sensitivity Analysis

The /Data Table options allow you to quickly substitute a range of values in one or two cells referenced by formulas and to record the results of worksheet calculations at the same time. In other words, /Data Table automates the "what-if" analysis you may have been doing with the package as you individually plugged in new variable values and tried to remember the results from previous iterations. The advantage of this automated approach is that 1-2-3 will do all the work, plug in the values, and remember the results for you. The results will be recorded in a table, as you might guess from the command's name.

The /Data Table command provides three options: a one-way table, a two-way table, and a Reset option that eliminates settings you have made through either of the other choices.

### One-Way Data Tables

A one-way data table allows you to choose a set of values for one variable and record them in a worksheet column. Above and to the right of this column of values you place formulas that you wish to have evaluated for each value of the variable. The results are recorded below the formulas to form a complete table.

Let's look at two examples of a one-way table. The first will be used with the worksheet data shown in Figure 10-2. This worksheet computes commissions using the quarterly sales figure for each salesman times the commission percentage in D1. If you were considering changing the commission percentage, you might be interested in what you would have paid out if that commission structure was in existence in prior periods. You could plug individual values into D1 and monitor the effect on the total commission calculation in C20, but it will be faster to have 1-2-3 do the work for you.

```
         A            B            C         D        E        F        G
1              Sales Commissions Assuming A  1.50% Commission
2
3                    Quarterly
4    Salesman        Sales        Commission
5    Rich Roberts    $1,200,987    $18,015
6    Jim Jolson      $2,134,567    $32,019
7    Mike Moore      $1,987,600    $29,814
8    Harry Harm      $3,278,965    $49,184
9    Tom Torn        $3,456,123    $51,042
10   Roy Roberts     $2,134,987    $32,025
11   Paul Peters     $1,897,626    $28,464
12   Ken Kolson      $1,750,890    $26,263
13   Herb Horst      $2,345,910    $35,189
14   Frank Folly     $3,890,152    $58,352
15   Ivan Imers      $3,186,450    $47,797
16   Will Walker     $2,134,567    $32,019
17   Norm Nait       $1,678,932    $25,184
18   Ed Edens          $540,900     $8,114
19
20   TOTAL          $31,618,656   $474,280
04-Oct-86   06:47 AM
```

**Figure 10-2.**　　Commission schedule

The first step is to set up the framework for the table. This step must be completed before you enter /Data Table. The values you want to substitute for D1 must be recorded in a column. The example uses I4..I19, but any empty location could be selected. If you are using values in even increments, you can have /Data Fill generate these values for you. Step 2 in the setup process is to record the formula or formulas you wish to evaluate. They should be placed one column to the right of the values and one row above them. To evaluate total commission, a reference to C20 will suffice. This entry would be made in J3. After entering +C20, you can format the cell as text to display the formula. The table format at this time looks like the display in Figure 10-3. After completing these two preliminary steps, you are ready to use the /Data Table command.

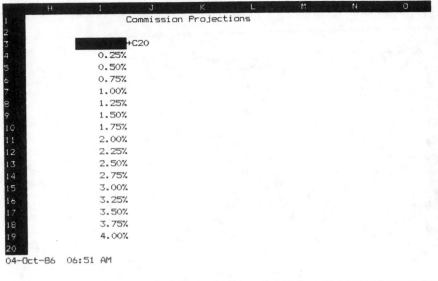

Figure 10-3.    Outline of one-way table

Move your cursor to I3, the blank cell to the left of the formulas and immediately above the values. Enter /**Data Table** and then select 1 for a one-way table. Select the range I3..J19 for the table location. You can use cell addresses, pointing, or a range name for this task.

1-2-3's next prompt is for the input cell. This is the cell into which you want to plug the values in the left column one by one. For our example this will be D1. When you press ENTER, 1-2-3 will take the first value in the input column and plug it into D1 in the model. After the first calculation is completed, 1-2-3 records the value in the table and repeats the process for each of the remaining values. Figure 10-4 shows the level of commissions at a variety of percentages. Be aware that if you change the formulas in your model, the

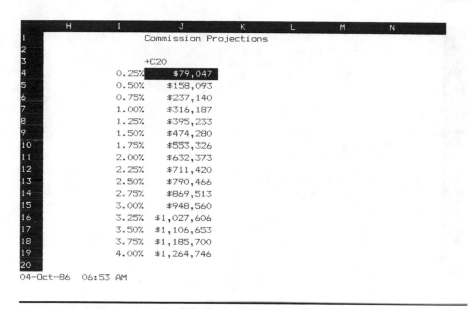

**Figure 10-4.**     Commission output

table will not be updated to reflect these changes. To update the table values, you will need to issue the /Data Table command again.

Now let's look at a second example of a one-way table, this time using more than one formula. Figure 10-5 shows the model and the completed table. The model projects sales, cost of goods sold, and profit through 1991, using a 9% fixed growth rate for sales and 45% as the cost of goods sold percent. Suppose you want to look at the impact on sales, costs, and profits of variations in the sales growth factor. You could place the variable values in A11..A20. References to the cells containing the formulas you wish to evaluate could be placed in B10..D10 as +G4, +G2, and +G3. You could define the table as being in A10..D20 after entering /**Data Table 1**.

| | A | B | C | D | E | F | G |
|---|---|---|---|---|---|---|---|
| 1 | | 1986 | 1987 | 1988 | 1989 | 1990 | 1991 |
| 2 | Sales | $23,500 | $25,615 | $27,920 | $30,433 | $33,172 | $36,158 |
| 3 | Cogs | $10,575 | $11,527 | $12,564 | $13,695 | $14,927 | $16,271 |
| 4 | Profit | $12,925 | $14,088 | $15,356 | $16,738 | $18,245 | $19,887 |
| 5 | | | | | | | |
| 6 | | | | | | | |
| 7 | Sales Growth: | | 9.00% | | | | |
| 8 | Cogs % | | 45.00% | | | | |
| 9 | | | | | | | |
| 10 | | +G4 | +G2 | +G3 | | | |
| 11 | 8.00% | $18,991 | $34,529 | $15,538 | | | |
| 12 | 8.25% | $19,212 | $34,931 | $15,719 | | | |
| 13 | 8.50% | $19,435 | $35,336 | $15,901 | | | |
| 14 | 8.75% | $19,660 | $35,745 | $16,085 | | | |
| 15 | 9.00% | $19,887 | $36,158 | $16,271 | | | |
| 16 | 9.25% | $20,116 | $36,574 | $16,458 | | | |
| 17 | 9.50% | $20,347 | $36,995 | $16,648 | | | |
| 18 | 9.75% | $20,580 | $37,419 | $16,838 | | | |
| 19 | 10.00% | $20,816 | $37,847 | $17,031 | | | |
| 20 | 10.25% | $21,053 | $38,279 | $17,226 | | | |

04-Oct-86   08:08 AM

**Figure 10-5.**    One-way table with multiple formulas

The input cell is defined as C7. The results are shown in cells B11..D20 of the figure.

### Two-Way Data Tables

The /Data Table 2 command lets you build a table in which you supply input values for two variables and have 1-2-3 apply these values when recalculating the worksheet and recording the result of one of the worksheet formulas in the table. This kind of table is frequently referred to as a two-way table. It differs from a one-way table in its use of two sets of variable values and its ability to record the results of only one formula. This command allows you to see which variable the formula being evaluated is most sensitive to.

Like the one-way table, the two-way table requires a significant amount of preliminary work. The example uses a two-way table in connection with the following model for payment calculations.

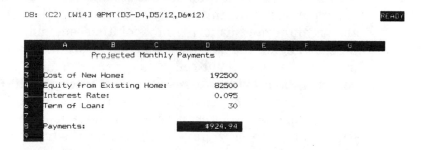

D8: (C2) [W14] @PMT(D3-D4,D5/12,D6*12)                                   READY

The payment calculation is dependent on the amount borrowed, the interest rate, and the term of the loan, since the amount borrowed will be equal to the cost of the new home minus the equity from the sale of the existing home. While holding the loan term constant, you can use /Data Table 2 to vary the equity received from the sale of an existing home and the interest rate.

Values for the first input variable are stored in one column of the worksheet. If the values are spaced at equal intervals, /Data Fill can be used to generate the column of values. Values for the second input value are placed one row above the top value for input 1 and one cell to the right. The values for the second input variable are placed across the row. A formula or a reference to a worksheet formula is then placed in the cell at the top of the column used for input variable 1.

For the payment example you might use column H for the input values for variable 1 and enter values in H2..H17, beginning with 9%, adding increments of .25%, and ending with 12.75%. The equity figures would start in I1 with 75000 and proceed at increments of 2500, ending with the value of 90000 in O1. Cell H1 would contain the formula reference, +D8, to show the payment calculated. If you want this cell to display as a formula, format the cell as text with /Range Format Text.

With all these preliminaries accomplished, you could enter /**Data Table** and choose 2 from the submenu. The first prompt asks for the location of the table, which would be H1..O17. This can be entered as a range, as a range name, or by pointing. The next prompt asks for the cell to use for the first input value. In this example the input cell is D5. You can communicate this to 1-2-3 by pointing, entering a range name, or keying the address. The same procedure will work for D4, the second input cell. After you respond to this last prompt, 1-2-3 provides the results shown in Figure 10-6. You can use this table of results to determine the monthly payment as long as the interest rate and the amount of money borrowed are in the ranges established for the table. You can follow across whichever row of the table has the interest rate you feel you can obtain for a loan and can determine your payments at different levels of borrowing. Similarly, you can

H1:  (T) +D8                                                                    READY

|     | H      | I       | J       | K       | L       | M       | N       | O       |
|-----|--------|---------|---------|---------|---------|---------|---------|---------|
| 1   | +D8    | 75000   | 77500   | 80000   | 82500   | 85000   | 87500   | 90000   |
| 2   | 9.00%  | $945    | $925    | $905    | $885    | $865    | $845    | $825    |
| 3   | 9.25%  | $967    | $946    | $926    | $905    | $884    | $864    | $843    |
| 4   | 9.50%  | $988    | $967    | $946    | $925    | $904    | $883    | $862    |
| 5   | 9.75%  | $1,010  | $988    | $967    | $945    | $924    | $902    | $881    |
| 6   | 10.00% | $1,031  | $1,009  | $987    | $965    | $943    | $921    | $900    |
| 7   | 10.25% | $1,053  | $1,031  | $1,008  | $986    | $963    | $941    | $919    |
| 8   | 10.50% | $1,075  | $1,052  | $1,029  | $1,006  | $983    | $960    | $938    |
| 9   | 10.75% | $1,097  | $1,074  | $1,050  | $1,027  | $1,003  | $980    | $957    |
| 10  | 11.00% | $1,119  | $1,095  | $1,071  | $1,048  | $1,024  | $1,000  | $976    |
| 11  | 11.25% | $1,141  | $1,117  | $1,093  | $1,068  | $1,044  | $1,020  | $996    |
| 12  | 11.50% | $1,164  | $1,139  | $1,114  | $1,089  | $1,065  | $1,040  | $1,015  |
| 13  | 11.75% | $1,186  | $1,161  | $1,136  | $1,110  | $1,085  | $1,060  | $1,035  |
| 14  | 12.00% | $1,209  | $1,183  | $1,157  | $1,131  | $1,106  | $1,080  | $1,054  |
| 15  | 12.25% | $1,231  | $1,205  | $1,179  | $1,153  | $1,126  | $1,100  | $1,074  |
| 16  | 12.50% | $1,254  | $1,227  | $1,201  | $1,174  | $1,147  | $1,121  | $1,094  |
| 17  | 12.75% | $1,277  | $1,250  | $1,223  | $1,195  | $1,168  | $1,141  | $1,114  |
| 18  |        |         |         |         |         |         |         |         |
| 19  |        |         |         |         |         |         |         |         |
| 20  |        |         |         |         |         |         |         |         |

04-Oct-86   07:11 AM

**Figure 10-6.**     Two-way table for payment calculation

follow down the column for any given borrowing level and determine your payments, given a variation in the interest rate paid.

## Using /Data Table With Database Statistical Functions

The /Data Table command can also be used effectively with the database statistical functions covered in Chapter 9. For example, you could use the variable values to supply different criteria values to be used with the database functions. These values can be numeric or label entries, depending on the search criteria you are using.

The database this example will use is shown in Figure 10-7. It contains employee records for a variety of locations and job codes. You can use the /Data Table 2 command to

---

A1: [W12] 'Last Name ⬛READY

| | A | B | C | D | E | F |
|---|---|---|---|---|---|---|
| 1 | Last Name | First Name | SS# | Job Code | Salary | Location |
| 2 | Larson | Mary | 543-98-9876 | 23 | $12,000 | 2 |
| 3 | Campbell | David | 213-76-9874 | 23 | $23,000 | 10 |
| 4 | Campbell | Keith | 569-89-7654 | 12 | $32,000 | 2 |
| 5 | Stephens | Tom | 219-78-8954 | 15 | $17,800 | 2 |
| 6 | Caldor | Larry | 459-34-0921 | 23 | $32,500 | 4 |
| 7 | Lightnor | Peggy | 560-55-4311 | 14 | $23,500 | 10 |
| 8 | McCartin | John | 817-66-1212 | 15 | $54,600 | 2 |
| 9 | Justof | Jack | 431-78-9963 | 17 | $41,200 | 4 |
| 10 | Patterson | Lyle | 212-11-9090 | 12 | $21,500 | 10 |
| 11 | Miller | Lisa | 214-89-6756 | 23 | $18,700 | 2 |
| 12 | Hawkins | Mark | 215-67-8973 | 21 | $19,500 | 2 |
| 13 | Hartwick | Eileen | 313-78-9090 | 15 | $31,450 | 4 |
| 14 | Smythe | George | 560-90-8645 | 15 | $65,000 | 4 |
| 15 | Wilkes | Caitlin | 124-67-7432 | 17 | $15,500 | 2 |
| 16 | Deaver | Ken | 198-98-6750 | 23 | $24,600 | 10 |
| 17 | Kaylor | Sally | 312-45-9862 | 12 | $32,900 | 10 |
| 18 | Parker | Dee | 659-11-3452 | 14 | $19,800 | 4 |
| 19 | Preverson | Gary | 670-90-1121 | 21 | $27,600 | 4 |
| 20 | Samuelson | Paul | 219-89-7080 | 23 | $28,900 | 2 |

04-Oct-86  08:22 AM

---

**Figure 10-7.**    Employee database

Data Management Features with Spreadsheets

systematically vary the values for these two variables and obtain an employee count for each job code at each location. The table is created in B22..E28, as shown here:

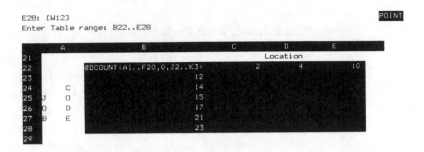

The job codes are placed in B23..B28, with the values 12, 14, 15, 17, 21, and 23 listed. Locations are in C22..E22 as 2, 4, and 10. The formula is @DCOUNT(A1..F20,0,J2..K3). The first argument references the database. The second references the first column of the database, which contains last name. That field is a good choice because it is unlikely to be missing from any record. The third argument references a criteria area that you must set up by entering Job Code and Location in J2 and K2 respectively. You should specify the two cells immediately below these as input cells. Initially these two cells will be blank, but as the /Data Table 2 command executes, it will supply values for criteria to compute the selective counts of database records.

With all the preliminary work accomplished, enter **/Data Table 2** and specify the table location as B22..E28, the first input cell as J3, and the second input cell as K3. 1-2-3 will then produce the following output:

B22: (T) [W26] @DCOUNT(A1..F20,0,J2..K3)                        READY

|    | A | B | C | D | E |
|----|---|---|---|---|---|
| 21 |   |   |   | Location |   |
| 22 |   | @DCOUNT(A1..F20,0,J2..K3) | 2 | 4 | 10 |
| 23 |   | 12 | 1 | 0 | 2 |
| 24 | C |  | 14 | 0 | 1 | 1 |
| 25 | J O | 15 | 2 | 2 | 0 |
| 26 | O D | 17 | 1 | 1 | 0 |
| 27 | B E | 21 | 1 | 1 | 0 |
| 28 |   | 23 | 3 | 1 | 2 |

From this table you can tell how many employees in each job code work at each location.

## Regression Analysis

The /Data Regression command is new with release 2. You can use it to perform a simple regression with one independent variable or a multiple regression with as many as 16 independent variables. You can have up to 8192 observations (that is, values) for each of your variables. All variables must have the same number of observations, however; you could not have 8192 values for one independent variable and 50 values for the dependent variable or another independent variable.

The purpose of this statistical technique is to determine whether changes in the independent variables can be used to predict changes in the dependent variable. This potential interrelationship is described quantitatively with regression analysis. Details of the theory behind regression analysis can be found in any business statistics book.

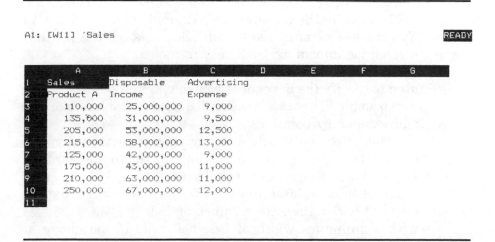

**Figure 10-8.** Regression variables

The first step in using regression analysis is recording the values for the dependent and independent variables in columns on your worksheet. Figure 10-8 shows the dependent variable—the sales of product A—in column A. You could use regression analysis to see whether the independent variables for which you have historic data for the same period had an impact on the sales figures for the period. If these variables do seem to have a relationship to the values for sales, you may be able to predict sales for future periods if you know the values for these other variables during the periods.

Suppose the two independent variables selected are disposable income and advertising expense. Disposable income is in column B, and advertising expense is in column C.

You are now ready to enter /**Data Regression**. When you do so, the following menu will be displayed.

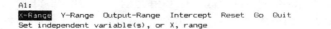

A1:                                                    MENU
X-Range  Y-Range  Output-Range  Intercept  Reset  Go  Quit
Set independent variable(s), or X, range

You will need to make a number of selections from this menu. These are summarized for you in the box called "Creating a Regression Analysis." Your first step should be to select the independent variables with the X-Range option. You can specify up to 16 columns of values, with as many as 8192 entries in the columns. This example will use B3..C10. You can use a range name, cell addresses, or the pointing method for informing 1-2-3 of your choice.

Your next selection should be Y-Range. This selection, used to specify the dependent variable, would be A3..A10 in our example. This can be specified as a range name or cell addresses or by pointing.

Output-Range should be your third selection. You can specify the upper left cell in the range or the complete range. If you choose to explicitly specify the range, keep in mind that it must be at least nine rows from top to bottom and two columns wider than the number of independent variables, with a minimum width of four columns. If you choose to specify only the left corner, be sure that the space under and

## Creating a Regression Analysis

A number of steps are required to create a regression analysis. They are as follows:

1. Enter values for the dependent and independent variables in spreadsheet columns.

2. Enter /**Data Regression**.

3. Choose X-Range to select the range containing the independent variables.

4. Choose Y-Range to select the column containing the dependent variable.

5. Choose an output range 9 rows by at least 4 columns. The number of columns should be equal to the number of independent variables plus 2.

6. Select Intercept and choose Zero for a 0 intercept or Compute if you wish 1-2-3 to compute the intercept. If you have not previously done a regression with a Zero intercept during the current session, you can omit this entry if you wish the intercept to be computed, since Compute is the default.

7. Choose Go to create the regression output.

to the right of that cell is free, or 1-2-3 will overwrite it with your regression results. A21 was chosen for our example.

The fourth menu choice is Intercept. If you wish to have 1-2-3 compute the Y intercept, you can leave this choice blank, since Compute is the default. If you want the intercept set to zero, you can select Zero rather than Compute.

Once the preliminary setup is finished, you can enter Go to have 1-2-3 tabulate the regression statistics. The result of the regression for our two variables when 1-2-3 computes the intercept is shown in Figure 10-9. After your analysis is finished, you can use the Reset option to remove previous settings for the command. The Quit option allows you to exit the /Data Regression menu.

In general, the higher the R value, the greater the correlation, although you will want to be aware of the number of observations and the degrees of freedom when determining the reliability of your results. All this is explained in more detail in a book on statistics. The results shown include a computed intercept of −60493.6, a standard error of the estimated Y values, R squared (if you want to know what R is, you can use @SQRT with R squared as the argument), the number of observations for your variables, the coefficients or slopes for the independent variables, and the standard error for the X coefficients.

You can use the same variable values to do two simple regressions. The variable with the highest R squared value will have the closest relationship to the dependent variable. Figure 10-10 presents two regression output areas. The upper regression output is for disposable income, and the

**Figure 10-9.** Multiple regression analysis

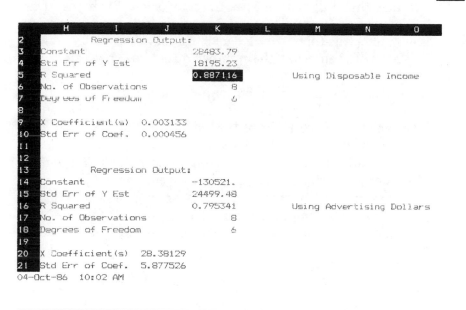

|   | H | I | J | K | L | M | N | O |
|---|---|---|---|---|---|---|---|---|
| 2 | | Regression Output: | | | | | | |
| 3 | Constant | | | 28483.79 | | | | |
| 4 | Std Err of Y Est | | | 18195.23 | | | | |
| 5 | R Squared | | | 0.887116 | | Using Disposable Income | | |
| 6 | No. of Observations | | | 8 | | | | |
| 7 | Degrees of Freedom | | | 6 | | | | |
| 8 | | | | | | | | |
| 9 | X Coefficient(s) | 0.003133 | | | | | | |
| 10 | Std Err of Coef. | 0.000456 | | | | | | |
| 11 | | | | | | | | |
| 12 | | | | | | | | |
| 13 | | Regression Output: | | | | | | |
| 14 | Constant | | | -130521. | | | | |
| 15 | Std Err of Y Est | | | 24499.48 | | | | |
| 16 | R Squared | | | 0.795341 | | Using Advertising Dollars | | |
| 17 | No. of Observations | | | 8 | | | | |
| 18 | Degrees of Freedom | | | 6 | | | | |
| 19 | | | | | | | | |
| 20 | X Coefficient(s) | 28.38129 | | | | | | |
| 21 | Std Err of Coef. | 5.877526 | | | | | | |

04-Oct-86  10:02 AM

**Figure 10-10.**　　Two simple regression analyses

lower regression output is for advertising dollars. The R squared value for disposable income is higher, which indicates that disposable income is a better predictor of sales than advertising dollars. Since the R squared value in Figure 10-9 is higher than either output in Figure 10-10, you can assume that both variables together are stronger predictors than either one individually.

You can also use the regression output to help you determine estimated Y values and the best fitting regression line. The formula you would use to estimate the Y values is as follows:

Constant +Coefficient of X1 ∗ X1 +Coefficient of X2 ∗ X2

You can use this formula to project sales values, assuming that historic relationships are being maintained.

Data Management Features with Spreadsheets      **551**

## Frequency Distribution

A frequency distribution allows you to count the number of values that fall within specific categories. With the /Data Distribution features that 1-2-3 provides, you can set up whatever intervals (bins) for categorizing your data that you want. 1-2-3 will then count the number of entries that fall within each of these intervals.

The frequency distribution table is set up prior to using the command by placing the categories in a location where the column to the right of the categories and the table cells below the last interval are blank. The two cells at the bottom of the table location must be blank to record frequencies greater than the largest specified frequency. All category entries must be numeric and in ascending sequence.

When you enter /**Data Distribution** and tell 1-2-3 the location of the data to be categorized and of the frequency

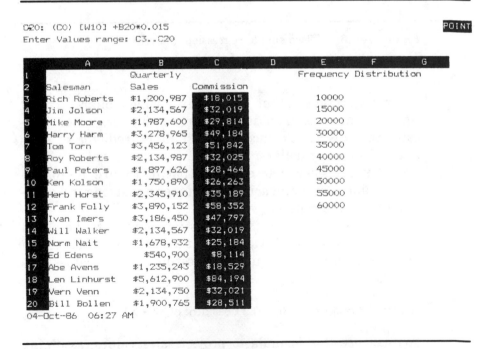

**Figure 10-11.** Commission data

table, 1-2-3 will place each entry within the range you selected into the smallest category that is equal to or greater than the value in your data. In other words, it will add 1 to the frequency count for that bin. With bin values of 3, 7, and 10, a value of 4 would be counted in bin 7. Each time a value is counted for a category, it increments that category's counter by 1.

The entries ERR and NA are numeric values. ERR has a numeric value higher than any regular number, and NA has a value less than any number. Cells that contain a label or a blank are considered to have a value of zero.

Figure 10-11 presents a worksheet that contains commission data in C3..C20. The categories for the frequency count are located in E3..E12. These are arbitrary settings and could have been any set of ascending numbers. The area to the right of these categories is blank, as are cells E13 and

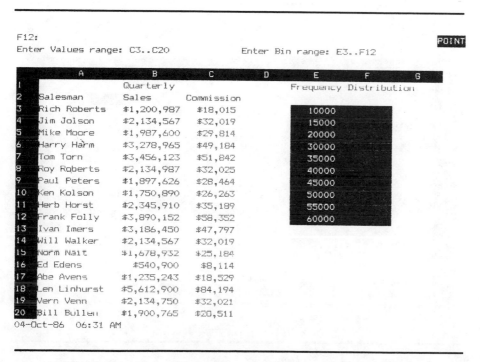

F12:                                                                    POINT
Enter Values range: C3..C20              Enter Bin range: E3..F12

|   | A | B | C | D | E | F | G |
|---|---|---|---|---|---|---|---|
| 1 | | Quarterly | | | Frequency Distribution | | |
| 2 | Salesman | Sales | Commission | | | | |
| 3 | Rich Roberts | $1,200,987 | $18,015 | | 10000 | | |
| 4 | Jim Jolson | $2,134,567 | $32,019 | | 15000 | | |
| 5 | Mike Moore | $1,987,600 | $29,814 | | 20000 | | |
| 6 | Harry Harm | $3,278,965 | $49,184 | | 30000 | | |
| 7 | Tom Torn | $3,456,123 | $51,842 | | 35000 | | |
| 8 | Roy Roberts | $2,134,987 | $32,025 | | 40000 | | |
| 9 | Paul Peters | $1,897,626 | $28,464 | | 45000 | | |
| 10 | Ken Kolson | $1,750,890 | $26,263 | | 50000 | | |
| 11 | Herb Horst | $2,345,910 | $35,189 | | 55000 | | |
| 12 | Frank Folly | $3,890,152 | $58,352 | | 60000 | | |
| 13 | Ivan Imers | $3,186,450 | $47,797 | | | | |
| 14 | Will Walker | $2,134,567 | $32,019 | | | | |
| 15 | Norm Nait | $1,678,932 | $25,184 | | | | |
| 16 | Ed Edens | $540,900 | $8,114 | | | | |
| 17 | Abe Avens | $1,235,243 | $18,529 | | | | |
| 18 | Len Linhurst | $5,612,900 | $84,194 | | | | |
| 19 | Vern Venn | $2,134,750 | $32,021 | | | | |
| 20 | Bill Bullen | $1,900,765 | $20,511 | | | | |

04-Oct-86  06:31 AM

**Figure 10-12.**    Bin range

F13 immediately below it. /Data Distribution has already been entered, and cells C3..C20 are highlighted in response to 1-2-3's prompt for the range of values requiring categorization. When you press ENTER, 1-2-3 will prompt you for the location of the frequency table or bin range. This is shown in Figure 10-12. You may enter either just the column bin values or the entire table area as your range. When you press ENTER, the completed table in Figure 10-13 will appear. You can interpret the first entry in the table as meaning that there was one entry less than or equal to 10,000. The last 1, in F13, says that there was one entry greater than the largest bin of 60,000.

/Data Distribution provides a quick way to condense data. It is ideal when you want an overall picture of the data within a category. You can also show the result of a frequency distribution in a bar chart or line graph very effectively.

F3: 1                                                                    READY

|    | A | B | C | D | E | F | G |
|----|---|---|---|---|---|---|---|
| 1 |  | Quarterly |  |  | Frequency Distribution |  |  |
| 2 | Salesman | Sales | Commission |  |  |  |  |
| 3 | Rich Roberts | $1,200,987 | $18,015 |  | 10000 | 1 |  |
| 4 | Jim Jolson | $2,134,567 | $32,019 |  | 15000 | 0 |  |
| 5 | Mike Moore | $1,987,600 | $29,814 |  | 20000 | 2 |  |
| 6 | Harry Harm | $3,278,965 | $49,184 |  | 30000 | 5 |  |
| 7 | Tom Torn | $3,456,123 | $51,842 |  | 35000 | 4 |  |
| 8 | Roy Roberts | $2,134,987 | $32,025 |  | 40000 | 1 |  |
| 9 | Paul Peters | $1,897,626 | $28,464 |  | 45000 | 0 |  |
| 10 | Ken Kolson | $1,750,890 | $26,263 |  | 50000 | 2 |  |
| 11 | Herb Horst | $2,345,910 | $35,189 |  | 55000 | 1 |  |
| 12 | Frank Folly | $3,890,152 | $58,352 |  | 60000 | 1 |  |
| 13 | Ivan Imers | $3,186,450 | $47,797 |  |  | 1 |  |
| 14 | Will Walker | $2,134,567 | $32,019 |  |  |  |  |
| 15 | Norm Nait | $1,678,932 | $25,184 |  |  |  |  |
| 16 | Ed Edens | $540,900 | $8,114 |  |  |  |  |
| 17 | Abe Avens | $1,235,243 | $18,529 |  |  |  |  |
| 18 | Len Linhurst | $5,612,900 | $84,194 |  |  |  |  |
| 19 | Vern Venn | $2,134,750 | $32,021 |  |  |  |  |
| 20 | Bill Bollen | $1,900,765 | $28,511 |  |  |  |  |

04-Oct-86  06:34 AM

**Figure 10-13.**    Frequency output

Frequency distribution can be performed for a category of numeric values or on the results of a formula calculation like the one found in our example. The frequency count will not be updated as changes occur in the data that was categorized, however. If the data is changed, /Data Distribution should be executed again to update the frequency table.

## Matrix Arithmetic

The /Data Matrix commands were added to release 2 because Lotus needed them to develop the regression analysis features. They can be used to multiply and invert matrices according to the rules of matrix arithmetic. Since matrices are tabular arrangements of data, you will have to organize your information into a table before using the commands.

Matrices can be used to solve econometric modeling problems, market share, and population study problems. The rules of matrix algebra and application details are well beyond the scope of this book; our discussion will focus merely on the procedures for using the two /Data Matrix commands.

### Matrix Multiplication

If you are to multiply the values in two matrices, one matrix must have the same number of rows as the other has columns. The dimensions of these matrices are always specified as the number of rows followed by the number of columns. Thus a 5 by 2 matrix would be a matrix with five rows and two columns. To conform to the rule for the size of the two matrices, one could be a 2 by 3 matrix and the other could be 3 by 2. Figure 10-14 provides an example of two appropriately sized matrices, one in B2..D3 and the other in B6..C8.

To multiply these two matrices, you would enter /**Data Matrix Multiply**. When 1-2-3 requests the location of the first matrix, you would enter B2..D3. When the prompt for the second is displayed, you would enter B6..C8. Output can be specified as B11, if you would like it to begin at that loca-

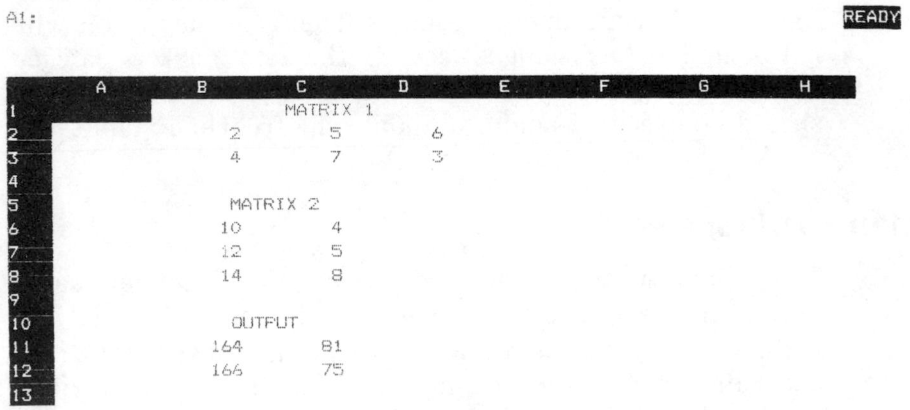

```
        A        B        C        D        E        F        G        H
1                       MATRIX 1
2                 2        5        6
3                 4        7        3
4
5                 MATRIX 2
6                10        4
7                12        5
8                14        8
9
10                OUTPUT
11               164       81
12               166       75
13
```

**Figure 10-14.**   Matrix multiplication

tion, or B11..C12. The result will be the 2 by 2 matrix shown in the same figure.

### Matrix Inversion

Only square matrices (those with the same number of rows as columns) can be inverted. Figure 10-15 shows a matrix originally entered in B3..D5. If you enter /**Data Matrix Invert**, you will be prompted to define the location of this matrix. Specifying B10 for an output area will be sufficient, since that is the upper left corner of the output area. After you make these selections, 1-2-3 will produce the results shown in B10..D12 of the figure.

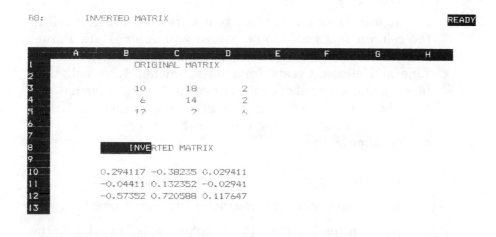

|   | A | B | C | D | E | F | G | H |
|---|---|---|---|---|---|---|---|---|
| 1 | | ORIGINAL MATRIX | | | | | | |
| 2 | | | | | | | | |
| 3 | | 10 | 18 | 2 | | | | |
| 4 | | 6 | 14 | 2 | | | | |
| 5 | | 12 | 2 | 6 | | | | |
| 6 | | | | | | | | |
| 7 | | | | | | | | |
| 8 | | INVERTED MATRIX | | | | | | |
| 9 | | | | | | | | |
| 10 | | 0.294117 | −0.38235 | 0.029411 | | | | |
| 11 | | −0.04411 | 0.132352 | −0.02941 | | | | |
| 12 | | −0.57352 | 0.720588 | 0.117647 | | | | |
| 13 | | | | | | | | |

**Figure 10-15.**    Matrix inversion

## Splitting Long Labels
## Into Individual Cell Entries

The /File Import command can be used to bring information
from an ASCII text file into your 1-2-3 worksheet, as described in Chapter 8. However, it imports this information as
a column of long labels, which may not be what you want.
Fortunately, release 2 has the /Data Parse command, which
allows you to split these long labels into various components.
These individual pieces can be labels, numbers, or serial
time or date numbers.

Using /Data Parse is a multistep process. The steps are
summarized for you in the box called "Splitting Text Entries
Into Cell Values." The options in the /Data Parse submenu
are as follows:

To use /Data Parse, place your cursor on the first cell in the column that needs to be parsed and enter **/Data Parse**. When the command options are presented, select Format-Line and choose Create from its submenu. 1-2-3 will then insert a blank row above your cursor and create a format line that shows how it will split the label into component pieces.

The characters used in the format line generated by 1-2-3 are as follows:

D     marks the first character of a date block.

L     marks the first character of a label block.

S     indicates that the character below should be skipped during the parse operation. This character is never generated by 1-2-3, but you can enter it manually through the Edit option.

T     marks the first character of a time block.

V     marks the first character of a value block.

>     indicates that the block started by the letter that precedes it is continued. The entry that began with the letter will continue to be placed in one worksheet cell until a skip or another letter is encountered.

*     represents a blank space immediately below the character. This position can become part of the block that precedes it.

The pattern established in the format line will be followed in the parsing operation to determine where to split the labels and what type of data is needed for each block. Although you can generate a format line in multiple locations within your column of labels, you will need some consistency in the format of the column in order for this command to be useful.

If you are not pleased with the format line generated by 1-2-3, you can edit it with /Data Parse Format-Line Edit. You

## Splitting Text Entries Into Cell Values

**1**
**2**
**3**

After importing text into your worksheet, you may want to use /Data Parse to split long labels into individual entries. You will need to follow these steps after using /File Import:

1. Move your cursor to the top of the column containing the labels to be parsed and enter /**Data Parse**.

2. Choose Format-Line, then Create to have 1-2-3 generate a suggested format line.

3. If the generated formatted line requires changes, choose Format-Line Edit and make your changes.

4. Select Input-Range and choose the column of labels to be altered (including the format line in the range).

5. Select Output-Range and choose the top left cell in a blank area large enough to hold the output, or else select a range large enough to hold each of the parsed entries. The width of this area is determined by the number of individual fields in the output. The length is the same as the number of labels being parsed.

6. Select Go.

can add, replace, or delete any part of the format line after entering the Edit option.

Once the format has been established, the remaining steps for using /Data Parse are quite easy. Choose Input-Column and then either highlight the cells to be parsed or type in the address of this column of label entries. Be sure to include the Format line in the range. Then select Output Range and enter either the upper left cell or the complete range of cells required. If you choose to supply only the upper left cell, 1-2-3 will determine the space requirements, overwriting data if necessary. If you enter a complete range but do not supply one that is large enough. 1-2-3 will produce an error message on the screen rather than overwriting data beyond the range. With the first three menu selections set, choose Go to have 1-2-3 restructure the long labels into individual cell entries according to the pattern established by the format line.

The other two options in the Parse menu are Reset and Quit. Reset eliminates any settings you have established for the parsing operation. Quit removes the "sticky" Parse menu and returns you to READY mode. (Pressing ESC does the same thing.)

A few examples should help you clarify the workings of /Data Parse. In the illustration, the entries in A1..A3 are long labels.

```
A1: 'Jason Roberts       23    45000      23-Sep-82                           READY

        A      B       C       D       E           F        G        H
            erts        23    45000     23-Sep-82
      Pete Bradon        12    24500      3-Oct-81
      Mary Hanson.       23    34600     12-Dec-84
```

Although at first glance the components of each line may appear to be in separate cells, the control panel shows that each line is in fact a single label entry. The steps you would use to parse these labels are as follows:

1. Move the cursor to A1 and enter /**Data Parse Format-Line Create**. 1-2-3 will generate this format line.

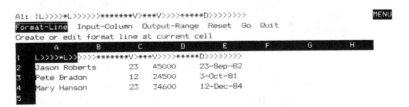

```
A1: !L>>>>*L>>>>>*******V>***V>>>*****D>>>>>>>                                MENU
Format-Line  Input-Column  Output-Range  Reset  Go  Quit
Create or edit format line at current cell
        A       B       C       D       E         F        G        H
1  L>>>>*L>>>>>>*******V>***V>>>*****D>>>>>>>
2  Jason Roberts        23    45000     23-Sep-82
3  Pete Bradon          12    24500      3-Oct-81
4  Mary Hanson          23    34600     12-Dec-84
5
```

Notice that first name and last name have been treated as separate entries because of the space between them.

2. Choose Input-Column and select A1..A4.

3. To duplicate our example, choose A9 as Output-Range.

4. Select Go, and the output shown in Figure 10-16 will be produced.

If you did not want the two name components treated as separate entries, you would choose **Format-Line Edit**. You would then change the format line to agree with the one in Figure 10-17 and issue Go. You will notice that the entry Jason Roberts is now placed in A9. The display is initially truncated due to the column width, but you can change this easily with /Worksheet Column Set-Width.

## Sequencing Spreadsheet Data

Although the /Data Sort commands were designed primarily for use in the data management environment, they can sometimes be used successfully when your worksheet contains data used solely for calculations. Let's look at examples of a

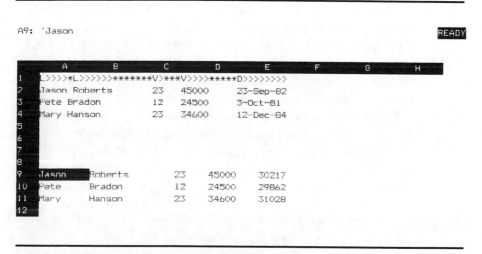

**Figure 10-16.** Output from /Data Parse

```
        A         B         C         D         E         F         G         H
1   L>>>>>>>>>>>>*******V>***V>>>>*****D>>>>>>>>>
2   Jason Roberts      23     45000      23-Sep-82
3   Pete Bradon        12     24500       3-Oct-81
4   Mary Hanson        23     34600      12-Dec-84
5
6
7
8
9   Jason Rob          23     45000     30217     30217
10  Pete Brad          12     24500     29862     29862
11  Mary Hans          23     34600     31028     31028
12
```

**Figure 10-17.**     Output after editing format line

successful and an unsuccessful sort for a spreadsheet application. If you are not familiar with the /Data Sort command, you should review its features as described in Chapter 9 before using it with your data.

Before using this command, you will need to assess whether your spreadsheet is organized in such a manner that sorting the data will not cause problems with your formulas. It would be advisable to save your worksheet file prior to the sort, just in case you make a mistake and sort formulas that cannot be shuffled without causing an error. Since /Data Sort does not have an undo feature, your only recourse in the event of a problem will be to retrieve your file from disk.

As a worksheet is sorted, the rows of your model will be placed in a different order. As long as the formulas within each row reference only other variables in that row, the sort cannot cause a problem. When formula references point outside the row, however, potential problems can occur. If you look at these inventory calculations for six months, you will see that for each month the new beginning inventory is equal to the inventory at the end of the last period.

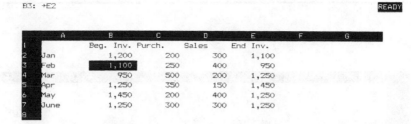

To obtain the beginning inventory figures, the formula in each month references the appropriate address in the previous month (that is, the prior line of the model). These formulas are as follows:

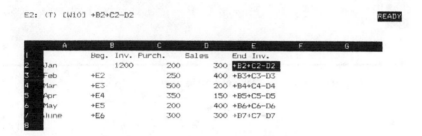

If you wanted to sequence the data by sales figure rather than month, you might decide to try the /Data Sort command. You would enter **/Data Sort Data-Range** and then specify the range as A2..E7. You would select a primary key of D2 (sales) and then choose Go. The results shown here indicate a problem with the references to previous lines.

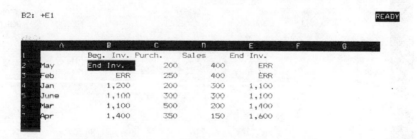

The reason the errors are confined to the top rows is that the 1200 entry for January is a numeric constant rather than a reference to a previous line.

|   | A | B | C | D | E | F | G | H |
|---|---|---|---|---|---|---|---|---|
| 1 |  |  |  |  |  |  |  |  |
| 2 |  |  |  |  |  |  |  |  |
| 3 |  | LODGING | TRAVEL | # | LODGING/ |  |  | TOTAL |
| 4 | LOCATION | CLASS | COST | TRIPS | MEALS | AIRFARE | MISC. | COST |
| 5 |  |  |  |  |  |  |  |  |
| 6 | Akron | 2 | 2 | 2 | $300.00 | $600.00 | $90.00 | $990.00 |
| 7 | Atlanta | 2 | 2 | 4 | $600.00 | $1,200.00 | $180.00 | $1,980.00 |
| 8 | Chicago | 3 | 1 | 3 | $525.00 | $750.00 | $150.00 | $1,425.00 |
| 9 | Dallas | 1 | 2 | 12 | $1,500.00 | $3,600.00 | $420.00 | $5,520.00 |
| 10 | Denver | 2 | 2 | 12 | $1,800.00 | $3,600.00 | $540.00 | $5,940.00 |
| 11 | New York | 3 | 2 | 6 | $1,050.00 | $1,800.00 | $300.00 | $3,150.00 |
| 12 | Phoenix | 2 | 3 | 5 | $750.00 | $1,750.00 | $225.00 | $2,725.00 |
| 13 | Portland | 2 | 4 | 3 | $450.00 | $1,500.00 | $135.00 | $2,085.00 |
| 14 |  |  |  |  |  |  |  |  |

**Figure 10-18.**    Travel worksheet

|   | A | B | C | D | E | F | G | H |
|---|---|---|---|---|---|---|---|---|
| 1 |  |  |  |  |  |  |  |  |
| 2 |  |  |  |  |  |  |  |  |
| 3 |  | LODGING | TRAVEL | # | LODGING/ |  |  | TOTAL |
| 4 | LOCATION | CLASS | COST | TRIPS | MEALS | AIRFARE | MISC. | COST |
| 5 |  |  |  |  |  |  |  |  |
| 6 | Dallas | 1 | 2 | 12 | $1,500.00 | $3,600.00 | $420.00 | $5,520.00 |
| 7 | Akron | 2 | 2 | 2 | $300.00 | $600.00 | $90.00 | $990.00 |
| 8 | Chicago | 3 | 1 | 3 | $525.00 | $750.00 | $150.00 | $1,425.00 |
| 9 | Denver | 2 | 2 | 12 | $1,800.00 | $3,600.00 | $540.00 | $5,940.00 |
| 10 | Phoenix | 2 | 3 | 5 | $750.00 | $1,750.00 | $225.00 | $2,725.00 |
| 11 | Atlanta | 2 | 2 | 4 | $600.00 | $1,200.00 | $180.00 | $1,980.00 |
| 12 | New York | 3 | 2 | 6 | $1,050.00 | $1,800.00 | $300.00 | $3,150.00 |
| 13 | Portland | 2 | 4 | 3 | $450.00 | $1,500.00 | $135.00 | $2,085.00 |
| 14 |  |  |  |  |  |  |  |  |

**Figure 10-19.**    Sorted travel worksheet

To avoid this problem, you have two options for sorting the original inventory data. First, you could use /Range Values to freeze the values in column B before sorting. Your other option would be to use /File Extract Values to save the portion you wanted to sort as another file that could be retrieved and sorted.

Figure 10-18 shows another worksheet that, at first glance, may appear to have the same kind of problem as the formula in E6. The formula references a table located outside the row of the worksheet. You will notice, however, that the formula references the table with absolute addresses. References that are absolute will not change when the sort is performed, so these formulas can be sorted without being changed. When /Data Sort is entered and a data range of A6..H13 is specified with a primary key of A6 for location, the results in Figure 10-19 will be produced.

Another situation to watch for is data placed at the side of the data range like a new field for the database. This data will not be moved, since /Data Sort will move only the specified data range.

# SPREADSHEETS

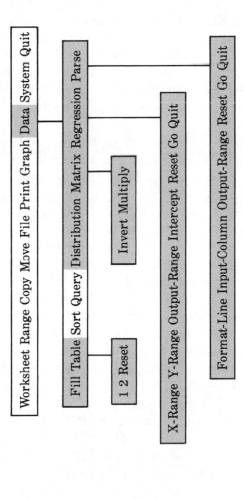

Worksheet Range Copy Move File Print Graph Data System Quit

Fill Table Sort Query Distribution Matrix Regression Parse

1 2 Reset

Invert Multiply

X-Range Y-Range Output-Range Intercept Reset Go Quit

Format-Line Input-Column Output-Range Reset Go Quit

© The Lotus Corporation 1986. Used with permission.

### Description

The /Data Distribution command permits you to create a frequency distribution table from the values in a range on your worksheet. This will tell you how many values in the range fall within each of the intervals you establish. An area of the worksheet must be set aside to record the frequency intervals (bins) against which your data will be analyzed. The frequency for each bin will be placed in an adjacent column.

Using the /Data Distribution command requires some preliminary work. First, you must select a location on your worksheet for the bins. 1-2-3 will use the column to the right of the bins for the frequency numbers for each interval and the row immediately below the last bin for a count of all the values that exceed the last bin value. Second, the values you place in the bins must be in ascending sequence from the top to the bottom of the column you are using.

An example should clarify the way 1-2-3 assigns values to the bins. If you were to create bin values of 5, 10, and 20, the first bin would contain a count of the values in your list that are less than or equal to 5, the second bin would contain a count of values greater than 5 and less than or equal to 10, and the third bin would be for values greater than 10 and less than or equal to 20. 1-2-3 would create a fourth bin for a count of all values greater than 20.

Cells containing labels or blanks will be categorized as cells that have a value of zero. Both ERR and NA are regarded as numeric values. ERR will be counted in the highest interval, since it is considered greater than all numeric values, and NA will be categorized in the first (lowest) interval, since it is considered to be lower than any other numeric value.

Once /Data Distribution has classified the values in the specified range, a change in one of the values will not cause a reclassification. To reclassify data after a change, you must enter /**Data Distribution** again, but this time all you have to do is press ENTER in response to 1-2-3's prompts, since 1-2-3 will suggest the same ranges as were used last time.

### Options

The only options you have with this command are the size of the intervals you enter in the bin range and the number of values in the values range.

## /Data Fill

The /Data Fill command will generate a numeric sequence in any contiguous range of cells on your worksheet. The command offers you your choice of a start number, an end number, and an even interval between each pair of values in the range. Each new value in the range is generated by adding the increment to the previous value.

The /Data Fill command could be used to generate values for the frequency bins for a /Data Distribution table. It could also be used to generate sequential invoice numbers, serial date or time numbers, or purchase order numbers. Whenever you need a sequence of numbers with a defined beginning and equal intervals, /Data Fill can supply it quickly.

### Options

When you enter /Data Fill, 1-2-3 prompts you for several choices. The first prompt asks what range of cells the /Data Fill operation should use. Next, to specify the start value for the series, you can enter a number, or you can accept 1-2-3's zero default by pressing ENTER. The next value is the increment or interval between series values. The default is 1, but you may choose any positive or negative number. The last option is the stop value. The default is set at 8191 for release

2 and 2047 for release 1A. You may use a default higher than the highest value needed to fill the selected range, or you may specify a stop value less than what is needed to fill the range. Whichever is reached first will determine the actual stop value for the range.

# /Data Matrix

## Description

The /Data Matrix command is new in release 2. It allows you to perform multiplication and inversion on large matrices up to 90 rows by 90 columns.

Matrices are tabular arrangements of data with a number in each cell. They are specified by their size. The number of rows is specified before the number of columns. Thus, a matrix with 5 rows and 6 columns is a 5 by 6 matrix. A square matrix has the same number of rows as it has columns.

With 1-2-3's matrix multiplication and inversion options you can solve problems relating to market share, projecting receivable aging, inventory control, and other modeling problems for the natural and social sciences. The specifics of these applications and the theory behind matrix operations are beyond the scope of this volume, however.

## Options

The /Data Matrix command provides options for two algebraic matrix operations, multiplication and inversion.

**Multiply**    This option multiplies the individual components of two matrices according to the rules for matrix arithmetic. It assumes that only two matrices will be multiplied and that the number of columns in one matrix will be equal to the number of rows in a second matrix.

When the Multiply option is chosen, 1-2-3 will prompt you for the location of the two matrix ranges. You can choose to type the cell addresses, reference the matrices with range names, or use the pointing method for specifying the ranges. When prompted for the output range, you can choose to enter the complete range or a reference to it or just enter the upper left cell.

**Invert**     This option inverts any square matrix according to the rules for matrix algebra. 1-2-3 will prompt you for the range of the matrix to invert and the output range. When prompted for the output range, you can enter the complete range or a reference to it or just enter the upper left cell.

### Note

Addition and subtraction on matrices can be handled with the /File Combine Add and /File Combine Subtract options, which are covered in Chapter 8.

## /Data Parse

### Description

The /Data Parse command is new in release 2. It creates individual field values from the long labels stored in worksheet cells. You will need to use this command after you use /File Import to bring long labels from text files created by your word processor or other program into a column of cells. This column of long labels is limited to descriptive use or a string formula without the /Data Parse command. Once the /Data Parse command is used to split the long labels into individual fields, however, you can use the results in numeric formulas and graphs.

Assuming some consistency in the format of the labels, /Data Parse can divide each label into a row of individual values, including label, value, date, and time entries. 1-2-3 will make a suggestion for splitting the label into its individual components, but you have the option of changing this recommendation.

### Options

When you enter **/Data Parse**, 1-2-3 presents a submenu of six choices, as follows:

Format-Line Input-Column Output-Range Reset Go Quit

**Format-Line**     This is the most important option in the /Data Parse command, since it determines how 1-2-3 will split the long labels into individual cell entries. You can use it to create a new format line or edit an existing one.

**Creating a Format Line**     Selecting the Create option under Format-Line will create a format line above the cursor location at the time you make the selection. Position your cursor one cell above the first long label in your column to be parsed before entering /Data Parse Format-Line Create to ensure that the format line is positioned correctly.

1-2-3 will place letters and special symbols in the format line to present its interpretation of the way the long label should be split. The letters and symbols used are as follows:

D     marks the first character of a date block.

L     marks the first character of a label block.

S     indicates that the character below should be skipped during the parse operation. This character is never generated by 1-2-3, but you can enter it manually through the Edit option.

T     marks the first character of a time block.

V    marks the first character of a value block.

>    indicates that the block started by the letter that precedes it is continued. The entry that began with the letter will continue to be placed in one worksheet cell until a skip or another letter is encountered.

*    represents a blank space immediately below the character. This position can become part of the previous block.

**Editing a Format Line**    After you have 1-2-3 create a format line, you can use the Edit option to make changes in it if you wish.

## Input-Column

This is the location for the column of long labels imported from an ASCII text file. The range you specify should include the Format line.

## Output-Range

This is the location you wish to use for the individual entries generated from the long labels. You have the option of entering the upper left cell in an area of the worksheet large enough for the output or entering the complete range for the area. Each approach offers a different advantage. If you specify the complete range and it is not large enough, 1-2-3 will provide an error message rather than expand it. This prevents data stored near the output range from being destroyed if additional space is needed. If you specify only the upper left cell of the output range, 1-2-3 will determine how much space is required and will write over cells containing entries if it needs the space.

### Reset

This option eliminates the format line if you have generated it, along with any settings for input or output area, so you can start over.

### Go

The Go option tells 1-2-3 that you have created and verified the accuracy of the format line and have defined the location of the input and output areas. It causes the long labels to be parsed according to the specifications given.

### Quit

This option tells 1-2-3 that you have finished with /Data Parse and want to be returned to READY mode. You will have to either make this selection or press ESC to get rid of the /Data Parse menu.

## /Data Regression

### Description

The /Data Regression command was added to release 2 to allow you to perform a statistical analysis to see whether two or more variables are interrelated. This command allows you to use from 1 to 16 independent variables for your regression analysis. It will estimate the accuracy with which these independent variables can predict the values of a specified dependent variable.

As an example, your dependent variable may be the sales of hot chocolate at a football concession stand. You may wish to look at outdoor temperature and pregame ticket sales as possible predictors of the number of cups of hot chocolate that will be sold at a game. These two factors would be your independent variables. By applying regression analysis to historic data for the three variables, you could determine how effective the independent variables are as predictors of the dependent variable. When the regression analysis has been completed, 1-2-3 will display the number of observations, the Y intercept or constant, the standard error of estimated Y values and X coefficients, R squared, the X coefficients, and the degrees of freedom.

As with many of the other data commands, using /Data Regression involves a few preliminary steps. First, your dependent and independent variable values must be placed in columns on the worksheet. Each column should have the same number of entries, and all of them should contain numeric values. You can have a maximum of 8192 values with release 2 and 2048 with release 1A; this is one value for each row of the worksheet. Second, you will need to choose a blank area of the worksheet for 1-2-3 to use for output. This area must be at least nine rows in length and four columns wide. The width will need to exceed the number of independent variables by two. After these preliminary steps are completed, you will need to use several of the /Data Regression options to complete your analysis.

### Options

The /Data Regression submenu has the following options.

**X-Range**    This is the column or columns (16 maximum) that contain the values for your independent variables. X-Range can be specified by entering cell addresses or a range name or by pointing with your cursor to highlight the selected area.

**Y-Range**    This is the column containing the values for your dependent variable. It may be specified as a range name or cell addresses or by pointing.

**Output-Range**    This is the area that will contain the results of the analysis. It must be at least nine rows deep and four columns wide, and it must be at least two columns wider than the number of independent variables you are using. You have the option of specifying the entire range or just the upper left corner. If you use the latter approach, 1-2-3 will decide the size of the area to use for the output of the regression analysis. Any data within cells of the output range will be overwritten.

**Intercept**　　This is the Y intercept. You have the option of having 1-2-3 compute this value or setting it to zero. Compute is the default setting.

**Reset**　　This option eliminates all the settings you have established for /Data Regression.

**Go**　　This option completes the regression analysis after you have chosen X-Range, Y-Range, Output-Range, and Intercept.

**Quit**　　This option exits the /Data Regression menu and returns you to READY mode.

# /Data Sort

### Description

This command allows you to sequence information in worksheet cells. The command is covered fully in Chapter 9, since its primary application is for data management. It is mentioned again here because there are selected instances where it can be used in the spreadsheet environment. These are described in the chapter.

### Options

The options for /Data Sort are covered in Chapter 9.

### Description

The /Data Table 1 command allows you to use different values of a variable in formulas. This command provides a structured what-if feature that substitutes various values in your formulas and records the result of each value.

The /Data Table 1 command builds what is called a one-way table. The table will have one set of input values running down its left side. It can evaluate many formulas.

The /Data Table 1 command requires that you set up a table area in your worksheet. The purpose of the table is to structure the input values that you would like to plug into an input cell one by one while recording the impact of these values on the formulas that are also part of the table. To set up the table, place the input values you wish to use in a column in a blank area of your worksheet. The formulas you wish to have evaluated should begin one row above the first value and one column to the right. You may place new formulas in these cells, or you may reference other cells in the worksheet that contain the desired formulas. For example, to have a formula in A3 evaluated, you would place +A3 in one of the cells in this formula row. You may also wish to format the formula cells as text for documentation purposes. The two sets of entries just discussed will create the framework for the table. The value cells form the left edge of the table, with the last entry determining the bottom edge of the table. The row of formulas forms the top of the table, with the last entry in the row marking the right edge.

After the initial setup, you are ready to respond to 1-2-3's prompts to define the location of your table and the cell you wish to reference for input.

### Options

After you enter /**Data Table 1**, you will need to tell 1-2-3 the location you have selected for the table. The best way to do this is to position your cursor at the upper left edge of the table before you enter the command. The table should be a rectangular area that includes all the formulas and all the values you are concerned with. You can use cell addresses, a range name, or the pointing method to communicate the table location.

Next, 1-2-3 will ask you what worksheet cell you want to use as an input cell. This is the cell into which 1-2-3 will place the values in the table column one by one. Using a given value for the input cell, 1-2-3 will evaluate each of the table formulas and place the result of the formula in the column beneath the formula on the row for the input value being used. When 1-2-3 has used each of your values, the table will be filled in with the formula results. Depending on the size of your table, this may take up to several minutes. When 1-2-3 has completed the table, the input cell will still have its original value; 1-2-3 makes its substitutions behind the scenes without affecting the cell entry. A change to a value in the input table will not cause the table to recalculate. To get recalculation, you must reuse /Data Table. If you wish to reset the table location and input cell before using the command again, you can use /Data Table Reset to eliminate your previous settings.

## /Data Table 2

### Description

The /Data Table 2 command allows you to pick any two cells on the worksheet that contain numeric variable values and set up substitution values for these cells so that the impact of the changes can be measured in the result of a particular worksheet formula. This feature provides a structured approach to "what-if" analysis, in which 1-2-3 does most of the work.

The /Data Table 2 command produces a table that is similar to a one-way table except that you can substitute values for two variables at once and can evaluate only one formula. It allows you to see whether the formula result is more sensitive to changes in variable one or variable two, which provides an easy-to-use sensitivity analysis feature.

The /Data Table 2 command requires that you set up a table area in your worksheet. The purpose of the table is to structure values that you would like to plug into the two input cells one by one while recording the impact of these values on the result of a formula that is also part of the table. To set up the table, place the input values for the first variable you wish to use in a column in a blank area of your worksheet. The values for the second input cell you wish to use should begin one row above the first value and one column to the right. Place the values for this second variable across the row. You can use the /Data Fill command to supply these values if the increment between values is evenly spaced. The formula you wish to have evaluated for each value of the input variable should be placed in the blank cell at the intersection of the row and column of variable values. You may enter either an actual formula or a reference to a worksheet cell containing a formula. For example, to have a formula in A3 evaluated, you would place +A3 in the formula cell. You may also wish to format the formula cell as text for documentation purposes.

The two sets of entries just discussed will create the framework for the table. The column of value cells forms the left edge of the table, with the last entry determining the bottom edge of the table. The row of value entries form the top of the table, with the last entry in the row marking the right edge. To have 1-2-3 complete the table entries for you, enter /**Data Table 2** and respond to 1-2-3's requests for specifications.

### Options

After you enter /**Data Table 2**, you will need to tell 1-2-3 the location you have selected for the table. To facilitate this process, position your cursor at the upper left edge of the table before entering /Data Table 2. The table should be a rectangular area that includes the formula and all the values you are concerned with. You can use cell addresses, a range name, or the pointing method to communicate the table location.

Next, 1-2-3 will ask you what worksheet cell you want to use as an input cell for the column of values you entered. This is the cell into which 1-2-3 will place the values in the table column one by one. 1-2-3 will then ask what input cell will be used for the row of values. 1-2-3 will evaluate the formula shown at the upper left corner of the table, using each of the possible value combinations for input cell 1 and input cell 2.

When 1-2-3 has used each of your values, the table will be filled in with the formula results. Depending on the size of your table, this may take up to several minutes. When 1-2-3 has completed the table, the input cell will still have its original value, since 1-2-3 alters the values of the input cell only internally. A change to a value in the input table will not cause the table to recalculate. To get recalculation, you must reuse /Data Table. If you wish to reset the table location and input cell before using the command again, you can use /Data Table Reset to eliminate your previous settings.

## /Data Table Reset

### Description

The /Data Table Reset command eliminates the settings you have established for the table location and input cell. Since 1-2-3 will suggest the previous setting the next time you use the command, Reset can be a convenience when the next table location or input cell setting is far removed from the last use. If you select /Data Table before canceling your previous settings, you will have to press ESC and move your cursor to the new location in order to establish new settings. Once Reset is used, your cursor will remain in its current location.

# ELEVEN

# Working With 1-2-3's Graphics Features

E
L
E
V
E
N

The graphics features of 1-2-3 allow you to present your spreadsheet information in a format that is easy to interpret. Rather than presenting all the specific numbers, graphs can summarize the essence of your data so that you can focus on general patterns and trends. When you notice something that warrants further analysis, you can return to the supporting spreadsheet numbers and look at them more closely.

1-2-3's graphics features are popular because they do not require that data be reentered. You can use the data already entered for your spreadsheet without any changes. You also do not need to transfer data to another program or learn a new system in order to plot a graph. 1-2-3's graphics menus are just like the other 1-2-3 menus, so you need only learn a few new 1-2-3 commands in order to use them. The graphics features are an integral part of 1-2-3, available from the main menu. After creating your spreadsheet model, you simply make a few more menu selections to project the data onto a chart.

If you have a color monitor or a graphics card, you will be able to view your graph or chart on the screen. If you have only a monochrome monitor without a graphics card, you will not be able to view your graph, but you will be able to save the graphic image to disk and print it with the Lotus PrintGraph program. After viewing a graph, you can add enhancements such as legends, titles, patterns, and grid lines. You can save the definition of the graph to use again, or you can print the graph itself on your printer or plotter.

Since 1-2-3's print options for graphs are so extensive, they have been placed in a separate program. After saving a graph on the screen, you can transfer to the PrintGraph program to create a printed copy tailored to your needs. Different fonts are available as well as different sizes of output and support for a variety of printers and plotters.

This chapter will explore the various options available through the /Graph command. It will also look at the PrintGraph program and describe the choices you will have after your graphic image is saved and ready to print.

All the commands you will need to create, modify, display, and save graphs are located under the /Graph option, available from 1-2-3's main menu. When you select /Graph, you will be presented with a menu that looks like this:

```
A1:
Type  X  A  B  C  D  E  F  Reset  View  Save  Options  Name  Quit
Set graph type
```

Under Type, this menu presents the options for selecting the type of graph you wish to see. The specific data to be shown in your graph is accessed through options X and A through F. You can use the Options selections to enhance your graph. Various other selections permit you to view, save, and name your graph.

## Selecting a Graph Type

To create a graph for the first time, you will need to make several menu selections. These specify the type of graph you wish to see and tell 1-2-3 which data to show in the graph.

1-2-3 offers a choice of five different types of graphs, as shown in the following menu:

```
A1:
Line  Bar  XY  Stacked-Bar  Pie
Line graph
```

A list of these graph types is presented when you select Type from the main Graph menu. You can easily change from one type of presentation to another by returning to the Type selection and choosing another graph type. This flexibility allows you to look at your data in a number of presentation formats and select the one that seems to show the data most effectively. Figure 11-1 presents an example of each of the different graph formats. A description of each graph type,

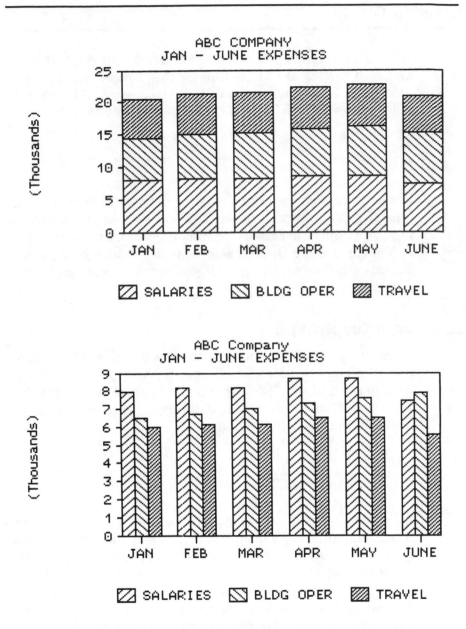

**Figure 11-1.** The five graph types

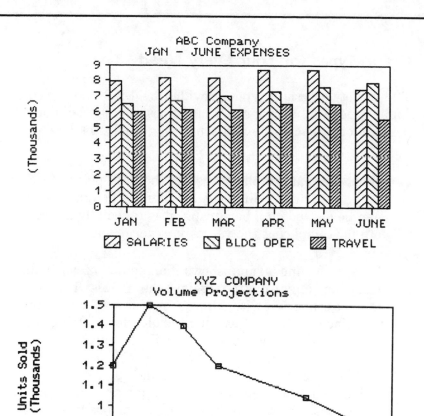

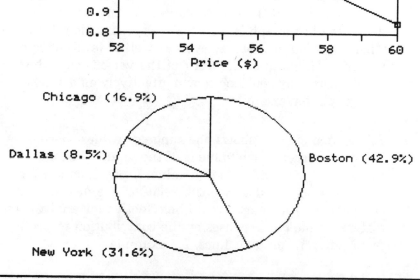

# Graph Types for Your Every Need

The variety of graph types provided by 1-2-3 allows you to find a type suitable for presenting almost any kind of data. A description of each type and some suggested uses follow.

Bar    A bar graph represents the data points in your series by bars of different heights. Although any data can be plotted on a bar graph, it is especially appropriate for comparing the values in several series.

Line    A line graph shows the points of your data range or ranges plotted against the Y axis. The points may be connected with a line, shown as symbols, or both. The line graph is an excellent choice for plotting trend data over time, such as sales, profit, or expenses.

Stacked Bar    A stacked bar graph places the values in each series on top of each other for any one point on the X axis. The total height of a bar thus represents the total values in all the series plotted for any given point. A stacked bar graph is an effective presentation vehicle when you wish to see total levels as well as levels of components. Contribution to profit of the various subsidiaries of a company could be shown effectively on a stacked bar graph, for example.

Pie    A pie chart shows one range of values. It represents the percent each value is of the total by the size of the pie wedge assigned to that value. A pie chart is effective when you need to see the relative size of different components. Pie charts would be effective for analyzing different kinds of expenses or the contribution to profit from different product lines, for example.

> **XY**  An XY graph plots the values in one series against those in another. An XY graph could be used to plot age against salary, machine repairs by age, or time against temperature, for example.

along with some suggested uses, is found in the box called "Graph Types for Your Every Need."

To select any of the graph types from the menu, simply point to the format you want and press ENTER. Alternatively, you can type the first letter of the selection.

## Labeling the X Axis

After selecting the graph type, you will need to define the data to be shown on your graph. The X option in the main Graph menu permits you to specify a range of cells containing labels to be placed along the points on the X axis for line and bar graphs. These labels may mark the points for years, months, or other data values. For the example in Figure 11-2, the cells containing the words Jan through June were selected as the range after choosing /Graph X. The words in the range will be placed along the X axis, as shown in Figure 11-3.

For pie charts, the X range is used to label the sections of the pie. It might list regions, expense categories, or something similar. X range data for a pie chart must be in the same sequence as the data you provide for the A range, which gives the values for the chart.

For XY charts, the X data is plotted against corresponding Y values provided by the ranges A through F. You will again use /Graph X to specify the range of cells that contains

|   | A | B | C | D | E | F | H | I | J |
|---|---|---|---|---|---|---|---|---|---|
| 1 | | | | | | ABC Company | | | |
| 2 | | | | | | | | | |
| 3 | | | | | | | | | |
| 4 | | | | JAN | FEB | MAR | APR | MAY | JUNE |
| 5 | Salaries | | | $8,000 | $8,200 | $8,200 | $8,700 | $8,700 | $7,500 |
| 6 | Building Operations | | | 6,500 | 6,760 | 7,030 | 7,312 | 7,604 | 7,908 |
| 7 | Travel | | | 6,000 | 6,150 | 6,150 | 6,525 | 6,525 | 5,625 |
| 8 | Supplies | | | 500 | 500 | 500 | 500 | 500 | 500 |
| 9 | Depreciation | | | 1,200 | 1,200 | 1,200 | 1,200 | 1,200 | 1,200 |
| 10 | Equipment Maintenance | | | 750 | 750 | 750 | 750 | 750 | 750 |
| 11 | Shipping Expense | | | 400 | 400 | 400 | 400 | 400 | 400 |
| 12 | Data Processing Costs | | | 2,100 | 2,100 | 2,100 | 2,100 | 2,100 | 2,100 |
| 13 | Printing & Duplicating | | | 640 | 640 | 640 | 640 | 640 | 640 |
| 14 | Other | | | 1,030 | 1,030 | 1,030 | 1,030 | 1,030 | 1,030 |
| 15 | Total Expenses | | | $27,120 | $27,730 | $28,000 | $29,157 | $29,449 | $27,653 |

**Figure 11-2.**     ABC Company expenses

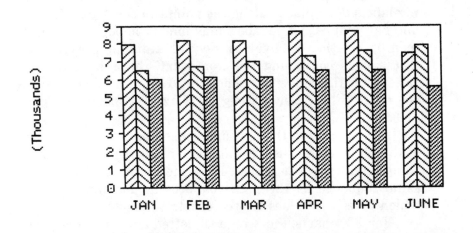

**Figure 11-3.**     Bar chart showing X range data

the entries you wish to use for the X axis. For this type of chart, the entries should be values rather than labels.

If the range you select for X contains too many characters, they will overlay each other, creating an unreadable display like the one shown in Figure 11-4. This problem can be corrected by using fewer or shorter names or by using /Graph Options Scale Skip and entering a skip factor that will cause 1-2-3 to skip some of the labels in the range. A skip factor of 3 will cause every third label in the X range to be used for labeling, for example.

In contrast to the X axis, the Y axis is labeled automatically once you have selected the data you wish to show on your graph. If 1-2-3 needs to represent your data values in thousands or millions to place them on the graph effectively, it will make the conversion and label the Y axis appropriately.

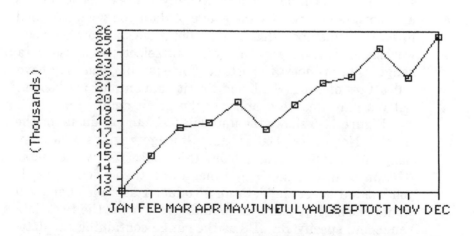

**Figure 11-4.** Overlapping X data values

## Selecting Data for a Graph

1-2-3 permits you to show up to six sets of data values on all graph types except the pie chart. A set of data values might represent the sales of a product for a period of months or years, or it might be the number of rejects on a production line for each of the last 16 weeks, to give two examples. Any series of values can be used, as long as they all pertain to the same thing and are organized according to the points labeled on the X axis. The six different sets of data values will be specified for the chart in ranges A through F. To expand our two examples, they might represent sales figures for six different products or production line rejects from six different factories.

Pie charts are special in that they show what percentage each value is of the total. They therefore would not be appropriate for multiple sets of data. With a pie chart you will use only the A range for your data values. As mentioned earlier, you use the X range to label the sections of the pie.

The A through F options on the main Graph menu represent the six possible ranges of data values to be shown on a graph. If you plan to show only one set of data values, choose A and specify the range of cells containing the numeric values you wish to have plotted on the graph. If you wish to show other sets of data, select as many of the other letters as appropriate and specify the range of data you wish assigned to each. Remember that you do not have to show all your worksheet data on a graph; you can select just those data ranges that are most important. For example, you may have Sales, Cost of Goods Sold, and Profit data on your worksheet, but you may elect to graph just the profit data.

Figure 11-5 shows the unit sales of four products for the Boston, New York, Dallas, and Chicago regions of a company. To create a graph from this data, you would enter **/Graph** to invoke the Graph menu and then select Type. If you wanted to see the data for Product 1 as a pie chart, you would choose Pie. Next you would select A for the first data range and specify B5..B8 as the range containing the data. You can specify this range by entering a range name, pointing after moving to the beginning of the range and locking it

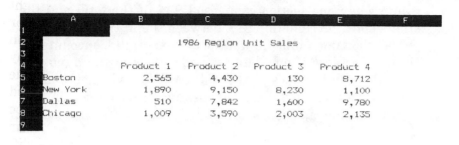

|        |   A    | B | C | D | E | F |
|--------|--------|---|---|---|---|---|
| 1      |        |   |   |   |   |   |
| 2      |        |   | 1986 Region Unit Sales | | | |
| 3      |        |   |   |   |   |   |
| 4      |        | Product 1 | Product 2 | Product 3 | Product 4 | |
| 5      | Boston | 2,565 | 4,430 | 130 | 8,712 | |
| 6      | New York | 1,890 | 9,150 | 8,230 | 1,100 | |
| 7      | Dallas | 510 | 7,842 | 1,600 | 9,780 | |
| 8      | Chicago | 1,009 | 3,590 | 2,003 | 2,135 | |
| 9      |        |   |   |   |   |   |

**Figure 11-5.**    Region sales data

in place with a period, or typing the range reference. You would select X next and specify A5..A8 as the range.

With the basic graph defined, you could select View from the main Graph menu to see a display like the one shown in Figure 11-6. This is all that is required to create a basic graph. It is wise to view the graph before proceeding

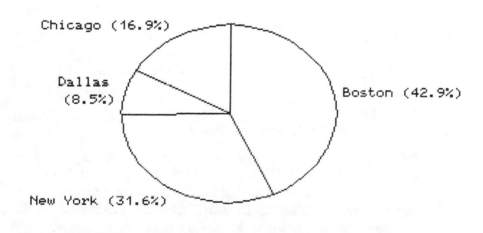

**Figure 11-6.**    Basic pie chart

further. You might find that the data ranges you have selected are too dispersed to be shown on one graph, for instance. As an extreme example, this would occur in a pie graph when one section comprised 99% of the total and the others split the remaining 1% between them. In a bar or line graph showing multiple data sets, you would encounter a similar problem if one data set had values in the hundreds and others had values in the millions. You will not want to spend time creating titles, legends, and other enhancements if your basic graph is not usable.

## Enhancing the Basic Display

Once you are sure that your data can be shown effectively with the graph type you selected, you will most likely want to make some changes to improve its appearance. (If you do not like your basic graph, you may want to try some of the other graph types.) 1-2-3 offers plenty of enhancement options, from shading and exploding a pie chart to adding titles and legends to any type of graph. To select these options, you will need to remove the graph from the screen and return to the Graph menu by pressing ESC. (You can call back the graph display at any time by pressing F10 (GRAPH).) Most of the commands needed to produce graph enhancements are shown on the Graph Options menu, which follows; others are options on the main Graph menu.

```
A1:
Legend  Format  Titles  Grid  Scale  Color  B&W  Data-Labels  Quit
Specify data-range legends
```

### Shading and Exploding Pie Charts

Normally the B data range is used to specify a second set of data for your chart. With a pie chart, however, the B range can be used to specify shading for the individual pieces of the pie. The numbers from 0 through 7 represent different shading patterns, as shown in Figure 11-7.

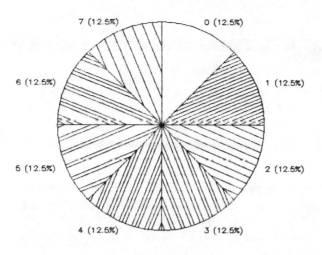

**Figure 11-7.**    Hatch mark patterns

The B data range can also be used to explode a section from the pie. Any pattern can be changed to an exploded section by adding 100 to the shading code selected.

Figure 11-8 shows the same data found in Figure 11-5, except that an extra column has been added for the codes to be specified as the B data range. These codes are stored in F5 through F8 and will correspond to the data values shown in the pie chart. When B is selected and F5..F8 is used as the range, the pie chart will change its appearance, as you would see if you chose View again. Figure 11-9 shows the pie chart exactly as it would appear in your display after you made these changes. You will notice that the section for Boston has ragged edges because of the shading. 1-2-3 will correct this when a copy of the chart is printed with PrintGraph, since printed graphs have sharper details than those shown on the screen.

READY

| | A | B | C | D | E | F |
|---|---|---|---|---|---|---|
| 1 | | | | | | |
| 2 | | | 1986 Region Unit Sales | | | |
| 3 | | | | | | |
| 4 | | Product 1 | Product 2 | Product 3 | Product 4 | Codes |
| 5 | Boston | 2,565 | 4,430 | 130 | 8,712 | 1 |
| 6 | New York | 1,890 | 9,150 | 8,230 | 1,100 | 2 |
| 7 | Dallas | 510 | 7,842 | 1,600 | 9,780 | 103 |
| 8 | Chicago | 1,009 | 3,590 | 2,003 | 2,135 | 4 |
| 9 | | | | | | |

**Figure 11-8.**    Shading and explosion codes added in column F

### Adding Descriptive Labels

Figure 11-10 shows a graph created by selecting Bar from the Type menu. This graph has been enhanced with titles at the top, values along the Y axis, X data labels, and a legend. Adding this type of extra description to a chart can allow it to convey your message much more effectively.

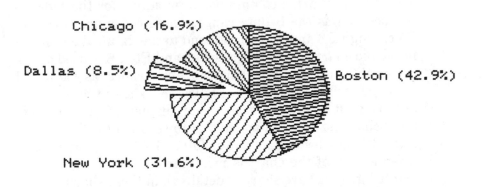

**Figure 11-9.**    Shaded pie chart

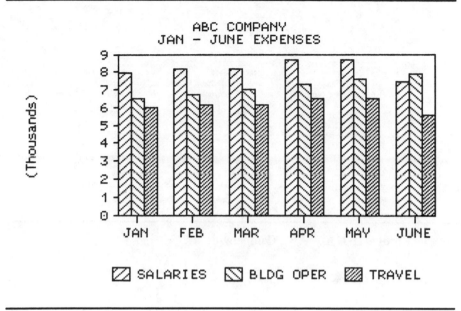

**Figure 11-10.** Bar graph with titles and legends added

The data used to create this graph is shown in Figure 11-11. Of the data in the worksheet, only Salaries, Building Operations, and Travel were selected to be shown. This was done by assigning the numeric values for January through June to the A, B, and C ranges respectively. You would have to make three separate selections from the Graph menu to do this. Each time, you would need to specify the appropriate range.

### Adding Legends

A legend provides a description for each of the ranges shown on a graph. (You saw an example in Figure 11-10.) If you are creating a line graph with symbols marking the data points in the range, the legend will show the markers at the bottom of your chart along with a description of what each repre-

| | A | B | C | D | E | F | H | I | J |
|---|---|---|---|---|---|---|---|---|---|
| 1 | | | | | | ABC Company | | | |
| 2 | | | | | | | | | |
| 3 | | | | | | | | | |
| 4 | | | | JAN | FEB | MAR | APR | MAY | JUNE |
| 5 | Salaries | | | $8,000 | $8,200 | $8,200 | $8,700 | $8,700 | $7,500 |
| 6 | Building Operations | | | 6,500 | 6,760 | 7,030 | 7,312 | 7,604 | 7,908 |
| 7 | Travel | | | 6,000 | 6,150 | 6,150 | 6,525 | 6,525 | 5,625 |
| 8 | Supplies | | | 500 | 500 | 500 | 500 | 500 | 500 |
| 9 | Depreciation | | | 1,200 | 1,200 | 1,200 | 1,200 | 1,200 | 1,200 |
| 10 | Equipment Maintenance | | | 750 | 750 | 750 | 750 | 750 | 750 |
| 11 | Shipping Expense | | | 400 | 400 | 400 | 400 | 400 | 400 |
| 12 | Data Processing Costs | | | 2,100 | 2,100 | 2,100 | 2,100 | 2,100 | 2,100 |
| 13 | Printing & Duplicating | | | 640 | 640 | 640 | 640 | 640 | 640 |
| 14 | Other | | | 1,030 | 1,030 | 1,030 | 1,030 | 1,030 | 1,030 |
| 15 | Total Expenses | | | $27,120 | $27,730 | $28,000 | $29,157 | $29,449 | $27,653 |

**Figure 11-11.**    ABC Company data

sents. If you are creating a shaded chart, the legend will show what each of the shaded areas represents by placing a small box filled with the shading pattern on the chart and adding a description next to the box.

Legends are added by selecting /Graph Options Legend. The menu shown here will be displayed.

```
E2: [W9]
A  B  C  D  E  F
Set legend for A range
```

Enter the letter corresponding to the data range to specify a legend for that range.

When you enter a range letter, 1-2-3 will prompt you for the description to be stored for the data range you selected. The legends used for Figure 11-10 were SALARIES, BLDG OPER, and TRAVEL for the A, B, and C ranges respectively. If you are working with release 2 and the legend you wish to use appears in a worksheet cell, you have an alternative entry method. Rather than typing the legend at the prompt, you can enter a backslash (\) and the address of the cell containing the data you wish to use as a legend. For example, entering \C10 would tell 1-2-3 to use the text in C10 as the legend. A legend typed at the prompt may not exceed 19 characters; a legend in a cell reference may be longer.

### Adding Titles

1-2-3 has four title options, all accessible through the /Graph Options Titles command. They place titles at the top of the chart or along either the X or Y axis. The menu you will see when you enter **/Graph Options Titles** is shown here.

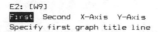

```
E2: [W9]
First  Second  X-Axis  Y-Axis
Specify first graph title line
```

The first title will be shown at the top of the graph. For example, the characters ABC COMPANY were added to the graph in Figure 11-10 by entering **/Graph Options Titles First** and then entering the characters shown. If this label were already in your worksheet, you could enter a backslash (\) and a reference to the cell containing the label.

A line for a second label is also reserved at the top of the graph. To place an entry in this location, enter **/Graph Options Titles Second**. JAN - JUNE EXPENSES was entered at the prompt for the second line title. If you want to reference a label in a worksheet cell for this title, you can use a backslash (\) and the cell address. This method will also let you use a label with more than 39 characters, 1-2-3's normal limit for the first or second line of the graph title. Simply store the long label in a cell and reference this stored value by a backslash in front of the cell address in response to the prompt.

Titles can also be given to the X or Y axis. These labels normally describe the quantities being measured. The Y axis title might be Dollars and the X axis title might be Sales, for example. If you enter a value for the Y axis title, it will be placed vertically on the graph to the left of the Y axis. (The 39-character limit applies to this title at all times.) If you choose X axis, the entry you make will be stored horizontally below the X axis.

### Enhancing an XY Graph

Data for the volume projections for XYZ Company is shown here:

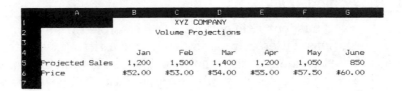

An XY graph can be used to plot the unit sales at different prices. To produce such a graph, you would first enter /Graph Type XY. Then you would enter /Graph X and specify B6..G6 as the X axis values. The A data range would be specified as B5..G5.

After viewing the graph, you might want to add first and second line titles like the ones shown in Figure 11-12. You could enter the first line title with /Graph Options Titles

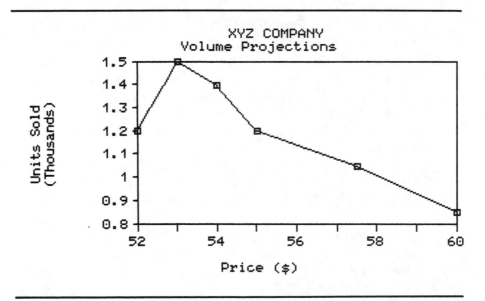

**Figure 11-12.**    XY graph

First followed by \C1 and handle the second line title in the same way, using the /second option and \C2. This graph also has X axis and Y axis titles. To enter these, you would select /Graph Options Titles Y-Axis and then enter Units Sold from the keyboard. This title will be displayed vertically, as shown in the figure. Similarly, you could enter the X axis title of Price ($) from the keyboard after selecting /Graph Options Titles X-Axis. Both of these titles could have been taken from worksheet cells by entering a backslash and the address of the cell containing the entry in response to the prompt.

### Adding Grid Lines

If you have a number of points on a graph, it may be difficult to identify the exact X and Y values for each point on the line. To make such identification easier, 1-2-3 allows you to add vertical and horizontal lines that originate at the axis markers and extend upward and to the right. These lines are called grid lines, since using them in both directions forms a grid pattern across your graph.

The menu for Grid is obtained by entering /Graph Options Grid. The Grid options can be used with all graph types except the pie chart, since grid lines across a pie chart would detract from your ability to interpret the graph. The Grid menu contains these four options:

Choosing the first option will add horizontal lines across the graph. This choice is especially effective for bar graphs, since it enables you to more accurately interpret the tops of the bars. Figure 11-13 presents a bar graph to which horizontal lines were added by entering **/Graph Options Grid Horizontal**.

Vertical bars extend upward from the X axis points. They are more effective on a line or XY graph than on a bar graph. They are added by entering **/Graph Options Grid Vertical**.

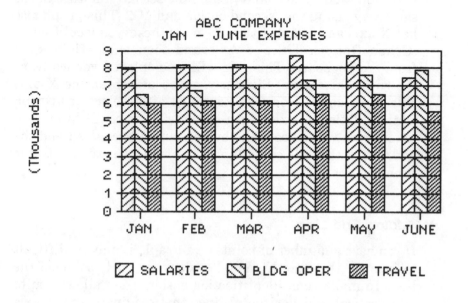

**Figure 11-13.** Horizontal grid lines

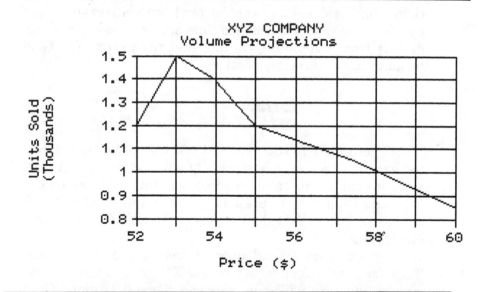

**Figure 11-14.** Grid lines in both directions

To add grid lines in both directions, enter **/Graph Options Grid Both**. Figure 11-14 shows a line graph with grid lines in both directions.

You can remove grid lines without changing the rest of your graph. To take off the grid lines, simply enter the command sequence **/Graph Options Grid Clear**.

### Choosing Line and Symbol Options

1-2-3 allows you to show line graphs and XY graphs in a variety of formats by using the options under /Graph Options Format. You can show the graph as a smooth line connecting the points, as symbols marking the points with lines connecting them, or just as symbols. The options are shown in the following menu:

`Lines` Symbols Both Neither

You will need to specify the range for the command to apply to as either Graph (everything on the graph) or one of the range letters, A through F.

The first option, Lines, connects the points for a data range with a line. The points are not marked by symbols when this option is chosen. The next option, Symbols, omits the line and just marks the data points with the six different symbols that 1-2-3 provides. The third option is Both. As the name states, it provides both lines and symbols for your display. The last option, Neither, may seem useless, since it means that neither lines nor symbols are shown. However, it can be used with the Data-Labels option (covered later in this chapter) to mark the points with actual data values. The default setting for /Graph Options Format is Both.

### Choosing Color or Black and White

If you have a color monitor, you will want to select /Graph Options Color to take advantage of the color display capabilities of your monitor in distinguishing the different data ranges shown on your graph. When you save this image for later printing with /Graph Save, however, you will want to change to /Graph Options B&W. This option will distinguish the different bars on your chart with hatch mark patterns when it prints.

1-2-3 uses the following color assignments for your graph when Color is selected:

A   White
B   Red
C   Blue
D   White
E   Red
F   Blue

Selecting /Graph Options B&W will display your chart if you have a monochrome monitor. It is also the choice to use for retaining hatch mark patterns when you have a color monitor. In this latter situation, all the data ranges in a pie or bar chart will be shown as the background color of the monitor, but the hatch mark patterns will make the various categories distinguishable.

### Selecting Scaling Options

1-2-3's scaling options allow you to override the selections that 1-2-3 makes when constructing your graph. You always have the option of letting 1-2-3 make the scaling decisions, and you are likely to use the /Scale command only when you feel you can improve upon the selections made by 1-2-3. You can use this command to change the scaling for the X or Y axis or to specify a skip factor for x data labels shown on the X axis. /Graph Options Scale Skip was discussed earlier in this chapter in the section called "Labeling the X Axis."

You specify the scale to be changed by choosing either /Graph Options Scale X-Axis or /Graph Options Scale Y-Axis. The menu presented for either of these selections looks like this:

Automatic  Manual  Lower  Upper  Format  Indicator  Quit

The Automatic option is the default setting. It is also the method for returning to automatic scaling after requesting Manual.

Manual permits you to decide what the upper and lower limits of your scale should be. If you choose this option, you should also plan to choose Upper and Lower to define the limits of your scale. With a manual setting, 1-2-3 does not display values outside the established limits unless you are displaying bar graphs, in which case the entire bar will be displayed regardless of the height of the bars.

The Format option on the Scale menu allows you to use any of the numeric formats on the scale markers for the X and Y axis. You can format the numbers as currency, percent, or any of the other formats acceptable for the /Range Format command covered in Chapter 5. When you are working with the X axis, the Format option will be meaningful only for XY graphs, since in the other types of graphs, the markers on the X axis are treated as labels, not numbers.

The Indicator option is available only in release 2. It permits you to turn off the label indicator that specifies size. As an example, if you were showing sales in thousands of dollars, 1-2-3 would generate the label thousands for use along the Y axis. If you did not wish this to appear, you could request Indicator No. Yes is the default setting for this option.

When you are finished with the Scale menu, enter /Graph Options X-Axis or Y-Axis Quit. This returns you to the Graph Options menu.

### Using Data to Label Your Graph

You can use the contents of worksheet cells to label the points in a graph. 1-2-3 will allow you to assign data labels to any one of the data ranges involved in your graph. Simply choose /Graph Options Data-Labels and then enter the letter of your range choice (A through F). After entering the range of cells containing the labels, you will need to choose the location for them relative to your data points. Your options are Center, Left, Above, Right, and Below. Figure 11-15 presents a bar

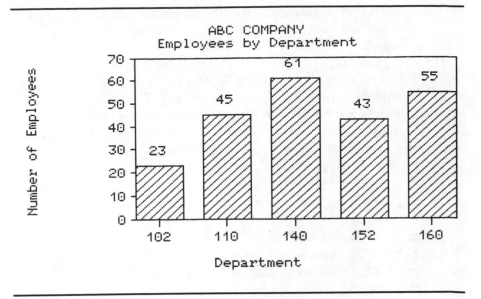

**Figure 11-15.** Data points marked with data labels

chart where data labels are shown above the data points to provide a clear description of the height of each bar.

To use data labels as the only marker on a graph, you will need to create a line graph. You can then enter **/Graph Options Format Neither**, which will keep lines and symbols from being displayed, and center the data labels on the chart with /Graph Options Data-Labels Center to create a display similar to the one shown in Figure 11-16.

### Resetting Graph Options

After specifying particular options for a graph, you might change your mind about some of them. Labels can be changed by entering the appropriate command again and deleting the label from the prompt. As an example, if you have a first line title of ABC Company and wish to remove it, you can enter **/Graph Options Title First** and delete the title XYZ Company from this entry. If a cell reference was used

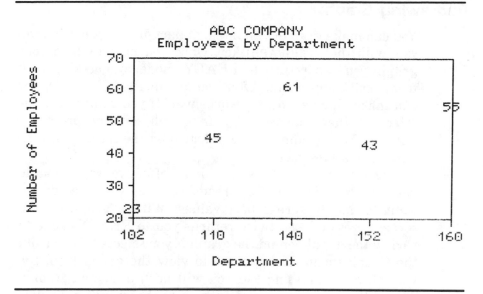

**Figure 11-16.** Data labels displayed without lines or symbols

to supply the label, you can delete the cell reference and backslash from the entry.

If you want to eliminate all the graph settings, however, you will want to use /Graph Reset Graph. This command will eliminate all graph settings, including ranges. It permits you to start defining a new graph from the beginning.

The Reset command also allows you to remove just some of the graph settings. The following menu provides a number of options for removing particular settings.

Graph X A B C D E F Quit

You can remove the X data range by choosing X, or you can remove any of data ranges A through F by choosing the letter of the range you wish to eliminate. Since the Reset menu remains after you make a selection, you will have to choose Quit or press ESC when you want to exit from this command.

## Redrawing Graphs

You can make graphics an integral part of your what-if analysis with the F10 (GRAPH) key. Once you have defined your graph, you can return to READY mode by choosing Quit from the Graph menu. After you are in READY mode, you can make changes to your worksheet. If you want to see the effect of the changes on your graph, simply press F10 (GRAPH). Your graph will be redrawn on the screen with the new data values shown.

The F10 and ESC keys provide an effective way to toggle between graphics and the spreadsheet even when you do not want to update spreadsheet values. With a graph on the screen, pressing ESC twice returns you to READY mode to review the detail behind the graph if you selected View from the Graph menu. If you chose to view the graph from the worksheet by pressing F10, you will need to press ESC only once. When you are ready to return to the graphics display, just press F10 again. This takes you from the worksheet READY mode to the graph display, where current worksheet figures will be reflected in the graph.

## Naming Graphs for Later Use

1-2-3 uses all the settings you enter for a graph to define the current graph. Since only one graph can be current at a time, you will lose the original settings if you start choosing different ones for a new graph. If you want to retain the definition of the current graph while you begin a new graph, use the /Graph Name Create command to save the settings for the existing graph. When 1-2-3 prompts you for the name of the graph to save, you can enter any name up to 15 characters in length. To eliminate all of the settings after saving the first graph, use /Graph Reset Graph. You can then start defining the new graph, and, when the definition is complete, you can name it, too. When you save your worksheet, the graph names and definitions will be saved along with the other data.

A graph whose settings have been saved can be used again by making its settings current. To make the settings of a named graph current, enter /**Graph Name Use** and specify the name you assigned to the desired graph with /Graph Name Create in an earlier session. The settings that were current at the time the graph was saved will now be in effect, and pressing View will recreate the graph on your screen.

The ability to name and use graphs at will allows you to create a number of graphs on one worksheet. You can define all the graphs you need for an application and name each one. Then, when you update your spreadsheet figures, you can create a slide show of graphic results by using and viewing each of the named graphs. You will not have to recreate each of the graphs and make menu selections for settings and other options.

## Deleting Graphs

The /Graph Name Delete option permits you to eliminate stored graph settings that you no longer need. When you enter this command, 1-2-3 will prompt you with a list of all existing graph names. Selecting a name from the list or typing in a name will cause all the settings for that graph to be eliminated. If you change your mind and wish to reproduce the graph, you will have to enter all the options for it again.

1-2-3 also provides a quick delete feature. This can be dangerous, since it eliminates all the graph names you created with one command. If you do want to eliminate all the graph names and their associated settings, enter /**Graph Name Reset**. Since 1-2-3 does not provide a confirmation step for this command, be sure you do not accidentally press R while working with the /Graph Name menu.

## Saving Graphs for Later Printing

1-2-3 does not permit you to print graphs directly from the 1-2-3 program. You can print by loading a screen dump program like Domus, which will reproduce the graphic screen image when you press SHIFT and PRT SC. Such packages are not part of 1-2-3; they can reside in part of memory while 1-2-3 is active, however, and wait for your request. The normal process for printing 1-2-3 graphs, though, is to save the graphic image on disk and then use the PrintGraph program to produce your printed output. This approach also provides a number of enhancement options for your graph.

You should be aware that you cannot save a graphic image with /File Save. This command can save only worksheet data, the current graph setting, and the graph settings stored with any graph names you have created. It creates a .WKS or .WK1 file, not the .PIC file that PrintGraph requires. To create a .PIC file, you will need to use the /Graph Save. After you enter **/Graph Save**, you can provide a file name up to 8 characters in length. 1-2-3 will then save the current graph as a .PIC file for later use with Print-Graph. If you want to save a graph other than the current graph, you must first make the desired graph current with /Graph Name Use.

## Quitting the Graph Menu And Accessing PrintGraph

The main Graph menu and several of its submenus remain on your screen until you choose the Quit option at the end of the menu. Your other option for quitting to press ESC the number of times required to return to READY mode.

To print your graphs, you will normally choose Quit from the 1-2-3 menu to return to either the Access menu or DOS. You can then choose the PrintGraph option from the Access menu or enter **Pgraph** at the DOS prompt. If you are using floppy diskettes, you will have to place the PrintGraph disk in your drive before finalizing the entry.

You have one additional option under release 2, provided that you have available the approximately 140K of memory needed to keep 1-2-3, your current worksheet and graph, and PrintGraph all in memory together. If you have sufficient memory, you can enter **/System** to leave 1-2-3 temporarily, enter **Pgraph** at the DOS prompt, use PrintGraph for your printing, exit back to the DOS prompt, and then type **Exit** to return to 1-2-3.

As previously noted, the Lotus PrintGraph program is the tool you will usually use to obtain printed copies of your graphs. The program requires that the graph has been saved on disk as a .PIC file. PrintGraph should have been configured for your system at the same time that 1-2-3 was configured. If it was not, you will need to return to Install to add the necessary drivers to the program.

This section will discuss the options from release 2 of PrintGraph. Most of the release 1A options are similar, though the main menu appears quite different because the Settings option in release 2 is covered by two different menu selections, Options and Configure, in release 1A. With release 1A, Options gives you access to colors, paper size, and action settings, and Configure makes changes to hardware configurations such as directories and devices.

Since the PrintGraph program is separate from 1-2-3, Lotus was able to add many sophisticated print options beyond the standard features. The program has a menu structure similar to 1-2-3's. The main menu for PrintGraph is shown in Figure 11-17.

## Selecting Graphics Files

If you choose Image-Select from the main PrintGraph menu, 1-2-3 will read the names of all the .PIC files from the disk listed under Graph Directory onto the left side of the main PrintGraph screen, as shown in Figure 11-18. If the graph directory is set as A:\, 1-2-3 will expect you to place the disk with graph files on it in drive A or else change the setting for the graph directory. Simply follow the instructions on the right side of the screen to use the different options.

To mark a file to be printed, press the space bar while the cursor is positioned on the file name. If you change your mind, pressing the space bar again will undo your selection. You can specify as many files as you like, since 1-2-3 is able to

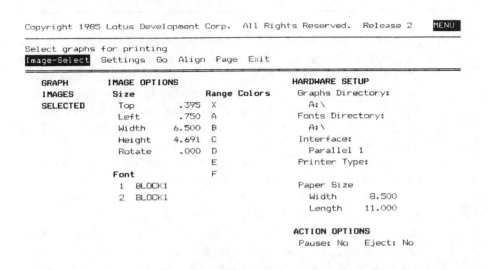

**Figure 11-17.** PrintGraph menu

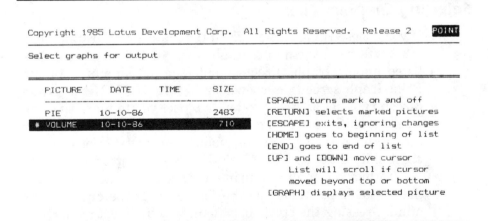

**Figure 11-18.** Selecting .PIC files to print

print graphs sequentially in the order you select them. If you wish to view a graph, press F10 (GRAPH) while pointing to the graph name. 1-2-3 will recreate the chosen graph on the screen with PrintGraph's special type fonts for your review. Pressing ESC will return you to the selection screen.

## Making Setting Selections

The Settings menu provides access to all the options for PrintGraph, including hardware and image settings. This menu appears as follows:

Image Hardware Action Save Reset Quit

### Changing the Image Settings

The settings you select for the Image option will apply to all the graphs selected for printing. You can change the size of the printed graph, the fonts, and the range colors.

**Selecting Size**     PrintGraph provides an option for using a full page to print each graph, which you can access by selecting Full from the PrintGraph Settings Image menu. The chart shown in Figure 11-19 was printed with this option. When 1-2-3 prints a full-page graph, it automatically rotates the graph 90 degrees to a vertical orientation. You can also choose a half-page size by selecting Half. Figure 11-20 shows two half-page graphs printed on a single page. (Notice the greater clarity produced with the PrintGraph image, as compared to the screen dump images shown earlier.) If neither of these sizes meets your needs, you can create your own size by selecting Manual.

The Manual selection under Size presents a whole new submenu. From this menu you can select settings for the top and bottom spacing to allow blank space at the top and bottom of your page. There are also height and width settings to specify the printed area of the graph. Because of the aspect ratio or size relationship between the X and Y axes, it is easy

*1-2-3's Graphics Features*                                                **611**

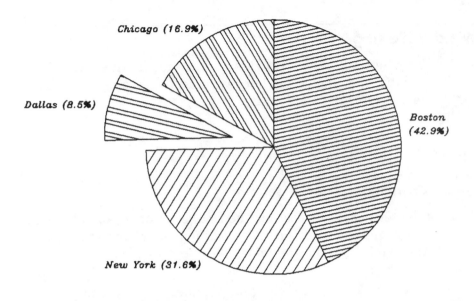

ABC COMPANY

*Sales — Product A*

*Chicago (16.9%)*

*Dallas (8.5%)*

*Boston (42.9%)*

*New York (31.6%)*

**Figure 11-19.** Full-page graph

to distort a graph when you select a new height and width. A little experimentation should help you establish suitable settings for these values, however. A good starting point is to try a ratio of 1 to 1.385 between the sizes of the X and Y axes.

Rotation is the last size option. It permits rotation or turning of the graph as an alternative to changing its size. A rotation of 0 to 90 degrees can be specified.

**Selecting Fonts**    You can choose a particular font for use with the PrintGraph program. The various fonts have characters with different sizes, shapes, and thicknesses. Your font selection will affect the text printed on the graph for titles

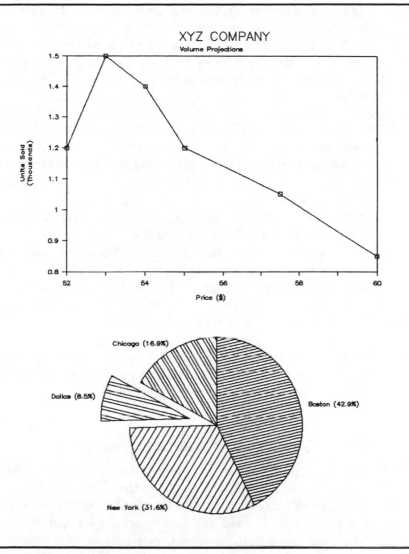

**Figure 11-20.**    Two half-page graphs

and legends but not the graph itself. Options like Roman, Block, Script, and Italic are available. If you see a font name listed more than once, look at the number that follows each listing. This number determines how dark the font prints; high numbers print darker than low numbers. You have the option of choosing either one or two fonts. If only one is selected, it will be used for the entire graph. If two fonts are specified, the first line of the graph title will be printed with font 1 and the other lines will use font 2. You specify your font settings with PrintGraph Settings Image Font.

**Selecting Colors**    PrintGraph assigns a default color of black to every range in the graph. With a dot-matrix printer, black is the only option. If you are printing on a color printer or plotter, PrintGraph will allow you to set the colors for your various data ranges. After selecting Settings Image Range-Colors you can choose from blue, brown, gold, green, lime, orange, red, turquoise, and violet, assuming you have an output device that supports these options.

When you select Range-Colors, 1-2-3 will ask you to select a range and provide X and A through F for choices. Once you specify the range, 1-2-3 will list the colors for you to choose from. With nine colors available, you may assign a different color to each range if you wish.

**Quitting the Settings Image Menu**    The Quit option under Settings Image tells 1-2-3 that you are finished with this menu. It returns you to the Settings menu.

### Changing Hardware Settings

The Settings Hardware options allow you to establish the disk drive that 1-2-3 will read for the files it needs to print your graph. You also use the Hardware options to establish the printer to be used and the interface for the connection. The Hardware Settings menu remains on the screen until you choose Quit. The menu looks like this:

Graphs-Directory  Fonts-Directory  Interface  Printer  Size-Paper  Quit

**Changing the Directories for Graphs and Fonts**    Both the graph and the font directories have a default setting of A:\. This means that 1-2-3 is expecting to read both the font and the .PIC files that you want to print from drive A. If you have

PrintGraph installed on your hard disk, you can set the font directory to the directory in drive C, where the information is stored. You also have the option of reading your graphs (that is, from .PIC files) from any drive.

To change the setting for the graph directory, enter **Settings Hardware Graphs-Directory**. You then need to specify the pathname for your files, for example, C:\123\graphs. The pathname you enter here will be what 1-2-3 uses when you choose Image-Select from the main PrintGraph menu, since it will assume that your .PIC files are stored in this directory.

To change the font directory, enter **Settings Hardware Fonts-Directory**. When prompted for the directory, enter the pathname that tells 1-2-3 where the .FNT files are stored, for example, C:\123\FONT. When you choose the Go option from the main PrintGraph menu, 1-2-3 will attempt to read the required fonts from the pathname you specified.

**Choosing the Interface**    With release 2, you can choose up to eight different interface settings for your printer. You can access the various Interface options by entering **Settings Hardware Interface**. Options 1 and 3 are parallel settings, which are used for a printer that has a parallel connection. Options 2 and 4 are serial printer interfaces and require that you specify the transfer or baud rate supported. The baud rate is a measure of the speed with which your printer can accept input. There are nine different baud rate codes in the manual, ranging from 1 for 110 baud to 9 for 19,200 baud. The remaining four interface codes are for devices on a local area network. Each of them represents a particular DOS device. An interface setting of 5 is used for LPT1, 6 for LPT2, 7 for LPT3, and 8 for LPT4.

The default setting for a parallel device is option 1. For a serial device, the interface default is option 2.

**Selecting a Printer**    You can use any of the graphics printers you installed with 1-2-3's original Install program while you are working with PrintGraph. To make your selection, enter **Settings Hardware Printer**. 1-2-3 will display the names of the graphics printers you selected during installation and will provide the options of high and low density for the different printers. A sample printer selection screen might look like this:

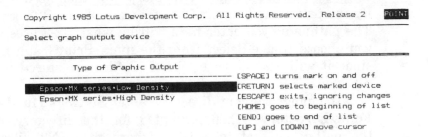

High density will produce better print quality but will take longer to print.

Make your selection by pointing to the printer of your choice and pressing the space bar. If you change your mind, you can press the space bar again, since it functions as a toggle switch. Unlike the case with graphs, where many can be chosen at once, you can select only one printer at a time. You will have to return to this menu even while you continue to use the same printer if you wish to change density.

### Specifying Paper Size

1-2-3 allows you to specify the size of paper you are using. This allows you to take full advantage of wide-carriage printers that can use 14-inch paper. In this case you would leave the length setting as it is and change the width setting to 14. You use Settings Hardware Page-Size to specify the size of your paper.

### Changing the Action Settings

1-2-3's default action after printing one graph is to continue with the next one. The default setting is also not to advance the paper to the next page after printing. This allows you to print two half-page graphs on one sheet.

The three options for the PrintGraph Settings Action command are Pause, Eject, and Quit, as shown in the menu.

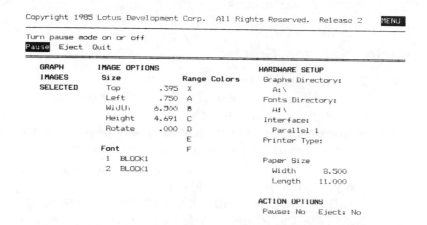

Pause provides a choice of Yes or No. Choose Yes when you want a pause for changing the paper after each graph. Choose No when you are using continuous-form paper. The Eject option automatically pages between graphs if it is set to Yes. If you choose Eject No, 1-2-3 will not automatically page between graphs. Choosing Quit tells 1-2-3 that you do not need to make further changes to the Action settings.

## Making Changes Permanent

All the changes you make to the PrintGraph program are temporary. Unless you save the new settings, they will revert to the defaults the next time you use PrintGraph. To make the current settings the new default values, use the Settings Save command. 1-2-3 will save the new settings to your PrintGraph disk in a file named PGRAPH.CNF.

## Resetting the Settings Options

Choosing Reset from the Settings menu returns all the PrintGraph settings to their default values. The default values are the ones stored in the file PGRAPH.CNF.

### Leaving the Settings Menu

The Quit option will remove the Settings menu. It returns you to the main menu for PrintGraph.

## Printing Selected Graphs

1-2-3 will begin printing the graphs you listed under Image-Select when you choose the Go option from the main Print-Graph menu. It will use the format settings established as it prints the graph. The CTRL-BREAK key provides a way to stop the printing if an emergency arises. (The stop will not take effect for a few seconds because information already sent to the printer must be processed.)

If you are working with a one-drive system, you should have both the graph and the font directory set to drive A. You should have the PrintGraph disk in drive A when you initially request the program. After the fonts have been read into memory, you will be prompted to insert the disk containing your data files. With a two-drive system or a hard drive, it will not be necessary to transfer disks.

Two options on the main PrintGraph menu allow you to affect the paper in your printer. The Page option advances the paper in y ur printer one full page. This option is useful for ejecting your paper after a graph is printed.

The second option, Align, asks 1-2-3 to consider the current cursor location as the top of a form. It is your responsibility to have the paper positioned at the top of a form when you issue the Align command.

## Ending Your PrintGraph Session

To end your PrintGraph session, select Exit from the main menu. Be sure to save configuration settings changes before leaving the program.

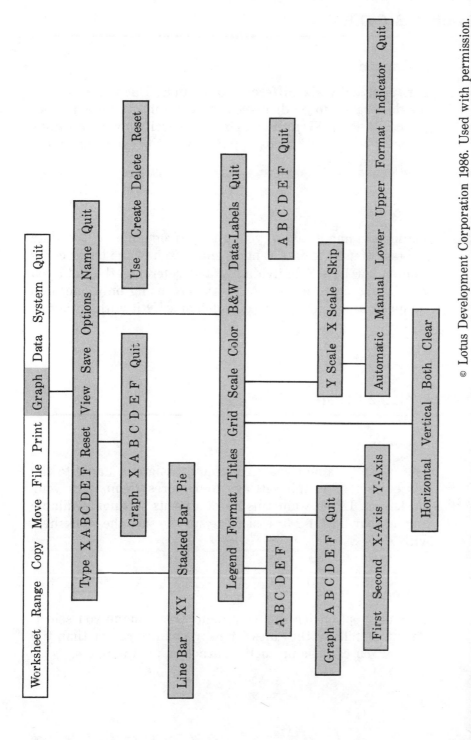

© Lotus Development Corporation 1986. Used with permission.

# Graph A B C D E F

### Description

This is actually six different commands. Each one assigns one data range to be displayed on a graph. As an example, you could enter /**Graph A** and then specify your first data range by entering the range, pointing to the range, or entering a range name.

### Options

These commands allow you to use from one to six data ranges. To use six data ranges, enter each of the letter codes from A through F individually and reference the data you want assigned to each one. If you are using only one data range (in a pie chart, for example), specify it with option A.

# /Graph Name Create

### Description

The /Graph Name Create command assigns a name to the current set of graph settings and stores them with your worksheet. If you want this name and its settings available during your next 1-2-3 session, be sure to save the worksheet with /File Save.

### Options

Your only option for this command is the name you select. The name follows the rules for range names rather than file names. You can use up to 15 characters for the name.

1-2-3 does not warn you if you select a name that has already been assigned to another graph. If you do this, it will over-write the existing settings with the current settings without asking you.

# /Graph Name Delete

### Description

The /Graph Name Delete command removes unneeded graph names individually from the worksheet. Since this process frees up some memory space, it is useful to purge graph names and their associated settings with this command when you no longer need them.

### Options

There are no options for this command.

# /Graph Name Reset

### Description

This command removes all graph names and their settings from the worksheet. Since there is no prompt before the actual deletion, you risk losing all your graph definitions if you accidentally choose Reset from the Graph Name menu.

### Options

There are no options for this command.

## /Graph Name Use

### Description

The /Graph Name Use command allows you to choose a graph name from the list associated with the current worksheet. The graph whose name is selected will become the current graph.

### Options

You can either type the graph name or point to it in the list that 1-2-3 displays.

## /Graph Options B&W

### Description

This command displays graphs in one color. To differentiate between a group of bars on a bar chart, 1-2-3 will automatically add hatch mark patterns when the B&W option is in effect. You can elect to use hatch mark patterns for a pie chart by adding the codes for the patterns you wish to use. The codes should be placed on the worksheet and referenced as the B data range.

### Options

There are no options for this command.

## /Graph Options Color

### Description

This command displays your graphs in color.

## Options

There are no options for this command.

## Note

Never save a graph for printing with Color chosen unless you have a color printer or plan to use a plotter. If you choose Color and have a standard printer, you will not get the hatch mark patterns that differentiate between parts of pie charts and bar graphs when you choose B&W.

# /Graph Options Data-Labels

## Description

The /Graph Options Data-Labels command permits you to add specific labels to a range of data points. 1-2-3 will obtain these data labels from the range of worksheet cells you specify.

## Options

You can choose where to place the data labels in relation to your data points. Your options are Center, Above, Left, Right, and Below.

## Note

With a line graph you can use data labels as the only markers for your data points. To do this, choose /Graph Options Format Neither to remove lines and symbols.

# /Graph Options Format

### Description

The /Graph Options Format command allows you to select the type of line or XY graph you will create. This command will determine whether data points are shown as symbols, are connected with a line, or are marked with both symbols and a line (or neither).

### Options

Your first choice is the range that the format will apply to. You can specify Graph as the range if you want your selection used for all ranges on the graph, or you can select a specific data range by entering a letter from A through F.

After selecting the range for the format, you have the choice of specifying Lines, Symbols, Both, or Neither. A choice of Lines will show the data points connected by a line without the data points being marked. Symbols will show only symbols, with no connecting line. (1-2-3 uses a different symbol for each of the ranges.) A choice of Both will show both the symbols and a connecting line. A choice of Neither shows neither lines nor symbols. It is useful in conjunction with the Data-Labels option when you center a data label on a point to mark it and do not want any other marking on the graph.

# /Graph Options Grid

### Description

The /Graph Options Grid command will add vertical lines, horizontal lines, or both to a graph. These lines start at the markers on the X or Y axis and extend upward or to the right, depending on whether you choose Vertical, Horizontal, or Both. The lines can greatly aid in the interpretation of points on the graph.

### Options

The options for /Graph Options Grid determine whether the grid lines are generated in one or both directions. The choices are as follows:

**Horizontal**    This option adds horizontal lines that extend across from the Y axis. These lines are effective with bar graphs, since they help you interpret the value for the top of each bar.

**Vertical**    Vertical lines are added by this option. They start at the X axis and extend upward. They are most effective with an XY or line graph; they tend to detract from the clarity of a bar graph.

**Both**    This option adds lines in both directions at once. The lines form a grid pattern on the graph.

**Clear**    This option eliminates grid lines that you have added to a graph.

## /Graph Options Legend

### Description

This command displays legends at the bottom of your graph to describe the data represented by the different data ranges.

### Options

You can choose any one of the ranges from A through F each time you request this command. You can either enter a legend of up to 19 characters or reference a cell address containing the legend you wish to use. If you use the latter approach, the legend may exceed 19 characters.

### Note

If you use a cell reference for the legend and later move this cell on the worksheet, 1-2-3 will not adjust the legend reference. This problem can be eliminated by using a range name for the referenced cell.

## /Graph Options Scale Skip

### Description

This command permits you to remove the congestion and overlap that can occur when you assign labels to be displayed along the X axis. The skip factor you specify will let you use only some of the labels in the range. If you specify a skip factor of 3, for example, only every third label will be used.

### Options

You can specify any number from 1 to 8191 for the skip factor. The default is 1, meaning that 1-2-3 uses every label in the range.

## /Graph Options Scale Y-Scale

### Description

This command permits you to let 1-2-3 choose the scale for the Y axis or, alternatively, to choose the scale yourself.

### Options

The options for the /Graph Options Scale Y-Scale command are as follows:

**Automatic**     This setting is the default. It lets 1-2-3 determine the proper scale.

**Manual**     This option informs 1-2-3 that you want to determine the scale range.

**Lower**     This is the lower limit or the smallest value that can be shown on your scale. You define it when you select Manual.

**Upper**     This is the upper limit or the highest value that can be shown on your scale. You define it when you select Manual.

**Format**     This option allows you to select a display format (currency, percent, or the like) for the numeric values represented on the scale.

**Indicator**     This option, available only in release 2, permits you to turn off the display of the size indicator for the scale. The default is Yes, allowing 1-2-3 to display indicators like thousands.

**Quit**     This option exits the command and returns you to the Graph Options menu.


## /Graph Options Scale X-Scale

### Description

This command permits you to let 1-2-3 choose the scale for the X axis or, alternatively, to choose the scale yourself.


### Options

The options for the /Graph Options Scale X-Scale command are as follows:

**Automatic**     This setting is the default. It lets 1-2-3 determine the proper scale.

**Manual**     This option informs 1-2-3 that you want to determine the scale range.

**Lower**     This is the lower limit or the smallest value that can be shown on your scale. You define it when you select Manual.

**Upper**     This is the upper limit or the highest value that can be shown on your scale. You define it when you select Manual.

**Format**     This option allows you to select a display format (currency, percent, or the like) for the numeric values represented on the scale. You will want to use it only for XY graphs.

**Indicator**     This option, available only in release 2, permits you to turn off the display of the size indicator for the scale. The default is Yes, allowing 1-2-3 to display indicators like thousands.

**Quit**     This option exits the command and returns you to the Graph Options menu.


## /Graph Options Titles

### Description

This command permits you to add titles to your graph to improve its clarity and readability. Your titles will be limited to 39 characters if you enter them at the prompt for the command. If you use references to a worksheet cell instead, you can exceed the 39-character limit for all but the vertical option. Referencing a stored title requires that you enter a backslash (\) and a cell address containing the title.

## Options

You can add titles at the top of your graph or along the axes with the options available. Your choices are as follows:

**First**    The label you enter after this choice will be centered at the top of your graph.

**Second**    Your entry for this option will be centered and placed immediately below the label shown by the First option.

**X-Axis**    This option places a title below the X axis.

**Y-Axis**    This option places your entry vertically to the left of the Y axis.

## Note

If you use a cell reference for the legend and later move the referenced cell on the worksheet, 1-2-3 will not adjust the title reference. This problem can be eliminated by using a range name for the referenced cell.

# /Graph Quit

## Description

This command exits the Graph menu and returns you to the worksheet READY mode.

## Options

There are no options for this command.

# /Graph Reset

## Description

The /Graph Reset command cancels graph settings that you selected previously.

## Options

You can choose to cancel all or some of the graph settings with the options for this command. Your choices are as follows:

**Graph**    This option cancels all graph settings.

**X**    This option cancels the X data values.

**A-F**    Choosing one of this set of options cancels the data range for the letter code selected.

**Quit**    This option tells 1-2-3 that you have canceled all the settings you wanted to eliminate and returns you to the previous menu.

# /Graph Save

## Description

The /Graph Save command saves the current graph picture in a .PIC file. This file is separate from your worksheet. It can be used by the PrintGraph program but not by 1-2-3.

## Options

After selecting this command, you have the choice of entering a file name or choosing one from the list that 1-2-3 presents. If you choose to use an existing .PIC file name, 1-2-3 will prompt you to determine whether you really want to reuse (and therefore overwrite) that file or cancel your request.

## /Graph Type

### Description

The /Graph Type command allows you to pick a format for displaying your data. You have five different graph formats to choose from. You can easily change from one to another without any alterations other than selecting another type.

### Options

This command provides five options, as follows:

**Line**    This choice plots the points of a data range and connects them with a line. The default is to use both symbols and a line on the graph. Symbols mark each point, and a line joins the data points. You can use the /Graph Options Format command to change the display so that it uses just a line or just symbols if you prefer. Up to six separate lines, displaying six data ranges, can be generated on one graph.

**Bar**    This uses up to six sets of vertical bars to represent the data ranges selected. 1-2-3 will use hatch mark patterns to distinguish the different data ranges unless you select /Graph Options Color and show the bars in different colors.

**XY**    This option pairs X range values with values from the A to F data ranges. You can use the /Graph Options Format command to connect the points with a line or display them as symbols. With this kind of graph, 1-2-3 generates a numeric scale for the X as well as the Y axis.

**Stacked-Bar**    For one data range a stacked bar graph will appear the same as an ordinary bar graph. When additional data ranges are graphed, however, a difference can be noticed. Rather than adding the second set of bars to the right of the first, the stacked bar graph option stacks the second set on top of the first, the third on top of the second, and so on. The total height of a bar thus indicates the total of the values for that category. The different bars in a stack will be distinguished by hatch mark patterns unless you choose /Graph Options Color.

**Pie**    A pie chart is used to show the size of each of several categories relative to the whole. Each category shown in the chart will be represented by a wedge whose size is proportional to its value in comparison with the values for the other categories shown in the chart. Only one set of data, the A range, can be shown. A B range can be used to indicate colors or hatch mark patterns with a number code from 0 to 7. If 100 is added to the code in the B range, the piece of the pie represented by that code will be exploded (removed from the pie and shown as a separate slice).

## /Graph View

### Description

The /Graph View command displays the graph that you have defined by selecting data ranges and a graph type. If you have not defined a graph, the screen will appear blank when you select this command. To return to the Graph menu when you are through with the View option, press ESC.

## Options

This command does not have any options.

## Note

If your 1-2-3 package is installed for a graphics device different from the one you are using, your screen will appear blank when you press View. To correct the problem, go back to the installation process described in Chapter 1. Similarly, if you attempt to use the package on a system without graphics support, entering /Graph View will cause the screen to appear blank. In both cases you can press ESC to return to the Graph menu.

# /Graph X

## Description

The /Graph X command is used to label the points on the X axis for a line or bar graph. For a pie chart the X values provide labels for the pie segments, and for an XY chart they provide values to plot against the Y values. The labels assigned to the points must be stored in worksheet cells and specified with a range name, a range address, or pointing to the cells you wish to use.

## Options

There are no options for this command. If the labels you choose contain too many characters, they will overlap in the display, causing this area of the graph to be unreadable. You can use /Graph Options Scale Skip to tell 1-2-3 not to use every label.

## PRINTGRAPH
## COMMAND REFERENCE

### PrintGraph Align

#### Description

The PrintGraph Align command tells 1-2-3 that you have your printer paper at the top of a form.

#### Options

There are no options for this command.

### PrintGraph Exit

#### Description

A selection of Exit from the PrintGraph menu exits the PrintGraph program.

#### Options

There are no options for this command.

### PrintGraph Go

#### Description

Selecting PrintGraph Go will cause 1-2-3 to print the graphs chosen with Image-Select. The settings selected on the

PrintGraph menu will be used when printing the selected graphs. Pressing CTRL-BREAK will stop the printing of a graph as soon as the printer buffer is empty. When a plotter is specified as the device, you will receive a message prompting you to change plotter pens.

### Options

There are no options for this command.

## PrintGraph Image-Select

### Description

Image-Select will present a list of all the .PIC files in the directory established as the graphs directory. The default setting for this directory is A:\. You can select files by pointing to them and pressing the space bar to mark the file names with a #. You can choose as many files as you wish. Your selection order will control the print order when Go is selected.

### Options

If you press F10 while pointing to a file name, 1-2-3 will display the graph on your screen.

## PrintGraph Page

### Description

This command advances the paper in your printer by the number of lines in one page.

### Options

There are no options for this command.

## PrintGraph Settings Action

### Description

This command allows you to determine the actions Print-Graph will take after each graph is printed.

### Options

This command has three options:

**Pause**    When this option is set to Yes, PrintGraph will pause for a paper change between graphs. When it is set to No, PrintGraph expects continuous forms and will continue printing graphs without pause.

**Eject**    When set to Yes, this option ejects the page after each graph is printed. When this option is set to No, Print-Graph will print two half-page graphs on one page.

**Quit**    The Quit option returns you to the Settings menu.

## PrintGraph Settings Hardware

### Description

The Settings Hardware option provides access to the commands that change graph and font directories, the interface with the printer or plotter, the print device, and the paper size.

### Options

The options for this command are as follows:

**Graphs-Directory**    This option allows you to specify the pathname for the .PIC files that you plan to print.

**Fonts-Directory**    This option allows you to specify the pathname for the .FNT files that contain the fonts Print-Graph will need to produce your graphs.

**Interface**    This option defines the type of connection between your system and your printer or plotter (serial, parallel, or local area network device).

**Printer**    This option permits you to select one of the graphics printers defined during installation.

**Page-Size**    This option permits you to define the length and width of the paper you are using.

**Quit**    This option returns you to the Settings menu.

## PrintGraph Settings Image

### Description

The Settings Image command permits you to determine the appearance of the graphics image. You can choose fonts, size, and range colors with this command.

### Options

PrintGraph Settings Image has four options: Size, Font, Range-Colors, and Quit.

**Size**    This option permits the choice of a full-page graph, a half-page graph, and manual page size definition. It also permits you to rotate the graph from 0 to 90 degrees before printing. The Manual option has a separate submenu.

**Font**    This option permits you to select either one or two fonts from a list of fonts displayed by PrintGraph. Fonts with a 2 after the font name will be darker than fonts with a 1. The first font you specify will be used for the first title of the graph, and the second font will be used for the remainder of the text.

**Range-Colors**     With this option you can choose ranges from A through F or X and select a color for each range by either highlighting the color name or typing the first character of the name. Naturally, this command will be effective only if you have a color printer or a plotter.

**Quit**     This option returns you to the settings menu.


## PrintGraph Settings Quit

### Description

Selecting the Quit option from the Settings menu returns you to the main PrintGraph menu.

### Options

There are no options for this command.


## PrintGraph Settings Reset

### Description

The Settings Reset command returns your settings to the ones in the PGRAPH.CNF file (the default settings).

### Options

There are no options for this command.

# PrintGraph Settings Save

### Description

This command saves the current settings in the PGRAPH. CNF file, making them the default settings for all subsequent sessions.

### Options

There are no options for this command.

# Keyboard Macros

**T W E L V E**

Many people are intimidated by macros because they have tried unsuccessfully to work with them. Macros, however, are a powerful and flexible feature of 1-2-3, and they can be quite simple if you master them with a step-by-step approach and learn the simplest type before attempting the more sophisticated variety. You will also be able to improve your success ratio if you follow the procedures for creating macros outlined in this chapter and Chapter 13.

## Types of Macros

1-2-3's macros can be used to automate printing, formatting, or any other task that can be completed with menu selections. This type of macro provides an alternative to typing from the keyboard and is therefore called a keyboard alternative macro. These macros are a good type to begin with if you are new to macros, since they contain familiar keystroke commands. They can also provide a wealth of time-saving features. If you follow the instructions in this chapter, you will find yourself creating keyboard alternative macros that are successful the first time you try them.

The second type of macro uses commands beyond menu selections. These commands are available as keyword options from 1-2-3's command language. With this type of macro you can read and write records to a file, create your own menus, utilize iterative loops, and alter the order in which commands are processed. 1-2-3's command language is a full programming language that functions like other programming languages to allow you to develop complete applications. Chapter 13 will cover all the features of 1-2-3's command language.

## Keyboard Macros

Like all macros, a keyboard alternative macro is nothing more than a column of label entries that have a special name assigned to them. The contents of the labels are the sequence of keystrokes that you want 1-2-3 to execute for you.

After all your label entries are stored in a column, you will name the top cell in the column with the /Range Name Create command. The name of the macro will consist of the backslash and a single letter key. Once the macro is named in this manner, you can execute it by pressing ALT and the letter code assigned to the macro.

## Recording the Keystrokes

To prevent 1-2-3 from executing macro commands immediately, begin the macro sequence with a single quotation mark so it will be treated as a label. Then record the keystrokes. Indicate a request for a menu command with a slash, and record each of the menu commands as the first letter of the menu choice. To enter the keystrokes necessary to get a worksheet status report, you would type '/ws or '/WS in the cell, for example (case is not important).

In addition to specifying menu selections, you will sometimes have to indicate the need to press the ENTER key. This key is represented in a macro by the tilde mark (~). File names or range names should be entered in full. As an example, to store the characters needed to retrieve a file named SALES from the default drive, you would enter '/frSALES~ in the macro cell.

## Recording Special Keys

There are a number of special keyboard keys, like the function and cursor movement keys, that you will want to include in your macros. These keys and the macro keywords that stand for them are listed in the box called "Special Keys in Macro Commands." You will note that all the keywords are enclosed in curly brackets or braces ({}). There is no representation for the NUM LOCK or the SCROLL LOCK keys because they must be requested from outside a macro. CAPS LOCK is not represented either, since cell entries are typed right into a macro and you have your choice of typing either upper-case or lower-case letters. Case is also unimportant in operator entries made while a macro is executing.

## Special Keys in Macro Commands

1-2-3 has a keyword to represent each of the special keyboard keys, except for the NUM LOCK key and the SCROLL LOCK key. The keyword symbol for each of the keys is shown in the following table.

| Cursor Movement Keys | Keywords |
|---|---|
| Up arrow | {UP} |
| Down arrow | {DOWN} |
| Right arrow | {RIGHT} |
| Left arrow | {LEFT} |
| HOME | {HOME} |
| END | {END} |
| PGUP | {PGUP} |
| PGDN | {PGDN} |
| CTRL-RIGHT | {BIGRIGHT} |
| CTRL-LEFT | {BIGLEFT} |

| Editing Keys | |
|---|---|
| DEL | {DEL} or {DELETE} |
| INS | {INSERT} |
| ESC | {ESC} or {ESCAPE} |
| BACKSPACE | {BACKSPACE} or {BS} |

| Function Keys | |
|---|---|
| F2 (EDIT) | {EDIT} |
| F3 (NAME) | {NAME} |
| F4 (ABS) | {ABS} |
| F5 (GOTO) | {GOTO} |
| F6 (WINDOW) | {WINDOW} |
| F7 (QUERY) | {QUERY} |
| F8 (TABLE) | {TABLE} |
| F9 (CALC) | {CALC} |
| F10 (GRAPH) | {GRAPH} |

```
Special Keys
Input from keyboard during
    macro                        {?}
ENTER key                        ~
Tilde                            {~}
{                                {{}
}                                {}}
```

## Cursor Movement Keys

In a macro, movement of the cursor to the right is represented by {RIGHT}. Movement to the left is {LEFT}, movement down is {DOWN}, and movement up is {UP}. In release 1A, if you want to move the cursor up three times, you must record {UP}{UP}{UP}. In release 2, you can record it in the same fashion, or you can use a shortcut approach and enter it as {UP 3}.

The effect of specifying {HOME} for a worksheet or a cell will depend on whether the macro is in READY mode or EDIT mode. If in READY mode, it will return you to A1. If in EDIT mode, it will move you to the beginning of your entry.

The END and arrow key combination is supported in macros. You can enter {END}{RIGHT} to have your cursor move you to the last occupied cell entry on the right side of the worksheet. {BIGLEFT} and {BIGRIGHT} are also supported under release 2. They will shift you a whole screen to the left or the right, respectively. To specify paging up or paging down, use the entries {PGUP} and {PGDN}.

## Function Keys

With the exception of the F1 (HELP) key, all the function keys can be represented by special macro keywords. To represent

F2 (EDIT), you would enter {EDIT}. To use the F3 (NAME) key, enter {NAME} in the macro. {ABS} is used to convert the reference type of a formula entry while the formula is being constructed and is equivalent to F4 (ABS). The F5 (GOTO) key is used frequently to control cursor movement while the macro is executing and is represented by {GOTO}. To move the cursor into the opposite window, use {WINDOW}, which stands for F6 (WINDOW). {QUERY} will perform the same query operation as long as your input range and criterion are the same size. This keyword takes the place of F7 (QUERY). F8 (TABLE) is synonymous with {TABLE}. To recalculate your worksheet you can press F9 (CALC), and using {CALC} in your macro performs the same function. In both cases, if you are in EDIT mode, {CALC} performs the calculation on the current worksheet cell and eliminates the formula when you press ENTER.

### Edit Keys

In addition to F2 (EDIT), which places you in the EDIT mode, there are several special keys that you use when correcting worksheet entries. The ESC key can remove an entry from a cell and can delete a menu default, such as a previous setup string, so you can make a new entry. The ESC key is represented as {ESC} or {ESCAPE} in macros.

To delete the character in front of the cursor while in EDIT mode or to delete the last character entered, you can use the BACKSPACE key when making your entries from the keyboard. To represent this key in a macro, use {BS} or {BACKSPACE}.

The DEL key will delete the character above the cursor while you are in EDIT mode. This is represented in a macro as {DEL} or {DELETE}. As an example, you could request a change of the prefix for a label entry to center justification with the following sequence of macro entries:

{EDIT}{HOME}{DEL}^~

The repeat factors can also be used with the editing keys in release 2. {DELETE 4} will delete the character above the cursor and the next three characters. {BACKSPACE 7} will delete seven characters to the left of the cursor.

### Other Special Keys

As mentioned earlier, the tilde represents ENTER. To actually use a macro to place a tilde in a cell, you would type {~}. If you need to place curly brackets (braces) in a cell with a macro, you would enter either {{} or {}}. These features can be useful in a macro that builds another macro.

The symbols {?} can be used in a macro to let 1-2-3 know that you want the operator to input something from the keyboard. 1-2-3 will then sit and wait for the entry to be made and ENTER to be pressed. Chapter 13 will cover two additional methods for keyboard input that offer greater sophistication in that they allow you to present a message to the operator regarding the data you wish to have entered.

## Creating a Keyboard Macro

The following step-by-step procedure for creating a macro is not the fastest way of doing it, but it should more than pay for itself in time savings during the testing and debugging phase as you are trying to get your macro to execute correctly.

• The first step in creating a keyboard macro is planning the task you wish to accomplish. Without a plan, you are not likely to create a macro that is well organized and successful.

• After you have made your plan, test it by entering the proposed keystrokes for immediate execution by 1-2-3. As you enter each keystroke directly into the menu, record it on a sheet of paper.

- If the menu selections handled your task correctly, you can use your sheet of paper as a script when you record the keystrokes as labels in the worksheet cells.

- Choose an out-of-the-way location on your worksheet for recording your macro. With release 1A you must make sure that it is not too far out of the way, however, because of this release's memory management problems.

- You can record up to 240 keystrokes in one label cell, but it would not be advisable to do so, since you could never read the entire entry at one time. At the other extreme, you can enter a single keystroke in a cell and continue your entry by placing the next keystroke in the cell below it. 1-2-3 will continue reading down the column until it reaches a blank cell, but this second approach is also not advisable because you would need so many cells to create even a short macro. The best approach is to select some reasonable upper limit for the number of characters to be entered in one macro cell and then, within that limit, move to a new cell whenever you reach a logical breaking place in your keystroke entries.

## Naming Your Macro

Once you have entered all the keystrokes, you are ready to name your macro. Before doing this, position your cursor on the top cell in the macro, since this is the only cell that will be named. Then enter /**Range Name Create**. At the prompt for the range name, enter a backslash and any single alphabetic character and press ENTER. Since you positioned your cursor before requesting the range command, simply press ENTER in response to the prompt for the range address. When you save the worksheet, the macro and its name will be saved as well and will be available whenever you retrieve the worksheet.

The naming conventions for 1-2-3's macros allow you to create 26 unique macro names with the letters of the alphabet. 1-2-3 will not distinguish between upper- and lower-case characters in a macro name.

If you have release 2, you can obtain a list of all your current macro names and the range addresses they are assigned to with the /Range Name Table command. To get such a list, enter **/Range Name Table** and respond to 1-2-3's prompt for a table range by entering the address of the upper left cell in any blank section of the worksheet where 1-2-3 can write the macro name assignments. This command is described more fully in Chapter 6. It is not available in release 1A. If you are using release 1A, you can use /Range Name Create and specify a particular macro name to see the cell to which that name is assigned, but there is no way to check the assignment of all macro names in one step.

## Documenting Your Macro

As you create a macro, you are aware of the name you have assigned to it and the function of each step in it. A month from now, however, when you look back at the macro cells, it may take some thought to remember what you were attempting to accomplish. You can make your work with macros much easier if you record information like the macro name and the function of each step on the worksheet as you create the macro. The time investment involved in this extra step will more than pay for itself later on.

A good strategy to use for documentation is to place the macro name in the cell immediately to the left of the top macro cell. If the macro is named a, you would enter ' \a in the name cell. The ' is needed to prevent 1-2-3 from interpreting the backslash as the repeating label indicator and filling your cell with the letter a. The cell to the left of your top macro cell is an especially appropriate choice because if you place the macro name there before naming the macro itself, you can use the /Range Name Labels Right command to name the macro cell without typing the name in again. In other words, you would type the name in the empty cell to the left of the macro, ensure that your cursor remains on the

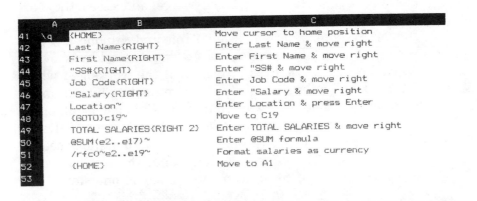

READY

**Figure 12-1.**   Macro with documentation

name, enter /**Range Name Labels Right**, and press ENTER.

A good area to use for documenting macro instructions is a column of cells to the right of the actual instructions. Depending on the length of your macro entries, this may be one or several cells to the right of the macro column. A brief description of every command will make the function of the macro clearer and will save a significant amount of time if it is necessary to modify the macro later. Figure 12-1 shows a macro with documentation entries for both the macro name and the individual macro instructions.

## Executing Your Macro

Once you have entered and named a macro, you can use it whenever you wish. If your macro requires the cursor to be positioned in a certain cell, put the cursor there before executing the macro. The cursor does not need to be on the macro cell to execute the macro. After your cursor is in place, press the ALT key and, while the key is pressed, touch the letter key that you used in your macro name. Then release both keys.

## Creating a Macro Library

A macro library is nothing more than a worksheet that contains all of your macros. Place the macros in an out-of-the-way location on the worksheet. Whenever you create a new worksheet, retrieve the macro library worksheet from disk and build your application on it. Save the completed worksheet to disk, under a new name. That way, your original macro library still contains nothing but macros, and your new application will be able to access all the macros from the library as well.

When you wish to add a new macro to your library file, simply call up the macro sheet, enter the new macro, and save the sheet under its original file name. To add a macro from another worksheet to the library, use the /File Xtract command to extract the macro from the other sheet, saving it to another file temporarily. Then retrieve your macro library file and use the /File Combine Copy command to place the new macro in the library. This approach also works for copying a single macro from the macro library to any of your other worksheets. Be sure to name the entire range for each macro and include the documentation to the right and left of the macro in this range. Then, when you use /File Combine, you will be able to specify Named-Range and copy in just the one macro. You will need to name the macro again once it is on the new worksheet, since the range name used for the macro will not be copied.

## Debugging Macros

The debugging process involves testing and correcting macros to ensure that you are obtaining the desired results. One of the most common mistakes made when creating keyboard macros is forgetting to enter the tilde mark to represent each time the ENTER key needs to be depressed.

1-2-3 has a STEP mode of execution that executes a macro one keystroke at a time so you can follow its progress and spot any area of difficulty. The SHIFT and F2 keys used simultaneously will activate STEP mode in release 2; in release 1A, use SHIFT plus F1. Since this is a toggle operation, holding the keys down too long will turn STEP mode off again. When this mode is operational, you will see the word STEP on the bottom line of your screen.

When the STEP indicator is on, any macro you invoke will be executed one instruction at a time. Press the space bar whenever you are ready to move on to the next instruction. The menu selections invoked will display in the control panel to provide information on the operation of the macro, but you will not be able to input direct commands while the macro is executing. While the macro is executing, SST will appear at the bottom of the screen.

To stop a malfunctioning macro, press the CTRL and BREAK keys simultaneously. This cancels macro operation immediately and presents an ERROR indicator at the upper right corner of the screen. Pressing ESC will return you to READY mode so you can make corrections to your macro.

## Automatic Macros

1-2-3 has a unique feature that allows you to create an automatic macro for a worksheet. Every time a worksheet containing an automatic macro is retrieved, 1-2-3 will immediately execute this macro. This feature has more application with the advanced macro commands discussed in Chapter 13, but there may be situations where you want to do, say, a file combine or a range erase as soon as a worksheet is retrieved.

The only difference in creation between an automatic macro and one that you must execute is the name that you assign it. An automatic macro must have a name of \0 (\zero). There can be only one automatic macro on a worksheet.

Figure 12-2 shows an automatic macro that is designed to erase a range of input cells in the worksheet shown in

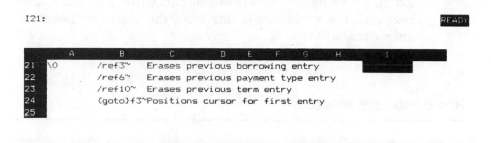

```
       A     B        C       D      E     F    G     H         I
21  \0        /ref3~   Erases previous borrowing entry
22            /ref6~   Erases previous payment type entry
23            /ref10~  Erases previous term entry
24            {goto}f3~Positions cursor for first entry
25
```

**Figure 12-2.**　　Automatic macro to erase worksheet cells

Figure 12-3 every time the worksheet is retrieved. That way, each new user can enter new values for the principal interest and time. To create this macro, type your instructions into a

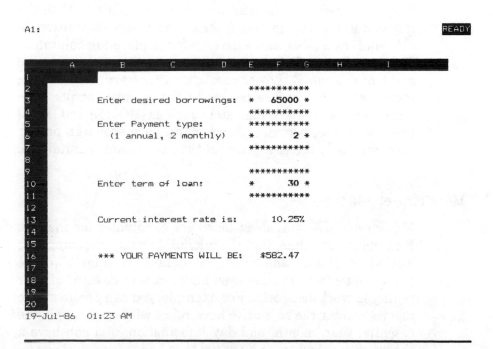

```
       A     B        C       D      E     F    G     H         I
1
2                              ***********
3          Enter desired borrowings:  *   65000 *
4                              ***********
5          Enter Payment type:  ***********
6            (1 annual, 2 monthly)  *       2 *
7                              ***********
8
9                              ***********
10         Enter term of loan:   *      30 *
11                             ***********
12
13         Current interest rate is:   10.25%
14
15
16         *** YOUR PAYMENTS WILL BE:  $582.47
17
18
19
20
19-Jul-86  01:23 AM
```

**Figure 12-3.**　　Worksheet example with cells that macro erases

column of worksheet cells and assign the special name to the top cell. Then save the worksheet file with /File Save. The next time the worksheet is retrieved, the macro will execute immediately.

## Ready-to-Use Macros

The macros in the sections that follow are ready to use in the sense that they are complete macros designed to perform the tasks described. Since it is likely that data on your worksheet will be located in different cells than on the worksheets used to create these examples, you probably will have to make minor modifications to the cell addresses referenced in the macros. Each macro description will include guidelines for its use and a section on potential modifications.

The same conventions have been used for all the macros. The name used for the macro is shown in column A, to the left of the top cell in the macro. The macro is written in column B as a label, and a description is placed in column C. This description frequently continues in the columns to the right of column C. Lower-case characters are used for the menu selections and responses to the menu prompts. File names and special key indicators such as {HOME} and {ESC} are shown in upper case. Range names are shown in proper case, with only the first letter of the range name capitalized.

## Worksheet Macros

Many repetitive worksheet tasks are candidates for macros. Examples are changing the global format, checking the worksheet status, and changing default settings like the printer interface. You can even have a macro do some of your typing in worksheet cells. For example, you can create a date macro to enter the repetitive keystrokes while you supply the essential year, month, and day information. You can have a macro make changes to an entry to enhance it or to cover up existing errors.

## A Macro to Display Formulas

1-2-3 will print the formulas behind your worksheet results when you specify /Print Printer Options Other Cell-Formulas, but it creates one line of printed output per cell. If you would like to display or print out formulas while maintaining the integrity of your worksheet design, you will have to change the format of each formula cell to text. These steps can be placed in a macro to simplify the task.

The macro to perform this task is as follows:

```
        A        B                    C
1      \t       /wgft     Request global format as text
2               /rfr      Request range format reset
3               A1..Z60~  Specify range as A1..Z60
```

The instructions in the first line request /Worksheet Global Format Text. If there were no range formats for your worksheet cells, you could end the macro at this point. Since most worksheets do use a range format to override the global setting, our macro is designed to operate under this condition. It uses /Range Format Reset to make all the cells conform to the global format setting of text. This command is specified in B2. It is followed by a range that contains all the entries on the worksheet that the macro is designed to work with.

**Guidelines for Use**    It is important that you save your worksheet before executing this macro. You will not want to save your worksheet afterward, since all your regular formats will have been destroyed.

**Modifying the Macro**    You may want to add an instruction at the beginning to save your current worksheet file to ensure that you do not lose your established formats. The only risk with this addition is that you might execute the macro a second time and overlay your existing file with the text-formatted version. Another option is adding the commands necessary to print the file. These instructions could be placed at the end of the macro. You could add a /Worksheet Erase command after the Print commands to ensure that the formatted version is not saved to disk after the macro ends. You could also add a command to increase the column width so that complete formulas can display.

### A Macro to Insert Blank Rows

Many people do not like 1-2-3's requirement that you not leave blank rows between column headings and data if you wish to perform Data Query operations. It is possible to create macros that will add and delete blank rows for you. When you plan to use the worksheet for calculations and printed reports, you can use the macro that inserts blank rows. When you wish to perform a query, you can invoke the macro that deletes the blank rows. In fact, this latter macro could be made a part of a query macro.

The macro that follows will insert blank rows.

```
              A          B                     C
1       \i         /wi             Request worksheet insert
2                  r               Specify rows
3                  {DOWN}{DOWN}~    Move down to insert 3 rows
```

The macro is currently set to add three blank rows, but it can easily be modified to add any number you choose. The first macro instruction, in B1, requests a worksheet insert. The next instruction specifies that rows rather than columns should be inserted. Using a repeated keyword to represent the down arrow, the third instruction expands the insertion to three rows. If you are using release 2, you can use the shortcut approach for moving the cursor and write this instruction as {DOWN 2}.

**Guidelines for Use**    This macro requires that you position your cursor where you want to insert the blank rows, since they will be added above the cursor. When you invoke the macro, the cursor row will be shifted down to make room for the new rows. Just as with a keyboard entry of the same command, your formulas will be adjusted to reflect the addition, but insertions at the top or bottom of a range will not expand the range.

**Modifying the Macro**     By changing the entry in B2 to c, you could make a macro that inserts columns. You may also wish to modify the last instruction to allow for the addition of extra rows (or columns). A third option is to end the macro after line 2 and allow the operator to specify the number of rows or columns to be added.


## A Macro to Change
## The Global Default Directory

When you are working with completed worksheet models, you may want your directory set at drive C if all your completed models are stored on the hard drive. If you have a number of new models to create and wish to store them on a floppy disk, you may want the directory set at drive A. You may also wish to change the directory if you use 1-2-3 on two systems that have different configurations. Making the change with a macro eliminates the need for remembering the command path required.

The macro shown is set to change the existing directory to drive \B.

```
            A          B              C
1      \d          /wg         Request worksheet global change
2                  d           Specify default change
3                  d           Specify directory
4                  {ESC}       Escape to clear existing entry
5                  b:\~        Set directory to drive b
6                  q           Quit default menu
```

The first instruction requests a Worksheet Global change. A Default change and Directory are specified in the next two instructions. B4 causes the macro to generate an ESCAPE to remove the current directory setting. The instruction in B5 generates the new directory setting and finalizes it, and the last instruction leaves the Default menu and returns to READY mode.

**Guidelines for Use**     When you change the directory, both the old and the new directories must be available on the system you are using to change the settings. If you are changing the directory to a floppy drive, you will want to place a data disk in the drive before executing the macro, since 1-2-3 attempts to read the directory for the selected device. You can also use this macro to change the subdirectory for model storage and retrieval if you are using a hard disk.

**Modifying the Macro**     B5 is the cell you are likely to want to modify in this macro. It should contain the pathname of the device and directory you plan to use for data storage. As an example, if you are currently using drive A and want to change to a subdirectory on drive C, you might change this cell to read C:\123\Dallas\Sales\.

## A Macro to Change
## The Global Printer Default Setup

When you install your 1-2-3 package, you have the option of installing more than one printer. It is possible that you may have both a dot matrix and a letter-quality printer coupled to your system. You may want to use the letter-quality printer for printing most worksheets and use the dot matrix for printing quick drafts of a model and graphs.

If you want to change the default printer that 1-2-3 uses when you request print and your second printer is cabled to another port, you will have to change both the printer requested and the interface. The printer will be the device requested, and the interface specification will tell 1-2-3 whether you have it cabled to a serial or parallel device or wish to access one of the DOS devices on your local area network. This latter option is available only on release 2.

A macro for changing the default printer is as follows:

|   | A | B | C |
|---|---|---|---|
| 1 | \s | /wg | Request worksheet global change |
| 2 |   | d | Specify default |
| 3 |   | p | Choose printer |
| 4 |   | i1 | Set interface to parallel 1 |
| 5 |   | n1 | Set name to first printer install |
| 6 |   | s\015~ | Create default setup string for Epson |
| 7 |   | q | Quit printer default menu |
| 8 |   | q | Quit default menu |

The first line requests a Worksheet Global change. The next two lines tell 1-2-3 that you wish to use the Default Printer option. The instruction in B4 tells 1-2-3 that you wish to set the interface to the first parallel interface. The Name option is selected next, and the first name in the list of printers is specified. For our system this was an Epson LX printer.

You can change other default print settings at the same time you change the specified printer. B6 shows the entry of a default setup string for compressed print on the Epson. The current entry is correct for a first use of the setup string. If a setup string entry is present already, B6 in the macro should be changed to read s{ESC}\015~. The last two instructions quit the Printer submenu and the Default menu.

**Guidelines for Use**    Before creating this macro, you will need to familiarize yourself with the settings for the eight interfaces available under release 2 and the four options available under release 1A. Interfaces 1 and 3 are parallel interfaces, and 2 and 4 are serial. The extra four options available under release 2 are the DOS devices LPT1, LPT2, LPT3, and LPT4.

The printer names you use in the macro will depend on the options you selected during installation. You cannot access printer types that were not selected then, since the necessary driver files will not be available. If you plan to use a new printer device, you will need to go back to the installation program and add it there.

**Modifying the Macro**    B4 would be modified to a 2 or a 4 if you planned to use a serial connection for your printer. If you wanted a different setup string, you would modify the 015 in B6.

You could also expand this macro to include a change to the default settings for other print characteristics, such as margins and page length. If you wanted to have these new settings available the next time you used the package, you would have to add a command to select the Update option after exiting the Printer Default menu. This would save your changes to the file 123.CNF.

## A Macro to Enter
## A Date in a Worksheet Cell

When you enter dates in worksheet cells, you should enter them as values. If you were to enter a date as a label, you would not be able to use it in date arithmetic operations, since it would not have a serial date number behind the date displayed. Entering a date so that you can use it in arithmetic formulas requires that you use the @DATE function, so a substantial number of additional keystrokes would be required if you enter many dates. A macro can solve this problem by making most of the entries for you, including @DATE, the parentheses, and the argument separators. The only entries you will have to make are the year number, the month number, and the day number.

A macro to enter dates is shown in Figure 12-4. It is designed to make its entries in the current cell and begins by entering the keystrokes @DATE(. When the macro executes the first input instruction, {?}, it will wait for the operator to make an entry and will store those keystrokes in the cell. It will then add a comma to the cell and wait for additional input. Another comma is added next, after which the third input instruction is executed. The cell entry is completed with an entry of the closing parenthesis.

---

A1: '\d                                                                    `READY`

```
        A       B        C       D       E       F       G
1   \d          @DATE(   Enter @DATE in current cell
2               {?}      Wait for operator to enter year & press Enter
3               ,        Enter comma in current cell after year
4               {?}      Wait for operator to enter month & press Enter
5               ,        Enter comma in current cell after month
6               {?}      Wait for operator to enter day & press Enter
7               )~       Enter closing parenthesis in current cell & finalize
8               /rfd1~   Format as date format 1
9               /wcs10~  Set column width to 10
10
```

---

**Figure 12-4.**    Macro to enter dates

B8 contains the /Range Format Date 1 request for the cell in which the entry was just made. The column that contains the cell is set to a width of 10 with a request for /Worksheet Column Set-Width 10. The result of using the macro three times to enter dates in worksheet cells is shown in Figure 12-5.

**Guidelines for Use**     The {?} method of input does not provide a prompt telling the operator what it is waiting for. It is important that the operator knows to enter the year number and press ENTER, enter the month number and press ENTER, and then enter the day number and press ENTER, since that is the argument order that the @DATE function requires.

**Modifying the Macro**     This macro can be modified to use any of 1-2-3's built-in functions. The beginning of the macro would be altered to show a different keyword. The number of input statements will depend on the number of arguments in the particular function.

In Chapter 13, you will learn how you can make a macro like this fill a complete column of cells. As it exists now, you would have to move to another cell and reexecute the macro if you wished to enter additional dates.

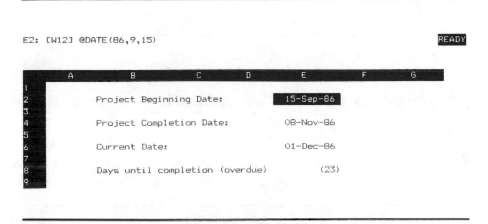

**Figure 12-5.**     Worksheet with dates entered

## A Macro to Round Formulas

When you format worksheet cells, you may choose a format that displays less than the full number of decimal places in a number. 1-2-3 will round the displayed number to the number of decimal places specified for your display. The internal storage of the number is not changed and still retains its full accuracy, however. Calculations will use the stored number, not the displayed one. This can result in a total at the bottom of a column seemingly not being in agreement with the figures in the cells above it.

The @ROUND function can handle this problem by rounding the internally stored number to the number of decimal places you specify. The catch is that you have to enclose your numbers or formulas in @ROUND and supply the position in the entry at which rounding should take place. When a number of formulas must have @ROUND added, this can be a tedious process. You can create a macro to relieve the tedium and make most of the entry for you.

The macro is shown in Figure 12-6. The first instruction edits the current cell. The cursor is then moved to the front of the entry. The keystrokes @ROUND( are added at the front of the entry. The cursor is moved to the end of the entry with the instruction in B4. The keystrokes ,0) are placed at the end of the entry to complete the arguments for @ROUND, and the entry is finalized with the tilde (~).

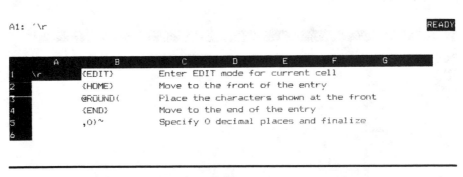

**Figure 12-6.** Round macro

**Guidelines for Use**     This macro is position dependent. It will round only the formula or number at the cursor location to the specified number of decimal places. You must move the cursor to each new cell and reexecute the macro to round additional cells.

**Modifying the Macro**     The macro can be modified easily to round to any number of decimal places. Simply change the number in B5 to reflect the place at which you want rounding to occur. The places for rounding are described under the @ROUND function in Chapter 7.

You could also change this macro so that it uses the input statement {?} to allow the operator to enter the place of rounding each time it is executed. The operator would input a number and press ENTER to have 1-2-3 include it in the instruction.

When you learn how to create a loop with the macro instructions in Chapter 13, you will be able to modify this macro to round a whole column of numbers with one execution of the macro.

### A Macro to Handle Data Entry Errors

Macros can be used to correct a variety of data input errors. They are especially valuable for this purpose in release 2, since that version of 1-2-3 gives you access to all the string functions. For example, if you had employees' names entered in the following format in your database:

Jim Jones

it would be considered proper case, since only the first letter of each word is capitalized. String functions are case sensitive, so if someone else updates your database and enters names as BOB BROWN or bill smith, you are likely to have trouble with these functions. It could be time consuming to enter corrections to make all the entries match in format. However, you can create a macro that will change any entry into proper case. It is shown in Figure 12-7.

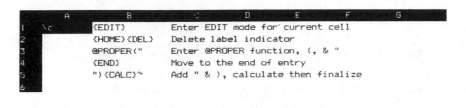

```
        A        B              C         D        E       F       G
1   \c      {EDIT}         Enter EDIT mode for current cell
2           {HOME}{DEL}    Delete label indicator
3           @PROPER("      Enter @PROPER function, (, & "
4           {END}          Move to the end of entry
5           "){CALC}~      Add " & ), calculate then finalize
6
```

**Figure 12-7.**     Proper case macro

The macro begins by preparing to edit the current cell. It then moves to the home position and deletes the label indicator in the first position. The @PROPER function is entered and is followed by a ( and a double quotation mark ("), since the string entry from the current cell must be enclosed in double quotes. The instruction in B4 moves the cursor to the end of the entry. The last instruction adds the double quote at the end and follows it with a closing parenthesis. Before finalizing the entry, the macro recalculates the formula so it can be stored in the cell as a string constant rather than as a formula.

**Guidelines for Use**     This macro is position dependent. It will change only the label entry at the cursor location to proper case. You must move the cursor to each new cell and reexecute the macro to change additional cells.

**Modifying the Macro**     If you want your data in upper case, you can use the @UPPER function in place of @PROPER. For lower case, use @LOWER.

### A Macro to Enter a Worksheet Heading

If you need to create a whole series of worksheets that use the same heading, you can place the heading instructions in a macro and copy them into each worksheet. Since the macro is designed to begin the heading at the cursor location, the headings will not need to start in the same position in each worksheet.

The following macro will place headings for the quarters of the year across a worksheet.

```
          A            B                        C
1      \h        ^QTR1{RIGHT}       Enter QTR1 & move 1 cell to the r
2                ^QTR2{RIGHT}       Enter QTR2 & move 1 cell to the r
3                ^QTR3{RIGHT}       Enter QTR3 & move 1 cell to the r
4                ^QTR4{RIGHT}       Enter QTR4 & move 1 cell to the r
5                ^TOTAL^            Enter TOTAL & press Enter
6                {END}{LEFT}        Move to the leftmost entry
7                {DOWN}             Move down 1 cell
```

The first four macro instructions each place one of the quarter headings in a worksheet cell and move one cell to the right. The instruction in B5 places the heading TOTAL in a cell and finalizes the entry with ENTER. The cursor is then moved to the left of this section. It will be on the first heading as long as the cell to its left is blank or it is in column A. The last instruction moves the cursor down one cell.

**Guidelines for Use**    The macro places the first heading in the cell at the cursor location and moves to the right with subsequent entries, so it is important that you position your cursor before executing the macro.

**Modifying the Macro**    The macro can be modified to create any series of headings, including the months of the year, weeks of the month, multiple years, or account numbers. All you need to change are the headings themselves. You can easily modify the label prefix that begins each heading entry as well, if you wish different justification.

This same macro can be modified to create account names down a column. The only difference is that the cursor will be moved down after each entry and the caret symbol (^) for center justification will not be used.

## Range Macros

You can create macros for all the range commands you use frequently. They can be either open-ended macros or closed ones. An open-ended macro is one that returns control to the operator before the range is selected. As an example, if you wanted a macro to format cells as currency with zero decimal places, you would have to record the following keystrokes:

/rfc0~

If you end the macro at this point, it is open-ended, since the operator can complete the range specification. It would be a closed macro if you supplied the range as part of the formula, for example by entering

/rfc0~{DOWN 5}~

or

/rfc0~A1..D12~

Closed macros are more limited in their application, since they function only under one particular set of circumstances.

If you are developing macros for yourself, you will probably want to create open-ended macros to increase their flexibility. If you are developing them for someone else and want to maintain as much control over the application as possible, you might want to create closed macros.


### A Macro to Create a Range Name Table

The /Range Name Table command lists all the range names and their cell addresses in a table on your worksheet if you are using release 2. This table is not updated automatically as you add new range names, however; you must execute the command sequence again to have 1-2-3 update the table. A macro can easily handle this task for you.

The short macro needed reads as follows:

| | A | B | C |
|---|---|---|---|
| 1 | \t | {GOTO}G5~ | Position cursor at range table |
| 2 | | /rnt~ | Request Range Name Table at curre |

The first instruction in the macro positions the cursor in the upper left corner of the area where you wish your table to appear—cell G5, in this example. The second instruction requests the /Range Name Table command.

**Guidelines for Use**     This macro is dependent on the area to the right and below G5 (or wherever you send the cursor) being empty, since it will overwrite any data that is stored there. If you plan to print the table of range names, you will always want to execute this macro before printing in order to ensure that your table of names is current.

**Modifying the Macro**     The macro can be modified to supply a complete range address or range name for the table. If a range address is supplied instead of the upper left corner, 1-2-3 will use only the area within the specified range for the table. Specifying the upper left cell allows 1-2-3 to use as much space as it needs below the cell specified. When building the table of range names, 1-2-3 will always use the column of cells to the right of the cell specified for the storage of the range addresses for the various range names, just as the /Range Name Table command would when executed from the keyboard.

## File Macros

You can automate any of the file commands with a macro. Although the /File Save and /File Retrieve commands do not require a significant number of keystrokes, they are still possible candidates for a macro because they are used so frequently. Other File commands, such as Combine and Xtract, also can be automated. This may cut down on typing errors, since the same keystrokes will be executed each time.

### A Macro to Save Files

A file save does not require many keystrokes, but it should be done frequently so you do not risk the loss of your data. A macro can be created to save your file with one keystroke.

A macro for saving a file reads as follows:

```
              A          B                    C
1        \s        /fs              Request file save
2                  ~                Specify existing file name
3                  r                Specify replace file
```

The first line of the macro invokes the /File Save command. The tilde (~) in line 2 indicates that you want to retain the file's existing name. The final line tells 1-2-3 to replace the file on disk with the current contents of memory.

**Guidelines for Use**    This macro is designed to save a file that has been saved previously. It cannot be used if a file has never been saved to disk or if you want to use a new name for the file.

**Modifying the Macro**    The macro can easily be modified to allow you to input the file name. Simply use an input statement between the current line 1 and line 2. If you prefer, a file name to use for storage can be placed in the macro in the same location.

## A Macro to Retrieve Files

A file retrieve macro will call a new file into memory. The worksheet containing the macro will no longer be resident in memory when the retrieve operation has completed. Such a macro is normally used as part of a much larger macro that chooses the task you wish to have performed and retrieves the appropriate file.

A retrieve macro might look like this:

```
              A          B                    C
1        \r        /fr              Request file retrieve
2                  SALES~           Specify SALES file
3                  r                Specify replace file
```

The first line of the macro issues the request to retrieve a file. The second line contains the file name and the tilde (~) to finalize the file name entry. The third line causes the current file to be replaced by the one you specified.

**Guidelines for Use**     The macro will erase the worksheet containing the macro when it is executed. If you made changes to the current worksheet, you will want to save it before executing this macro.

**Modifying the Macro**     You can modify the macro to add a file save before it does a file retrieve. You could also change the name of the file being saved.

   If you want, you can modify the macro so it has a name of \0. This would cause it to do an immediate retrieve of a second file as soon as the first one is retrieved. In this situation you would probably want to add some macro instructions at the beginning to perform a few tasks before retrieving the new file.

### A Macro to Extract Files

The File Xtract command is used to save a section of a worksheet in a separate worksheet file. This process can be used to transfer end-of-period totals to a new worksheet for the next period, for example. If you need to extract files frequently, you will want to consider the time-saving features of a macro that does the job.

   Our macro is as follows:

```
         A          B                    C
1        \x        /fxv                 Request file extract of values
2                  TOTALS~              Specify file name of TOTALS
3                  Year_End_Total~      Enter range name to extract
4                  r                    Specify replace
```

The first line contains a request to perform a File Xtract Values operation to save the values from the original file. The next step contains the name of the file in which you want the new material saved. In our example macro, the file name is TOTALS. The next response tells 1-2-3 what to place in the new file. You can specify a range address or a range name. The example macro uses the range name Year__End__Total. The r in the last instruction tells 1-2-3 to replace the TOTALS file with the current contents of Year__End__Total.

**Guidelines for Use**    This macro operates on two assumptions. First, it assumes that the range name Year__End__ Total has already been created. Second, it assumes that the file TOTALS has already been created, since it requests that 1-2-3 replace it.

**Modifying the Macro**    The macro can be modified easily to use a range address rather than a range name for the extract area. The file name used can also be modified. Either of these can be input by the operator while the macro is executing if you use an input instruction.

### A Macro to Combine Files

The /File Combine command allows you to add data from files on disk to the current worksheet without erasing the current worksheet the way a File Retrieve operation would do. A macro to handle the combining operation is shown in Figure 12-8. The final product of the macro is shown in Figure 12-9, where each figure represents the combined totals of each of the four company regions. Each of the detail worksheets contains a 1 in column H in the row number that corresponds to the region number. After the macro has added all four regions to the total company template, the four cells in column H should each contain a 1, as they do in Figure

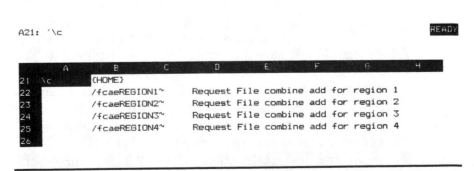

**Figure 12-8.**    Macro to combine files

12-9. These 1's are your check that each detail sheet has been combined with the total worksheet only once, since each detail sheet has a 1 in a different location. In addition to saving keystrokes, this macro can ensure that the combining process is handled consistently and accurately. When you are entering these commands from the keyboard to consolidate many worksheets, it is easy to forget which combining operations have been completed.

After moving to the Home position to ensure correct cursor placement, the macro executes the File Combine instructions that follow. The four combine instructions are the same except for the file names being combined. Each requests /File Combine Add Entire-File for the appropriate region file.

**Guidelines for Use**    The region files are assumed to be in the current directory at the time you execute this macro. Each of the region files is also assumed to have a format identical to that of the file in memory. The region file should contain a 1 in column H in the row that corresponds to the region number, that is, 1 through 4. As previously noted, these serve as flags to indicate that each region has been combined into the total worksheet. This is a good strategy to use with /Combine Add even if you are not using a macro.

A1:                                                                READY

| | A | B | C | D | E | F | G | H |
|---|---|---|---|---|---|---|---|---|
| 1 | | | | | | | | 1 |
| 2 | | | ABC COMPANY SALES | | | | | 1 |
| 3 | | | | | | | | 1 |
| 4 | | | Q1 | Q2 | Q3 | Q4 | TOTAL | 1 |
| 5 | | | | | | | | |
| 6 | Sales Product 1 | | 26,610 | 31,807 | 32,239 | 34,918 | 125,575 | |
| 7 | Sales Product 2 | | 10,301 | 12,057 | 13,666 | 16,281 | 52,305 | |
| 8 | Sales Product 3 | | 50,600 | 46,948 | 51,149 | 55,874 | 204,571 | |
| 9 | | | | | | | | |

**Figure 12-9.**    Worksheet after file combining

**Modifying the Macro**     The macro can be modified to combine any number of files. Although each of the region files is combined with the Add option in this case, you can easily change the macro to use the Subtract option instead.

After you learn to add more sophistication to macros in Chapter 13, you may want to return to this macro and make it check for the 1's in column H using the {IF} and {BRANCH} instructions.

## Print Macros

Since 1-2-3 can retain only one set of print specifications at a time and many worksheets contain more than one printed report, you may find that you are reentering print specifications each month as you print your worksheet reports. This wastes time and could lead to errors that might require the reprinting of a report.

You can avoid such problems by using macros to record the commands needed to print your reports. Once you have worked out the details, you can have the macro print as many reports as you like with one keystroke. Also, since the macro is tested, you can be assured that you will not have to reprint reports because of errors in print specifications.

### A Macro to Create Printed Reports

Most of your reports are likely to be sent directly to the printer. It is possible that the margins, setup strings, header, and other specifications for the printed page may differ between two reports printed from the same worksheet. If you store the different print specifications in a macro, you need only position your paper at the top of a form and turn your printer on. 1-2-3 can handle everything else.

The macro shown will print two different reports from one worksheet.

| | A | B | C |
|---|---|---|---|
| 1 | \p | /pp | Request print |
| 2 | | rA10..C15~ | Specify range of A1..C15 |
| 3 | | oml20~ | Request options & left margin of 20 |
| 4 | | mr55~ | Set right margin to 55 |
| 5 | | mt15~ | Set top margin to 15 |
| 6 | | h||Today's Date : @ | Create header with date at far right |

```
7          q                    Quit options
8          g                    Print requested range
9          pa                   Page & align
10         rA1..H20             Specify range of A1..H20
11         oml5~                Set left margin to 5
12         mr75~                Set right margin at 75
13         s\015~               Send Epson compressed set-up string
14         q                    Quit options
15         g                    Print requested range
16         pa                   Page & align
17         q                    Quit print menu
```

The first instruction in the macro tells 1-2-3 that you want the Print commands and would like your output sent directly to the printer. The first print range, A10..C15, is requested in B2.

The Options changes come next. The first request is to change the left margin to 20. Next, the right margin is set to 55. The top margin is set to 15. B6 specifies the header to be used at the top of each page of the report. There is no entry on the left or in the center of the header, so the line contains only two vertical bars to mark the positions. The rightmost portion of the header contains the constant Today's Date:. It also contains a @, which will cause 1-2-3 to substitute the current date. Since this is the last change through the Options menu, a q is used to quit this menu. Printing is requested with the g for Go in the next cell.

The Page and Align request will be processed as soon as 1-2-3 finishes printing. This request causes 1-2-3 to page to the top of the next form and align its internal line count with the appropriate setting for a new page.

B10 contains the first instruction for the second report. Since the Print menu remains on the screen until you choose Quit, there is no need to make a new request for this menu. The first Options request for the second report is found in B11. The left margin is set at 5 and the right margin is set at 75. B13 contains an instruction that transmits the Epson compressed print string to the printer so it will use small characters.

B14 quits the Options menu. The second report is printed by the g in B15. Page and Align are issued again to position the paper and 1-2-3's line count for your next print request, and the Print menu is quit with the q in the last macro instruction.

**Guidelines for Use**    The critical success factor for use of the macro is positioning your paper before turning your printer on. Wherever your paper is at the time you turn your printer on is where 1-2-3 will assume the top of the form to be. The macro will assume that the paper is at the top of a form when you start.

**Modifying the Macro**    You will want to modify this macro to conform to the specific ranges you need to print your report. These instructions are found in B2 and B10. They can be edited to supply a new range. Depending on the range you select and your exact printing requirements, you may need to modify Options parameters such as margins and setup strings. You may also wish to add options besides those listed in this macro. If you have additional reports to create, you can insert new lines before line 17 to include specifications for them. This way you will be able to have one macro print all your reports.

You may also want to modify this macro to clear all the Print options between reports, depending on how much your specifications change from report to report. If they stay almost the same, you might prefer to change just one or two options by including the appropriate commands and new values in your macro. On the other hand, if there are substantial changes, you might want to include /Print Printer Clear All in the macro. This could be accomplished by adding ca for Clear All after the g in B8.

## A Macro to Store
## Print Output in a File

If you have never printed to a file, you may wonder why anyone would want to store printed output on a file. There are several good reasons. First, your printer may be out for repair and you may want to save the printed output until later. Alternatively, you may want to continue with your current task and wait until later to print. If you are using a print utility that prints your output across the page sideways,

you may need to supply that program with print output
stored on a .PRN file.

The macro presented here will write worksheet formulas
to a file with one formula per line. The macro reads as
follows:

```
          A        B                      C
1        \f       /wgc20˜        Set global column width to 20
2                 /pf           Request print to file
3                 FORMULAS˜      Write to file FORMULAS
4                 rA1..C20˜      Specify range of a1..C20
5                 oo            Request options other
6                 u             Request unformatted
7                 oc            Other cell-formulas
8                 q             Quit options
9                 g             Write requested range to file
10                ca            Clear all print specifications
11                q             Quit print menu
```

The first line in the macro sets columns to a width of 20.
The macro then requests the Print menu and selects File as
the output destination. B3 contains the file name that will be
supplied in response to 1-2-3's prompt. The range to be
printed is shown next and includes the cells in A1..C20.

The Options menu is requested next, and the Other
selection from this menu is chosen. Unformatted output is
requested to remove any formatting specifications in the current print settings. While still in the Options menu, the
macro requests Other again, and Cell-Formulas is chosen to
print each cell in the range on a line by itself and print the
formulas. B8 contains a request to quit the Options menu,
and the following cell writes the output to disk. All print
specifications are cleared with the ca in B10, and the Print
menu is exited via the q in B11.

**Guidelines for Use**     When your computer writes disk files,
it writes data to the disk in blocks. When you request Go,
most of your print output is written to the disk. It is not until
you request Quit from the Print menu that you can be sure
that all of your output is written to the file, however. Also, the
end-of-file indicator is not placed on the file until after you
choose Quit. You will want to be sure to quit the Print menu
with Quit rather than pressing ESC, and you will want to

make sure you leave your disk in the drive until after quitting to ensure that all your data is in the file.

**Modifying the Macro**    This macro will work for any set of reports. You should eliminate the request for Other Cell-Formulas from B7 if you want regular print rather than the formula print the macro requests. The range in B4 will need to be modified to print other reports.

If you want to print multiple reports to one file, you can begin the range specification process again after B9 or B10, depending on whether or not you want the existing print parameters cleared. If you want the output in a second file, you should place your second request after B10 and begin again with /Print File so you can request a new file name.

## Graph Macros

Graphs normally require numerous settings. You have to add titles, data labels, grid lines, legends, and other options to create appealing graphs. You can save time and reduce errors by capturing the required keystrokes in a macro and making it available for use with departmental budgets or other worksheets where a number of managers are using the same formats.

### A Macro to Create a Bar Graph

The following macro is designed to work with the sales worksheet used with the File Combine example earlier in the chapter (Figure 12-9). It can be used for any of the region budgets or the total company worksheet. The only change you may wish to make is in the first line title.

The macro looks like this:

|    | A | B | C |
|----|---|---|---|
| 41 | \g | /grg | Request graph and reset all options |
| 42 |   | tb | Select bar graph for type |
| 43 |   | xc4..f4~ | x range for labels below axis points |
| 44 |   | ac6..f6~ | First data range |
| 45 |   | bc7..f7~ | Second data range |
| 46 |   | cc8..f8~ | Third data range |
| 47 |   | ogh | Options grid lines horizontal |

```
48              tf\d2~              First line title with contents of d2
49              ty$ Sales~          Y axis title
50              laProduct 1~        Legend for first product
51              lbProduct 2~        Legend for second product
53              lcProduct 3~        Legend for third product
54              cq                  Request color and quit options
55              v                   View graph
```

The macro begins in line 41 with a request for the graph menu. This instruction also resets all the graph values. A bar graph is selected in the next instruction, after which the ranges for the different series used to create the graph are specified. The labels below the X axis will be the entries in cells C4..F4. The next three instructions assign values to data ranges A, B, and C.

The Options menu is requested next, and horizontal grid lines are added by the gh option in B47. The first line title is set to use the contents of cell D2. A Y axis title of $ Sales is entered as the next option. Legends for data ranges A, B, and C are then added. Last, color is requested and the Options menu is quit. The graph is viewed with the v in B55.

**Guidelines for Use**   This macro can be used every time you update your worksheet. Of course, if you have just displayed a graph and simply want to see it again, the F10 (GRAPH) key is a quicker approach, since the graph specifications will not be changed. This macro is most useful when you are in a new 1-2-3 session and find that someone else has been using the graphics features and has deleted the definition of your graph.

**Modifying the Macro**   This macro could be modified to save the graph specifications under a graph name. A second, shorter macro could issue a /Graph Name Use command to make the specifications current at a later time.

The macro can also be modified to specify settings for any type of graph you wish. You can use as many options as you need to enhance your basic data.

## Data Macros

Macros can save you time when you use them to automate functions in the data environment. Most of the data commands require that you make a number of selections before you complete your task. Some, like /Data Table, require that you complete preliminary steps before requesting the command. Also, since you must reissue the data commands if you want a sort, data table, frequency analysis, regression analysis, or data fill operation performed again, you could be executing them frequently. With the macro approach, you can enter them once and check their accuracy, then store them in worksheet cells and use them as much as you want.

## A Macro to Create a Data Table

A data table can perform a sensitivity analysis for you by systematically plugging values into your input variables. Before you ask 1-2-3 to perform this analysis, you must build a table shell on the worksheet. Since a macro to do this is a little more complicated than our other macros, you will want to take a look at the worksheet in Figure 12-10 before you study the macro listing. Projections for products A and B use the growth rates in C10 and C11 and the previous year's sales

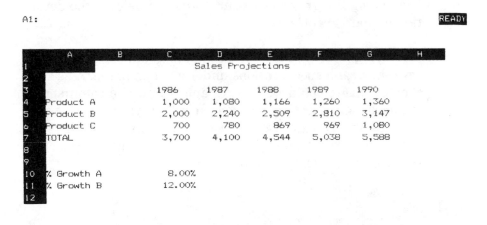

**Figure 12-10.**     Worksheet for use with /Data Table

to project future periods. Product C is calculated as a percentage of products A and B sales. The completed table is shown in Figure 12-11. The rules for working with tables are found in Chapter 10; you will want to look at this chapter if you are not familiar with the /Data Table command. The table in this macro is calculated by having 1-2-3 substitute the values in column B for the growth of product A in C10 each time the table performs a new calculation. The percentages in row 22 will be substituted as new growth factors for product B. The table contains the result of the formula in G7, which is the total sales in 1990.

The first macro instruction is found in B41, as shown here.

```
          A        B                    C
41       \t       /df                 Request Data Fill
42                B23..B31~            Set range
43                .05~                 Enter start value
44                .01~~                Enter increment & accept stop value
45                /df                  Request Data Fill
46                C22..H22~            Set range
47                .09~                 Enter start value
48                .01~~                Enter increment & accept stop value
49                /dt2                 Request Data Table 2
50                B22..H31~            Set range
51                C10~                 Set input value 2
52                C11~                 Set input value 1
53                {GOTO}B22~           Move cursor to B22 to view table
```

A21:                                                                    READY

| | A | B | C | D | E | F | G | H |
|---|---|---|---|---|---|---|---|---|
| 21 | | | | | PRODUCT B | | | |
| 22 | | +B7 | 9.00% | 10.00% | 11.00% | 12.00% | 13.00% | 14.00% |
| 23 | P | 5.00% | 5,007 | 5,144 | 5,284 | 5,428 | 5,576 | 5,728 |
| 24 | R | 6.00% | 5,059 | 5,195 | 5,336 | 5,480 | 5,628 | 5,780 |
| 25 | O | 7.00% | 5,112 | 5,249 | 5,389 | 5,533 | 5,681 | 5,833 |
| 26 | D | 8.00% | 5,167 | 5,303 | 5,444 | 5,588 | 5,736 | 5,888 |
| 27 | U | 9.00% | 5,223 | 5,359 | 5,500 | 5,644 | 5,792 | 5,944 |
| 28 | C | 10.00% | 5,281 | 5,417 | 5,557 | 5,702 | 5,850 | 6,002 |
| 29 | T | 11.00% | 5,340 | 5,477 | 5,617 | 5,761 | 5,909 | 6,061 |
| 30 | | 12.00% | 5,401 | 5,538 | 5,678 | 5,822 | 5,970 | 6,122 |
| 31 | A | 13.00% | 5,464 | 5,600 | 5,741 | 5,885 | 6,033 | 6,185 |
| 32 | | | | | | | | |

**Figure 12-11.**   Completed table

This starting location deviates from those in our other examples, showing that you need not begin macros in A1. This first instruction requests /Data Fill to start building the shell for the table. A location for filling is established with the second instruction. Then a start value of .05 and an increment of .01 are specified. When the stop value prompt is displayed, the second tilde in B44 will accept the default, since it is greater than the stop value needed.

The second data fill operation supplies the values across row 22. A start value of .09 is used, along with the same increment as the first range. The default stop value is accepted again.

The request for the /Data Table 2 command is made in B49. The table location is defined in B50 as B22..H31. The first input value is the value for the growth factor for product A, stored in C10. The second input value is the growth factor for product B, which is stored in C11. When this second input value is entered, the macro calculates the new values for G7 and places them in the table.

**Guidelines for Use** This macro is designed to handle most of the setup as well as the call for /Data Table to do the calculations. The only tasks it does not take care of are the entry of the formula in cell B22 and the formatting of the table cells. This is to ensure that the values you want are always placed in the table as input values. You will want to be sure not to store information in the cells the table uses, since executing the macro would overlay these cells.

**Modifying the Macro** The macro can be modified to create a table of different size or with different input values generated by the Data Fill operation. You could also modify the instructions in B43, B44, B47, and B48 to contain {?} so that the operator could enter the fill parameters and therefore the input values every time the macro is executed.

You could also modify the macro to handle the remaining preliminary steps for preparing the table. It would be easy to handle the entry of the formula in B22 and the Range Format statements that would be required to display the table as shown.

## A Macro to Sort a Database

Sorting a database requires the definition of the data range. This does not have to be done every time you sort, but it must be done if you have added a new field or new records to your database. Since it is easy to forget to do this, you can make a macro handle this precautionary step to ensure that you do not sort just a section of your database.

The database this example will use is shown in Figure 12-12. You will notice that the names are in random sequence. The macro will sort the file into sequence by last name and will use the first name as a secondary key. The result of using the macro is shown in Figure 12-13.

A1: [W12] 'Last Name

READY

| | A | B | C | D | E | F |
|---|---|---|---|---|---|---|
| 1 | Last Name | First Name | SS# | Job Code | Salary | Location |
| 2 | Chambers | Sally | 817-66-1212 | 15 | $54,600 | 2 |
| 3 | Wilkes | Caitlin | 670-90-1121 | 21 | $27,600 | 4 |
| 4 | Stephens | Tom | 659-11-3452 | 14 | $19,800 | 4 |
| 5 | Smythe | George | 569-89-7654 | 12 | $32,000 | 2 |
| 6 | Samuelson | Paul | 560-90-8645 | 15 | $65,000 | 4 |
| 7 | Preverson | Gary | 560-55-4311 | 14 | $23,500 | 10 |
| 8 | Patterson | Lyle | 543-98-9876 | 23 | $12,000 | 2 |
| 9 | Parker | Dee | 459-34-0921 | 23 | $32,500 | 4 |
| 10 | Miller | Lisa | 431-78-9963 | 17 | $41,200 | 4 |
| 11 | McCartin | John | 313-78-9090 | 15 | $31,450 | 4 |
| 12 | Lightnor | Peggy | 312-45-9862 | 12 | $32,900 | 10 |
| 13 | Larson | Mary | 219-89-7080 | 23 | $28,900 | 2 |
| 14 | Kaylor | Sally | 219-78-8954 | 15 | $17,800 | 2 |
| 15 | Justof | Jack | 215-67-8973 | 21 | $19,500 | 2 |
| 16 | Hawkins | Mark | 214-89-6756 | 23 | $18,700 | 2 |
| 17 | Hartwick | Eileen | 213-76-9874 | 23 | $23,000 | 10 |
| 18 | Deaver | Ken | 212-11-9090 | 12 | $21,500 | 10 |
| 19 | Campbell | David | 198-98-6750 | 23 | $24,600 | 10 |
| 20 | Campbell | Keith | 124-67-7432 | 17 | $15,500 | 2 |

18-Jul-86  03:30 AM

**Figure 12-12.**    Unsorted database

|    | A | B | C | D | E | F |
|----|---|---|---|---|---|---|
| 1 | Last Name | First Name | SS# | Job Code | Salary | Location |
| 2 | Campbell | David | 198-98-6750 | 23 | $24,600 | 10 |
| 3 | Campbell | Keith | 124-67-7432 | 17 | $15,500 | 2 |
| 4 | Chambers | Sally | 817-66-1212 | 15 | $54,600 | 2 |
| 5 | Deaver | Ken | 212-11-9090 | 12 | $21,500 | 10 |
| 6 | Hartwick | Eileen | 213-76-9874 | 23 | $23,000 | 10 |
| 7 | Hawkins | Mark | 214-89-6756 | 23 | $18,700 | 2 |
| 8 | Justof | Jack | 215-67-8973 | 21 | $19,500 | 2 |
| 9 | Kaylor | Sally | 219-78-8954 | 15 | $17,800 | 2 |
| 10 | Larson | Mary | 219-89-7080 | 23 | $28,900 | 2 |
| 11 | Lightnor | Peggy | 312-45-9862 | 12 | $32,900 | 10 |
| 12 | McCartin | John | 313-78-9090 | 15 | $31,450 | 4 |
| 13 | Miller | Lisa | 431-78-9963 | 17 | $41,200 | 4 |
| 14 | Parker | Dee | 459-34-0921 | 23 | $32,500 | 4 |
| 15 | Patterson | Lyle | 543-98-9876 | 23 | $12,000 | 2 |
| 16 | Preverson | Gary | 560-55-4311 | 14 | $23,500 | 10 |
| 17 | Samuelson | Paul | 560-90-8645 | 15 | $65,000 | 4 |
| 18 | Smythe | George | 569-89-7654 | 12 | $32,000 | 2 |
| 19 | Stephens | Tom | 659-11-3452 | 14 | $19,800 | 4 |
| 20 | Wilkes | Caitlin | 670-90-1121 | 21 | $27,600 | 4 |

18-Jul-86   03:40 AM

**Figure 12-13.**     Sorted database

The macro shown here begins in B22 with a request for /Data Sort Data-Range.

```
        A        B                          C
22   \s    /dsd                    Request sort data-range
23         {ESC}{HOME}{DOWN}       Remove old range; set A2 as beginning
24         .                       Lock in beginning of range
25         {END}{DOWN}             Move to last entry in first field
26         {END}{RIGHT}~           Move to last field on right
27         pA2~a~                  Set last name as primary key
28         sB2~a~                  Set first name as secondary key
29         g                       Complete sort
30         {HOME}                  Move to A1 to display sorted records
```

Since the range is set from the previous use, ESC is needed to unlock the beginning of the range. The cursor is moved to A1 with the HOME key and then moved down one row to A2. This cell is locked in place as the beginning of the sort range by typing a period. The cursor is moved to the last entry in the column and then is moved across to the last column to complete the range specification.

A2 is defined as the primary key, on which the records will be sorted in ascending sequence. The secondary key will be B2, the first name, which will also be applied in ascending sequence. The g in B29 requests that the sort begin. The macro ends by moving to the Home position so you can review your results.

**Guidelines for Use**     The macro makes several assumptions about the worksheet. First, it assumes that the worksheet has been sorted at some time in the past. Otherwise, the ESC in B23 would exit you from the Data-Range request. Second, the macro assumes that the first and last data field will have values for every record. The instructions in B25 and B26 would not work if some of the fields were blank.

**Modifying the Macro**     The macro can be modified to sort on any field. You can enter the range address for the macro, though this approach would require modification to the macro as the database expands.

# Command Language
# Macros

Differences Between Command Language Macros and
Keyboard Macros
Constructing and Using Command Language Macros
Macro Commands

# THIRTEEN

Command language macros are even more powerful than
the keyboard alternative macros described in the last
chapter. Command language macros allow you to perform
repetitive tasks with ease and automate applications so
that even novice users can handle complex worksheet
tasks. They also allow you to use features that are not part
of the 1-2-3 menu structure. The macro command set in
release 2 is substantially enhanced over that in release 1A.
The release 1A commands are found in the /X command
section near the end of this chapter. With both releases,
you can alter the execution flow of a macro by branching
to a new location. You can also create your own custom
menus patterned after 1-2-3's.

Command language macros are not for everyone,
however. They are built with 1-2-3's command language,
which is essentially a programming language. As with
any programming language, you are likely to have moments
of frustration and exasperation as you strive to make 1-2-3
understand your needs. If you plan to be successful in
creating command language macros, you must be willing
to work at the detail level in defining your needs exactly.
You will need blocks of uninterrupted time so you can concentrate fully on these details. Finally, you will need per-

sistence to stick with the task until the macro works correctly. Given these things, you can learn to create macros you will be proud of.

This chapter is designed to provide strategies for creating command language macros with as little pain as possible. The first part of the chapter will cover some general strategies for creating macros and discuss some specific techniques used by programmers working in other programming languages to ensure the correct operation of their programs. Since the 1-2-3 macro command language is also a programming language, you are likely to find some of these techniques helpful when writing your macros. The second section of this chapter will cover each macro command separately. It will provide a description and a working example that incorporates each macro command.

## Differences Between Command Language Macros And Keyboard Macros

Command language macros are entered in the same way as the keyboard variety covered in Chapter 12. Like keyboard macros, they are label entries stored in a column of worksheet cells and are named with a backslash and a single letter key. Just as you needed to follow rigid rules when entering a menu selection sequence, you will also have to follow rules when entering instructions from 1-2-3's macro command language. The command key word and any arguments it expects must always be enclosed in braces { } —for example, {BRANCH A9}. Arguments must always be entered in the prescribed order.

How will you know when to use command language macros and when to use the keyboard variety? It is really quite easy. When a keyboard macro will work, use it. When you want to accomplish things that menu commands cannot handle, however, it is time to look beyond keyboard macros.

Your first command language macros may use only a few statements, as in the following macro, which enters a date all the way down a column instead of just once the way the example in the last chapter did.

```
         A            B
 1    \d     {LET Z1,0}
 2    Top    {IF Z1=5}{BRANCH End}
 3           @DATE(
 4           {?}
 5           ,
 6           {?}
 7           ,
 8           {?}
 9           )~
10           {DOWN}
11           {LET Z1,Z1+1}
12           {BRANCH Top}
13    End    {QUIT}
```

After you have mastered the simpler variety of command language macro, you can begin to think of more sophisticated tasks you would like to delegate to 1-2-3. Many of these will require the use of command language instructions, but they are likely to employ the familiar built-in functions, formulas, and menu options as well. As long as you are working with the 1-2-3 package, you will want all its features at your disposal.

## Constructing and Using Command Language Macros

A command language macro normally consists of a number of detailed steps that must be executed in a logical order. When you communicate instructions to another person, you can often be less than fully specific and still get the desired results. Human beings can interpret directions and make assumptions about the exact way a task should be performed. If someone knows your way of doing business and has worked for you in the past, his or her interpretations and assumptions about the way you want a particular task done are likely to be correct.

When you ask a computer to do your bidding, however, there will be no interpretation and no assumptions. You will get exactly what you ask for, whether it is what you want or not. If you leave out a step or provide the steps in the wrong sequence, you will get results different from what you expect.

Since you can't change the way computers do their processing, you will have to learn to set up tasks in a way that a computer can handle. You need to create a road map showing what you want the computer to do for you. You should create this road map on paper so you can separate logic and syntax. Logic refers to the steps in the task you wish the computer to perform, and syntax refers to the detailed instructions in the 1-2-3 macro command language and the arguments they need to execute successfully. If you do not have all the logic of your macro worked out, you will never be able to solve the problem by entering specific instructions. You need to know where you are going and the general route you plan to follow before you start.

## Planning Command Language Macros

You can use a variety of techniques to map out your logic flow. Programmers frequently use flowcharts or pseudocode (statements written in something like computer code but without concern for precise syntax) to map out their programs. The following subsections will describe these techniques in more detail. You can use one of them, or you can develop your own technique. The important thing is to completely think through the steps needed to complete your tasks before you get involved with the command language syntax. If you attempt to tackle both logic and syntax in one step and your macro does not work, you will not know where to begin the correction process.

### Flowcharts

Flowcharts are diagrams of the detailed logic in a macro or other program that are constructed with special symbols. These symbols are joined with lines to form a pictorial representation of the logic flow. A standard set of symbols is used so that any programmer can understand a flowchart created by any other individual. In fact, a programmer often asks another programmer to review the flowchart of a problem solution before it is coded to help identify logic errors early in the testing process.

In most flowcharts, the diamond represents a decision to be made, the small circle is a connector, the parallelogram marks input and output operations, and the rectangle indicates arithmetic operations and other processes. Figure 13-1 presents a flowchart using these symbols. It describes the logic required to combine a variable number of region files into one worksheet. This would allow someone to create division or total company reports with one worksheet. Ctr1 and Ctr2 are counters.

If you choose to use flowcharts for mapping your program logic, there is no need to buy a special flowchart template to create the special symbols. Drawing them by hand is just as effective. You can even use a different set of symbols if you prefer.

## Pseudocode

Pseudocode is a shortcut method of documenting your logic with everyday English words. It can be quicker to use than flowcharts, since there are no figures to be drawn, and it is closer to the final form of program code that you will use. When writing pseudocode, don't concern yourself with spelling, grammar, or complete sentences; phrases are best, in fact, as long as they are clear.

The following lines of pseudocode describe the same process that was pictured in the flowchart in Figure 13-1.

|         |                               |
|---------|-------------------------------|
|         | Initialize Ctr2 to 1          |
|         | Position cursor               |
|         | Enter number of regions to combine |
|         | Set Ctr1 = # regions          |
| Combine | Use file combine add          |
|         | If Ctr1 = Ctr2 branch to End  |
|         | Add 1 to Ctr2                 |
|         | Branch to Combine             |
| End     | Quit                          |

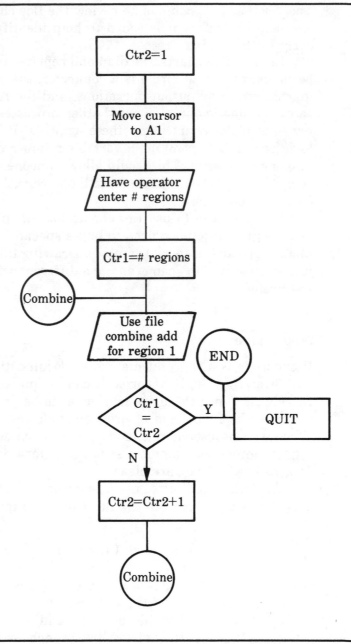

**Figure 13-1.** Flowchart for combining files

## Strategies for Designing Complex Macros

A three- or four-line command language macro is no more difficult to create than a keyboard macro. It is so small that you can keep track of its entire logic flow mentally. More sophisticated command language macros, however, need more careful structuring and planning.

### Branching Versus Straight-Line Code

It is easy to create macro code that branches all over the place. Programmers refer to this as "spaghetti bowl" code. It usually results from lack of planning. New instructions are simply added as the programmer thinks of them. If there is not enough room to insert all the instructions needed, the program branches away to a blank location and then branches back again to execute the remaining instructions. The result is confusion. It may be quicker to code a program or a macro in this fashion, but it is definitely not quicker to make it work correctly.

Straight-line code is at the opposite end of the spectrum. Wherever possible, it proceeds from the top to the bottom of the logic flow without branching. Of course, branching need not be forbidden entirely. A little common sense can go a long way in creating macros that are both workable and correct. Straight-line code, however, offers the advantage of allowing you to read from the top to the bottom of the code to get a picture of what it is accomplishing.

### Main Code and Subroutines

You can write a large macro that contains, say, 400 instructions and list them consecutively down a column on your worksheet. To get a picture of what this macro is designed to accomplish, someone would have to read all 400 lines of code.

A better approach is to separate your macros into a main code section and subroutines. Properly planned, this structure combines the advantages of branching and straight-line code.

Fifty lines of code has been found to be a manageable upper limit for the length of the main section. Detail tasks are taken out of this section and placed in subroutines, which are referenced by instructions in the main section. Because the main section is short, it can be scanned quickly to learn the essence of the macro. This form of organization also makes it easier to test the macro a section at a time and thereby trace errors to particular sections of code.

When a main program calls a subroutine, the subroutine instructions will be executed until a {RETURN} is encountered or the end of the subroutine is reached. At that time, control will return to the main program that called the subroutine. The instruction immediately following the subroutine call will be executed next. A subroutine call is always indicated by enclosing the routine name in braces. To call a subroutine named Print, for example, you would enter {Print}.

The following example shows how a main program and its subroutines might be structured.

*Main Routine*
    . . .
    . . .
    {Update}
    {Print}
*Subroutines*
*Update* . . .
    . . .
    . . .
    . . .
    {RETURN}
*Print*   . . .
    . . .
    {RETURN}

The ... entries represent macro instructions appropriate for the routines. You will notice that with this structure, you can read down the main code and see that an update operation will be performed, followed by a print operation. You need not read the precise instructions in either subroutine to understand the program's basic structure.

When you call a subroutine, you can pass arguments to it. This will allow you to tailor the routine to each particular situation. Passing arguments to a subroutine requires that the arguments be included in the instruction that calls the subroutine. In addition, the subroutine must contain a {DEFINE} instruction that provides a storage location for each argument passed to it.

You can have a main program that calls the same subroutine multiple times and passes different arguments to it each time. For example, you might want to print your worksheet with three different setup strings and have defined an argument to pass a setup string to the print subroutine. Your main program might appear as follows:

```
{Print K1}
{Print K2}
{Print K3}
```

Each time a call is executed, whatever is stored in the specified cell (that is, K1, K2, K3) is passed to the subroutine.

The subroutine would require a storage place for only one argument, since only one argument is passed to it each time it is executed. Assuming Setup was defined as a range name, the subroutine might appear like this:

```
Print          {DEFINE Setup:string}
               . . .
               . . .
```

Setup is defined as a string argument; it will contain the value of K1, K2, and K3 from each execution of the Print routine.

## Entering Command Language Macros

Having mapped out a plan for your macro, you are ready to begin entering actual code. Command language macros are entered in the same manner as keyboard alternative macros. As with keyboard macros, it is a good idea to place command macros in an out-of-the-way location that has a blank column on both sides of the column you plan to use for the macro instructions. Then you can use the column to the left of the macro to document the macro name as well as any range names you might assign to different sections of the macro.

You can use either upper or lower case for macro commands, argument names, cell address references, keyboard commands, and macro names. Each cell in the column where you make your entries can contain up to 240 characters, since each macro instruction is entered as a label. It is not recommended that you use entries that even approach this upper limit, however. Forty or fifty characters is a reasonable upper limit if you want your macros to be readable.

### Naming Command Language Macros

Command language macros are named in the same fashion as keyboard macros. The name of any command language macro that you wish to execute directly from the keyboard should consist of a single letter preceded by a backslash ( \ ). Upper and lower case are equivalent, so you can have 26 unique macros that can be executed from the keyboard. Just as with keyboard macros, you can have a special automatic macro that will begin execution as soon as the worksheet containing it is retrieved. This macro must have the special name of \0.

Since command language macros have branching instructions as well as subroutine calls to execute other macros, you can have macros named with regular range names. These macros will be able to be executed only when invoked by another macro.

In all cases, you will need to name only the top cell in a

macro. 1-2-3 considers a macro to continue until a blank cell or a {QUIT} instruction is encountered.

### Creating a Macro Shell

If you like, you can code all your macro instructions at once. It often works better, however, to code just the major instructions first. As an example, if you have a macro that branches to one of four main subroutines depending on an operator input, you might code only the instructions to process the operator's input and the beginning instructions for each of the four main subroutines. At the beginning of each subroutine you would place an instruction that informs you that you have reached that particular routine. In this manner you can check out the upper-level logic of your macro without investing time in creating detailed code. This kind of "framework" code is called a shell.

This approach to program construction is referred to as top-down programming. It can save considerable time by allowing you to detect major logic problems before you bother with detailed coding. If a problem arises, there will be far fewer instructions to change or move.

You might construct a shell that consists of little more than subroutine calls and instructions to display messages, for example. You can use a "dummy" input statement with the {GETNUMBER} on {GETLABEL} command for the sole purpose of displaying a message on the screen. The {INDICATE} instruction provides another option to inform you of a macro's progress.

This method can speed up your testing process significantly, since you can test the program's basic logic by invoking each subroutine and checking the special message it displays. Once you have checked the execution flow, you can add the detailed code needed to complete the subroutines.

Figure 13-2 provides an example of this shell structure. At this point, each subroutine contains only an instruction to let you know that you have arrived at that location in the macro. Once this program pattern checks out as correct, you can add instructions to do the processing for each routine.

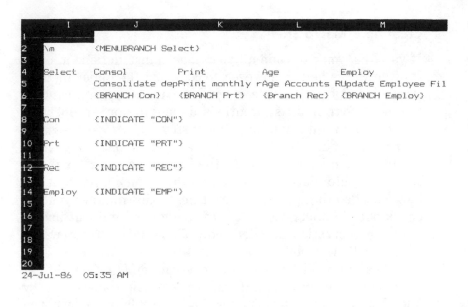

**Figure 13-2.** Macro shell with menu

## Creating Interactive Macros

Interactive macros are macros that change as they are executed. They can change logic flow in response to entries by the operator. They can even change entries in instructions, such as file names.

### Macros That Respond to Operator Input

As you look through the various macro commands in this chapter, you will find several that accept operator input. These include {?}, {GETLABEL}, {GETNUMBER}, {GET}, and {LOOK}. You can use the information obtained from these entries to control {BRANCH} instructions and subroutine calls as well as other processing within the macro.

### Dynamically Altered Macros

Dynamically altered macros are macros that store the information that is input or calculated during execution as part of the macro itself. For example, you might wish to do a file retrieve and change the file retrieved depending on the application you are working on. To do this, you may use a menu selection to determine the application and have this instruction alter the following macro instruction sequence:

```
/fr
blank
~
```

In this example, the cell that contains the word *blank* would actually be an empty cell. You want to have the macro make an appropriate entry in this cell, using either a {PUT} or a {LET} instruction. Thus the macro would be altering itself to perform the exact action you want.

A simpler form of this dynamic alteration will be seen in the example under {GETLABEL}, where dates are being temporarily entered in macro cells for later storage in a different area of the worksheet. Depending on your entries, the macro is altered to create a variety of date entries.

## Documenting Command Language Macros

Documentation consists of comments added to the worksheet to explain your macro. Its main purpose is to make each step clear to someone who was not involved in the macro's operation. However, you also are likely to find it very helpful when you look back at a macro you wrote, say, three months previously.

Variables in your macro should be given meaningful names. This will minimize the need for supplemental documentation and will make formulas in your macro easier to read.

You can document the names in your macro by placing them in the column to the left of the top macro instruction. When naming subroutines, place the name to the left of the top cell in each subroutine. Other macro instructions should be documented by placing a description to the right of each instruction. Be as brief as possible, but make sure you clearly describe all formulas or other entries that may not seem clear at a later time.

Since macro instructions are only label entries, any references to cell addresses they contain will not be updated if cells are moved or deleted. You may want to flag macro cells containing cell address references with an asterisk to the far left or right of the macro column to make sure you check these entries any time you reorganize the worksheet.

You may want to consider the use of section names within your macro. Section names are names placed in the column to the left of a macro; they simply name sections of the macro. Even when you have not created range names for these locations, section names can make your macro more readable.

If you are like most people, you are likely to not want to bother with the documentation step. You have to learn to think of documentation as a worthwhile investment that can save you time in the future and make it possible to delegate the maintenance of your applications to others as you move on to new responsibilities. A few extra minutes spent documenting a macro when you have just finished creating it can pay off in hours of saved time later.

## Testing Command Language Macros

You cannot assume that a macro will work correctly unless you have tested it. A multiple-step testing process is the most efficient and will ensure that your macro will work under all conditions.

The steps you follow should probably be something like this.

1. Your first test should be an easy one. If the macro performs calculations, use nice, even numbers so you can check its answers mentally. If you choose a complicated number, you might make arithmetic mistakes yourself while testing it.

2. If your macro is an iterative one, that is, one that is executed numerous times, test only two or three iterations of its cycle. This saves time and makes it easier to check results.

3. Now try to see what the macro does with exceptions or unusual conditions that occur only sporadically.

4. Check for error conditions next. If the macro prompts you for the number of times you wish to execute a certain routine, respond with −25. If it asks for a number of vacation days, respond with 560. If it asks for a salary increase, respond with 1500%. See whether it responds to each of these error conditions as you expect.

5. If your macro fails at any step along the way, correct the error condition and go back to the first step for a quick recheck after the change. Never assume that a change to one part of a macro will not affect another part. It often does, and the only way you will know for sure is to test it.

6. If your macro will be used by others in the organization, involve them in the testing process. No one knows better the type of data that will be entered into the macro than the person who will use the program every day. This approach will also help you discover whether you have to change your macro because you have misinterpreted the user's needs. As an example, you may have allowed for the entry of an invoice amount, not realizing that the user expected your macro to compute the total invoice amount based on entry of detail figures.

## Executing Command Language Macros

Executing a completed command language macro is easy. Just as with keyboard macros, press the ALT key and the letter key of the macro's name simultaneously. There are several other things you should be aware of before executing a macro, however.

## Updating the Worksheet

When you execute macros, you will find that some of the macro commands can update worksheet cells. They do not always update these cells immediately, and sometimes the worksheet must be recalculated before the update takes place. For some commands, pressing the ENTER key may be sufficient to cause the updating. You will want to follow these commands with a tilde (~) if immediate update is critical to the successful execution of the macro. Other commands require that the worksheet be recalculated.

The following commands will update the worksheet if you follow them with a tilde (~):

{BLANK}
{GETLABEL}
{GETNUMBER}
{LET}

These commands require a {CALC} instruction if you want immediate update:

{CONTENTS}
{DEFINE}
{FILESIZE}
{GET}
{GETPOS}
{LOOK}
{ONERROR}
{PUT}
{READ}
{READLN}

## Stopping a Macro

Unless you have disabled the Break function by including {BREAKOFF} in your macro, you will be able to interrupt the macro in midstream by pressing CTRL-BREAK. This will present an ERROR indicator on the screen. If you press ESC, you can acknowledge the error and return to READY mode.

## Macro Commands

### Syntax of Macro Commands

1-2-3's command language has two separate types of macro commands, those that do not have arguments and those that do. Both types will include a keyword in braces. Subroutine calls are exceptions. See "The Macro Language Commands" for a list of macro commands and their functions.

The format of the first type is nothing more than a keyword enclosed in braces. Examples are {RETURN}, {RESTART}, and {QUIT}.

The format of the second type consists of the keyword followed by a blank space and a list of arguments separated by commas. As with function arguments, no spaces are allowed between or within arguments. The entire entry is enclosed in braces. Here are two examples:

{GETLABEL "Enter your name :",A2}
{FOR Counter,1,20,1,Loop}

The following discussion will describe all the arguments for each command and will specify which of the arguments are optional.

### Conventions for Macros in This Chapter

The same conventions have been used for all the example macros whenever possible. The name used for the macro is shown in column A to the left of the top cell in the macro. The macro instructions are written in column B as labels, except for the menu macros, which extend to the right.

When possible, documentation has been placed in column

# 1 2 3 The Macro Language Commands

| Macro Command | Function | Type of Macro |
|---|---|---|
| {?} | Accepts keyboard input | Keyboard |
| {BEEP} | Sounds bell | Screen |
| {BLANK} | Erases cell or range | Data |
| {BRANCH} | Changes execution flow to a new location | Flow |
| {BREAKOFF} | Disables BREAK key | Keyboard |
| {BREAKON} | Restores BREAK key function | Keyboard |
| {CLOSE} | Closes an open file | File |
| {CONTENTS} | Stores the numeric contents of a cell as a label in another cell | Data |
| {DEFINE} | Specifies location and type of arguments for a subroutine call | Flow |
| {DISPATCH} | Branches to a new location indirectly | Flow |
| {FILESIZE} | Determines number of bytes in a file | File |
| {FOR} | Loops through a macro subroutine multiple times | Flow |
| {FORBREAK} | Cancels current {FOR} instruction | Flow |
| {GET} | Halts macro to allow single-keystroke entry | Keyboard |
| {GETLABEL} | Halts macro to allow label entry | Keyboard |
| {GETNUMBER} | Halts macro to allow number entry | Keyboard |

## The Macro Language Commands

| Macro Command | Function | Type of Macro |
|---|---|---|
| {GETPOS} | Returns pointer position in a file | File |
| {IF} | Causes conditional execution of command that follows | Flow |
| {INDICATE} | Changes mode indicator | Screen |
| {LET} | Stores a number or label in a cell | Data |
| {LOOK} | Checks to see if entry has been made | Keyboard |
| {MENUBRANCH} | Allows the construction of a customized menu | Keyboard |
| {MENUCALL} | Executes a customized menu as a subroutine | Keyboard |
| {ONERROR} | Branches to an error-processing routine | Flow |
| {OPEN} | Opens a file for read or write access | File |
| {PANELOFF} | Eliminates control panel updating | Screen |
| {PANELON} | Restores control panel updating | Screen |
| {PUT} | Stores a number or label in one cell of a range | Data |
| {QUIT} | Ends the macro and returns to READY mode | Flow |
| {READ} | Reads characters from file into cell | File |
| {READLN} | Reads a line of characters from a file | File |
| {RECALC} | Recalculates formulas in a range row by row | Data |

## The Macro Language Commands

| Macro Command | Function | Type of Macro |
|---|---|---|
| {RECALCCOL} | Recalculates formulas in a range column by column | Data |
| {RESTART} | Clears subroutine pointers | Flow |
| {RETURN} | Routines to the instruction after the last subroutine call or {MENUCALL} | Flow |
| {routine} | Calls the subroutine specified by routine | Flow |
| {SETPOS} | Moves file pointer to a new location in the file | File |
| {WAIT} | Waits until a specified time | Keyboard |
| {WINDOWSOFF} | Suppresses window updating | Screen |
| {WINDOWSON} | Restores window updating | Screen |
| {WRITE} | Places data in a file | File |
| {WRITELN} | Places data in file and adds a carriage return/line feed at the end | File |
| /XC | Calls a subroutine | /X |
| /XG | Branches to a new location | /X |
| /XI | Tests a logical condition | /X |
| /XL | Gets a label entry from the keyboard | /X |
| /XM | Creates a user-defined menu | /X |
| /XN | Gets a number from the keyboard | /X |
| /XQ | Quits the macro | /X |
| /XR | Returns control to the main macro code from a subroutine | /X |

C. Each description extends to the right and frequently displays in the columns to the right of column C. It is often not possible to show complete macro documentation in the book due to width restrictions. Macros that lack descriptions would be documented on your worksheet in the same manner as those that show them.

Lower-case characters are used for menu selections and responses to menu prompts. File names, command keywords, and special key indicators, such as {HOME}, {ESC}, {IF}, and {MENUBRANCH}, are shown in upper case. Range names, which also serve as subroutine names, are shown in proper case, with only the first letter of each word in the name capitalized.

The macro commands in the sections that follow will be grouped according to the categories in which they are placed in your 1-2-3 manual. Every macro command in each of the sections will be covered. For each command you will find a description and format, descriptions of arguments, if any, suggestions for use, and an example. Special setup procedures are also described, if any are required.

## Macro Commands That Affect the Screen

Macro commands that affect your screen can handle such tasks as updating the window and control panel. If you leave such commands set as on, you have an indication of where the macro is at any particular moment, but the macro's quick progress can cause a flicker as the screen is updated. These macros also provide the ability to create your own mode indicator and to beep your computer's bell to get the operator's attention.

### {BEEP}

The {BEEP} command will sound your computer's bell.

**Format**    The format for the {BEEP} command is

{BEEP *number*}

where *number* is an optional argument that you can use to affect the tone of the bell. The number argument can have any value from 1 to 4, with 1 as the default value when no number is specified.

**Use**     You can use the beep to alert the operator to an error, indicate that you expect input, show periodically that the macro is still functioning during a long-running macro, or signify the conclusion of a step. In this example, it is used to indicate that an input instruction follows.

```
{BEEP 3}
{GETNUMBER "Enter your account number",F2}
```

The {BEEP} instruction will cause the computer's bell to ring with the third tone right before the input message is displayed.

**Example**     The following macro uses the {BEEP} instruction to alert the operator that a significant response is being requested.

```
        A                                    B
1    \B        {GETLABEL "Do you wish to erase your work? ",H1}
2              {IF H1="Y"}{BRANCH Erase}
3              {QUIT}
4
5    Erase     {BEEP}
6              {GETLABEL "Confirm erase request by typing a Y ",H2}
7              {IF H2="Y"}/wey
8              {QUIT}
```

The worksheet is about to be erased, and confirmation is being requested that this step is desired. The first macro instruction uses {GETLABEL} to request a response concerning whether or not the worksheet should be erased. If the operator responds with a Y, the condition test {IF H1="Y"} will be true, and the instruction from the same line that branches to the Erase subroutine will be executed. If any other response is provided, the macro quits.

When Erase is executed following the {BRANCH} instruction, its first step is to issue the {BEEP} warning. It then asks for confirmation of the erase request. If the request to erase is confirmed, the macro erases the worksheet and then quits.

### {INDICATE}

The {INDICATE} command provides the ability to customize the mode indicator in the upper right corner of the screen.

**Format**    The format of the {INDICATE} command is

{INDICATE **string**}

when *string* is any character string (although {INDICATE} will use only the first five characters). Using an empty string, that is, {INDICATE " "}, will remove the indicator light from the control panel. Using no string, that is, {INDI-CATE}, returns the indicator to READY mode.

**Use**    The indicator you select with this command will remain until you use the command again to establish a new setting. The setting will continue beyond the execution of the macro. If you set the indicator at FILE, FILE will remain on the screen even if you are in READY mode. You will want to include {INDICATE} without any argument at the end of any macro that has used this instruction in its body. Doing so will restore 1-2-3's normal indicator display at the conclusion of the macro.

The {INDICATE} command is useful when you are designing automated applications. If you have a series of menu selections for the operator to use, you can have an {INDICATE} instruction for each path that will supply a string related to the selection the operator has made. This command can also be useful in testing macro shells. Each subroutine can be represented initially by nothing more than an {INDICATE} with a suitable character string to allow you to check the logic flow. If you have a budget subroutine, for example, you might represent it in your shell with

{INDICATE "BUDG"}

**Example**    The macro shown here will change the mode indicator several times.

```
         A           B                      C
1    \i       {INDICATE "SETUP"}   Change indicator to SETUP
2             /wcs15~               Change column width to 15
3             /rfc0~{DOWN 5}~       Format as currency 0 decimals
4             {INDICATE "SPLIT"}    Change indicator to SPLIT
5             {DOWN 5}              Move down 5 cells
6             /wwh                  Create horizontal window
7             {INDICATE}            Eliminate indicator setting
```

You may want to try this macro in STEP mode, since it does not remain in any one mode for very long. You will just see the indicators flash on the screen briefly while the macro executes unless you slow it down.

The first step in the macro changes the indicator to SETUP. The macro then performs worksheet commands to set up the worksheet with a new column width adjustment and currency format.

The instruction in A4 changes the indicator to SPLIT. A horizontal second window is then created. Finally, the {INDI-CATE} command is used without an argument to return to the default setting of READY mode when the macro ends. Without this last instruction, the mode indicator would still read SPLIT when the macro ends. This indicator instruction is most useful in a long macro when you stay in a set mode for a large section of the macro. Its use there is the same as shown here.


## {PANELOFF}

The {PANELOFF} command prevents 1-2-3 from redrawing the control panel while the command is in effect.

**Format**    The format for the {PANELOFF} command is

{PANELOFF}

This command has no arguments.

**Use**    This command reduces the flicker that can occur when macro instructions are executed. It is also useful if you do not want the operator to be aware of the exact instructions executed. Even if the operator sets the STEP mode on to slow down the operation of the instructions so they can be read, the control panel will not be updated while {PANELOFF} is in effect. This command affects only the execution of the menu commands, since 1-2-3 does not use the control panel for advanced macro commands like {BRANCH} and {IF}.

**Example**     The following macro lets you determine whether you want the control panel updated as you execute the macro.

```
        A                       B
1   \p          {GETLABEL "Update Control Panel? ",Update}
2               {IF Update="Y"}{BRANCH Yes}
3               {PANELOFF}
4               {BRANCH Finish}
5   Yes         {PANELON}
6   Finish      {GOTO}D1~
7               /rfc2~~
8               /wcs12~
9               {GOTO}F3~
10              /rfp3~{DOWN 3}~
11              {QUIT}
```

This macro will provide an opportunity to see the effect of updating the panel as compared to disabling it. The first instruction expects a Y if you want to update the control panel and an N if you do not. The entry you make is stored in a range (cell) called Update, which is checked by the {IF} statement in B2. If the entry in Update is a Y, control passes to B5. If it is any other value, control passes to B3, where {PANELOFF} disables updating of the control panel. B4 branches to the subroutine called Finish to bypass the instruction that turns the control panel on. The remainder of the macro moves the cursor to D1, then invokes a format and a Column Set-Width command. The cursor is moved to F3, and another format instruction is issued before the {QUIT} instruction ends the macro.

Using this macro with the two alternative responses shows you what both ways look like to the user. You can then select the approach you think would be most appropriate for your application.

**Setup**     In addition to entering the macro instructions and naming the macro \p, you must select a cell to contain the response to the {GETLABEL} instruction. This cell should be assigned the range name Update. Range names must also be assigned to two sections of the macro. B5 is assigned the range name Yes, and B6 is assigned the range name Finish. You may wish to enter these labels in column A as documentation and assign the names with /Range Name Labels Right.

## {PANELON}

The {PANELON} command restores the default setting of having 1-2-3 update the control panel with each instruction executed.

**Format**    The format for the {PANELON} command is

{PANELON}

This command has no arguments.

**Use**    This command is useful when you want to return to control panel updating in the middle of a macro.

**Example**    The example for the {PANELOFF} instruction shows the effect of both {PANELOFF} and {PANELON} on the control panel.

## {WINDOWSOFF}

The {WINDOWSOFF} command freezes the entire screen, with the exception of the control panel.

**Format**    The format for the {WINDOWSOFF} command is

{WINDOWSOFF}

The command has no arguments.

**Use**    Using this command reduces the flicker that occurs on the screen with each new instruction executed. It also reduces execution time for long macros, since it means that 1-2-3 does not have to redraw the screen every time you move the cursor or manipulate data.

Like {PANELOFF}, {WINDOWSOFF} is also useful when you do not want the operator to be aware of each activity performed. You can change the indicator light to WAIT and return control at an appropriate point in the macro.

**Example**    The following macro will allow you to monitor the effect of updating the window or freezing it during the execution of the macro.

```
        A                              B
1   \w          {GETLABEL "Do you wish to have window updated? ",Update}
2               {IF Update="Y"}{BRANCH Yes}
3               {WINDOWSOFF}
4               {BRANCH Finish}
5   Yes         {WINDOWSON}
6   Finish      {GOTO}D1~
7               /rfc2~~
8               /wcs~
9               {GOTO}F3~
10              /rfp3~{DOWN 3}~
11              {QUIT}
```

With just one entry in response to a prompt message you will be able to change the window updating option, enabling you to see the difference between updating and freezing.

The first instruction expects a Y if you want to update the bottom portion of the screen while the macro executes and an N if you do not. The entry you make is stored in the cell range Update, which is checked by the {IF} statement in B2. If the entry is a Y, control passes to B5, where {WINDOWSON} is executed. If it is any other value, control passes to B3, where {WINDOWSOFF} disables updating of the bottom portion of the screen. B4 branches to the subroutine called Finish to bypass the instruction that turns window updating on. The remainder of the macro moves the cursor to D1, then invokes a format and a column set-width command. The cursor is moved to F3, and another format instruction is issued before the {QUIT} instruction ends the macro.

Using this macro with the two alternative responses

shows you what both ways look like to the user. You can then select the approach you think would be most appropriate for your application.

**Setup**    In addition to entering the macro instructions and naming the macro \w, you must select a cell to contain the response to the {GETLABEL} instruction. This cell should be assigned the range name Update. Range names must also be assigned to two sections of the macro. B5 is assigned the range name Yes, and B6 is assigned the range name Finish. You may wish to enter these labels in column A as documentation and assign the names with /Range Name Labels Right.

### {WINDOWSON}

The {WINDOWSON} instruction returns to the default mode of having the screen updated.

**Format**    The format of the {WINDOWSON} command is

{WINDOWSON}

This command has no arguments.

**Use**    You would use this command when you want to return to the normal mode of constant screen updates. It could be inserted near the end of a macro to have the screen updated with the current results.

**Example**    The example found under {WINDOWSOFF} provides a look at the {WINDOWSON} command as well. Take a look at this example to see the impact of both settings on the execution of a macro.

This extract from a macro shows how {WINDOWSOFF} can be used at the beginning of a macro in which entries for labels are made in a number of cells.

```
          A              B                        C
 1   \w        {WINDOWSOFF}           Turn off window updates
 2             {GOTO}K1~              Move cursor to K1
 3             /wcs20~                Set column to 20
 4             Cash~                  Enter title in K1
 5             {DOWN}                 Move cursor down
 6             Accts. Receivable      Enter next title
 7             {DOWN}                 Move cursor down
 8             Mkt. Securities        Enter title
 9             {DOWN 2}               Move down 2 cells
10             Total Current Assets~  Enter title
11             {GOTO}L1~              Move cursor to L1
12             {WINDOWSON}            Turn window updating on
```

The macro involves a considerable amount of movement
on the screen, which would show as a flicker to a watching
operator. Once the instruction in B11 is completed, the screen
is set up as shown in Figure 13-3. There will not be a significant amount of cursor movement again, so window updating
is turned back on in B12 before the remainder of the macro
proceeds.

## Macro Commands That Involve Keyboard Entries

### {?}

The {?} command is actually an advanced macro instruction,
although it was introduced in Chapter 12. As you know, it is

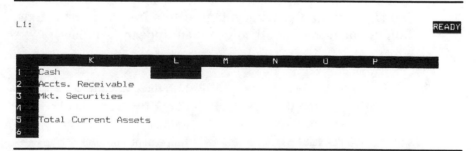

**Figure 13-3.**    Completed screen for {WINDOWSON} example

used to allow the operator to enter information from the keyboard.

**Format**    The format for the {?} command is

{?}

This command has no arguments.

**Use**    The {?} command is useful when you need to obtain a few pieces of information from the operator. If you have more extensive needs, {GETNUMBER} and {GETLABEL} are more useful, since they allow you to supply prompts as part of the instruction to clarify the exact information you want.

   If you do use the {?} instruction, you can use an instruction before it to place a prompt message in the current cell, as follows:

Enter your department number~
{?}

The number entered by the operator would replace the message placed in the current cell by the previous instruction.

**Example**    Let's enhance a macro from the last chapter that allowed you to enter a date in a cell. Frequently when you need to enter dates in cells, you want to enter an entire column of dates. The basic macro shown in Chapter 12 under the {?} command can be enhanced to add a loop for a fixed number of iterations. It might then appear as follows:

| | | |
|---|---|---|
| \d | {LET A1,0} | Initialize A1 to 0 |
| Top | {IF A1=10}{BRANCH End} | Check for max value in counter |
| | {LET A1,A1+1} | Increment counter |
| | @DATE( | Enter first part of function |
| | {?} | Pause for the entry of year |
| | , | Generate comma separator |

|          |                | |
|----------|----------------|------------------------------------|
|          | {?}            | Pause for the entry of month       |
|          | ,              | Generate comma separator           |
|          | {?}            | Pause for the entry of day         |
|          | )~             | Generate close & finalize          |
|          | {DOWN}         | Move cursor down 1 cell            |
|          | {BRANCH Top}   | Begin loop again                   |
| End      | {QUIT}         | End macro after 10 entries         |

This macro follows the basic format of the earlier one but shows how the {?} can be enhanced with the use of other instructions to produce multiple dates rather than a single entry. The {?} command will appear again in the example for {GETNUMBER}, where further flexibility will be provided by letting you enter the number of dates you wish to produce each time the macro is executed.

**Setup**     In addition to entering the macro instructions and a range name assignment of \d, you will need to assign the range names End and Top to two sections of the macro. These range names should be assigned to the appropriate cells with either /Range Name Create or /Range Name Labels Right.

## {BREAKOFF}

The {BREAKOFF} command is used to disable the BREAK key function, thereby preventing the interruption of a macro.

**Format**     The format of the {BREAKOFF} command is

{BREAKOFF}

This command has no arguments.

**Use**     Normally, CTRL-BREAK can be used to stop a macro. It will display ERROR as a mode indicator. When you press ESC, you can proceed to make changes to the worksheet from

READY mode. When you have designed an automated application and want to ensure its integrity by maintaining control throughout the operator's use of the worksheet, however, you will want to disable the Break feature by placing {BREAKOFF} in your macro. Be sure you have tested the macro before doing this, since a macro that contains an infinite loop and {BREAKOFF} can be stopped only by turning off the machine.

**Example**     Since the {BREAKOFF} command disables the ability of the CTRL-BREAK sequence to stop a runaway macro, it is dangerous. It is even more dangerous with a \0 macro that executes automatically, since there is then no way to interrupt the macro.

This may be exactly what you want if you have enabled the protection features and wish to ensure that the operator's entries are restricted to the cells you choose. Without disabling the Break function, you can prevent accidental destruction to the contents of cells, but you cannot prevent malicious destruction, since an operator can turn protection off. If you allow worksheet updating only through a controlled access macro with /Range Input statements, disable Break, and save the file at the end before erasing the worksheet, the operator cannot do anything other than what you have established. The only problem is that you cannot do anything else, either—but a correction for that problem will be presented after a discussion of what is needed to lock the operator out of illegal changes.

The macro reads as follows:

```
         A                                          B
23  \0          Insert {BREAKOFF} here
24              {GETLABEL "Do you wish to update employee names? ",R1}
25              {IF R1<>"Y"}{BRANCH Address}
26              /riA2..B20~
27  Address     {GETLABEL "Do you wish to update employee addresses? ",R2}
28              {IF R2<>"Y"}{BRANCH Phone}
29              /riC2..F20~
30  Phone       {GETLABEL "Do you wish to update employee phone numbers? ",R3}
31              {IF R3<>"Y"}{BRANCH Salary}
32              /riG2..G20~
33  Salary      {GETLABEL "Enter password to update salaries ",R4}
34              {IF R4=Z1}{BRANCH Update}
35  End         {BREAKON}{QUIT}
36
37  Update      /riH2..H20~
38              {BREAKON}{QUIT}
```

The first instruction, in B23, will eventually contain {BREAKOFF}, but it is best not to add this until you have tested the macro. From here the macro controls the updating of various sections of an employee database. Certain fields will not be able to be changed, others can be changed as desired, and salaries are updateable only with the correct password.

The {GETLABEL} instruction in B24 checks to see if the operator wishes to update the section of the database that includes employee names. If the response is Y, the macro will proceed to the /Range Input instruction in B26. The names in the database for our example are located in columns A and B, and this instruction will allow the operator to change any of them.

If the operator did not wish to alter any names and responded with N, the Address section of the macro would be executed next. Again the operator would respond to the {GETLABEL} prompt, and if he or she wished to make updates to this section, a new range input instruction would be established.

The next section is Phone, which will allow the updating of phone numbers in the same manner. When the operator is finished with this section, salary will be next. This section functions a little differently in that the {GETLABEL} instruction expects a password. This password must match with the one stored in cell Z1. Since Break is disabled, the operator must know the password because it is impossible to interrupt the macro to look at the contents of Z1. If the operator's entry matches the entry stored in Z1, the macro branches to Update and allows updates to the section of the worksheet where salaries are stored. In our example, this is H2..H20, but of course it could be changed to any appropriate range.

{BREAKOFF} is cancelled with {BREAKON} before ending, although this is not mandatory, since ending a macro automatically disables it. This macro leaves the worksheet vulnerable to unauthorized changes after the update is completed, since the worksheet would still be on the screen and anything could be changed. To prevent this, the two {BREAKON}{QUIT} instruction sequences could be replaced with /fsemploy~r/wey to both save the worksheet and erase memory. If you do this, you have forever locked both the operator and yourself out of this worksheet. A fix for this problem is to store another password in a different cell and request the password right before the file save. If the password is entered correctly, {BREAKON} is executed and another instruction asks if you have further changes. The changed ending for the macro might appear like this:

```
{GETLABEL "Enter special password for further updates ",R10}
{IF R10<>Z2}/fsemploy~r/wey
{BREAKON}
{QUIT}
```

**Setup**    There are a number of steps to be completed in addition to the entry and naming of the macro. These are as follows:

• The cells where you wish to allow entries must be unprotected with /Range Unprotect.

• Worksheet protection should be enabled with /Worksheet Global Protection Enable.

• Range names of Address, Phone, Salary, End, and Update must be assigned to B27, B30, B33, B35, and B37 respectively.

• The password to allow salary updates must be stored in Z1. Although you can assign any password you wish, LOCK was used when this macro was tested.

• You may wish to freeze titles on the screen, since this will affect the display when the /Range Input statements are executed. Test the macro once and then decide. If you wish to make this change, use the command /Worksheet Titles. You may decide to incorporate this command into the macro to allow the area of frozen titles to change for each section.

## {BREAKON}

The {BREAKON} command restores the Break function so that you can press CTRL-BREAK to interrupt a macro.

**Format**    The format of the {BREAKON} command is

{BREAKON}

This command has no arguments.

**Use**    You may elect to disable the Break function during part of a macro and then restore its operation for a later section such as printing or data entry. The Break function is always restored at the end of a macro.

**Example**    The example found under {BREAKOFF} should be reviewed for an explanation and example of the {BREAK-ON} instruction. Since {BREAKON} is the default setting, this instruction is needed only to restore the default after using {BREAKOFF}.

## {GET}

The {GET} command is designed to accept the entry of a single character from the keyboard.

**Format**    The format of the {GET} command is

{GET *location*}

where *location* is the storage location for the single character you enter from the keyboard. Your entry can be an alphabetic character, a numeric digit, or any other key, including one of the special function keys such as F9 (CALC) or F2 (EDIT).

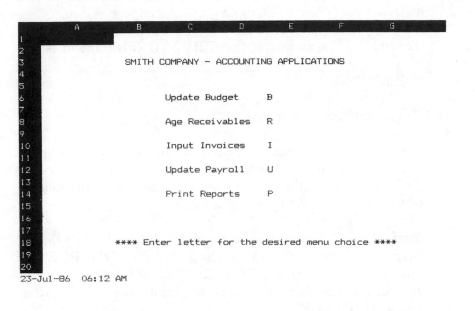

Figure 13-4.     Menu for {GET} example

**Use**    This command provides another option for keyboard input. It offers an advantage over commands like {?}, {GET-LABEL}, and {GETNUMBER} in that it can restrict the entry to a single character. It lacks the ability to display a prompt message as {GETNUMBER} and {GETLABEL} can, however. It can be the ideal solution for situations where you wish to build your own full-screen menu and expect a one-letter code for each selection.

**Example**    The screen in Figure 13-4 presents a full-screen menu that offers selections in Smith Company's accounting application. Letter selections represent a budget update, aging of receivables, and other accounting functions. Instructions at the bottom of the screen tell the operator to enter the letter representing his or her menu choice.

The following macro works with this menu.

```
        J                                    K
1     \g          {BLANK A20}
2                 {INDICATE}
3                 {GOTO}A1~
4                 {GET Choice}
5                 {IF Choice="B"}{BRANCH Budget}
6                 {IF Choice="R"}{BRANCH Rec}
7                 {IF Choice="I"}{BRANCH Inv}
8                 {IF Choice="U"}{BRANCH Payroll}
9                 {IF Choice="P"}{BRANCH Report}
10                {INDICATE "ERROR"}
11                {LET A20,"Incorrect entry re-execute macro"}{CALC}
12
13    Budget      {GOTO}Q1~
14                {GETLABEL "Budget routine",Z1}
15                {CALC}
16
17    Rec         {GOTO}Q1~
18                {GETLABEL "Receivables Routine",Z1}
19                {CALC}
```

The macro begins with a {BLANK} instruction that makes sure that A20 has been erased. This cell must be erased because it is the cell that will be used to present an error message to the user when incorrect entries have been made. You will want to start each new selection process without an entry in this cell.

The {INDICATE} instruction in J2 is used to ensure that the mode indicator is in its default state, without any previous displays in this area of the screen. Again, this is important because the mode indicator will be set to ERROR if an incorrect response is made.

The cursor is next moved to A1 to ensure that it is positioned correctly to allow the display of the entire screen. The {GET} instruction accepts a single-character response and stores it in a cell that has previously been assigned the range name Choice.

The next five instructions check the value of Choice and branch to appropriate subroutines. Only two of these subroutines are shown in the listing, but they all would follow the same pattern. They have been established as shell routines that do nothing more at this time than move the cursor and display a message letting the operator know what routine has been reached. These shells would be expanded later to include a full set of instructions to do the appropriate processing.

If none of the branches is taken, this means that the

operator entered an unacceptable character. If this happens, the mode indicator is set to ERROR in K10, and an error message is placed in A20 with the {LET} instruction, which assigns a string value to A20. This produces the display shown in Figure 13-5.

### {GETLABEL}

The {GETLABEL} command is used to permit the entry of a character string from the keyboard in response to a prompt message.

**Format**     The format for the {GETLABEL} command is

{GETLABEL *prompt message,location*}

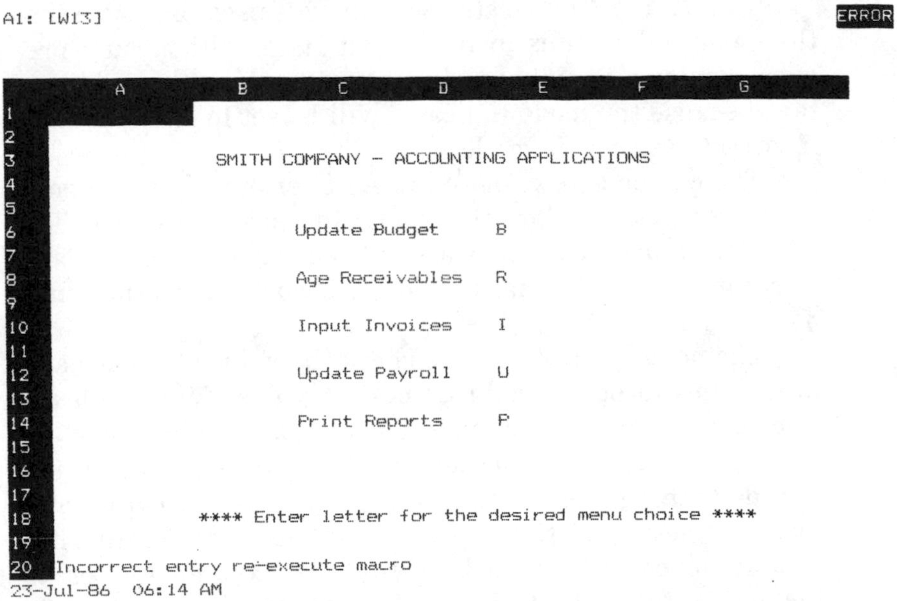

---

A1: [W13]                                                                 ERROR

```
       A          B          C          D          E          F          G
 1
 2
 3              SMITH COMPANY - ACCOUNTING APPLICATIONS
 4
 5
 6              Update Budget       B
 7
 8              Age Receivables     R
 9
10              Input Invoices      I
11
12              Update Payroll      U
13
14              Print Reports       P
15
16
17
18          **** Enter letter for the desired menu choice ****
19
20 Incorrect entry re-execute macro
23-Jul-86  06:14 AM
```

---

**Figure 13-5.**     Error message due to incorrect entry for {GET}

The argument *prompt message* is a string that must be enclosed in double quotation marks if it contains a character that can be used as an argument separator (, or ;). The string will display in the control panel. Its length is limited to the 72 characters at the top of the control panel. If you supply a longer string, it will scroll off the screen. The string must be stored in the macro itself; it cannot be stored in a cell and referenced.

The argument *location* is a reference to a cell, range, or range name where the information entered from the keyboard will be stored. Up to 80 characters will be accepted as input. If a range is supplied for the argument, the character string entered will be stored in the upper left cell of the range.

**Use**     The {GETLABEL} command stores your entry as a left justified label in the location specified. This feature makes this command appropriate for numeric entries as well when you want them placed at the left edge of the cell so they can be read as macro keystrokes.

You might use this command to obtain the name of a vendor with the following instruction:

{GETLABEL "Enter Vendor Name...",A2}~

The name you enter will be stored as a left justified label in A2 in this instance.

**Example**     Figure 13-6 shows a screen that might be used to capture data entry information. The following instructions are an extract from a macro that might be used with this data entry screen.

```
        J                           K
1    \e        {GOTO}C3~
2              {GETLABEL "Enter Name (Last, First) ",C3}
3              {GOTO}C5~
4              {GETLABEL "Enter Street Address ",C5}
5              {GOTO}C7~
6              {GETLABEL "Enter City ",C7}
7              {GOTO}C9~
8              {GETLABEL "Enter State ",C9}
9              {GOTO}C11~
10             {GETLABEL "Enter Zip ",C11}~
```

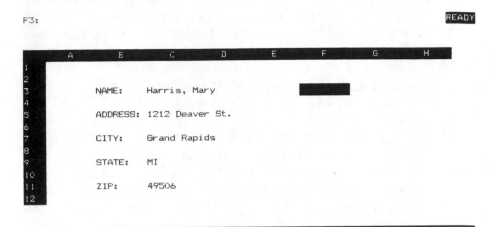

**Figure 13-6.**    Data entry screen for {GETLABEL} example

The first macro instruction moves the cursor to C3. The {GETLABEL} instruction that follows presents a prompt and stores the information in C3. The cell address was added for clarity. The remaining instructions all follow the same pattern, providing a prompt for each new piece of information required and storing it in the current cell. At the end of these instructions, you might wish to add further instructions to move this data to the next available database record within the worksheet or perform some additional manipulations with the data.

The second example for the {GETLABEL} command shows its use with numeric data that you wish stored as a left justified label. The macro reads as follows:

```
        H                               I
18    \l          {LET P1,0}
19                {GETNUMBER "How many dates would you like to enter? ",P2}
20    Begin       {IF P1=P2}{BRANCH End}
21                {LET P1,P1+1}
22                {GETLABEL "Enter month number ",I28}
23                {GETLABEL "Enter day number ",I30}
24                {GETLABEL "Enter year number, e.g. 86 ",I26}
25                @DATE(
26                86
27                ,
28                1
29                ,
30                12
31                )~
32                {DOWN}
33                {BRANCH Begin}
34    End         {QUIT}
```

**724**

The first instruction initializes a counter to zero. The {GETNUMBER} instruction that follows asks how many dates you wish to enter. The response you make will control the number of iterations performed by the macro. As soon as the counter is equal to the number of iterations you have requested, the {IF} instruction in the third line will branch to End.

Until then, each cycle will increment the counter by 1. The cycle includes three {GETLABEL} instructions that you can use to obtain the date components in a convenient sequence. Since you are storing these components in worksheet cells, you are not restricted to the year, month, and day sequence required by the @DATE function. The current instructions obtain month, day, and year, respectively. These pieces of information are stored in a different sequence than they are entered so they will be in the correct order for the @DATE function. The macro then shows the entry of a date into a cell. The cells referred to in the macro (I26, I28, and I30) show the year, month, and day number from the last time the macro was executed.

After the date entry is finalized, the cursor is moved down one cell and control branches to the top of the loop, which is named Begin. The macro will end when the {IF} instruction at the top of the loop encounters the equal condition and branches to End, which will execute {QUIT}.

**Setup**    The first macro example would need to have the menu created before the macro was executed. The macro also assumes that the cursor is positioned in A1 before the macro begins. You could add a {GOTO} instruction at the top of the macro to eliminate this assumption if you choose.

The second macro described in this section requires that range names be established for Begin and End before the macro is executed.

### {GETNUMBER}

The {GETNUMBER} command is used to permit the entry of numeric information from the keyboard in response to a prompt message.

**Format**    The format for the {GETNUMBER} command is

{GETNUMBER *prompt message,location*}

The argument *prompt message* is a string that must be enclosed in double quotation marks if it contains a character that can be used as an argument separator (, or ;). The string will display in the control panel. Its length is limited to the 72 characters at the top of the control panel. If you supply a longer string, it will scroll off the screen. The string must be stored in the macro itself; it cannot be stored in a cell and referenced.

The argument *location* is a reference to a cell, range, or range name where the information entered from the keyboard will be stored. A numeric value, formula, or range name referencing a numeric value can be entered. If a range is supplied for the argument, the numeric value entered will be stored in the upper left cell of the range.

**Use**    You might use this pair of instructions to obtain the price and quantity for a purchase order:

{GETNUMBER "Enter the price.....",Price}~
{GETNUMBER "Enter the quantity.....",Quantity}~

The values you enter in response to these two instructions would be stored in the cells with the range names Price and Quantity.

**Example**    The following macro is another macro that can be used to enter a built-in function like @DATE.

```
          H                          I
1    \D        {LET P1,0}
2              {GETNUMBER "How many dates would you like to enter? ",P2}
3    Top       {IF P1=P2}{BRANCH End}
4              {LET P1,P1+1}
5              @DATE(
6              {?}
7              ,
8              {?}
9              ,
10             {?}
11             )~
12             {DOWN}
13             {BRANCH Top}
14   End       {QUIT}
```

This macro uses the {?} form of entry, which does not provide prompts. You can still choose the number of iterations you want, however. The first instruction initializes a counter. Next, the number of iterations is determined by requesting input from the operator. The iterative section or loop begins with the label Top. An {IF} instruction checks for equality between the counter and the number of iterations requested. If they are equal, a branch to End executes a {QUIT} to stop the macro.

Until the equal condition is reached, the macro stays within the loop and enters the @DATE function in worksheet cells. The operator provides the year, month, and day numbers, and the macro adds the fixed characters needed for each function. At the end of the loop, the cursor is moved down a cell and control branches to the top of the macro.

### {LOOK}

The {LOOK} command checks the keyboard buffer for characters and places the first character in this buffer as an entry in location. It is similar to {GET}, except that with {LOOK} the operator can type the entry ahead and the macro will still find it.

**Format**    The format of the {LOOK} command is

{LOOK *location*}

where *location* is a cell address or range name used to store the character from the type-ahead buffer. If {LOOK} finds the buffer blank, it erases the location cell.

**Use**    {LOOK} does not suspend macro execution waiting for an entry, as the {GET} instruction does. Normally you will use {LOOK} within a loop, allowing a certain amount of time for an entry before canceling the application. You may or may not wish to update the file before canceling.

**Example**    The following macro uses the {LOOK} instruction to process a menu request from the same application designed for {GET} earlier in this section.

```
               I                    J
1    \ l                 {INDICATE}{GOTO}A1~
2                        {LET Time,@NOW}
3    Keep_Looking        {LOOK Selection}
4                        {IF Selection<>""}{BRANCH Process}
5                        {IF @NOW<{Time+@TIME{10,10,0}}}{Branch Keep_Looking}
6                        {INDICATE "ERROR"}
7                        {LET A20, "No selection made - Reexecute macro"}
8                        {QUIT}
9
10   Process             Macro instructions to process menu selection
```

Unlike the example with {GET}, this macro will not wait beyond a specific amount of time. It uses a loop to control the time it will wait if the selection is not in the type-ahead buffer.

The macro begins by setting the indicator to its default setting and moving the cursor to A1. It then places the current date and time in a cell named Time.

The next instruction begins the loop for checking the type-ahead buffer. {LOOK} is executed and stores the first character from the type-ahead buffer, if present, in Selection. The next instruction, in J4, checks to see if anything has been placed in Selection. If anything is stored there, the macro branches to Process. If the cell is empty, the macro continues to the {IF} instruction in J5. This {IF} instruction compares the current time against the time stored at the beginning in Time plus an acceptable wait interval. For this example, the wait time was set at 10 minutes. If the current time is less than 10 minutes after the beginning time, the macro will keep looking for an entry by branching to the Keep—Looking subroutine. If the chosen time interval has elapsed, the macro will set the indicator to ERROR and display an error message in A20. Alternative strategies might be to save the file, clear memory, and quit 1-2-3. The Process section of this macro has not been completed but would contain instructions similar to those in the {GET} example shown earlier.

**Setup**    The macro requires that cells for the storage of variables be named Time and Selection. The range names Keep—Looking and Process must be assigned to locations in the macro as shown.

## {MENUBRANCH}

The {MENUBRANCH} command allows you to branch to a location containing information required to build a customized menu. Once this branch occurs, the instructions the macro will execute will depend on your menu selections.

**Format**    The format of the {MENUBRANCH} command is

{MENUBRANCII *location*}

where *location* is a cell address or range name that represents the upper left cell in the area for menu storage. This area must be a minimum of three rows deep and two columns wide. You may have up to eight columns of menu information.

**Use**    Information for the customized menu must be organized according to a specific set of rules. These rules are as follows:

• The top row of the menu area will contain the menu selection words that you wish to use. Each of these words should begin with a different character, just as in 1-2-3's menus. This allows you to enter the first letter of an option to make your selection as well as to point to the options. Menu selection words are entered one to a cell, should not exceed eight characters each, and may use up to eight cells across, providing eight menu options.

• The second row of the menu area contains the expanded description for each menu choice that will display when you point to the menu selection. As you make one label entry in each cell and move across, it is likely that the entries will appear truncated, since they are long labels. Although you will want to keep your descriptions brief, do not be concerned about this apparent overlap. Each description should be put in the appropriate column for the menu choice.

The last step is placing the remainder of the macro instructions appropriate for each choice in the column with the menu item and description. These instructions should begin in the cell immediately under the expanded description and can extend as far down the column as you want. They can also contain a branch to a subroutine.

**Example**    Figure 13-7 shows a menu. There are four different selections in the menu, and it is duplicated four times in the figure so that you can see the expanded description for each of the four choices.

The macro that created this custom menu is shown in Figure 13-8. The macro begins with the {MENUBRANCH} instruction and has all the menu options stored at a location named Select. The cell J3 is the one to which this name was

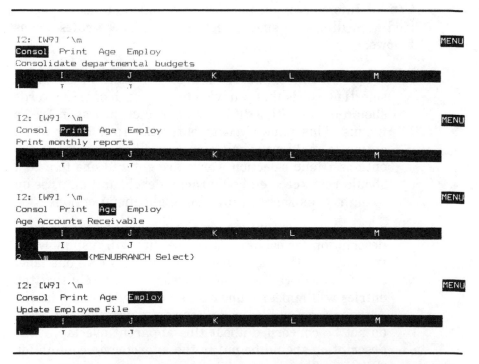

**Figure 13-7.**    Custom menu with expanded descriptions

```
          I         J            K          L          M
  1    \m     {MENUBRANCH Select}
  2
  3    Select  Consol       Print       Age        Employ
  4            Consolidate depPrint monthly rAge Accounts RUpdate Employee File
  5            {BRANCH Con}  {BRANCH Prt}  {Branch Rec}  {BRANCH Employ}
  6
  7    Con     {INDICATE "CON"}
  8
  9    Prt     {INDICATE "PRT"}
 10
 11    Rec     {INDICATE "REC"}
 12
 13    Employ  {INDICATE "EMP"}
```

**Figure 13-8.** Macro for creation of custom menu

attached, although the menu selections extend down from
there and to the right.

The menu selections are shown in J3..M3 with the
words Consol, Print, Age, and Employ. As required, each
word begins with a different letter. The expanded descriptions appear in cells J4..M4. They are as follows:

J4    Consolidate department budgets
K4    Print monthly reports
L4    Age Accounts Receivable
M4    Update Employee File

As you enter the second through the fourth descriptions, it
will appear that you are writing on top of previous ones, but
you need not be concerned. Each description is stored as a
label in the appropriate cell.

The last step in creating a menu macro is to fill in the
cells underneath the descriptions with all the instructions for
each choice. In our example these instructions occupy only
row 5, but the selections could extend down in the column to
row 50 or longer.

In our example each option has a branch to a different
subroutine. At this time the routines are simply shells to

allow you to check the logic. The only action taken in each shell is to change the indicator to the entry specified.

**Setup**     The entire menu section must be entered before a macro like this can be tested. It is the only example of a macro that can extend across as many as eight columns. Actually, it is eight individual macros in adjacent columns.

All the names listed in column I must be assigned to the respective cells in column J. /Range Name Labels Right is the easiest way to handle this task.

### {MENUCALL}

The {MENUCALL} command displays the same custom menu as {MENUBRANCH}, but it executes the menu as a call rather than as a branch. This affects the execution flow at the end of the menu processing. With {MENUBRANCH}, the macro ends when the code for the selected option completes. With {MENUCALL}, control returns to the statement following {MENUCALL} in the main code for the macro, and execution begins again at that location.

**Format**     The format of the {MENUCALL} command is

{MENUCALL *location*}

where *location* is a cell address or range name that represents the upper left cell in the area for menu storage. This area must be a minimum of three rows deep and two columns wide. You may have up to eight columns of menu information.

**Use**     Information for the menu must be organized according to a specific set of rules. These rules are as follows:

• The top row of the menu area will contain the menu selection words that you wish to use. Each of these words should begin with a different character, just as in 1-2-3's menus. This allows you to enter the first letter of an option to make your selection as well as to point to the options. Menu selection words are entered one to a cell, should not exceed eight characters each, and may use up to eight cells across, providing eight menu options.

• The second row of the menu area contains the expanded description for each menu choice that will display when you point to the menu selection. As you make one label entry in each cell and move across, it is likely that the entries will appear truncated, since they are long labels. Although you will want to keep your descriptions brief, do not be concerned about this apparent overlap. Each description should be put in the appropriate column for the menu choice.

The last step is placing the remainder of the macro instructions appropriate for each choice in the column with the menu item and description. These instructions should begin in the cell immediately under the expanded description and can extend as far down the column as you want. They can also contain a branch to a subroutine.

**Example**    The example would be exactly the same as the one for {MENUBRANCH}, except that you would expect to see statements after {MENUCALL} in the main code. These would be executed after the menu processing had completed.

## {WAIT}

The {WAIT} command will halt the execution of a macro until a specified time.

**Format**    The format of the {WAIT} command is

{WAIT *time_serial_number*}

where *time_serial_number* is a decimal value that represents the serial time number for the time of day when you wish execution to continue. This value can be computed by adding a time value to the value computed with @NOW to create a fixed delay. You may, as an example, want to display information on the screen for 30 seconds to allow time for it to be read. You could use this instruction to accomplish that:

{WAIT @NOW+@TIME(0,0,30)}

This will add 30 seconds to the current time and wait until that time is reached before continuing execution. While 1-2-3 is waiting, the mode indicator will say WAIT.

**Example**  If you want an operator to read the instruction screen shown in Figure 13-9, you have several choices for proceeding after the information is displayed. You can have the operator enter a character to proceed and use the {GET} instruction to process this. In this situation, that operator may move hurriedly past the screen without reading it. Using {WAIT} allows you to freeze the screen containing this information for a period of time, increasing the chance that

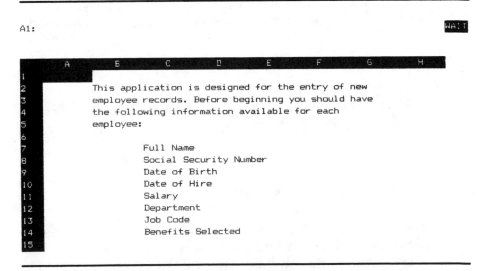

**Figure 13-9.**    Instruction screen for {WAIT} example

the information will be read. If you elect to use this approach, these instructions might appear in your macro:

```
{GOTO}A1                          Position cursor at the display
{WAIT @NOW+@TIME(0,0,25)}   Wait 25 seconds

. . .
        Macro instructions to be executed after wait
. . .
```

## Macro Commands That Affect Flow of Execution

### {BRANCH}

The {BRANCH} command allows you to move the flow of execution in your macro to a new location.

**Format**    The format of the {BRANCH} command is

{BRANCH *location*}

where location is a cell address or a range name that tells 1-2-3 where the next keystroke to be executed by the macro is stored. If you specify a range name that refers to a range of cells, 1-2-3 will begin execution with the keystrokes in the upper left cell of the range.

**Use**    {BRANCH} is frequently used with a condition test to change the flow of execution. As an example, you might have the following entry in your macro:

```
{IF A1>10}{BRANCH End}
  . . .
  . . .
End {QUIT}
```

In this case you may have been using A1 as a counter, and when A1 exceeds 10, your task is finished. This sequence of instructions would branch to End at that time and execute the {QUIT} instruction stored there.

**Example**    The following listing is an excerpt from a macro that combines the data in four files.

```
        A                      B
1    \c           {GETLABEL "Begin combine? ",H21}
2                 {IF H21<>"Y"}{BRANCH Stop}
3                 {HOME}
4                 /fcaeREGION1~
5                 /fcaeREGION2~
6                 /fcaeREGION3~
7                 /fcaeREGION4~
8    Stop         {CALC}{QUIT}
```

The excerpt begins by asking the operator whether to proceed with the consolidation. The logical {IF} in the next line checks for any value other than Y and uses the {BRANCH} instruction to alter the execution flow to Stop if such a value is found. Stop recalculates the worksheet and ends the macro.

Assuming a Y was entered, the cursor is moved to the Home position, and the four files are combined with the Add option. The worksheet is then recalculated, and the macro ends.

**Note**    {BRANCH} is frequently confused with {GOTO}, but they are not the same. {GOTO} repositions the cursor without affecting the execution of the macro. {BRANCH} alters the macro's execution flow but does not move the cursor.

## {DEFINE}

The {DEFINE} command allocates space for arguments to be passed to subroutines and establishes the type of information they will contain.

**Format**    The format of the {DEFINE} command is

{DEFINE *location1:type1,location2:type2.....locationn:typen*}

The argument *location* is a cell where the value being passed to the subroutine can be stored. This cell can be specified with a cell address or a range name. A range name is preferable, since it will automatically be updated when the worksheet is restructured. If you specify a range name that references a group of cells, the upper left cell in the range will be used for storage.

The argument *type* tells 1-2-3 whether value or label data is to be passed to the subroutine. Type may be entered as either value or label, like this:

{DEFINE *Price:value,Supplier:label*}

where *Price* and *Supplier* are range names that will be used for passing the arguments to the subroutine. Price will contain value data, and Supplier will contain labels.

**Example**     If you wanted to call a subroutine and pass it three numeric arguments, the subroutine would require a {DEFINE} statement to specify storage locations for the three arguments. Since you will want these arguments treated as values, you will want to specify the type, because string is the type default. If you specify nothing for type, the values will be placed in their locations as labels. Your {DEFINE} statement for this example might appear as follows:

{DEFINE Z1:*value,*Z2:*value,*Z3:*value*}

If any of the arguments passed to these locations are arithmetic formulas, they will be evaluated before storage, since the value type has been specified.

For an additional example, look at the description of {*routine*} later in this section.

### {DISPATCH}

The {DISPATCH} command allows you to use the contents of a cell to determine the location to which to branch.

**Format**    The format of the {DISPATCH} command is

{DISPATCH *location*}

where location is a cell address or a range name that refers to a single cell. This cell in turn should contain a cell address or a range name of another cell. {DISPATCH} will read this information from the cell and branch to the location represented by its contents.

**Use**    This command is useful when you need to set up a variable branching situation based on the contents of data fields or other worksheet results. It differs from the {BRANCH} command in that {BRANCH} immediately executes the instructions in the cells beginning at location, whereas {DISPATCH} reads the location cell to determine the final branch location at which it will execute instructions.

**Example**    The macro shown here provides an example of {DISPATCH}.

```
         A                        B
1    \d          {IF Due_Date>@NOW}{LET Routine,"Not_Due"}
2                {IF Due_Date<=@NOW}{LET Routine,"Over_Due"}
3                {CALC}{DISPATCH Routine}
4
5    Not_Due  {GETLABEL "Account not yet due",A18}
6
7
8    Over_Due {GETLABEL "*** Account Overdue ***",A18}
```

The macro is designed to take two different paths, depending on whether the date in Due—Date is greater than today's date. The first instruction checks Due—Date against @NOW. If Due—Date is greater, it places the value Not— Due in the cell named Routine. If the opposite condition is true, the value Over—Due is placed in Routine.

The worksheet is calculated to place these values in Routine, so you can see them display if you use the STEP mode for this macro. {DISPATCH} is the next instruction. It reads the entry in Routine and then branches to the appropriate location. Again the two routines have been set up here as shells, but they could be expanded easily to handle whatever tasks you require.

## {FOR}

The {FOR} command permits you to execute the code at a given location numerous times through a loop that it establishes.

**Format**     The format of the {FOR} command is

{FOR *counter,start,stop,increment,starting—location*}

The argument *counter* is a location within the worksheet that the {FOR} instruction can use to count the number of iterations performed. {FOR} will initialize this location with the value you specify for start.

The argument *start* is the initial value for counter.

The argument *stop* is the stopping value for counter. Counter will never exceed this value.

The argument *increment* is the amount that should be added to counter for each iteration of the loop.

The argument *starting—location* is a cell address or range name that specifies the location of the routine to be executed repetitively.

None of these values should be altered from within the subroutine. Start, stop, and increment are maintained internally by 1-2-3.

**Use**     You have seen examples earlier in this chapter of loops created without the {FOR} statement. Using {FOR} can make looping tasks easier, since it automatically handles initialization of the counter, increments it with each iteration, and checks for the last execution of the loop. When you create an iterative process outside of {FOR}, you must manage these tasks yourself.

The rules used by {FOR} for processing a loop are as follows:

• Before each pass through the loop, {FOR} compares counter and stop. If counter is less than or equal to stop, the loop is processed. If counter is greater than stop, control passes to the instruction following {FOR}.

- At the end of the starting location routine or at a {RETURN}, control will pass to the top of the loop. At this time, counter will be increased by increment.

- If stop is less than start, the loop will not be executed. A loop with an increment of 0 is an infinite loop; it can be stopped only by pressing CTRL-BREAK.

- If {QUIT} or {FORBREAK} is used at the end of the loop rather than {RETURN}, the loop will end after the first pass.

**Example** The following macro is designed to enter a column of numbers from the numeric keypad and to sum the numbers once they are entered. An arbitrary limit of 20 numbers was established, but if you want to stop sooner, enter **z**.

The macro instructions are as follows:

```
         A                      B
1    \f        {FOR Counter,1,20,Numbers}
2              /re~
3              @SUM(
4              {UP}{END}{UP}.{END}{DOWN}
5              )~
6
7    Numbers   {?}~
8              {IF @CELLPOINTER("contents")="z"}{FORBREAK}
9              {DOWN}
```

The first instruction sets up the loop with an initial value of 1, an increment of 1, and a stop value of 20. A cell named Counter is used to store the number of iterations performed, and Numbers is the location of the code that begins the loop.

Numbers will be executed next. In every iteration, it will expect you to enter a value. You may use the numeric keypad, since the directional movement keys will have been disabled with NUM LOCK.

The next instruction checks to see whether the current cell contains a z. If it does, the {FOR} loop ends, regardless of the number of iterations completed, and control returns to B2.

Assuming a z was not entered, the cursor moves down one cell. The counter is incremented by 1, and the loop begins again.

When control returns to B2, the current cell is erased. It will either be blank already or contain a z, depending on how the loop ended. The @SUM instruction is added to this cell. The complete list of numbers you entered will then be added and the @SUM function finalized.

**Setup**    The range name Numbers must be assigned to B7. You must also assign a range name to Counter. Before executing the macro, you should position your cursor in the desired location for the column of numbers to be entered and turn on NUM LOCK, since this cannot be done from the macro.

## {FORBREAK}

The {FORBREAK} command can be used to cancel processing of a {FOR} loop before the stop value is reached.

**Format**    The format of the {FORBREAK} command is

{FORBREAK}

This command has no arguments.

**Use**    Normally {FORBREAK} is used in conjunction with an {IF} statement that checks the value a variable and, on a certain condition, exits the loop. As an example, you may want to process a loop 20 times or until the account balance is zero. {FORBREAK} could be executed based on a test of the account balance.

**Example**    The {FOR} example also contains an example of a {FORBREAK} instruction that is capable of ending the loop early.

## {IF}

The {IF} command will execute the command on the same line with {IF} conditionally.

**Format**   The format of the {IF} command is

{IF *condition*}

where condition is any expression with either a numeric or a string value.

**Use**   The statement on the same line as the {IF} statement is treated as a THEN clause: "IF the expression is true, THEN the instruction following is executed." Any numeric expression is considered true as long as it is not the numeric value zero. A False condition, blank cells, ERR, NA, and string values all evaluate as zero.

The instructions on the line after {IF} are regarded as the ELSE clause. Normally the THEN clause will contain a {BRANCH}; otherwise, the macro will execute the instructions in the ELSE clause after completing the THEN instructions.

**Example**   The macro shown here provides an example of the {IF} command.

```
        A              B                              C
1   \h       {GOTO}I1~                    Move cursor to read directions
2            {GET K1}                     Get type
3            {IF K1="C"}{LET C15,I20}     Check Budget Year/Set heading
4            {IF K1="P"}{LET C15,I19}     Set heading for previous year
5            {GOTO}B16~                   Move cursor to B16
6            ~QTR 1                       Enter ~QTR 1
7            {RIGHT}QTR 2                 Move cursor right & enter ~QTR 2
8            {RIGHT}QTR 3                 Move cursor right & enter ~QTR 3
9            {RIGHT}QTR 4                 Move cursor right & enter ~QTR 4
10           {RIGHT}~TOTAL                Move cursor right & enter ~TOTAL
11           {END}{LEFT} .                Move to end on left (i.e. B16)
12           {DOWN}                       Move down 1 cell
```

The macro establishes a heading for a budget report and uses the {IF} command to determine which budget year to print at the top of the report.

At the beginning of the macro the cursor is moved to I1, where directions are displayed. The macro uses {GET} to wait for a single-character entry of C for current or P for previous.

The {IF} statements in B3 and B4 check the character entered to determine the proper heading to use and then place it in C15. The statement following each {IF} on the same line will be executed only if the condition shown for that {IF} is true.

The macro then proceeds to complete the remainder of the heading after the variable portion is entered. At the end of the macro, the cursor is positioned immediately beneath the first quarter heading to be ready for your first entry.

**Setup**    The macro expects to find headings for the previous and current budget years in I19 and I20, respectively.


## {ONERROR}

The {ONERROR} command allows you to intercept errors, or process them yourself, during macro execution.

**Format**    The format of the {ONERROR} command is

{ONERROR *location,message—location*}

The argument *location* is the location you wish 1-2-3 to branch to for error processing when an error is encountered.

The argument *message—location* is a cell containing the message that 1-2-3 will display at the bottom of the screen when an error occurs. This argument is optional, but if you do not supply it, you will not be able to determine what type of error occurred.

**Use**    Since the {ONERROR} command will not be effective until 1-2-3 has executed it within the flow of the macro, you will want to place it near the beginning of your macro. It will remain in effect until another {ONERROR} command is executed, an error is encountered, CTRL-BREAK is pressed, or the macro ends. Since CTRL-BREAK registers as an error, you can intercept Break requests without using {BREAKOFF}. Once {ONERROR} is used to intercept an error, it will not normally be available to be used again in the same macro. If you want to reinstate {ONERROR} after using it, the routine at location should contain another {ONERROR} command.

## {QUIT}

The {QUIT} command is used to terminate a macro.

**Format**  The format of the {QUIT} command is

{QUIT}

This command has no arguments.

**Example**  The {QUIT} command can be used as a value at the end of a condition test, for example, {IF A1>10}{QUIT}. When the condition evaluates as True, the macro, including all its subroutines, will end.

## {RESTART}

The {RESTART} command cancels the execution of the current subroutine and eliminates all pointers to routines that called it so it cannot return.

**Format**  The format of the {RESTART} command is

{RESTART}

This command has no arguments.

**Example**  You can include this command anywhere within a called subroutine and it will immediately cancel the call, complete the routine, and continue executing from that point downward. All upward pointers to higher-level routines are canceled.

## {RETURN}

The {RETURN} command is used to return from a subroutine to the calling routine. It is used in conjunction with {MENUCALL} and {routine}. A blank cell or one containing a numeric value will have the same effect as {RETURN} when it is encountered in a subroutine.

**Format**   The format for the {RETURN} command is

{RETURN}

This command has no arguments.

**Example**   Placing {RETURN} anywhere in a called subroutine sends the flow of control back to the instruction beneath the one that called the subroutine. Unlike {RESTART}, {RETURN} does not cancel upward pointers. Check the example under the {routine} command for further information on the use of {RETURN}.

**Note**   Do not confuse {RETURN} with {QUIT}. {RETURN} continues processing after returning to the calling routine. {QUIT} ends the macro at the point it is encountered. With {QUIT}, no further instructions are processed.

### {routine}

This command calls a specified subroutine. Its format is different from that of all the other commands in that it does not contain a keyword, only the argument routine and any optional value arguments you may choose to use.

**Format**   The format of the *{routine}* command is

*{routine argument1,argument2,argumentn}*

The *routine* is a range name assigned to a single cell. This name should not be the same as any of the function key or cursor movement key names, such as {UP}, {EDIT}, or {CALC}.

The *arguments* are optional values or strings passed to the subroutine. They must have corresponding entries in a {DEFINE} statement.

**Example**   The following macro provides an example of the use of a subroutine call.

```
                  A                B
1      \r                 {GETNUMBER "How many items did you buy? ",K1}
2                         {LET Counter,0}
3                         {LET K5,0}{LET K6,0}
4                         {Purchase K1}
5                         {INDICATE "DONE"}
6                         {GOTO}Q1~The total purchased is :~
7                         {RIGHT 3}+K6~/rfc2~~
8                         {QUIT}
9
10     Purchase           {DEFINE K2:value}
11                        {IF Counter=K2}{BRANCH End}
12                        {GETNUMBER "Enter Purchase Amount ",K5}
13                        {LET K6,K6+K5}
14                        {LET Counter,Counter+1}
15                        {BRANCH Purchase}
16     End                {RETURN}
```

The macro is designed to allow you to enter as many purchase amounts as you wish and to total them for you.

The first instruction prompts you for the number of items purchased. This number is stored in K1. The next two instructions do some housekeeping by zeroing counters that the macro will use.

The subroutine call is in B4. You will notice that the optional argument is used to pass the value in K1 to the subroutine.

The subroutine that begins in B10 is the next focus of attention. It uses a {DEFINE} statement to set aside K2 for the information passed to it and declares this information to be a numeric variable. It uses Counter to loop within the subroutine until Counter is equal to the number of purchases specified. Until that time, it increments cell K6 by the purchase amount each time, increments Counter by 1, and then branches back to the top of the subroutine.

When all purchases are processed, the subroutine branches to End, where a {RETURN} statement is located. This statement returns control to B5 in the main routine. The mode indicator is then changed to DONE, and the total amount purchased is displayed.


## Macro Commands (Release 1A)

The /X commands and {?} are the only macro commands available in release 1A. These commands are still available in release 2 for compatibility, but all of them have corresponding keyword commands in the new release 2 macro language. A brief description and example for each of the /X commands follow. In addition, you will find a reference to the corresponding release 2 keyword command. Refer to the section describing the keyword command for an expanded example of the command's use. You may substitute the /X command in the example if you are using release 1A. If you have release 2, however, you will want to use the keyword commands, since they are self-documenting.

Note that the /X commands, unlike the keyword commands, are preceded by a slash and are not enclosed in braces. Note, too, that there is no space between the command and its arguments.

## /XC

The /XC command corresponds to the {routine} command, which is described in the section on macro commands that alter the flow of execution.

**Format**     The format for /XC command is

/XClocation~

where *location* is the address or range name of a cell containing a routine that you wish executed.

**Use**     After /XC executes the routine or when it encounters the /XR or {RETURN} statement at the end of the routine, control will return to the instruction following the /XC instruction.

An excerpt from a macro using the /XC command might look like this:

```
/XCTotal~
/pprA1..F20~~
gpaq
```

These lines would appear in the main macro. You would also need a subroutine named Total with an /XR or {RETURN} at the end of it, as follows:

```
Total {GETLABEL "Enter first amount",B5}
    . . .
    . . .
    /XR
```

When the /XR instruction is executed, control will return to the Print instruction following the initial call.

## /XG

The /XG command alters the execution flow in a macro by branching to a new location. This new location contains the keystrokes that will be entered next.

**Format**    The format of the /XG command is

/XG*location*~

where *location* is the cell address or range name containing the keystrokes that you want executed next. If a range name is used and it refers to a range of cells, the upper left cell in the range will be used.

**Use**    You might use this instruction with a condition test, like this:

```
/XICounter>10~/XGS3~
    . . .
```

The instruction will transfer control to S3 only if the condition Counter>10 is true. If this condition is false, control will pass to the macro instruction in the cell below the condition test.

The /XG command is equivalent to the release 2 macro command {BRANCH}. {BRANCH} is described in the section on macro commands that alter the flow of execution.

## /XI

The /XI command allows you to test a condition and take one action if it is true and another if it is false.

**Format**    The format for the /XI command is

/XI*condition~keystrokes for true condition*
*keystrokes for false condition*

The argument *condition* is a comparison of two values in cells or a formula.

The argument *keystrokes* is any valid macro instruction. It can be a menu selection, an /XG instruction, or any other instruction you wish executed.

**Use**    You might use this instruction to check for the end of a repetitive operation by checking the value of a counter, like this:

```
         /XICounter<>10~/XGContinue~
         /XGEnd~
Continue ....
         ...
End      /XQ
```

This command is equivalent to the {IF} command in the release 2 macro commands. That command is described in the section on macro commands that control the flow of execution.

## /XL

The /XL command causes 1-2-3 to wait for the operator to input a character string from the keyboard and then stores the entry in a specified location.

**Format**      The format for the /XL Command is

*/XLprompt message~location~*

The argument *prompt message* is a message of up to 39 characters that prompts the operator for the information you expect to be entered.

The argument *location* is an address or range name for a cell that will contain up to the 240-character limit that the instruction permits the operator to enter from the keyboard. If the range name supplied pertains to a range of cells, the information will be stored in the upper left cell in the range.

**Use**      An example of this command's use might look like this:

/XLEnter your name :~A10~

This instruction would display the prompt "Enter your name :" and then wait for the operator to enter something and finalize it with the ENTER key. The entry would be stored in A10. If you wish, you can leave off the location, and 1-2-3 will store the entry in the current cell. In other words, /XLEnter your name :~~ will enter the information in the current cell.

This command is equivalent to the {GETLABEL} command in the release 2 macro commands. It is described in the data entry section of this chapter.

## /XM

The /XM command permits you to construct a custom 1-2-3 menu at the top of the screen, with up to eight menu choices and the same expanded descriptions that 1-2-3 provides when you point to a selection.

**Format**      The format of the /XM command is

*/XMlocation~*

where *location* is the range name or address of the cell that begins the description of the menu. The upper left cell in the menu area is specified.

**Use**     The location that contains the menu conforms to the area used by the {MENUBRANCH} command, which is the equivalent command to /XM in the release 2 macro language. {MENUBRANCH} is described in the section of this chapter that covers macro commands that affect the keyboard.

## /XN

The /XN command causes 1-2-3 to wait for the operator to input a numeric value from the keyboard and then stores the entry in a specified location.

**Format**     The format for the /XN command is

/XN*prompt message~location~*

The argument *prompt message* is a message of up to 39 characters that prompts the operator for the information you expect to be entered.

The argument *location* is an address or range name for a cell that will contain up to the 80-character limit that the instruction permits the operator to enter from the keyboard. If the range name supplied pertains to a range of cells, the information will be stored in the upper left cell in the range.

**Use**     You may specify numeric values, range names referencing numeric values, formulas, or built-in functions in response to the prompt.

An example of the use of the /XN command follows:

/XNEnter your age :~A10~

This instruction would display the prompt "Enter your age :" and then wait for the operator to enter something and finalize it with the ENTER key. The entry would be stored in A10. If you wish, you can leave off the location, and 1-2-3 will store the entry in the current cell. In other words, /XNEnter your age :~~ will enter the information in the current cell.

This command is equivalent to the {GETNUMBER} command in the release 2 macro commands. It is described in the data entry section of this chapter.

### /XQ

The /XQ command stops execution of a macro.

**Format**     The format for the /XQ is

/XQ

This command has no arguments.

**Use**     This command is equivalent to the {QUIT} command in the release 2 macro commands. It is described in the section on macro commands that control the flow of execution.

### /XR

The /XR command causes a return from the execution of a macro subroutine. An /XR instruction must have a corresponding /XC instruction in the main macro program in order to function.

**Format**     The format for the /XR command is

/XR

This command has no arguments.

**Use**     This command may be used as follows:

```
Main Routine
   . . .
   . . .
   /XCSub~
   /XLEnter next selection :~AI~
Subroutine
Sub . . .
   . . .
   . . .
   . . .
   /XR
```

When the /XC instruction calls Sub, this subroutine will be executed until /XR is reached. Control will then return to the /XL statement following /XC in the main routine.

The /XR statement is equivalent to the {RETURN} statement in the release 2 macro language. {RETURN} is described in the section on macro commands that control the flow of execution.

## Macro Commands
## That Manipulate Data

The macro commands in this section allow you to manipulate values and strings stored in worksheet cells. You can use these commands to blank out a section of the worksheet or store a value or string in a cell. Commands from this section can also be used to recalculate the worksheet in row or column order.

### {BLANK}

The {BLANK} command is functionally equivalent to /Range Erase, since it erases a range of cells on the worksheet.

**Format**     The format of the {BLANK} command is

{BLANK *location*}

**Figure 13-10.** Data entry screen containing old data

where *location* is a range of cell addresses or a range name associated with one or more worksheet cells.

**Use**   This command can be used to clear data from previous uses of the worksheet. You might want to clear a data entry area with this command.

**Example**   Figure 13-10 presents a data entry screen that might be used with a macro. The screen contains the data from the previous entry, which may confuse the operator when a new record is entered. To clear the screen, you can add these lines of code to an existing macro, placing them so they will be executed following the processing of the current record.

```
        P              Q
1
2     \b            {BLANK C3..C11}
3                    {CALC}
```

The lines are shown with a macro name so they could be executed from the keyboard without incorporating them into another macro if desired. The first line requests that the range C3..C11 be erased. The second line calculates the worksheet to ensure that these cells are blanked immediately, as shown in Figure 13-11.


## {CONTENTS}

The {CONTENTS} command stores a numeric value in a cell as a label with a specified format.

**Format**    The format for {CONTENTS} is

{CONTENTS *destination,source,width,format*}

The argument *destination* is the location where you wish the label to be stored. You may specify it as a cell address or a range name.

The argument *source* is the location of the value entry you want stored in another cell as a string (label). You may specify this location as a cell address or a range name.

The argument *width* is an optional argument unless you choose to specify format, in which case this argument will be required. Width determines the width of the string entry if

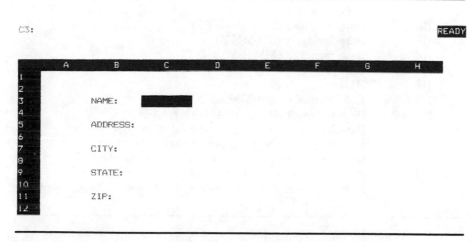

**Figure 13-11.**    Data entry screen cleared with {BLANK}

you elect to specify it. If you do not specify width, it is obtained from the source location.

The argument *format* is an optional argument that allows you to determine the exact manner in which the source value is formatted in the destination string. Figure 13-12 shows a list of the values you may select for this argument.

**Example**   You may want to display the formula behind a cell at a destination location. The {CONTENTS} command will allow you to do this. Let's say that the source location is D1, and it contains the formula +Z1*Z3, although a 30 displays in the cell. The formula behind D1 can be displayed in D5 with the following macro statement:

{CONTENTS D5,DI,9,117}~

| | |
|---|---|
| 0 to 15 | Fixed format with 0 to 15 decimal places, depending on the number. 0 will be 0 decimal places, and 15 will be 15 decimal places |
| 16 to 32 | Scientific format with 0 to 15 decimal places |
| 33 to 47 | Currency format with 0 to 15 decimal places |
| 48 to 63 | % format with 0 to 15 decimal places |
| 64 to 79 | Comma (,) format with 0 to 15 decimal places |
| 112 | +/− format |
| 113 | General format |
| 114 | Date format 1 (DD-MMM-YY) |
| 115 | Date format 2 (DD-MMM) |
| 116 | Date format 3 (MMM-YY) |
| 117 | Text display |
| 118 | Hidden |
| 119 | Date format 6 (HH:MM:SS AM/PM) |
| 120 | Date format 7 (HH:MM AM/PM) |
| 121 | Date format 4 - Full international date display |
| 122 | Date format 5 - Short international date display |
| 123 | Date format 8 - Full international time display |
| 124 | Date format 9 - Short international time display |
| 127 | Default numeric display format for the worksheet |

**Figure 13-12.**   Codes and associated formats for the Contents command

In this statement, D5 represents the destination location and D1 represents the source. A width of 9 is established, and the format represented by 117 is selected. The number 117 specifies text display, so the formula behind D1 will display in D5. Remember that it is no longer a formula but a string once it is stored in the destination location.

### {LET}

The {LET} command permits the assignment of a number or a string to a location on the worksheet.

**Format**     The formats for the {LET} command are

{LET *location,number*}

or

{LET *location,string*}

The argument *location* is the address or range name of the cell that you wish to store the value or label in. If you specify location as a range, only the upper left cell in the range will be used.

The argument *number* is a numeric value or a formula that evaluates to a numeric value.

The argument *string* is a string or a string formula.

**Use**     This command is useful whenever you wish to control the value in a worksheet cell. It can be used with a loop to increment a counter. Since it can be used with either strings or values, it is extremely flexible. Here are several examples:

{LET A1,10}~ stores 10 in A1
{LET A1,A1+1}~ increments A1 by 1
{LET A1,"ABC "&"COMPANY"}~ places ABC
COMPANY in A1

You also have the option of using an indicator for numeric values that tells 1-2-3 whether you wish them treated as numbers (values) or as strings. The examples that follow show the proper format:

{LET A1,5+1:value} places a 6 in A1

{LET A1,5+1:string} places '5+1 in A1

**Example**    The {LET} command can be used to initialize and increment a counter when you want to set up your own loops. The following shell shows the format of a loop using {LET} in this way.

```
\s        {LET Counter,1}
Top—Loop {IF Counter>Stop}{BRANCH End—Loop}
          . . .
          . . .
          . . .
          {LET Counter,Counter+1}
End—Loop {QUIT}
```

If you choose to build your own loop rather than use the {FOR} instruction, you will always need to initialize your counter, increment it, and test it to see that it is within an acceptable range. In this example, Stop is a range name used to contain the ending value for this range.

## {PUT}

The {PUT} command allows you to put a value in a location within a range. Unlike {LET}, which accepts only a cell address, {PUT} allows you to select a row and column offset within a range.

**Format**    The formats for the {PUT} command are

{PUT *location,column,row,number*}

or

{PUT *location,column,row,string*}

The argument *location* is a range of cells identified by cell addresses or a range name.

The argument *column* is the column number within the range. The first column in the range is column 0.

The argument *row* is the row number within the range. The first row in the range is row 0.

The argument *number* is the value you wish to have stored at the specified location.

The argument *string* is the string you wish to have stored in the specified location.

**Use**     This command is similar to {LET} but has additional flexibility, since it lets you store values within a range. A few examples and their results follow:

{PUT A1..B5,0,3,4} places a 4 in A4

{PUT A1..B5,1,0,3} places a 3 in B1

{PUT A1..B5,0,15,0} causes an error, since a row number of 15 is not within the range specified.

**Example**     This command could be used to supply the values for a table. You might have entries like this in your macro:

{PUT Table,0,0,100}~
{PUT Table,0,1,D5/2}~

The tilde at the end of each instruction causes the table entry to be updated immediately.

**Note**     The row and column offsets must be within the range you establish with the location argument. When they are not, an error occurs. This error cannot be processed with {ONERROR}.

**{RECALC}**

The {RECALC} command recalculates the formulas within the range you specify, proceeding row by row within this range.

**Format**    The format for the {RECALC} command is

{RECALC *location,condition,iteration*}

The argument *location* is the range of the worksheet that you wish to have recalculated.

The argument *condition* is an optional argument specifying a condition that must be true before the range selected is no longer recalculated. As long as the condition is false, 1-2-3 will continue to recalculate the worksheet. This argument is used in conjunction with iteration, which specifies a maximum number of iterations.

The argument *iteration* is an optional argument that allows you to specify the number of times that formulas within the range will be recalculated as long as condition is false. When condition is true, recalculation stops, even though you may not have used all the iterations. With each iteration the count is reduced by 1. When it is zero, no further recalculations will occur.

**Use**    When you use {CALC}, the entire worksheet is recalculated. This can be unnecessarily time consuming if you need just a section of it recalculated. The {RECALC} and {RECALCCOL} commands are designed to recalculate a section. You should use {RECALC} when the area you are recalculating is below and to the left of the cells the formulas in this area reference. You should use {RECALCCOL} when the area you are recalculating is above and to the right of the cells the formulas in this area reference. If the formula is both above and to the left of cells with new values, you must use {CALC} and recalculate the entire worksheet.

**Example**    If you have a macro that changes the value of cell AB10 and you are interested in the value of cell Z12, which is affected by AB10, you can use a {RECALC} instruction in your macro, as follows:

{RECALC Z1..AB12}

1-2-3 will recalculate row by row to obtain the correct result for Z12. If you want to add a condition and iteration count to this instruction, you might get this:

{RECALC Z1..AB12,Z3>20,10}

The recalculation of the specified range will now continue until either Z3 is greater than 20 or 10 iterations are performed.

## {RECALCCOL}

The {RECALCCOL} command recalculates the formulas within the range you specify, proceeding column by column within this range.

**Format**     The format for the {RECALCCOL} command is

{RECALCCOL *location,condition,iteration*}

The argument *location* is the range of the worksheet that you wish to have recalculated.

The argument *condition* is an optional argument specifying a condition that must be true before the range selected is no longer recalculated. As long as the condition is false, 1-2-3 will continue to recalculate the worksheet. This argument is used in conjunction with iteration, which specifies a maximum number of iterations.

The argument *iteration* is an optional argument that allows you to specify the number of times that formulas within the range will be recalculated as long as condition is false. When condition is true, recalculation stops, even though you may not have used all the iterations. With each iteration the count is reduced by 1. When it is zero, no further recalculations will occur.

**Use**     When you use {CALC}, the entire worksheet is recalculated. This can be unnecessarily time consuming if you need just a section of it recalculated. The {RECALC} and {RECALCCOL} commands are designed to recalculate a section. You should use {RECALC} when the area you are recalculating is below and to the left of the cells the formulas in this area reference. You should use {RECALCCOL} when the area you are recalculating is above and to the right of the cells the formulas in this area reference. If the formula is both above and to the left of cells with new values, you must use {CALC} and recalculate the entire worksheet.

**Example**     {RECALCCOL} follows the same syntax rules as {RECALC}. You decide which one to use depending on whether a row or a column order of recalculation fits best with your application. Refer to the example under {RECALC} for additional information.

### Macro Commands That Handle Files

The file macro commands provide sequential file handling capabilities equivalent to the ones you find in the BASIC programming language. You can use these commands in macros to read and write records to text files. If you have never worked with files, you will want to review a section from a data processing text that overviews records, file size concepts, file input and output procedures, and other basic terminology connected with the use of files before you try to use these macros.

The commands in this section are used in groups. For example, it is not possible to use {READLN}, {READ}, {WRITE}, or {WRITELN} unless you have first opened the file with {OPEN}. Short examples dealing with the syntax will be provided with each command. Examples showing the commands in this section used in context with other required commands are found under {WRITE}, {WRITELN}, {READ}, {READLN}, and {FILESIZE}.

## {CLOSE}

The {CLOSE} command closes the file you opened with the {OPEN} command. You must close one file before opening a second one.

**Format**    The format for the {CLOSE} command is

{CLOSE}

This command has no arguments.

**Use**    If you use this command when there are no open files, 1-2-3 will ignore it.

## {FILESIZE}

This command allows you to determine the number of bytes or characters in your file.

**Format**    The format for the {FILESIZE} command is

{FILESIZE *location*}

where *location* is the cell address or range name of the cell where you want 1-2-3 to store the number representing the length of your file.

**Use**    The file must be open before you use this command. You should also remember that the character for the end-of-file condition will be included in the count for {FILESIZE}. If you know the length of the records on the file, you can use {FILESIZE} to determine how many records the file contains.

**Example**    The following macro uses the {FILESIZE} command:

```
            A                          B
22   \F               {OPEN "B:TEST.PRN",R}
23                    {FILESIZE G21}
24                    {CALC}
25                    {CLOSE}
```

The first step in the macro is to open the file, since a file must be opened before {FILESIZE} can be used. The entry in B23 determines the number of bytes in the file and places this number in G21. A {CALC} is included to update the worksheet cell immediately, after which the file is closed.


## {GETPOS}

The {GETPOS} command determines the current position in a file.

**Format**    The format for the {GETPOS} command is

{GETPOS *location*}

where *location* is the address or range name of the cell where you wish the current position number stored. Remember that the first character in a file is considered position 0.

**Example**    You can use this command to monitor your progress through a file, comparing the current position to the file size to be sure that you do not attempt to read beyond the end of the file. After reading a record, you might include a {GETPOS} instruction, like this:

{READLN A10}
{GETPOS Current}

You could then compare Current and the result from the {FILESIZE} command and determine the number of records yet to read.

## {OPEN}

The {OPEN} command allows you to open a file and specify whether you plan to read the file, write to it, or do both.

**Format**  The format for the {OPEN} command is

{OPEN *file,access*}

The argument *file* is a string or a range name referring to a single cell that contains a string or string formula that references the name of the file you want to open. The string has an upper limit of 64 characters and can include the entire pathname and subdirectory as well as the filename extension.

The argument *access* is a single character that controls the type of access you have to the file. The possible code characters are as follows:

R  means read only. You cannot write to the file if your access mode is R.

W  means write only. Opens a new file or recreates an existing file. You cannot read from the file if your access mode is W.

M  allows modifications to the file, permitting both read and write access. It can be used only on existing files.

**Use**  If you wish to use an error routine in the event {OPEN} fails, you can place it on the same line as {OPEN} as a subroutine call—for example, {OPEN SALES,R}{Fix—Err}.


## {READ}

The {READ} command reads the number of characters specified into the location you define, starting at the file pointer's present location.

**Format**    The format for the {READ} command is

{READ *bytes,location*}

The argument *bytes* is the number of characters you wish to have read from the file, beginning at the current position in the file. If bytes is larger than the number of remaining characters in the file, {READ} will take the amount of data remaining. Bytes must be a numeric value or an expression that evaluates to one. The number should be between 0 and 240. If bytes is negative, 240 is used.

The argument *location* is the address or range name for the cell where you would like the string of characters to be stored. The data will be stored in this location as a left justified label.

**Example**    The following macro shows the use of the {READ} instruction:

```
              A                              B
30    \r              {OPEN "B:TEST.PRN",R}
31                    {SETPOS 6}
32                    {READ 9,G22}
33                    {CALC}
34                    {CLOSE}
```

The file is opened for reading in the first instruction. The file pointer is then set at 6, which would be the seventh character in the file. Nine bytes (characters) are read from the file and stored in G22. The worksheet is recalculated immediately to show this entry, after which the file is closed.

## {READLN}

The {READLN} command copies a line of characters (a record) from a file and places it at the location specified.

**Format**    The format for the {READLN} command is

{READLN *location*}

where *location* is the cell address or range name that specifies the cell where you wish the line of data stored.

**Use**    The {READ} command works on the basis of number of bytes. {READLN}, by contrast, looks for a carriage return/ line feed to know how many characters to read. Like {READ}, it uses the current file pointer position as the starting point and can be used with {SETPOS}.

**Example**    The following macro shows code that will read one line from a text file.

```
         A                              B
1    \z            {OPEN "B:TEST.PRN",R}
2                  {READLN Place}
3                  ~
4                  {RIGHT}
5                  {CLOSE}
```

The file is opened. {READLN} then reads the first line from the file and places these characters in Place. A tilde rather than {CALC} is used to update the worksheet, since the tilde is just as effective and more efficient. The cursor is moved to the right, and the file is closed.


## {SETPOS}

The {SETPOS} command positions the file pointer at the location you specify.

**Format**    The format for the {SETPOS} command is

{SETPOS *number*}

where *number* is a numeric value or expression that results in a numeric value that tells 1-2-3 which character you want the pointer set on. Remember that the first character in the file is considered to be position 0.

**Use**    1-2-3 does not prevent you from setting the pointer at a location beyond the end of the file. You should always use {FILESIZE} to ensure that this does not occur.

**Example**    Given the following information stored in a file:

ABC Company, LaCrosse, MI

setting the pointer to 4 would place it on the C in Company.

## {WRITE}

The {WRITE} command places a set of characters in a file that you have opened.

**Format**     The format for the {WRITE} command is

{WRITE *string*}

where *string* is a character string, an expression evaluating to a character string, or a range name assigned to a single cell that contains a string.

**Use**     When you use this command, 1-2-3 writes a string to the file at the current location of the file pointer. It then moves the pointer to the end of this entry to place it in position for writing the next set of characters.

**Example**     If you have a column of worksheet cells that contains the days of the week, you could use this command to write this list of names to a file. If you use {WRITE}, they will all be in one line (record) of the file.

Assuming that you position your cursor at the top of the list, the macro that follows will write all seven names for you.

```
               A                        B
1      \z           {OPEN "B:TOGETH.PRN",W}
2                   {LET Ctr,1}
3      Top          {IF Ctr>7}{BRANCH End}
4                   {WRITE @CELLPOINTER("contents")}
5                   {DOWN}
6                   {Let Ctr,Ctr+1}
7                   {BRANCH Top}
8      End          {CLOSE}
```

The file is opened for Write access in the first instruction. A counter is initialized in B2. The first statement in the iterative loop of the macro checks the counter to see whether it is greater than 7. If it is, the macro ends by closing the file.

If the counter is not greater than 7, the loop continues. The contents of the current cell are written to the file using the built-in function @CELLPOINTER. The cursor is moved down, and Ctr is incremented. The execution flow then branches to the top of the loop. The macro continues in this cycle until it has written all seven entries to the file.

Since entries are written sequentially on the same line, the result of using {WRITE} would be

MondayTuesdayWednesdayThursdayFridaySaturdaySunday

assuming that the first cell contained Monday and the days proceeded in order throughout the week as you moved down the column.

**Setup**    The macro requires that the range names Top, End, and Ctr be assigned to appropriate cells. Also, the days of the week must already be in the worksheet and your cursor must be positioned on the first one before you execute the macro.

### {WRITELN}

The {WRITELN} command places characters in an open file. In contrast to {WRITE}, it adds a carriage return/line feed to the end of each character string written, so a new line or record is created in the file each time the command is used.

**Format**    The format for the {WRITELN} command is

{WRITELN *string*}

where *string* is a character string, an expression evaluating to a character string, or a range name assigned to a single cell that contains a string.

**Use**    When you use this command, 1-2-3 writes a string to the file at the current location of the file pointer. It then moves the pointer to the beginning of the next line to place it in position for writing the next set of characters.

Using {WRITELN " "} will generate a carriage return/line feed at the current position in the file. You might want to build a record with a series of {WRITE} commands, then use {WRITELN} to add a line feed before beginning the next record.

**Example**     Let's look at two examples. The first writes a series of string literals to a file named DAYS. It reads as follows:

```
          A                           B
1    \z        {OPEN "B:DAYS",W}
2              {WRITELN "Monday"}
3              {WRITELN "Tuesday"}
4              {WRITELN "Wednesday"}
5              {WRITELN "Thursday"}
6              {WRITELN "Friday"}
7              {WRITELN "Saturday"}
8              {WRITELN "Sunday"}
9              {CLOSE}
```

The file is opened. Seven individual {WRITELN} statements are then used to write character strings to the file, after which the file is closed.

If you import the text file created with this macro into the worksheet with your cursor in Z1, Z1..Z7 will contain the following:

Monday

Tuesday

Wednesday

Thursday

Friday

Saturday

Sunday

Since each day was written to a separate line when the file was imported, each record is written to a different cell.

A second macro that achieves the same end results is this:

```
                A                              B
1    \z          {OPEN "B:TOGETH.PRN",W}
2                {LET Ctr,1}
3    Top         {IF Ctr>7}{BRANCH End}
4                {WRITELN @CELLPOINTER("contents")}
5                {DOWN}
6                {LET Ctr,Ctr+1}
7                {BRANCH Top}
8    End         {CLOSE}
```

This macro uses a loop construction and writes the days of the week, which are stored in worksheet cells, to the file. It follows the same format as the example discussed under {WRITE} except that each day of the week appears in a separate line (record) of the file.

# Software Add-ons That Extend 1-2-3's Power

# Using 1-2-3 Report Writer

**FOURTEEN**

1-2-3 Report Writer is a companion product to 1-2-3 that can produce customized reports and forms from 1-2-3 files. It is not part of the 1-2-3 package, though it is marketed by Lotus Development Corporation.

1-2-3 Report Writer is a valuable tool for experienced 1-2-3 users and novices alike.

## The Experienced 1-2-3 User

Since 1-2-3 Report Writer allows users to extract reports from their 1-2-3 databases with ease and can remember the exact report definitions from period to period so it is not necessary to define them each time, it provides real time-saving features. It allows greater sophistication in certain areas than the standard 1-2-3 package. It will permit up to four sort keys and a break on any of the sort keys for a count, average, minimum, or maximum calculation. In addition to subtotals, the package provides a grand total feature and a page containing report statistics. Special print attributes can be selected from menus for any field value, field name, or total.

Selected fields and records can be chosen for a report, and fields can be printed in any sequence. Multiple lines can be printed for one record, or a mailing label format can be chosen. If mailing labels are selected, you can print from one to four labels across a page, depending on the width of your printer and the type of label stock you are using.

Since most of the Report Writer menu selections are similar to 1-2-3 menu selections, you will feel familiar with the menu structure from the outset. Those menus that differ provide a list of options, and it will be clear what each selection means.

## The 1-2-3 Novice

Even those users in your organization who have not mastered the details of spreadsheet model creation can benefit from Report Writer. Since the Report Writer package does not modify existing worksheet files, you can make it available to users who have no knowledge of 1-2-3 without risking the integrity of your models. These users will be able to define their needs to 1-2-3 Report Writer and extract data from your files with ease.

Report Writer is even easier to use than 1-2-3. As an example, records for a report are specified through criteria just as in 1-2-3, but with Report Writer your specifications are defined with menu selections that allow you to pick the field, the condition, and the value. Records are also sorted via menu definitions of the fields to be used as the four sort keys. When you want to add special print features to your report, you do not need to use 1-2-3's compose character sequences or setup strings. Your requirements can be defined with plain English descriptions of print features selectable from menus. You can apply these options globally or to a single field. The help features of Report Writer are also easier to use than those of 1-2-3. They are comprehensive and provide references to pages in the Report Writer manual for expanded descriptions.

## The Package Components

The 1-2-3 Report Writer package includes a manual, a command card, a Report Writer program disk, and an Installation and Tutorial Disk. You may copy the disks, but you will most likely need the original disk every time you start your system.

The manual consists of seven chapters. It provides step-by-step coverage of everything from installation to printing a series of batch reports. It is easy to follow and has chapters on the program's basic as well as more sophisticated features, including restructuring reports, sorting reports, selecting records for a report, and creating mailing labels. Chapters 3 through 6 are tutorial chapters; there is information on the Installation and Tutorial Disk for the examples in these chapters. The last chapter contains over 60 pages of reference material on the commands used by Report Writer. The manual also contains ten pages of error messages in alphabetical order. This makes it easy to find a description of your error if you make a mistake while using the package.

## Installing Report Writer

Report Writer can be installed on your system if it is an IBM PC, PC/XT, AT, or 3270 portable; a Compaq Portable, Deskpro, or Compaq Plus; or an AT&T 6300. You should have DOS 2.0 or higher on your system and have worksheet files in 1-2-3 release 1A or 2 format or in Symphony 1.0, 1.01, or 1.1.

The installation procedure for Report Writer is more limited than 1-2-3's but very similar. Since 1-2-3 works with graphic images as well as text, you must define information about both aspects of system support for it. Report Writer works in the text environment only, however, and thus is interested only in the text printer or printers you will be using. Under the Advanced Options feature, you will see a selection for collating sequence something like the one that 1-2-3 provides. Rather than 1-2-3's three options, though, Report Writer allows you to choose only numbers first or numbers last. It does not provide the ASCII code option found in release 2 of 1-2-3.

The Report Writer installation process is menu driven and extremely easy to perform using the directions on the screen. Depending on whether your installation is on a hard- or floppy-based system, you may need to insert the Installation and Tutorial Disk before starting. The menu options on the screen will tell you exactly which order to use for your selections.

## Getting Started

Once Report Writer is installed, you can access it by placing the original system disk in drive A and typing REPORT at the DOS prompt. The insertion of this disk is normally

```
                1-2-3 Report Writer

                     Release 1
                  1200054-0975312
    Software Authored by Concentric Data Systems, Inc.

     (C) Copyright 1985 Concentric Data Systems, Inc.
     (C) Copyright 1985 Lotus Development Corporation
                  All Rights Reserved
```

```
          **  Press [RETURN] to begin  **
```

**Figure 14-1.**    Report Writer entry screen

necessary even if your report program is stored on a hard
disk. If you fail to insert your original disk, you will get a
Load Error message, and Report Writer will not operate. To
avoid this nuisance, Lotus has recently made available the
same permanent hard disk copy program that is available
for 1-2-3. It will allow you to make one executable copy of
Report Writer on your hard disk. You must copy both the
RCOPYON and RCOPYHRD programs, which are provided
on your Installation and Tutorial Disk. They are described in
Chapter 2 of the Report Writer manual.

Figure 14-1 shows the entry screen that appears when
Report Writer is loaded successfully. This screen displays
copyright information, your disk serial number, and the current release of the product. Pressing ENTER will take you to
the first usable screen. This screen prompts you for the name
of the worksheet file to use for your report. It reads the
names of the .WK1 and .WKS files on your 1-2-3 data disk
and displays them at the top of the screen. You can select a
file by pointing or by typing in the file name. Just as in 1-2-3,
the first letter of the file name is not sufficient to have Report
Writer retrieve it. You will have no opportunity to look at the

worksheet itself from Report Writer, but you will be shown Report Writer's guess at the field names to use for the file and the type of data for each field, based on the top row of the worksheet.

Figure 14-2 shows some example worksheet data that can be used in Report Writer. It also shows a format that Report Writer does not handle well. The field names in this file are several rows from the top of the worksheet, but Report Writer will expect to find them in row 1. Report Writer also expects that these field names will be unique. You may have up to 100 field names and may have entries as long as 50 characters in any field as long as the column is wide enough to display the entire entry.

If you choose not to use the top line of your database for field names, you will want to use the /Range Name Create option from 1-2-3 to name your database area on your work-

A1: [W9]                                                                      READY

|   | A | B | C | D | E | F |
|---|---|---|---|---|---|---|
| 1 | | | Consolidated Financial, Inc. | | | |
| 2 | | | August 1986 Orders | | | |
| 3 | | | | | | |
| 4 | Order # | Date | Supplier | Price | Quantity | Description |
| 5 | K5607 | 01-Aug-86 | Arkins Supply | $12.50 | 4 | Metal trash can |
| 6 | K5500-9 | 01-Aug-86 | Cheap Paper | $7.80 | 14 | Box legal pads |
| 7 | F4310 | 02-Aug-86 | Office News | $5.50 | 10 | Magazine storage box |
| 8 | K5501 | 02-Aug-86 | Borman Lumber | $3.59 | 12 | Shelf brackets |
| 9 | R6789 | 03-Aug-86 | Merideth's | $349.00 | 1 | Credenza |
| 10 | F5502 | 04-Aug-86 | Rinko Printing | $124.00 | 1 | Credit report forms |
| 11 | R6790 | 05-Aug-86 | TY Office Inc. | $14.50 | 4 | Staplers, heavy duty |
| 12 | F5503 | 06-Aug-86 | Morris Catering | $625.75 | 1 | Office picnic |
| 13 | F5504 | 07-Aug-86 | Merideth's | $25.00 | 2 | File cabinets |
| 14 | R6791 | 12-Aug-86 | Cheap Paper | $12.50 | 15 | Box envelopes letter |
| 15 | R6792 | 13-Aug-86 | Cheap Paper | $17.60 | 10 | Box legal envelopes |
| 16 | R6793 | 14-Aug-86 | Computer Supply | $7.80 | 10 | Ark ribbons |
| 17 | R9906-2 | 15-Aug-86 | Beacon | $120.00 | 1 | Monthly coffee order |
| 18 | C1109 | 18-Aug-86 | Computer Supply | $0.79 | 1000 | DS/DD diskettes |
| 19 | C1110 | 20-Aug-86 | ABC Computers | $75.00 | 3 | Printer stands |
| 20 | F5505 | 14-Aug-86 | Arkins Supply | $14.50 | 5 | Envelopes legal size |

19-Jul-86   12:17 AM

**Figure 14-2.**     Worksheet data with first row blank

sheet before saving the worksheet file with 1-2-3. Report Writer gives you the option of printing a report for a named range, and you will be able to direct it to the exact location for your field names and data with the range name you have assigned.

If you do not want to assign a range name, you can eliminate the heading in a worksheet like the one shown by deleting the heading lines or moving the data up in the file while you are still in 1-2-3. The worksheet shown earlier had the top three rows deleted with /Worksheet Delete Rows before it was saved to disk. It is shown in its final form in Figure 14-3. When Report Writer brings it into memory, it will use the field names found in the record for its own field names and will use the first record to determine the data type for the report. You are directed to type a slash to see the menu, which is shown here in the box called "The Report Writer

A1: [W9] 'Order #                                                                  READY

| | A | B | C | D | E | F |
|---|---|---|---|---|---|---|
| 1 | Order # | Date | Supplier | Price | Quantity | Description |
| 2 | K5607 | 01-Aug-86 | Arkins Supply | $12.50 | 4 | Metal trash can |
| 3 | K5500-9 | 01-Aug-86 | Cheap Paper | $7.80 | 14 | Box legal pads |
| 4 | F4310 | 02-Aug-86 | Office News | $5.50 | 10 | Magazine storage box |
| 5 | K5501 | 02-Aug-86 | Borman Lumber | $3.59 | 12 | Shelf brackets |
| 6 | R6789 | 03-Aug-86 | Merideth's | $349.00 | 1 | Credenza |
| 7 | F5502 | 04-Aug-86 | Rinko Printing | $124.00 | 1 | Credit report forms |
| 8 | R6790 | 05-Aug-86 | TY Office Inc. | $14.50 | 4 | Staplers, heavy duty |
| 9 | F5503 | 06-Aug-86 | Morris Catering | $625.75 | 1 | Office picnic |
| 10 | F5504 | 07-Aug-86 | Merideth's | $25.00 | 2 | File cabinets |
| 11 | R6791 | 12-Aug-86 | Cheap Paper | $12.50 | 15 | Box envelopes letter |
| 12 | R6792 | 13-Aug-86 | Cheap Paper | $17.60 | 10 | Box legal envelopes |
| 13 | R6793 | 14-Aug-86 | Computer Supply | $7.80 | 10 | Ark ribbons |
| 14 | R9906-2 | 15-Aug-86 | Beacon | $120.00 | 1 | Monthly coffee order |
| 15 | C1109 | 18-Aug-86 | Computer Supply | $0.79 | 1000 | DS/DD diskettes |
| 16 | C1110 | 20-Aug-86 | ABC Computers | $75.00 | 3 | Printer stands |
| 17 | F5505 | 14-Aug-86 | Arkins Supply | $14.50 | 5 | Envelopes legal size |
| 18 | F5506 | 25-Aug-86 | Merideth's | $17.60 | 10 | Box legal envelopes |
| 19 | F5509 | 27-Aug-86 | Cheap Paper | $7.80 | 10 | Ark ribbons |
| 20 | F5511 | 28-Aug-86 | TY Office Inc. | $120.00 | 1 | Small File |

19-Jul-86    12:27 AM

**Figure 14-3.**    Worksheet data with first record in row 1

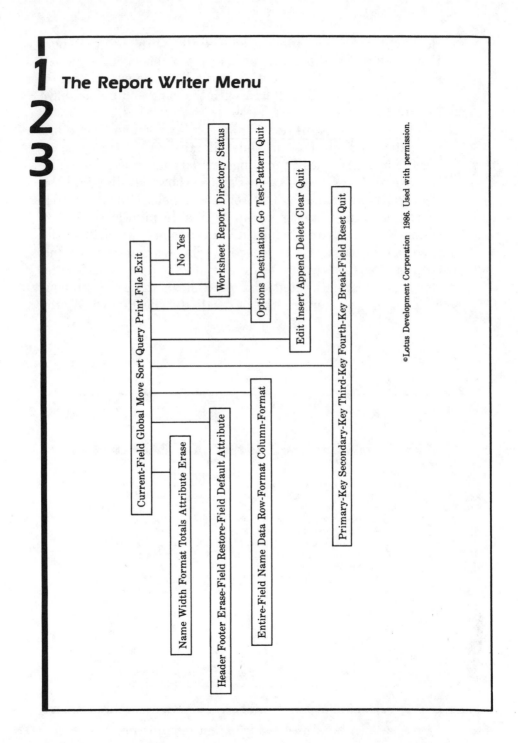

# 1
# 2
# 3

## The Report Writer Menu

©Lotus Development Corporation 1986. Used with permission.

Menu." The field names, the codes for the field type, and the menu invoked by the / are shown in Figure 14-4.

Report Writer classifies data into three types. If you see rectangular boxes under a field name, this means that Report Writer assumes the data is label data with alphanumeric entries. In our example, this is the case with Order #, Supplier, and Description. If the field is marked by #s, Report Writer is assuming that the field contains value or numeric entries, as shown here for Price and Quantity. Date entries are marked D, M, and Y in a combination representative of the date format encountered in the first database record, here Date.

## Understanding the Mode Indicators

Report Writer has ten different mode indicators. As in 1-2-3, these indicators are found in the upper right corner of the control panel, which is in the first three lines at the top of your screen. They inform you of the package's current status and let you know what actions you can or should be performing. A summary of Report Writer's mode indicators is found in the box called "The Report Writer's Mode Indicators."

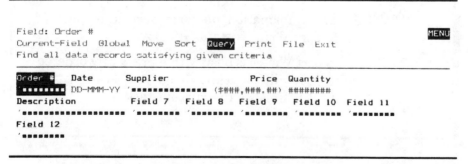

**Figure 14-4.** Display of Report Writer layout

## The Report Writer's Mode Indicators

Just as with 1-2-3, the mode indicators that Report Writer displays can help you follow its actions. The mode indicators and their meanings are as follows:

EDIT      You can enter data onto the screen or edit existing data.

ERROR      Report Writer has encountered an error. Check the error message on the last line of the screen against the list in your manual for directions.

FILES      Report Writer expects you to select a file name from the list.

HELP      The information on your screen is part of Report Writer's help facility.

MENU      Report Writer is waiting for you to select a menu item.

MOVE      You can move a report field or the name or data portion of a field.

POINT      You can specify part of a query by pointing.

READY      Report Writer is waiting for your next command. You can change the current field with the arrow keys or type a / to get a menu.

STATUS      The information on your screen is part of Report Writer's status display.

WAIT      Report Writer is busy with a previously ordered task. It will not acknowledge your next request until it finishes the current task.

## Using the Menus

Most of the Report Writer menus are like the one shown earlier in Figure 14-4. They are identical to 1-2-3's menus in appearance and operation. They always appear in the top line of the control panel. A list of the suboptions available under the menu option where the cursor rests will be found on the second line of the control panel. You can select an option by typing its first letter or by pointing to it and pressing ENTER.

This chapter will cover each of Report Writer's menu options. You will need only a small number of these to create any one report. To clarify the steps, the process for creating a simple report is summarized in the box called "Essential Steps for Creating a Report."

## Changing the Characteristics
## Of the Current Field

After you have selected a worksheet file and the main Report Write menu is displayed, you are ready to begin the creation of a report. The first option in the main menu is Current-Field. It permits you to change characteristics of the fields shown below it. The field that is highlighted will be the one affected by the changes. In the example in Figure 14-4, this is Order #. To change to a different field, you must press ESC to leave the menu, move the cursor to the right to select a new field, and then type / to invoke the menu again.

Selecting Current-Field displays the following submenu:

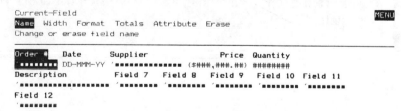

## 1  Essential Steps for Creating a Report

**2**

**3**

Report Writer has so many options that creating a report may seem difficult. Actually, creating a simple report is a quick process that requires only a few selections. The following list presents the steps involved in a typical report.

1. Save your worksheet file and load Report Writer.

2. Select your file name from the Report Writer screen after bypassing the copyright screen by pressing ENTER.

3. Examine the report layout and point to any field for which you wish to change the format or attribute. Type a slash, then select Current-Field and the options you wish.

4. If you need to make more widespread changes, type a slash and select Global.

5. If you want only selected records in the file, type a slash, select Query, and enter your specifications.

6. If you want to change the record order, type a slash, select Sort, and enter your sort keys.

7. Select Print and request Go unless you need to change the page length or some other printing characteristic first.

If you do not require a query or a sort, steps 5 and 6 can be omitted. Steps 3 and 4 can also be omitted if Report Writer's defaults are acceptable.

You can choose options to change any of the characteristics named.

## Changing the Current Field Name

Choosing the Name option from the Current-Field menu allows you to enter a new name for the current field. This name will be used in all subsequent reports. It may be made more descriptive, conformed with organizational standards, or changed in any other way you wish. For Order #, the screen at this point will appear as follows:

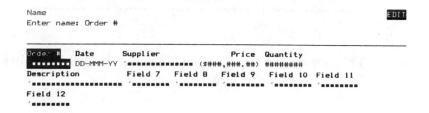

You could use the backspace to remove the # and type No. so that the field name would become Order No.

## Changing the Width of a Field

The Width option allows you to reserve either more or less space for a field than Report Writer has suggested in its format. A maximum of 50 characters is allowed for label fields and 20 for value fields. The number of characters you specify for numeric fields with Width reserves space for that number of integer positions. You will learn to specify decimals later under the Current-Field Format option. Whatever number of positions is left after the number of integers is subtracted from 20 will determine the maximum number of decimal positions you may use. In other words, if you specify a width of 15 for a value field, no more than 5 decimals can be specified with Format, since 20 minus 15 equals 5. The width of date fields is not changeable with Width.

You have the option of changing the width by typing in a new width, as shown here, or using the right and left arrow keys to expand and contract the width on the screen.

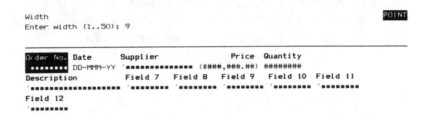

This command works the same way as 1-2-3's /Worksheet Column-Width Set-Width command.

## Using the Format Options

The Format options available through Current-Field are dependent on the field type of the current field. Here are the options for a label field like Order No.:

You are first presented with the options Alignment and Word-Order. Selecting Alignment allows you to choose whether the data should be right, left, or center justified in the cell. Selecting the Word-Order option presents the following menu:

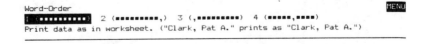

These selections are appropriate for label data that has an

embedded comma, such as Smith, John. You can choose to print the entry as shown, in reverse order without the comma, as only the first word of the entry, or as only the last word of the entry. The descriptions below the menu guide you into making the correct selection by providing an example of each option as you point to the different menu selections.

With value fields the Format command provides a different list of options. You can choose from Fixed, Scientific, Currency, Comma, General, and Percent formats. For all the format options except General you will be prompted for the number of decimal places and may enter from 0 to 15. Each of the options functions the same as in 1-2-3 except Fixed, which here has two subchoices, Spaces and Zeros. A choice of Zeros will include leading 0's, and a choice of Spaces will eliminate them. The appearance of the currency display can be affected further by selections made under the Global Default International menu.

When Format is selected for a date field, the five format options that display with /Range Format Date under release 2 of 1-2-3 are presented. The formats for options 4 and 5, the international date formats, can be altered further with choices in the Global Default International menu.

## Deciding What Totals to Compute

The Current-Field Totals option permits you to count the number of items found in a label field. If you choose this option, you will be shown a menu like the one that follows so that you can select the type of total you want.

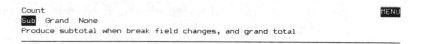

Choosing Sub will create a subtotal if the report has a break field. (The break field controls the sequence of your report, and when its value changes, a subtotal will be produced.) Choosing Sub will also produce a grand total at the end of your report. Choosing Grand produces a total at the end of your report but no subtotals. A choice of None cancels any totals that may have been selected previously.

Choosing the Totals option while a numeric field is highlighted presents a different set of options. You can calculate a sum, count, or average, or you can identify the minimum and maximum values in the field. A choice of None will eliminate any options selected previously. You will still be able to select Sub, Grand, or None for the type of total you desire. The control panel will contain abbreviations for the types of calculations selected for a column. The abbreviations used are as follows:

| | |
|-----|---------------------------------|
| AG  | Average Grand Total             |
| AS  | Average Subtotal                |
| CG  | Count Grand Total               |
| CS  | Count Subtotal                  |
| MG  | Minimum/Maximum Grand Total     |
| MS  | Minimum/Maximum Subtotal        |
| SG  | Sum Grand Total                 |
| SS  | Sum Subtotal                    |

## Choosing Attributes to Affect Appearance

The Report Writer package makes it easy to use a variety of print attributes. Attributes selected under the Current-Field menu will affect the appearance of the current field only. Under the Attributes option you can choose to change the appearance of the field name, the field contents or data, or the field total. The Attributes menu with the Name option chosen looks like this:

```
Attribute                                                    MENU
Name  Data  Totals
Apply attribute to name portion
```

After you determine what aspect of the current field you wish to change the attribute for, you will be presented with the list of options shown in Figure 14-5. Any option you select through this menu will override the global setting, just as 1-2-3's range commands override the global settings for that package. You will also notice that the menu of print attributes is more like a list than like the normal menu. You can select from it with the up and down arrow keys. When your cursor is positioned over the desired attribute, press ENTER. Naturally your printer must support the option selected if you expect your choice to affect the printed output.

## Erasing the Current Field

The Erase option in the Current-Field menu is a quick delete option that requires no confirmation. Choosing this option eliminates the current field from the report. You can restore the field with the Global Restore-Field command. Your worksheet data will be unaffected by any deletions that occur with this command, since it affects only the report format.

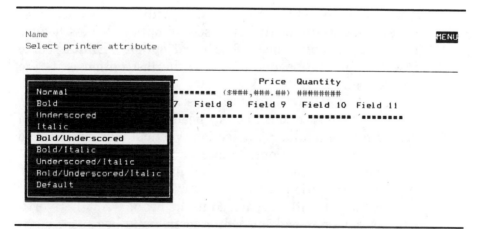

**Figure 14-5.**   Attribute options for Current-Field

The Global command structure is shown in Figure 14-6. Choosing Global from the main menu permits you to change the defaults that apply to the entire report as well as add headers and footers. The Global options also allow you to erase every field except the current field and to restore fields previously erased from the report format.

## Adding Headers and Footers

1-2-3 permits you to have a one-line header at the top of every page. Report Writer permits you to have as many as five header lines at the top of every page. This will let you present a page number, date, company name, and multiple-line field headings in the header area if you wish.

The menu that is presented when you select the Header option from the Global menu looks like this:

The first option allows you to put in additional header lines up to a maximum of five. The second option deletes header lines you no longer need. The third option permits you to insert a / in the header line, and the last option exits the Header option.

Headers follow the same rules as in 1-2-3. Specifically, there are three sections to every header line: a left section, a center section, and a right section. Vertical bars are used to divide the three sections. Whatever you type in response to the header prompt will be placed in the left section of the header. This section can be ended with a vertical bar. What follows the bar will be centered in the header. Another vertical bar is used to end the center section and begin the right section. The same special symbols that 1-2-3 recognizes can be used in the Report Writer header. The # represents the current page number, and the @ accesses the system date.

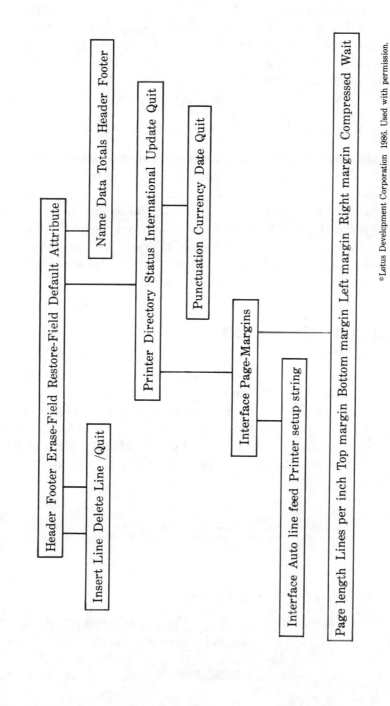

**Figure 14-6.** Global command structure

When either symbol is included in the header, its current value will print.

The Footer option is similar to Header. From zero to five lines of footer are allowed at the bottom of each page. Like headers, footers are divided into three sections. They recognize the same symbols as headers.

## Erasing and Restoring Fields

The Erase-Fields option on the Global menu erases all fields from the current report format except the current field. This option will not affect your data on the 1-2-3 worksheet. It merely prevents the data from appearing in the report.

The Global Restore-Field option will present a list of all the fields deleted from the report. You can type the first letter of any field name that you want to restore to select it quickly.

## Changing the Global Default Options

The Default command on the Global menu allows you to change the global default settings maintained by the package. There is a similar command in the 1-2-3 package. When you select the Default command, you will have the choice of changing the Printer, Directory, or International options. You can also check the status of the global settings, update the global settings, or quit the Global Default menu, as shown here:

```
Default                                                      MENU
Printer  Directory  Status  International  Update  Quit
Save default settings in configuration file
```

## Changing the Printer Settings

When you choose to change the global default printer settings, you will be presented with two options, as follows:

```
Printer
Interface  Page-Margins
```

When Interface is selected, it presents additional choices for Printer, Interface number, Auto line feed, and Printer setup string, as shown here:

```
Interface                                                              MENU
Select option.  Press ESC to return to the Options menu.

_____

      DEFAULT INTERFACE OPTIONS

      Printer: Epson MX-100

      Interface: Parallel 1
      Auto line feed: No
      Printer setup string:
```

If you have installed more than one printer, you can select the Printer option from the list and specify another printer. You also have the option of selecting any of eight interfaces. Options 1 and 3 are parallel interfaces, and options 2 and 4 are serial interface connections. Options 5 through 8 are DOS device types, from LPT1 through LPT4, that are used with a local area network printer. If you choose one of the serial connections, you will also have to choose a baud rate setting. Settings from 110 to 19200 are represented by codes from 0 through 9.

The automatic line feed option is next. If you choose Auto line feed Yes, you are telling Report Writer that your printer automatically advances the paper in the printer. No has the opposite effect.

You can supply a setup string to use for the entire report if you choose Setup. This string must always begin with a backslash. The backslash may be followed with the letter representing the desired option or the three-character ASCII code.

Page-Margins is the second Global Default Printer option. The menu listing for this choice is shown in Figure 14-7. It permits you to choose the page length and the lines per inch. It also permits you to choose top, bottom, right, and left margin settings. Margin settings are measured in inches. Compressed print is available as a menu option. Yes indicates that you wish to use it, and No indicates that you do not want it. You can choose to wait between pages if you use single-feed paper.

```
DEFAULT PAGE-MARGIN OPTIONS


Page length (inches): 11.0
Lines per inch: 6
Top margin (inches): .0.5
Bottom margin (inches): 0.5
Left margin (inches): 0.5
Right margin (inches): 8.0
Compress print? Yes
Wait between pages? No
```

**Figure 14-7.**     Page-Margins menu

### Changing the Default Directory

Global Default Directory will allow you to change the current directory to a different drive or to a different pathname on your hard disk. After using this option, you may want to select Global Default Update to make the change permanent.

### Displaying the Current Default Options

Selecting Global Default Status will display all the current default settings. These include settings for the Printer, Directory, and International options, as shown in Figure 14-8.

### Changing the International Settings

The Global Default International command permits you to change the standard punctuation indicators, the currency symbol and its placement, and the appearance of the international date formats. The selections in this section are almost the same as those found in 1-2-3 under /Worksheet Global

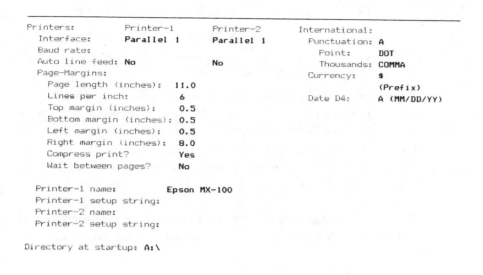

**Figure 14-8.**    Global Default Status screen

Default International. Report Writer's International menu options are as follows:

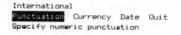

**Punctuation**    1-2-3 permits you to change the point, thousands, and argument separators. It has eight rather than Report Writer's four settings for this command. Report Writer lets you change only the point and the thousands separator, since built-in functions are not used with the package. These options affect the appearance of currency and comma fields. The designators—the symbols used for the point and thousands—and their effect on numeric entries are as follows:

| Setting | Point Separator | Thousands |
|---|---|---|
| A (.,) default | $512.57 | 7,800 |
| B (,.) | $512,57 | 7.800 |
| C (. ) | $512.57 | 7800 |
| D (, ) | $512,57 | 7800 |

**Currency**     This option allows you to specify up to 15 characters as the currency symbol. You may use 1-2-3's Compose sequence, described in Chapter 6, to create your own symbols from the LICS character set. The default is $. After selecting the symbol, you can elect to use it as a suffix or prefix for your entry.

**Date**     You have the choice of four different international date display options with this command. They are as follows:

A   MM/DD/YY

B   DD/MM/YY

C   DD.MM.YY

D   YY-MM-DD

### Updating the Default Settings

Selecting the Update option from the Global Default menu will save the changes you have made for the Printer, Directory, and International default settings so they will be available during your next Report Writer session.

## Changing Global Attributes

The Global Attribute command permits you to add special print attributes to all the field names in a report, all the data, all the totals, the header area, or the footer area. To make your specification, select Name, Data, Totals, Header, or Footer, respectively, from the menu shown.

Then select the special option you want from the list that Report Writer presents. The print options you can choose from are the same as those found under Current-Field Attribute, as you can see from the following list:

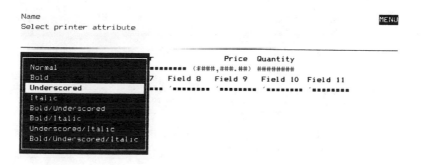

```
Name                                                            MENU
Select printer attribute
```

```
                                             Price   Quantity
        ┌────────────────────────┐  ======= ($###,###.##)  ========
        │ Normal                 │
        │ Bold                   │ 7  Field 8  Field 9  Field 10  Field 11
        │ Underscored            │ === '======== '======== '======== '========
        │ Italic                 │
        │ Bold/Underscored       │
        │ Bold/Italic            │
        │ Underscored/Italic     │
        │ Bold/Underscored/Italic│
        └────────────────────────┘
```

## Restructuring a Report
## With the Move Command

You can make the Move command operate on an individual field or all the fields in your report by selecting options from the menu shown.

```
Move                                                           MENU
Entire-Field  Name  Data  Row-Format  Column-Format
Position entire field
```

When working with the current field, this command allows you to reposition the field within the report. When working with all the fields, it gives you the choice of using a row or column orientation for your data.

As you attempt to restructure your report, you may want to consult some of the help material that Report Writer offers. Figure 14-9 presents one of the help screens for the Move command. You will note that the help screens provide even more extensive support than 1-2-3 does in many

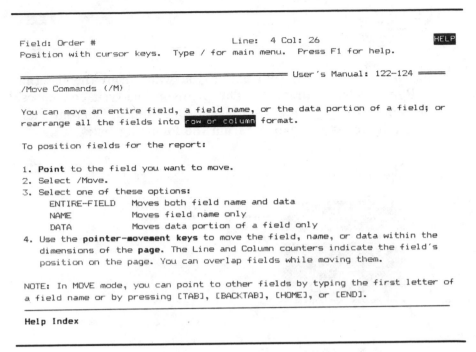

========================================== User's Manual: 122-124 =====

/Move Commands (/M)

You can move an entire field, a field name, or the data portion of a field; or
rearrange all the fields into `row or column` format.

To position fields for the report:

1. **Point** to the field you want to move.
2. Select /Move.
3. Select one of these options:
   ENTIRE-FIELD   Moves both field name and data
   NAME           Moves field name only
   DATA           Moves data portion of a field only
4. Use the **pointer-movement keys** to move the field, name, or data within the
   dimensions of the **page.** The Line and Column counters indicate the field's
   position on the page. You can overlap fields while moving them.

NOTE: In MOVE mode, you can point to other fields by typing the first letter of
a field name or by pressing [TAB], [BACKTAB], [HOME], or [END].

Help Index

**Figure 14-9.**    Help instructions for Move

instances, with reference to pages in the user manual and
step-by-step directions for a command's use.

The choices Entire-Field, Name, and Data are all
designed to work with one report field at a time. You can
select a field with the first letter of the field name, the TAB
key, or the END or HOME keys. After selecting the field, you
can use the arrow keys and the CTRL-arrow key combination
to move the field on your report. You may allow two fields to
overlap temporarily as you reposition entries. If this situation
remains at the time you print the report, however, you will
get an error message.

As an example, suppose you want to move Order No. to
the right of Date and Supplier. First, choose Entire-Field
and highlight Order No.

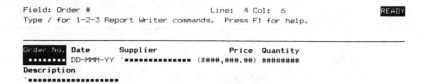

The appearance of the report layout changes as Order No. is moved to the right, partly covering Supplier.

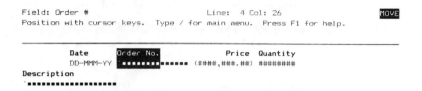

Date and then Supplier are then moved left, producing the following display:

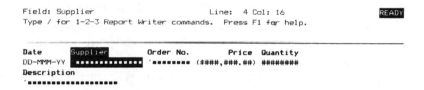

Choosing Column-Format will rearrange all the fields so that they have a column orientation, after which each entry in the report will display on multiple lines, as shown:

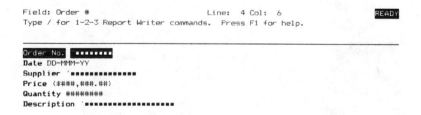

A choice of Row-Format will eliminate the Column-Format setting and change the format back to the default setting.

# Sorting Data for a Report

Report Writer's sort features are easier to use than those of 1-2-3 options and provide expanded functionality. Choosing Sort from the main menu will produce the menu shown.

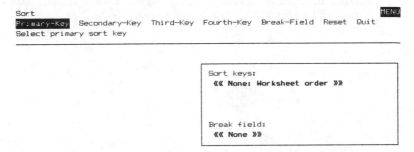

From this menu you can see that you can sort on up to four fields. As in 1-2-3, Primary-Key will always be the controlling sequence; the other keys will be used only when the higher-level keys contain duplicates. As you select each key, it will display in the box to the right of your screen. Choosing a sort key is easy because 1-2-3 provides a list of field names for you to select from, as shown in Figure 14-10. Simply

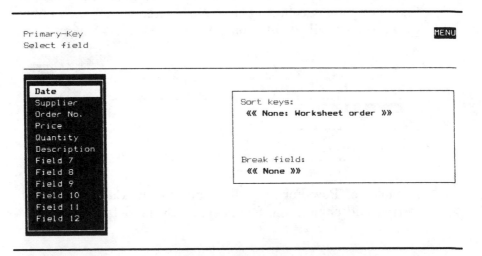

**Figure 14-10.**    Selecting a primary key

point to the field name you wish to control the sequence at that level and press ENTER. For each key selected you will have to tell Report Writer whether your sort sequence is ascending (A) or descending (D).

The Break-Field option permits you to determine the level at which you want to insert report subtotals. Every time the value of the break field changes, Report Writer will present the subtotal calculation or calculations you have defined. Figure 14-11 shows the screen after the selection of three sort keys and a break key.

Like 1-2-3's Sort Reset option, the Reset option in this menu cancels all the selections you have made with the Sort command. This means that you will have to define the sort fields and the break key again if you plan to execute another sort.

## Selecting the Records You Want

Report Writer's Query command allows you to define the rules for selecting the database records that will appear in your report. The records that you define for selection will be used when your report is printed with the Print command.

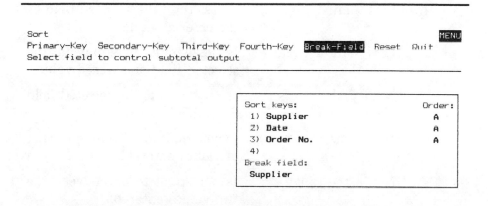

Sort                                                                    MENU
Primary-Key  Secondary-Key  Third-Key  Fourth-Key  Break-Field  Reset  Quit
Select field to control subtotal output

```
                              Sort keys:              Order:
                               1) Supplier              A
                               2) Date                  A
                               3) Order No.              A
                               4)
                              Break field:
                               Supplier
```

**Figure 14-11.**    Screen with three sort keys and a break key

## Entering a Basic Query

Creating a Report Writer query is much easier than creating a query with 1-2-3. You define three separate components of the selection rule. Each part can be selected from a menu. The first part of the selection rule is the field name you wish to use in the comparison. Figure 14-12 shows the way Report Writer allows you to select your field name from a list. There is no need to type it into a criteria area, as you must with 1-2-3; simply point to the field you wish to use. The second part of every selection rule is the condition or comparison operator. Report Writer will select comparison operators appropriate for the type of field you have chosen for the comparison. The complete list of options is as follows:

| | |
|---|---|
| Equal | Equals the selected field or the value entered. |
| Greater than | Is greater than the selected field or entered value. |
| Greater than or equal | Is greater than or equal to the selected field or entered value. |
| In the list | Equals a value in the list of values entered. |
| In the range | Is equal to or between the two values entered. |
| Less than | Is less than the selected field or the entered value. |
| Less than or equal | Is less than or equal to the selected field or entered value. |
| Not equal | Is not equal to the selected field or entered value. |
| Not in the list | Is not equal to a value in the list of values entered. |
| Not in the range | Is not equal to or between the two values entered. |

Select·all·records·where

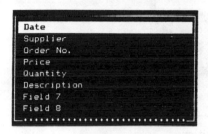

**Figure 14-12.** Selecting a field name

Report Writer makes the selection of the appropriate condition simple, since it presents the possible conditions on the screen alongside your first selection, as shown in Figure 14-13.

The last part of the selection rule will be a choice from a list of fields or an entry for you to fill in. 1-2-3 will present a list of fields that are of the same type as your first selection. You also have the option of entering a value or a list of values. If there are no other fields of the same type, the third box on the screen will be blank, and you will be expected to enter one or more values, depending on the comparison operator you chose. Figure 14-14 presents the third box when Date and less than were the first two selections. In this situation your only alternative would be to enter a date value in the format MM/DD/YY. Report Writer will supply the slashes, and you must supply the proper numeric values.

Select•all•records•where

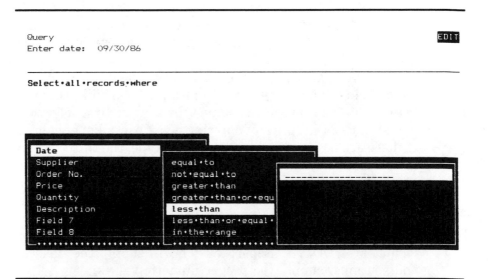

**Figure 14-13.**　　Selecting a condition

Select•all•records•where

**Figure 14-14.**　　The last query entry

## Using Wildcard Characters in a Query

Report Writer supports the same wildcard characters in a query as 1-2-3 does. You may use them with the following comparison operators: equal to, not equal to, in the list, and not in the list. The wildcard characters are as follows:

* Matches any number of upper-case or lower-case characters. Sm* would match with Sm, Smith, Smithfield, Smothers, and so on.

? Matches any single upper-case or lower-case character. Sm?th would match with Smith, Smath, Smeth, and so on but would not match with Smithfield.

These characters can be combined for more sophisticated wildcard operations. For example, Sm?th* would match with Smith, Smithfield, or Smath but would not match with Smouth.

## Using Connectors for Compound Queries

After you enter your first complete query, Report Writer will display a fourth box at the side of your screen. It contains the options AND, OR, and DONE. The last option tells Report Writer that you are finished with your query. The other two tell Report Writer that you wish to create a compound query, using either AND or OR to join the current query with a second query. A compound query might read, Supplier equal to ABC Company AND Price greater than 25.50. In this case, both conditions would need to be true before a record in the database would be considered to match the selection criteria and be placed in your report when it is printed. When you use OR, a record will be selected for your report if it meets either condition specified.

## Using the Query Menu

Report Writer has a complete menu that is displayed after you have entered an initial query. The options in the Query menu are Edit, Insert, Append, Delete, Clear, and Quit. Edit allows you to change one of your selection rules or the connector without retyping the entire entry. Insert allows you to insert a selection rule or connector in your current criteria. Append is similar to Insert except that it adds selection rules or connectors to the end of your entry. Delete eliminates the highlighted portion of your selection without destroying the entire entry. Clear completely eliminates the current selection rules so that you can start over. Quit returns you to the report layout and prompts you with an error message if the current query is incomplete.

## Printing Your Report

The Print commands produce a printed copy of your report. They actually do much more, since the menus for Print contain many options. The main Print menu is shown in Figure

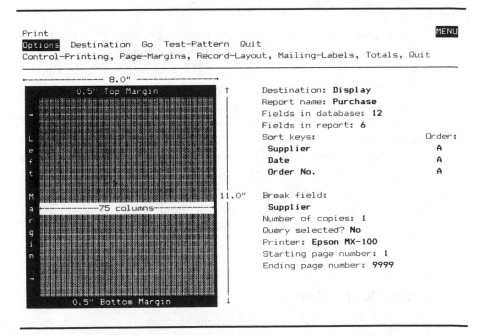

**Figure 14-15.**    The Print menu

14-15. Note the graphic representation of the print layout, which minimizes errors in selecting your options.

## Selecting Print Options

Print Options presents a submenu from which you can elect to set page margin, change printing options such as whether to print field names and separate records, define your record layout, and select totals placement for your report. This menu also provides access to the mailing label commands. These let you create mailing labels that are placed one, two, three, or four across the page.

### Using Control-Printing Options

Figure 14-16 presents the options available under Control-Printing, the first choice under Options. As you can see from

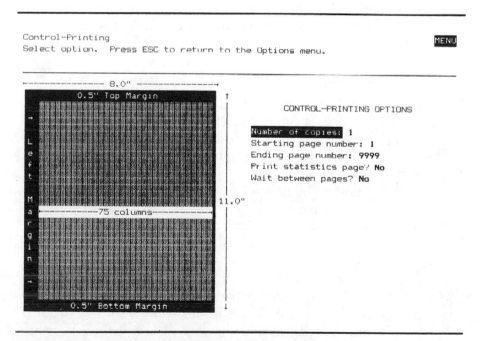

**Figure 14-16.** Control-Printing options

the figure, these options for changing the printed output are presented in a vertical list. You can select the number of copies you wish to print, specifying from 1 to 99 copies, as long as your output is sent to the printer and not the screen. The starting page number option can be used to print an extra page of a report or to replace a page containing errors. If you specify 10 as the starting page number and the report has 15 pages, for example, pages 10 through 15 will be printed. The ending page number permits you to stop printing before the end of the report. It can be used in conjunction with the starting page number to reprint a single page or section of a report.

The statistics page is an optional page that can be placed in any report. It shows the name of the worksheet file used for the report and other information such as the date, time, sort key, and starting and ending pages for the report. Choosing Yes will print it. No will suppress the printing.

The last option in the Control-Printing list allows you to adjust the settings for both single sheet and continuous form paper. If you select Yes for Wait between pages?, 1-2-3 will stop after each page and ask whether you wish to continue. The No option prints from beginning to end without stopping.

### Setting the Page Margins

The screen in Figure 14-17 shows the options available for the Page-Margins command. It also shows the page display that appears when the Compress print option is set at Yes.

The first Page-Margins option is the page length. Report Writer will accept any entry from .5 to 14 inches. The second option, lines per inch, can be set at either 6 or 8.

The Top margin setting is next. It can be any number from 0 to 4 inches. Its default setting is .5 inches. You may include from 0 to 99 blank lines after the header line. The Bottom margin setting, like that for Top margin, can be any number from 0 to 4, with a default of .5.

The Left and Right margin options are next. The Left margin default is .5 inches, with acceptable settings from 0 to 3 inches. The Right margin default is 8 inches, but this

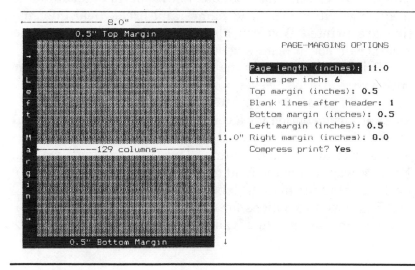

Page-Margins
Select option.   Press ESC to return to the Options menu.

MENU

PAGE-MARGINS OPTIONS

Page length (inches): 11.0
Lines per inch: 6
Top margin (inches): 0.5
Blank lines after header: 1
Bottom margin (inches): 0.5
Left margin (inches): 0.5
Right margin (inches): 0.0
Compress print? Yes

**Figure 14-17.**    Page-Margins options

margin can be set at any value from 5 through 14 inches.

As you choose your right and left margin, keep in mind that the minimum width allowed for a report line is 50 characters. This will be 5 inches when compressed print is set at No.

Regular print is 10 characters to the inch. The package also supports the smaller (compressed) print available on many printers, although the number of characters to the inch with Compressed will vary somewhat with different printer models. Setting the last Page-Margins option to Yes will cause your report to be printed in compressed print. Using the default setting of No will print it in regular print. When you select Compressed, Report Writer adjusts the page display on the screen to increase the number of characters across the screen and to change other selections such as headers.

### Selecting Record Layout Commands

Figure 14-18 shows the Record-Layout options at the right side of the screen. These options allow you to determine the frequency with which field names and break field information are printed. You can also choose spacing options and whether or not to print a separator character.

Print Field Names is the first option on this menu. Your options are Always, Never, and Once. Choosing Always will cause field names to be printed in each record. This may be an appropriate option for a columnar report, where you want each piece of data labeled. Once will print the field names only at the top of each column. This is the default setting. Never always omits the field names. This would be an appropriate setting for mailing labels.

You have two options for spacing at the end of a record. You can choose Page to advance to the next page or Lines to

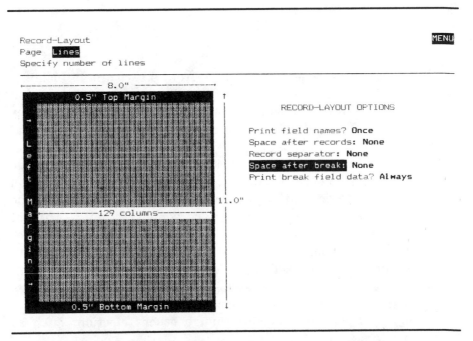

Record-Layout                                                    MENU
Page  Lines
Specify number of lines

**Figure 14-18.**    Record-Layout options

use blank lines to separate the records. If you choose Lines, you can use from 0 to 99 blank lines as a separator.

The Record Separator option permits the use of a line of characters to separate records. You can choose None to leave the separator line blank. If you choose Character, Report Writer will expect you to enter a character as a separator.

Space After Break allows the insertion of blank lines after a change in the break field. If you choose Page, the next record will print at the top of the next page. If you choose Lines, you can specify from 0 to 99 blank lines after the break.

Print Break Field Data allows you to print the data for the break field in every record if you choose the Always option. If you choose the Once option, it will print the data only when the value in the break field changes.

### Printing Mailing Labels

There is a special menu under Print Options for mailing labels. The Mailing-Labels menu is your vehicle for telling Report Writer that you wish to print mailing labels and specifying what they should look like. This menu is shown in Figure 14-19.

The first option in the menu is Print Labels. The default value for this option is No. This will cause Report Writer to follow the format of the report layout. Changing this option to Yes eliminates field names and any lines that do not contain data.

Label Height is the distance from the top of one label to the top of the next. It can be any value from .1 inch to 4 inches. Its default value is 1 inch.

Labels Across tells Report Writer whether you will print one, two, three, or four labels across the page. The choice you make should be consistent with your margin settings and your choice of compressed or regular print.

Label Width can be any number between 1 and 6 inches, in increments of .1 inch. The default value for this option is 4 inches. Label width is measured as the distance from the left edge of one label to the left edge of the next label on the right.

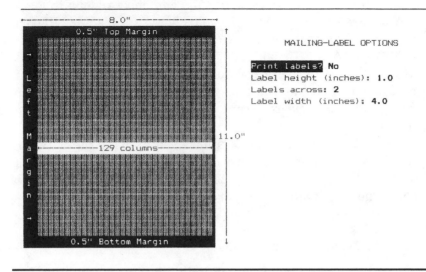

**Figure 14-19.**      Mailing-Labels menu

### Specifying Totals Options

The Totals options allow you to specify the pattern for label placement and the separator characters for grand totals and subtotals. They also give you the ability to create a summary report containing just totals.

The Totals menu is another list. If you select Placement Type, you will see the three different formats presented on the screen in Figure 14-20. The first placement type is valid for either row-format or column-format reports. The other two types can be used only for column-format reports.

You can also select the totals separator characters. At present the subtotal separator is - and the grand total separator is *. You may change the setting of either of these options by selecting the option and typing a new character. The default value for the subtotal is -. The default for the grand total is =.

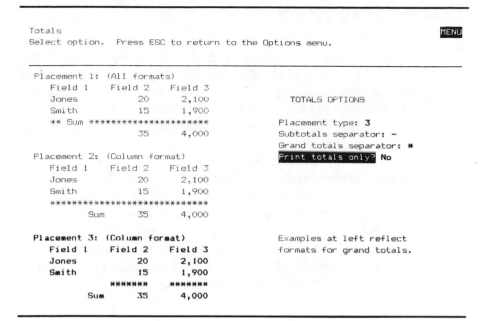

```
Totals                                                                    MENU
Select option.  Press ESC to return to the Options menu.


  Placement 1: (All formats)
     Field 1      Field 2      Field 3
     Jones              20        2,100                TOTALS OPTIONS
     Smith              15        1,900
     ** Sum ***********************        Placement type: 3
                        35        4,000        Subtotals separator: -
                                              Grand totals separator: *
  Placement 2: (Column format)                Print totals only? No
     Field 1      Field 2      Field 3
     Jones              20        2,100
     Smith              15        1,900
     ******************************
              Sum       35        4,000

  Placement 3: (Column format)                Examples at left reflect
     Field 1      Field 2      Field 3        formats for grand totals.
     Jones              20        2,100
     Smith              15        1,900
                   *******      *******
              Sum       35        4,000
```

**Figure 14-20.**    Totals options

The last option on the Totals menu permits you to print only totals if you choose. If you set the Totals Only option to Yes, both Total and Subtotal information will be printed. If you set it to No, only the total information will be printed.

## Selecting Print Destination

The Print Destination menu provides you the choice of three different print destinations. You can choose to print your report to the screen (Display), your printer, or a disk file, as you can see:

```
Destination                                                               MENU
Display  Printer  File
Output report to display
```

If you choose File, you will need to specify the file name you want 1-2-3 to use.

## Obtaining a Test Pattern

The Print Test-Pattern command will display or print a report with special characters rather than your actual data. This option is useful for aligning mailing labels or ensuring that you have formatted your report correctly before requesting a printout of the complete report. The Test-Pattern option will print the pattern to the current destination device, using selections from the menu shown in Figure 14-21.

If the current destination is the screen, the pattern will fill your screen and then present the menu below. If you choose Line, it will display a new line of pattern at the bottom of your screen while scrolling an old one off the top. Selecting Screen will present another screen of information. Restart displays the test pattern from the beginning, and Quit ends this option. Figure 14-22 shows a sample of the test pattern for the worksheet shown earlier in the chapter.

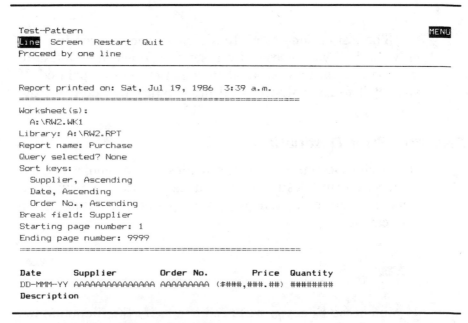

```
Test-Pattern                                                    MENU
Line  Screen  Restart  Quit
Proceed by one line


Report printed on: Sat, Jul 19, 1986  3:39 a.m.
=================================================================
Worksheet(s):
  A:\RW2.WK1
Library: A:\RW2.RPT
Report name: Purchase
Query selected? None
Sort keys:
  Supplier, Ascending
  Date, Ascending
  Order No., Ascending
Break field: Supplier
Starting page number: 1
Ending page number: 9999
=================================================================

Date       Supplier        Order No.      Price  Quantity
DD-MMM-YY AAAAAAAAAAAAAAA AAAAAAAAA ($###,###.##) ########
Description
```

**Figure 14-21.**     Test-Pattern menu

```
Date      Supplier          Order No.        Price Quantity Description
DD-MMM-YY AAAAAAAAAAAAAAA AAAAAAAA ($###,###.##) ######## AAAAAAAAAAAAAAAAAAAA
DD-MMM-YY AAAAAAAAAAAAAAA AAAAAAAA ($###,###.##) ######## AAAAAAAAAAAAAAAAAAAA
DD-MMM-YY AAAAAAAAAAAAAAA AAAAAAAA ($###,###.##) ######## AAAAAAAAAAAAAAAAAAAA
DD-MMM-YY AAAAAAAAAAAAAAA AAAAAAAA ($###,###.##) ######## AAAAAAAAAAAAAAAAAAAA
DD-MMM-YY AAAAAAAAAAAAAAA AAAAAAAA ($###,###.##) ######## AAAAAAAAAAAAAAAAAAAA
DD-MMM-YY AAAAAAAAAAAAAAA AAAAAAAA ($###,###.##) ######## AAAAAAAAAAAAAAAAAAAA
DD-MMM-YY AAAAAAAAAAAAAAA AAAAAAAA ($###,###.##) ######## AAAAAAAAAAAAAAAAAAAA
DD-MMM-YY AAAAAAAAAAAAAAA AAAAAAAA ($###,###.##) ######## AAAAAAAAAAAAAAAAAAAA
DD-MMM-YY AAAAAAAAAAAAAAA AAAAAAAA ($###,###.##) ######## AAAAAAAAAAAAAAAAAAAA
DD-MMM-YY AAAAAAAAAAAAAAA AAAAAAAA ($###,###.##) ######## AAAAAAAAAAAAAAAAAAAA
DD-MMM-YY AAAAAAAAAAAAAAA AAAAAAAA ($###,###.##) ######## AAAAAAAAAAAAAAAAAAAA
DD-MMM-YY AAAAAAAAAAAAAAA AAAAAAAA ($###,###.##) ######## AAAAAAAAAAAAAAAAAAAA
DD-MMM-YY AAAAAAAAAAAAAAA AAAAAAAA ($###,###.##) ######## AAAAAAAAAAAAAAAAAAAA
DD-MMM-YY AAAAAAAAAAAAAAA AAAAAAAA ($###,###.##) ######## AAAAAAAAAAAAAAAAAAAA
DD-MMM-YY AAAAAAAAAAAAAAA AAAAAAAA ($###,###.##) ######## AAAAAAAAAAAAAAAAAAAA
DD-MMM-YY AAAAAAAAAAAAAAA AAAAAAAA ($###,###.##) ######## AAAAAAAAAAAAAAAAAAAA
DD-MMM-YY AAAAAAAAAAAAAAA AAAAAAAA ($###,###.##) ######## AAAAAAAAAAAAAAAAAAAA
DD-MMM-YY AAAAAAAAAAAAAAA AAAAAAAA ($###,###.##) ######## AAAAAAAAAAAAAAAAAAAA
DD-MMM-YY AAAAAAAAAAAAAAA AAAAAAAA ($###,###.##) ######## AAAAAAAAAAAAAAAAAAAA
```

**Figure 14-22.** Actual test pattern

## Printing the Report

The Go option in the Print menu is the culmination of all the selections made in the Report Writer menus. It is the command that actually produces your report. It writes the report to the currently selected destination device.

When the destination device is the screen, selecting Go produces another menu, with options of Line, Screen, Restart, and Quit. Choosing Line prints the next line of the report to the screen. Choosing Screen prints the next full screen of the report. Restart begins the print display from the beginning. The last option, Quit, cancels the printing of the report.

Figure 14-23 shows a page of a report produced with Report Writer. This particular report provides an average unit price for purchases from different suppliers. Figure 14-24 provides a simpler report with the same data; it essentially just lists data from the records. A sample of a report statistics page is shown in Figure 14-25.

```
Order #   Date       Supplier          Price    Quantity Description
C1110     20-Aug-86  ABC Computers     $75.00        3 Printer stands
-- Average ------------------------------------------------------------------
                                       $75.00


K5607     01-Aug-86  Arkins Supply     $12.50        4 Metal trash can
F5505     14-Aug-86  Arkins Supply     $14.50        5 Envelopes legal size
-- Average ------------------------------------------------------------------
                                       $13.50


R9906-2   15-Aug-86  Beacon            $120.00       1 Monthly coffee order
-- Average ------------------------------------------------------------------
                                       $120.00


K5501     02-Aug-86  Borman Lumber     $3.59        12 Shelf brackets
-- Average ------------------------------------------------------------------
                                       $3.59


K5500-9   01-Aug-86  Cheap Paper       $7.80        14 Box legal pads
R6791     12-Aug-86  Cheap Paper       $12.50       15 Box envelopes letter
R6792     13-Aug-86  Cheap Paper       $17.60       10 Box legal envelopes
F5509     27-Aug-86  Cheap Paper       $7.80        10 Ark ribbons
-- Average ------------------------------------------------------------------
                                       $11.43


R6793     14-Aug-86  Computer Supply   $7.80        10 Ark ribbons
C1109     18-Aug-86  Computer Supply   $0.79      1000 DS/DD diskettes
-- Average ------------------------------------------------------------------
                                       $4.29


R6789     03-Aug-86  Merideth's        $349.00       1 Credenza
F5504     07-Aug-86  Merideth's        $25.00        2 File cabinets
F5506     25-Aug-86  Merideth's        $17.60       10 Box legal envelopes
-- Average ------------------------------------------------------------------
                                       $130.53


F5503     06-Aug-86  Morris Catering   $625.75       1 Office picnic
-- Average ------------------------------------------------------------------
                                       $625.75


F4310     02-Aug-86  Office News       $5.50        10 Magazine storage box
-- Average ------------------------------------------------------------------
                                       $5.50


F5502     04-Aug-86  Rinko Printing    $124.00       1 Credit report forms
-- Average ------------------------------------------------------------------
                                       $124.00


R6790     05-Aug-86  TY Office Inc.    $14.50        4 Staplers, heavy duty
F5511     28-Aug-86  TY Office Inc.    $120.00       1 Small File
```

**Figure 14-23.**     Report page with averages

```
Date      Supplier       Order No.    Price  Quantity Description
20-Aug-86 ABC Computers   C1110       $75.00        3 Printer stands
01-Aug-86 Arkins Supply   K5607       $12.50        4 Metal trash can
14-Aug-86 Arkins Supply   F5505       $14.50        5 Envelopes legal size
15-Aug-86 Beacon          R9906-2    $120.00        1 Monthly coffee order
02-Aug-86 Borman Lumber   K5501        $3.59       12 Shelf brackets
01-Aug-86 Cheap Paper     K5500-9      $7.80       14 Box legal pads
12-Aug-86 Cheap Paper     R6791       $12.50       15 Box envelopes letter
13-Aug-86 Cheap Paper     R6792       $17.60       10 Box legal envelopes
27-Aug-86 Cheap Paper     F5509        $7.80       10 Ark ribbons
14-Aug-86 Computer Supply R6793        $7.80       10 Ark ribbons
18-Aug-86 Computer Supply C1109        $0.79     1000 DS/DD diskettes
03-Aug-86 Merideth's      R6789      $349.00        1 Credenza
07-Aug-86 Merideth's      F5504       $25.00        2 File cabinets
25-Aug-86 Merideth's      F5506       $17.60       10 Box legal envelopes
06-Aug-86 Morris Catering F5503      $625.75        1 Office picnic
02-Aug-86 Office News     F4310        $5.50       10 Magazine storage box
04-Aug-86 Rinko Printing  F5502      $124.00        1 Credit report forms
05-Aug-86 TY Office Inc.  R6790       $14.50        4 Staplers, heavy duty
28-Aug-86 TY Office Inc.  F5511      $120.00        1 Small File
```

**Figure 14-24.**    Record listing report

```
Report printed on: Sat, Jul 19, 1986  3:56 a.m.
=======================================================
Worksheet(s):
  A:\RW2.WK1
Library: A:\RW2.RPT
Report name: Purchase
Query selected?
  Select all records where (Date is not equal to
  "__/__/____")
Sort keys:
  Supplier, Ascending
  Date, Ascending
  Order No., Ascending
Break field: Supplier
Starting page number: 1
Ending page number: 9999
Number of copies: 1
Left margin (inches): 0.5
Right margin (inches): 8.0
Page length (inches): 11.0
Lines per inch: 6
Printer: Epson MX-100
=======================================================
```

**Figure 14-25.**    Report statistics page

Report Writer's File command permits you to work with worksheet, report, and library files. You can retrieve worksheet files with this option. You can also save or retrieve report files or create them from a newly retrieved worksheet. You can use, rename, and erase library files as well. The menu for the File command is as follows:

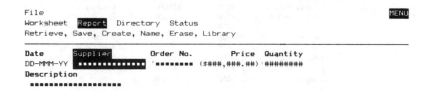

```
File                                                    MENU
Worksheet  Report  Directory  Status
Retrieve, Save, Create, Name, Erase, Library

Date        Supplier         Order No.       Price   Quantity
DD-MMM-YY   ■■■■■■■■■■■■■    '■■■■■■■■  ($###,###.##) '########
Description
■■■■■■■■■■■■■■■■■■
```

## Using Worksheet Options

Since Report Writer cannot update worksheet files, the only option it permits is to retrieve a worksheet file. Since retrieving a new worksheet will erase the current report options, you will want to save your current report before invoking Worksheet Retrieve.

## Using Report Options

The Report options provide the heart of the File command. They allow you to create, save, retrieve, erase, and rename report layouts. The Create option lets you create a new report layout from a worksheet or a named range within a worksheet. Selecting this option will automatically create a new report layout when you first start Report Writer or retrieve a worksheet. If a worksheet is already in memory, you will be asked to select Yes after Create to get a new report layout.

The Report Save option allows you to assign an 18-character name to a report layout and save it in the current library. If you are saving an existing file, you will be prompted to choose Cancel or Replace to ensure that you really wish to replace the existing report layout with the current report description.

The Retrieve option permits you to make a saved report current. The Name option allows you to rename an existing report. The Erase option deletes a saved report.

The Library option provides three choices. You can use this command to specify a report library from the current directory. You can also use it to rename a library or erase a library from the current directory.

## Changing the File Directory

The File Directory command changes the default location that 1-2-3 uses to read files. It can be used in conjunction with the other File commands to alter the current drive or directory. Changes you make with it will be in effect only for the remainder of the current session or until you issue the File Directory command again. This command overrides the global default directory.

## Examining File Status

The File Status display is shown in Figure 14-26. It tells you the worksheet drive and the percentage of the disk that is currently filled. The current worksheet directory and file name are also listed. So are the range name, the name of the current report library file, and the report name.

## Exiting Report Writer

Choosing the Exit command tells Report Writer that you would like to end your current session. Be sure to save your worksheet before responding Yes to Report Writer's confirmation prompt when you request Exit. If you have not saved, choose the No option and save before selecting Exit again.

```
                           ┌─File Status─┐
          Worksheet drive:     A

             Percent full:     18%

      Worksheet directory:     A:\

          Worksheet name:      A:\RW2.WK1

             Range name:       Entire worksheet

          Report library:      A:\RW2.RPT

            Report name:       Purchase

```

**Figure 14-26.**     File Status screen

## Creating a Batch of Reports

Report Writer allows you to access predefined reports through batch files. You create the batch file instructions through your word processor, the DOS editor, or some other text processor. These instructions allow Report Writer to produce a whole series of reports with one command. You can process up to 12 worksheets with one report definition using this method, and you may request multiple reports. Complete directions for using this feature are found in the Report Writer manual.

# FIFTEEN

# Extending 1-2-3
# With Add-on Products

**Reflex: The Analyst**
**Note-It**
**SQZ!**
**Manager Mouse**
**Sideways**
**The Spreadsheet Auditor**
**SuperKey**
**Freelance**

An entire market of third-party products that work with or enhance 1-2-3's features has developed because of the package's popularity. These products run the gamut from dedicated 1-2-3 templates for specialized applications to utility packages that enhance the features of 1-2-3 along with other popular software packages. This chapter will look briefly at several of these products. The ones that were chosen meet one or more of the following criteria:

• Utility package that can support the needs of users in various business disciplines rather than being limited to a specific business application.

• Package that provides significant enhancements to 1-2-3's features.

• Package currently in widespread use among 1-2-3 business users.

Within these criteria, only one package of each type was selected—that is, one print utility, one database package, and so on.

The packages selected for coverage are the following:

• Freelance, a free-form graphics package capable of enhancing 1-2-3 graphics with text, symbols, and other options.

• Note-It, a memory-resident program that lets you create file notes or call notes for better documentation.

• Manager Mouse, a mouse product that allows you to make selections with a mouse rather than the keyboard.

• Reflex, an analytical database system that can read and write 1-2-3 files and has found widespread use for generating 1-2-3 reports.

Sideways, a print utility package that can print wide spreadsheet reports sideways on your paper.

• The Spreadsheet Auditor, a package that audits worksheet entries to reduce worksheet errors.

• SQZ!, a package that compresses worksheet files to reduce their size by 85% to 90% for disk storage or electronic transmission.

• SuperKey, a keyboard enhancement with macro recording features as well as a file security package.

This chapter is not designed to function as a tutorial for the use of these packages or to cover all their features. It will simply point out one or two of the key features of each that may be of interest to a 1-2-3 user. You can then select the package or packages you wish to examine in more detail.

Reflex is a database package that works equally well with text and numeric data. Once your data is entered into Reflex, you can look at it in several ways through the package's various views. Reflex provides the following views:

- Form View provides a close-up look at one record in your file.

- List View, similar to the worksheet format used by 1-2-3, allows you to look at many records at once.

- Graph View provides a visual summary of your data.

- Crosstab View provides a numeric summary of your data by category.

- Report View allows you to design custom-printed output for your data.

Although Reflex can be used alone, it has gained popularity as a report generator for 1-2-3 and other packages. It is capable of analyzing data stored in its files to provide new perspectives on your worksheet data. It is extremely easy to use and is reasonably priced compared to other database packages with the same level of features.

## The Reflex Menu Structure

Reflex's menus are a little different from 1-2-3's. Reflex has two main programs, each with its own menu. The opening screen, which appears after you load Reflex from the System disk, is shown in Figure 15-1. The Form, List, Crosstab, and

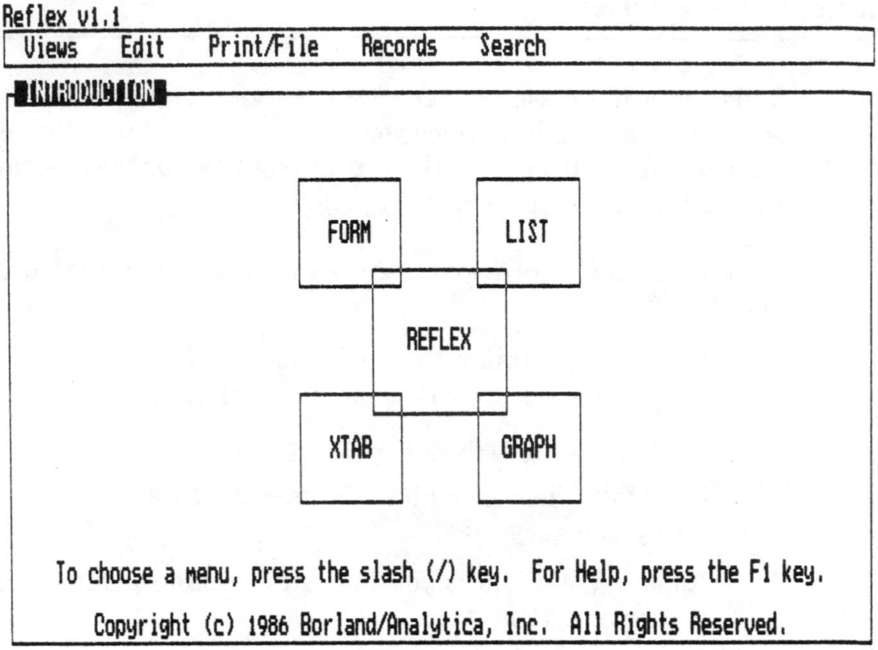

| Views | Edit | Print/File | Records | Search |
|-------|------|------------|---------|--------|

**INTRODUCTION**

```
        ┌──────────┐      ┌──────────┐
        │   FORM   │      │   LIST   │
        │          │      │          │
        └────┬─────┘      └────┬─────┘
         ┌───┴────────────────┴───┐
         │         REFLEX         │
         └───┬────────────────┬───┘
        ┌────┴─────┐      ┌────┴─────┐
        │   XTAB   │      │  GRAPH   │
        │          │      │          │
        └──────────┘      └──────────┘
```

To choose a menu, press the slash (/) key.  For Help, press the F1 key.

Copyright (c) 1986 Borland/Analytica, Inc.  All Rights Reserved.

**Figure 15-1.**    Reflex entry screen

Graph features can be accessed from this screen by typing a slash to call up the appropriate menu. The Report disk contains Reflex2 and provides access to the features shown in Figure 15-2. From this screen you can call up the Report features, Translate to bring in files from 1-2-3 and other sources, Graph Print, and File Merge. You select from this initial screen by pointing to the box of your choice and pressing ENTER. You must insert a second disk to get these files when working with a floppy disk system, but when working with a hard disk you will be able to copy all the files to your hard disk without the need for a key disk to start the program.

After entering the menu structure for any of the Reflex options, you will find a first-level menu that resembles 1-2-3's.

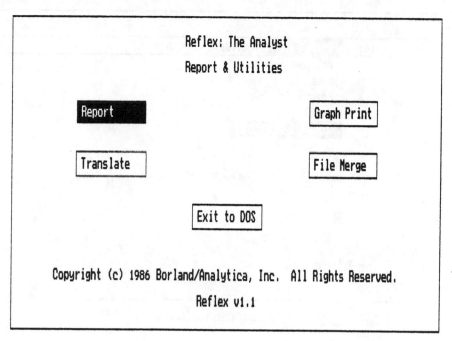

**Figure 15-2.** Entry screen for Reflex Report and Utilities

You will see options across the top of the screen, each beginning with a different letter so that they can be selected by entering the first letter of the name as well as by pointing. When you select an option, a submenu something like this will appear on the screen.

```
 Views   Edit   Print/File   Records   Search
        Delete
        Insert
        Set Column Width
        Row Select
        Column Select
        Window Clear
```

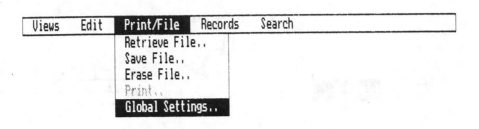

```
   Views    Edit    Print/File   Records    Search
                   Retrieve File..
                   Save File..
                   Erase File..
                   Print..
                   Global Settings..
```

Global System Settings

**Figure 15-3.**    Selection highlighted on menu

This type of menu is ideally suited for a mouse, and Reflex supports several varieties, though you do not need a mouse product to use the package. To select from the keyboard, use the down arrow key to reach the selection you want. The choice you make will be highlighted as shown in Figure 15-3. Press ENTER to finalize a selection.

You will notice a difference in the intensity of the print listing the menu options in Figure 15-3. Selections that are not available appear less intense than currently available selections. In this situation, Print is not available because a database has not yet been retrieved or created.

What happens after you make your selection depends on the option chosen. Some selections immediately begin the requested task. Others require further selections and present screens like the one shown in Figure 15-4 for global settings.

```
A:\
   Views    Edit    Print/File    Records    Search    Global Settings

┌─────────────────────────────────────────────────────────────────────┐
│                         GLOBAL SETTINGS                                │
│                                                                        │
│  Status:  Memory Available:  184/184K Working,   0/0K Expanded        │
│           Records:  0 in Filter,   0 Total in Database                 │
│  ──────────────────────────────────────────────────────────────       │
│                                                                        │
│  System Directory  ▐ A:\                    ▌                          │
│  Recalculation:    ☐ Manual  ☒ Automatic                             │
│  Printer Connection:  Serial ☐ 1   ☐ 2   Parallel ☒ 1    ☐ 2        │
│  Printer Has Auto-LineFeed:  ☒ No   ☐ Yes                            │
│                                                                        │
│                     ┌─────────┐   ┌────────┐                          │
│                     │ Proceed │   │ Cancel │                          │
│                     └─────────┘   └────────┘                          │
│                                                                        │
└─────────────────────────────────────────────────────────────────────┘
```

**Figure 15-4.**    Global settings options

This screen provides some status information as well as
options that can be changed. At the top you see information
on the amount of memory available and the number of
records in the database. At the bottom you see that you can
change the directory for reading and writing data, set recalculation to the mode desired, change the printer interface, or
modify the linefeed characteristics. Use your arrow keys to
make the required selections and type the new values if
working from the keyboard, or click your mouse button if you
are using a mouse.

There are many other menus to choose from, but all
work in basically the same fashion as the series you just followed. A help feature is available to provide additional
information at many points along the path.

## Interfacing Reflex With 1-2-3 Data

The Report disk contains the program that handles translating 1-2-3 files into a Reflex database. It can translate both release 1A and release 2 worksheet files. Before beginning you will want to have available the disk containing the worksheet files you wish to translate, unless they are stored on your hard disk. As an example, let's use use the worksheet shown in Figure 15-5. It is an employee listing that contains only the data shown on the screen. It is organized in what might be thought of as 1-2-3's database format, with field names at the top and data records on the lines below. This is the format you will need for data transfer to Reflex.

---

A1: [W12] 'Last Name                                                          READY

|    | A | B | C | D | E | F |
|----|---|---|---|---|---|---|
|    | Last Name | First Name | SS# | Job Code | Salary | Location |
| 1  | Last Name | First Name | SS# | Job Code | Salary | Location |
| 2  | Larson | Mary | 543-98-9876 | 23 | $12,000 | 2 |
| 3  | Campbell | David | 213-76-9874 | 23 | $23,000 | 10 |
| 4  | Campbell | Keith | 569-89-7654 | 12 | $32,000 | 2 |
| 5  | Stephens | Tom | 219-78-8954 | 15 | $17,800 | 2 |
| 6  | Caldor | Larry | 459-34-0921 | 23 | $32,500 | 4 |
| 7  | Lightnor | Peggy | 560-55-4311 | 14 | $23,500 | 10 |
| 8  | McCartin | John | 817-66-1212 | 15 | $54,600 | 2 |
| 9  | Justof | Jack | 431-78-9963 | 17 | $41,200 | 4 |
| 10 | Patterson | Lyle | 212-11-9090 | 12 | $21,500 | 10 |
| 11 | Miller | Lisa | 214-89-6756 | 23 | $18,700 | 2 |
| 12 | Hawkins | Mark | 215-67-8973 | 21 | $19,500 | 2 |
| 13 | Hartwick | Eileen | 313-78-9090 | 15 | $31,450 | 4 |
| 14 | Smythe | George | 560-90-8645 | 15 | $65,000 | 4 |
| 15 | Wilkes | Caitlin | 124-67-7432 | 17 | $15,500 | 2 |
| 16 | Deaver | Ken | 198-98-6750 | 23 | $24,600 | 10 |
| 17 | Kaylor | Sally | 312-45-9862 | 12 | $32,900 | 10 |
| 18 | Parker | Dee | 659-11-3452 | 14 | $19,800 | 4 |
| 19 | Preverson | Gary | 670-90-1121 | 21 | $27,600 | 4 |
| 20 | Samuelson | Paul | 219-89-7080 | 23 | $28,900 | 2 |

27-Jul-86   03:04 AM

---

**Figure 15-5.**     Employee worksheet from 1-2-3

Once you have your data file available, select Translate from Reflex's main Report menu. Reflex will prompt you for the file type you plan to translate, such as DIF, dBASE, or 1-2-3. File type options are shown in Figure 15-6. You can enter the type directly into the box provided or use the F10 (CHOICES) key to see the options. Once you have used F10 (CHOICES), your selection process is the same as from any menu. The option of using this key will be available for most of your entries with Reflex.

The next prompt on your screen is for the file to use. You can use F10 (CHOICES) again to have Reflex display the names of the worksheet files on the current directory. The example selection was EMPLOY, the name of the .WK1 file created with release 2 of 1-2-3 that contains the employee database shown in Figure 15-5. Reflex generates a file name for the destination file that is the same as the name of your worksheet but has a different suffix. You can change this name if you wish.

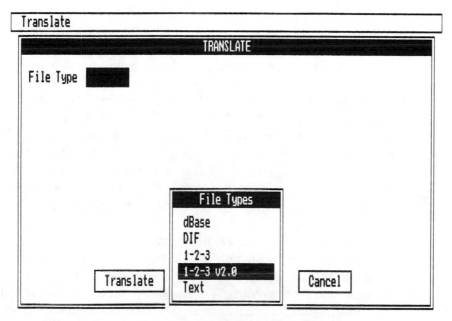

**Figure 15-6.** Selecting a file type for Translate

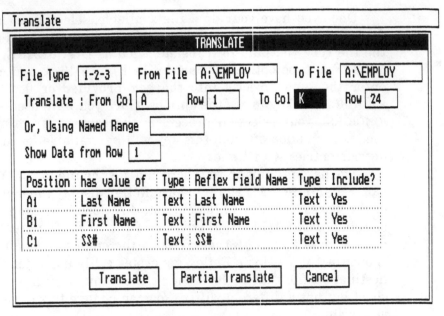

**Figure 15-7.**     Reflex's default settings for translating the file
EMPLOY.WK1

The main Translate screen is shown in Figure 15-7. It
shows the selections already made as well as Reflex's "best
guess" about the way you wish the file to be translated. As
Reflex read file EMPLOY.WK1, it determined that the area
from A1 to K24 should be translated, since that range
included the criteria cells from the 1-2-3 application. The
data is only in A1..F20, so we will change the To Col and
Row entries by moving with the arrow keys and typing new
entries in the appropriate boxes. If you wish, you can specify
a named range from your worksheet rather than cell
coordinates.

The entry Show Data from Row determines what row
will be used for field names. Below this is an area where
your individual fields are listed. The area on the left is the
information from your 1-2-3 file, and the area on the right is
the information for the Reflex file to be generated. You can

change the way your Reflex file will look by altering the field names or types on the right. You can also elect to delete a field during the translation process by changing Include? to No. To see fields that are not currently visible, you can use the down arrow key to scroll down the list. When you have finished making your selections, choose Translate to proceed.

## Reflex Options

Reflex has a wide variety of options, ranging from creating multiple windows to performing complex searches of database records. The two options this section will look at are report writing and the crosstab feature.

### Report

Reflex is often used as a report writer for 1-2-3. If you select the Report option from the main menu on the Report disk, you will be shown a menu that lists reporting features and will also be presented with a blank report layout. Your first step in preparing a report will be to select Print/File and retrieve a Reflex database to work with. Our example will use the EMPLOY file translated earlier. You might then decide to sort your file. Reflex provides up to five sort keys.

There are two sections in the report layout screen, a blank column on the left and a wider area on the right. The area on the left is used for defining the type of entry for each row of the report. The entries in this column are called row flags. Some of the row flag options and their meanings are as follows:

| | |
|---|---|
| Body | Row to the right will print once for every detail record selected. |
| Conclusion | Row to the right will print at the end of the report. |
| Header | Row to the right will print once at the top of every page. |

Intro        Row to the right will print once at the top of the report.

Sort fields 1..5    Displays as an abbreviation of the field name and is used to print subtotals when there is a break in the sort field specified.

Each line you define for your report must have a row flag to tell Reflex when to print it. The layout of the report itself is completely free-form. You can use the F10 (CHOICES) key to reduce your typing time in designing the report.

Figure 15-8 shows a report format for the EMPLOY file.

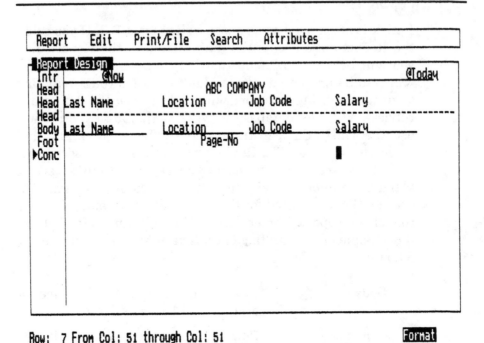

**Figure 15-8.**    Design of a report

The Reflex functions for time and date have been stored in an introductory line that will print on the first page of the report. The three lines of heading will print at the top of each page. The body of the report consists of a single row for each record, although additional rows could be added easily with the Edit Insert option. The page number will be used as the footer of the report. A conclusion flag has been set, but there is no entry as yet for this row.

One of the strongest features of the Reflex package is the ability it provides for you to preview your report with real data. Figure 15-9 shows the report that has been designed up to this point. As you review it, you may decide that you would

```
 Report    Edit    Print/File    Search    Attributes

   2:02:35 am                                      July 27, 1986
                          ABC COMPANY
   Last Name        Location        Job Code        Salary
   -------------------------------------------------------------
   Campbell         2               12              32000
   Kaylor           10              12              32900
   Patterson        10              12              21500
   Lightnor         10              14              23500
   Parker           4               14              19800
   Hartwick         4               15              31450
   McCartin         2               15              54600
   Smythe           4               15              65000
   Stephens         2               16              17800
   Justof           4               17              41200
   Wilkes           2               17              15500
   Hawkins          2               21              19500
   Preverson        4               21              27600
   Caldor           4               23              32500
   Campbell         10              23              23000
   Continue previewing page 1?    Continue    Quit
```

**Figure 15-9.**    Initial report preview

like to format the salaries as currency and add a subtotal for the breaks in job code.

Changing the salary display requires a selection from the Attribute menu to alter the format of the entry. Once you have chosen the command, F10 (CHOICES) will provide the selections. Adding subtotals requires adding another row with a row flag of Job Code 1 for the primary sort field. The effect of these changes can be seen in Figure 15-10, which shows a second preview. You can continue to make changes and preview until you have the format you want. When you have finished, you can save the report layout for subsequent use or print your report immediately.

```
 Report    Edit    Print/File    Search    Attributes


  2:36:11 am                                        July 27, 1986
                             ABC COMPANY
 Last Name          Location        Job Code       Salary
 -------------------------------------------------------------
 Campbell           2               12             $32,000
 Kaylor             10              12             $32,900
 Patterson          10              12             $21,500
            Total for Job Code:     12             $86,400
 Lightnor           10              14             $23,500
 Parker             4               14             $19,800
            Total for Job Code:     14             $43,300
 Hartwick           4               15             $31,450
 McCartin           2               15             $54,600
 Smythe             4               15             $65,000
 Stephens           2               15             $17,800
            Total for Job Code:     15             $168,850
 Justof             4               17             $41,200
 Wilkes             2               17             $15,500
            Total for Job Code:     17             $56,700
 Continue previewing page 1?   [Continue]   Quit
```

**Figure 15-10.**    Second preview after adding subtotals and currency format

### Crosstab

Reflex's Crosstab features allow you to look at a summary view of your data based on values in your data categories. Let's use it with the EMPLOY file to determine how many employees in each job code category are in each location.

To work with the Crosstab features, choose Xtab from the main system menu. To create the Crosstab, you will need to define the summary statistic to be computed and the field to be used in the computation. The choice in our example was @COUNT for the Last Name field, since we want a count of all the employees by job code and location. Other options are @SUM, @AVG, @MIN, @MAX, @STD, and @VAR. You would need to use a numeric field like Salary for any of these summaries.

The first result Reflex will provide is a total count of all employees, since categories have not been defined yet. To split your analysis into smaller categories, you can choose the Crosstab menu option for each and define the field you wish to use. Reflex will list each unique value for that field across the top or side of the tabulation area, depending on which you have selected. You also have the option of deleting some categories or using a set of ranges for the values if the fields are numeric.

Figure 15-11 shows the Crosstab created for the EMPLOY file. The ALL categories for both options were deleted to show just the entries for each category. This tabulation makes it easy to see that, for example, location 10 has two employees in job code 12, whereas location 4 has none. The power of the Crosstab feature becomes more apparent as you work with larger files and see how easy it is to change the categories, field, and summary statistic. You can also save your Crosstab definition for later use.

## Instant Applications

Borland has just introduced a companion product for Reflex called the Reflex Workshop, which provides 22 instant applications for Reflex. These applications include database designs for instructions for further customization, graphs, crosstab,

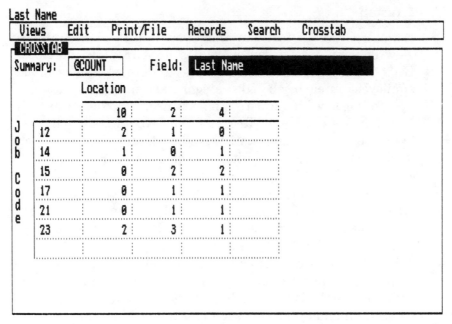

**Figure 15-11.** Crosstab for the employee file

and report definitions. Specific applications include the following:

Appointment Scheduling

Project Management

Inventory

Accounts Receivable Analysis

Purchasing

Manufacturing Quality Assurance

Reflex Workshop comes with a disk containing all of the templates and a book that describes each of them in detail.

The Note-It program is a documentation aid that can be resident in memory while you work with 1-2-3. You can use it to create file notes that describe information in your files, special archive procedures, or file retention information. You can create as many file notes as you require. Later you can look at these notes rather than having to retrieve the file and review its contents.

Note-It also creates cell notes that can be attached to an individual cell. Cell notes can be used to describe assumptions, explain the logic behind formulas, or flag cells that will need to be updated when projections are redone. Up to 100 individual cell notes can be used with a worksheet file. Each cell note can contain as many as 500 characters, displayed as 10 lines with 50 characters in each. If you elect to use all 100 notes, you will have the equivalent of 25 pages of documentation for your worksheet.

## Using Note-It With 1-2-3

Note-It is placed in memory with 1-2-3. The method used to load the programs depends on whether you use a hard or a floppy disk. With a floppy disk, place Note-It in drive B and 1-2-3 in drive A with the DOS A> prompt on your screen. Then enter **B:NOTE 123** to have the Note-It program begin. You will see a screen display like this.

```
Note-It     for Lotus 1-2-3 Worksheets
            Turner Hall Publishing   Version 2.0

(C) Copyright 1985 Access Learning Technology Corp.
            All Rights Reserved
```

[ press any key to start program ]

When you follow Note-It's direction to push any key, 1-2-3 will be loaded for you. Both programs are then resident in memory.

## Entering a File Note

You don't need to retrieve a file in order to enter a file note. Simply execute one of the 1-2-3 commands that displays file names on your screen, such as /File Retrieve or /File List. Then point to the file name you wish to create the note for and invoke Note-It with the ALT/RIGHT SHIFT key combination.

Figure 15-12 shows a note created for the file EMPLOY. WKS. It describes the contents of the file as well as retention information. You will notice that the right side of the screen shows the date in the DOS directory, the file size, and the directory. Once you have made your entries on the file note screen, use F6 to save your note.

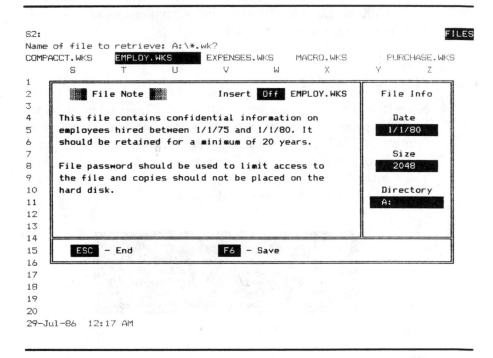

**Figure 15-12.**    A file note

## Entering a Cell Note

Entering a cell note requires a preliminary step. Any work-sheet that will contain cell notes must have a special entry added to an out-of-the-way location on the worksheet. The procedure for making this addition is to position your cursor on the location, enter **/File Combine Copy**, and select PAD. Your Note-It disk should be in the default drive at this time unless you have already copied PAD to your data disk.

The PAD file is nothing more than a four-cell worksheet file with special entries. You will not need to be concerned with their contents; just make sure you do not **erase** them. They will look like this:

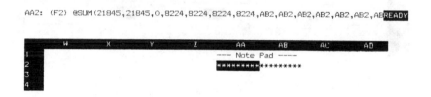

Once you have added the necessary cells, save the worksheet with /File Save.

With this preliminary task accomplished, you can move to any cell to which you would like to add a note and enter the ALT/RIGHT SHIFT key combination. A screen like that shown in Figure 15-13 will display for the entry of your cell note. To make your entry, press F2 and add your description. When you are finished, save the cell note with F6. You can continue to add further notes or edit existing ones with the same process.

Once you have created your notes, you can print them or review them on the screen. You may not remember which cells have notes, so Note-It has provided a feature to identify them. Simply press ALT/RIGHT SHIFT/LEFT SHIFT simultaneously to have each cell with a note highlighted, as shown in Figure 15-14.

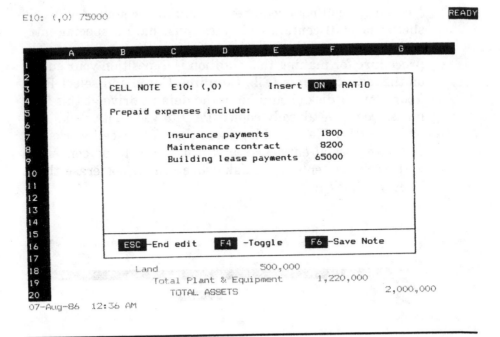

READY

```
        A        B        C        D        E        F        G
1
2
3    CELL NOTE  E10: (,0)              Insert  ON  RATIO
4
5    Prepaid expenses include:
6
7           Insurance payments           1800
8           Maintenance contract         8200
9           Building lease payments     65000
10
11
12
13
14
15
16    ESC -End edit     F4  -Toggle     F6 -Save Note
17
18    Land                     500,000
19    Total Plant & Equipment          1,220,000
20    TOTAL ASSETS                             2,000,000
07-Aug-86  12:36 AM
```

**Figure 15-13.**    A cell note

# SQZ!

The SQZ! (pronounced squeeze) program is designed to provide a data compression feature for 1-2-3 worksheets and other files. This compression can significantly increase the number of files your diskette or hard disk can store. SQZ! can store a worksheet file in an average of 15% of the regular worksheet storage space.

SQZ! is resident in memory simultaneously with 1-2-3. To load both packages with a floppy disk system, enter **B:SQZ 123** in response to the DOS A> prompt. The SQZ!

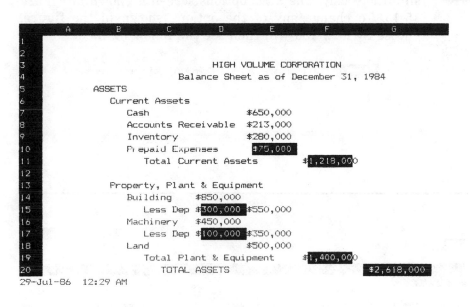

|   | A | B | C | D | E | F | G |
|---|---|---|---|---|---|---|---|
| 3 | | | HIGH VOLUME CORPORATION | | | | |
| 4 | | | Balance Sheet as of December 31, 1984 | | | | |
| 5 | | ASSETS | | | | | |
| 6 | | Current Assets | | | | | |
| 7 | | Cash | | $650,000 | | | |
| 8 | | Accounts Receivable | | $213,000 | | | |
| 9 | | Inventory | | $280,000 | | | |
| 10 | | Prepaid Expenses | | $75,000 | | | |
| 11 | | Total Current Assets | | | $1,218,000 | | |
| 12 | | | | | | | |
| 13 | | Property, Plant & Equipment | | | | | |
| 14 | | Building | $850,000 | | | | |
| 15 | | Less Dep $300,000 | $550,000 | | | | |
| 16 | | Machinery | $450,000 | | | | |
| 17 | | Less Dep $100,000 | $350,000 | | | | |
| 18 | | Land | | $500,000 | | | |
| 19 | | Total Plant & Equipment | | | $1,400,000 | | |
| 20 | | TOTAL ASSETS | | | | $2,618,000 | |

29-Jul-86  12:29 AM

**Figure 15-14.**    Highlighting for cells with notes

program will be loaded first and present the following
screen:

▶▶▶  SQZ!  ◀◀◀

THE DATA SQUEEZER FOR LOTUS

Turner Hall Publishing
Software Copyright (C) 1986
Synex Systems Corporation
All Rights Reserved
Version 1.10

( Press Any Key To Continue )

Pressing any key will automatically load 1-2-3.

Once loaded, SQZ! is always active while you are running 1-2-3, but you can check its current settings by pressing ALT-! simultaneously. The SQZ! options screen is shown in Figure 15-15. To change any of the options shown in the figure, choose Switch. You will then see the following menu:

Squeeze  Values  Blanks  Communication  Password

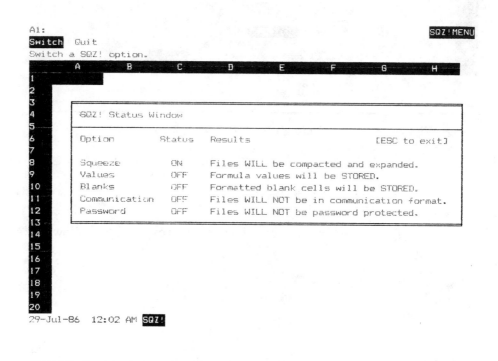

**Figure 15-15.**     SQZ! status window

The options are all toggle switches. They represent the following features:

| | |
|---|---|
| Squeeze | Offers choice of working with **regular file storage and retrieval features** or compaction and expansion when files are saved and retrieved |
| Values | Permits storage of formulas only or formulas and their current **results** |
| Blanks | Offers choice of storing formatted blank cells or deleting them |
| Communication | Allows storage of files in special communication format (uses more space than regular SQZ! format) |
| Password | Provides password protection for files (SQZ! does not support 1-2-3 release 2's file password features) |

Whatever SQZ! features are in effect when you use 1-2-3's file commands will be applied. SQZ! acts as an interface between 1-2-3 and DOS for file save and retrieve commands. It does not need to be invoked separately once it is loaded.

## Manager Mouse

Manager Mouse is a mouse product that can reduce the need for entries from your keyboard as you work with 1-2-3 and other products. The mouse works with a standard RS-232-C interface and has an independent suspension system and self-contained drive mechanism. The independent suspension system makes it possible to use the mouse on a variety of surfaces and at any angle. The self-contained drive mechanism makes this mouse relatively maintenance free as compared to the roller-ball type of mouse device. The mouse can easily be connected to your serial connector port and does not require an external power source.

The mouse is shown in Figure 15-16. As you can see, it has three buttons on the top rather than using the standard one-button design. Certain programs will make use of these additional buttons. Although 1-2-3 does not directly support a mouse product, the mouse can be purchased and used with either KeyFree or TelePaint for 1-2-3 applications.

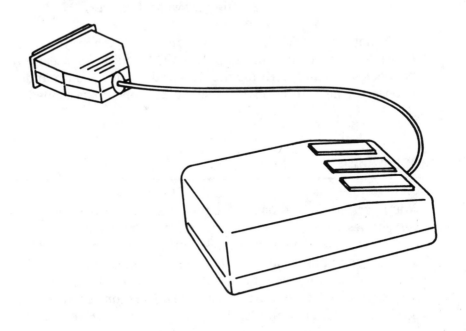

**Figure 15-16.**    Manager Mouse

## Using Manager Mouse
## And KeyFree With 1-2-3

The combination of the KeyFree program and Manager Mouse makes it possible to enter 1-2-3 selections with the mouse rather than through the keyboard. The following character sequences are assigned to the three mouse buttons:

Left button          / for menu

Right button         ESC

Middle button        ENTER

The up, down, right, and left arrow key movements are simulated by moving the mouse in the corresponding direction. If you click the right mouse button as you move, you can make menu selections.

## Enhancing 1-2-3 Graphs
## With Manager Mouse and TelePaint

The combination of TelePaint and Manager Mouse provides a MacIntoshlike interface that you can use to enhance 1-2-3's graphics. This combination allows you to make free-form entries to retrace 1-2-3 line graphs, add logos, modify titles, change colors, or perform any number of other modifications. You will work from the graph file you saved under 1-2-3 and use the mouse to define the changes you wish to make.

The TelePaint program supports a wide variety of standard and sophisticated output devices. You can use a printer, a plotter, or even the Polaroid palette for your output.

## Sideways

Sideways is a print utility program that allows you to enhance your printed output and print it sideways on a sheet of paper so you can fit a wide report on one piece of paper.

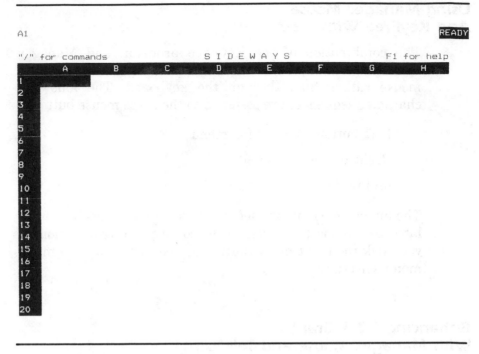

**Figure 15-17.**     Sideways entry screen

Sideways is capable of reading 1-2-3 worksheet files. Unless you look closely at the initial Sideways screen, shown in Figure 15-17, you might even think you were in 1-2-3.

The main menu and the default settings for Sideways are shown in Figure 15-18. The menu has a structure similar to 1-2-3's and, like 1-2-3, allows you to make selections by entering the first letter of the selection or pointing. Your first step should be to use the File selection to retrieve a worksheet file. Figure 15-19 shows a section of a 1-2-3 worksheet retrieved in this manner. This is a screen from the Sideways program, not from 1-2-3, although they appear the same. This worksheet is too wide for the screen and is also too wide to print on 8 1/2 by 11 paper using the standard orientation across the page, even if compressed print is invoked. Sideways will allow you to print it on one page.

Range Go Options Clear File Interface Defaults Quit
Enter print range

```
Form-size                    Range:              [      0 pages long ]
  Vertical:      11.00                           [    0.00 inches wide]
  Horizontal:     8.00
Character
  Font:         Normal     [ 5 x 15 dot matrix]
  Density:      Single
  Char-spacing:    1        [12.00 chars/inch]
  Line-spacing:    3        [ 6.66 lines/inch]
Margins
  Top:           0.00
  Bottom:        0.00       [    53 lines/page]
  Left:          0.00
  Perf-skip:     0.00
Borders
  Top:
  Bottom:
  Left:
Special-effects: No
```

Print Settings

**Figure 15-18.** Sideways menu

A1

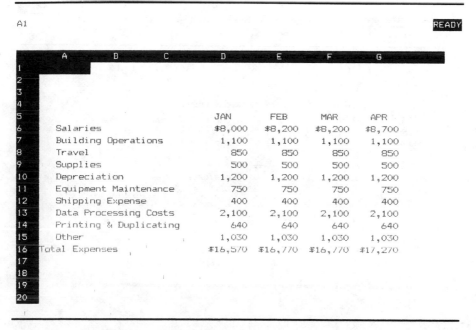

| | | | JAN | FEB | MAR | APR |
|---|---|---|---|---|---|---|
| 6 | Salaries | | $8,000 | $8,200 | $8,200 | $8,700 |
| 7 | Building Operations | | 1,100 | 1,100 | 1,100 | 1,100 |
| 8 | Travel | | 850 | 850 | 850 | 850 |
| 9 | Supplies | | 500 | 500 | 500 | 500 |
| 10 | Depreciation | | 1,200 | 1,200 | 1,200 | 1,200 |
| 11 | Equipment Maintenance | | 750 | 750 | 750 | 750 |
| 12 | Shipping Expense | | 400 | 400 | 400 | 400 |
| 13 | Data Processing Costs | | 2,100 | 2,100 | 2,100 | 2,100 |
| 14 | Printing & Duplicating | | 640 | 640 | 640 | 640 |
| 15 | Other | | 1,030 | 1,030 | 1,030 | 1,030 |
| 16 | Total Expenses | | $16,570 | $16,770 | $16,770 | $17,270 |

**Figure 15-19.** Worksheet retrieved with Sideways

Extending 1-2-3 With Add-on Products

**849**

You can change any of the settings on the Sideways menu. For our example, Formsize and Borders were not altered. Range was set at A1..P16. Under Character, the font size was reduced to Tiny, which has characters composed on a 4-dot by 12-dot grid. The top margin was set at 1 1/2 inches, and the left margin was set at 1/4 inch.

The Special-effects option allows you to use bold, enlarged, and underlined characters. The top two lines of the heading were given the special effect of bold, and the range for the month names was selected to be underlined. The altered options are shown in Figure 15-20.

Once all the changes are made, select Go to produce output across the page, as shown in Figure 15-21.

```
                                                              MENU
Range  Go  Options  Clear  File  Interface  Defaults  Quit
Form-size, Character, Margins, Borders, Clear

  Form-size                   Range: A1..P16        [     1 pages long ]
     Vertical:      11.00                           [   10.59 inches wide]
     Horizontal:     8.00
  Character
     Font:          Tiny      [ 4 x 12 dot matrix]
     Density:       Single
     Char-spacing:   1        [14.40 chars/inch]
     Line-spacing:   3        [ 8.00 lines/inch]
  Margins
     Top:           1.50
     Bottom:        0.00      [   51 lines/page]
     Left:          0.25
     Perf-skip:     0.00
  Borders
     Top:
     Bottom:
     Left:
  Special-effects: Yes
                                                         =Print Settings=
```

**Figure 15-20.**    Modified Sideways options

Friendly Bank of Richmond
Department 123 - Expense Projections

29-Jul-86

| | JAN | FEB | MAR | APR | MAY | JUNE | JULY | AUG | SEPT | OCT | NOV | DEC | TOTAL |
|---|---|---|---|---|---|---|---|---|---|---|---|---|---|
| Salaries | $8,000 | $8,200 | $8,200 | $8,700 | $8,700 | $7,500 | $7,500 | $10,000 | $10,000 | $10,000 | $10,000 | $10,000 | $106,800 |
| Building Operations | 1,100 | 1,100 | 1,100 | 1,100 | 1,100 | 1,100 | 1,100 | 1,100 | 1,300 | 1,300 | 1,300 | 1,300 | $14,000 |
| Travel | 850 | 850 | 850 | 850 | 850 | 850 | 850 | 850 | 850 | 850 | 850 | 850 | $10,200 |
| Supplies | 500 | 500 | 500 | 500 | 500 | 500 | 500 | 500 | 500 | 500 | 500 | 500 | $6,000 |
| Depreciation | 1,200 | 1,200 | 1,200 | 1,200 | 1,200 | 1,200 | 1,200 | 1,200 | 1,200 | 1,200 | 1,200 | 1,200 | $14,400 |
| Equipment Maintenance | 750 | 750 | 750 | 750 | 750 | 750 | 750 | 750 | 750 | 750 | 750 | 750 | $9,000 |
| Shipping Expense | 400 | 400 | 400 | 400 | 400 | 400 | 400 | 400 | 400 | 400 | 400 | 400 | $4,800 |
| Data Processing Costs | 2,100 | 2,100 | 2,100 | 2,100 | 2,100 | 2,100 | 2,100 | 2,100 | 2,100 | 2,100 | 2,100 | 2,100 | $25,200 |
| Printing & Duplicating | 640 | 640 | 640 | 640 | 640 | 640 | 640 | 640 | 640 | 640 | 640 | 640 | $7,680 |
| Other | 1,030 | 1,030 | 1,030 | 1,030 | 1,030 | 1,030 | 1,030 | 1,030 | 1,030 | 1,030 | 1,030 | 1,030 | $12,360 |
| Total Expenses | $16,570 | $16,770 | $16,770 | $17,270 | $17,270 | $16,070 | $16,070 | $18,570 | $18,770 | $18,770 | $18,770 | $18,770 | $210,440 |

**Figure 15-21.** Printout created with Sideways

The Spreadsheet Auditor is a documentation and diagnostics tool for 1-2-3 and Symphony. It permits you to check for errors in cells, formulas, and ranges. It also provides a means of documenting worksheet formulas and highlighting X-Ref and other relationships in your data. The new Spreadsheet Auditor (version 3.0) permits you to work interactively with the product as you test error conditions and highlight specific cells. It also has a Sideprint feature that provides a sideways printout, in addition to five different font features and special characteristics like underlining and bold. Spreadsheet Auditor also includes Noter to attach notes to worksheet cells. The following description will focus on the audit features of the package.

The entry screen for The Spreadsheet Auditor is shown in Figure 15-22. As with many of the other utility packages,

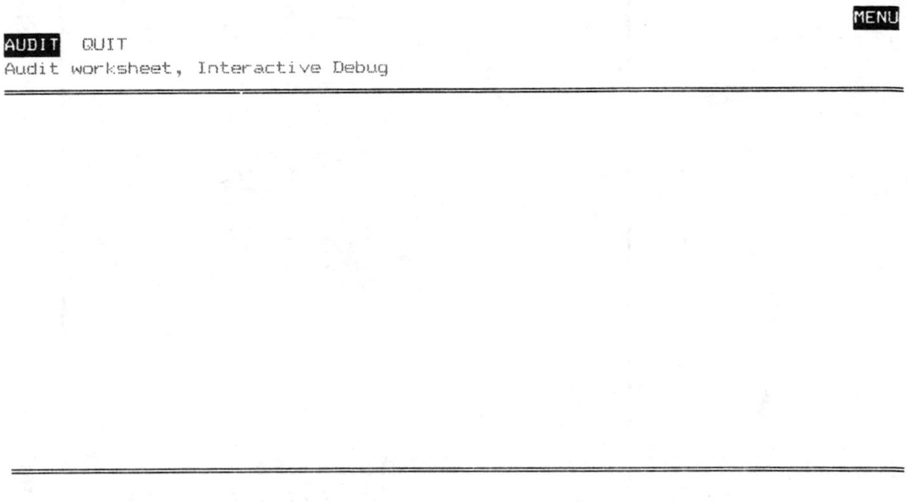

```
                                                                    MENU
AUDIT  QUIT
Audit worksheet, Interactive Debug
```

**Figure 15-22.**    Entry screen for The Spreadsheet Auditor

the first step in using The Spreadsheet Auditor is to retrieve
a worksheet file. You will use a screen that looks something
like this.

The worksheet is initially displayed in the same format as
with 1-2-3. The bottom line of the display as well as the menu
options will remind you that you are not in 1-2-3, however, as
Figure 15-23 shows. At this point your choices include the

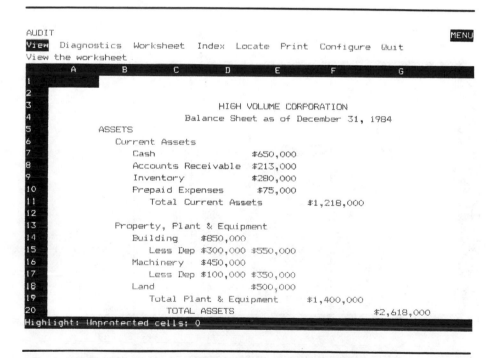

**Figure 15-23.**   The Spreadsheet Auditor menu and a 1-2-3 work-
sheet

following menu selections:

View          Allows you to look at the contents of your worksheet in new ways, including a variety of display modes. One option is the formula view shown in Figure 15-24. View can also provide a map of the worksheet, showing the location of different types of entries so you know where to focus your attention when auditing the worksheet. Query commands allow you to search interactively for information of specific interest. Several cross-reference

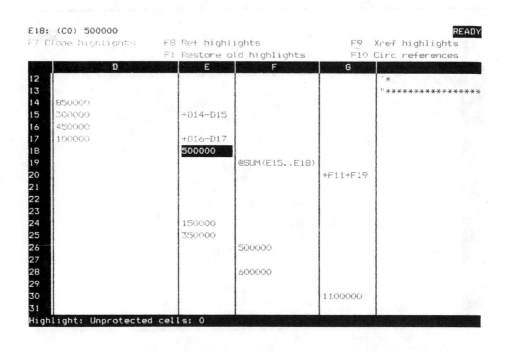

**Figure 15-24.**     The Spreadsheet Auditor formula view

commands permit you to determine relationships between cells. Figure 15-25 shows the X-Ref display with the cursor on E18. The display shows that only one cell references this cell value and highlights that cell.

Diagnostics    Helps you track down errors within your worksheet. It provides the options of Range Tests, Cell Tests, and Formula Tests, as well as a printed copy of any results you choose. Range tests include tests for overlapping ranges, multiple

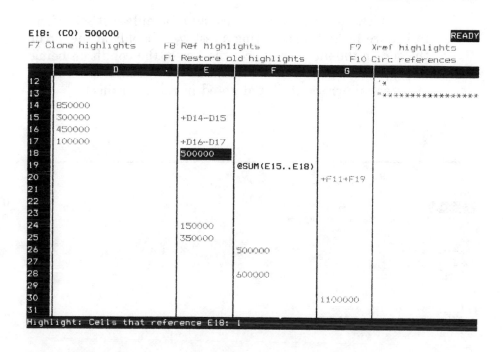

**Figure 15-25.**    Highlighting cells that reference a particular cell

names, reversed ranges, and unused ranges. Some of the cell tests are for unused cells, cells containing errors, and unprotected cells. Formula tests include tests for formulas referencing labels, formatted blank cells with no entries, cells outside the worksheet boundaries, and unused formulas.

Worksheet     Permits changes to the appearance of the worksheet display, including a two-window split and column width changes.

Print     Allows you to print any section of the worksheet. Also includes special reports such as a macro extract, circular references, cross-reference, and worksheet settings.

You can see from the cell test and formula test selections in Figure 15-26 that selecting a test will display at the top of the screen the number of occurrences of the condition being tested for. Although it is not shown in the figure, these sources of potential errors are highlighted in the worksheet.

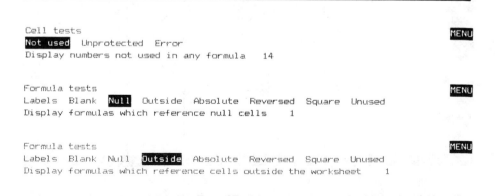

**Figure 15-26.**    The results of cell and formula tests

SuperKey is a product that allows you to use your keyboard more efficiently. It is designed to be memory resident with 1-2-3 and other programs so it will always be available during your use of the packages. One of its features is a macro recorder option. Others include the following:

- A type-ahead buffer that can hold 128 characters rather than the standard 10.

- Data encryption for file storage or data transmission.

- Features that allow cutting and pasting from one stand-alone program to another.

- Redefinition of the keyboard layout.

- A screen protection feature to turn off your monitor after a specific amount of time.

- A command stack capable of replaying the last 10 to 30 DOS commands.

SuperKey comes with some ready-to-use 1-2-3 macros, as shown in Figure 15-27. You can also use the program to design your own macros. SuperKey uses the following menu structure:

```
Macros  Commands Functions  Options   Defaults Encryption Layout  Setup
```

This menu is activated with ALT /. The options for each main choice are shown on a pull-down menu when you select that choice. For example, selecting M for Macros displays the pull-down menu shown in Figure 15-28.

Recording a macro is as easy as selecting Begin and entering the key you wish to attach this macro to. From this point on, every keystroke you enter will be processed by 1-2-3 immediately and will also be recorded by SuperKey. Super-Key gives you visual verification of the macro's accuracy while you are recording it. When you have finished recording your macro, type ALT /**Macro** again and select End.

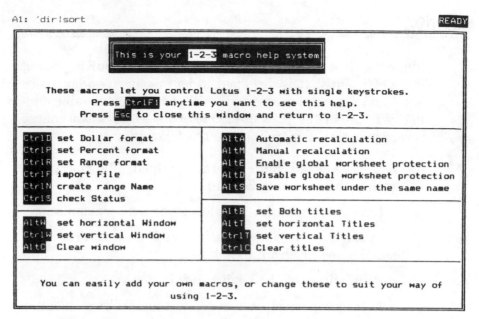

**Figure 15-27.** SuperKey's ready-to-use 1-2-3 macros

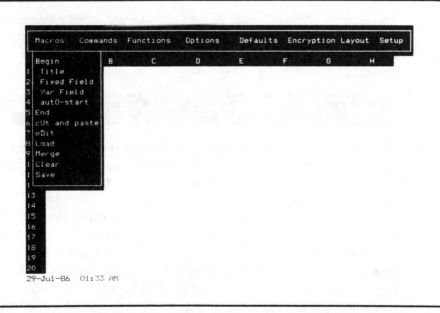

**Figure 15-28.** SuperKey's macro menu

## Freelance

Freelance is a free-form graphics package that allows you to create your own charts by using either the package's predrawn shapes or your own imagination. You can create word graphs, diagrams, or any other type of drawing you wish. Freelance also has the ability to edit 1-2-3 charts and make enhancements. You can add text, underline a key point, merge charts, or add a logo to your 1-2-3 graphs, for example.

### Starting Freelance

Figure 15-29 presents the Freelance access menu. This menu provides access to all of the Freelance features, including a batch plotting feature, installation options through

```
Freelance  Batch  Setup  Help  Done
Run Freelance

    Freelance Access Manager

    Instructions:

        Use the cursor keys to highlight
        the program you want to run.
        Press <ENTER>.

        or

        Press the first letter of the
        program you want to run.

        (Press <F1> at any time for Help.)


    Copyright 1985
    Graphic Communications, Inc.
```

**Figure 15-29.**     Freelance access menu

Setup, and help information. If you have not used Freelance before, you should select the Setup option before attempting to work with your 1-2-3 files. Setup allows you to define three different output devices. This means you can have plotter specifications as well as two printer options at your fingertips and can select different output devices for different charts. If you do not enter Setup initially, your first output may not be legible, since codes for completely different devices could be sent to your hardware when you request a plot.

When you have finished with Setup, you are ready to enter Freelance. The menu screen you will see at that point is shown in Figure 15-30. Make selections from it in the same way you make 1-2-3 menu selections, by typing the first

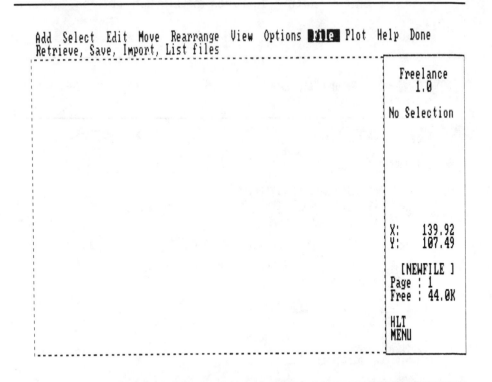

**Figure 15-30.** Main Freelance menu

letter of an item or by pointing. You will be presented with submenus to further refine your selections. Freelance is then ready for you to begin a new chart or to work with an existing one. The 1-2-3 /File Retrieve command will allow you to access any Freelance charts you may have saved, but a special process is required for 1-2-3 graph files.

## Working With 1-2-3 .PIC Files

1-2-3 can save your charts as graphic images in .PIC files if you use the /Graph Save option after defining your graph. Freelance supports the use of the raw data in these files as well as the use of an enhanced converted version that improves the resolution of the image. To access such data, select /File Import and choose PIC, Raw Pic, or ASCII as the file type to import. Any file can be chosen by pointing to it and pressing ENTER. Once your 1-2-3 chart is in memory, you can edit it or add text and other symbols. Since Freelance can have two pages of graphic information in memory at once, you can even copy sections of one graph to another or merge two or more charts on one page.

## Adding Text and Arrows
## To Your 1-2-3 Graph

With 1-2-3 you have six places where text can be used. You can use a first- or second-line title for the graph, X and Y axis labels, a legend, and an X range to label the points on the X axis. You cannot enhance the graph with text entries outside these fixed locations. With Freelance you can add text in any area you wish, however. You might be interested in flagging specific data points that represent extremely high or low values, for example, or you might want to add the creator's name and date in a corner of the graph in small letters. You might also wish to add a second line of text to an axis label.

To add text, you must first choose Add from the main Freelance menu and then choose Text. Freelance will then prompt you to type the characters you wish to add. After they are entered, specify the location for entry by moving with your arrow keys (several mouse devices are also supported) until you get the best placement on your chart. You can make one text entry after another, placing each entry in a new location. When you have finished adding text, you can press ESC and make another selection from the menu.

Adding arrows is just as easy but works a little differently. Choose Add Arrow, move your cursor to the origination point you wish the arrow to have, and press ENTER. Then move to the arrow's termination point and enter space ENTER to complete the arrow. Its head will point toward the destination selection.

Figure 15-31 shows a 1-2-3 graph that was imported with the .PIC option. This chart has had a point added to

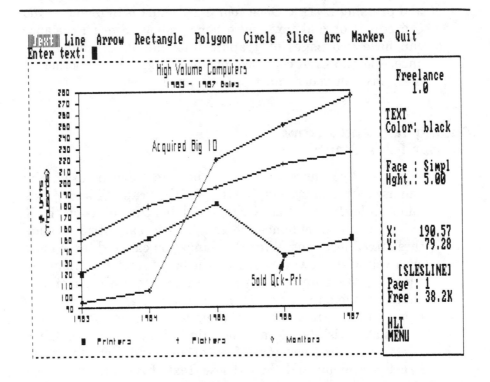

**Figure 15-31.**    Adding text to a 1-2-3 chart

note the acquisition of Big 10, a large distributor for 10-inch monitor screens. This text entry explains the large increase in sales for 1985. The other point marked is the sales figure for printers in 1986. The added text shows that Qck-Prt, a retail outlet specializing in printer and plotter sales, was sold that year. An arrow was also added at this point, using the middle of the text entry as the origination point and the symbol marking the data point as the destination.

Freelance's output is of extremely high quality. You can select fonts, font size, and a rainbow of colors if your output device supports such choices. Figure 15-32 shows the output from the chart in Figure 15-31, using the Freelance default settings.

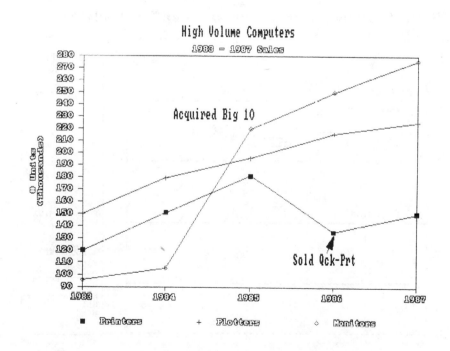

**Figure 15-32.**    Freelance output

## Adding Symbols to Your 1-2-3 Graph

Freelance will allow you to add symbols to your graph from one of its many libraries or to create your own symbols, representing your logos or those of your customers. These created symbols can be stored in library files as well and can be added to any chart. To read in a library of symbols to use with a chart in the first graphics page, press PG DN to get to the second page and retrieve the library of symbols with a /File Retrieve command. Figure 15-33 shows one of the libraries, which contains computer equipment. Some of the other libraries are Human Forms, Maps, Office Objects, Space Planning, Common Objects, Geometric Shapes, Arrows, and Text Banners.

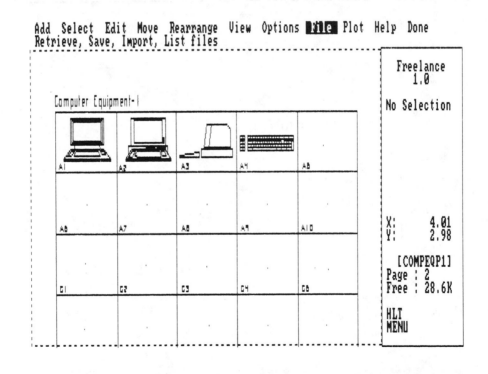

**Figure 15-33.**    Freelance computer equipment symbol library

Once the symbol you want is in memory, you can select it and use the Rearrange Copy option to place it in window one at the location you want on your 1-2-3 chart. Figure 15-34 shows a computer symbol placed in the upper right corner of a chart. You will notice that the computer image has been customized by adding the letters HVC to represent High Volume Computers. These letters were added with the Add Text option and moved to the center of the monitor screen. You have the option of placing the symbol in any location you wish. Figure 15-35 shows the computer symbol printed as a background entry on the page, with the chart image superimposed on it.

Freelance's Lotus-style menus make this package easy to use. If you work with graphics on a regular basis and would

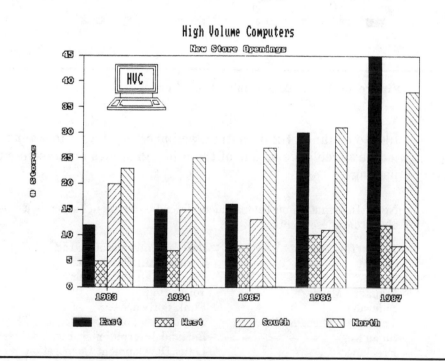

**Figure 15-34.**    Computer logo added to graph

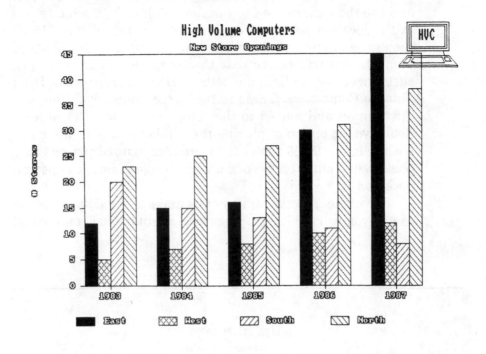

**Figure 15-35.** Logo printed behind graph

like to enhance 1-2-3's output, you are very likely to want to look at Freelance or one of the other graphics enhancement packages.

**Note:** Information on the products described in this chapter is available from these companies:

| | |
|---|---|
| Reflex:The Analyst | Borland International, Inc. |
| Note-It | Turner Hall Publishing |
| SQZ! | Turner Hall Publishing |
| Manager Mouse | Torrington |
| Sideways | Funk Software |
| The Spreadsheet Auditor | Consumer's Software Inc. |
| SuperKey | Borland International, Inc. |
| Freelance | Lotus Development Corporation |

# A History of 1-2-3

**Computers Enter the Business World**
**Changes in the 1970s**
**The First Micros**
**VisiCalc: The First Generation**
**The Growth of Business Software for Micros**
**Integrated Packages: The Second Generation**
**Reasons for 1-2-3's Popularity**

Although the first computer was introduced in the 1940s, computers began to find their way into the business world only in the early 1960s. At this time large universities and corporations began to tap into the power of computers to automate business tasks such as payroll calculations, accounts payable, and record keeping.

The first computers were big enough to fill a large room or even a small building. Even so, their capabilities were very limited compared to those of today's machines. These early machines often had memory sizes of 16K or less. Since most business systems of that era were oriented around punched paper cards and did little more than provide an ability to read and tabulate the data in these cards, that memory capacity was adequate. Error checking and correction in these early days consisted of a failed job followed by the correction of the faulty card and a rerun of the entire job.

If business users wanted a new report from the data contained in their cards, they had to define their needs to someone in the business' data processing group. The technical guru from data processing then had to translate the users' needs into a language the computer could understand. Autocoder was one popular language of this era. One of a number of machine-level languages, it had instructions that looked something like this:

```
SIO     (Start I/O)
MVC     MoVe Character
LR      Load Register
```

These assembly language instructions were combined with a reference to a machine register or a numeric address location to give instructions to the computer. It is easy to see that it must have been quite time-consuming to define a business problem and solution in this way. Furthermore, these programs often did not work correctly the first time they were executed. It was not unusual for a lengthy debugging process to be required to eliminate errors.

Obtaining desired output often meant changing the sequence of data or merging data in two different card files. Supporting equipment known as unit record equipment was often used to reorganize the data files prior to reading the cards into the computer. To complete these sorting and merging operations, a data processing person had to rewire the boards of the unit record devices. In short, no computer-related processing could ever be completed by the business user. Users were completely dependent on the technical experts to obtain the limited, inflexible output produced by the business programs of the '60s.

## Changes in the 1970s

The early to middle 1970s brought changes on some fronts in business computing and adherence to the status quo on others. The size and price of computing power changed greatly, for example. Mainframe computers began to shrink in size and grow in capabilities and features. Cycle speed for computations became measurably shorter, and price/performance ratios fell rapidly. Replacing the punched paper cards of the past, magnetic tape units, large disk drives, and mass storage devices become the norm. Businesses placed more and more of their information in these new storage media as per-character storage costs continued a rapid decline.

The location of equipment was also changing during this era. The centralized computer room of the '60s had evolved into increasing placement of computing equipment in the user's environment. Smaller computers called minicomputers were installed on the shop floor of manufacturing facilities and in some offices with specialized applications. Terminals were located throughout the business organization to allow users to enter data and access the files stored on a mainframe computer. Although these terminal devices did not have enough intelligence to handle application processing, they did have sufficient intelligence to check errors as the operator entered data. This improved error checking greatly reduced aborted processing caused by incorrect data entry. In some instances, data was processed on a real-time basis and the mainframe files were updated immediately. In other, less time-critical applications, the data was stored so that files could be updated during off hours.

Software was growing more sophisticated as well. Users had begun to expect more than just a printed listing and total for their transactions. There was a demand for exception reporting to bring potential problems to management's attention and also for the automation of more complex tasks. Faster machines with larger memory lent popularity to programming languages like COBOL and PL/1. These languages were much closer to everyday English and sped up the application development process markedly. For example, a line from a COBOL program might look like this:

```
COMPUTE GROSS__PAY = HOURS * RATE
```

In addition to readable commands, COBOL provided a program structure with divisions for different functions and "paragraphs" within the main body of the program. These divisions made it easy to create a logical, well-organized program that others could follow as easily as the program's developer. This feature was especially important when modifications had to be made in a program.

Software packages to handle business functions such as accounts receivable, payroll, personnel, general ledger, and inventory control were being marketed by a number of vendors. If a package was flexible enough to meet a user's needs, a new system could be available in a matter of weeks as compared to the months that had been required in earlier years even if high-level languages were used.

Database management was also a popular focus for the '70s. A number of mainframe packages for this purpose were introduced, such as IMS and Adabas. These packages allowed an organization to build a repository of corporate information. They also provided the ability to separate the data structure from the application programs. Alterations in file structures thus no longer required changes in application programs. In theory, this change eliminated the need for major program overhauls every time a new field was added. Unfortunately, building a corporate database took much longer than anyone had ever envisioned—in most companies, a period of years.

Throughout all these changes, the end-user's dependence on the data processing staff remained the same. Although the transition to a database environment helped, most new reports and all new calculations required the expertise of the programming staff to make necessary changes. Some organizations had as much as 80 percent of their data processing staff working on maintenance activities. This meant that few resources were available to implement new applications. Some organizations had a backlog of three years or more for new requests. By the time a new request made its way to the top of the backlog list, the user's needs had often changed.

Not surprisingly, users felt increasingly frustrated by the time lag between defining requirements and actually seeing the change or new system in production. Users felt that with all the computer claimed to offer, there should be a way for them to change storage requirements without major work, query their data files at will, create new reports on the spur of the moment, and have flexible computation capabilities. Their current systems were not meeting these needs.

Users were aware of efforts to build corporate databases, and they had been promised that such databases would provide some of the options for which they were searching. Once a database was in place, query languages and report writers supposedly would allow users to tap into their information with only minimal involvement of DP personnel. The problem was that this effort was taking much longer than most organizations had bargained for, and users were not seeing the results they had been promised. Although a solution seemed in sight, most users found it to be still out of reach, and many blamed the DP staff for not delivering the tools they needed.

## The First Micros

As technology continued to bring down the size and cost of computing power, the first microcomputer was introduced in

1974. This small machine could fit on a desktop like a terminal, yet, unlike that of a terminal, all its computing power was self-contained. The micro or personal computer even had data storage capabilities, so it could truly function as a stand-alone machine.

The early micros manufactured by Altair were not intended for the office. These machines were available only in kit form, for one thing. Even after they had been soldered and otherwise assembled, there was no software available for them. They were designed to be programmed with assembly language and thus required a time investment that was not practical in the business environment. At $400, the cost of these early micros was reasonable, but the time had not yet arrived for their introduction to business.

The Apple II was developed by Stephen W. Wozniak and Steven J. Jobs not too long after the Altair. It offered the advantage of preassembly and opened the possibility of owning a micro to many individuals. Tandy and countless other companies quickly followed Apple's lead, introducing micros like the TRS-80 and the Vector Graphic. The fact that these new machines could be programmed with a relatively easy-to-learn language like BASIC made them acceptable to at least a small group of end-users.

Since most business users did not have the time or inclination to become programmers even with BASIC, however, these early machines generally remained relegated to the computer hobbyist. Furthermore, data processing departments, already buried by requests for work on mainframes and minicomputers, tended to ignore micros in the hope that they would go away. Thus users initially found little support for programming the micro within the DP ranks. Besides, many data processing professionals thought of the microcomputer merely as a toy. Surely a "real computer" could not fit on a desktop!

Flexible, easy-to-use software was the missing component required for micros to make a significant contribution to the business world. Public domain software was free but was useful only if you were interested in playing games or generating pictures of trees or cars on your computer screen. These programs certainly did not provide the tools business users were looking for. Users thus might purchase an Apple or TRS-80 for around $2,000 and then have to spend $5,000 or more to have someone develop a custom program for their application, since little or no commercial business software for micros existed.

## VisiCalc: The First Generation

In 1978, VisiCalc, the first successful business software for microcomputers, entered the marketplace. Dan Bricklin, its creator, was an end-user, not a computer professional. Dan was motivated to develop a solution for the tedium of calculations involved in case studies in his program at the Harvard Business School. The solution he developed for his problems resulted in a tool that was soon welcomed by thousands of users.

VisiCalc was actually one of the first packages for any computer that offered complete flexibility in the tasks it could be used for. It was able to produce reliable computations whether the user's needs were for loan amortization schedules, income projections for a legal practice, salary calculations, or a ratio comparison of potential investments.

Another advantage VisiCalc offered was that it could operate with a limited instruction set selectable from menus at the top of the display screen. Although these menus were a bit cryptic, they were still easier to use than a programming language. Essentially, VisiCalc provided a large electronic sheet of paper that the end-user could work with in a variety of ways. Numbers, labels, and formulas could be placed anywhere on the sheet to create a model tailored to the user's exact needs. Other features such as windows, printing, and built-in functions made this product an even better solution for tasks that involved projections and calculations.

VisiCalc's commands were so easy to master that any user willing to learn them could escape dependence on data processing. This was just as well, for in most organizations, data processing departments chose to ignore VisiCalc. They were so backlogged with work on mainframes and minis that they did not have the resources to get involved at the beginning in any case. Also, as with the microcomputer itself, many data processors felt that this innovation was only a passing fad.

Many microcomputers were purchased for the sole purpose of gaining access to VisiCalc software. In particular, VisiCalc gained immediate and widespread acceptance among accounting and finance professionals. Since these individuals were constantly making projections and other financial analyses, a package like this could save them an immense amount of valuable time. The payback period for the cost of hardware, software, and model development became extremely short.

Before the availability of tools like VisiCalc, most financial projections were done with a pencil and paper. A change in one worksheet number meant that the entire worksheet had to be totaled and cross-footed again. This slow process made it very difficult to evaluate a series of assumptions in a reasonable period of time. With VisiCalc, users could define the required calculations once and then have the software handle the recalculations whenever a number was changed. Since the recalculation normally required only a few seconds, users could evaluate dozens of assumptions in the time it formerly took to perform one recalculation by hand.

Although accountants and financial analysts immediately adopted VisiCalc, their corporate colleagues lagged in their support. In fact, accountants sometimes had to smuggle an Apple and a copy of VisiCalc into the office under the guise of purchasing a typewriter or a calculator. This secrecy was due to the fact that in most corporations the purchase of computer equipment or software had to be approved by a central committee, and such groups often doubted the usefulness of micros. More and more micros nonetheless came in "through the back door." Users were deciding what they needed and finding money in their budgets to acquire these low-cost machines.

# The Growth of Business Software for Micros

IBM was an established leader in the mainframe and mini-computer marketplace, and this company's entry into the personal computer market in the early 1980s convinced many organizations that micros were not merely a passing fad. IBM's action also encouraged third-party vendors to develop business software for microcomputers. A number of VisiCalc clones appeared, each providing some old and some new features.

New packages to handle word processing, data management, and graphics were introduced as well. Many were marketed by the same companies that were marketing spreadsheet packages. As an example, VisiCorp offered Visi-File for data management and VisiTrend/VisiPlot for statistics and graphics. Many of these new packages even allowed data transfer between the various offerings of a given company.

The biggest flaw in the design of these new offerings was the user interface. Users who had mastered one product felt that they were starting all over again when they attempted to learn a new package because there was no consistency in the user interface from product to product, even when the products were manufactured by the same company. This frustration, along with the increasing sophistication of end-users, led to a demand for a second generation of microcomputer business software with additional sophistication and integrated features.

## Integrated Packages: The Second Generation

The demand for additional features and sophistication as well as the need to use multiple environments led to the development of Lotus 1-2-3, Context MBA, and other integrated software packages. The computer memory needed to effectively utilize integrated packages was now reasonably priced; companies began offering add-on cards to boost the basic memory of a PC at a nominal cost.

Lotus 1-2-3 became the distinct leader among these second-generation offerings. It offered support for spreadsheet, data management, and graphics work in one package. It also possessed a consistent and easy-to-use user interface spanning all three environments. Lotus had a strong management team with in-depth experience in the microcomputer field and the backing of financial leaders. The management team was headed by Mitch Kapor, a former VisiCorp employee and developer of the VisiTrend/VisiPlot package. Financial backers included heavyweights like Ben Rosen. The excellence of both management and support convinced corporate buyers that this new company was planning to be a major factor in microcomputer software then and in the years to come.

## Reasons for 1-2-3's Popularity

Within just a few months of its introduction, Lotus 1-2-3 zoomed to the top of Softsel's best-seller chart. Sales were spurred by a full-scale publicity campaign with ads in the popular computer and business publications. Word of mouth was another strong sales factor. Business users who had tried the product were impressed with its features, and they did not hesitate to tell their associates about it.

Corporations had been hesitant to adopt the products of many microcomputer firms because they feared that dependence on a small firm that might fail could result in later problems with updates and support. Because of its instant success, Lotus was able to convince the corporate decision makers that it had long-term viability. It was also one of the first software companies to provide online phone support at no additional fee. Whenever users had questions, they could call one of the support lines and have one of 1-2-3's staff provide quick answers.

Success in the corporate arena led to volume sales for the 1-2-3 product. Unlike Apple products, which were typically purchased by single users or small businesses, 1-2-3 was often bought by Fortune 500 companies that purchased hundreds or thousands of copies for their employees.

Lotus quickly began to plan enhancements to its original offering. Small changes were made between release 1 and release 1A. Release 2, introduced in the fall of 1985, made major enhancements to the product, including new options and commands that do everything from suppressing zero entries to performing regression analyses. These new features were the result of user requests and helped to keep the product current amid a sea of integrated packages.

In 1985 Lotus further strengthened support for the 1-2-3 package with two new products. The first is a monthly magazine called *Lotus Magazine.* It has a business emphasis and provides information both on using Lotus products and on microcomputers in general. A free six-month subscription is given with each purchase of 1-2-3 or Symphony. The second new product is 1-2-3 Report Writer. This product allows users to produce a wide variety of reports from a 1-2-3 database or spreadsheet. It is also useful in the corporate setting where many people may share a 1-2-3 file. It means that some individuals can have access to the full features of 1-2-3, while others in the same organizational unit may be restricted to the features offered in 1-2-3 Report Writer.

Even more important is the fact that Lotus has committed itself to continuing support for the 1-2-3 product line. The latest release of 1-2-3 provides full compatibility with Lotus' Symphony software. There is little doubt that other new products added to the Lotus product line will either support or offer full compatibility with 1-2-3.

# 1-2-3 Keyboard Guides

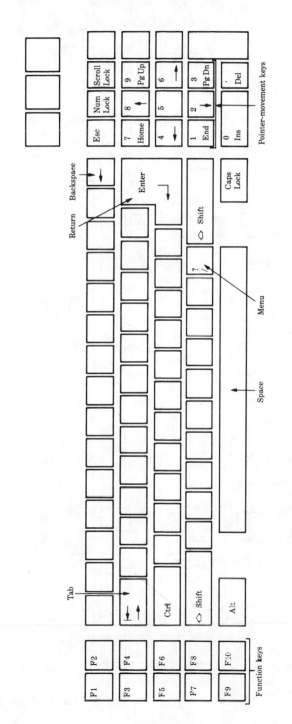

**Figure B-1.** IBM PC AT keyboard guide

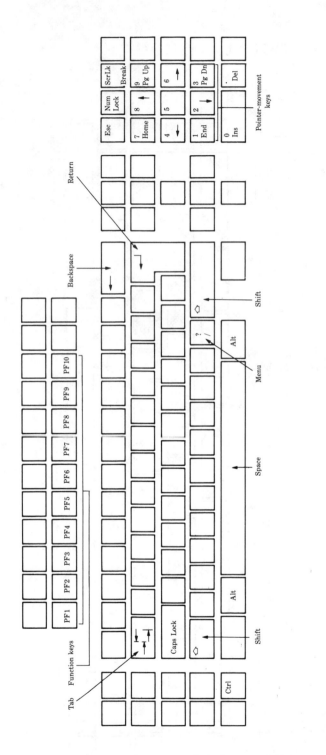

**Figure B-2.** IBM 3270-PC, PC/G, PC/GX keyboard guide

Note: Function keys are activated by first pressing Fn and then the appropriate number key:

Fn then Home for Home
Fn then End for End
Fn then PgDn for Page Down
Fn then PgUp for Page Up
Fn then Break for Break

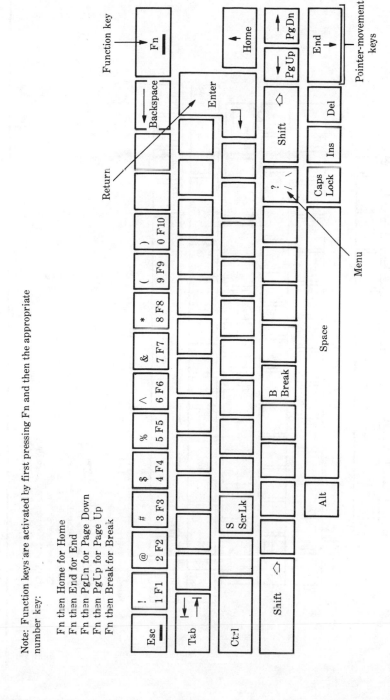

**Figure B-3.** IBM PCjr keyboard guide

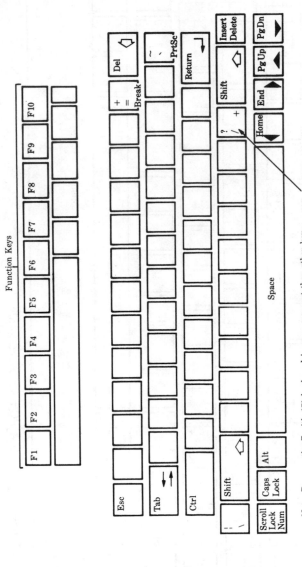

Function Keys

Note: Because the Zenith 171 keyboard is more compact than other keyboards, several keys needed for 1-2-3 must be used in combination with other keys to peform their task:

PtrSc plus Ctrl for Print Screen
Scroll Lock plus Right Shift for Scroll Lock
Insert plus Right Shift for Insert
Home plus Right Shift for Home
End plus Right Shift for End
PgUp plus Right Shift for Page Up
PgDn plus Right Shift for Page Down

**Figure B-4.** Zenith 171 Portable keyboard guide

The following names are trademarked products of the corresponding companies.

| | |
|---|---|
| 1-2-3® | Lotus Development Corporation |
| Above Board™ | Intel Corporation |
| Adabas™ | Software AG |
| Apple® | Apple Computer, Inc. |
| Apple II® | Apple Computer, Inc. |
| Anadex® | Anadex |
| C. Itoh™ | C. Itoh & Company, Ltd. |
| Compaq® | Compaq Computer Corporation |
| Context MBA™ | Context Management Systems |
| dBASE II® | Ashton-Tate |
| dBASE III® | Ashton-Tate |
| DEC™ | Digital Equipment Corporation |
| Diablo® | Xerox Corporation |
| DIF™ | Software Arts, Inc. |
| Epson™ | Epson America, Inc. |
| Hercules™ | Hercules Computer |
| HP™ | Hewlett-Packard Company |
| IBM® | International Business Machines Corporation |
| IMS® | International Business Machines Corporation |
| Intel® | Intel Corporation |
| Jazz® | Lotus Development Corporation |
| LICS® | Lotus Development Corporation |
| Lotus® | Lotus Development Corporation |
| Manager Mouse™ | Torrington |
| NEC® | NEC Corporation |
| Note-It™ | Turner Hall Publishing |
| Plantronics Color Plus™ | Plantronics |
| Radio Shack® | Tandy Corporation |
| Reflex™ | Borland International, Inc. |
| Reflex Workshop™ | Borland International, Inc. |
| Sideways™ | Funk Software |
| Sofsel® | Sofsel Computer Products |
| SQZ!™ | Turner Hall Publishing |
| Symphony® | Lotus Development Corporation |
| TI® | Texas Instruments |
| TRS-80® | Tandy Corporation |
| Vector™ | Vector Graphic |
| VisiCalc® | VisiCorp, Inc. |
| VisiFile® | VisiCorp, Inc. |
| VisiTrend/ VisiPlot® | VisiCorp, Inc. |
| Wang® | Wang Laboratories, Inc. |
| WordStar® | MicroPro International |
| Zenith™ | Zenith Radio Corporation |

Note that this index is separated into four sections: (1) 1-2-3 commands, (2) macro commands, (3) 1-2-3 functions, and (4) general entries.

**Macro Commands**

{WRITE}, 768
{WRITELN}, 769

## 1-2-3 Functions

@@, 363
@ABS, 328
@ATAN, 332
@ATAN2, 333
@AVG, 389
@CELL, 365
@CELLPOINTER, 367
@CHAR, 400
@CHOOSE, 371
@CLEAN, 401
@CODE, 402
@COLS, 373
@COS, 334
@COUNT, 390
@CTERM, 309
@DATE, 291, 536
@DATEVALUE, 293
@DAVG, 510
@DAY, 294
@DCOUNT, 511
@DDB, 310
@DMAX, 513
@DMIN, 514
@DSTD, 517
@DSUM, 518
@DVAR, 520
@ERR, 374
@EXACT, 403
@EXP, 336
@FALSE, 351
@FIND, 404
@FV, 211
@HLOOKUP, 375, 384
@HOUR, 296
@IF, 352
@INDEX, 379
@INT, 336
@IRR, 314
@ISERR, 357
@ISNA, 358
@ISNUMBER, 359
@ISSTRING, 361

@LEFT, 406
@LENGTH, 408
@LN, 338
@LOG, 338
@LOWER, 409
@MAX, 391
@MID, 410
@MIN, 392
@MINUTE, 298
@MOD, 301, 339
@MONTH, 298
@N, 413
@NA, 381
@NOW, 301, 337
@NPV, 315
@PI, 340
@PMT, 317
@PROPER, 414
@PV, 320
@RAND, 341
@RATE, 321
@REPEAT, 415
@REPLACE, 416
@RIGHT, 418
@ROUND, 288, 342
@ROWS, 383
@S, 420
@SECOND, 302
@SIN, 345
@SLN, 323
@SQRT, 346
@STD, 393
@STRING, 421, 490
@SUM, 288, 395
@SYD, 324
@TAN, 347
@TERM, 326
@TIME, 303
@TIMEVALUE, 304
@TRIM, 288, 423
@TRUE, 362
@UPPER, 424
@VALUE, 425
@VAR, 396
@VLOOKUP, 375, 384
@YEAR, 307

## General Entries

@ symbol, 287
? character, 497
* character, 497
+/− format, 105
1-2-3 menu option, 31
1-2-3 Report Writer, 776-822
1-2-3, history of, 867-878

Absolute references, 237
Absolute value, 328
Access system, 29-52
    menu choices, 31-36
Action settings, 616
Adding rows and columns, 219
Add-on products, 775-866
Align option, 142
ALT key, 650
Archive option, 454
Arctangent, 333
Arguments, 288
    passing, 736
ASCII text, 447
ASCII/LICS code, 400, 402
Asterisks, 65
Automatic line feed, 167
Averages, calculating, 389, 510
Axes, graph, 587

Bar graph, 595
Blank rows, macro to insert, 656
Blanks, stripping away, 423
Borders, 150-156
Branching, 691, 735
BREAK key function, 715

CALC indicator, 42
Capitalization conversion, 414
CAPS indicator, 41
Cell display, 261
Cell ranges, 192-211. See also Ranges
Cells
    examining characteristics of, 365
    protecting, 211-216
Character strings
    duplicating, 415
    replacing, 416
    searching, 404

CHKDSK equivalent, 453
CIRC indicator, 42
Circular reference, 261
Clock display, 116
CMD indicator, 42
Color options, 601
Column borders, 150
Column commands, 87
Column width, changing the, 93
Columns, counting, 373
Comma format, 102
Command language macros,
    685-771
    creating, 695
    creating interactive, 696
    documenting, 696
    executing, 699
    naming, 694
    stopping, 699
    testing, 698
Commands, map of 1-2-3, 46
Comparing disks, 453
Computer bell, 706
Computer requirements, 2-3
Control panel, 38, 708
Copy options, 229-242
Copyhard, 23
Copying formulas, 234
Copyon and Copyoff, 21
Cosine, 334
Criteria, database query, 495
Currency, international format for, 114
Currency format, 89, 101
Cursor movement, 50
Cutting and pasting, 216-228

Data disks, 27
Data entry, 53-84
    errors, macro to handle, 663
Data macros, 677
Data management, 475-534
    with spreadsheets, 535-580
Data ranges, 593
Data table, macro to create, 678
Data value sets for graphs, 590
Database
    adding a second, 509

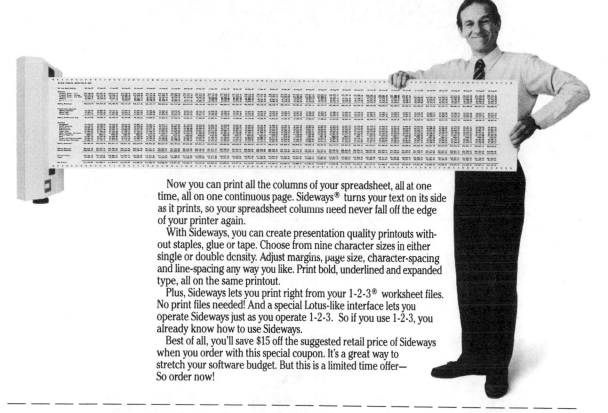

# The SIDEWAYS Specifics

**Printers Supported:**

C. Itoh Prowriter (8510/1550)
Epson MX/RX/FX-80/100
  or LQ-1500
Hewlett Packard ThinkJet
IBM Graphics, Color, Proprinter
  or Quietwriter-2
IDS Prism (Dataproducts P-80/132)
Mannesmann Tally Spirit,
  MT160/180

MPI Sprinter
NEC 8023
Okidata ML 82A/83A/92/93/84
Step 2, 182/183/192/193, or 2350/2410
Printek 910/920/930
Printronix MVP 150B
Star Gemini 10X/15X
Texas Instruments 850/855/865
Toshiba 1340/1350/1351

**System Reqirements:** IBM® PC/XT/AT or compatibles, DOS 1.1 or higher.

**Character Set:** IBM Extended ASCII Character Set 2. Bold, underlined, and expanded type are recognized if printer control sequences are embedded in the print file using IBM/Epson protocol. For 1-2-3 and Symphony, you may specify within Sideways which ranges are to be printed bold, underlined, and expanded.

**Compatibility:** Sideways works with all programs that can create ASCII print files. Instructions are included for use with Framework, Javelin, VisiCalc, Multiplan, SuperCalc, Smart Software, Electric Desk, TimeLine, Microsoft Word, Multi-Mate, WordStar, Volkswriter Deluxe, WordPerfect, dBase II and III. Sideways reads .WKS and .WK1 files from Lotus 1-2-3 Versions 1, 1A, and 2. Sideways occupies approximately 75K when used as a Symphony "add-in".

© 1986 Funk Software, Inc. 222 Third Street, Cambridge, MA 02142.
Sideways is a registered trademark of Funk Software.

**FUNK
SOFT
WARE**

## 30-YEAR FINANCIAL PROJECTION BY WEEK

| For the Week Ending: | 03-Jan-87 | 10-Jan-87 | 17-Jan-87 | 24-Jan-87 | 31-Jan-87 | 07-Feb-87 | 14-Feb-87 | 21-Feb-87 | 28-Feb-87 | 07-Mar-87 | 14-Mar-87 | 21-Mar-87 | 28-Mar-87 |
|---|---|---|---|---|---|---|---|---|---|---|---|---|---|
| **Revenues** | | | | | | | | | | | | | |
| Product Sales - U.S. | $23,432.00 | $24,837.92 | $23,619.46 | $24,720.76 | $24,439.58 | $25,775.20 | $25,540.88 | $26,009.52 | $26,478.16 | $26,712.48 | $25,775.20 | $27,649.76 | $27,415.44 |
| Product Sales - Europe | $10,125.44 | $10,732.96 | $10,206.44 | $10,682.33 | $10,560.83 | $11,137.98 | $11,036.73 | $11,239.23 | $11,441.74 | $11,543.00 | $11,137.98 | $11,948.01 | $11,846.76 |
| Product Sales - Far East | $5,673.36 | $6,013.76 | $5,718.74 | $5,985.39 | $5,917.31 | $6,240.69 | $6,183.96 | $6,297.42 | $6,410.89 | $6,467.63 | $6,240.69 | $6,694.56 | $6,637.83 |
| Rentals | $4,838.71 | $5,129.03 | $4,877.42 | $5,104.84 | $5,046.77 | $5,322.58 | $5,274.19 | $5,370.97 | $5,467.74 | $5,516.13 | $5,322.58 | $5,709.68 | $5,661.29 |
| Maintenance Fees | $2,541.20 | $2,693.67 | $2,561.53 | $2,680.97 | $2,650.47 | $2,795.32 | $2,769.91 | $2,820.73 | $2,871.56 | $2,896.97 | $2,795.32 | $2,998.62 | $2,973.20 |
| **Weekly Revenues** | $46,610.70 | $49,407.34 | $46,983.59 | $49,174.29 | $48,614.96 | $51,271.77 | $50,805.66 | $51,737.88 | $52,670.09 | $53,136.20 | $51,271.77 | $55,000.63 | $54,534.52 |
| **Promotional Expenses** | | | | | | | | | | | | | |
| Agency Expenses | $2,720.55 | $2,883.78 | $2,742.31 | $2,870.18 | $2,837.53 | $2,992.60 | $2,965.40 | $3,019.81 | $3,074.22 | $3,101.43 | $2,992.60 | $3,210.28 | $3,183.04 |
| Media Cost | $1,909.71 | $2,024.29 | $1,924.99 | $2,014.74 | $1,991.83 | $2,100.68 | $2,081.58 | $2,119.78 | $2,157.97 | $2,177.07 | $2,100.68 | $2,253.46 | $2,234.36 |
| Direct Mail | $1,813.29 | $1,922.09 | $1,827.80 | $1,913.03 | $1,891.27 | $1,994.62 | $1,976.49 | $2,012.76 | $2,049.02 | $2,067.16 | $1,994.62 | $2,139.69 | $2,121.55 |
| **Weekly Promotional Exp.** | $6,443.55 | $6,830.16 | $6,495.10 | $6,797.95 | $6,720.62 | $7,087.91 | $7,023.47 | $7,152.34 | $7,281.21 | $7,345.65 | $7,087.91 | $7,603.39 | $7,538.96 |
| **Overhead** | | | | | | | | | | | | | |
| Management | $3,710.22 | $3,932.84 | $3,739.90 | $3,914.29 | $3,869.76 | $4,081.25 | $4,044.14 | $4,118.35 | $4,192.55 | $4,229.65 | $4,081.25 | $4,378.06 | $4,340.96 |
| Staff Salaries | $4,745.54 | $5,030.27 | $4,783.51 | $5,006.55 | $4,949.60 | $5,220.10 | $5,172.64 | $5,267.55 | $5,362.46 | $5,409.92 | $5,220.10 | $5,599.74 | $5,552.28 |
| Engineering | $2,981.31 | $3,160.19 | $3,005.16 | $3,145.28 | $3,109.50 | $3,279.44 | $3,249.63 | $3,309.25 | $3,368.88 | $3,398.69 | $3,279.44 | $3,517.94 | $3,488.13 |
| Depreciation | $2,465.05 | $2,612.95 | $2,484.77 | $2,600.62 | $2,571.04 | $2,711.55 | $2,686.90 | $2,736.20 | $2,785.50 | $2,810.15 | $2,711.55 | $2,908.75 | $2,884.10 |
| Legal Fees | $1,663.67 | $1,763.49 | $1,676.96 | $1,755.17 | $1,735.21 | $1,830.74 | $1,813.40 | $1,846.60 | $1,879.95 | $1,896.59 | $1,830.04 | $1,963.13 | $1,946.50 |
| Other Profess. Services | $1,016.95 | $1,077.97 | $1,025.08 | $1,072.80 | $1,060.60 | $1,118.64 | $1,108.47 | $1,128.81 | $1,149.15 | $1,159.32 | $1,118.64 | $1,200.00 | $1,189.83 |
| Office Supplies | $288.21 | $305.51 | $290.52 | $304.07 | $300.61 | $317.03 | $314.15 | $319.92 | $325.68 | $328.56 | $317.03 | $340.09 | $337.21 |
| Rent | $4,051.39 | $4,294.48 | $4,083.80 | $4,274.22 | $4,225.60 | $4,456.53 | $4,416.02 | $4,497.05 | $4,578.07 | $4,618.59 | $4,456.53 | $4,780.64 | $4,740.13 |
| Travel and Entertainment | $2,462.18 | $2,631.12 | $2,502.04 | $2,618.70 | $2,586.92 | $2,730.40 | $2,705.50 | $2,755.23 | $2,804.87 | $2,829.69 | $2,730.40 | $2,928.98 | $2,904.16 |
| Honorariums (Foreign) | $1,061.47 | $1,125.16 | $1,069.96 | $1,119.85 | $1,107.11 | $1,167.62 | $1,157.00 | $1,178.23 | $1,199.46 | $1,210.08 | $1,167.62 | $1,252.53 | $1,241.92 |
| **Weekly Overhead** | $24,466.00 | $25,933.96 | $24,661.73 | $25,811.63 | $25,518.04 | $26,912.60 | $26,667.94 | $27,157.26 | $27,646.58 | $27,891.24 | $26,912.60 | $28,869.88 | $28,625.22 |
| **Weekly Revenues** | $46,610.70 | $49,407.34 | $46,983.59 | $49,174.29 | $48,614.96 | $51,271.77 | $50,805.66 | $51,737.88 | $52,670.09 | $53,136.20 | $51,271.77 | $55,000.63 | $54,534.52 |
| **Weekly Expenses** | $30,909.55 | $32,764.13 | $31,156.83 | $32,609.58 | $32,238.66 | $34,000.51 | $33,691.41 | $34,309.60 | $34,927.79 | $35,236.89 | $34,000.51 | $36,473.27 | $36,164.18 |
| Pre-tax Profit | $15,701.15 | $16,643.22 | $15,826.76 | $16,564.71 | $16,376.30 | $17,271.26 | $17,114.25 | $17,428.27 | $17,742.30 | $17,899.31 | $17,271.26 | $18,527.35 | $18,370.34 |
| Taxes | $3,925.29 | $4,160.80 | $3,956.69 | $4,141.18 | $4,094.07 | $4,317.82 | $4,278.56 | $4,357.07 | $4,435.57 | $4,474.83 | $4,317.82 | $4,631.84 | $4,592.59 |
| **Net Profit** | $11,775.86 | $12,482.41 | $11,870.07 | $12,423.53 | $12,282.22 | $12,953.45 | $12,835.69 | $13,071.20 | $13,306.72 | $13,424.48 | $12,953.45 | $13,895.52 | $13,777.76 |

# SPECIAL DISCOUNT
## From Consumers Software Inc.

THE SPREADSHEET
AUDITOR™
FOR SPREADSHEETS YOU CAN COUNT ON

Now you can save $50.00 on your purchase of the new Spreadsheet Auditor 3.0, the only utility that combines Error Checking, Cell Notation, Worksheet Documentation, and Sideways Printing into one easy to use package.

**You pay only—** # $99 Regularly $149

To order, just clip this coupon from your copy of **1-2-3: The Complete Reference** and mail to:

### CONSUMERS SOFTWARE INC.
**8315 Monterey Street, Suite A, Gilroy, CA 95020**

- - - - - - - - - - - - - - - - - - - - - - -

Please rush me_____copies of the **Spreadsheet Auditor 3.0** at $99.00 each (CA residents please add local sales tax).

☐ **Check enclosed** (make checks payable to: Consumers Software Inc., 8315 Monterey Street, Suite A, Gilroy, CA 95020)

☐ Visa

☐ MasterCard

☐ American Express

If credit order, please provide the following information:
Card #:_____
Exp. date:_____
Signature:_____

Ship to:  Name:_____

Address:_____

City:_____State:_____Zip:_____

Coupon expires 10/31/87

# For spreadsheets you can count on.

This coupon is solely the offering of Consumers Software Inc., Osborne McGraw-Hill takes no responsibility for fulfillment of this offer

# DataPrep
## The Format Manager

**Data Extract** – lets you separate the data you want to analyze from useless information.

**Data Convert** – reformats files into Lotus 1-2-3™, dBase II™, dBase III™, DIF and other program formats.

**Data Exchange** – lets you easily exchange data, formulas, etc. between Lotus 1-2-3, Symphony, dBase II and dBase III.

**Data Export** – converts selected spreadsheet and data base information into ASCII file format.

**Application Interface** – lets you organize and execute the programs you use every day from one master menu.

# SAVE 50% ON
# SCHEDULE GRAFIX

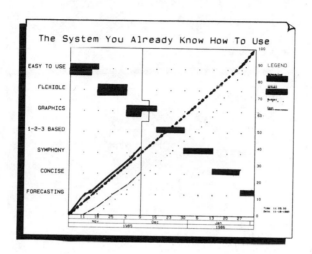

From now until August 31, 1987 you can save 50% on Schedule Grafix from **Digital Engineering**.  Just clip this coupon from your copy of **1-2-3: The Complete Reference** (no duplicating machine copies will be accepted) and mail to:

> Digital Engineering
> P.O. Box 6076
> Glendale, Az.   83512-6076

The package provides templates for Lotus(tm) 1-2-3 Rev. 1A* and Rev. 2.0 and Symphony Rev. 1.1.  If you have any questions about this offer, call (602) 439-3245.

This coupon is solely the offering of Digital Engineering. Osborne/McGraw-Hill takes no responsibility for fulfillment of this offer.

# ORDER FORM

SCHEDULE GRAFIX  (Regular price $200)          $100.00

VISA/MASTERCHARGE Orders
Please add $5.00 for shipping and handling     _____

Arizona Residents add 6.5%   ($6.50)     _____

Total     _____

_____ My check is enclosed
_____ My money order  is enclosed
_____ Charge to my VISA account
_____ Charge to my MasterCard account

IF CREDIT CARD ORDER, PLEASE PROVIDE THE FOLLOWING INFORMATION.

Exp. Date _____ Card# _____

Name (as it appears on your card).............. _____

Authorized Signature............................. _____

Ship to:    Name........ _____

               Address.... _____

               City.......... _____

               State/Zip... _____

**NEW!!**

**Ready-to-Run Accounting** turns Lotus 1-2-3 into the most flexible accounting system ever developed!

You already know how powerful Lotus 1-2-3 is. Now imagine dozens of macro-driven templates all integrating to create a menu-driven professional accounting system. That's Ready-to-Run Accounting.

**"About as easy as bookkeeping will ever get . . . An excellent buy."**
Lotus Magazine

This growing system now consists of the following modules:

**GENERAL LEDGER** — with budgeting, full financial reporting, and complete audit trails
Only $69.95

**ACCOUNTS PAYABLE** — with check printing and job costing
Only $49.95

**ACCOUNTS RECEIVABLE** — with invoice printing and customer aging/histories
Only $49.95

**PAYROLL** — a complete system featuring check and W-2 printing
Only $49.95

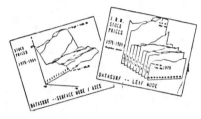

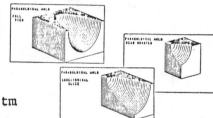

# DATASURF™

DATASURF is a very sophisticated yet simple-to-use surface-sketching utility. Using electronic data tables, DATASURF produces three-dimensional graphic images in two forms: as a continuous two-dimensional surface; or as a series of sheets or "leaves" shown in three-dimensional perspective. These plots can be rotated, translated, and rescaled to suit the user's needs. A full range of characters is provided in a full range of sizes so that labels of any size can be inserted anywhere on the plot. The **PrinterPack** feature produces **high-resolution (960 x 1056), plotter-quality printouts using a standard dot-matrix printer.**

Among its many features, **DATASURF:**

o has a conversion utility that allows it to work with data table files generated by:

**All** versions of **all** Lotus products prepared for the IBM PC and its compatibles.
Most other numerical tables generated in ASCII code readable by MS-DOS including tables from a wide variety of programs including WordStar, MultiMate, VisiCalc, SuperCalc, as well as files created using Pascal, BASIC, FORTRAN, etc.

o permits logarithmic scaling for both business and scientific plots
o supports the 8087, if one has been installed
o is easy-to-use and comes with complete, usable, readable documentation that contains several Workshop examples plus information for programmers.
o can handle rectangular tables with over 32,000 entries, if sufficient memory (RAM) is available.

## DATASURF HARDWARE AND SOFTWARE REQUIREMENTS

o IBM-PC, XT, AT, PCjr, or compatibles with/without an 8087.
o **The IBM color/graphics adapter,** the IBM EGA and compatibles or the Hercules monochrome graphics card.
o 320K if high resolution printed output is desired. At least 512K is suggested for optimal operation.
o **Printers:** Epson MX, FX, and RX, IBM Graphics, C. Itoh Prowriter, Panasonic, Okidata 92/93 with "Plug and Play", the IDS Prism, the Mannesmann Tally and the Gemini X.
If you have another type of printer, please contact us. We will try to accommodate you. H-P plotter and laser-jet printer support is not available at this writing but will soon be.
o **Operating Systems:** PC-DOS or MS-DOS 2.0 or later.

**SPECIAL PROMOTIONAL DISCOUNT OFFER FOR DATASURF APPEARS ON NEXT PAGE**

BRIDGE SOFTWARE  EDUCATIONAL
                 SCIENTIFIC WARE

## SPECIAL DISCOUNT ON
## BRIDGE SOFTWARE'S DATASURF tm

From now until September 30, 1987, you can save 10% off the regular $125.00 price of Bridge Software's DATASURF tm **Version 1.1.**

You pay only $112.50 plus $3. for shipping and handling.

**And** we'll give you a twenty-day, money-back guarantee.

Just cut this coupon from your copy of **1-2-3:** The Complete Reference, by Campbell and Campbell (no duplicating machine copies will be accepted), and mail it to:

Sales Promotions Department
**BRIDGE SOFTWARE**
P. O. Box 118
**New Town Branch**
Boston, MA 02258

If you have any questions about this offer or the program, call (617) 527-1585.

This coupon is solely the offering of Bridge Software. Osborne **McGraw-Hill** takes no responsibility for fulfillment of this offer.

---

Please send me one **DATASURF** tm **Version 1.1** program prepared for use on the following equipment:

Computer: _____

Graphics Card: _____

Printer: _____

◇ My check in the amount of $115.50 ($112.50 plus $3.00 for shipping and handling) is enclosed.

◇ **Massachusetts residents** add $5.63 for 5% sales tax. Check in the amount of $121.13 is enclosed.

**U.S. Funds only. For overseas shipments, call or write to determine shipping and handling costs.**

Ship to:

Name _____

Address _____

City _____

State/Zip _____

**No P. O. boxes, please. We ship via UPS ground which requires a delivery address.**

Save $20 on PREVIEW
Buy the software that makes it simple to
generate picture perfect reports from
LOTUS 1-2-3 every time!

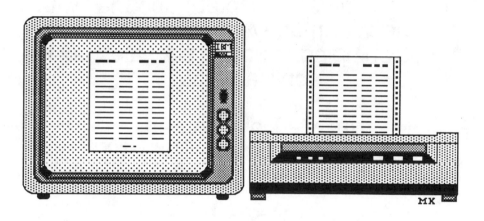

PREVIEW's the software that lets you
preview your page to your screen before
printing, lets you reformat or edit (including
wrap around of up to 5 columns).
PREVIEW works in either a memory
resident mode (so you don't have to leave
1-2-3 to use it) or stand alone.

From now until September 1987, you can save $20 off the $54.95 suggested retail price of InSyte Development's PREVIEW.

Just cut this coupon out (no duplicating machine copies accepted) and mail with your check or money order for $34.95 plus $3.00 shipping (plus 6% CA sales tax if applicable) to:

InSyte Development
9842 Hibert Street, Suite 137
San Diego, CA 92131

(619) 566-3973

Name _____
Address _____
City _____
State/Zip _____

This coupon is solely the offering of InSyte Development.  Osborne McGraw-Hill takes no responsibility for fulfillment of this offer.

# Templates of Doom

## A learning adventure on Computer Spreadsheets

Templates of Doom is an interactive adventure **game** learning tutorial **on Lotus 1-2-3 spreadsheets**. It is a tongue-in-cheek James Bond satire that challenges the player into using many spreadsheet commands and formulas. It is a **lot of fun** for experienced users, yet can be played by beginners who may elect to use the extensive selection of hints and helps available at the price of penalty points.

In the process of playing the game, **the player is faced with challenges** like finding the weapon of the hero. In order to find it, the player might have to delete rows or columns, reformat cells or use any one of the many Lotus commands.

A player can choose up to four levels of hints or helps with four corresponding levels of penalty points. The basic idea of the program is to give just enought help to cause the player to **experiment** and in the process **learn.**

The game can be played alone, however it also makes an excellent **classroom exercise** and special instructions are available to teachers. **Site licenses** and volume discounts are available to non-profit learning institutions.

It is not copy protected and runs on Lotus 1-2-3 release 1a and 2, as well as VP-planner, and the TWIN.

## LISTEN TO WHAT THE REVIEWERS ARE SAYING

*PC MAGAZINE, OCT 85*

**...an ingenious idea...enjoyed the puzzles...recommend.**

*LOTUS MAGAZINE, OCT 85*

**...TRULY ENJOYABLE,  (AND VERY FUNNY).**

Fold here, place check inside (If that is your method of payment), tape on three sides, stamp and mail.

Please place
stamp here

SOLAR SYSTEMS SOFTWARE
8105 SHELTER CREEK
SAN BRUNO,CA 94066

(415) 952-2375

# COMMAND CARD

## WORKSHEET COMMANDS

/Worksheet Global
Format
Fixed
Scientific
Currency
,
General
+/-
Percent
Date
Time
Text
Hidden
Label-Prefix
Left
Right
Center
Column-Width
Recalculation
Natural
Automatic
Manual
Iteration
Columnwise
Rowwise
Protection
Enable
Disable
Default
Printer
Interface
Auto-LF
Left

## WORKSHEET COMMANDS

Right
Top
Bottom
Pg-Length
Wait
Setup
,
General
Name
Quit
Directory
Status
Update
Other
International
Punctuation
Currency
Date
Time
Quit
Help
Clock
Quit
Zero
/Worksheet Insert
Column
Row
/Worksheet Delete
Column
Row
/Worksheet Column
Set-Width
Reset-Width
Hide
Display

## WORKSHEET COMMANDS

/Worksheet Erase
/Worksheet Titles
Both
Horizontal
Vertical
Clear
/Worksheet Window
Horizontal
Vertical
Sync
Unsync
Clear
/Worksheet Status
/Worksheet Page

## RANGE COMMANDS

/Range Format
Fixed
Scientific
Currency
,
General
+/-
Percent
Date
Time
Text
Hidden
Reset
/Range Label

## RANGE COMMANDS

Left
Right
Center
/Range Erase
/Range Name
Create
Delete
Labels
Reset
Table
/Range Justify
/Range Protect
/Range Unprotect
/Range Input
/Range Value
/Range Transpose

## COPY COMMAND

/Copy

## MOVE COMMAND

/Move

## FILE COMMANDS

/File Retrieve
/File Save
Cancel
Replace
/File Combine

## FILE COMMANDS

Copy
Entire-File
Named-Range
Add
Entire-File
Named-Range
Subtract
Entire-File
Named-Range
/File Xtract
Formulas
Values
/File Erase
Worksheet
Print
Graph
Other
/File List
Worksheet
Print
Graph
Other
/File Import
Text
Numbers
/File Directory

## PRINT COMMANDS (Printer or File)

/Print Printer Range
/Print Printer Line

## PRINT COMMANDS (Printer or File)

/Print Printer Page
/Print Printer Options
Header
Footer
Margins
Left
Right
Top
Bottom
Borders
Columns
Rows
Setup
Pg-Length
Other
As-Displayed
Cell-Formulas
Formatted
Unformatted
Quit
/Print Printer Clear
All
Range
Borders
Format
/Print Printer Align
/Print Printer Go
/Printer Printer Quit

© 1987 Osborne McGraw-Hill
1-2-3: The Complete Reference

# GRAPH COMMANDS

/Graph Type
- Line
- Bar
- XY
- Stacked Bar
- Pie

/Graph X
/Graph A
/Graph B
/Graph C
/Graph D
/Graph E
/Graph F

/Graph Reset
- Graph
- X
- A
- B
- C
- D
- E
- F

/Graph View
/Graph Save
/Graph Options
- Legend
  - A through F
- Format
  - A through F
  - Graph
  - Quit

/Graph Name
- Use
- Create

Titles
- First
- Second

X-Axis
Y-Axis
Grid
- Horizontal
- Vertical
- Both
- Clear

Scale
- Y Scale
- Automatic
- Manual
- Lower
- Upper
- Format
- Indicator
- Quit

X Scale
- Same options as Y Scale

Skip
Color
B&W
Data-Labels
- A through F
- Quit

Quit

Delete
Reset
/Graph Quit

# DATA COMMANDS

/Data Fill
/Data Table
- 1
- 2
- Reset

/Data Sort
- Data-Range
- Primary-Key
- Secondary-Key
- Reset
- Go
- Quit

/Data Query
- Input
- Criterion
- Output
- Find
- Extract
- Unique
- Delete
- Cancel
- Delete
- Reset
- Quit

/Data Distribution
/Data Matrix
- Invert
- Multiply

/Data Regression
- X-Range
- Y-Range
- Output-Range
- Intercept
  - Compute
  - Zero
- Reset
- Go
- Quit

/Data Parse

**Note:** Release 2 commands are highlighted

© 1987 Osborne **McGraw-Hill**
1-2-3: The Complete Reference